Birnbaum's 94
Ireland

A BIRNBAUM TRAVEL GUIDE

Alexandra Mayes Birnbaum
EDITORIAL CONSULTANT

Lois Spritzer
Executive Editor

Laura L. Brengelman
Managing Editor

Mary Callahan
Senior Editor

Patricia Canole
Gene Gold
Jill Kadetsky
Susan McClung
Beth Schlau
Associate Editors

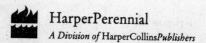 HarperPerennial
A Division of HarperCollins*Publishers*

To Stephen, who merely made all this possible.

BIRNBAUM'S IRELAND 94. Copyright © 1993 by HarperCollins Publishers. All
rights reserved. Printed in the United States of America. No part of this book
may be used or reproduced in any manner whatsoever without written permission except in the case of brief quotations embodied in critical articles and
reviews. For information address HarperCollinsPublishers, 10 East 53rd Street,
New York, NY 10022.

FIRST EDITION

ISSN 0749-2561 (Birnbaum Travel Guides)
ISSN 0896-8691 (Ireland)
ISBN 0-06-278130-8 (pbk.)

93 94 95 96 97 CC/CW 10 9 8 7 6 5 4 3 2 1

Cover design © Drenttel Doyle Partners
Cover photograph © George Munday/Leo de Wys

BIRNBAUM TRAVEL GUIDES

Bahamas, and Turks & Caicos
Berlin
Bermuda
Boston
Canada
Cancun, Cozumel & Isla Mujeres
Caribbean
Chicago
Disneyland
Eastern Europe
Europe
Europe for Business Travelers
France
Germany
Great Britain
Hawaii
Ireland
Italy
London

Los Angeles
Mexico
Miami & Ft. Lauderdale
Montreal & Quebec City
New Orleans
New York
Paris
Portugal
Rome
San Francisco
Santa Fe & Taos
South America
Spain
United States
USA for Business Travelers
Walt Disney World
Walt Disney World for Kids, By Kids
Washington, DC

Contributing Editors

Frederick H. Brengelman
Karlys Daly Brown
Helen Lucy Burke
Kevin Causey
Karen Cure
Michael Finlan
Brian Geraghty
Tom Glennon
Judith Glynn
Jody Gould
Elizabeth Healy

H. Constance Hill
Joanne McGrath
Maxine Moore
Winkie Nixon
Breandon O'Heithir
Mary O'Sullivan
John Preston
Patricia Tunison Preston
Tracy Smith
Colin Toibin

Maps

B. Andrew Mudryk

Contents

Getting Ready to Go

Practical information for planning your trip.

The Cities

Thorough, qualitative guides to each of the 13 cities most often visited by vacationers and businesspeople. Each section offers a comprehensive report on the city's most compelling attractions and amenities — highlighting our top choices in every category.

Diversions

A selective guide to active and/or cerebral vacation themes, pinpointing the best places in which to pursue them.

Unexpected Pleasures and Treasures

For the Experience

For the Mind

For the Body

Directions

Foreword

The first night my husband, Steve Birnbaum, ever spent in Ireland included several hours at *Bofey Quinn's* pub in the village of Corofin in the west of Ireland. He'd been at the bar there for about 15 minutes, sipping his first ever "jar" of stout from a keg, when a man of the town came up beside him and put his hand on Steve's shoulder. He was dressed in a well-worn tweed jacket, and an equally old tweed cap was on his head.

"Tell me, Boy-o," he began, in a brogue as thick as peat, "where in Ireland is your family from?"

"Poland," Steve replied, feeling he had scored with a laser-like bon mot.

"Not to worry," the Irishman said, not missing a beat, "it's our easternmost county!"

There were lots of lessons to learn from this first encounter on Irish soil. The first, clearly, was not to challenge the wit of the Old Country on its own turf. Second, and perhaps most important, was the depth of hospitality the Irish feel toward visitors, especially those from America.

Hospitality is not a sometime thing in Ireland; it is perhaps the island's single most valuable commodity. Whether in the North or in the Republic, Irish men and women seem to take great delight in making a visitor feel supremely comfortable, and the Irish talent for warmth and welcome has no equal in this wide world.

Ireland was one of Steve's favorite destinations. And for me, it holds a high place in my romantic recollections: Steve proposed to me in the middle of Dublin's O'Connell Street. A month later, I was married in a suit of handwoven Donegal tweed; the fabric purchased in a tiny shop near one of the bridges spanning the Liffey. The shop is gone; I've still got the suit. Ireland is a place to which I return again and again, often inventing excuses to visit with Irish people and to dine out on fine Irish fare.

Obviously, any guidebook to Ireland must keep pace with and answer the real needs of today's travelers. That's why we've tried to create a guide that's specifically organized, written, and edited for the more demanding modern traveler, one for whom qualitative information is infinitely more desirable than mere quantities of unappraised data.

For years, dating back as far as Herr Baedeker, travel guides have tended to be encyclopedic, much more concerned with demonstrating expertise in geography and history than in any analysis of the sorts of things that actually concern a typical modern tourist. That's exactly what we've tried to do in this series. I think you'll notice a different, more contemporary tone to our text, as well as an organization and focus that are distinctive and more functional. Early on, we realized that giving up the encyclopedic approach precluded our listing every single route and restaurant, a realization that helped define our overall editorial focus. Similarly, when we discussed the possibility of presenting certain information in other than strict geographic order, we found that the new format enabled us to arrange data in a way that best answers the questions travelers typically ask.

Travel guides are, understandably, reflections of personal taste, and putting one's name on a title page obviously puts one's preferences on the line. But I think I ought to amplify just what "personal" means. I don't believe in the sort of personal guidebook that's a palpable misrepresentation on its face. It is, for example, hardly possible for any single travel writer to visit thousands of restaurants (and nearly as many hotels) in any given year and provide accurate appraisals of each. And even if it were physically possible for one human being to survive such an itinerary, it would of necessity have to be done at a dead sprint, and the perceptions derived therefrom would probably be less valid than those of any other intelligent individual visiting the same establishments. It is, therefore, impossible (especially in a large, annually revised and updated guidebook *series* such as we offer) to have only one person provide all the data on the entire world.

I also happen to think that such individual orientation is of substantially less value to readers. Visiting a single hotel for just one night or eating one hasty meal in a random restaurant hardly equips anyone to provide appraisals that are of more than passing interest. We have therefore chosen what I like to describe as the "thee and me" approach to restaurant and hotel evaluation and, to a somewhat more limited degree, to the sites and sights we have included in the other sections of our text. What this really reflects is personal sampling tempered by intelligent counsel from informed local sources, and these additional friends-of-the-editor are almost always residents of the city and/or area about which they are consulted.

In addition, very precise editing and tailoring keep our text fiercely subjective. So what follows is purposely designed to be the gospel according to Birnbaum, and it represents as much of our own taste and instincts as we can manage. It is probable, therefore, that if you like your cities stylish and prefer hotels with personality to high-rise anonymities, we're likely to have a long and meaningful relationship.

I also should point out something about the person to whom this guidebook is directed. Above all, he or she is a "visitor." This means that such elements as restaurants have been specifically picked to provide the visitor with a representative, illuminating, stimulating, and, above all pleasant experience. Since so many extraneous considerations can affect the reception and service accorded a regular restaurant patron, our choices can in no way be construed as an exhaustive guide to resident dining. We think we've listed all the best places, in various price ranges, but they were chosen with a visitor's enjoyment in mind.

Other evidence of how we've tried to tailor our text to reflect modern travel habits is in the section we call DIVERSIONS. Where once it was common for travelers to spend a foreign visit seeing only obvious sights, the emphasis today is more likely to be directed toward pursuing some special interest. Therefore, we have collected these exceptional experiences so that it is no longer necessary to wade through a pound or two of superfluous prose just to find unexpected pleasures and treasures.

Finally, I also should point out that every good travel guide is a living enterprise; that is, no part of this text is carved in stone. In our annual revisions, we refine, expand, and further hone all our material to serve your travel needs better. To this end, no contribution is of greater value to us than your personal reaction to what we have written, as well as information reflecting your own experiences while using this book. Please write to us at 10 E. 53rd St., New York, NY 10022.

We sincerely hope to hear from you.

Alexandra Mayes Birnbaum

ALEXANDRA MAYES BIRNBAUM, editorial consultant to the *Birnbaum Travel Guides*, worked with her late husband, Stephen Birnbaum, as co-editor of the series. She has been a world traveler since childhood and is known for her lively travel reports on radio on what's hot and what's not.

Ireland

IRELAND

How to Use This Guide

A great deal of care has gone into the organization of this guidebook, and we believe it represents a real breakthrough in the presentation of travel material. Our aim is to create a new, more modern generation of travel books, and to make this guide the most useful and practical travel tool available today.

Our text is divided into four basic sections in order to present information in the best way on every possible aspect of a vacation to Ireland. Our aim is to highlight what's where and to provide basic information — how, when, where, how much, and what's best — to assist you in making the most intelligent choices possible.

Here is a brief summary of the four sections of this book, and what you can expect to find in each. We believe that you will find both your travel planning and en route enjoyment enhanced by having this book at your side.

GETTING READY TO GO

A mini-encyclopedia of practical travel facts with all the precise data necessary to create a successful journey to and through Ireland. Here you will find how to get where you're going, plus selected resources — including useful publications, and companies and organizations specializing in discount and special-interest travel — providing a wealth of information and assistance useful both before and during your trip.

THE CITIES

Individual reports on the 13 cities most visited by travelers and business-people offer a short-stay guide, including an essay introducing each city as a historic entity and a contemporary place to visit; *At-a-Glance* material is a site-by-site survey of the most important, interesting, and sometimes most eclectic sights to see and things to do; *Sources and Resources* is a concise listing of pertinent tourism information, such as the address of the local tourist office, which sightseeing tours to take, when special events and holidays occur, where to find the best museums and theaters or where to hail a taxi, which shops have the finest merchandise and/or the most irresistible bargains, and where the best golf, tennis, fishing, and hiking are to be found. *Best in Town* lists our choices of the best places to eat and sleep on a variety of budgets.

DIVERSIONS

This section is designed to help travelers find the best places in which to engage in a variety of exceptional — and unexpected — experiences for the mind and body without having to wade through endless pages of unrelated text. In every case, our particular suggestions are intended to guide you to that special place where the quality of experience is likely to be highest.

DIRECTIONS

Here are 12 itineraries that range all across the countryside, along the most beautiful routes and roads, past the most spectacular natural wonders, through the most historic cities and countryside. DIRECTIONS is the only section of this book that is organized geographically, and its itineraries cover the touring highlights of both Northern Ireland and the Republic of Ireland in short, independent journeys of 3 to 5 days' duration. Itineraries can be "connected" for longer sojourns or used individually for short, intensive explorations.

To use this book to full advantage, take a few minutes to read the table of contents and random entries in each section to get a firsthand feel for how it all fits together. You will find that the sections of this book are building blocks designed to help you put together the best possible trip. Use them selectively as a tool, a source of ideas, a reference work for accurate facts, and a guidebook to the best buys, the most exciting sights, the most pleasant accommodations, the tastiest food — *the best travel experience* you can possibly have.

Getting
Ready to Go

When to Go

Ireland's temperate climate makes it a multi-seasonal travel destination. Summers are cool and winters are relatively mild. The island's small size ensures fairly uniform temperatures throughout, although skies frequently are overcast and there is a fair amount of rain — especially in winter.

Mid-May to mid-September generally is the peak travel period, but travel during the off-season (roughly November to *Easter*) and shoulder seasons (the months immediately before and after the peak months) also offers relatively fair weather and smaller crowds. During these periods, travel also is less expensive.

The *Weather Channel* (2600 Cumberland Pkwy., Atlanta, GA 30339; phone: 404-434-6800) provides current weather forecasts. Call 900-WEATHER from any touch-tone phone in the US; the 95¢ per minute charge will appear on your phone bill.

Traveling by Plane

SCHEDULED FLIGHTS

Leading airlines offering flights between the US and Ireland include *Aer Lingus, American, British Airways, Continental, Delta, Northwest, TWA, United,* and *USAir.*

FARES The great variety of airfares can be reduced to the following basic categories: first class, business class, coach (also called economy or tourist class), excursion or discount, and standby, as well as various promotional fares. For information on applicable fares and restrictions, contact the airlines listed above or ask your travel agent. Most airfares are offered for a limited time period. Once you've found the lowest fare for which you can qualify, purchase your ticket as soon as possible.

RESERVATIONS Reconfirmation is strongly recommended for all international flights. It is essential that you confirm your round-trip reservations–*especially the return leg* — as well as any flights within Europe.

SEATING Airline seats usually are assigned on a first-come, first-served basis at check-in, although you may be able to reserve a seat when purchasing your ticket. Seating charts often are available from airlines and are included in the *Airline Seating Guide* (Carlson Publishing Co., PO Box 888, Los Alamitos, CA 90720; phone: 310-493-4877).

SMOKING US law prohibits smoking on flights scheduled for 6 hours or less within the US and its territories on both domestic and international carriers. These rules do not apply to nonstop flights between the US and international destinations. A free wallet-size guide that describes the rights of nonsmokers is available from *ASH (Action on Smoking and Health;*

DOT Card, 2013 H St. NW, Washington, DC 20006; phone: 202-659-4310).

SPECIAL MEALS When making your reservation, you can request one of the airline's alternate menu choices for no additional charge. Call to reconfirm your request 24 hours before departure.

BAGGAGE On a major international airline, passengers usually are allowed to carry on board one bag that will fit under a seat or in an overhead bin. Passengers also can check two bags in the cargo hold, measuring 62 inches and 55 inches in combined dimensions (length, width, and depth) with a per-bag weight limit of 70 pounds. There may be charges for additional, oversize, or overweight luggage, and for special equipment or sporting gear. Note that baggage allowances may vary for children (depending on the percentage of full adult fare paid) and on domestic and intra-European routes abroad. Check that the tags the airline attaches are correctly coded for your destination.

CHARTER FLIGHTS

By booking a block of seats on a specially arranged flight, charter operators frequently offer travelers bargain airfares. If you do fly on a charter, however, read the contract's fine print carefully. Charter operators can cancel a flight or assess surcharges of 10% of the airfare up to 10 days before departure. You usually must book in advance (no changes are permitted, so invest in trip cancellation insurance); also make your check out to the company's escrow account. For further information, consult the publication *Jax Fax* (397 Post Rd., Darien, CT 06820; phone: 203-655-8746).

DISCOUNTS ON SCHEDULED FLIGHTS

COURIER TRAVEL In return for arranging to accompany some kind of freight, a traveler may pay only a portion of the total airfare and a small registration fee. One agency that matches up would-be couriers with courier companies is *Now Voyager* (74 Varick St., Suite 307, New York, NY 10013; phone: 212-431-1616).

Courier Companies

Courier Travel Service (530 Central Ave., Cedarhurst, NY 11516; phone: 516-763-6898).

Discount Travel International (169 W. 81st St., New York, NY 10024; phone: 212-362-3636; and 940 10th St., Suite 2, Miami Beach, FL 33139; phone: 305-538-1616).

Excaliber International Courier (c/o *Way to Go Travel*, 6679 Sunset Blvd., Hollywood, CA 90028; phone: 213-466-1126).

F.B. On Board Courier Services (10225 Ryan Ave., Suite 103, Dorval, Quebec H9P 1A2, Canada; phone: 514-633-0740).

Halbart Express (147-05 176th St., Jamaica, NY 11434; phone: 718-656-8279).

International Adventures (60 E. 42nd St., New York, NY 10165; phone: 212-599-0577).

Midnight Express (925 W. High Park Blvd., Inglewood, CA 90302; phone: 310-672-1100).

Publications

Insider's Guide to Air Courier Bargains, by Kelly Monaghan (The Intrepid Traveler, PO Box 438, New York, NY 10034; phone: 212-304-2207).

Travel Secrets (PO Box 2325, New York, NY 10108; phone: 212-245-8703).

Travel Unlimited (PO Box 1058, Allston, MA 02134-1058; no phone).

World Courier News (PO Box 77471, San Francisco, CA 94107; no phone).

CONSOLIDATORS AND BUCKET SHOPS These companies buy blocks of tickets from airlines and sell them at a discount to travel agents or to consumers. Since many bucket shops operate on a thin margin, before parting with any money check the company's record with the Better Business Bureau.

Bargain Air (655 Deep Valley Dr., Suite 355, Rolling Hills, CA 90274; phone: 800-347-2345).

Council Charter (205 E. 42nd St., New York, NY 10017; phone: 800-800-8222 or 212-661-0311).

International Adventures (60 E. 42nd St., New York, NY 10165; phone: 212-599-0577).

Travac Tours and Charters (989 Ave. of the Americas, New York, NY 10018; phone: 800-872-8800 or 212-563-3303).

Unitravel (1177 N. Warson Rd., St. Louis, MO 63132; phone: 800-325-2222 or 314-569-0900).

LAST-MINUTE TRAVEL CLUBS For an annual fee, members receive information on imminent trips and other bargain travel opportunities. Despite the names of these clubs, you don't have to wait until literally the last minute to make travel plans.

Discount Travel International (114 Forest Ave., Suite 203, Narberth, PA 19072; phone: 215-668-7184).

Last Minute Travel (1249 Boylston St., Boston, MA 02215; phone: 800-LAST-MIN or 617-267-9800).

Moment's Notice (425 Madison Ave., New York, NY 10017; phone: 212-486-0500, -0501, -0502, or -0503).

Spur-of-the-Moment Cruises (411 N. Harbor Blvd., Suite 302, San Pedro, CA 90731; phone: 800-4-CRUISES in California; 800-343-1991 elsewhere in the US; or 310-521-1070).

Traveler's Advantage (3033 S. Parker Rd., Suite 900, Aurora, CO 80014; phone: 800-548-1116 or 800-835-8747).

Vacations to Go (1502 Augusta, Suite 415, Houston, TX 77057; phone: 713-974-2121 in Texas; 800-338-4962 elsewhere in the US).

Worldwide Discount Travel Club (1674 Meridian Ave., Miami Beach, FL 33139; phone: 305-534-2082).

GENERIC AIR TRAVEL These organizations operate much like an ordinary airline standby service, except that they offer seats on not one but several scheduled and charter airlines. One pioneer of generic flights is *Airhitch* (2790 Broadway, Suite 100, New York, NY 10025; phone: 212-864-2000).

BARTERED TRAVEL SOURCES Barter is a common means of exchange between travel suppliers. Bartered travel clubs such as *Travel World Leisure Club* (225 W. 34th St., Suite 909, New York, NY 10122; phone: 800-444-TWLC or 212-239-4855) offer discounts to members for an annual fee.

CONSUMER PROTECTION

Passengers with complaints who are not satisfied with the airline's response can contact the US Department of Transportation (DOT; Consumer Affairs Division, 400 7th St. SW, Room 10405, Washington, DC 20590; phone: 202-366-2220). If you have a complaint against a local travel service, contact the Irish tourist authorities. Also see *Fly Rights* (Publication #050-000-00513-5; US Government Printing Office, PO Box 371954, Pittsburgh, PA 15250-7954; phone: 202-783-3238).

Traveling by Ship

Your cruise fare usually includes all meals, recreational activities, and entertainment. Shore excursions are available at extra cost, and can be booked in advance or once you're on board. An important factor in the price of a cruise is the location and size of your cabin; for information on ships' layouts and facilities, consult the charts issued by the *Cruise Lines International Association* (*CLIA;* 500 Fifth Ave., Suite 1407, New York, NY 10110; phone: 212-921-0066).

Most cruise ships have a doctor on board, plus medical facilities. The US Public Health Service (PHS) also inspects all passenger vessels calling at US ports; for the most recent summary or a particular inspection report, write to Chief, Vessel Sanitation Program, National Center for Environmental Health (1015 N. America Way, Room 107, Miami, FL 33132; phone: 305-536-4307). For further information, consult *Ocean and Cruise News* (PO Box 92, Stamford, CT 06904; phone: 203-329-2787). And for a free listing of travel agencies specializing in cruises, contact the *National Association of Cruise Only Agencies* (*NACOA;* PO Box 7209, Freeport, NY 11520; phone: 516-378-8006). In addition to the companies listed below, a good source of information on inland waterway cruises is the Irish Republic's Office of Public Works, Waterways Division (51 St. Stephen's Green, Dublin 2, Ireland; phone: 1-613111). Numerous ferries link Ireland with Great Britain and the rest of Europe. Nearly all of them carry both passengers and cars, and most routes are in service year-round.

International Cruise Lines

Classical Cruises (132 E. 70th St., New York, NY 10021; phone: 800-252-7745 in the US; 800-252-7746 in Canada; or 212-794-3200).

Cunard (555 Fifth Ave., New York, NY 10017; phone: 800-5-CU-NARD or 800-221-4770).

Ocean Cruise Lines (6301 NW 5th Way, Suite 4000, Ft. Lauderdale, FL 33309; phone: 800-556-8850).

Princess Cruises (10100 Santa Monica Blvd., Los Angeles, CA 90067; phone: 800-421-0522).

Royal Viking Line (95 Merrick Way, Coral Gables, FL 33134; phone: 800-422-8000).

Seabourn Cruise Line (55 Francisco St., Suite 710, San Francisco, CA 94133; phone: 800-929-9595).

SeaQuest Cruises (600 Corporate Dr., Suite 410, Ft. Lauderdale, FL 33334; phone: 800-223-5688 or 305-772-7552). British Isles cruises.

Special Expeditions (720 Fifth Ave., New York, NY 10019; phone: 800-762-0003 or 212-765-7740).

Inland Waterway Cruise Companies

Bargain Boating, Morgantown Travel Service (PO Box 757, Morgantown, WV 26507-0757; phone: 800-637-0782 or 304-292-8471).

Blakes Vacations (4918 Dempster St., Skokie, IL 60077; phone: 708-982-0561 in Illinois; 800-628-8118 elsewhere in the US).

Le Boat (PO Box E, Maywood, NJ 07607; phone: 800-922-0291 or 201-342-1838).

Destination Ireland (250 W. 57th St., Suite 2511, New York, NY 10107; phone: 212-977-9629 in New York State; 800-832-1848 elsewhere in the US).

Shannon Bargelines (represented in the US by: *Cruise Company of Greenwich*, 31 Brookside Dr., Greenwich, CT 06830; phone: 800-825-0826 or 203-622-0203; *European Waterways*, 140 E. 56th St., Suite 4C, New York, NY 10022; phone: 800-438-4748 or 212-688-9538; and *Skipper Travel Services*, see below).

Skipper Travel Services (9029 Soquel Ave., Suite G, Santa Cruz, CA 95062; phone: 408-462-5333).

Ferry Companies

B & I Line and *Irish Ferries* (c/o *Lynott Tours*, 350 Fifth Ave., Suite 2619, New York, NY 10118; phone: 212-760-0101 in New York State; 800-221-2474 elsewhere in the US).

Norse Irish Ferries and *Swansea Cork Car Ferries* (c/o *P & O European Ferries* — address below).

P & O European Ferries (Channel House, Channel View Rd., Dover, Kent CT17 9TJ, England; phone: 44-304-203388).

Sealink (c/o *BritRail Travel International,* 1500 Broadway, Suite 1000, New York, NY 10036-4015; phone: 212-575-2667).

Traveling by Train

In the **Irish Republic**, the government-owned *CIE (Córas Iompair Eireann, National Transport Company)* operates the railroads. Main rail routes radiate from Dublin to Belfast in Northern Ireland, and to Cork, Galway, Limerick, Sligo, Tralee, Waterford, Westport, and Wexford. There also are trains between Dublin and the ferry ports of Dún Laoghaire and Rosslare and between Rosslare and Limerick. Shannon Airport is connected by bus with Limerick, from which several trains run daily to Dublin and Cork.

Because of the relatively short distances between Irish cities, there is no need for sleeping cars on Irish trains, but on main routes there often is a dining car or some other kind of food service. The two classes of travel in the Irish Republic are called standard (second) and super-standard (first), but most routes have only standard class. Reservations usually are not necessary, except for travel on weekends or bank holidays. A round-trip ticket (called a "return" ticket) costs less than two one-way (or "single") tickets. Reduced-rate weekend fares and extended return tickets also are available.

In **Northern Ireland,** *Northern Ireland Railways* operates the following routes: Belfast to Londonderry via Ballymena and Coleraine; Belfast to Bangor; and Belfast to Larne. Travel is standard class only. As in the Republic, reservations generally are not required. Fares include round-trip, weekend return (available for *InterCity* trains only), and weekly tickets. Cross-border (Northern Ireland to Irish Republic) fares include a variety of daily and monthly round-trip excursions. Rail tickets can be bought in conjunction with a through ticket to Great Britain by ferry. Connections can be made at Larne Harbour for ferries to Stranraer and Cairnryan, Scotland, and at Belfast Harbour for ferries to Douglas on the Isle of Man and Stranraer, Scotland.

Irish rail passes include the BritIreland Pass, available from *BritRail* (1500 Broadway, Suite 1000, New York, NY 10036-4015; phone: 212-575-2667), and the Rambler Ticket, available from *CIE Tours International* (108 Ridgedale Ave., PO Box 2355, Morristown, NJ 07962-2355; phone: 800-CIE-TOUR or 201-292-3438) or *Rail Europe* (226-230 Westchester Ave., White Plains, NY 10604; phone: 800-438-7245). Other sources of rail passes for use in Northern Ireland include *NIR Travel Limited* (2830 Wellington Pl., Belfast BT1 6GE, Northern Ireland; phone: 232-230671; and Ferry Terminal, Larne Harbour, Larne BT40 1AW, Northern Ireland; phone: 574-270517) and *Ulsterbus* (10 Glengall St., Belfast BT12 5AH,

Northern Ireland; phone: 232-333000). A company offering packaged rail tours throughout Ireland is *Accent on Travel* (112 N. 5th St., Klamath Falls, OR 97601; phone: 503-885-7330 in Oregon; 800-347-0645 elsewhere in the US).

FURTHER INFORMATION

For information on train travel in the Irish Republic, contact *CIE Tours International* (address above), which provides a timetable of the main intercity train services. For information on train travel in Northern Ireland, contact the Northern Ireland Tourist Board (551 Fifth Ave., Suite 701, New York, NY 10176; phone: 212-922-0101).

Rail Europe's *Travel Guide* and various brochures on the Eurail system are available from *Rail Europe* (PO Box 10383, Stamford, CT 06904-2383) and from the *Rail Europe Distribution Centre* (PO Box 4000, Station A, Mississauga, Ontario L5A 9Z9, Canada). The *Thomas Cook European Timetable,* a compendium of European rail services, is available in bookstores and from the *Forsyth Travel Library* (PO Box 2975, Shawnee Mission, KS 66201-1375; phone: 800-367-7984 or 913-384-3440). Other useful resources include the *Eurail Guide,* by Kathryn Turpin and Marvin Saltzman (Eurail Guide Annuals, 27540 Pacific Coast Hwy., Malibu, CA 90265) and *Europe by Eurail,* by George Wright Ferguson (Globe Pequot Press, PO Box 833, Old Saybrook, CT 06475; phone: 203-395-0440).

> **NOTE** For security reasons, you cannot check baggage through to your destination either within or between the Republic and Northern Ireland, or between Ireland and Great Britain. Since you will have to keep all your luggage with you, travel light.

Traveling by Bus

A map of Ireland's bus routes is not much different from a road map; the network of express buses (called "coaches") — traveling long distances with few stops en route — is only slightly less extensive. Bus passes and other discount tickets and cards make travel by bus quite reasonable in Ireland. These can be purchased in advance in the US, or once you arrive in Ireland.

In the **Irish Republic,** *CIE,* which operates the trains, also runs the long-distance or provincial buses, and the city buses of Cork, Dublin, Galway, Limerick, and Waterford. In the US, the *Expressway Bus Timetable* of *CIE* routes in the Irish Republic is available from *CIE Tours International* (address above). Timetables, maps, information, and tickets are available at *CIE*'s main booking office (35 Lower Abbey St., Dublin 1, Ireland; phone: 1-771871) and at the Central Bus Station, or *Busáras* (Store St., Dublin 1, Ireland; phone: 1-366111). All long-distance buses leave from the Central Bus Station. *CIE* also operates a series of half-day or full-day tours by sightseeing bus from major cities.

In **Northern Ireland,** *Ulsterbus* operates all bus service. For information on routes, schedules, and fares, contact *Ulsterbus* (10 Glengall St., Belfast BT12 5HA, Northern Ireland; phone: 232-333000). Specify a region of interest or ask for the complete package of timetables.

Seats cannot be reserved on Irish buses — tickets are sold on a first-come, first-served basis at bus stations or (in towns where there are none) at local stores acting as ticket agents. The ticket usually is good only for that ride on that day. Toilet facilities are likely to be provided only on long-distance coach trips, and air conditioning or heating are the exceptions rather than the rule — particularly on rural routes. Bus passes and other discount tickets and cards are available in both the Republic and Northern Ireland and can be purchased both in the US and abroad.

Traveling by Car

Driving is the most flexible way to explore Ireland. To drive in either the Republic or Northern Ireland, a US citizen needs a valid US driver's license. Proof of liability insurance also is required and is a standard part of any car rental contract. (To be sure of having the appropriate coverage, let the rental staff know in advance about the national borders you plan to cross.) Most rental agencies in the Republic allow cars to be driven to Northern Ireland. Some also allow cars to be ferried to England and Scotland, but you must obtain an International Insurance Certificate (called a Green Card) to do so. A Green Card also is required if you plan to purchase and use a car abroad. You can obtain a Green Card in the US from your insurance agent or the *American Automobile Association (AAA)*.

The Irish drive on the left-hand side of the road and pass on the right, and the steering wheel is on the right-hand side of the car. Pictorial direction signs are standardized under the International Roadsign System and their meanings are indicated by their shapes: Triangular signs indicate danger; circular signs give instructions; and rectangular signs provide information.

Unlike most of Europe, distances are measured in miles in Northern Ireland. Speed limits are the same as in Great Britain: 70 mph on motorways (expressways) and dual carriageways (four-lane highways), 60 mph on single carriageways (dual-lane highways), and 30 mph in towns or built-up areas — unless otherwise indicated. In the Republic, distances are measured in both kilometers and miles; speed limits are 70 mph (approximately 113 kph) on highways, 60 mph (about 97 kph) on the open road, and 30 to 40 mph (48 to 64 kph) in towns.

Throughout Ireland, seat belts are compulsory for the driver and front seat passenger, and children under 12 must travel in the back seat. In some cities and towns honking is forbidden; flash your headlights instead. Pay particular attention to parking signs in large cities. If you park in a restricted zone, you may return to find one of the car's wheels "clamped," a procedure that renders your car inoperable and involves a tedious — and costly — process to get it freed.

MAPS

In the US, free maps can be obtained from Irish tourist offices. The best road maps for touring are available from Michelin Guides and Maps (PO Box 3305, Spartanburg, SC 29304-3305; phone: 803-599-0850 in South Carolina; 800-423-0485 elsewhere in the US). Useful maps published by the Irish government are available from the Ordnance Survey Office (Phoenix Park, County Dublin 8, Ireland; phone: 1-8-206100), the *Government Bookstore* (16 Arthur St., Belfast BT1 4GD, Northern Ireland; phone: 232-234488), and bookstores and newsstands in Ireland. The *AA Touring Map of Ireland* is published by Britain's *Automobile Association (AA;* Fanum House, Basing View, Basingstoke, Hampshire RG21 2EA, England; phone: 256-20123) and also can be ordered from the *British Travel Bookshop* (551 Fifth Ave., New York, NY 10176; phone: 800-448-3039 or 212-490-6688). HarperCollins-Bartholomew (12 Duncan St., Edinburgh EH9 1TA, Scotland; phone: 31-667-9341) publishes maps of Ireland, available in the US through Hammond, Inc. (515 Valley St., Maplewood, NJ 07040; phone: 201-763-6000). Freytag & Berndt maps cover most major destinations, and can be ordered from *Map Link* (25 E. Mason St., Suite 201, Santa Barbara, CA 93101; phone: 805-965-4402). The *American Automobile Association (AAA;* address below) provides several useful reference sources, including a map of Ireland and Great Britain, an overall planning map of Europe, the *Travel Guide to Europe,* and *Motoring in Europe*. Another invaluable guide, *Euroad: The Complete Guide to Motoring in Europe,* is available from VLE Ltd. (PO Box 444, Ft. Lee, NJ 07024; phone: 201-585-5080 or 212-580-8030).

AUTOMOBILE CLUBS AND BREAKDOWNS

To protect yourself in case of breakdowns while driving to and through Ireland, and for travel information and other benefits, consider joining a reputable automobile club. The largest of these is the *American Automobile Association (AAA;* 1000 AAA Dr., Heathrow, FL 32746-5063; phone: 407-444-7000). Before joining this or any other automobile club, check whether it has reciprocity with Irish clubs such as the *Automobile Association (AA;* Fanum House, Basing View, Basingstoke, Hampshire RG21 2EA, England; phone: 256-20123; or 23 Rock Hill, Black Rock, County Dublin, Ireland; phone: 1-283355).

GASOLINE

Called "petrol" in Ireland, gasoline is sold primarily by the British or "imperial" gallon, which is 20% larger than the American gallon (1 imperial gallon equals about 1.2 US gallons). Due to the ongoing metric conversion, gasoline also may be sold by the liter (approximately 3.7 liters to 1 US gallon). In both Northern Ireland and the Republic, leaded, unleaded, and diesel fuel are available.

RENTING A CAR

You can rent a car through a travel agent or international rental firm before leaving home, or from a local company once in Ireland. Reserve in advance.

Most car rental companies require a credit card, although some will accept a substantial cash deposit. The minimum age to rent a car is set by the company; some impose special conditions on drivers above a certain age. Electing to pay for collision damage waiver (CDW) protection will add to the cost of renting a car, but releases you from financial liability for the vehicle being rented. Additional costs include drop-off charges or one-way service fees. One way to keep down the cost of car rentals is to deal with a car rental consolidator, such as *Connex International* (phone: 800-333-3949 or 914-739-0066).

Car Rental Companies

Auto Europe (phone: 800-223-5555).

Avis (phone: 800-331-1084).

Budget (phone: 800-472-3325).

Dollar Rent A Car (known in Europe as *Eurodollar Rent A Car;* phone: 800-800-4000).

Europe by Car (phone: 212-581-3040 in New York State; 800-223-1516 elsewhere in the US).

European Car Reservations (phone: 800-535-3303).

Foremost Euro-Car (phone: 800-272-3299).

Hertz (phone: 800-654-3001).

Kemwel Group (phone: 800-678-0678).

Meier's World Travel (phone: 800-937-0700).

National (known in Europe as *Europcar;* phone: 800-CAR-EUROPE).

Thrifty (phone: 800-367-2277).

Package Tours

A package is a collection of travel services that can be purchased in a single transaction. Its principal advantages are convenience and economy — the cost is usually lower than that of the same services bought separately. Tour programs generally can be divided into two categories: escorted or locally hosted (with a set itinerary) and independent (usually more flexible).

When considering a package tour, read the brochure *carefully* to determine what is included and other conditions. Check the company's record with the Better Business Bureau. The *United States Tour Operators Association* (*USTOA;* 211 E. 51st St., Suite 12B, New York, NY 10022; phone: 212-944-5727) also can be helpful in determining a package tour operator's reliability. As with charter flights, always make your check out to the company's escrow account.

Many tour operators offer packages focused on special interests such as the arts, nature study, sports, and other recreations. *All Adventure Travel* (PO Box 4307, Boulder, CO 80306; phone: 800-537-4025 or 303-499-1981) represents such specialized packagers; some also are listed in the *Specialty Travel Index* (305 San Anselmo Ave., Suite 313, San Anselmo, CA 94960; phone: 415-459-4900 in California; 800-442-4922 elsewhere in the US).

Package Tour Operators

Abercrombie & Kent (1520 Kensington Rd., Oak Brook, IL 60521; phone: 708-954-2944 in Illinois; 800-323-7308 elsewhere in the US).

Academic Travel Abroad (3210 Grace St. NW, Washington, DC 20007-3600; phone: 202-333-3355).

Adventure Golf Holidays (815 North Rd., Westfield, MA 01085; phone: 800-628-9655 or 413-568-2855).

Adventures in Golf (29 Valencia Dr., Nashua, NH 03062; phone: 603-882-8367).

Aer Lingus (122 E. 42nd St., New York, NY 10168; phone: 800-223-6537).

American Express Vacations (offices throughout the US; phone: 800-241-1700 or 404-368-5100).

Atlantic Golf (c/o *European Travel Management*, address below).

AutoVenture (425 Pike St., Suite 502, Seattle, WA 98101; phone: 800-426-7502 or 206-624-6033).

Brendan Tours (15137 Califa St., Van Nuys, CA 91411; phone: 800-421-8446 or 818-785-9696).

Brian Moore International Tours (116 Main St., Medway, MA 02053; phone: 800-982-2299 or 508-533-6683).

British Airways Holidays (phone: 800-AIRWAYS).

British Coastal Trails (California Plaza, 1001 B Ave., Suite 302, Coronado, CA 92118; phone: 800-473-1210 or 619-437-1211).

BritRail Travel International (1500 Broadway, New York, NY 10036; phone: 212-575-2667).

Caravan Tours (401 N. Michigan Ave., Chicago, IL 60611; phone: 800-CARAVAN or 312-321-9800).

Catholic Travel (4925 St. Elmo Ave., Bethesda, MD 20814; phone: 800-284-4681 or 301-654-4681).

Celtic International Tours (161 Central Ave., Albany, NY 12206; phone: 800-833-4373 or 518-463-5511).

Chieftain Tours (c/o *European Travel Management*, address below).

CIE Tours International (108 Ridgedale Ave., PO Box 2355, Morristown, NJ 07962-2355; phone: 800-CIE-TOUR or 201-292-3438).

Classic Adventures (PO Box 153, Hamlin, NY 14464-0153; phone: 800-777-8090 or 716-964-8488).

Delta's Dream Vacations (phone: 800-872-7786).

Destination Ireland (250 W. 57th St., Suite 2511, New York, NY 10107; phone: 212-977-9629 in New York State; 800-832-1848 elsewhere in the US).

Earthwatch (680 Mt. Auburn St., PO Box 403, Watertown, MA 02272; phone: 800-776-0188).

Easy Rider Tours (PO Box 1384, E. Arlington, MA 02174; phone: 800-488-8332 or 617-643-8332).

English Wanderer (13 Wellington Court, Spencers Wood, Reading RG7 1BN, England; phone: 44-734-882515; and 6 George St., Ferryhill, County Durham DL17 0DT, England; phone: 44-740-653169).

Equitour (PO Box 807, Dubois, WY 82513; phone: 307-455-3363 in Wyoming; 800-545-0019 elsewhere in the US).

European Travel Management (237 Post Rd. W., Westport, CT 06880; phone: 203-454-0090 in Connecticut; 800-992-7700 elsewhere in the US).

Extra Value Travel (683 S. Collier Blvd., Marco Island, FL 33937; phone: 800-336-4668 or 813-394-3384).

Fishing International (PO Box 2132, Santa Rosa, CA 95405; phone: 800-950-4242 or 707-539-3366).

FITS Equestrian (685 Lateen Rd., Solvang, CA 93463; phone: 805-688-9494).

Forum Travel International (91 Gregory La., Suite 21, Pleasant Hill, CA 94523; phone: 510-671-2900).

Frames Rickards (11 Herbrand St., London WC1N 1EX, England; phone: 44-71-837-3111; in the US, contact *Trophy Tours,* 1810 Glenville Dr., Suite 124, Richardson, TX 75081; phone: 800-527-2473 or 214-690-3875; or *California Parlor Car Tours,* 1101 Van Ness Ave., San Francisco, CA 94109; phone: 800-331-9259 or 415-474-7500).

Globus and Cosmos (5301 S. Federal Circle, Littleton, CO 80123; phone: 800-221-0090 or 800-556-5454).

Golf International (275 Madison Ave., New York, NY 10016; phone: 800-833-1389 or 212-986-9176).

Golfing Holidays (231 E. Millbrae Ave., Millbrae, CA 94030; phone: 800-652-7847 or 415-697-0230).

Golfpac (PO Box 940490, 901 N. Lake Destiny Dr., Suite 192, Maitland, FL 32794-0490; phone: 800-327-0878 or 407-660-8277).

Grasshopper Golf Tours (403 Hill Ave., Glen Ellyn, IL 60137; phone: 800-833-1389 or 708-858-1660).

The Hidden Ireland (PO Box 40034, Mobile, AL 36640-0034; phone: 800-868-4750 or 205-433-5465).

In Quest of the Classics (316 Mission Ave., Oceanside, CA 92054; phone: 800-227-1393 or 619-721-1123 in California; 800-221-5246 elsewhere in the US).

Insight International Tours (745 Atlantic Ave., Suite 720, Boston, MA 02111; phone: 800-582-8380 or 617-426-6666).

Ireland Golf Tours (251 E. 85th St., New York, NY 10028; phone: 800-346-5388 or 212-772-8220).

Irish American Cultural Institute (2115 Summit Ave., University of St. Thomas, St. Paul, MN 55105; phone: 800-232-ERIN or 612-962-6040).

Isle Inn Tours (113 S. Washington St., Alexandria, VA 22314; phone: 800-237-9376 or 703-739-2277).

ITC Golf Tours (4134 Atlantic Ave., Suite 205, Long Beach, CA 90807; phone: 800-257-4981 or 310-595-6905).

Lismore Tours (106 E. 31st St., New York, NY 10016; phone: 212-685-0100 in New York State; 800-547-6673 elsewhere in the US).

Lynott Tours (350 Fifth Ave., Suite 2619, New York, NY 10118; phone: 212-760-0101 in New York State; 800-221-2474 elsewhere in the US).

Marathon Tours (108 Main St., Charlestown, MA 02129; phone: 800-783-0024 or 617-242-7845).

Marsans International (19 W. 34th St., Suite 302, New York, NY 10001; phone: 800-777-9110 or 212-239-3880).

Matterhorn Travel Service (2450 Riva Rd., Annapolis, MD 21401; phone: 410-224-2230 in Maryland; 800-638-9150 elsewhere in the US).

Maupintour (PO Box 807, Lawrence, KS 66044; phone: 800-255-4266 or 913-843-1211).

Olson Travelworld (970 W. 190th St., Suite 425, Torrance, CA 90502; phone: 800-421-2255 or 310-354-2600).

O'Mara Travel (c/o STS Travel, 795 Franklin Ave., Franklin Lakes, NJ 07417; phone: 800-752-6787 or 201-891-4143).

Owenoak International (3 Parklands Dr., Darien, CT 06820; phone: 800-426-4498 or 203-655-2531).

Perry Golf (8302 Dunwoodie Pl., Suite 305, Atlanta, GA 30350; phone: 800-344-5257 or 404-641-9696).

Scottish Golf Holidays (9403 Kenwood Rd., Cincinnati, OH 45242; phone: 800-284-8884 or 513-984-0414).

Showcase Ireland (586 Roma Court, Naples, FL 33963; phone: 800-654-6527 or 813-591-3447).

Take-A-Guide (11 Uxbridge St., London W8 7TQ, England; phone: 800-825-4946 in the US).

Trafalgar Tours (11 E. 26th St., Suite 1300, New York, NY 10010-1402; phone: 800-854-0103 or 212-689-8977).

Travcoa (PO Box 2630, Newport Beach, CA 92658; phone: 800-992-2004 in California; 800-992-2003 elsewhere in the US; or 710-476-2800).

Travel Concepts (62 Commonwealth Ave., Suite 3, Boston, MA 02116; phone: 617-266-8450).

Travent International (PO Box 305, Waterbury Center, VT 05677-0305; phone: 800-325-3009).

TWA Getaway Vacations (phone: 800-GETAWAY).

Value Holidays (10224 N. Port Washington Rd., Mequon, WI 53092; phone: 800-558-6850).

Voyagers International (PO Box 915, Ithaca, NY 14851; phone: 800-633-0299 or 607-257-3091).

Wilderness Travel (801 Allston Way, Berkeley, CA 94710; phone: 800-368-2794 or 510-548-0420).

Insurance

The first person with whom you should discuss travel insurance is your own insurance broker. You may discover that the insurance you already carry protects you adequately while traveling and that you need little additional coverage. If you charge travel services, the credit card company also may provide some insurance coverage (and other safeguards).

Types of Travel Insurance

Baggage and personal effects insurance: Protects your bags and their contents in case of damage or theft anytime during your travels.

Personal accident and sickness insurance: Covers cases of illness, injury, or death in an accident while traveling.

Trip cancellation and interruption insurance: Guarantees a refund if you must cancel a trip; may reimburse you for the extra travel costs incurred in catching up with a tour or traveling home early.

Default and/or bankruptcy insurance: Provides coverage in the event of default and/or bankruptcy on the part of the tour operator, airline, or other travel supplier.

Flight insurance: Covers accidental injury or death while flying.

Automobile insurance: Provides collision, theft, property damage, and personal liability protection while driving your own or a rented car.

Combination policies: Include any or all of the above.

Disabled Travelers

Make travel arrangements well in advance. Specify to all services involved the nature of your disability to determine if there are accommodations and facilities that meet your needs. Regularly revised hotel and restaurant guides, such as the *Michelin Red Guide to Ireland* (Michelin Guides and Maps, Box 3305, Spartanburg, SC 29304-3305; phone: 803-599-0850 in South Carolina; 800-423-0485 elsewhere in the US), use a symbol of access (person in a wheelchair) to point out accommodations suitable for wheelchair-bound guests.

Organizations

ACCENT on Living (PO Box 700, Bloomington, IL 61702; phone: 309-378-2961).

Access: The Foundation for Accessibility by the Disabled (PO Box 356, Malverne, NY 11565; phone: 516-887-5798).

American Foundation for the Blind (15 W. 16th St., New York, NY 10011; phone: 800-232-5463 or 212-620-2147).

Disability Action Office (2 Annadale Ave., Belfast BT7 3UR, Northern Ireland; phone: 44-232-491011).

Disability Federation of Ireland (2 Sandyford, Office Park, Dublin 18, Ireland; phone: 1-353-295-9344).

Holiday Care Service (2 Old Bank Chambers, Station Rd., Horley, Surrey RH6 9HW, England; phone: 44-293-774535).

Information Center for Individuals with Disabilities (Ft. Point Pl., 1st Floor, 27-43 Wormwood St., Boston, MA 02210; phone: 800-462-5015 in Massachusetts; 617-727-5540 or 617-727-5541 elsewhere in the US; TDD: 617-345-9743).

Mobility International USA (*MIUSA;* PO Box 3551, Eugene, OR 97403; phone: 503-343-1284, both voice and TDD; main office: 228 Borough High St., London SE1 1JX, England; phone: 44-71-403-5688).

National Rehabilitation Board (24-25 Clyde Rd., Dublin 4, Ireland; phone: 1-684181 or 1-689618).

National Rehabilitation Information Center (8455 Colesville Rd., Suite 935, Silver Spring, MD 20910; phone: 301-588-9284).

Paralyzed Veterans of America (*PVA;* PVA/ATTS Program, 801 18th St. NW, Washington, DC 20006; phone: 202-872-1300 in Washington, DC; 800-424-8200 elsewhere in the US).

Royal Association for Disability and Rehabilitation (*RADAR;* 25 Mortimer St., London W1N 8AB, England; phone: 44-71-637-5400).

Society for the Advancement of Travel for the Handicapped (*SATH;* 347 Fifth Ave., Suite 610, New York, NY 10016; phone: 212-447-7284).

Travel Information Service (MossRehab Hospital, 1200 W. Tabor Rd., Philadelphia, PA 19141-3099; phone: 215-456-9600; TDD: 215-456-9602).

Tripscope (The Courtyard, Evelyn Rd., London W4 5JL, England; phone: 44-81-994-9294).

Publications

Access Travel: A Guide to the Accessibility of Airport Terminals (Consumer Information Center, Dept. 578Z, Pueblo, CO 81009; phone: 719-948-3334).

Accommodation Guide for Disabled Persons (The Irish Tourist Board, 757 3rd Ave., New York, NY 10017; phone: 212-418-0800).

Air Transportation of Handicapped Persons (Publication #AC-120-32; US Department of Transportation, Distribution Unit, Publications Section, M-443-2, 400 7th St. SW, Washington, DC 20590).

The Diabetic Traveler (PO Box 8223 RW, Stamford, CT 06905; phone: 203-327-5832).

Directory of Travel Agencies for the Disabled and *Travel for the Disabled,* both by Helen Hecker (Twin Peaks Press, PO Box 129, Vancouver, WA 98666; phone: 800-637-CALM or 206-694-2462).

The Disabled Tourist in Northern Ireland: Things to See, Places to Stay (*Disability Action Office* — address above — and the Northern Ireland Tourist Board, 551 Fifth Ave., Suite 701, New York, NY 10176; phone: 212-922-0101).

Guide to Traveling with Arthritis (Upjohn Company, PO Box 989, Dearborn, MI 48121).

The Handicapped Driver's Mobility Guide (*American Automobile Association,* 1000 AAA Dr., Heathrow, FL 32746; phone: 407-444-7000).

Handicapped Travel Newsletter (PO Box 269, Athens, TX 75751; phone: 903-677-1260).

Handi-Travel: A Resource Book for Disabled and Elderly Travellers, by Cinnie Noble (*Canadian Rehabilitation Council for the Disabled,* 45 Sheppard Ave. E., Suite 801, Toronto, Ontario M2N 5W9, Canada; phone: 416-250-7490, both voice and TDD).

Incapacitated Passengers Air Travel Guide (*International Air Transport Association,* Publications Sales Department, 2000 Peel St., Montreal, Quebec H3A 2R4, Canada; phone: 514-844-6311).

Ticket to Safe Travel (*American Diabetes Association,* 1660 Duke St., Alexandria, VA 22314; phone: 800-232-3472 or 703-549-1500).

Travel for the Patient with Chronic Obstructive Pulmonary Disease (Dr. Harold Silver, 1601 18th St. NW, Washington, DC 20009; phone: 202-667-0134).

Travel Tips for Hearing-Impaired People (*American Academy of Otolaryngology,* 1 Prince St., Alexandria, VA 22314; phone: 703-836-4444).

Travel Tips for People with Arthritis (*Arthritis Foundation,* 1314 Spring St. NW, Atlanta, GA 30309; phone: 800-283-7800 or 404-872-7100).

Traveling Like Everybody Else: A Practical Guide for Disabled Travelers, by Jacqueline Freedman and Susan Gersten (Modan Publishing, PO Box 1202, Bellmore, NY 11710; phone: 516-679-1380).

Where to Stay in Northern Ireland (*Disability Action Office,* address above).

Package Tour Operators

Accessible Journeys (35 W. Sellers Ave., Ridley Park, PA 19078; phone: 215-521-0339).

Accessible Tours/Directions Unlimited (Lois Bonnani, 720 N. Bedford Rd., Bedford Hills, NY 10507; phone: 800-533-5343 or 914-241-1700).

Beehive Business and Leisure Travel (1130 W. Center St., N. Salt Lake, UT 84054; phone: 800-777-5727 or 801-292-4445).

Classic Travel Service (8 W. 40th St., New York, NY 10018; phone: 212-869-2560 in New York State; 800-247-0909 elsewhere in the US).

Dialysis at Sea Cruises (611 Barry Pl., Indian Rocks Beach, FL 34635; phone: 800-775-1333 or 813-596-4614).

Evergreen Travel Service (4114 198th St. SW, Suite 13, Lynnwood, WA 98036-6742; phone: 800-435-2288 or 206-776-1184).

Flying Wheels Travel (143 W. Bridge St., PO Box 382, Owatonna, MN 55060; phone: 800-535-6790 or 507-451-5005).

Good Neighbor Travel Service (124 S. Main St., Viroqua, WI 54665; phone: 608-637-2128).

The Guided Tour (7900 Old York Rd., Suite 114B, Elkins Park, PA 19117-2339; phone: 800-783-5841 or 215-782-1370).

Hinsdale Travel (201 E. Ogden Ave., Hinsdale, IL 60521; phone: 708-325-1335 or 708-469-7349).

MedEscort International (ABE International Airport, PO Box 8766, Allentown, PA 18105; phone: 800-255-7182 or 215-791-3111).

Prestige World Travel (5710-X High Point Rd., Greensboro, NC 27407; phone: 800-476-7737 or 919-292-6690).

Sprout (893 Amsterdam Ave., New York, NY 10025; phone: 212-222-9575).

Weston Travel Agency (134 N. Cass Ave., PO Box 1050, Westmont, IL 60559; phone: 708-968-2513 in Illinois; 800-633-3725 elsewhere in the US).

Single Travelers

The travel industry is not very fair to people who vacation by themselves—they often end up paying more than those traveling in pairs. Services catering to singles match travel companions, offer travel arrangements with shared accommodations, and provide useful information and discounts. Also consult publications such as *Going Solo* (Doerfer Communications, PO Box 123, Apalachicola, FL 32329; phone: 904-653-8848) and *Traveling on Your Own*, by Eleanor Berman (Random House, Order Dept., 400 Hahn Rd., Westminster, MD 21157; phone: 800-733-3000).

Organizations and Companies

Club Europa (802 W. Oregon St., Urbana, IL 61801; phone: 800-331-1882 or 217-344-5863).

Contiki Holidays (300 Plaza Alicante, Suite 900, Garden Grove, CA 92640; phone: 800-466-0610 or 714-740-0808).

Destination Ireland (250 W. 57th St., Suite 2511, New York, NY 10107; phone: 212-977-9629 in New York State; 800-832-1848 elsewhere in the US).

Gallivanting (515 E. 79th St., Suite 20F, New York, NY 10021; phone: 800-933-9699 or 212-988-0617).

Globus and Cosmos (5301 S. Federal Circle, Littleton, CO 80123; phone: 800-221-0090 or 800-556-5454).

Insight International Tours (745 Atlantic Ave., Boston, MA 02111; phone: 800-582-8380 or 617-482-2000).

Jane's International and Sophisticated Women Travelers (2603 Bath Ave., Brooklyn, NY 11214; phone: 718-266-2045).

Marion Smith Singles (611 Prescott Pl., N. Woodmere, NY 11581; phone: 516-791-4852, 516-791-4865, or 212-944-2112).

Partners-in-Travel (11660 Chenault St., Suite 119, Los Angeles, CA 90049; phone: 310-476-4869).

Singles in Motion (545 W. 236th St., Riverdale, NY 10463; phone: 718-884-4464).

Singleworld (401 Theodore Fremd Ave., Rye, NY 10580; phone: 800-223-6490 or 914-967-3334).

Solo Flights (63 High Noon Rd., Weston, CT 06883; phone: 203-226-9993).

Suddenly Singles Tours (161 Dreiser Loop, Bronx, NY 10475; phone: 718-379-8800 in New York City; 800-859-8396 elsewhere in the US).

Travel Companion Exchange (PO Box 833, Amityville, NY 11701; phone: 516-454-0880).

Travel Companions (Atrium Financial Center, 1515 N. Federal Hwy., Suite 300, Boca Raton, FL 33432; phone: 800-383-7211 or 407-393-6448).

Travel in Two's (239 N. Broadway, Suite 3, N. Tarrytown, NY 10591; phone: 914-631-8301 in New York State; 800-692-5252 elsewhere in the US).

Older Travelers

Special discounts and more free time are just two factors that have given older travelers a chance to see the world at affordable prices. Many travel suppliers offer senior discounts — sometimes only to members of certain senior citizen organizations, which provide other benefits. Prepare your itinerary with one eye on your own physical condition and the other on a topographical map, and remember that it's easy to overdo when traveling.

Publications

Going Abroad: 101 Tips for Mature Travelers (*Grand Circle Travel,* 347 Congress St., Boston, MA 02210; phone: 800-221-2610 or 617-350-7500).

The Mature Traveler (GEM Publishing Group, PO Box 50820, Reno, NV 89513-0820; phone: 702-786-7419).

Take a Camel to Lunch and Other Adventures for Mature Travelers, by Nancy O'Connell (Bristol Publishing Enterprises, PO Box 1737, San Leandro, CA 94577; phone: 510-895-4461 in California; 800-346-4889 elsewhere in the US).

Travel Tips for Older Americans (Publication #044-000-02270-2; Superintendent of Documents, US Government Printing Office, PO Box 371954, Pittsburgh, PA 15250-7954; phone: 202-783-3238).

Unbelievably Good Deals & Great Adventures That You Absolutely Can't Get Unless You're Over 50, by Joan Rattner Heilman (Contemporary Books, 180 N. Michigan Ave., Chicago, IL 60601; phone: 312-782-9181).

Organizations

American Association of Retired Persons (*AARP;* 601 E St. NW, Washington, DC 20049; phone: 202-434-2277).

Golden Companions (PO Box 754, Pullman, WA 99163-0754; phone: 208-858-2183).

Mature Outlook (Customer Service Center, 6001 N. Clark St., Chicago, IL 60660; phone: 800-336-6330).

National Council of Senior Citizens (1331 F St. NW, Washington, DC 20004; phone: 202-347-8800).

Package Tour Operators

Elderhostel (PO Box 1959, Wakefield, MA 01880-5959; phone: 617-426-7788).

Evergreen Travel Service (4114 198th St. SW, Suite 13, Lynnwood, WA 98036-6742; phone: 800-435-2288 or 206-776-1184).

Gadabout Tours (700 E. Tahquitz Canyon Way, Palm Springs, CA 92262; phone: 800-952-5068 or 619-325-5556).

Grand Circle Travel (347 Congress St., Boston, MA 02210; phone: 800-221-2610 or 617-350-7500).

Grandtravel (6900 Wisconsin Ave., Suite 706, Chevy Chase, MD 20815; phone: 800-247-7651 or 301-986-0790).

Insight International Tours (745 Atlantic Ave., Suite 720, Boston, MA 02111; phone: 800-582-8380 or 617-482-2000).

Interhostel (UNH Division of Continuing Education, 6 Garrison Ave., Durham, NH 03824; phone: 800-733-9753 or 603-862-1147).

OmniTours (104 Wilmont Rd., Deerfield, IL 60015; phone: 800-962-0060 or 708-374-0088).

Saga International Holidays (222 Berkeley St., Boston, MA 02116; phone: 800-343-0273 or 617-262-2262).

Money Matters

The basic unit of currency in both Northern Ireland and the Republic is the **pound** — the **British pound sterling** in Northern Ireland and the **Irish pound** (or **punt**) in the Republic — which is divided into 100 **pence.** In Northern Ireland, there are £1, 50p, 20p, 10p, 5p, 2p, and 1p coins. (You also may occasionally find shillings and 2-shilling coins — equal to 5p and 10p, respectively — leftovers of the pre-decimal currency system.) Paper money is issued in denominations of £100, £50, £20, £10, and £5. In the

Republic, coin denominations are £1, 50p, 20p, 10p, 5p, 2p, and 1p, and paper money is issued in IR£100, IR£50, IR£20, IR£10, and IR£5. The currencies of Northern Ireland (British currency) and the Republic of Ireland are not interchangeable, and each has a different rate of exchange with the US dollar.

Exchange rates are posted in international newspapers such as the *International Herald Tribune.* Foreign currency information and related services are provided by banks and companies such as *Thomas Cook Foreign Exchange* (for the nearest location, call 800-621-0666 or 312-236-0042); *Harold Reuter and Company* (200 Park Ave., Suite 332E, New York, NY 10166; phone: 212-661-0826); and *Ruesch International* (for the nearest location, call 800-424-2923 or 202-408-1200). In Ireland, you will find the official rate of exchange posted in banks, airports, money exchange houses, hotels, and some shops. Since you will get more pounds for your US dollars at banks and money exchanges, don't change more than $10 for local currency at other commercial establishments. Ask how much commission you're being charged and the exchange rate, and don't buy money on the black market (it may be counterfeit). Estimate your needs carefully; if you overbuy, you lose twice — buying and selling back.

TRAVELER'S CHECKS AND CREDIT CARDS

It's wise to carry traveler's checks while on the road, since they are replaceable if stolen or lost. You can buy traveler's checks at banks and some are available by mail or phone. Although most major credit cards enjoy wide domestic and international acceptance, not every hotel, restaurant, or shop in Ireland accepts all (or in some cases any) credit cards. When making purchases with a credit card, note that the rate of exchange depends on when the charge is processed; most credit card companies charge a 1% fee for converting foreign currency charges. Keep a separate list of all traveler's checks (noting those that you have cashed) and the names and numbers of your credit cards. Both traveler's check and credit card companies have international numbers to call for information or in the event of loss or theft.

CASH MACHINES

Automated teller machines (ATMs) are increasingly common worldwide. Most banks participate in one of the international ATM networks; cardholders can withdraw cash from any machine in the same network using either a "bank" card or, in some cases, a credit card. At the time of this writing, most ATMs belong to the *CIRRUS* or *PLUS* network. For further information, ask at your bank branch.

SENDING MONEY ABROAD

Should the need arise, it is possible to have money sent to you via the services provided by *American Express* (*MoneyGram;* phone: 800-926-9400 or 800-666-3997 for information; 800-866-8800 for money transfers) or *Western Union Financial Services* (phone: 800-325-4176). If you are down to your last cent and have no other way to obtain cash, the nearest US Consulate will let you call home to set these matters in motion.

Accommodations

For specific information on hotels and other selected accommodations, see *Best in Town* in THE CITIES and *Checking In* in DIRECTIONS. The Irish Tourist Board's annual *Accommodation Guide* details regularly inspected accommodations that are registered with the tourist board. Hotels, guesthouses, and other accommodations in Northern Ireland are listed in the annual *Where to Stay* guide, available from the Northern Ireland Tourist Board.

BED AND BREAKFAST ESTABLISHMENTS

Commonly known as B&Bs, these are a staple of the lodging scene in Ireland and range from humble country cottages to elegant manor houses. The homes listed in the Irish Tourist Board's annual *Farm Holidays in Ireland* guide consist of extra rooms in private homes that have been modified to meet the tourist board's inspection standards. The illustrated *Town and Country Homes* guide, published by the *Town and Country Homes Association* and distributed by the Irish Tourist Board, also provides detailed information on B&B-type accommodations. For information on B&Bs in Northern Ireland, see the "Approved Accommodation" and "Farm & Country Houses" headings in the *Where to Stay* guide mentioned above, as well as *Farm & Country Holidays,* both available from the Northern Ireland Tourist Board.

RENTAL OPTIONS

An attractive accommodations alternative for the visitor content to stay in one spot is to rent one of the numerous properties available throughout Ireland. For a family or group, the per-person cost can be reasonable. To have your pick of the properties available, make inquiries at least 6 months in advance.

The Irish Tourist Board publishes *Self Catering,* a region-by-region guide to properties for rent that meet the tourist board's standards. *Irish Cottage Holiday Homes,* a supplement dedicated to thatch-roofed cottage rentals alone, is contained in this guide and can also be ordered separately. For information on rentals in Northern Ireland, see the Northern Ireland Tourist Board's information bulletin on self-catering or the "Self-Catering Accommodation" section of *Where to Stay.* The *Worldwide Home Rental Guide* (369 Montezuma, Suite 297, Santa Fe, NM 87501; phone: 505-984-7080) lists rental properties and managing agencies.

Rental Property Agents

At Home Abroad (405 E. 56th St., Suite 6H, New York, NY 10022-2466; phone: 212-421-9165).

Castles, Cottages and Flats (7 Faneuil Hall Marketplace, Boston, MA 02109; phone: 617-742-6030).

> **Heritage of Ireland** (22 Railroad St., Great Barrington, MA 01230; phone: 413-528-6610).
>
> **Hideaways International** (PO Box 4433, Portsmouth, NH 03802-4433; phone: 800-843-4433 or 603-430-4433).
>
> **The Independent Traveller** (Thorverton, Exeter EX5 5NT, England; phone: 392-860807).
>
> **Rent a Vacation Everywhere** (*RAVE;* 383 Park Ave., Rochester, NY 14607; phone: 716-256-0760).
>
> **Sterling Tours** (2707 Congress St., Suite 2G, San Diego, CA 92110; phone: 800-727-4359).
>
> **Villas International** (605 Market St., Suite 510, San Francisco, CA 94105; phone: 800-221-2260 or 415-281-0910).

HOME EXCHANGES

For comfortable, reasonable living quarters with amenities that no hotel could possibly offer, consider trading homes with someone abroad. The following companies provide information on exchanges:

> **Home Base Holidays** (7 Park Ave., London N13 5PG, England; phone: 44-81-886-8752).
>
> **Intervac US/International Home Exchange** (PO Box 590504, San Francisco, CA 94159; phone: 800-756-HOME or 415-435-3497).
>
> **Loan-A-Home** (2 Park La., Apt. 6E, Mt. Vernon, NY 10552; phone: 914-664-7640).
>
> **Vacation Exchange Club** (PO Box 650, Key West, FL 33041; phone: 800-638-3841 or 305-294-3720).
>
> **Worldwide Home Exchange Club** (138 Brompton Rd., London SW3 1HY, England; phone: 44-71-589-6055; or 806 Brantford Ave., Silver Spring, MD 20904; phone: 301-680-8950).

HOME STAYS

The *United States Servas Committee* (11 John St., Room 407, New York, NY 10038; phone: 212-267-0252) maintains a list of hosts throughout the world willing to accommodate visitors free of charge. The aim of this nonprofit cultural program is to promote international understanding and peace, and *Servas* emphasizes that member travelers should be interested mainly in their hosts, not in sightseeing, during their stays. Another organization, *In the English Manner* (PO Box 936, Alamo, CA 94507; phone: 510-935-7065 in California; 800-422-0799 elsewhere in the US), specializes in home stays in Great Britain, but also arranges stays with Irish families (mainly in the Republic).

Time Zones

Ireland is in the Greenwich Mean Time zone, which means that the time in Ireland is 5 hours later than it is in east coast US cities. Like most western European nations, Ireland moves its clocks ahead an hour in the spring and back an hour in the fall, corresponding to daylight saving time, although the exact dates of the changes are different from those observed in the US. Irish timetables use a 24-hour clock to denote arrival and departure times, which means that hours are expressed sequentially from 1 AM.

Business Hours

Most businesses in Ireland are open weekdays from 9 AM to 5 or 5:30 PM. Shops follow roughly the same schedule, staying open until 5:30 or 6 PM on weekdays, and usually opening on Saturdays as well. In small towns and villages, some shops may close for an hour at lunchtime, and on at least 1 weekday they close at 1 PM. Some stores in Dublin may skip the early closing and simply not open on Mondays; others may close completely or early on Saturdays. Larger stores in shopping centers stay open until 8 or 9 PM at least 1 day a week (usually on Thursdays, but sometimes also on Fridays).

Banks in Northern Ireland are open weekdays from 10 AM to 3:30 PM. In the Irish Republic, banking hours are from 10 or 10:30 AM to 3 PM (or 5 PM in some cities). In both Northern Ireland and the Republic, bank branches at major airports are open 7 days a week.

Holidays

In Ireland, the public holidays this year are as follows:

Republic of Ireland
New Year's Day (January 1)
St. Patrick's Day (March 17)
Good Friday (April 1)
Easter Monday (April 4)
June Holiday (June 6)
August Bank Holiday (August 1)
October Holiday (October 31)
Christmas Day (December 25)
St. Stephen's Day (December 26)

Northern Ireland
New Year's Day (January 1)
St. Patrick's Day (March 17)
Good Friday (April 1)
Easter Monday (April 4)
May Day (May 2)
Spring Holiday (May 30)
Orange Day or *Battle of the Boyne Holiday* (July 11)

Summer Bank Holiday (August 29)
Christmas Day (December 25)
Boxing Day (December 26)

Mail

There are post offices in almost every city, town, and hamlet in Ireland, as well as in many train stations and airports. In Northern Ireland, post offices are open weekdays from 9 AM to 5:30 PM; major post offices in large cities also are open on Saturdays from 9 AM to 12:30 PM. In the Republic, post offices usually are open weekdays from 9 AM to 5 PM; the main post office in Dublin also is open on Saturday mornings. Stamps are sold at post offices, authorized tobacconists, shops, and hotels. Letters can be mailed in letter boxes on the street — red in Northern Ireland, green in the Republic — but it is better to mail them (and certainly packages) directly from post offices.

Delivery from Ireland can be slow — to speed up the process, use express mail (called *Swift Post* in Ireland) and air mail. Important letters should be sent by registered mail or via one of the international courier services, such as *Federal Express* or *DHL Worldwide Express*.

You can have mail sent to you care of your hotel (marked "Guest Mail, Hold for Arrival") or to a post office (the address should include *Post Restante* — the Irish equivalent of "General Delivery"). *American Express* offices also will hold mail for customers ("c/o Client Letter Service"); information is provided in the pamphlet *American Express Travelers' Companion*. US Embassies and Consulates abroad will hold mail for US citizens *only* in emergency situations.

Telephone

Direct dialing within Ireland, to other European countries, and overseas is possible in both Northern Ireland and the Republic, but note that the number of digits in Irish phone numbers may vary. The procedure for calling both Northern Ireland and the Republic from the US is to dial 011 (the international access code) + the country code + the city code + the local number. (The country code for Northern Ireland — as for the rest of the United Kingdom — is 44; the country code for the Irish Republic is 353.) The procedure for making a direct call from Ireland to the US is as follows: From Northern Ireland, dial 010 (the international access code) + 1 (the US country code) + the area code + the local number; from the Irish Republic, dial 00 (the international access code) + 1 (the US country code) + the area code + the local number. Calls between the Irish Republic and Northern Ireland are not dialed like other international calls: To make a call from the Republic to Northern Ireland, dial 08 (a special access code)

+ the city code + the local number; to make a call from Northern Ireland to the Republic, dial 010 (the international access code) + 353 (the country code for the Irish Republic) + the city code + the local number. To call between cities, either within the Irish Republic or within Northern Ireland, dial 0 + the city code + the local number. For calls within the same city code coverage area, just dial the local number.

Public telephones are widely available. Although the majority of Irish pay phones still take coins, phones that take specially designated phone cards are increasingly common. Phone cards are sold at post offices, transportation and other commercial centers, and at some shops.

Long-distance telephone services that help you avoid the surcharges that hotels routinely add to phone bills are provided by *American Telephone and Telegraph* (*AT&T Communications,* International Information Service, 635 Grant St., Pittsburgh, PA 15219; phone: 800-874-4000), *MCI* (323 3rd St. SE, Cedar Rapids, IA 52401; phone: 800-444-3333), *Metromedia Communications Corp.* (1 International Center, 100 NE Loop 410, San Antonio, TX 78216; phone: 800-275-0200), and *Sprint* (offices throughout the US; phone: 800-877-4000). Some hotels still may charge a fee for line usage.

Also useful are the *AT&T 800 Travel Directory* (available at *AT&T Phone Centers* or by calling 800-426-8686), the *Toll-Free Travel & Vacation Information Directory* (Pilot Books, 103 Cooper St., Babylon, NY 11702; phone: 516-422-2225), and *The Phone Booklet* (*Scott American Corporation,* PO Box 88, W. Redding, CT 06896; phone: 203-938-2955).

Important Phone Numbers

In the Irish Republic

Local operator and information: 10
International operator: 114 (a local operator also can connect you)
Emergency assistance: 999

In Northern Ireland

Local operator and information: 100
International operator: 100 (for a local operator who will connect you)
Emergency assistance: 999

Electricity

Like most other European countries, both Northern Ireland and the Irish Republic run on 220-volt, 50-cycle alternating current (AC). Travelers from the US will need electrical converters to operate the appliances they use at home, or dual-voltage appliances, which can be switched from one voltage standard to another. (Some large tourist hotels may offer 110-volt current or may have converters available.) You also will need a plug adapter set to deal with the different plug configurations found in Ireland.

Staying Healthy

For information on current health conditions, call the Centers for Disease Control and Prevention's *International Health Requirements and Recommendations Information Hotline:* 404-332-4559.

Travelers to Ireland — and to Western Europe in general — do not face the same health risks entailed in traveling to many other destinations around the world. Tap water generally is clean and potable throughout the country, although in rural areas, the water supply may not be thoroughly purified. Ask if the water is meant for drinking, but if you're at all unsure, bottled water is readily available in stores. You also should avoid drinking water from freshwater streams, rivers, or pools, as they may be contaminated. Milk is pasteurized throughout Ireland, and dairy products are safe to eat, as are fresh fruit, meat, poultry, and fish.

Ireland has some good beaches, but it's important to remember that the sea can be treacherous. When you are swimming, be careful of the undertow (a current running back down the beach after a wave has washed ashore), which can knock you down, and riptides (currents running against the tide), which can pull you out to sea. If you see a shark, swim away quietly and smoothly. Also beware of eels and Portuguese man-of-war (and other jellyfish).

In Northern Ireland, the United Kingdom's National Health Service (NHS) provides free medical care to US travelers *only* in hospital accident and emergency wards and for the diagnosis and treatment of certain communicable diseases. In the Irish Republic, the General Medicine Service (GMS) requires travelers from the US to pay for all treatment, even in emergencies.

Ask at your hotel for the house physician or for help in reaching a doctor or contact the US Consulate. There should be no problem finding a 24-hour drugstore ("chemist") in any major Irish city. Chemists who close post in the window the addresses of the nearest all-night drugstore or the evening's on-call pharmacy (night duty may rotate among pharmacies in some areas). A call to the emergency room of the local hospital also may produce this information.

In an emergency: Go directly to the emergency room ("casualty department") of the nearest hospital, dial the emergency number given above, or call an operator for assistance. Note that in some areas (particularly in the Republic) night emergency service may rotate among hospitals, so call ahead to find out which one is on duty.

Additional Resources

International Association of Medical Assistance to Travelers (*IAMAT;* 417 Center St., Lewiston, NY 14092; phone: 716-754-4883).

International Health Care Service (440 E. 69th St., New York, NY 10021; phone: 212-746-1601).

International SOS Assistance (PO Box 11568, Philadelphia, PA 19116; phone: 800-523-8930 or 215-244-1500).

Medic Alert Foundation (2323 Colorado Ave., Turlock, CA 95380; phone: 800-ID-ALERT or 209-668-3333).

TravMed (PO Box 10623, Baltimore, MD 21285-0623; phone: 800-732-5309 or 410-296-5225).

Consular Services

The American Services section of the US Consulate is a vital source of assistance and advice for US citizens abroad. If you are injured or become seriously ill, the Consulate can direct you to sources of medical attention and notify your relatives. If you become involved in a dispute that could lead to legal action, the Consulate is the place to turn. In cases of natural disasters or civil unrest, Consulates handle the evacuation of US citizens if necessary.

In the Irish Republic, the US Embassy is located at 42 Elgin Rd., Ballsbridge, Dublin 4, Ireland (phone: 1-688777). In Northern Ireland, the US Consulate is at Queens House, 14 Queen St., Belfast BT1 6EQ, Northern Ireland (phone: 232-328239).

The US State Department operates a 24-hour *Citizens' Emergency Center* travel advisory hotline (phone: 202-647-5225). **In an emergency, call 202-647-4000 and ask for the duty officer.**

Entry Requirements and Customs Regulations

ENTERING IRELAND

The only document a US citizen needs to enter Northern Ireland or the Irish Republic, or to re-enter the US, is a valid US passport. As a general rule, a US passport entitles a visitor to remain in Northern Ireland for up to 6 months and in the Irish Republic for up to 3 months.

In Northern Ireland, visas are required for study, residency, or work, and are good for up to 1 year. US citizens should inquire at the British Embassy or the nearest British Consulate well in advance of a proposed trip. Proof of substantial means of independent financial support during the stay is pertinent to the acceptance of any long-term–stay application.

In the Irish Republic, visas for study, residency, or work are no longer required. Instead, the following procedures apply: To study in Ireland, you must have an acceptance letter and/or proof of registration from the school; to work, you must obtain a work permit from your employer prior to your arrival in Ireland. Permits for study, residency, or work are valid for 90 days, after which time you must re-register and show proof of financial independence to the appropriate authorities.

You are allowed to enter Northern Ireland with the following duty-free: 200 cigarettes or 50 cigars, up to 2 liters of wine and 1 liter of hard liquor, 2 fluid ounces of perfume, 9 fluid ounces of cologne, and items designated as gifts valued at less than £32 (about $50 at press time) for adults or £16 (about $25) for children 16 and under. The Irish Republic permits the following items: A combination of cigars and/or cigarettes not to exceed 200, 2 liters of wine and 1 liter of hard liquor, 2 fluid ounces of perfume, a quarter liter (approximately 7.25 fluid ounces) of cologne, and items designated as gifts and valued at less than IR£32 (about $50) for adults or IR£16 (about $25) for children 16 and under.

RETURNING TO THE US

You must declare to the US Customs official at the point of entry everything you have acquired in Ireland. The standard duty-free allowance for US citizens is $400; if your trip is shorter than 48 continuous hours, or you have been out of the US within 30 days, it is cut to $25. Families traveling together may make a joint declaration. Antiques (at least 100 years old) and paintings or drawings done entirely by hand are duty-free.

A flat 10% duty is assessed on the next $1,000 worth of merchandise; additional items are taxed at a variety of rates (see *Tariff Schedules of the United States* in a library or any US Customs Service office). With the exception of gifts valued at $50 or less sent directly to the recipient, items shipped home are dutiable. Some articles are duty-free only up to certain limits. The $400 allowance includes 1 carton of (200) cigarettes, 100 cigars (not Cuban), and 1 liter of liquor or wine (for those over 21); the $25 allowance includes 10 cigars, 50 cigarettes, and 4 ounces of perfume. To avoid paying duty unnecessarily, before your trip, register the serial numbers of any expensive equipment you are bringing along with US Customs.

Forbidden imports include articles made of the furs or hides of animals on the endangered species list. In addition, archeological finds or other original artifacts may not be taken out of Northern Ireland without the permission of the Department of Trade and Industry (Export Licensing, Kingsgate House, 66-74 Victoria St., London SW1E 6SW, England; phone: 44-71-215-8086). You also can contact the Customs Department in Belfast (H. M. Customs and Excise, Customs House, Belfast 1, Northern Ireland; phone: 232-234466). Similarly, historical documents or cultural objects over 100 years of age cannot be taken out of the Irish Republic without written permission from the Department of Taoiseach (Arts and Cultural Section, Government Buildings, Upper Merrion St., Dublin 2, Ireland; phone: 1-689333).

For further information, consult *Know Before You Go; International Mail Imports; Travelers' Tips on Bringing Food, Plant, and Animal Products into the United States; Importing a Car; GSP and the Traveler; Pocket Hints; Currency Reporting;* and *Pets, Wildlife, US Customs;* all available from the US Customs Service (PO Box 7407, Washington, DC 20044). For tape-recorded information on travel-related topics, call 202-927-2095 from any touch-tone phone.

DUTY-FREE SHOPS AND VALUE ADDED TAX Located in international airports, duty-free shops provide bargains on the purchase of foreign goods. But beware: Not all foreign goods are automatically less expensive. You *can* get a good deal on some items, but know what they cost elsewhere.

Value Added Tax (VAT) is a levy added to the purchase price of most goods and services, and for most purchases, visitors are entitled to a refund. For information about minimum purchase requirements and refund procedures, contact the Irish tourist authorities.

For Further Information

In the US, the **Irish Tourist Board** (for the Republic) and the **Northern Ireland Tourist Board** are the best sources of travel information. Both generally are open on weekdays, during normal business hours.

The Irish Tourist Board is located at 757 Third Ave., New York, NY 10017 (phone: 212-418-0800). The Northern Ireland Tourist Board is located at 551 Fifth Ave., Suite 701, New York, NY 10176 (phone: 212-922-0101).

The Cities

Belfast

As the capital of Northern Ireland, Belfast has been making international headlines for many years. Since 1969, the city has received more than its share of attention because of political, religious, and economic upheaval, as well as terrorist activity. Although the most recent episodes have been directed toward specific targets in the city center, tourists should be aware of increased measures to foil such violent attacks: A security check on vehicles approaching Belfast International Airport is usual, and cars entering the city center may have to undergo a quick inspection (the trunk is opened). Shoppers may be subject to a parcel inspection when entering stores, as well.

For travelers trying to appreciate the origins of "the troubles," a look at Belfast's history proves invaluable. Belfast, or *Béal Feirste* in Irish, means "mouth of the Farset," a stream that flows into the River Lagan. It was the natural harbor and strategic defense position formed by the Lagan and Belfast Lough that prompted various marauders over the centuries — Anglo-Norman, Scottish, and Irish — to establish fortified strongholds or castles here. By the 16th century, the area was controlled by the O'Neills, Earls of nearby Tyrone. After the defeat of the great Irish chieftain Hugh O'Neill at Kinsale in 1601, the lands were confiscated by the English Crown. Under the so-called Plantation policy, which supplanted the native Irish with English and Scottish colonists, the area was given to Sir Arthur Chichester, Governor of Carrickfergus, by Elizabeth I. In 1613, Belfast was granted a charter of incorporation and was allowed two (Protestant) representatives to the British Parliament. In the years that followed, the Catholic Irish rose up in revolt several times, with no success; they suffered under harsh penal codes, which usurped their property, outlawed their religion, and denied their civil rights.

Soon after the revocation of the Edict of Nantes in France in 1685, Belfast was washed by a new wave of settlers — this time French Huguenots fleeing religious persecution. They brought with them improved weaving methods, which spurred the town's fledgling linen industry into rapid expansion throughout the 18th century. In addition to the linen industry, the development of rope making, engineering, tobacco, and sea trade boosted Belfast's economy, causing the town to double in size every 10 years throughout the 1700s. During this period, Roger Mulholland, a local architect, drew up a plan dividing the town into a grid of streets for construction and development. Along these avenues — Great Victoria, May, and Howard Streets — many elegant Georgian buildings were erected by Belfast's prosperous linen merchants.

In 1791, Wolfe Tone, the son of a Protestant Dublin tradesman who was inspired by the American and French revolutions and influenced by radical Belfast Presbyterians, formed the Society of United Irishmen in Belfast. Espousing social as well as political reforms, the society's goal was "to substitute the common name of Irishmen in place of the denominations of Protestant, Catholic, and Dissenter." As Belfast became a center of dissent against the British, the United Irishmen supported an effort by both Presbyterians and Catholics to rid Ireland of English rule. Uprisings in 1798 proved unsuccessful. But with the uprisings and Wolfe Tone's Belfast-born ideas of an Irish republic for all the Irish, the concept of a united Ireland took hold. Unfortunately, the idea collapsed under the weight of sectarianism soon after.

Economically, Belfast continued to flourish during the 19th century, aided by the Act of Union (which made Ireland part of Great Britain) and by the growth of its shipbuilding industry. Belfast was fancifully called the "Athens of the North" for its patronage of the arts, and most of its gracious architecture (designed by Sir Charles Lanyon) dates from this era. Unfortunately, the city's prosperity was not shared by all its citizens; the Irish Catholics were still excluded from representation in London, from decent housing, and sometimes even from employment.

In 1920, after a long and bloody struggle by the Irish for self-government, Britain enacted the Home Rule Bill, which established two new Parliaments — one each in Dublin and Belfast. In 1921, a treaty was signed that formally created an Irish Free State (the Republic of Ireland) consisting of 26 mostly southern counties and left the six northern counties to choose between union with the new republic or with Britain. The Protestant-dominated Belfast Parliament chose the latter course, and the new entity called Northern Ireland was born.

Today, Belfast, second in size on the Emerald Isle only to Dublin, is a sturdy, red brick, industrial city ringed by beautiful bluish-purple hills that shelter ancient castles and echo with Irish folklore. Although the city is bothered by continued high unemployment, a visit to downtown Belfast reveals few visual remnants of prior urban renewal projects or overt terrorist activity. Its basically prosperous appearance reflects the city's role as commercial and cultural capital of Northern Ireland. However, until the smoldering internecine conflicts are finally resolved, there will be shadow as well as sun in Belfast's future.

Belfast At-a-Glance

SEEING THE CITY

The best views of Belfast are from the top of Cave Hill, 2 miles north of the city. To the south is City Center (the Old City), dominated by the copper-domed City Hall in Donegall Square, to the west is Lough Neagh, the largest lake in Ireland. To the northeast, the towns of Carrickfergus, Holywood, and Bangor can be seen from the hill, and on a clear day the Isle of Man may be visible in the Irish Sea to the southeast.

SPECIAL PLACES

Many of Belfast Center's 18th-century streets have been converted to pedestrian walkways and shopping arcades, and automobiles are prohibited. This poses no problem to the tourist, as central Belfast is a compact area best seen on foot. Five walking tours are described in the *Belfast Civic Festival Trail* brochures available free at the Northern Ireland Tourist Board's Tourist Information Centre (TIC; see *Tourist Information* below).

CITY CENTER

CITY HALL A statue of Queen Victoria stands in front of this imposing pillared and corniced gray stone structure capped by a 173-foot-high copper dome. Completed in 1906, its interior is richly decorated in the elaborate Edwardian style with stained glass and marble. It is one of Ireland's most outstanding buildings. Free tours, which last about 45 minutes, are offered at 10:30 AM on Wednesdays, the only time the building is open to tourists. Reservations (best made a day ahead) are required; contact the information officer (phone: 320202, ext. 2227). Donegall Sq. S.

ST. MALACHY'S CHURCH This is a fine example of the lavish Gothic Roman Catholic churches built in Ireland during the 19th century. Especially remarkable is the fan-vaulted ceiling, virtually dripping with intricate plasterwork, similar to that found in Henry VII's Chapel at Westminster Abbey in London. 24 Alfred St. (phone: 321713).

ALBERT MEMORIAL Looking a little incongruous among parking lots and office buildings, this 116-foot memorial honoring Prince Albert, Queen Victoria's consort, is often called Belfast's Big Ben since it bears a striking resemblance to London's famous tower. This clock tower, however, has settled slightly to one side, which has also earned itself the nickname "Belfast's Leaning Tower." At the river end of High St.

CUSTOM HOUSE This squarish, solid-looking building was designed by the architect Sir Charles Lanyon in the richly corniced, somewhat grand Italianate style that was popular in Ireland in the mid-19th century. Sculptures of Britannia, Neptune, and Mercury decorate the pediment on the seaward side. Custom House Sq.

ST. ANNE'S CATHEDRAL Belfast's principal Anglican church, it took 86 years to build — from 1899 to 1985 — and therefore combines many architectural styles. It is distinguished by some fine Irish Romanesque carving and sculpture. Lower Donegall St. (phone: 328332).

ST. PETER'S CATHEDRAL Completed in 1866, this Roman Catholic church is noted for its soaring twin spires and a circular carving by the doorway depicting angels freeing St. Peter from prison. St. Peter's Sq.

FIRST PRESBYTERIAN CHURCH John Wesley preached here in 1789, 6 years after the church was completed. It has a lovely interior. Rosemary St.

PORT OF BELFAST Numerous ocean liners have been constructed or repaired here, and shipbuilding remains a primary occupation. The noted Harland & Wolff (H&W) shipyard grew from 2 acres in 1858 to 300 in the mid-20th century. Once the world's largest shipyard and long renowned for innovative ship design and sophisticated engine and hull construction, H&W today boasts the world's largest dry dock. On April 2, 1912, the *Titanic* set out from its H&W birthplace to Southampton, England, for her maiden transatlantic voyage. Because government defense contracts make them a potential terrorist target, the shipyards are no longer open to the public.

STORMONT A mile-long road leads uphill through this landscaped estate to the erstwhile Parliament House, once the seat of Northern Ireland's legislature, now a government office building. Two statues on the grounds remind visitors of Ulster's political reality. One, at the juncture of the approach avenues, is of Lord Carson, the Dublin lawyer who kept Belfast British during and after World War I; the other, in the main entrance hall of the Parliament building, is of Lord Craigavon, Northern Ireland's first prime minister, best known for his anti-Republican slogans "Not an inch" and "No surrender." The building is not open to the public, but is visible from the road. Upper Newtownards Rd., just east of the city.

BELFAST CASTLE Of relatively recent vintage (1870), this mansion — with its turrets, tower, gables, and ornate carving — is a fine example of the romantic Scottish baronial style imported to this area during the 17th-century Plantation period. Given to the city in 1934 by a former Mayor of Belfast, the castle has been extensively restored. It houses a restaurant offering a splendid view of the city. Antrim Rd., north of the city on Cave Hill (phone: 776925).

CAVE HILL About 2 miles north of the city, Cave Hill is a lovely afternoon's diversion. Stroll through the Hazelwood Gardens, climb to the craggy hill's summit (1,188 feet) and MacArt's Fort (an ancient earthwork), or visit the Belfast Zoo (see below). Easiest access is from the parking lot of Belfast Castle.

BELFAST ZOO Recently expanded and improved, the zoo features an African House, a sea lion pool, a penguin exhibit, and a large free-flight aviary. Renowned for its excellent climate for breeding and conservation, it has a visitors' center with audiovisual exhibits. There's also a restaurant. Open daily, April through September, from 10 AM to 5 PM; October through March from 10 AM to 3:30 PM. Admission charge. Take city bus routes 2, 3, 4, 5, or 6 from Donegall Square W., Antrim Rd. (phone: 776277).

QUEEN'S UNIVERSITY When founded in 1845, the school was associated with colleges in Galway and Cork; it became independent in 1909. The original red brick Tudor buildings, designed by Sir Charles Lanyon, are now only a fraction of the many structures that make up the university complex. The university hosts the *Belfast Festival at Queen's* each November (see *Special Events*). The *Queen's Music Society* holds free 45-minute lunchtime concerts each Thursday during the school year beginning at 1:15 PM sharp; concert programs and locations are posted at the main university gate. The *Queen's Film Theatre* (phone: 244857, evenings only) is open to the public. University Rd. (main university phone: 245133).

ULSTER MUSEUM Housed in a 1920s neo-classical building with a well-designed modern addition that stands right in the city's delightful Botanic Gardens (see *Extra Special,* below), this museum's collections are broad ranging: early Christian and medieval antiquities, including facsimiles of the 8th- and 9th-century *Book of Kells* and *Book of Armagh;* a superb group of contemporary paintings and sculpture; prehistoric artifacts including the only surviving pair of late Bronze Age trumpets that can still be played; a display of minerals and gemstones, including the largest group of quartz crystals in Britain and Ireland, a display of fluorescent and phosphorescent minerals in a darkened central vault, and a full-size cave; plus the fabulous collection of jewelry, coins, and other items recovered from the *Girona,* a galley of the Spanish Armada that went down off the Antrim Coast in 1588. The Living Sea exhibit abounds with realistic models of marine creatures, and the Dinosaur Show, a gallery designed with children in mind, features a near-complete skeleton of *Anatosaurus annecteus.* Open weekdays from 10 AM to 5 PM, Saturdays from 1 to 5 PM, and Sundays from 2 to 5 PM. No admission charge. Stranmillis Rd. (phone: 381251).

ULSTER FOLK AND TRANSPORT MUSEUM Created in 1958, this 136-acre, 19-building complex offers a glimpse of how Ulster folk lived back at the turn of the century. Townhouses, farmhouses, mills, a church, and schools were moved here, then furnished with the everyday objects of the appropriate period, and landscaped as they might have been originally. A farm from mid-Antrim has been reconstructed right down to the stone walls, hedges, and ditches around the fields. An assortment of galleries are filled with domestic and agricultural artifacts and vehicles used in Irish transport over the ages. In fact, the museum is the home of the finest and most comprehensive collection of vehicles in Ireland, with sleighs, elegant horse-drawn carriages, automobiles (including a De Lorean sports car prototype), and even a vertical-takeoff plane. (A collection of railway cars is kept in Belfast, on Witham Street, off the Lower Newtownards Road.) Open April through June, and September, weekdays 9:30 AM to 5 PM, Saturdays from 10:30 AM to 6 PM, and Sundays from noon to 6 PM; July through August, Mondays through Saturdays from 10:30 AM to 6 PM, and Sundays from noon to 6 PM; October through March, weekdays from 9:30 AM to 4 PM, weekends from 12:30 to 4:30 PM. Admission charge. Off Bangor Rd. in Cultra, 7 miles northeast of Belfast. Bangor buses depart from Oxford St. Station every half hour (phone: 428428).

| EXTRA SPECIAL | Between Queen's University and the *Ulster Museum* lie Belfast's charming Botanic Gardens. |

The showpiece of these 28 verdant acres is the Palm House, a famous Victorian-era Belfast landmark and one of the earliest examples of a curvilinear cast-iron glasshouse (greenhouse). Begun in 1839, it predates London's Kew Gardens conservatory. The colorful floral displays in the cool left wing, tropical right wing, and 37-foot-high center dome are open to the public year-round. From April through September, the Palm House is open weekdays from 10 AM to 5 PM, and on weekends and holidays from 2 to 5 PM; October through March, it's open weekdays from 10 AM to 4 PM, weekends and holidays from 2 to 4 PM. The rest of the Botanic Gardens are open daily from dawn to dusk. No admission charge. University Rd. (phone: 324902).

Sources and Resources

TOURIST INFORMATION

The Northern Ireland Tourist Board and Tourist Information Centre (St. Anne's Court, 59 North St.; phone: 246609; fax: 240960) offers information, maps, and leaflets, and sells books, postcards, stamps, posters, and slides of the area. The *Belfast City Council Reference Guide* and other informational publications are available at City Hall (Donegall Sq. S.), and *The Visitor's Guide to Northern Ireland* (Hunter Publishing; $18) by Rosemary Evans is available at bookshops. For help in tracing ancestral roots, contact the *Ulster Historical Foundation* (68 Balmoral Ave., Belfast BT9 6NY; phone: 681365).

LOCAL COVERAGE The *Belfast Telegraph,* the *Newsletter,* and the *Irish News* are all published daily. The *Belfast Telegraph* carries entertainment listings.

FOOD The Northern Ireland Tourist Board publishes a booklet, updated yearly, called *Where to Eat in Northern Ireland* that includes an extensive list of eating places in Belfast and throughout the province.

TELEPHONE The area code for Belfast and the immediate vicinity is 232. When calling from within Northern Ireland, dial 0232 before the local number.

GETTING AROUND

Walking is the best way to tour Belfast's inner core since it is off limits to private cars. Travel outside the city is possible by bus, car, or train.

AIRPORT Belfast International Airport is 19 miles northwest of the city, off M2 (phone: 8494-22888). Eight flights daily depart for and arrive from London on *British Airways' Super Shuttle. British Airways* also has frequent daily flights between Belfast and Glasgow, Scotland; Manchester and Birmingham, England; and Amsterdam, Holland. *Air France* has service between Belfast and Paris.

BUS Buses to the airport and points south depart from the *Ulsterbus Europa Travel Centre* (Great Victoria St.). Those to points north leave from the station on Oxford Street. For schedule information, call *Ulsterbus* (phone: 333000, 320011 for day tours).

CAR RENTAL Several car rental agencies are represented at Belfast International Airport, including *Avis* (173 Airport Rd.; phone: 8494-22333); *Hertz* (phone: 8494-22533); and *McCauslands* (phone: 8494-22022), which also has an office in the city (21-31 Grosvenor Rd.; phone: 333777). *Dan Dooley* (phone: 8494-52522) charges no drop-off fee for one-way rentals between the North and the Republic on rentals of more than 10 days.

SIGHTSEEING TOURS *Citybus* conducts 3½-hour tours of greater Belfast and Carrickfergus Castle at 1:30 PM, Tuesdays through Thursdays, in June through September. The colorful commentary provided by the drivers is a treat in itself. Highlights include city center landmarks, the Queen's University district, Stormont, and the Belfast Zoo. Departure is from Castle Place, outside the general post office. Other *Citybus* offerings include a parks and gardens tour, a tour of the historic buildings of North Down, and an evening Belfast architecture tour. Call for tour rates (phone: 246485, ext. 130).

TAXI There are taxi stands at the main bus and rail terminals and at City Hall. These taxis are the familiar old London-type black cabs and have a yellow disk on the windshield. Other taxis may not have meters, so passengers are advised to ask the fare to their destination before setting off. Don't be surprised if you are asked to share a cab when there is a long waiting line — it will cost you less. Or call *Fast Taxi* (phone: 458011), *Dial-A-Cab* (phone: 797777), *Able Taxi* (phone: 241999), or *Fon A Cab* (phone: 233333).

TRAIN The Belfast Central Station (East Bridge) provides service to all destinations in Northern Ireland and in the Republic. Trains to Larne for the car ferry to Stranraer, Scotland, leave from York Road Station (phone: 327525). A special *Rail-Link* bus runs frequently between the two stations, Mondays through Saturdays from 7:30 AM to 8:30 PM. For information on train schedules and fares call *Northern Ireland Railways* passenger services (phone: 230310).

SPECIAL EVENTS

Established more than 30 years ago, the *Belfast Festival at Queen's* is an extraordinary occasion not to be missed.

Belfast Festival at Queen's One of the two biggest cultural events in the United Kingdom (the other is the *Edinburgh Festival*), this November event has, since its beginnings in the early 1960s, created excitement on the cultural scene that even "the troubles" have not been able to undermine. Although it covers the entire spectrum of the arts, the emphasis traditionally has been on classical music. But the jazz and film programs are excellent, and folk and popular music are well represented, as is a spectrum of drama, opera, and ballet, with visiting companies from the Republic and the rest of Europe. Such luminaries as Cleo Laine and Dame Janet Baker, James Galway and Yehudi Menuhin, and Billy Connolly and Michael Palin have performed here. The setting is the Victorian campus of Queen's University; concerts are also presented in the *Grand Opera House,* the *Ulster Hall,* and the *Arts, Lyric,* and *Group* theaters (phone: for schedule information, 667687; to make reservations, 665577).

Also, the *Ulster Harp National,* Northern Ireland's most important steeplechase, is held at *Downpatrick Racecourse* (phone: 369-612054) in February. A boisterous parade commemorating the Battle of the Boyne — in which the Catholic King James II lost his throne to Protestant William III — marches through Belfast every July 12. It is often the occasion for much Protestant politicking and speech making. In late summer the city holds its *International Rose Trials* at Sir Thomas and Lady Dixon Park, an event that draws rose aficionados from around the world (call the tourist office for dates).

MUSEUMS

Belfast's major museums are listed under *Special Places*. In addition, the *Arts Council Gallery* features exhibits of contemporary Irish and international art. Closed Sundays. No admission charge. Bedford House, 56 Dublin Rd. (phone: 321402).

SHOPPING

The highlights of Belfast's shopping scene are china, crystal, linen, woolens, and antiques. The city's major stores are in a pedestrian shopping mall that encompasses several streets off Donegall Pass in the center of town. *Queen's Arcade,* although small, has a fine selection of shops. Nearby Howard Street (between Donegall Sq. W. and College Sq. E.) has the newer trendy boutiques. The *Castle Court* complex on Royal Street in the center of Belfast offers the city's latest selection of shops.

In addition, there's an antiques market with stalls on Donegall Pass in the university area on Saturdays from 9 AM to mid-afternoon. Some of the city's best antiques shops also can be found in this area. A few good bets include *Alexander the Grate* (128 Donegall Pass; phone: 232041), which sells antique fireplaces, and *Dara Antiques* (135 Donegall Pass; phone: 248144), featuring furniture, clocks, silver, and porcelain.

Handicrafts are displayed and sold at *Craftworks* (13 Linenhall St., 1 block from City Hall; phone: 236334), a centralized retail outlet for craftspeople from throughout the province. Also available here is *Crafts in Northern Ireland,* a free booklet with the names, addresses, and specialties of artisans in the six counties of Northern Ireland, as well as Belfast.

For last-minute gifts and souvenirs, the shops at Belfast International Airport sell favorite local food items: cheese, wheat bread, smoked salmon, and Old Bushmill's whiskey, as well as linen and crafts. Irish crafts and other local specialties also may be found in the following shops. Most stores in Belfast are closed on Sundays.

BELL GALLERY Paintings, mainly by Irish artists from the 19th century to the present. 13 Adelaide Pk. (phone: 662998).

HOGGS A large selection of Northern Ireland's Tyrone crystal, which is less expensive than Waterford and of comparable quality. There also is a variety of English china and figurines. Seconds sometimes are available. 10 Donegall Sq. W. (phone: 243898).

IRISH LINEN SHOP Fine linen goods. 46 Fountain Centre, College St. (phone: 322727).

JOHN AND CHARLOTTE LAMBE Eighteenth- and 19th-century furniture, paintings, and silver. 41 Shore Rd. (phone: 370761).

JOHNSTON'S UMBRELLA SHOP The place to buy Irish blackthorn walking sticks. 33 Ann St. (phone: 320729).

MARKS & SPENCER Northern Ireland's largest department store is known for its lamb's wool and Shetland sweaters. Men's woolen suits are of excellent quality and moderately priced. Credit cards are not accepted. 48 Donegall Pl. (phone: 235235).

SMYTH'S IRISH LINEN/SIMPSON BROS. Top-quality linen along with needlework and textile crafts. 14 Callender St. (phone: 322983).

TOM JONES Ireland's best crystal and England's finest china are sold at this elegantly designed shop. Two locations: 9 Wellington Pl. (phone: 325932) and in the downtown *Castlecourt* shopping complex (phone: 237475).

SPORTS AND FITNESS

FISHING Despite all the commercial shipping in and out of Belfast, fishing can be very good in Belfast Lough. It is best known for its coalfish, pollack, and whiting, but small skate are sometimes taken at Ballymaconnell Point, near Bangor, and it's worth trying for cod from the rocks around Blackhead Lighthouse. The area is best fished from a small boat with an outboard motor. The required game fishing licenses can be obtained from the Northern Ireland Tourist Board, tackle shops, or local hotels. There is no closed season in Northern Ireland. The nearest fishing boat charters are in Bangor; contact Brian Meharg (25 Holborn Ave., Bangor; phone: 247-455321). For additional details, see *Gone Fishing* in DIVERSIONS.

GOLF There are numerous 18-hole courses in the Belfast area, among them *Balmoral* (518 Lisburn Rd.; phone: 381514); *Malone* (240 Upper Malone Rd., Dunmurry; phone: 612758); *Helen's Bay* (Golf Rd., Helen's Bay; phone: 247-852815); *Fortwilliam* (Downview Ave.; phone: 370770); *Knock* (Summerfield, Dundonald; phone: 483251); *Belvoir Park* (73-75 Church Rd., Newtonbreda; phone: 491693); *Royal Belfast* (Craigavad, Holywood; phone: 428165); and *Bangor* (Broadway, Bangor; phone: 247-270922).

SAILING *Bangor Sailing School* offers boats for hire, instruction in cruising, and skippered sails around Lough Belfast. Contact John Irwin, 13 Gray's Hill Rd., Bangor, County Down (phone: 247-455967).

TENNIS Municipal courts abound in Northern Ireland; check local tourist information for locations. In addition, the *Culloden* hotel in nearby Holywood (see *Checking In*) is one of Northern Ireland's few first class hotels with tennis facilities. It has one all-weather court. Also try the tennis and squash courts at the *Maysfield Leisure Centre* (E. Bridge St.; phone: 241633).

THEATER

The performing arts know no boundaries and — as in the Irish Republic — theater is very much a way of life here. We begin with Belfast's finest theater.

CURTAIN CALL

Grand Opera House When architect Robert McKinstry first went into the deserted building of Belfast's *Grand Opera House and Cirque* in the summer of 1975, he found the house manager's black jacket still hanging on the back of his office door. In a drawer in the projection room lay a single copy of a pamphlet entitled *How to Emigrate*. But now the *Opera House* has come back to life. The brass rails that once reflected the footlights that illuminated Pavlova and the Divine Sarah (Bernhardt) glisten again, and the turn-of-the-century theater has been restored to its full plush and stucco glory. *Christmas* pantomimes share the bill with drama companies from all over Britain and Ireland; international orchestral, opera, and dance companies; and major popular entertainers. In July and early August, the house usually is dark. Great Victoria St. (phone: 249129 for recorded information; 241919 for advance booking).

Among the city's other theatrical venues is the *Lyric Players Theatre* (Ridgeway St.; phone: 381081), which features Irish drama, the classics, and new works. The *Arts Theatre* (41 Botanic Ave.; phone: 324936) and the *Old Museum Arts Centre* (College Sq.; phone: 235053) offer popular plays and musicals. The *Group Theatre* (Bedford St.; phone: 329685) presents mostly amateur theatricals, some of which are quite good.

MUSIC

The *Ulster Orchestra* gives concerts at *Ulster Hall* (30 Bedford St.; phone: 233240 for tickets). Jazz is featured at the *Europa* hotel (see *Checking In*) on Saturday nights, and at *Cutter's Wharf* (Lockview Rd., near the university; phone: 663388) during Sunday brunch.

NIGHTCLUBS AND NIGHTLIFE

Belfast's nightlife has improved dramatically, although many non-hotel bars still shutter at 11:30 PM. The *Paradise Lost* disco (phone: 330055) is located behind the *Europa* hotel. *Pips International* nightclub and restaurant (45 Dublin Rd.; phone: 233003) is open Monday though Saturday nights until 1 AM.

Best in Town

CHECKING IN

Belfast, like other Irish cities, offers a range of accommodations, from modern hotels to Victorian hostelries to cozy guesthouses. Expect to pay over $150 to $200 for a double room (including a full Irish breakfast, VAT, and service charge) in a hotel listed as expensive, between $100 and $150 in the moderate category, and $145 or less in an inexpensive place. All telephone numbers are in the 232 area code unless otherwise indicated.

For an unforgettable experience, we begin with our favorite hostelry in the Belfast area, followed by our cost and quality choices of hotels, listed by price category.

SPECIAL HAVEN

Culloden A splendid Scottish baronial structure on 12 acres of secluded gardens and woodlands, once a bishop's palace, this is possibly the most luxurious hotel in Northern Ireland. Its 94 handsomely decorated guestrooms are full of velvet and silk, and the lovely dining room and public areas are embellished with fine plasterwork ceilings, Louis XV chandeliers, paintings, and other beautiful antiques. The former bishop's chapel is now the bar. Belfast's most expensive hotel also has a pair of squash courts, table tennis, exercise equipment, a putting green, tennis, and croquet. 142 Bangor Rd., Holywood, 6 miles from downtown Belfast (phone: 425223; fax: 426777).

Dukes Situated in renovated buildings in a pleasant, tree-lined Victorian neighborhood near Queen's University, convenient to museums, the Botanic Gardens, galleries, and restaurants, and less than a mile from the city center, it offers the atmosphere of a small hotel with some of the amenities of larger properties. The 21 small, modern guestrooms have direct-dial phones in both bedrooms and bathrooms, cable TV and free movie channel, hair dryers, and tea/coffee makers. There's also a health club and sauna, a pleasant restaurant, and a lounge for lighter meals. 65 University Ave. (phone: 236666; fax: 237177).

Dunadry Inn Not far from the airport, just 12 miles from downtown Belfast, this atmospheric inn was a linen mill and then a paper mill in past lives. Beetling machines can be seen in the bar and old mill cottages provide the lodging space (67 rooms, all with private baths). 2 Islandreagh Dr., Dunadry, County Antrim (phone: 8494-32474; fax: 8494-33389).

Europa Damaged in the past by IRA bombings, most recently last year, this 200-room, high-rise hotel is one of the city's most centrally located. Its restaurants and bars serve fare from traditional Ulster breakfasts to post-theater refreshments. *Harper's Bar* is an English-style pub with live music nightly, except Sundays. Upstairs is an à la carte restaurant, which serves daily specialties in an elegant library-like atmosphere. Nonsmoking rooms are available. Great Victoria St. (phone: 327000; fax: 327800).

Wellington Park In the attractive Queen's University neighborhood, this modern building has 50 rooms and a restaurant. It's a good choice during the *Belfast Festival at Queen's*. 21 Malone Rd. (phone: 381111; fax: 665410).

MODERATE

Old Inn The thatch-roofed portion of this place was built about 1614, and smugglers were said to have used the inn until the close of the 18th century. Many handsome, old pieces of furniture are scattered throughout, and what the rooms lack in size they make up for in charm. The Old English Suite has twin brass four-poster beds, and the Azalea Suite has cupboard beds with drapes. All 33 rooms have private baths. In the back of the inn is a tea garden overlooking Crawfordsburn Glen. About 11 miles from Belfast just off the Bangor road, 15 Main St., Crawfordsburn (phone: 247-853255; fax: 247-852775).

Plaza Located in central Belfast, this 83-room establishment, opened in 1990, is situated near the shopping, cultural, and business hubs of the city. The small but pleasantly decorated rooms have private baths, cable TV, tea/coffee makers, and complimentary daily newspapers. Nonsmoking rooms are available. There's a business services center, a restaurant with wide-window views onto a bricked square, and a bar/lounge. 15 Brunswick St. (phone: 333555; 800-228-5151 from the US; fax: 232999).

Ash-Rowan Guest House This comfortable house on a quiet residential street is 3 blocks from the *Ulster Museum* and Queen's University, and within walking distance of restaurants, theaters, and shops. The 4 rooms have private baths. Breakfasts and dinners are prepared by the owners, who are former proprietors of an award-winning restaurant. 12 Windsor Rd. (phone: 661758; fax: 663227).

EATING OUT

Belfast has experienced a downtown restaurant boom. New eateries serving fare from Mexican to Mongolian have opened in the past few years. The average cost of a three-course meal for two, including VAT and 10% service charge (but not beverages), will be $50 or more at a restaurant listed as expensive, $35 to $50 at places described as moderate, and under $35 at eateries in the inexpensive category. In general, midday meals cost less than evening meals. Most Belfast hotels have their own dining rooms, and most pubs offer light, inexpensive lunches; some serve evening meals and/or pub grub. All telephone numbers are in the 232 area code unless otherwise indicated.

EXPENSIVE

Restaurant 44 Conveniently located next to *Ulster Hall,* this place, which has a British colonial tropical decor, is a good choice for an after-theater dinner. The specialty is fresh seafood, including such dishes as scallops in garlic, brill, lemon sole in ginger sauce, and fried mussels. There's a moderately priced wine bar annex called *Bananas.* Open weekdays for lunch and dinner; Saturdays for dinner only. Reservations necessary. Major credit cards accepted. 44 Bedford St. (phone: 244844).

Roscoff With a bright white modern atmosphere and an imaginative menu, this spot has burst onto the Belfast restaurant scene with outstanding success. Specialties include crispy duck *confit,* pork medallions, terrine of peaches, and French pastries. This one-Michelin-star restaurant offers a table d'hôte menu for lunch and dinner as well as à la carte choices. Open weekdays for lunch and dinner; Saturdays for dinner only. Reservations necessary. Major credit cards accepted. Lesley House, Shaftsbury Sq. (phone: 331532).

MODERATE

Nick's Warehouse Housed in a restored warehouse with pine floors and brick walls, this trendy French bistro-style wine bar serves homemade soups, appetizers, and cakes. A more formal restaurant is upstairs. Open weekdays for lunch and dinner. Reservations advised. Diners Club, MasterCard, and Visa accepted. 35-39 Hill St. (phone: 439690).

Saints and Scholars Small and cozy, with a conservatory section decorated with plants, this eatery features an eclectic menu: stir-fried vegetables, deep-fried brie, cassoulet. Open for lunch and dinner; dinner only on Sundays. Reservations necessary. Major credit cards accepted. 3 University St., in the Queen's University area (phone: 325137).

Strand Located in a brick row house near Queen's University, this popular spot is divided into intimate small rooms decorated with stained glass windows, detailed woodwork, and creative lighting. The excellent fare includes crabmeat, stuffed courgettes (zucchini), chicken roulade, and salmon. Open daily for lunch and dinner. Reservations necessary. Major credit cards accepted. 12 Stranmillis Rd. (phone: 682266).

INEXPENSIVE

Skandia Centrally located, this informal restaurant has extensive hours from early morning to after-theater supper. The menu features traditional dishes, and grills, salads, and sandwiches. Open daily for breakfast, lunch, and dinner; closed Sundays. Major credit cards accepted. 50 Howard St. (phone: 240239).

SHARING A PINT

It seems everywhere you look there's a pub to be explored. We begin with our Belfast favorite, followed by some other congenial spots.

HIGH SPIRITS

Crown Liquor Saloon This venerable, gaslit establishment on Great Victoria Street, opposite the *Europa* hotel and the *Grand Opera House,* has been extensively restored by the National Trust. The windows are stained glass, the floor is mosaic tile, the fireplace is stone, and all around are Victorian fancies — woodcarvings, glass mosaics, plasterwork curlicues, brocades, painted mirrors, and so much more that every nook and cranny seems filled with ornament. As for the snugs — where serious drinkers can hoist their pints in contented privacy — they are in the same good condition as when the place was built back in Victorian days. Open daily. 46 Great Victoria St. (phone: 325368).

Irish music can be heard at the *Errigle Inn* (320 Ormeau Rd.; phone: 641410), *Madden's* (74 Smithfield; phone: 244114), *Rotterdam* (54 Pilot St.; phone: 746021), *Duke of York* (11 Commercial St., off Lower Donegall St.; phone: 241062), *Front Page* on "newspaper row" (108 Donegall St.; phone: 324924), and *Kelly's Cellars* (30 Bank St.; phone: 324835). Also try *Drury Lane* (2 Amelia St.; phone: 238008), the *Beaten Docket* (48 Great Victoria St.; phone: 242986), and *Morning Star* (17 Pottinger's Entry; phone: 323976) for an old pub atmosphere. The *Queen's Bar* (Queen's Arcade; phone: 321347) is known locally for its tasty, good-value pub lunches. On Mondays through Saturdays, pub hours are 11:30 AM to 11 PM, with a half hour for "drinking up." A relaxation in licensing laws in Northern Ireland allows pubs to open on Sundays from 12:30 to 2:30 PM and from 7 to 10 PM. While many are taking advantage of the new rules, some publicans continue to observe the traditional Sabbath and remain closed on Sundays.

Cashel

The Rock of Cashel, with its spectacular grouping of historic ecclesiastical buildings, is one of Ireland's most striking landmarks and one of its most intriguing sights. Among the Irish, it was known as *Caiseal Mumhan,* "the stronghold of Munster" or "Cashel of the kings." For centuries the seat of the Munster kings, it also became the religious center of Ireland.

The small town of Cashel lies on the direct Dublin–Cork road and laps at the foot of the Rock on the south side. Approached from any direction, the 300-foot rocky outcrop — with its towers and battlements spiking out of the plain against the horizon — always jolts the vision and the imagination. Floodlit at night, it is spectacularly beautiful. The Rock of Cashel is no less than Ireland's Acropolis.

A warrior tribe called the Eoghanachta (which probably originated in the present-day Killarney area) arrived here about the 4th century and, after subjugating the original inhabitants, built their stronghold on the Rock and ruled for over 800 years.

During the 10th century, the fortress fell prey to Viking marauders, from whom it was rescued by the famous Brian Ború. Thereafter, the O'Briens — the descendants of Brian — held sway over Cashel and in 1101 made the magnanimous gesture of giving the Rock to the church. The Eoghanachta were at this time still lords of Cashel, although internecine warfare had reduced their status. Whatever they thought about the O'Briens' gesture, they obviously came to terms with it. The last of the Eoghanachta kings, Cormac, was responsible for the building of King Cormac's Chapel, the finest gem in the Rock's crown.

The Round Tower — the oldest of the structures on the Rock — has probably stood since the 10th century. Work on King Cormac's Chapel was begun in 1127. The large cathedral that now dominates the group of buildings was begun in the 13th century, some time after King Henry II of England had established — so he thought — his lordship over Ireland.

But things were not to be that simple for the English king and his successors. In the centuries of agitation that followed, Cashel had its share of "the troubles." The cathedral was burned down in 1495 by the tempestuous Earl of Kildare and again in 1647 by Cromwell's men, led by Lord Inchiquinn. All those inside, including 3,000 townspeople who had taken refuge there, perished.

After those terrible events, the buildings remained abandoned, except for a short period when they were partly repaired for Protestant use. They were abandoned completely in 1749, and the cathedral roof stripped. In 1874, the ruins were given to the state to be preserved as a national monument.

Compared with the importance and drama of the Rock, the town of

Cashel is subdued and modest. It has a population of only about 3,000 and consists of two thoroughfares, Main and Friar Streets, and a handful of side streets. Some 180,000 visitors come to the Rock in a season, but while tour buses draw up by the dozens, their comings and goings hardly impinge on the life of the town.

Cashel's real preoccupation is not the Rock and its great past, but horses. Cashel stands at the edge of the Golden Vale, a great sweep of fair and fertile lands bounded by the soft folds of Slievenamon, the Galtees, and the Knockmealdown Mountains. On these fertile acres graze some of Ireland's finest bloodstock. Up to a dozen stud farms or training stables are within 10 miles of the town. In this tiny town of two main streets there are four "turf accountants" (bookies) who provide a bit of excitement on local, national — and even international — race days.

Cashel At-a-Glance

SEEING THE CITY

To get the best view of the Rock from town, walk up Friar Street past both the Catholic church and the Protestant cathedral, and then look back. From here the Rock seems to sit on the roofs of the houses and shops. Guests at the *Cashel Palace* hotel (see *Checking In*), originally the bishop's palace, get the best view of all. A paved way known as the Bishop's Walk leads directly through the palace gardens to the gate of the Rock enclosure.

To see the town, ascend the Rock. Cashel is spread below, with its few modest 19th-century streets and handful of older buildings. Turn in the other direction and gaze over the miles of emerald grasslands that comprise the Golden Vale.

SPECIAL PLACES

ROCK OF CASHEL The Rock comprises, in chronological order, the Round Tower, King Cormac's Chapel, the cathedral, and the Hall of the Vicars Choral. Entrance is through the Hall of the Vicars Choral, which has been extensively renovated to create an exhibition area and visitors' center.

Hall of the Vicars Choral This complex of buildings is the most recent on the Rock, having been built in the 15th century to house the clergy of the cathedral. To the right of the entrance is a vaulted room in which various stone carvings and other local finds are displayed. Here, too, is the massive Cross of St. Patrick, which stood for 800 years outside on the Rock. For safety, it has been brought indoors, and a replica now stands outside. Tradition holds that the base of this cross was the coronation stone of the Kings of Munster. Upstairs is a restored dining hall with a minstrel gallery and kitchen, furnished with authentic 15th-century furniture.

Cathedral Outside, beyond the replica of the Cross of St. Patrick, is the doorway to the 13th-century cathedral, the largest of the buildings. It has a nave, a chancel, two transepts, a tower at the crossing, and a residential tower at the western end. Though roofless and much ruined, it offers interesting and attractive details, such as the fine arches of the center crossing and several tombs. Look for the humorous little carved heads peering from pillar tops and archways and for the tomb of Archbishop Miler Magrath, a cagey fellow who in the mid-17th century changed from Protestant to Catholic as politics dictated.

Round Tower Leave the cathedral by the doorway you entered, then walk to the right around the building to the Round Tower at the northeastern corner. As usual with such structures, its doorway is high above the ground because it was used as a refuge during attacks as well as a bell tower. The exact date of its construction is not known, but it was probably built in the late 10th century, certainly before the Rock was given to the church in 1101.

King Cormac's Chapel Continue to the right around the cathedral to the gem of the Rock — Cormac's Chapel. Even from a distance, this small, early 12th-century cathedral has a special glow; its warm-colored sandstone shows up golden against the cold gray limestone of the larger building. The chapel is regarded as the finest example of Irish Romanesque architecture. Remnants of paintings can just be discerned on the chancel walls, indicating that once the whole interior glowed with color. Attempts to preserve what's left of these frescoes, which are the only 12th-century paintings in Ireland, are ongoing. Unfortunately, visitors sometimes see more scaffolding than art. Note the superbly carved stone sarcophagus in which a crozier, now in the *National Museum* in Dublin, was found. The chapel was built in 1127, shortly after the Round Tower was completed. When the larger cathedral was begun more than a century later, it had to be carefully fitted between the two, which explains some of the odd connections and dislocations of line.

Buildings on the Rock are open daily 9:30 AM to 5:30 PM, mid-March to mid-June; 9 AM to 7:30 PM, mid-June through September; 10 AM to 4:30 PM, October through mid-March. Admission charge. Tours, which are about 45 minutes long, are generally conducted every hour on the hour. A 17-minute audiovisual presentation provides helpful background (phone: 61437).

BRÚ BORÚ Located at the foot of the Rock, this cultural center, a $3 million project developed under the auspices of the Society of Irish Musicians, opened in 1991. The attractive, modern complex is tucked unobtrusively at the foot of the Rock. The simple, but impressive theater inside was designed by Tomas Macanna, a former artistic director of the *Abbey Theatre* in Dublin. There is also an outdoor amphitheater. The resident *Brú Ború* group performs Irish music, song, and dance daily during summer (outdoors when possible) and winter (indoors). Tickets that include a traditional meal and a show are about $37; tickets for a show only are $9. A separate restaurant overlooks the Rock and serves traditional Irish fare. There is also a shop full of Tipperary crystal and other Irish goods, and a Heritage Centre with a computer linked to a national genealogical database that enables visitors to trace their Irish roots. Open daily from 9 AM to 5 PM in summers; from 9 AM to noon in winters. Admission charge for some performances (phone: 61122; fax: 62700).

HORE ABBEY The remains of this attractive abbey stand among the fields to the west of the Rock. It began as a Benedictine structure, but in 1272, when the local archbishop dreamed that the Benedictines were plotting to behead him, he banished them, replacing them with Cistercians from Mellifont Abbey in County Louth. The result, after various alterations, is the usual Cistercian plan (simple and utilitarian), except that here the cloisters lie on the north side. (Cloisters were usually on the south side so that monks could read and work warmed by the sun.) As it is not locked or guarded, visitors can stroll around the abbey at any time.

OLD PALACE First built in 1730 as the archbishop's "palace" and later the residence of the Protestant dean, the Old Palace is now the *Cashel Palace* hotel (see *Checking In*). It is a beautiful example of the Queen Anne style, with a fine hall, original paneling, and a red pine staircase. The gardens run from the back of the house to the slopes of the Rock, with a pathway known as the Bishop's Walk leading to the gate of the Rock enclosure. On the lawn are two sprawling mulberry trees, said to have been planted to celebrate Queen Anne's coronation in 1702. At the base of the Rock (phone: 61411).

CASHEL DIOCESAN LIBRARY (GPA-BOLTON LIBRARY) The library of Archbishop Bolton, who built the Old Palace (above) and who died in 1744, is now housed in the handsome Chapter House of the Protestant cathedral. Its treasures include 12th-century manuscripts, 15th-century printed books (incunabula), rare maps, and fine bindings. There is also an exhibition of books (including two leaves of a Caxton printing of Chaucer), manuscripts, and church silver. Most of the material relates to theological and historical themes. Open Mondays through Saturdays from 9:30 AM to 5:30 PM; Sundays from 2:30 to 5:30 PM. Closed December through February, and *Good Friday*. Admission charge. John St. (phone: 61232).

ST. DOMINIC'S ABBEY Now little more than a shell, this abbey, founded in 1243, was an important Dominican establishment in its day. Note the fine 13th-century window. To look inside the walls, get the key from the house adjacent to the abbey. The abbey is just below the Rock in the middle of Cashel.

| EXTRA SPECIAL | Ireland certainly has no shortage of ruined abbeys, their gray silhouettes standing

stark against the sky. But Holy Cross Abbey, on the shores of the River Suir, is among the country's most beautiful and best preserved. Founded in 1169 by Donal O'Brien, the King of Thomond, on the site of an earlier Benedictine property, the abbey came into possession of a fragment of the True Cross that Pope Pascal II had given to the founder's father, Donogh O'Brien, the grandson of none other than BrianBorú, in 1110. It has been a place of pilgrimage for centuries (the October pilgrimage still draws thousands). The glory of the abbey today is its church, which was reroofed with Irish oak and slate and otherwise restored for public worship beginning in 1971. It has magnificent stone carvings, lively Flamboyant traceries, an elaborately groined roof, and handsome windows and arches, along with one of the few wall paintings to be found in any Irish church. The chancel, with its ribbed vaulting and fine east window, is considered to be among the best examples of 15th-century architecture in Ireland. The cloisters are fairly well preserved, and there is a meditation garden by the river. The church proper is open daily year-round. A separate building provides facilities for pilgrims and visitors, including a souvenir shop (where an excellent booklet, *Holy Cross Abbey,* can be purchased), a tourist information center, an audiovisual center, and a museum. These facilities are open daily from 10 AM to 1 PM and 2 to 6 PM May through September (sometimes for a longer season, depending on traffic). Nine miles north on the Thurles road, R660 (phone: 504-43118).

Sources and Resources

TOURIST INFORMATION

The tourist board is in the Town Hall (Main St.; phone: 61333). It has information, maps, and leaflets — some free, others at nominal cost — and offers a reservation service, particularly useful for arranging on-the-spot bed and breakfast accommodations at local guesthouses. Open weekdays 10 AM to 6 PM from mid-March to early October.

LOCAL COVERAGE The *Nationalist,* which comes out on Thursdays, covers the Tipperary scene and contains a page focusing on people and events in Cashel. The *Tipperary Star* is another good weekly local newspaper. The tourist board, however, is probably the best source of information on activities and events.

TELEPHONE The area code for Cashel and the immediate vicinity is 62. When calling from within the Republic of Ireland, dial 062 before the local number.

GETTING AROUND

Cashel is a small town, best seen on foot.

BICYCLE The nearest bicycles to rent are available from *J. J. O'Carroll* (James St., Tipperary Town; phone: 51229) and at *Galtymore Adventure Holidays* (Cahir, County Tipperary; phone: 52-41314; fax: 52-41800). Most hotels will arrange for bicycle rentals.

BUS AND TRAIN Cashel is not on the railway network, but there is daily bus service to Dublin. There is also bus service to Cork City and to Waterford via Cahir. For more information, contact *CIE (Córas Iompair Eireann, National Transport Company)* in Dublin (phone: 1-78777) or the tourist board in Cashel.

CAR RENTAL There are no car rental agencies in town. It's best to pick up a car on your arrival in Ireland, usually at the airport in Shannon or Dublin, where all the major international and local rental companies are represented.

TAXI Taxis are unnecessary within the town, but to venture farther afield, there is a choice of three: *John Grogan* (phone: 61132), *Donal Feehan* (phone: 61088), or *Tom Devitt* (phone: 61030).

SPECIAL EVENTS

Cashel is a quiet town and has no celebrations beyond the standard holidays. But the town is horse-mad, and racing events at home and abroad bring the place to life. *Tipperary* racecourse (phone: 51000 or 51357), 18 miles away on N24, has a meet every week in summer, with the most important event taking place in July. For betting action, join the crowd at any of the four turf accountants (bookies) in town, especially on the days of the *Grand National* (April), *Cheltenham Gold Cup* (March), and the *Irish Derby* (late June). Check local listings for exact dates.

MUSEUMS

Apart from the *Hall of the Vicars Choral* on the Rock, there are two tiny, privately run museums in town. They pale in comparison to the Rock's buildings, however, and are likely to be of interest only to the most avid Irish history buffs.

SHOPPING

Most shops in Cashel are closed Sundays.

DAVEY ANTIQUES Mrs. Davey sometimes has old Belleek; her tiny shop is always interesting. Ladyswell St. (phone: 61267).

JOE BARRY ANTIQUES Another place to try your luck looking for old things. Bank Pl. (phone: 61319).

PÁDRAIG O MATHÚNA The shop/gallery of this master silversmith and enamelist is tucked inconspicuously into a corner almost behind Town Hall. Pádraig is a superb artist and craftsman, and his works have been featured in exhibitions in many countries. Items include unique silver and gold bowls, plaques, sculptures, and jewelry. Open usually from 9 AM to 6 PM. Ring the bell outside if the shop is closed. 98 Main St. (phone: 61741).

SARAH RYAN POTTERY Celtic themes and an engaging primitive look are characteristic of Ryan's work. A series of heads look like they descended from the ceiling of the cathedral on the Rock. Down a tiny road off Palmer's Hill, signposted off Ladyswell St. (phone: 61954).

SPORTS AND FITNESS

FISHING Good trout fishing is found on the lazy River Suir. The manager at the *Cashel Palace* hotel (phone: 61411) will make arrangements for hotel guests. Others should contact Frank Burke at Town Hall (phone: 61333).

FOX HUNTING County Tipperary is great hunt country. To join a fox hunt, contact Garrett Dooley in the village of New Inn, south of Cashel on N8 (phone: 52-62231), or Pierce Molony, secretary of the *Golden Vale Hunt* (*The Racecourse,* Thurles; phone: 504-22253). Either can make all the arrangements. Also see *Horsing Around* in DIVERSIONS.

THEATER

Folk theater, with traditional music, song, and dance, is offered every evening at *Brú Ború* (phone: 61122), a cultural center. Curtain at 8 PM; additional performances daily in summer, depending on demand. (See *Special Places.*)

MUSIC

In addition to the performances at *Brú Ború,* traditional Irish music can be heard at *Meaney's* (46 Main St.; phone: 62130), a venerable pub; weekends are the best time for music, but it's worth a stop mid-week as well. *O'Reilly's* (Main St.; phone: 61858) has a sing-along on Thursday evenings.

Best in Town

CHECKING IN

Cashel and its environs have a few excellent hotels. Otherwise the most reliable accommodations are the comfortable and homey bed and break-fast houses in and around town. Most are within walking distance of the town center, except perhaps for travelers carrying heavy baggage. The tourist board will make on-the-spot bookings (phone: 61333). In July or August, it is wise to make advance arrangements, either through the tourist board or directly with the establishment. Expect to pay over $85 to

$150 for two for accommodations classed as expensive, $50 to $85 for those listed as moderate, and less than $50 (sometimes far less) for inexpensive places. All telephone numbers are in the 62 area code unless otherwise indicated.

For an unforgettable experience, we begins with our Cashel favorites, followed by our cost and quality choices, listed by price category.

SPECIAL HAVENS

Cashel Palace A former Protestant archbishop's residence, this is now a "grand" hotel on a modest scale, with 20 bedrooms (one has a canopy bed, another a four-poster). Designed by Edward Lovett Pearce around 1730, it features fine gardens outside and beautiful paneling, columns, and a black marble mantelpiece in the lobby, one of the most gracious anywhere. The luxurious rooms include enormous suites and smaller beamed hideaways; fine period furnishings and attractive fabrics can be found throughout. There's a peat fire in the lobby on cold days. There also are 2 fine restaurants, the *Four Seasons* and *The Buttery* (see *Eating Out*). Open year-round. Main St. (phone: 61411; fax: 61521)

Dundrum House Built in 1730 on 2,400 acres, this gracious country manor has been extensively renovated and expanded by its present owners, Austin and Mary Crowe. The high ceilings, the ornate plasterwork, the carved mantelpieces, and the fine views over the tree-studded grounds make it a delightful place to stay. The manor house, a classic example of 18th-century Georgian architecture, features 55 guestrooms, all with private baths. Situated on wooded grounds where deer and red squirrels abound, it offers good trout fishing in the River Multeen (free for guests), horseback riding nearby, and an 18-hole golf course. The dining room (see *Eating Out*) gives guests an opportunity to sample some elegant Irish cooking. Open year-round. Located in Dundrum, 8 miles from Cashel on R505 (phone: 71116; fax: 71366).

EXPENSIVE

Rectory House This small, homey member of the Best Western chain is run by the Deegan family. Each of the 10 guestrooms has a private bath. Proprietor Paul Deegan prepares elegant meals (see *Eating Out*). Open March through November. Dundrum (phone: 71266; fax: 71115).

MODERATE

Bailey's of Cashel A friendly, family-run guesthouse in a Georgian townhouse. Some of the 8 guestrooms (all with private baths) look out on the Rock. Open year-round. Main St. (phone: 61937 or 62038).

INEXPENSIVE

Maryville Mary and Pat Duane look after guests solicitously in their comfortable, warm house in the center of town. There are 8 rooms, 3 with private baths.

The 13th-century walls of St. Dominic's Abbey adjoin the garden (phone: 61098).

Rahard Lodge Mrs. Foley's modern farmhouse and flowering gardens overlook the Rock. There are 8 guestrooms, 4 with private baths. Sheep nibble the surrounding lawn and green fields. Only a few minutes' walk from town (phone: 61052).

Thornbrook House Besides a pleasant rural setting, guests at Mrs. Kennedy's modern bed and breakfast establishment also enjoy peat fires, wide gardens, and a view of the Rock. There are 5 rooms, 3 with private baths. On the outskirts of town (phone: 61480).

EATING OUT

Cashel does not have a wide variety of dining places, but a few restaurants serve good food in congenial surroundings. In the listing below, expensive means $60 to $100 for two for dinner (excluding wine, drinks, and tips); and moderate, about $35 to $60. All telephone numbers are in the 62 area code unless otherwise indicated.

EXPENSIVE

The Buttery In the cellar of the fine old *Palace* hotel, with flagstone floors, stone walls, and lots of atmosphere, this is a lively and informal place to meet for food or drinks. It features a variety of flambéed dishes, and Irish specialties such as lamb stew and colcannon (mashed potatoes mixed with onions, cabbage, and thick cream). Open for lunch and dinner daily. Reservations advised. Major credit cards accepted. Main St. (phone: 61411).

Chez Hans This converted Anglican church, with pointed windows and an arched doorway, offers what the proprietor calls "honest French food with an Irish touch," such as lamb marinated in homegrown garden herbs and baked *en croûte*. Fish and shellfish also are specialties. Open for dinner only; closed Sundays, Mondays, and January. Reservations advised. MasterCard and Visa accepted. Next to the Rock (phone: 61177).

Dundrum House The dining room in the hotel of the same name offers delicious food in a gracious Georgian setting. Specialties include scallops served with their bright orange roe in a smoked salmon sauce, and Cashel blue cheese fritters. Presentation is elegant but unpretentious and the service is friendly. Sunday lunch is in the Irish tradition, featuring such simple, hearty fare as roast lamb or beef, and is popular with the locals. Open daily for dinner; lunch Sundays only. Reservations advised. Major credit cards accepted. Dundrum (phone: 71116; fax: 71366).

Four Seasons The main restaurant at the *Cashel Palace* hotel has a reputation for fine food. Try the Lobster Kathleen, with an Irish whiskey, cream, leek, and spring onion sauce. Open for dinner only; closed Sundays and Mondays. Reservations necessary. Major credit cards accepted. Main St. (phone: 61411).

MODERATE

Bailey's of Cashel Set in the basement of a Georgian house, this place specializes in traditional Irish dishes, superb homemade brown bread, and desserts. The "tourist menu" is an excellent value. Open daily for lunch (in summer) and dinner. Reservations advised. MasterCard and Visa accepted. Main St. (phone: 61937 or 62038).

Rectory House This charming old house has a Victorian-style dining room — a wonderful spot for a quiet, cozy, candlelit supper featuring Irish and French cuisine. The conservatory extension to the dining room is pleasant but not as cozy as the rest of the room. Open daily for dinner, March through November. Reservations advised. Major credit cards accepted. Dundrum (phone: 71266).

SHARING A PINT

The Buttery (in the *Palace* cellar; phone: 61411) and *Davern's* (20 Main St.; phone: 61121), across the road, are the obvious places for visitors to get a drink and a lunchtime snack. Also popular are *Brown's* (Main St.; no phone), a pub with lovely horse portraits; the *Golden Vale* (Dundrum St.; phone: 71218), a dance-hall pub with an Irish night every Monday; and the *Moor Lane Tavern* (Main St.; phone: 61719). Farther down the road toward Cork is *Meany's* (46 Main St.; phone: 62130), a little place with wood paneling, brass bars on the window, and a nice old-time air.

Cork City

The Irish Republic's second city is a bustling, zesty, highly individual place, quite different from Dublin in appearance and atmosphere. What it lacks in the capital's Georgian uniformity it makes up for with visual variety, mixing the romance of mock-Gothic silhouettes with the moderation and proportion of the classical style.

The making of Cork was the River Lee, which flows not just through but in and around the city as it approaches its great estuary. In its valley the river formed a great marsh with islands that became, as in Venice, the foundation of the town and the source of its Gaelic name, *Corcaigh,* meaning "a marshy place." The first settlement was a little Gaelic monastery founded in the 6th century by an obscure but beloved abbot-bishop named Barra of the Fair Hair, or Finbarre. The monastery, on a hill south of the river where the present St. Finbarre's Cathedral stands, grew in power, and its reputation for wealth was probably what enticed the Vikings in their longboats up the estuary and through the sinuous marsh. The Vikings first founded a trading post here in the 8th century, and within 50 years they had fortified one of the islands, creating the right and tight little city of Cork.

In time, the Vikings became subjects of MacCarthy Mor, the Gaelic prince of the area. However, they had their own *jarl* (ruler) and maintained a degree of independence in their island city until the Norman invasion in the 12th century forced them to switch allegiance. In the turbulent centuries that followed, the inhabitants of Cork City acquired a reputation for independent-mindedness even to rebellion. King John (as prince) gave them a charter in 1185; they were back under the rule of the MacCarthys by 1195; they were given a more prestigious charter by the king in 1199; and then another in 1241. In 1495 they nearly seized the crown itself when they received the pretender to the throne, Perkin Warbeck, and escorted him to England to proclaim him King of England and Lord of Ireland.

Within Cork's island walls are shops and warehouses and banks. It was and still is essentially a trading town. In the 18th century, it became the great supply port for the American colonies, sending out beef, bacon, and butter, and during the Napoleonic Wars it was the larder of the British Army and Navy. Gradually, Cork expanded beyond its walls and up the sides of the river valley.

As the merchants made money, they developed an appreciation of the accoutrements of civilized life. Cork silver and glass became tasteful and elegant, and a Cork school of painters developed. (Today the neo-classical works of James Barry and Robert Fagan, the townscapes of Nathaniel Grogan, and the historical panoramas of Samuel Forde and Daniel Maclise can be admired in the *Crawford Municipal Art Gallery.*) Talk has always been a strong art form in Cork. In the 19th century, wordsmiths met in drinking clubs and debating societies and produced a circle of essayists and poets, including the gentle lyric poet, J. J. Callanan; William Maginn, a Johnsonian schoolmaster and satirist; and Francis Sylvester O'Mahony (Father Prout), a mocking ex-priest.

The 19th century also produced some distinguished architecture in Cork. First the brothers Pain — James and George Richard — pupils of John Nash, came from London and built bridges, jails, a courthouse, some lovely townhouses with gentle Regency bowfronts, and the delightful Gothic fantasy Blackrock Castle at the end of the Marina Walk. They were succeeded by the Deane family, builders of churches, banks, and Cork's University College. From the Deane firm emerged Benjamin Woodward, a genius of the neo-Gothic whose best work is in Dublin and Oxford.

Cork in the 20th century is chronicled in the short stories of Seán O'Faoláin and Frank O'Connor, both natives. It is still a workaday city; shops, warehouses, and factories are the main fibers of its fabric. But it is also a good talking town, a great eating-out town, a sports-mad town. During the War of Independence (1919–21) it was a wellspring of nationalistic fervor, losing two mayors and many public buildings to the cause. Since then, it has withstood the worst assaults of modernization — though its cramped island site has given it some real traffic problems and the city's 136,000 inhabitants must cope with gridlock and congestion, albeit in their own spirited way. Cork residents are a most competent people whose response to good fortune and bad is a mocking laugh and a musical burst of anecdote. Their wit and vitality are sure to make any visit to Cork a memorable one.

Cork At-a-Glance

SEEING THE CITY

The north slope of the river valley is dominated by the tower of St. Anne's Church, better known simply as Shandon steeple. Cross the river and climb the tower to an outside balcony. The city is spread below, the flat marsh area with its busy streets surrounded by what Edmund Spenser called "The spreading Lee, that like an island fayre / Encloseth Corke with his divided floode." The Lee here forms a north channel and a south channel, and between them is the compact central island known as the "flat of the city." Patrick Street, or St. Patrick Street, the main artery crossing the island, was itself once an open river channel, as were the Grand Parade and the South Mall. By 1800 the waterways had been turned into thoroughfares for the traffic on foot, hoof, and wheel that crowded into the city's business district. Quieter, more reflective parts of Cork are found on the slopes that rise to the south and north of the central island. The Gothic towers of St. Finbarre's Cathedral and the graceful

Gothic quadrangles of the university are on the south slope, and churches, convents, and hospitals are to the right and left on the north slope.

SPECIAL PLACES

The "flat of the city" is the hub of activity in Cork, and a walk along Patrick Street (affectionately called "Pana" by residents) and its subsidiary arteries is as traditional an activity as the evening promenade in other European cities. Going east to west, the walk is properly done on the left path for a view of the better-preserved right side of the street, with its delicately bowfronted 18th-century houses. (The left side had to be replaced after being burned down by British troops in 1920.) Patrick Street leads to the Grand Parade, which runs straight to the south channel of the river and has some traditional slated bowfronts remaining from the 18th century. At the south channel, the Grand Parade meets the South Mall, now the financial district. Here, a few characteristic merchants' houses remain from the days when the South Mall was still an open waterway. Doors at street or water level opened onto basement storerooms so that boats could be unloaded easily, and high outside steps led up to the merchants' living quarters above their shops. Walking is the best way to see the flat of the city. Numerous bridges span the Lee's still-flowing channels providing access to the north and south banks.

FLAT OF THE CITY

FATHER MATTHEW STATUE This memorial to Father Theobald Matthew, the Apostle of Temperance, is the work of the celebrated 19th-century Irish sculptor John Henry Foley, who also created the monument to Daniel O'Connell in Dublin and was one of several artists responsible for the Albert Memorial in London. Father Matthew, a superior of the Capuchin order in Cork, was known not only for his crusade in the cause of temperance but also for his work among the poor, especially during the mid-19th-century famines. The statue is a central point of reference in Cork City. Patrick St. at Patrick Bridge.

CRAWFORD MUNICIPAL ART GALLERY Housed in a red brick building erected in the early 18th century as the city's custom house, the gallery contains a select collection of works by painters of the 20th-century Irish School: William Orpen, John Lavery, and Jack Yeats; a good representation by artists of the earlier Cork School: James Barry, Nathaniel Grogan, Samuel Forde, and Daniel Maclise; and some fine examples of Cork silver and glass. Open Mondays through Saturdays from 10 AM to 5 PM. No admission charge. Emmet Pl. (phone: 273377).

CHURCH OF SAINTS PETER AND PAUL Opened in 1868, this excellent Gothic Revival church by E. W. Pugin is typical of Cork in its casing of red sandstone and its dressing of white limestone. Off Paul St. (phone: 276573).

CITY MARKET Fruit, vegetables, fish, and meat — including local specialties such as *drisheen* (blood pudding or blood sausage) and tripe — are displayed and sold in a stylish late-18th-century market arcade under a cast-iron and glass roof. (It's also referred to by locals as the "English Market," reflecting its origins.) When the market is in full swing, daily except Sundays, the scene is animated and the stall holders are full of Cork esprit and chat. Entrances off Patrick St., Princes St., and Grand Parade.

COURT HOUSE The Pain brothers designed this stately building with Corinthian porticoes in 1835. Sir Walter Scott, among others, admired it. Washington St. (phone: 275321).

SOUTH AND NORTH MAIN STREETS When Cork was still enclosed by walls, its main gates were at the South Gate Bridge and the North Gate Bridge. Between the two ran the spine of the medieval city, worth walking today for its atmosphere and its food and housewares shops. The much-altered 18th-century Protestant Christ Church (South Main St.) is on the site of a medieval parish church that dated from the Normans and was probably the church in which Edmund Spenser married Elizabeth Boyle, his Irish bride, in the 16th century. The other Cork medieval parish church was off North Main Street. Nearby are many byways — such as Portney's Lane — where merchants and craftsmen once lived.

HOLY TRINITY CHURCH The church of the Capuchin friars, also known as Father Matthew Memorial Church, dates from the 1830s. Recently modernized, the interior still retains some of its former charming Regency Gothic decor, which was created by George Richard Pain. The lantern spire, a graceful later addition, is enhanced by the riverside setting. Father Matthew Quay (phone: 272631).

NORTH BANK

ST. PATRICK'S BRIDGE This mid-19th-century classical structure is constructed in white limestone. The view from the bridge — upriver over the city's churches, convents, and other institutions, and downriver to the ships — is quintessential Cork. Patrick's Hill, a precipitous street housing fashionable doctors, leads up the north bank from the bridge. It's worth the climb for another view over the city. End of Patrick St.

ST. ANNE'S CHURCH/SHANDON The quaint pepper-box tower of this Protestant church, built from 1722 to 1726, is the symbol of Cork. Shandon steeple rises in square tiers to its cupola and weather vane, which is crowned by a golden fish. The steeple has two red sides and two white sides, a combination that is a signature of many Cork buildings. From the top of the steeple, the source of the color scheme is apparent in the river valley: one slope of red sandstone and an opposite one of silvery white limestone. The Shandon churchyard is the last resting place of Francis S. O'Mahony, who, under the pen name Father Prout, wrote "The Bells of Shandon," a song that made both bells and church famous. Open daily from 9:30 AM to 6 PM in summer, 10:30 AM to 4:30 PM the rest of the year. Admission charge. Church St. (phone: 501672).

ST. MARY'S DOMINICAN CHURCH Kearns Deane, a member of the prominent family of Cork architects responsible for several of the city's classical buildings, designed this church with the solid portico in 1832. Inside is a tiny carved ivory Madonna of 14th-century Flemish origin. Pope's Quay (phone: 502267).

SOUTH BANK

ELIZABETH FORT The massive curtain walls are all that remain of a 17th-century fort that once housed the Cork garrison. Today, a modern police station stands incongruously within the walls. Off Barrack St.

ST. FINBARRE'S CATHEDRAL Though somewhat foreshortened on its confined site — where the city's patron saint chose to put his monastery in the 6th century — this Protestant cathedral is considered a brilliant essay in French Gothic by William Burges, an English architect who also designed Cardiff Castle and the quadrangle of Yale University. It was built between 1867 and 1879 to replace an earlier church, which itself replaced a medieval church damaged in the siege of 1690. (A cannonball found 40 feet above the ground in the tower is a reminder of that siege.) Burges's three spires are aesthetically most effective and his interior detail is rich and inventive. Bishop St. (phone: 964742).

UNIVERSITY COLLEGE The main quadrangle is a gem of 19th-century collegiate architecture (reminiscent of the colleges at Oxford) by Thomas Deane and his partner Benjamin Woodward. Later additions do not quite maintain the initial high standard, but the Honan Chapel, architect James J. McMullen's 1915 revival of 12th-century Irish Romanesque style (it's a copy of King Cormac's Chapel at the Rock of Cashel in Tipperary), has interesting exterior details and is stuffed with treasures: stained glass windows, embroideries, tabernacle enamels, and a joyous mosaic floor. The chapel is open daily, except during school holidays. Western Rd. (phone: 276871).

ENVIRONS

FOTA ISLAND The ornamental estate that belonged to the Smith-Barry family, once Earls of Barrymore, is now owned by University College Cork. Its centerpiece, Fota House, was built in the 1820s by Sir Richard Morrison, who created some of Ireland's finest neo-classical interiors, and it stands today as a splendid example of Regency architecture. The rooms are fully furnished with Irish pieces from the 18th and 19th centuries and decorated with rich period wallpapers and curtains. Most notable are the Irish landscape paintings, dating from the 1750s to the 1870s and constituting the most comprehensive private collection of its kind. On the grounds of the estate are an arboretum, a bee garden, and a wildlife park — home to giraffes, zebras, ostriches, antelopes, and other species — covering 70 acres of parkland, woods, and lagoons. At press time, Fota House was closed for repairs; no re-opening date has been announced. The wildlife park, however, is open daily from *St. Patrick's Day* (March 17) through September. On the main road to Cobh, about 10 miles southeast of Cork in Carrigtwohill (phone: 812555 for house; 812678 for the wildlife park).

BLARNEY Blarney Castle and the legendary Blarney Stone are a 10-minute drive from Cork City. The castle, which belonged to the MacCarthys, dates from 1446. Although other parts of it were demolished, the massive square keep, or tower, with a battlemented parapet, survived centuries of sieges by such notorious attackers as Oliver Cromwell and William III. The word "blarney" originated with Cormac MacDermot MacCarthy, a diplomat who was well known in the court of Elizabeth I for his "fair words and soft speech." Blarney has come to mean the ability to deceive without offending. Set in one of the castle walls is the stone that supposedly confers this gift on those who kiss it (leaning over backwards from the parapet). Also on the grounds is Blarney Castle House, a baronial mansion open to the public, and the Rock Close, a garden of ancient trees and stones, reputedly of druidical origin. The Blarney Castle Estate is open daily year-round except *Christmas Eve* and *Christmas Day.* The house is open from 10 AM to 5 PM, daily except Sundays, June through September. Admission charge. 5 miles north of Cork City, via R617 (phone: 385252).

QUEENSTOWN/COBH HERITAGE CENTRE This project, which opened in 1993, commemorates the days in the 19th and 20th centuries when Cobh (then known as Queenstown), the port city of Cork, was a vital link in transatlantic ocean liner traffic. So many people seeking a better life in America left Ireland from this port that the city became synonymous with emigration. Housed in the former railway station, the center tells the story of the city, its harbor, and the flow of Irish emigration through a series of displays and an audiovisual presentation. In the summer months, a steam railway ferries visitors from Cork City to Cobh. Open daily from 9:30 AM to 6 PM. Admission charge (phone: 813591).

JAMESON WHISKEY HERITAGE CENTRE Dating back to 1823, this landmark distillery — which is open to visitors — is the home of the largest pot still in the world (capacity over 30,000 gallons) and the main production center for John Jameson whiskey and other leading Irish spirits. Although the most modern techniques are now used in whiskey making at this 11-acre site, many of the original structures still remain — the mill building, corn stores, stillhouses, warehouses, kilns, and the original water wheel that provided power centuries ago. The complex also contains the last copper stills manufactured in Ireland and the associated receiver vats and storage vessels. The many steps in the production of whiskey are illustrated for visitors via a multilingual audiovisual presentation, photographs, graphic exhibits, demonstrations, and working models. Samples are provided at the end of the tour. Open daily 10 AM to 4 PM; admission charge. 15 miles northeast of Cork off the main Waterford Road. Main St., Midleton (phone: 631821).

Sources and Resources

TOURIST INFORMATION

The Cork–Kerry Tourism Office (Grand Parade; phone: 273251) offers information, maps, and leaflets; it also sells guidebooks on Cork City and County Cork and the excellent *Tourist Trail*, a walking guide to Cork. For books and pamphlets on the city's history and background, visit *Liam Ruiseal's* bookshop around the corner from the tourism office (49-50 Oliver Plunkett St.; phone: 270981).

LOCAL COVERAGE The *Cork Examiner* is the one they call "de payper." It's the morning daily, full of local color. The *Evening Echo,* essential for entertainment information, comes out every evening.

TELEPHONE The area code for Cork and the immediate vicinity is 21. When calling from within the Republic of Ireland, dial 021 before the local number.

GETTING AROUND

In the "flat of the city," walking is easier and faster than going by bus or car because of congested traffic, restricted parking, and one-way circuits. Drivers should observe the local disc parking system — it works. Books of 10 disc tickets cost about $7 at tobacco and newspaper shops, garages, and the tourist board. In addition, Cork has three multi-story parking garages along the banks of the river downtown — at Lavitt's Quay, Paul Street, and Merchants Quay. All are open Mondays through Saturdays.

BUS AND TRAIN A good city bus service radiates from the Father Matthew Statue. County buses, long-distance buses, and day tours leave from the bus station (Parnell Pl.), a block east of the statue. *Bus Eireann,* a division of *CIE (Córas Iompair Eireann, National Transport Company)*, operates summer bus tours of the city as well as excursions to Killarney, Bantry Bay, Limerick, and Tipperary (phone: 503399, ext. 318). Trains leave from Kent Station (Lower Glanmire Rd.; phone: 504422) on the north bank of the Lee.

CAR RENTAL All major international and national firms are represented, including *Avis/Johnson & Perrott* (phone: 800-331-1084 from the US), which has offices at Emmet Place (phone: 273295) and Cork Airport (phone: 963133);

Budget in the Cork-Kerry Tourism Office (Grand Parade; phone: 274755); and *Murrays/Europcar* (Patrick's Quay; phone: 509090). Consult the local yellow pages for more listings.

RIVER CRUISES From July through August or September there are afternoon and evening cruises around Cork Harbour and excursions to Fota Island. Schedules and rates are available from the tourist board or *Marine Transport,* Atlantic Quay, Cobh (phone: 811485).

TAXI Cabstands are at the stations, in the middle of Patrick Street, opposite the *Savoy Centre,* and at most hotels. Reliable firms for 24-hour service include *Tele-Cabs* (phone: 505050), *Cork Taxi Co-op* (phone: 272222), and *Shandon Cabs* (phone: 502255).

WALKING TOURS Half- and full-day tours are organized, for a fee, by *Discover Cork Guided Tours* (Belmont, Douglas Rd.; phone: 293873). The tourist office has itineraries and schedules for other shorter tours that are offered periodically.

SPECIAL EVENTS

Cork is a festive town with plenty to do.

FAVORITE FETES

Cork International Choral and Folk Dance Festival This event takes place annually at the beginning of May. Choirs and folk dance teams from all over the world participate, and each year several choral works are commissioned from distinguished composers. For information contact the *Cork International Choral and Folk Dance Festival,* City Hall (phone: 312296).

Guinness Jazz Festival A magnificent razzle for those passionate about their upbeats and downbeats, this popular October event attracts such international luminaries as Ella Fitzgerald, the *Heath Brothers,* and Cleo Laine, who — together with a circle of local swingers — keep the joints jumping on both banks of the stately River Lee. Don't expect to get too much sleep, and try to book the more important events in advance. For more details contact the *Cork Jazz Festival, Metropole Hotel,* MacCurtain St. (phone: 508122 or 545411).

In addition, during July, in even-numbered years, the *Royal Cork Yacht Club* organizes *Cork Week,* featuring a variety of contests, including the *European Offshore Team Championship.* The city's well-established *Film Festival* of short and feature-length films takes place in September or October; contact the tourist office for schedule information.

MUSEUMS

Paintings and sculpture by Irish artists and others are exhibited at the *Crawford Municipal Art Gallery* (see *Special Places*) and at the *Triskel Arts Centre* (Tobin St.; phone: 272022 or 272023). The *Cork Public Museum*

(Fitzgerald Park; phone: 270679) contains interesting displays of Cork history from the earliest times to the present, and the surrounding park has a pleasant riverside walk and sculptures by many local craftspeople, including Seamus Murphy, a well-known Cork stone carver who became a sculptor. The museum is open weekdays and Sunday afternoons; the park is open daily (contact the tourist board for the exact hours, which vary with the season). Off Mardyke Rd., a promenade parallel to Western Rd.

SHOPPING

As would be expected of the Republic's second-largest metropolitan area, Cork is an excellent shopping center. The major department stores are on Patrick Street. The *Merchant's Quay Shopping Centre* (Patrick St. and Merchant's Quay), Cork's newest shopping complex, offers a mix of large department stores, such as *Marks & Spencer* (phone: 275555); international boutiques, such as *Laura Ashley* (phone: 274070); and unique Irish specialty shops. There is also a food court and covered parking. The *Winthrop Arcade* (Winthrop St.) is especially alluring; be sure to visit *Eileen O'Connor's* knitwear shop, known for the owner's personalized service (8 Winthrop Arcade; phone: 271359). The *Savoy Centre* (Patrick St.) has a variety of large clothing stores, as well as specialty shops carrying Irish linen and fabric, greeting cards, and gift items. Small shops and boutiques abound on Princes and Oliver Plunkett Streets. *Queen's Old Castle* (Grand Parade), a former department store, now houses many shops and cafés. Paul's Lane, off Paul Street, is home to many antiques shops, including *Mills* (3 Paul's La.; phone: 273528), *Anne McCarthy* (2 Paul's La.; phone: 273755), and *O'Regan's* (4 Paul's La.; phone: 509141). The following are some of Cork's finest shops. All stores are closed Sundays unless otherwise indicated.

BLARNEY WOOLLEN MILLS One of the country's busiest craft emporiums, known for fine knits produced on the premises. Also stocks crystal, china, and other gift items. Open daily. In the village of Blarney, 5 miles north of Cork (phone: 385280).

CASH'S OF IRELAND Cork's equivalent of Dublin's *Switzer's* sells linen, woolens, tweeds, glassware, and other goods. 18 Patrick St. (phone: 964411).

CRAFTS OF IRELAND Conveniently situated at the corner of Oliver Plunkett Street opposite Cork's main post office, this shop features an "all Irish" collection of handmade items, from batik and baskets to candles, stained glass, leatherwork, pottery, toys, woolens, woodwork, and wrought-iron art. 11 Winthrop St. (phone: 275864).

FITZGERALD Established in 1860, this shop features Burberry coats and Bally shoes at considerably less than US prices, as well as Irish tweeds and cashmere knitwear. 24 Patrick St. (phone: 270095).

HERITAGE A variety of local glassware, plus the chance to see local glassblower Sean Murphy at work. 78 Oliver Plunkett St. (phone: 275914).

HOUSE OF DONEGAL The best source for classic trench coats and custom rainwear, with linings of Donegal tweed or silk, all fashioned on the premises. Tweed suits, coats, jackets, tartans, and capes also are made to order. 6-8 Paul St. (phone: 272447).

HOUSE OF JAMES Housed in a former tea warehouse and candy factory (original cogs and wheels are in evidence), this modern bi-level shop sells locally made pottery, as well as crafts by more than 50 Irish artisans. 20 Paul St. (phone: 272324).

IRISH HOME CRAFTS A tiny place chock-full of Irish crochet work, tweeds, hand-knits, pottery, art, jewelry, and patchwork. 7 Marlborough St. (phone: 273379).

LAVITT'S QUAY Frequent exhibitions of works for sale by local artists from the *Cork Arts Society*. Closed Sundays and Mondays. 16 Lavitt's Quay (phone: 505749).

QUEEN'S OLD CASTLE A traditional department store elegantly converted to a varied shopping mall that includes cafés for the weary. Grand Parade (phone: 275044).

QUILLS A super source of tweeds, woolens, and knits, this shop is a branch of the highly successful enterprise headquartered in nearby Ballingeary. 107 Patrick St. (phone: 271717).

WATERSTONE'S A bookshop par excellence, with an array of volumes on international topics, as well as shelves stacked ceiling high with books on Irish history, literature, language, politics, cookery, and crafts. Open daily. 69 Patrick St. (phone: 276522).

WILLIAM J. FRAZER The best hunting attire tailor on earth. He also makes men's and women's suits as fine as any from London's Savile Row. Main St. (phone: 83118).

SPORTS AND FITNESS

BICYCLING Raleigh touring bikes and all-terrain vehicles can be rented from the *AA Bike Shop* (68 Shandon St.; phone: 304154), *Cycle Repair Centre* (6 Kyle St.; phone: 276255), and *Cycle Scene* (396 Blarney St.; phone: 301183).

GOLF Several hospitable golf courses surround the city and welcome visitors. The 18-hole *Cork Golf Club* (phone: 353451) and the 18-hole *Harbour Point* golf complex (phone: 353094) are both at Little Island, about 6½ miles from the center. Others are the *Douglas Golf Club* (phone: 896297), about 3 miles away; the *Muskerry Golf Club* (phone: 385297), about 8 miles away; and *Monkstown Golf Club* (phone: 841376), at Monkstown, a village on the western shore of Cork Harbour, about 5 miles from Cork City. Call for hours. Greens fees average $17 to $45.

GREYHOUND RACING Betting is brisk Monday, Wednesday, and Saturday nights at the *Cork Greyhound Stadium* (Western Rd.; phone: 543013). Details are available in the *Cork Examiner*.

HURLING AND GAELIC FOOTBALL Cork's *Páirc Uí Chaoimh* stadium on the Marina Walk (phone: 963311), east of town, is the headquarters of Gaelic hurling and football in the south. Matches — of one or the other game — take place most summer Sunday afternoons. *Rebel Cork* is a power to be reckoned with, especially in hurling.

RIDING Three stables are convenient to the city: *Hitchmough Riding School* (Monkstown; phone: 371267); *Pine Grove Riding Centre* (White's Cross; phone: 303857); and *Skevanish Riding Centre* (Innishannon; phone: 775476). Rates average from $15 to $20 per hour.

RUGBY AND SOCCER Both are played at the *University Grounds* (Mardyke Walk; phone: 276871). See the sports pages of the *Cork Examiner* for match times.

SAILING Cork Harbour is a sailor's paradise and the *Royal Cork Yacht Club* (phone: 831440), with headquarters downriver in Crosshaven, welcomes visitors from other clubs.

TENNIS A local center offers excellent facilities, and is considered among the most advanced in Ireland.

CHOICE COURTS

Tennis Village Cork Two miles west of downtown, this modern sporting center offers 6 indoor courts and 8 outdoor courts; open year-round, 24 hours per day. The complex also includes a practice area, a tennis boutique, a restaurant, and a bar. Model Farm Rd. (phone: 342727).

THEATER

The *Cork Opera House* (Emmet Pl.; phone: 270022) is a modern replacement of a romantically decayed theater that burned down in the 1950s. Drama and musical comedies, opera, and ballet are all staged here. *Everyman Palace* (17 MacCurtain St.; phone: 501673) offers new plays, foreign and Irish. From May through December the *Triskel Arts Centre* (Tobin St., off S. Main St.; phone: 272022) hosts a wide variety of musical events, poetry readings, plays, films, and other performances. Check with the tourist board or the *Evening Echo* for details.

MUSIC

For a relatively small city, Cork is fairly rich in music. There are regular lunch-hour concerts of classical music in summer, evening concerts the rest of the year. Check at the tourist board, or call the *Cork School of Music* (phone: 965583). Irish ballads can be heard regularly at *DeLacy House* (74 Oliver Plunkett St.; phone: 270074); *An Bodhrán* (42 Oliver Plunkett St.; phone: 274544); the *Lobby Bar* (1 Union Quay; phone: 311113); the *Phoenix* (3 Union Quay; phone: 964275); and *An Spailpín Fánac,* also known as *The Loft* (28-29 S. Main St.; phone: 277949).

NIGHTCLUBS AND NIGHTLIFE

The disco scene is lively. Recommended are *Zoe's* (16 Oliver Plunkett St.; phone: 270870), *Mangan's* (16 Careys La.; phone: 279168), *Oscar's* (Coburg St.; phone: 501518), *The Pav* (13 Carey's La.; phone: 276330), and *Rearden's Mill* (26 Washington St.; phone: 271969). Check the hotels for cabaret and dancing and see the *Evening Echo* for other entertainment listings.

Best in Town

CHECKING IN

Cork can be jam-packed during high season, so reservations are recommended. Hotels vary from the sleek, modern edifices on the outskirts of town to the downtown dowagers that have been upgraded with bathrooms and coffee shops. Expect to pay $155 or more for a double room in the very expensive category (with Irish breakfast); $105 to $155 in the expensive range; from $70 to $100 in the moderate category; and $60 or less for a room listed as inexpensive. Visitors arriving without a reservation will not be left out in the cold. The tourist board will help find a hotel or a good, inexpensive guesthouse. All telephone numbers are in the 21 area code unless otherwise indicated.

For an unforgettable experience, we begin with our area favorites, followed by our cost and quality choices, listed by price category.

SPECIAL HAVENS

Ballymaloe House Beckoning across fields where ponies frolic and grassy lawns where plump sheep graze, this establishment (whose name is pronounced Bally-ma-*loo*) is a lesson in architecture and history enlivened by sumptuous food. While strolling around the premises, one can see the bare skull of rock on which the whole structure is founded and the wall of a castle built in 1500. Both the rock and the wall have been incorporated into the main building, and one corridor is flanked by the foundations of a 17th-century addition. But the star of the show here is the food. Everyone gathers in the restaurant to enjoy Myrtle Allen's first class meals, famed throughout Ireland (see *Eating Out*). All of this is an excellent recommendation for the hotel's cooking school, which offers a number of sessions of varying lengths throughout the year. There are 30 guestrooms (each with private bath) in the main house and in a contemporary modern wing adjoining the gardens and the heated outdoor swimming pool. Those who are able to waddle after breakfast and lunch can borrow some golf clubs from the management and make their way to the estate's small golf course, work off some calories at tennis or croquet, or wet a line in Ballycotton Bay, 6 miles distant. Open year-round, except for a few days at *Christmas*. About 20 miles east of Cork City in Shanagarry (phone: 652531; fax: 652021).

Longueville House Built in 1720, this Georgian mansion stands on a hill surrounded by some 500 acres of grounds scored by the River Blackwater. Inside, there's a lovely formality to the design (notably the noble double staircase) and an abundance of fine interior detail (inlaid mahogany doors, a marble Adam fireplace, Italian plasterwork ceilings). The 17 rooms will fulfill not a few fantasies — huge and old-fashioned, some with half-canopy beds muffled with curtains that can be used to shut out the Longueville Lady, a friendly shrouded ghost with a riveting history who occasionally appears to guests. Michael O'Callaghan and his wife, Jane, are the hosts, and their handsome Relais & Châteaux establishment is highly regarded for the food served in the magnificent *Presidents' Room* restaurant (see *Eating Out*). Between meals, guests fish for salmon and trout (though tackle is not supplied). It's also possible to ride at nearby stables and play golf in Mallow, 3 miles distant — or just sit and enjoy the sunshine in the palm-lined Victorian conservatory. Open early March to mid-December; prices drop with every story up since there is no elevator. In Longueville Mallow village about 20 miles north of Cork City; take the Limerick road to Mallow, then turn left on Killarney and drive 3 miles (phone: 22-47156; 800-223-6510 from the US; fax: 22-47459).

VERY EXPENSIVE

Imperial The grandmother of them all, stately in the middle of the South Mall and close to everything, took shape on the drawing board of 19th-century Cork architect Thomas Deane. The grande dame is not as starchy as she looks; in fact, most of the 101 rooms have been renovated with an Art Deco flair, and each has a private bath. Facilities include a French/Irish restaurant, a coffee shop, and 2 bars. For those who arrive by car, parking can be a problem. South Mall (phone: 274040; 800-223-6510 from the US; fax: 274040).

Morrison's Island Billed as Cork's first all-suite hotel, this 40-unit 6-story property sits beside the River Lee, adjacent to the South Mall and across from City Hall, within walking distance of all major sites. Each suite consists of a sitting room, dining area, kitchen, bathroom, and 1 or 2 bedrooms; all units are equipped with a TV set, phone, and fax machine. The rooms are tastefully decorated with contemporary furnishings and art, and many offer lovely views of the city, the river, and the bridges. Facilities include the *Riverbank* restaurant (see *Eating Out*), with views of Cork Harbour; a lounge; and an enclosed parking lot behind the hotel. Morrison's Quay (phone: 275858; 800-223-6510 from the US; fax: 275833).

EXPENSIVE

Arbutus Lodge The lodge is actually an elegant mansion set amid gardens overlooking the city and the river. There are 20 small but comfortable rooms, each with bath, and the Georgian decor is enhanced by a collection of modern Irish art. This place is a good choice if you want to be near what some consider the best restaurant in Cork, and perhaps in Ireland (see *Eating Out*). Montenotte (phone: 501237; fax: 502893).

Fitzpatrick Silver Springs Set on 42 acres overlooking the River Lee on the northeastern fringe of town, this modern 7-story lodging is owned and managed by the Fitzpatricks, one of Ireland's leading hotelier families. Like its sister properties in Dublin and Shannon, this place is always growing and improving. Currently, there are 150 rooms and suites (all with private baths) primarily decorated in contemporary style, although some of the suites feature European antiques or pieces of Asian art. Guest facilities include a restaurant with river views, a coffee shop, 2 lounges, and a unique glass-walled "skylift" that offers views of the surrounding countryside as it whisks guests to their floors. The grounds offer a 9-hole golf course and a hilltop activity center with an indoor Olympic-size pool, saunas, a steamroom, Jacuzzi, indoor and outdoor tennis courts, squash courts, a gym, and an aerobics room. There's plenty of parking, a rarity for Cork City hotels. Dublin Rd., Tivoli (phone: 507533; 800-367-7701 from the US; fax: 507641).

Jurys Situated on a well-landscaped 5-acre site beside the River Lee on the western edge of downtown, this modern 2-story hotel is only a 5-minute walk from the city's Grand Parade. The 200 guestrooms, which surround a central garden courtyard and a glass-enclosed atrium with an indoor-outdoor swimming pool, are decorated with dark wood furnishings, brass fittings, prints of Irish gardens and forests, and bright fabrics of autumn or rainbow hues. An in-room plus includes satellite TV. Unlike most hotels within the city, there is plenty of parking. In addition to the pool, facilities include a whirlpool, saunas, a squash court, a gym, and a patio/deck. There is also a Cork-themed pub overlooking the water, a coffee shop, and an award-winning seafood restaurant, the *Fastnet* (see *Eating Out*). Western Rd. (phone: 966377; 800-44-UTELL from the US; fax: 274477).

Rochestown Park Set on 7 acres of mature gardens in a mostly residential area about 2 miles south of the city center, this building was once the home of Cork's Lord Mayor. Restored and recently opened as a hotel, it offers 60 rooms with private baths and contemporary furnishings, TV sets, phones, hair dryers, trouser presses, and coffee/tea making facilities. There is a restaurant, a lounge, and an on-premises health club that includes an indoor swimming pool, sauna, steamroom, whirlpool spa, gym, and solarium. Douglas Rd. (phone: 892233; fax: 892178).

MODERATE

Fleming's Silver Grange House Nestled on its own grounds off the main road (N25) on the eastern fringes of the city, this 200-year-old Georgian country house presents a homey alternative to the city's larger hotels. There are 4 guestrooms with private baths; all are decorated with antiques and have the modern amenities of TV sets and telephones. The public areas include an Old World–style dining room and lounge, and a walled courtyard with a patio and garden. Tivoli (phone: 821621; fax: 821800).

INEXPENSIVE

Forte Travelodge With a modern 2-story brick façade, this 40-room motel is the first representative of the no-frills chain in Ireland, set on a hill 1½ miles south of the city center on the main road to Kinsale and the airport. Rooms are basic but can sleep up to four people for one flat rate; each unit has a double bed, sofa bed, private bath/shower, TV set, and coffee/tea making facilities, but no phone. There are no public areas or lounges, except for a small reception desk and the adjacent *Little Chef* restaurant (see *Eating Out*). Airport Rd., Blackash (phone: 310370; 800-CALL-THF from the US).

Lotamore House A sprawling Georgian residence, just a 5-minute drive from downtown Cork. All 20 rooms have private baths, orthopedic beds, TV sets, and telephones, while the public rooms retain an 18th-century aura — from a sweeping staircase, ornate plasterwork, and crystal chandeliers to the 1791 drawing room fireplace. Dublin Rd., Tivoli (phone: 822344; fax: 822219).

EATING OUT

Cork is a good eating-out town, largely because the residents eat out quite a bit. Do not ignore the hotel dining rooms; some offer very good value and one in particular (the *Arbutus Lodge*) is considered among the best in Ireland. In addition to the restaurants listed here, the natives frequent good dining places half an hour or so from Cork (see "Kinsale" in *West Cork,* DIRECTIONS). Dinner for two without wine, drinks, or tips will cost $100 and up in places listed as expensive; $50 to $100 at places in the moderate category; and under $50 at spots listed as inexpensive. All telephone numbers are in the 21 area code unless otherwise indicated.

For an unforgettable dining experience, we begin with our culinary favorites, followed by our cost and quality choices, listed by price category.

DELIGHTFUL DINING

Arbutus Lodge One of the great restaurants of Ireland, this place enfolds diners in luxury, cossets them with fine service, and feeds but does not fatten them with the absolute best of food. The Ryan family, who own and run it, have close alliances with the famous Troisgros brothers of France — the two staffs share secrets and inspirations — so the food is classically Franco-Irish, spiced with regional specialties like *drisheen,* a blood pudding native to Cork that is poached in milk. Those who are not inclined toward such ethnic fare can concentrate on the fish, hand-picked from the daily catch of four or five trawlers; the locally smoked salmon; or the game, brought in from the de Vesci estate. The hot oysters with herbs from the garden are especially memorable, and the wine list makes connoisseurs gasp. Open for lunch and dinner Mondays through Saturdays, with bar food on Sundays; closed *Christmas* week. Reservations necessary. Major credit cards accepted. Montenotte (phone: 501237).

Ballymaloe House Formally known as the *Yeats Room,* the food served here is simple and fresh, nearly everything is grown on the property. Begin with the watercress soup, smoked mackerel, or homemade Danish pâté, follow with summer turkey braised in butter and fresh herbs, roast beef with three sauces, or French casserole of roast pork with Normandy mustard, and top it all with a board of local cheese, fruit tarts, cake, and coffee with *Ballymaloe* chocolates. Open daily for lunch and dinner. Reservations necessary. Major credit cards accepted. Shanagarry, about 20 miles east of Cork (phone: 652531).

Lovetts Proprietor Dermot Lovett has brought a whole menu full of new culinary adventures to a peach-colored, late-19th-century house on an unobtrusive lane beside the sea, a few miles from the heart of Cork. Chief among those finds are sea urchins served raw in clusters on cracked ice with lemon wedges, as delicious as the best oyster. Diners will also relish the smoked eel, the Kenmare Bay oysters, and the brill — a small turbot, but better. High-cholesterol sinners can overdose on fried camembert in fresh tomato sauce. The wine list is impressive and a feature that deserves encouragement is the notice on the menu that says there is no service charge and discourages gratuities. Open weekdays for lunch and dinner, Saturdays for dinner only; closed for a week at *Christmas.* Reservations necessary. Major credit cards accepted. Churchyard La., off Well Rd., Douglas (phone: 294909).

EXPENSIVE

Clifford's French nouvelle cuisine is the mainstay at this small but trendy Art Deco–style eatery housed in the old County Library building, near *Jurys* hotel. Chef-owner Michael Clifford changes the menu daily and cooks all dishes to order. House specialties include medallions of monkfish with a prawn *coulis* sauce, breast of duck with baked chicory, and prime filet of beef with glazed shallots. Desserts, such as hot apple and almond tart or orange and lemon pancakes, are especially tempting. Open for lunch Tuesdays through Fridays; dinner Saturdays through Mondays. Reservations necessary. Major credit cards accepted. 18 Dyke Parade (phone: 275333).

Fastnet Named for a famous landmark rock and lighthouse off the southern coast of Ireland, this cozy restaurant focuses heavily on locally caught fish and shellfish, but meat and vegetarian selections are also available. Open for dinner only; closed Sundays and Mondays. Reservations advised. Major credit cards accepted. *Jurys Hotel,* Western Rd. (phone: 276622).

O'Keeffes Near *Jurys* hotel, this small family-run restaurant is one of Cork's culinary delights. It has a modern Art Deco ambience and a creative cooked-to-order menu including dishes such as chicken leg, boned and stuffed with a light mousse of chicken breast and sweet onion sauce; scallops in garlic butter with potato cake; monkfish, prawns, and squid in olive oil and flavored with shallots and pesto; and a house specialty of sirloin steak with Roquefort sauce. Open for dinner only; closed Sundays. Reservations necessary. MasterCard and Visa accepted. 23 Washington St. (phone: 275645).

Presidents' Room With a hand-painted ceiling, stained wood floor, and portraits of the Republic of Ireland's presidents hanging on the walls, this fine establishment at the *Longueville House* hotel serves French fare prepared with fresh ingredients from the 500-acre estate's garden, river, and farm. Menu items include lamb and a variety of fish. Summer dining can be enjoyed in the adjacent 18th-century conservatory. Lunch and dinner served daily from March to mid-December. Reservations necessary for dinner. Major credit cards accepted. Longueville Mallow, 20 miles from Cork; see *Checking In* for directions (phone: 22-47156).

MODERATE

Gallery Café Located on the ground floor of the *Crawford Municipal Art Gallery,* this spacious, high-ceiling dining room is appropriately decorated with fine artwork and sculpture. The fare, prepared by the Allen family of *Ballymaloe House* and its cooking school fame, offers a blend of the traditional and innovative, with such dishes as spinach and mushroom pancakes, potted crab, chicken pie with bacon and mushrooms, Scotch eggs, and shish kebab, all accompanied by *Ballymaloe* breads and scones. Open for lunch Mondays through Saturdays; dinner Wednesdays through Fridays. Reservations advised for dinner. MasterCard and Visa accepted. Emmet Pl. (phone: 274415).

Huguenot This popular bistro-style restaurant sits in the heart of the city between the busy shopping thoroughfares of Patrick and Paul Streets. It offers an

Old World setting with candlelight, mahogany fittings, and vintage paintings; but also has a modern menu of pasta, cold and warm salads, crêpes, curries, fish stews, and barbecue and stir-fry dishes, as well as steaks and chops. Open for lunch and dinner; closed Sundays. Reservations advised for dinner. Major credit cards accepted. French Church St. (phone: 273357).

Jacques A self-service eatery by day is transformed into a romantic bistro and wine bar each evening. The imaginative dinner menu ranges from cassoulet of shellfish to *noisettes* of lamb with apricot stuffing, roast quail, or chicken Dijon. Homemade desserts include a heavenly almond meringue filled with chocolate cream and rum. Closed Sundays and Mondays. Reservations necessary. Major credit cards accepted. 9 Phoenix St. (phone: 270634 or 277387).

Oyster Tavern An Old Cork favorite wedged in a narrow lane off the city's main thoroughfare, this dining place is known for its fresh seafood and fine steaks. Salmon is smoked in the restaurant's in-house smoke box; other specialties include shrimp scampi, lemon sole stuffed with prawns, and scallops with wine and cheese sauce. Open for lunch and dinner; closed Sundays. Reservations necessary. Diners Club, MasterCard, and Visa accepted. 4 Market La., off Patrick St. (phone: 27216).

Riverbank With its wide windows overlooking Cork Harbour, this hotel eatery lives up to its name. Besides expansive river views, it offers an innovative French/Irish menu in a contemporary setting enhanced by hand-painted oak furnishings and lots of greenery. Culinary choices include lamb cutlets with duxelle mushrooms and mint butter; filet of brill with prawn sauce; baked scallops rolled in thin salmon slices with lime and ginger sauce; and for strict vegetarians, pasta with spinach, cream, and garlic. Open daily for lunch and dinner. Reservations advised. Major credit cards accepted. *Morrison's Island Hotel,* Morrison's Quay (phone: 275858).

INEXPENSIVE

Beshoff A branch of the Dublin eatery, this is a contemporary version of an Irish "fish-and-chips" shop, in charming Edwardian surroundings. The menu focuses almost entirely on piscine delights from scampi and salmon to whiting, plaice, mackerel, trout, haddock, cod, and fish burgers. There are a few chicken dishes. Open daily from 11 AM to 11 PM. No reservations. No credit cards accepted. *Queens Old Castle* shopping complex (phone: 273635).

Bewley's Located within a half block of busy Patrick Street, this eatery serves breakfast, lunch, snacks, and freshly brewed coffee or tea at any time of day and is an ideal spot just to chat. Closed Sundays. No reservations. No credit cards accepted. 4 Cook St. (phone: 270660).

Gingerbread House Corkonians with a sweet tooth flock to this little pâtisserie, wedged between Patrick and Paul Streets. It offers a tempting selection of baked goods and confections, coffees and teas, with seating both indoors and outside. Closed Sundays. No reservations. No credit cards accepted. French Church St. (phone: 276411).

Little Chef Situated adjacent to the *Forte Travelodge*, 1½ miles south of the city center on the main airport road, this eatery serves burgers, sandwiches, and fast-food items in a spotless setting with swift service. Open daily from 7 AM to 10 PM. No reservations. Major credit cards accepted. Kinsale Rd. (phone: 310730).

SHARING A PINT

Cork's pub system is unusual for Ireland: As in Britain, it consists of independent houses and those linked, or "tied," to a particular brewery. Some pubs serve only Beamish stout, some only Murphy's (the local brews); the independent ones serve both, and Guinness as well. We begin with our favorite.

HIGH SPIRITS

HENCHY'S This century-old watering hole is a fine place to sip a pint and listen to the distinctive singsong local accent. All levels of Cork society are represented — even the odd poet, a regular, who is very odd indeed. The pub, a night place if ever there was one, with a fine snug, is owned by Michael Henchy and his mother, Catherine. 40 St. Luke's (phone: 501115).

Also in Cork is the *Long Valley* (10 Winthrop St.; phone: 272144), a traditional pub where you can sample both Beamish and Murphy's stouts. *Le Château* (right in the middle of Patrick St.; phone: 203701) is crowded but pleasant. Just beside the *Opera House,* audience and actors meet for good talk and the occasional song at the *Grand Circle* (15 Drawbridge St.; phone: 274546). *Beechers Inn* (Faulkners La.; phone: 273144) is convenient to the office of the *Cork Examiner,* so the usual liquids come with the customary quota of newspaper rumors. Across the river on the hill beside the old Elizabeth Fort, the *Gateway* (Barrack St.; phone: 968638) is supposed to be the oldest pub in Cork. It dates from the 17th century and it is credible that the Duke of Marlborough drank here; certainly legions of his military followers through the centuries did. Good lunchtime eating and drinking pubs include *Hourihan's* (Phoenix St.; phone: 273017), *Mutton Lane Inn* (Mutton La., off Patrick St.; phone: 273471), *Oyster Tavern* (see *Eating Out*), *Maguire's Pennyfarthing Inn* (Grand Parade; phone: 277825), *The Maltings* (Wood St., off Washington St.; phone: 271106), *Reidy's Vault Bar* (Washington St.; phone: 275751), and *Dan Lowrey's Seafood Tavern* (MacCurtain St.; phone: 505071).

Donegal Town

Cradled in the crook of a sheltered Atlantic inlet, near the nest of mountains called the Blue Stacks, Donegal is today a tiny town at peace with the world. But such was not always the case. Once the stronghold of the powerful O'Donnell clan, rulers of the northwestern kingdom of Tir Connaill (the country of Conall), now the county of Donegal, it was an arena for great and stirring events. In the glory days of that storied Gaelic era that began in the 13th century, Donegal Town attained a status that rivaled the larger, walled cities that had sprung up around the coast of Ireland, and for several centuries this bastion of the O'Donnells exerted a commanding influence on the course of Irish history. The O'Donnell dynasty became a towering symbol of Gaelic hegemony — during the English conquest of Ireland, the invaders had to vanquish the O'Donnells before they could claim a total victory.

In the Irish language, Donegal is *Dún na nGall* — fort of the foreigners. Some historians believe that the original "foreigners" were invaders from Gaul, who built a fort on the banks of the River Eske as many as 2,000 years ago. What is known with more certainty is that around the 9th century, the Vikings built a fortress on the river that was destroyed by the High King of Ireland in 1159. However, no trace of this fort has ever been found.

Toward the end of the 15th century, the O'Donnell chieftains erected a massive Norman-style stone tower on the site of the ancient Viking fort. Part of this tower is still standing, attached to the castle that burgeoned on the site over the centuries.

At about the same time they built the tower, the O'Donnells built a friary for the Franciscan order farther down on the estuary. Like the fortress, the friary of Donegal is closely identified with the heyday of Donegal history. It became an illustrious monastic school, attracting scholars from across Europe, and within its cloisters a monumental chronology of Irish history was inked out in scrupulous detail over a period of 4 years. This was the celebrated *Annals of the Four Masters.* The four masters — Franciscan Brother Michael O'Clery and three lay scholars — sat in their cells to pen what at first was intended to be a comprehensive history of the saints but somehow turned into a year-by-year narrative of the story of Ireland from 2242 BC to AD 1616. Completed in 1636, the *Annals* are now in Dublin's Royal Irish Academy Library.

For 400 years after the initial Anglo-Norman invasion, the O'Donnells defended their northwest kingdom from both native and foreign foes. Their fame was not founded solely on their prowess in war, however, for they were also bountiful patrons of education, religion, and the arts. In the late 16th century, Queen Elizabeth I finally succeeded in destroying the old

Gaelic dynasties that had ruled Ireland, and the O'Donnells were forced into exile.

To prevent Elizabethan forces from using their castle as a base, the O'Donnells deliberately removed the roof and floors and punched a gaping hole in one of the walls. However, when an English captain, Basil Brooke, took possession of it in 1603, he repaired the old tower and built extensive additions, using stone from the Franciscan friary, which had been laid to waste by the invaders (its tumbled remains are still visible). Toward the end of the 19th century, the castle was handed over to the state and declared a national monument.

With the departure of the O'Donnells at the turn of the 17th century, Donegal's heady hour in history ended, and the town's importance as a seat of power began to diminish. But even though the castle is deserted and the mighty sailing ships are no more than ghosts in the harbor, the memory of that glorious past still thrives.

Today Donegal's historic ruins still invite visitors to recall its storied past. Donegal also provides travelers with the opportunity to experience small-town life in contemporary Ireland and to enjoy a countryside of unchanging beauty. Verging Donegal is a majestic landscape of mountains and valleys, lakes and rivers, and vast expanses of lonely moorland, while the waters of the Atlantic forever lap at the edge of the town.

Donegal At-a-Glance

SEEING THE TOWN

The best way to see Donegal Town is on foot, and it is possible to cover nearly all of it in a few hours. The most commanding vantage point is atop Miller's Hill, behind the Roman Catholic church on Main Street. Another splendid viewing point is from the hill behind Drumcliffe Terrace, on the north side of the river estuary, where you can see a panoramic view of the town and Donegal Bay.

SPECIAL PLACES

Most of the places of interest in town are connected with Donegal's eventful past. A good way to embark on a tour is by starting at the harbor, where the Vikings stormed ashore during an earlier age.

THE DIAMOND Instead of the more conventional square, a diamond-shaped marketplace is a distinctive architectural feature of towns in the northern parts of Ireland. The Donegal Diamond was laid out by the Elizabethan captain Basil Brooke when he took over the town in 1603. Dominating the Diamond is a 25-foot-high, red granite obelisk erected in 1937 to commemorate the Four Masters, who in the nearby Franciscan friary, penned the monumental *Annals* of Irish history in the early 17th century. The architectural style of the obelisk is Irish Romanesque.

DONEGAL CASTLE This impressive keep stands as a symbol of both the lost Gaelic age and the Elizabethan Plantation. It is a combination of the original tower built by the native O'Donnell clan and the Elizabethan manse added on by Captain Brooke. The lower parts of the Norman-style tower house still remain, but the most striking feature of the castle is inside the great hall built by Brooke — a magnificent stone fireplace adorned with the arms of Brooke and of his wife's family, the Leicesters. At press time, visitors were not allowed within the castle, due to extensive renovations. Castle St.

CHURCH OF IRELAND This splendid cut-stone building, with a handsome steeple, has been a place of worship for the local Protestant community for more than 100 years. Before it was built, services were held in a small makeshift church amid the ruins of the old friary. Castle St.

STONE BRIDGE Built about 1840, this bridge beside the castle spans the River Eske. It bears a plaque commemorating a remarkable Catholic priest and writer, the Rev. Dr. John Boyce, who went to America during the Irish famine to care for Irish immigrants and who wrote a number of novels under the pseudonym Paul Peppergrass, one of which — *Shandy Maguire* — had considerable success. He died in the United States in 1864. Castle St.

METHODIST AND PRESBYTERIAN CHURCHES On the west bank of the Eske, these two 100-year-old churches are worth a visit. The Methodist church, the first on the right after crossing the Stone Bridge, is the focal point of a strong Methodist tradition in Donegal. A few steps beyond is the Presbyterian church. Presbyterianism in County Donegal has a close connection with the American sect: Francis Makemie, a minister from Donegal, established the religion in Maryland and is regarded as the virtual founder of the US Presbyterian church.

MEMORIAL CHURCH OF THE FOUR MASTERS Another architectural monument to the monastic authors of the *Annals,* this Catholic church was built in 1935. It is in the Irish Romanesque style and is constructed of red granite. Main St.

NAPOLEONIC ANCHOR On the quayside of the river estuary sits an enormous 15-foot-long, 1½-ton anchor believed to have come from the *Romaine,* a French frigate that was part of a flotilla dispatched by Napoleon and set to land in Donegal to join Irish revolutionaries in rebellion against the British in 1798. Tradition has it that the *Romaine* cut her anchor and fled back to France on the approach of British forces. Quay St.

FRIARY Built in 1474 by the first Red Hugh O'Donnell for the Franciscan order, this historic friary became a renowned seat of learning and monastic scholarship. Within its cloisters, the Four Masters penned their epic *Annals.* When the last of the O'Donnells and another great Irish tribe, the

O'Neills, were driven into exile in 1607, marking the demise of the ancient Gaelic order, the Franciscans departed the friary forever. On the south side of the Eske estuary, just beyond the quay.

Sources and Resources

TOURIST INFORMATION

The prime source of information and advice for visitors is the headquarters of the Donegal-Leitrim-Sligo Regional Tourism Organization (Temple St., Sligo, 40 miles south of Donegal Town on N15; phone: 71-61201). The organization's Donegal information office (Quay St.; phone: 21148) is open May through September. There's also a tourist office in Letterkenny (on the Derry road; phone: 74-21160) that's open year-round. The *Four Masters Bookshop* (see *Shopping*) has a good supply of books about Donegal.

LOCAL COVERAGE The *Donegal Democrat,* a weekly, is the principal purveyor of local news, announcements, and advertising. Other local weeklies are the *Derry People & Donegal News,* the *Derry Journal,* and the *Donegal People's Press.*

TELEPHONE The area code for Donegal Town and the immediate vicinity is 73. When calling from within the Republic of Ireland, dial 073 before the local number.

GETTING AROUND

In this little town, just about everybody walks. There's no municipal bus service, and people hire taxis only for journeys away from town.

BICYCLE During the summer it's pleasant to hire a bike and cycle around the streets, lanes, and byways. Bicycles can be rented from *D. A. McIntyre* (14 Castle St.; phone: 21942) and *C. J. Doherty* (Main St.; phone: 21119).

CAR RENTAL It's wisest to rent a car at the port of arrival — usually Shannon or Dublin airports — where the major rental companies have offices. The car rental closest to Donegal is in Sligo City, 40 miles south on N15: *John Gilbride & Co.,* Bridge St., Sligo (phone: 71-42091).

TAXI Call *James Anthony McGroary* (Orbeg; phone: 35162) or *Victor Kearney* (Doonan; phone: 21524).

SPECIAL EVENTS

Hundreds of card players flock to the town every November to take part in a major bridge congress, one of the most notable events in the calendar of the *Contract Bridge Association of Ireland.* For information contact Una Walsh (41 Friar's Hill, Rahoon, Galway; phone: 91-26502) or Mrs. Dee Crossin (Upper Main St., Donegal; phone: 21072).

SHOPPING

Donegal is the tweed capital of Ireland. There are a number of places that sell other traditional crafts and souvenir items as well. Shops generally are closed on Sundays and close early on Wednesdays.

THE ANTIQUE SHOP The scrupulous business policy of this quaint little establishment guarantees that all antiques on display are genuine. It's overflowing with vases, furniture, brass, and a plethora of paintings — with price tags ranging from bargain-basement to exorbitant. The Diamond (phone: 21144).

DONEGAL CRAFT CENTRE An attractive shopping village just outside town, where you'll will find a complete range of traditional Irish crafts, including Donegal crystal, as well as a pleasant tea shop. Donegal-Sligo Rd., N15 (phone: 22053, 22015, 22225, or 22228).

DONEGAL PARIAN CHINA FACTORY AND SHOW ROOMS Hand-crafted china that resembles Belleek in its delicacy is produced and sold at this nearby factory. Open April through October; factory tours offered weekdays from 9 AM to 4:30 PM. Ballyshannon (phone: 72-51826).

FOUR MASTERS BOOKSHOP This place features an excellent stock of Irish literature and books of local interest, as well as a pretty gift shop. The Diamond (phone: 21526).

THE GIFT SHOP An array of gifts and souvenirs including pottery, crystal, hand-crafted jewelry, paintings, and accessories. The Diamond (phone: 21168).

MAGEE Founded in 1881, this is the supreme tweed shop in Ireland. It displays endless varieties of the versatile fabric, unfinished or tailored to a customer's requirements. In summer there's often a weaver demonstrating the subtleties of tweed fashioning. The shop also has a particularly good selection of woolens and locally hand-knit Aran sweaters. Its café is an attractive place for lunch or tea. The Diamond (phone: 21100).

MCCREADY'S SWEATER SHOP Well-stocked with traditional and designer (mostly Irish) knitwear, most of it handmade. Adult's and children's sizes. The Diamond (phone: 22387).

MELODY MAKER A good place to buy tapes and CDs of traditional music, especially as performed by Donegal fiddlers. Owner Gerry Mehan is happy to assist customers in making a selection and will play tapes before you purchase. Castle St. (phone: 22326).

OVEN DOOR A pastry and cake shop loaded with toothsome take-away confections. The Diamond (phone: 21511).

SYLVESTER OF DONEGAL Tiny and unpretentious, this place sells handsome, custom-made vests and jackets fashioned from sturdy Donegal tweed. Tirconnell St. (phone: 21670).

WARD'S MUSIC SHOP Paddy Ward presides over this friendly studio crammed with musical instruments — *bodhráns,* flutes, bagpipes, fiddles — and songbooks. Upstairs from the *Melody Maker,* Castle St. (phone: 21313).

WILLIAM BRITTON & SONS A Donegal institution since 1874, this shop carries jewelry in traditional designs. Main St. (phone: 21131).

SPORTS AND FITNESS

BOATING For cruises around Donegal Bay, boats can be hired in Killybegs Port, 17 miles west of the town, at *Mooney Boats,* St. Catherine's Rd., Killybegs (phone: 31152).

FISHING A license is required to fish for salmon and all other species. March through September is open season for salmon and sea trout on the River Eske, and the biggest catches are made in mid-June. Six miles north of town is Lough Eske, which holds char, a rare fish in Ireland, along with salmon and trout. For angling information, contact Billy Johnston, *Northern Regional Fisheries Board* (Station Rd., Ballyshannon; phone: 72-51435). Rods and tackle are available at *Charles Doherty's* (Main St.; phone: 21119), where permits also can be obtained. For additional details, see *Gone Fishing* in DIVERSIONS.

GOLF The 18-hole course at *Donegal Golf Club* is set amid majestic scenery, overlooking the Atlantic. Six miles south on N15 at Murvagh, Ballintra (phone: 34054).

TENNIS There are outdoor hard courts at Ardeskin, beyond the Catholic church off Main Street.

SWIMMING There's no municipal pool, but a nice sandy beach is west of the town. The Atlantic waters in these parts, unfortunately, can be quite chilly unless a rare long, hot summer heats up the water. The beach is off the Mountcharles road, N56, and is signposted.

MUSIC

Some local pubs have traditional Irish music sessions. Local newspapers carry ads with the details. Also see *Sharing a Pint.*

NIGHTCLUBS AND NIGHTLIFE

Like so many small Irish towns, the nightlife of Donegal is largely focused on the revered pint of Guinness porter (stout) or "balls of malt" (glasses of Irish whiskey) sipped discreetly in shuttered pubs after dark. Lively dance parties are held until near dawn most nights in the *Abbey* hotel (see *Checking In*). *Nero's* (Main St.; phone: 21111) draws a younger crowd.

Best in Town

CHECKING IN

In the establishments rated as expensive expect to pay up to $150 a night for two. Places in the moderate category will cost between $90 and $120 for a double room. A great many excellent small guesthouses and bed and breakfast establishments in and around the town are of a very high standard and are absolutely great values. These often are inexpensive and cost $90 or less for two. The tourist board on Quay Street (phone: 21148) has information on vacancies. All telephone numbers are in the 73 area code unless otherwise indicated.

EXPENSIVE

Harvey's Point Country Hotel Four miles from Donegal Town on the shores of Lough Eske, this attractive country inn offers guests both a quiet getaway spot and lively entertainment. The sprawling 13-acre complex features 20 comfortable guestrooms in a separate building at a distance from the popular restaurant, bar, and cabaret. Country pleasures include hill walking, cycling, tennis, golf at a nearby course, and fishing on the lake, river, or sea. The resident Clydesdale horses are available for wagon rides. There are stables if guests would like to bring their own steeds, and a landing pad is available for those who arrive by helicopter from Sligo Airport. Open year-round. Lough Eske (phone: 22208; fax: 22352).

St. Ernan's House In sylvan surroundings on a small island joined to the mainland by a causeway, this 19th-century mansion offers a quiet and relaxed Old World atmosphere as well as first-rate food (see *Eating Out*). There are 13 rooms, many with views of the Atlantic. St. Ernan's Island, 2 miles south of town on N15, signposted (phone: 21065; fax: 22098).

MODERATE

Abbey A well-run hostelry with 49 comfortable rooms, excellent service, and a particularly good grill room (see *Eating Out*) with a view of the estuary. The Diamond (phone: 21014; fax: 21014).

Hyland Central A first class hotel, with a courteous staff that makes guests feel at home. There are 72 tastefully furnished rooms — some overlook the River Eske — with TV sets, radios, and phones. The leisure center has a heated indoor pool, a gym with instructor, a Jacuzzi, a steamroom, and sun beds. The food is good (see *Eating Out*). The Diamond (phone: 21027; fax: 22295).

INEXPENSIVE

Danby House This charming, 20-acre establishment is set on a bluff overlooking Donegal Bay. The house, built in 1820, has 5 spacious guestrooms, all

decorated with antiques. The restaurant is good (see *Eating Out*). In Ballyshannon, about 14 miles south of Donegal (phone: 72-51138).

EATING OUT

Options for eating out in Donegal Town are limited; restaurants in the
hotels recommended above are the best bets. At restaurants listed as
expensive, expect to pay $50 or more for dinner for two, excluding wine,
drinks, and tips; a dinner for two at a place described as moderate will cost
$30 to $50; and at places listed as inexpensive, expect to pay $30 or less.
All telephone numbers are in the 73 area code unless otherwise indicated.

EXPENSIVE

Danby House In the 1820 guesthouse of the same name, this excellent dining spot
is set on a bluff overlooking Donegal Bay. Specialties include mussels,
prawns, smoked salmon, and rack of lamb. The lettuce and herbs are
grown in a walled garden on the premises. Service is first-rate at this
friendly place. Open daily for dinner; closed Sundays. Reservations necessary. MasterCard and Visa accepted. In Ballyshannon, about 14 miles
south of Donegal (phone: 72-51138).

St. Ernan's House The decor in this handsome hotel dining room is pure 19th-
century Georgian, with antique furniture, gilt-framed paintings, heirloom
silver, and beautifully draped windows that overlook the water. The cuisine is continental and Irish, with an emphasis on seafood. Open for dinner
daily mid-March through mid-November. Reservations advised. Master-
Card and Visa accepted. St. Ernan's Island, 2 miles south of town on N15,
signposted (phone: 21065).

MODERATE

Hyland Central The restaurant at this eponymous hotel has the best and most
varied menu in town, with dishes such as Donegal mountain lamb, Lough
Eske salmon and trout, and lobsters from Killybegs. It's also famous for
its large portions. Open daily for dinner. Reservations advised. Major
credit cards accepted. The Diamond (phone: 21027).

Old Castle Bar and Restaurant A handsome series of wood-paneled rooms where
lunch is served daily, and dinner is offered on Saturday and Sunday
evenings. At the rear, *The Stables* serves light meals and snacks all day and
hosts traditional music performances in the evenings. Open daily. No
reservations. Major credit cards accepted. Castle St. (phone: 21062).

INEXPENSIVE

Abbey The grill room of the *Abbey* hotel offers first class food served cheerfully
and quickly. Open daily for lunch and dinner. Reservations advised.
Major credit cards accepted. The Diamond (phone: 21014).

McGinty's Also known as *Moll,* this clean and bright eatery serves such mainstays as burgers and pizza. Open daily from 9:30 AM to 9:30 PM. Reservations advised. No credit cards accepted. 11 Main St. (phone: 22416).

Magee Café Located upstairs in the *Magee* tweed shop, this café is excellent for lunches and snacks. Open 10 AM to 5 PM; closed Sundays. No reservations. No credit cards accepted. The Diamond (phone: 21100).

SHARING A PINT

The downstairs bar in the *Hyland Central* hotel (see *Checking In*) has softly lit Tudor decor and a roaring peat fire. In addition to the libations, it serves fine snacks. The *Schooner* (Ballybofey Rd., just off The Diamond; no phone) is the best place to hear traditional music. It also offers a cozy open fireplace and conversation in the musical Donegal brogue that is as exhilarating as the whiskey and stout. Also stop in at the *Star* (Main St.; phone: 21158), where locals mingle over a pint and listen to sounds of the fiddle.

Dublin

Dublin is a friendly city steeped in a history sometimes splendid, often troubled; a city of wide Georgian streets, elegant squares, and magnificent doorways; of ancient churches and cathedrals that thrust their hallowed spires and towers against the skyline; of memorable sunsets that bathe the 18th-century red brick façades in a fiery glow; a city where the English language acquires a special dimension and where dark, creamy-headed Guinness stout flows abundantly in companionable pubs. The city is set in the sweep of Dublin Bay, the Dublin hills and the Wicklow Mountains behind and to the south, and through the city the River Liffey — James Joyce's Anna Livia Plurabelle — wends its leisurely way to the sea, spanned as it passes by 11 bridges.

Once there was only one bridge. Indeed, it was not so much a bridge as a mere ford in the river, and it stood approximately where the Father Matthew Bridge stands today. It was built by the first Celtic inhabitants of what is now Dublin. When they came here, we cannot be sure; what is certain is that by AD 140 they were well established on this site. The Celts themselves probably referred to the spot by a name that endures to this day — the official Gaelic *Baile Atha Cliath* (town of the ford of the hurdles).

It was not, however, until the coming of the Vikings in the 9th century that Dublin as we now know it began to take shape. In AD 837, Viking settlers established themselves downstream from the old Celtic settlement, on a spot where the Poddle, which now flows underground, entered the Liffey, causing it to form a dark pool, or *dubh linn*. The Vikings referred to their settlement by those two Gaelic words, and the anglicized version became the city's modern English name. Dublin rapidly became the focal point of the Viking invasion of Ireland. Then, as the Vikings began to see that trading was ultimately more profitable than plunder, Dublin became a major center for their extensive European trade. Not long after their arrival, the Vikings were converted to Christianity, and in 1034 they erected a cathedral, which became the nucleus of modern Christ Church. The cathedral stood in the center of Viking Dublin and allows us to place the ancient city accurately.

Just over 3 centuries after the coming of the Vikings, new invaders swept Ireland. In 1169 the first contingent of Normans landed on the beach of Bannow, in County Wexford. Two years later, the powerful Baron Richard Gilbert de Clare, otherwise known as Strongbow, and his 1,000 men took Dublin by storm, forcing the city's Viking king and inhabitants to flee.

Not long afterward, Dublin Castle was built near the site of the old Viking cathedral, which the Normans had replaced with a new, larger edifice. City walls also were erected. (Their remains can be seen at St. Audoen's Arch, below Christ Church.) Thus medieval Dublin — a small area surrounded by walls — began to take form.

In shape and size Dublin did not alter greatly until the arrival of a new viceroy, or king's representative, in 1662 heralded the city's rise to definitive national importance. Dublin, under James Butler, Duke of Ormonde, became and remained the central arena for Ireland's social, political, and cultural life.

Butler, believing that the stability of a government should be reflected in public works, began municipal improvements almost immediately. The solitary, medieval Dublin Bridge was joined by four new bridges across the river; Phoenix Park was enclosed by a 7-mile wall; and several new streets were built.

Although Dublin's importance as a governmental center and seaport increased enormously in the late 17th century, it was during the 18th century that the city truly flourished, becoming one of the most vibrant and sparkling capitals in all of Europe. The strong movement toward parliamentary independence that took place at this time was reflected in the construction of the splendid Parliament House (now the Bank of Ireland in College Green). Begun in 1729, it was the first in a series of great public buildings built during this time. In addition, extensive rebuilding was carried out on Dublin Castle and Trinity College, and the Wide Streets Commission was set up. It was as if the city were proudly preparing for the new position of importance it would occupy when, in 1782, parliamentary independence was conceded to Ireland by the British Parliament.

Great buildings followed one another in dizzying succession — Leinster House, the Royal Exchange, the Mansion House, the Four Courts, the Custom House. Irish classical architecture, in all its gravity, beauty, and balance, reached full maturity. It flowered in public buildings and private houses, spacious squares and elegant streets. This was Georgian Dublin (various King Georges sat on the British throne during the period): the Dublin of Henry Grattan, Jonathan Swift, David Garrick, Peg Woffington, Oliver Goldsmith, Bishop Berkeley, and Edmund Burke. Handel himself conducted the world premiere of his "Messiah" in this glittering city, whose center was the area between Dublin Castle and the Parliament House.

Architecturally, Dublin reached its zenith in the 18th century. However, in the 19th century, with the dismantling of the Parliament, Dublin's political and social life suffered a blow from which it was not to recover easily. By contrast, the city's literary life began to flower in the late 19th and early 20th centuries with the birth of two great literary movements — the Irish literary renaissance and the Gaelic League. The two movements revived and romanticized the early legends and history of Ireland. The literary renaissance — spearheaded by William Butler Yeats, Lady Augusta Gregory, Douglas Hyde, and John Millington Synge, to name but a few — placed a splendid and indelible mark on 20th-century English literature. The movement found its greatest expression in the creation of Dublin's *Abbey Theatre,* associated forever with the brilliant plays of Sean O'Casey. For many years the *Abbey* was the most famous theater in the world. The Gaelic League had more popular appeal; with its dream of the restoration of the Gaelic language and the reestablishment of a separate Irish cultural nation, it provided a great deal of the inspiration for the Easter Rebellion of 1916. The Easter Rebellion, concentrated in Dublin, sparked the 5-year War of Independence, which culminated in the Anglo-Irish Treaty of 1921 (whereby Ireland gained the status of free state). The signing of the treaty was followed by civil war in 1922–23, during which many buildings that had escaped damage in the 1916 rebellion suffered badly. Happily, all the heirlooms of the 18th century have been restored to their original grandeur.

Dublin today, with a population of just over 1 million people, is far larger than it has been at any other stage of its history. Nevertheless, it still is an eminently walkable city. The crossroads of medieval and 18th-century Dublin remain the center of interest. Within a half-mile radius of the Bank of Ireland on College Green lie the cathedrals, museums, Dublin Castle, great Georgian public buildings, parks, and shops. All are neatly enclosed by the Royal Canal to the north and the Grand Canal to the south.

Thanks to the *Dublin Millennium* celebrations in 1988, the downtown area of the city now enjoys a number of permanent enhancements, including new sculptures by modern Irish artisans and, in the heart of the city on O'Connell Street, an elaborate fountain dominated by a larger-than-life sculpture of a reclining female nude, *Anna Livia Plurabelle,* who represents the River Liffey. Another urban improvement has been the transformation of Grafton Street into a pedestrian shopping area with rejuvenated shop façades, brick walkways, benches, and plants. The adjacent Temple Bar area also has been restored and is becoming Dublin's "Left Bank," with an assortment of avant-garde shops, bars, cafés, and restaurants.

In addition to seeing the city's numerous historic sites, and strolling through its streets, parks, and shopping areas, visitors should be sure to sample Dublin's ever-growing galaxy of theaters and concert halls, offering a year-round program of great dramatic, musical, literary, and artistic events.

But the focal point of Dubliners' social life is the pub, and it is in pubs that visitors will find the city's true spirit. Dublin can be a comfortable, "down home" kind of place, so slow down and enjoy it. It has an endearing earthiness, a quality that inspired James Joyce to refer affectionately to his native city as a "strumpet city in the sunset" and "dear, dirty Dublin."

Dublin At-a-Glance

SEEING THE CITY

Views of this essentially flat city are best from a number of restaurants in the surrounding hills; particularly nice is *Killakee House* in Rathfarnham (Killakee Rd.; phone: 493-2645 or 493-2917). Or see Dublin from the neighboring Wicklow Mountains.

SPECIAL PLACES

Central Dublin is very compact. Since traffic can move slowly, by far the best way to see the city is on foot by making full use of Dublin's splendid, signposted *Tourist Trail*. Walk the wide Georgian squares and avenues, meander down the cobblestone lanes near the Liffey Quays, stroll through the sylvan paths of St. Stephen's Green or along bustling Grafton Street — Dublin's shoppers' paradise — and stop at *Bewley's Café* (see *Shopping*) for a cup of coffee or at the *Shelbourne* hotel (see *Checking In*) for a proper afternoon tea.

SOUTH DOWNTOWN

MERRION SQUARE The loveliest of Dublin's Georgian squares, it is a study in balance and elegance that evokes the graciousness of a vanished age. Note particularly the variety of fanlights on doorways. At No. 1, the young Oscar Wilde lived with his celebrated parents, the surgeon Sir William Wills Wilde and the poetess Speranza; No. 42 was the home of Sir Jonah Barrington, an 18th-century barrister and raconteur; at No. 58 lived Daniel O'Connell, the "Liberator" who won Catholic emancipation in 1829; No. 70 was the home of tragic Sheridan Le Fanu, author of sinister tales such as *Uncle Silas* and *Through a Glass Darkly* (after his wife's death in 1858, he shut himself up there, appearing only after nightfall to walk in the shadows of Merrion Square); at No. 82 lived William Butler Yeats, poet and Nobel Prize winner. Today the only house in the square used as a private dwelling is No. 71, where well-known couturière Sybil Connolly has her home and studio.

NUMBER TWENTY-NINE Located on one of Dublin's most fashionable 18th-century streets, this 4-story brick building, restored and maintained by a joint effort of the *National Museum of Ireland* and the Irish Electrical Supply Board, gives visitors the opportunity to see the interior of a typical Georgian house. The furnishings are designed to reflect the home life of a middle class Dublin family during the late 18th and early 19th centuries. Open Tuesdays through Sundays year-round. No admission charge. 29 Lower Fitzwilliams St. (phone: 676-5831).

LEINSTER HOUSE When young Lord Kildare, Earl of Leinster, chose to build a mansion "on the other side of the River Liffey" in 1745, the location was questioned by many, for at that time, the north side of the city was considered more fashionable. Undaunted, he went ahead with his plan, asserting prophetically, "Where I go, fashion will follow." The house Lord Kildare built is said to resemble (and may have inspired) the White House, whose architect, James Hoban of Carlow, studied in Dublin after the completion of Leinster House. The building was purchased in the 19th century by the Royal Dublin Society, and in 1921 the Parliament of the new Irish Free State chose the building as its meeting place. Leinster House continues to be the meeting place of the Dáil (House of Representatives) and Seanad (Senate). When the Dáil is in session, visitors may watch from the visitors' gallery. Sessions are held Tuesdays through Thursdays, except in July, August, and September. Apply for tickets at the main gate or by writing in advance. No admission charge. Kildare St., Merrion Sq. (phone: 678-9911).

MUSEUM OF NATURAL HISTORY The first sight to greet visitors is an old favorite, a huge preserved shark that hangs from the ceiling. Also popular is the display of birds, as well as the three magnificent skeletons of giant Irish deer, believed to be about 10,000 years old. On the ground floor, the Irish Room displays Irish fauna and a new exhibition of Irish insects. An impressive collection of big-game heads and antlers from India and Africa in the galleries on the second floor transports museumgoers to late Victorian times. On the third floor are exotic shells, butterflies, and birds — plus skeletons of the extinct dodo, solitaire, and giant bird of Madagascar, with its 11.7-inch egg. A priceless assemblage of glass models of the invertebrates is also well worth seeing as is an impressive geological collection consisting of little-known Irish rocks and minerals. Admission charge. Closed Mondays. Merrion Sq. (phone: 661-8811).

NATIONAL GALLERY It has been called "the best small gallery in Europe" and, considering its chronic shortage of funds, it certainly has a remarkable collection, with some outstanding examples of works from all the major schools, particularly the Italian and Dutch. Andrea di Bartolo, Fra Angelico, Uccello, Signorelli, Perugino, Titian, Rembrandt, El Greco, and David are all represented; a collection of more than 30 Turner watercolors is shown every January. The Irish School is brilliantly represented by the works of Jack Yeats and earlier painters such as Nathaniel Hone, Walter Osborne, William Orpen, and James Arthur O'Connor. Though staff shortages often cause a number of its rooms to be closed, the gallery is lively and interesting. There's a good research library, a bookshop, and an inexpensive restaurant that has become a popular Dublin meeting place. Open daily. Admission charge. Merrion Sq. (phone: 661-5133).

NATIONAL MUSEUM The massive Thomas Deane building on Kildare Street houses a remarkable collection of Irish antiquities, among them priceless collections of prehistoric gold artifacts, such as solid gold dress fasteners, torques, and lunulae made by the skilled craftsmen of the Bronze and Iron ages. An exhibition area called The Treasury features the museum's important collection of early Christian metalwork, including the *Ardagh Chalice* and the *Cross of Cong*. The Georgian silver, Waterford crystal, and Belleek pottery on display are equally captivating. Visitors should not miss the collection of Irish harps, *uilleann* pipes, and other musical instruments, nor the Derrynaflan chalice, paten, and strainer, found in 1980 at Killenaule in Tipperary. Finds from the site of Viking Dublin are on display in the museum's exhibition center around the corner on Merrion Row. Closed Mondays. Admission charge for special exhibits. Kildare St. (phone: 661-8811).

GENEALOGICAL OFFICE AND HERALDIC MUSEUM Formerly in Dublin Castle, this is the domain of Ireland's chief herald (the official in charge of genealogy, heraldic arms, and the like) and the ideal starting point for an ancestry hunt. Open weekdays. No admission charge, but there is a fee for genealogical consultations. 2 Kildare St. (phone: 661-4877 or 661-1626).

ST. STEPHEN'S GREEN A couple of blocks southwest of Merrion Square lies St. Stephen's Green, the loveliest of Dublin's many public parks. Its 22 acres contain gardens, a waterfall, and an ornamental lake. In summer it's an excellent place to sit and watch working Dublin take its lunch; bands play on the bandstand in July and August.

NEWMAN HOUSE Composed of two 18th-century townhouses dating back to 1740, this is the historic seat of the Catholic University of Ireland, named for Cardinal John Henry Newman, the 19th-century writer and theologian and the first rector of the university. The recently restored plasterwork, marble tiled floors, and wainscot paneling are superb. The site also contains a basement restaurant called *The Commons* (see *Eating Out*), an outdoor terrace, and a "secret garden" tucked between the buildings in the back. Open June through September; closed Mondays. Admission charge. 85-86 St. Stephen's Green (phone: 475-7255 or 475-1752).

MANSION HOUSE Dublin preceded London in building a Mansion House for its lord mayor in 1715. The Round Room, which is usually open to the public, was the site of the adoption of the Declaration of Irish Independence in 1919 and the signing of the Anglo-Irish Treaty of 1921. No admission charge. Dawson St. (phone: 676-2852).

TRINITY COLLEGE Dawson Street descends to meet Trinity College, the oldest university in Ireland, founded by Elizabeth I of England on the site of the 12th-century Monastery of All Hallows. Alumni of the college include Oliver Goldsmith, Edmund Burke, Jonathan Swift, Bishop Berkeley (pronounced *Bark*-lee) — who also lent his name to Berkeley in California — William Congreve, Thomas Moore, Sheridan Le Fanu, Oscar Wilde, and J. P. Donleavy. No trace of the original Elizabethan structure remains; the oldest surviving part of the college dates from 1700. The Long Room, Trinity's famous library, is the longest single-chamber library in existence. It contains a priceless collection of 800,000 volumes and 3,000 ancient manuscripts and papyri. The area of the library known as the Colonnades is the setting for the library's chief treasure, the *Book of Kells,* an 8th-century illuminated manuscript of the four gospels that has been described as the "most beautiful book in the world." The Colonnades is open daily, year-round. Admission charge. College Green (phone: 677-2941).

Trinity College also is the home of "The Dublin Experience," a 45-minute multimedia program that traces the history of Dublin from earliest times to the present. In May through October it is shown daily, on the hour from 10 AM to 5 PM, in the *Davis Theatre.* Admission charge. Entrance on Nassau St. (phone: 677-2941, ext. 1177).

PARLIAMENT HOUSE Facing Trinity College is the monumental Parliament House, now the Bank of Ireland. Built in 1729 and regarded as one of the finest examples of the architecture of its period, this was the first of the great series of 18th-century public buildings in Dublin. As its name implies, it was erected to house the Irish Parliament in the century that saw the birth of Home Rule. Closed Sundays. No admission charge. College Green (phone: 677-6801).

TEMPLE BAR Situated just south of the River Liffey, this is an 8-block area in one of Dublin's oldest sections — stretching from Westmoreland to Fishamble Streets, between Trinity College and Christ Church Cathedral. The district, which has a distinctive blend of Georgian and Victorian ambience, owes its name to Sir William Temple, Provost of Trinity College, who maintained a house and gardens here in the early 17th century. Temple Bar is fast becoming Dublin's "Left Bank," with an assortment of avant-garde art galleries, shops, bars, cafés, and restaurants. The area is also the home of the *Irish Film Centre* (see below).

IRISH FILM CENTRE This recently opened complex is dedicated to the art of cinema culture — an exciting development for the Irish film industry, as well as for researchers, historians, students, and the general public. It houses two movie theaters, a National Film Archive, a film and television museum, a film information office, and film and video libraries, in addition to a restaurant and coffee shop. The center also hosts Film Trail tours to sites in Dublin that have been featured in major motion pictures. Film and video courses are conducted on site. Call for hours. Admission charge for films. 6 Eustace St. (phone: 677-8788).

DUBLIN CASTLE Dame Street leads westward from College Green toward the older part of the city, where the early Viking and Norman settlers established themselves. Fortresses have stood on the site of Dublin Castle since the time of the Celts. The current structure was the center of English rule in Ireland for 400 years; for much of this time it had as grim a reputation as the Tower of London. Although the present building dates primarily from the 18th century, one of the four towers that flanked the original moated castle survives as the Record Tower. The 15th-century Bedford Tower, later reconstructed in 1777, was used as a state prison from 1918 to 1920; the Georgian State Apartments, formerly the residence of the English viceroys, have been beautifully restored. They now are used for state functions. St. Patrick's Hall in the State Apartments was the scene of the inauguration of Ireland's first president, Douglas Hyde; here, too, President John F. Kennedy was declared a freeman of Dublin. Open daily. Admission charge for the Bedford Tower, and the State Apartments. Dame St. (phone: 677-7129).

CHRIST CHURCH CATHEDRAL Not far from Dublin Castle, the massive shape of Christ Church Cathedral crowns the hill on which the ancient city stood. Founded in 1038 by Viking King Sitric Silkenbeard of Dublin, Christ Church was demolished in the 12th century and rebuilt by the Norman Richard Gilbert de Clare (Strongbow), who is buried within its walls. Christ Church today is the Church of Ireland (Protestant) cathedral for the diocese of Dublin. The vaulted crypt remains one of the largest in Ireland. Dubliners traditionally gather in front of this cathedral to ring in the *New Year.* The cathedral and crypt are open daily. No admission charge, but a small donation is requested. Christ Church Pl. (phone: 677-8099).

ST. AUDOEN'S ARCH AND THE CITY WALLS The 13th-century Church of St. Audoen is Dublin's oldest parish church. It was founded by early Norman settlers, who gave it the name St. Ouen, or Audoen, after the patron saint of their native Rouen. Close to the church is a flight of steps leading down to St. Audoen's Arch, the sole surviving gateway of the medieval city walls. Open daily. No admission charge, but donations are welcome. High St. (phone: 679-1855).

"The Flame on the Hill," a multi-image show presented on the lower level of St. Audoen's Church, offers a look at Ireland before the coming of the Vikings, with particular emphasis on monastic life during the period when Ireland was known as the "land of saints and scholars." Open April through October; closed Sundays and Mondays. Admission charge (phone: 679-7099).

ST. PATRICK'S CATHEDRAL Although Christ Church stood within the old walled city, John Comyn, one of Dublin's 12th-century archbishops, felt that while he remained under municipal jurisdiction he could not achieve the temporal power for which he thirsted. Accordingly, he left the city walls and built a fine structure within a stone's throw of Christ Church. By the 19th century both cathedrals were in a state of considerable disrepair. Henry Roe, a distiller, came to the aid of Christ Church, restoring it at his own expense; Sir Benjamin Lee Guinness of the famous brewing family came to the assistance of St. Patrick's — hence the saying in Dublin that "Christ Church was restored with glasses, St. Patrick's with pints!"

The most interesting aspect of this quite beautiful cathedral is its association with Jonathan Swift, author of *Gulliver's Travels* and dean of the cathedral for 32 years. Within these walls he is buried, beside his loving Stella. On a slab near the entrance is carved the epitaph Swift composed for himself, which Yeats described as the greatest epitaph in literature: "He lies where furious indignation can no longer rend his heart." St. Patrick's now is used interdenominationally. Open daily. Admission charge. Patrick St. (phone: 475-4817).

MARSH'S LIBRARY Adjoining St. Patrick's, this library dates from 1702. Its collection of 25,000 rare and magnificently bound old volumes and maps includes a copy of Clarendon's *History of the Great Rebellion,* once owned and annotated by Jonathan Swift. Open year-round; closed Tuesdays and Sundays (phone: 543511).

GUINNESS BREWERY Founded in 1759 by Arthur Guinness, this is the largest exporting stout brewery in the world. The *Guinness Hopstore* (adjacent to the main brewery), once the storage building for the ingredients of the world-famous dark stout, is now a public hall that mounts temporary exhibits and art shows. In the same building is the *Guinness Museum,* which features old posters and other Guinness memorabilia, and the *Cooper's Museum,* which focuses on the casks and vats used in the brewing process. Next to the *Hopstore,* the visitors' center has an audiovisual presentation about the making of the famous brew, and offers free samples. Closed Saturdays and Sundays. Admission charge. Crane St. (phone: 536700).

IRISH MUSEUM OF MODERN ART (IMMA) Housed in one of Ireland's finest 17th-century structures is a permanent collection of contemporary and avant-garde works by such modern masters as Picasso, Miró, and Léger, as well as works by native artists including Jack Yeats and Louis le Brocquy. Originally the Royal Hospital, a home for retired soldiers, the museum building was restored at a cost of about $30 million and reopened in 1985 on its 300th anniversary. The galleries are set around a large courtyard in the style of Les Invalides in Paris. The museum often hosts visiting visual, theatrical, performance, and music exhibitions; check the Dublin newspapers for details. Closed Mondays. Admission charge (phone: 671-8666).

NORTH DOWNTOWN

FOUR COURTS Almost directly across the river from the Guinness Brewery lies the stately Four Courts of Justice, dating from the apogee of the 18th century. The design of the building was begun by Thomas Cooley and completed by James Gandon, the greatest of all the Georgian architects. Supreme and High Court sittings are open to the public on weekdays. No admission charge. Inns Quay (phone: 872-5555).

ST. MICHAN'S CHURCH Not far from the Four Courts is St. Michan's, a 17th-century church built on the site of a 10th-century Viking church. The

18th-century organ is said to have been played by Handel when he was in Dublin for the first public performance of "Messiah."

Of perhaps greater interest is the extraordinary crypt, with its remarkable preservative atmosphere: Bodies have lain here for centuries without decomposing, and visitors can, if they feel so inclined, shake the leathery hand of an 8-foot-tall Crusader. Open weekdays and Saturday mornings. Admission charge. Church St. (phone: 872-4154).

IRISH WHISKEY CORNER With numerous pubs on every street of the city, it's no wonder that Irish whiskey, like Guinness stout, is big business in Ireland. The story of the legendary liquid, known in Gaelic as *uisce beatha* (the water of life), is told at this former distillery warehouse. One-hour tours include a short introductory audiovisual presentation, a visit to an exhibition area with archival photographs and distillery memorabilia, and a whiskey making demonstration. The tour ends at a pub-style "tasting room," where visitors can sample the various brands being brewed today. Tours are available Mondays through Fridays at 3:30 PM. Admission charge. Bow St. (phone: 872-5566).

MOORE STREET On this thoroughfare near the historic General Post Office, among the fruit and flower sellers, the true voice of Dublin is audible — lively, warm, voluble, speaking an English that is straight out of Sean O'Casey.

MUNICIPAL GALLERY OF MODERN ART Lord Charlemont, for whom this house was designed by Sir William Chambers in 1764, was a great patron of the arts; it is fitting, therefore, that his home has become a museum. It has an outstanding collection of Impressionist paintings, as well as works by Picasso, Utrillo, Bonnard, and such prominent Irish painters as Sir William Orpen, John B. Yeats (the poet's father), and Jack Yeats (the poet's brother). Closed Mondays. No admission charge. Beyond the Garden of Remembrance (a memorial to those who died for Irish freedom), on the north side of Parnell Sq. (phone: 874-1903).

CUSTOM HOUSE This masterpiece of Georgian architecture — restored and newly illuminated in 1991, the year Dublin served as the European City of Culture — adorns the north bank of the Liffey, to the east of O'Connell Street. It was the *chef d'oeuvre* of James Gandon and is one of the finest buildings of its kind in Europe. Now occupied by government offices and closed to the public, it should nonetheless be seen at close range: The carved riverheads that form the keystones of the arches and entrances are splendid. Custom House Quay (phone: 874-2961).

CUSTOM HOUSE QUAY DEVELOPMENT There's something new on the Dublin skyline. This major urban renewal project — covering a 27-acre site adjacent to the historic Custom House in the city's dockside area — is scheduled to be completed in stages over the next few years. Architectural work is in the hands of Benjamin Thompson and Associates, the US firm that designed New York's *South Street Seaport* and Boston's *Faneuil Hall Marketplace*. At the core of the site is the Dublin Financial Services Centre, a network of more than 100 international banking, brokerage, and insurance firms. In addition to the financial and business hub, plans include a hotel and conference facility, shops, restaurants, museums, and entertainment outlets. Custom House Quay (phone: 363122).

SUBURBS

PHOENIX PARK Northwest of the city center, the park covers 1,760 acres, beautifully planted with a great variety of trees. Within its walls are the residences of the President of the Republic and the US Ambassador. Among the attractions are the lovely People's Gardens, a herd of fallow deer, and the Zoological Gardens. The charming Dublin Zoo has an impressive collection of animals and holds several records for lion breeding. The park and zoo are open daily. Admission charge for the zoo. Entrance on Park Gate St. (phone: 677-1425).

JAMES JOYCE MUSEUM Resembling other Martello towers that line the Irish coast, the one that houses this museum was built in 1804 to withstand a threatened Napoleonic invasion, and it would have remained an attractive but fairly anonymous pile of granite had it not been for James Joyce's *Ulysses,* one of the greatest novels in the English language. The author lived in the tower briefly with Oliver Joseph St. John Gogarty, and in the opening scene of *Ulysses,* Stephen Dedalus lives there with Buck Mulligan. For many a Joyce fan, June 16, the day when the events described in *Ulysses* took place, is marked with a *Bloomsday* tour, with the first stop at the tower. Sylvia Beach, *Ulysses'* first publisher, opened the tower as a museum in 1962, and it now holds an odd and varied collection of memorabilia: the writer's piano and guitar; his waistcoat, tie, and cane; and letters, manuscripts, photographs, and rare editions. But the chief exhibit is the tower itself, a squat structure looking across Dublin Bay to Howth that is one of the few of its type currently open to the public. Open year-round, but by appointment only from October through April. Sandycove (phone: 280-9265 or 280-8571).

CHESTER BEATTY LIBRARY Founded by an American-born, naturalized British resident in Ireland, this library houses what is considered to be the most valuable and representative private collection of Oriental manuscripts and miniatures in the world. The collection of Islamic art and manuscripts includes some 250 Korans; Persian, Turkish, and Indian paintings are also well represented. In addition, there's a unique collection of Chinese jade books, some 900 Chinese snuffboxes, and more than 220 rhinoceros horn cups. The collection of Japanese illuminated manuscripts *(nara-e)* ranks with the foremost in Europe, as does the collection of Japanese woodblock prints *(surimono)*. The superb group of Western manuscripts includes illuminated books of hours and a volume of gospels from Stavelot Abbey, executed in Flanders in about AD 1000. Eleven manuscript volumes of the Bible dating from the early 2nd to the 4th century are also on view. Closed Sundays and Mondays. No admission charge. 20 Shrewsbury Rd., Balls-bridge (phone: 269-2386).

NATIONAL BOTANIC GARDENS The largest garden of its kind in the world when it opened in 1800, it has since declined in importance, but its 46 acres of flowers, shrubs, and trees of some 20,000 species still make it one of the most pleasant places to pass a few hours in Dublin. Among the most notable features are a rose bush grown from a cutting of national poet Thomas Moore's original "Last Rose of Summer"; the curvilinear mid-19th-century glass conservatories designed by Dublin architect Richard Turner, who also built the Great Palm House at London's Kew Gardens; a specimen of the Killarney fern *Trichomanes speciosum,* virtually exter-minated in its native habitat by rapacious Victorian fern hunters; a charm-ing small rose garden reached by a bridge across a millstream; and a number of beds in which plants are arranged by scientific families, making for groupings that may surprise some gardeners. Known to Dubliners as the Botanics, the gardens also are rich in bird life and swarming with red squirrels and rabbits. Lovers of English literature will be interested to note that the property previously belonged to *Spectator* founder Joseph Addi-son, who was secretary to the Earl of Sutherland in Dublin for a short while. Lovers of Victorian cemeteries should wind up their visit with a stop next door, where the headstones are like a roll call of key figures in Irish history, with O'Connell and Parnell at the top of the list. Open daily, year-round. No admission charge. Glasnevin (phone: 377596 or 374388).

MALAHIDE CASTLE, PARK, AND GARDENS No other property in Ireland was occu-pied by a single family as long as this one overlooking the Broadmeadow estuary and the Irish Sea. The Talbot family lived here continuously from 1185 until 1973 (when the last Lord Talbot died), with a break of only a few years in Cromwellian times. Despite the pedigree, this is a smallish, easily managed castle, although many additions have been made to the oldest surviving section, a 15th-century tower. The paneled 16th-century Oak Room, one of the finest in the country, is still well preserved. Throughout the castle, a number of portraits from the valuable National Portrait Collection are on display, along with a fine collection of Irish period furniture.

The 270-acre gardens and park are superb. The last occupant, Lord Milo Talbot de Malahide, was a horticultural enthusiast who specialized in plants of the Southern Hemisphere; he also owned an estate in Tas-mania. Between 1948 and his death in 1973, he amassed a collection of some 5,000 species and varieties that flourished in the alkaline soil, the Gulf Stream–warmed climate, the fine breezes, and the low rainfall, including the world's largest collection of olearias, good specimens of euphorbia, eryngium, and ceanothus, and a significant assortment of ozothamnus. He also persuaded many extremely tender plants from South America and Africa to prosper in the open here. Open year-round during seasonally varying hours. Admission charge. Malahide, about 12 miles from Dublin on the Malahide road (phone: 845-2377 or 845-2337).

NEWBRIDGE HOUSE AND PARK Life upstairs and downstairs is the theme of this Georgian house designed by Edward Lovett Pearce's colleague Richard Castle and built from local stone in about 1740 for Charles Cobbe, Archbishop of Dublin. Although the house is now managed by the Irish government, Cobbe's descendants still live on a portion of the estate, among scores of curiosities from the lives of their forebears (furniture, portraits, dolls, and travel memorabilia upstairs; 18th-century kitchen and laundry implements downstairs). There are also some possessions of Jonathan Swift, who was dean of St. Patrick's in Dublin and a friend of the archbishop. The park surrounding the mansion is pleasant but not noteworthy, except for the remains of ancient and picturesque Landestown Castle. The grounds, continually enhanced with new attractions, now include Newbridge Farm, a 20-acre re-creation of a Victorian farm with indigenous Irish produce and livestock (Kerry cows, Jacob sheep, Shannon goats, and Connemara ponies). Open Mondays through Saturdays from 10 AM to 5 PM, Sundays from 2 to 6 PM in April through October and 2 to 5 PM in November through March. Admission charge. About 12 miles from Dublin center, off the Dublin–Belfast road, N1, at Donabate (phone: 843-6534 or 843-6535).

| EXTRA SPECIAL | The beautiful Boyne Valley is one of Ireland's most storied and evocative sites, and it makes an easy and interesting day trip. Leave Dublin by the Navan road, passing through Dunshaughlin. Six miles south of Navan, signposted to the left, is the Hill of Tara. This is where the High Kings of Ireland were crowned on the Lia Fail (Stone of Destiny) in prehistoric times. It was here, too, at the tribes' great triennial Feis of Tara, that laws were enacted and revised.

After returning to the Navan road, you will pass the striking ruins of 16th-century Athlumney Castle on the east bank of the Boyne, about 1½ miles from Navan. Continue through Donaghmore, with its remains of a 12th-century church and a round tower.

The village of Slane lies on one of the loveliest stretches of the Boyne. On the hill that overlooks the village, St. Patrick lit the paschal fire on *Holy Saturday*, AD 433, and drew upon himself the wrath of the high king's druids. Patrick emerged victorious from the ensuing confrontation, and

Christianity began its reign in Ireland. On the slopes of the hill are the remains of an ancient earthen fort and the ruins of a 16th-century church. The climb up Slane Hill is also rewarded with fine views across the tranquil Boyne Valley to Trim and Drogheda. Just outside the town lies the estate of Slane Castle, a 19th-century castellated mansion in which the present occupant, Lord Mountcharles, ran a fine restaurant until the castle suffered a disastrous fire in 1991. Restoration work is progressing well enough for a nightclub in the basement to operate on Saturday nights (phone: 41-24207).

Downstream from Slane is Brugh na Boinne (the Palace of the Boyne), a vast necropolis more than 4,000 years old. Here, beneath a chain of tumuli (ancient burial mounds), Kings of Ireland were laid to rest in passage graves of remarkable complexity. The tumuli of Dowth, Knowth, and Newgrange are of particular interest for both their extent and the amazing diversity of their sculptured ornamentation. Newgrange is one of the finest passage graves in all of Western Europe. There's a permanent archaeological exhibit on the site. Guided tours are available year-round; group reservations are necessary. Closed Mondays. Admission charge (phone: 41-24488). A mile down the road is Knowth, which after nearly 3 decades of excavation, is now open to the public from May through September and is drawing even more visitors than Newgrange. Admission charge (phone: 41-24824).

Farther down the Boyne Valley is Drogheda, an ancient town that has witnessed many dramatic scenes in the course of Irish history, most involving the contention of Royalists and Puritans for the English throne. Oliver Cromwell burned the city to the ground during a vicious siege in the 1640s, and James II was defeated by William of Orange on July 12, 1690. Reminders of Drogheda's past (all clustered in an area on the outskirts of town) include the 13th-century St. Laurence's Gate, the only survivor of the original ten gates in this once-walled city; the ruins of 13th-century St. Mary's Abbey; the Norman motte-and-bailey of Millmount Castle and the fine *Millmount Museum;* and St. Peter's Church, where the head of St. Oliver Plunkett, martyred Archbishop of Armagh, is enshrined.

Five miles north of Drogheda is Monasterboice, an ancient monastic settlement noteworthy for one of the most perfect high crosses in Ireland — the intricately carved 10th-century Cross of Muireadach. Southwest of Monasterboice are the impressive ruins of Mellifont Abbey. Dating from 1142, this was the first Cistercian structure in Ireland and heralded a whole new style of ecclesiastical architecture. Note especially the remains of the gate house and the octagonal lavabo (water basin).

Return to Dublin via N1.

Sources and Resources

TOURIST INFORMATION

For on-the-spot information and assistance, call the Dublin Tourism Office (at Dublin Airport; phone: 376387; or 14 O'Connell St.; phone: 874-7733). The tourist board personnel offer advice on all aspects of a stay in Ireland and can make theater bookings and hotel reservations anywhere in the country.

The Irish Tourist Board publishes several useful guides, which are available at tourist board offices and at most bookstores. They include *Dining in Ireland, The Dublin Guide,* and *Dublin Tourist Trail,* an excellent city walking guide (also see "Walking Tours," below). The best city map is the Ordnance Survey Dublin Map.

The US Embassy is at 42 Elgin Rd., Ballsbridge (phone: 668-8777).

LOCAL COVERAGE The *Dublin Event Guide,* published biweekly and distributed free of charge at hotels, shops, tourist offices, and other public places, includes the latest information on theater performances, exhibitions, clubs, live music venues, and films. In the summer months, the Dublin Tourism Office also publishes *What's On,* a weekly listing of major events. The city's large daily newspapers are the *Irish Times,* the *Irish Independent,* and the *Irish Press,* which come out in the morning, and the *Evening Herald* and the *Evening Press.*

TELEPHONE The city code for Dublin and the immediate vicinity is 01 if you are dialing within the Irish Republic and 1 if you are dialing from abroad. Be aware that Dublin phone numbers are being changed from 6 digits to 7 digits, a process that will continue through the end of this year. If you dial a number that has been changed since press time, a recording should inform you of the new number; otherwise, check with the local operator or the tourist office.

GETTING AROUND

AIRPORT Dublin Airport is north of the city at Collinstown. In normal traffic, a trip from the airport to downtown takes 35 to 40 minutes. *CIE (Córas Iompair Eireann, National Transport Company)* operates bus service (see below) between the airport and the central bus station.

BUS AND TRAIN *Bus Eireann* and *Irish Rail,* divisions of *CIE,* operate bus and rail services not only in Dublin but nationwide. *Dublin Bus,* the local division of *Bus Eireann,* offers extensive cross-city service. Passengers pay as they board (exact change is not required). Although Dublin has no subway, a commuter rail system, *Dublin Area Rapid Transit (DART),* runs from central Dublin along the bay as far north as Howth and as far south as Bray. It is swift, dependable, and safe at all hours. Traveling from one end of the line to the other makes a delightful sightseeing trip of the bay area for a modest fare. Train fare is collected at entry points.

For extended stays, purchase an Explorer Pass, which provides unlimited use of the *DART* system and of all buses and trains within a 20-mile radius.

All information regarding bus and rail travel throughout the republic can be obtained by calling 771871. Official *Bus Eireann, Dublin Bus,* and *Irish Rail* timetables are available at newsstands.

CAR RENTAL Many international companies, such as *Avis, Budget, Hertz,* and *National,* as well as a variety of local firms, offer excellent self-drive opportunities. *Dan Dooley* (42 Westland Row; phone: 677-2723; at the airport, 844-5156) and *Murray's/Europcar* (Baggot St. Bridge; phone: 668-1177; at the airport, 844-4179) are both dependable. Information and brochures are available from the tourist board.

TAXI There are taxi stands throughout the city, especially near main hotels, and cabs also can be hailed in the streets. Among the companies that have 24-hour radio service are *Blue Cabs* (phone: 676-1111), *Co-op Taxis* (phone: 676-6666), and *City Cabs* (phone: 286-8888).

BUS TOURS A good way to get one's bearings in Dublin is to take a guided tour. *Dublin Bus* operates half-day motorcoach tours through the city and the nearby countryside as well as full-day tours to more distant points, with very reasonable prices for a half-day or full-day trip. All tours leave from the Central Bus Station (Store St.; phone: 677-1871). *Gray Line* (3 Clanwilliam Ter.; phone: 661-9666) also offers a limited number of tours.

The bus tour that offers the greatest flexibility is *Dublin Bus*'s Heritage Trail, which provides continuous guided bus service connecting 10 major points of interest, available for a flat, per day rate. Passengers can get off the bus at whatever site they choose, take as much time as they like at each stop, and reboard another bus (they come by every 20 to 30 minutes) to continue the circuit at their own pace.

WALKING TOURS Small and easily navigated on foot, Dublin lends itself to walking tours. Stop at the Dublin Tourism Office (see above) for a copy of the *Dublin Tourist Trail.* This booklet outlines a signposted pedestrian route that offers a basic orientation to the city. The tourism office also has designed four special-interest walking tours, each outlined in a separate booklet. The *Georgian Trail* explores the city's most attractive 18th-century streets, squares, terraces, and public buildings; the *Old City Trail* traverses the most historic enclaves, dating back to Viking times; the *Cultural Trail* rambles around the leading museums, galleries, theaters, parks, quays, churches, markets, historic houses, and literary sites; and the *Rock 'n' Stroll Trail* traces Dublin's contemporary music scene, including places associated with performers such as *U2,* the *Chieftains,* and the *Dubliners.*

Walking tours are conducted by several individuals and small firms as well. *Old Dublin Walking Tours* offers 2-hour tours around the Liberties area, departing from Christ Church Cathedral daily during summer and on weekends the rest of the year. For reservations and information, call 532407. Babette Walsh, a guide registered with the Irish Tourist Board, knows every nook and cranny of the city and offers customized tours, including escorted shopping sprees. She is an irrepressible storyteller, and her often salty dialogue more than makes up for her occasionally creative view of Irish history. Walsh leads from 2 to 20 people on private half-day or full-day jaunts. Contact her in advance (at the *Cottage,* Balscaddon Rd., Howth, Co. Dublin; phone: 391869). The *Dublin Literary Pub Crawl* leads guests to haunts of the city's illustrious literary figures — Samuel Beckett, James Joyce, Brendan Behan, and Patrick Kavanaugh, a poet who wrote about the area. The tour begins at the *Bailey Pub* (Duke St.) on Mondays through Thursdays, June through August (phone: 540228).

Horse-drawn carriage tours are among Dublin's newest and most popular form of sightseeing. The carriages vary in size and style (some are open and others closed) and can accommodate from two to five passengers plus a driver/guide. Tours depart from the Grafton Street corner of St. Stephen's Green. Visitors have their choice of a quick trip around the Green; a half-hour Georgian tour past the *National Museum,* Mansion House, the government buildings, Merrion Square, Grand Canal, and Leeson Street; or an hour-long historic route that takes in St. Patrick's Cathedral, Christ Church Cathedral, the Four Courts, and Dublin Castle. Rides are available daily and some evenings, depending on the weather. No reservations necessary; tours are on a first-come, first-served basis. For more information, contact Bernard Fagan (phone: 872-6968) or Liam Stewart (phone: 661-3111); or ask at your hotel.

SPECIAL EVENTS

Throughout the year, Dublin is host to many outstanding festivals and celebrations.

FAVORITE FETES

Dublin Theatre Festival For the last week in September and the first in October, the Irish theater goes mad. Plays open daily — new plays by contemporary Irish authors, high classics by late Irish playwrights, productions by visiting theater companies, late-night revues, and mime shows. Those who like light comedies will be as gleeful as those who swear by experimental theater. A theater lover with stamina and eclectic taste could spend each day of the 2 weeks watching plays, topping off each night in a special festival club where all the casts, directors, and critics congregate. Increasingly, the festival seems to be functioning as a showcase for new works by Irish writers such as Tom Murphy, Hugh Leonard, Stewart Parker, Brian Friel, Frank McGuinness, and J. Graham Reid. Seats must be booked in advance — and the better the play, the bigger the queue. For details contact the *Dublin Theatre Festival,* 47 Nassau St., Dublin 2 (phone: 677-8439 or 679-2458).

Festival of Music in Great Irish Houses Held annually in early June, this festival pleases music and architecture enthusiasts alike. Scheduled events might include a Handel opera held in the beautifully restored 17th-century Royal Hospital, now home to the *Irish Museum of Modern Art;* a performance by singer Dame Janet Baker in stately Killruddery, a Tudor mansion just outside the city; or a *New Irish Chamber Orchestra* concert in splendid Castletown House, a mere carriage ride from Dublin for the 18th-century magnate who built it. This festival doesn't just want to sell tickets — it wants to provide music lovers with an opportunity to enjoy the period furniture, the damask curtains, and the perfumes of the herbaceous border laid down by her ladyship years before. For details contact Judith Woodworth, Festival Director, 4 Highfield Grove, Rathgar, Dublin 6 (phone: 962021).

Other special occasions include *St. Patrick's Day* (March 17) with a parade and many other festivities; the *Spring Show,* a social and agricultural gathering in May; *Bloomsday,* June 16, when James Joyce aficionados from the world over follow the circuitous path through Dublin that Leopold Bloom took from morning until late at night in *Ulysses;* the *Horse Show,* the principal sporting and social event of the year, held at the Royal Dublin Society grounds in Ballsbridge in July or August; and the *Dublin Marathon,* held the last Monday in October. For details about these and other events, inquire at any tourist office.

MUSEUMS

In addition to those described in *Special Places,* Dublin is the home of several smaller museums:

DUBLIN CIVIC MUSEUM Adjacent to the *Powerscourt Town House Centre,* it contains artifacts and memorabilia — from old maps and prints to street signs and wooden water mains — reflecting 1,000 years of Dublin history. Closed Mondays. No admission charge. 58 S. William St. (phone: 679-4260).

DUBLIN WRITERS' MUSEUM Dedicated to Dublin's rich literary heritage, this museum commemorates the work of some of its most famous native scribes, including Wilde, Swift, Shaw, Beckett, and Joyce. Set in two adjacent Georgian houses, the museum has a collection of rare editions and original manuscripts. It also houses a center for living writers, providing a place for them to work and meet with their peers. Open daily. Admission charge. 18-19 Parnell Sq. (phone: 874-7733).

IRISH JEWISH MUSEUM Housed in a former synagogue, this museum traces the history of Jews in Ireland over the last 500 years. Documents, photographs, and memorabilia are on display. Open Sundays, Tuesdays, and Thursdays; Sundays only in winter. No admission charge, but donations are welcome. 3-4 Walworth Rd., off Victoria St. (phone: 676-0737).

JAMES JOYCE CULTURAL CENTRE In Joyce's *Ulysses,* Professor Dennis J. Maginni held dancing classes at 35 North Great George's Street. The Georgian townhouse at that address became derelict in the 1970s, but now is being restored and refurbished by a group of Joyce enthusiasts. Plans include a library, lecture room, reading room, and bookshop. Though not yet fully operational, it is attended each weekday by Ken Monaghan, the writer's nephew. Guided tours are available by appointment. 35 North Great George's St. (phone: 873-1984).

MUSEUM OF CHILDHOOD Exhibits include dolls, dollhouses, and doll carriages from all over the world, dating from 1730 to 1940. There also are antique toys and rocking horses. Schedule varies, so call in advance. Admission charge. The Palms, 20 Palmerstown Park, Rathmines (phone: 497-3223).

NATIONAL WAX MUSEUM Life-size wax figures of important Irish historical, political, literary, theatrical, and sports figures, as well as international newsmakers from Pope John Paul II to Michael Jackson, are displayed. Open daily. Admission charge. Granby Row, off Parnell Sq. (phone: 872-6340).

ROYAL IRISH ACADEMY LIBRARY This small building houses a remarkable collection of ancient Irish manuscripts including the *Annals of the Four Masters,* a comprehensive history of Ireland from 2242 BC to AD 1616. Open daily from 10 AM to 5 PM. No admission charge. 19 Dawson St. (phone: 676-2570).

SHAW HOUSE George Bernard Shaw was born in this house in 1856 and lived here for the first decade of his life. The museum, which opened last year, includes original furnishings and memorabilia. Open daily May through September from 10 AM to 5 PM. Admission charge. 33 Synge St. (phone: 872-2077).

SHOPPING

Neatly balanced on both banks of the Liffey, Dublin has two downtown shopping areas: one around O'Connell and Henry Streets, the other centered in Grafton Street and its environs (stores on the south side are more elegant). *Arnott's* (phone: 872-1111), *Roche's* (phone: 873-0044 or 872-6500), and *Clery's* (phone: 878-6000) are reasonably priced department stores in the O'Connell and Henry Streets area; *Brown Thomas* (phone: 679-5666), *Marks & Spencer* (phone: 679-7855), and *Switzer's* (phone: 677-6821) are the main department stores on Grafton Street. *Powerscourt Town House Centre,* just off Grafton Street, has a number of clothing stores and crafts shops in a courtyard built around a pretty townhouse. The top floor houses the showrooms of the *Craft Council of Ireland.* The city's two newest shopping complexes are the *Royal Hibernian Way* on Dawson Street and *St. Stephen's Green Shopping Centre* on the Green. Good buys in Dublin include Aran sweaters, Donegal tweeds, Waterford and Galway crystal, and Belleek china.

Dublin is also famous for its hundreds of "old curiosity shoppes." Over the years, the antiques trade has developed great sophistication, particularly in the fields of furniture, glass and china, table silver, and certain kinds of jewelry. The city's antiques shops are clustered in several areas. Baggot, Clare, Duke, Kildare, Molesworth, and South Anne Streets are lined with long-established dealers; *Powerscourt Town House* has a number of antiques emporiums in addition to the purveyors of the new and trendy; and the Liffey Quays area, once a great source of underpriced treasures, still has quite a bit to see, mainly larger items. The antiques scene also has taken a firm hold on Francis and Patrick Streets, in the district known as The Liberties, among the city's oldest areas.

Some of our favorite antiques shops include *Anthony Antiques* (7-9 Molesworth St.; phone: 677-7222), for fine French and English furniture; *H.& E. Danker Antiques* (18 S. Anne St.; phone: 677-4009), featuring high-quality jewelry; *Kenyon Fine Art & Antiques* (10 Lower Ormond Quay; phone: 873-0488), a 200-year-old establishment that offers treasures, but not necessarily bargains; *Oriel Gallery* (17 Clare St.; phone: 676-3410), which specializes in early-20th-century art; *Jenny Vender* (20 Market Arcade; phone: 677-0406), for clothing from the turn of the century; *Bits and Pieces* (78 Francis St.; phone: 541178), specialists in Art Deco and Art Nouveau light fixtures; *Lantern Antiques* (57 Francis St.; phone: 44593), which carries old framed theatrical and advertising prints and posters; and *Timepiece Antiques* (58 Patrick St.; phone: 540774), for vintage clocks and watches.

The following are other recommended shops (unless otherwise indicated, the stores are closed on Sundays).

ANNCRAFT Situated at the back entrance of *Powerscourt Town House Centre,* this shop offers a wonderful assortment of products from the west of Ireland, including Claddagh rings, Foxford rugs, Kerry glass, and Connemara marble, as well as hand-knits, tweeds, crystal, china, oak carvings, and handmade toys. S. William St. (phone: 677-2609).

BEST OF IRISH A wide range of Irish goods — crystal, china, hand-knit goods, jewelry, linen, and tweeds. Open daily May through September; closed Sundays the rest of the year. Two locations: Next to the *Westbury Hotel,* on Harry St., off Grafton St. (phone: 679-1233); and 5 Nassau St. (phone: 679-9117).

BEWLEY'S CAFÉ LTD. A Dublin landmark, it's an emporium of coffees and teas of all nations, with a tempting candy selection, too. Sampling is encouraged. There are five shops in the Dublin area, but only the one on Grafton

Street has waitress service. Open daily. 78-79 Grafton St. (phone: 677-6761).

BLARNEY WOOLLEN MILLS A branch of the Cork-based family enterprise, this huge shop is known for its competitive prices. It stocks all the visitor favorites, from tweeds and hand-knits to crystal, china, pottery, and souvenirs. Open daily. 21-23 Nassau St. (phone: 671-0068).

CATHACH BOOKS Sheer joy for collectors, this shop has the most comprehensive selection of Irish literature and memorabilia in the country. The oldest book here was printed in the 17th century, while hand-drawn maps are from the 16th century. The shop also has first editions of W. B. Yeats and James Joyce. 10 Duke St. (phone: 671-8676).

CELTIC BOOKSTORE This shop focuses primarily on books about Irish history, language, and culture. It's housed on the ground floor of the Conrad na Gaeilge Building, a center of learning about all things Gaelic. 6 Harcourt St. (phone: 478-3814).

CLEO LTD. For more than 50 years, this has been one of Dublin's most fashionable sources for hand-knit and handwoven cloaks, caps, suits, coats, and shawls. 18 Kildare St. (phone: 676-1421).

DUBLIN WOOLLEN MILLS Beside the Ha'Penny Bridge, this place overflows with quality woolens. 41 Ormond Quay (phone: 677-5014).

DUNN'S The place to purchase excellent quality salmon at reasonable prices. 6 Upper Baggot St. (phone: 660-2688).

FERGUS O'FARRELL WORKSHOPS For more than 25 years, this has been a showcase for top-quality Irish crafts — from woodcarvings and brass door knockers to beaten copper art. 62 Dawson St. (phone: 677-0862).

FRED HANNA Bookseller to Trinity College and one of the finest bookstores in the country. It stocks new and used volumes, maps, and excellent books on Ireland. 28-29 Nassau St. (phone: 677-1255).

GAELIC DESIGN Wedged in the center of Dublin's Temple Bar district, this compact shop offers a wide array of colorful Irish-made sweaters, as well as heraldic jewelry and trendy sweatshirts and T-shirts. Asdills Row, Temple Bar (phone: 671-1146).

HERALDIC ARTISTS A good source for family crests, flags, scrolls, and genealogical books. 3 Nassau St. (phone: 676-2391).

H. JOHNSTON LTD. The place to purchase traditional blackthorn walking sticks. 11 Wicklow St. (phone: 677-1249).

HODGES FIGGIS A terrific bookstore, it has 4 stories stacked floor to ceiling with tomes on every subject. 57-58 Dawson St. (phone: 677-4764).

HOUSE OF IRELAND Top-quality Irish and European goods — from Aynsley, Lladró, Spode, Wedgwood, Hummel, and Waterford crystal and china to hand-knits, kilts, linen, and shillelaghs. Open daily in summer; closed Sundays the rest of the year. 64-65 Nassau St. and 6465 Dawson St. (phone: 671-4543).

HOUSE OF NAMES For high-quality genealogical items; sweaters can be custom-ordered with a family crest and name. Open daily. 26 Nassau St. (phone: 679-7287).

IB JORGENSEN Stunning fashions for women amid a gallery of 19th- and 20th-century Irish paintings and drawings. 29 Molesworth St. (phone: 661-9758).

JIMMY HOURIHAN Great ready-to-wear apparel for women, including stylish suits, capes, and coats. 28 Blackwater Rd. (phone: 300033).

KEVIN & HOWLIN LTD. Men's ready-to-wear and made-to-measure clothing. The store carries some women's tweeds as well. 31 Nassau St. (phone: 677-0257).

THE LACE LADY Owner Deirdre Ryan has scoured Ireland and other countries for yards of lace, antique and modern. She also stocks Irish linen tablecloths, bedcovers, pillowcases, handkerchiefs, and vintage clothes and accessories. 129 Upper Leeson St. (phone: 660-4537).

LOUIS COPELAND Dublin's best bespoke tailor. 18 Wicklow St. (phone: 677-7038).

MALTON GALLERY & BOOKSHOP Focusing on Ireland of old, this shop specializes in prints by 18th-century artist James Malton. His watercolor collection, titled "Views of Dublin," has been transformed into prints, engravings, placemats, coasters, greeting cards, and postcards. Also for sale here are hand-marked silver, pewterware, crystal, and books. 23 St. Stephen's Green (phone: 676-6333).

MARGARET JOYCE Women's sweaters, hand-knit in wool or cotton. *Powerscourt Town House Centre* (phone: 679-8037).

MCCULLOUGH PIGOTT In the music business for over 100 years, this shop offers 3 floors of records, tapes, CDs, and musical instruments. Suffolk St. (phone: 677-3138).

MULLINS OF DUBLIN Coats of arms emblazoned on parchment, plaques, and even door knockers. 36 Upper O'Connell St. (phone: 874-1133).

PATRICK FLOOD Silver and gold jewelry in traditional Irish designs. *Powerscourt Town House Centre* (phone: 679-4256).

LA POTINIERE Features a wide selection of Irish cheeses, mustards, and teas. *Powerscourt Town House Centre* (phone: 671-3000).

SHEEPSKIN SHOP High-quality sheepskin and lambskin coats are sold, along with leather trousers, suits, and jackets. 20 Wicklow St. (phone: 671-9585).

SLEATER'S A charming jewelry shop tucked in an alley between Grafton Street and *Powerscourt Town House Centre.* 9 Johnson's Court (phone: 677-7532).

SWEATER SHOP A good source of high-quality Irish knitwear of all kinds, colors, styles, fibers, and patterns. 9 Wicklow St., off Grafton St. (phone: 671-3270).

SYBIL CONNOLLY Ireland's reigning couturière; her romantic ball gowns of finely pleated Irish linen are special indeed. Open weekdays and by appointment. 71 Merrion Sq. (phone: 676-7281).

TOWER DESIGN CRAFT CENTRE Once a sugar refinery, this renovated 1862 tower houses the workshops of more than 30 craftspeople, with work ranging from heraldic jewelry, Irish oak woodcarvings, and hand-cut crystal to Irish chocolates, stained glass, toys, and fishing tackle. There's also a self-service restaurant. An ideal stop for a rainy day. Pearse St. (phone: 677-5655).

TRINITY COLLEGE LIBRARY SHOP Specializing in scholarly works and books on Irish subjects, this shop also carries reproductions, posters, and prints from the *Book of Kells.* Open daily. Nassau St. (phone: 677-2941).

TRINITY SHIRTMAKERS Distinctive linen shirts with mother-of-pearl buttons, many available with detachable collars. 13 S. Leinster St., 2nd Floor (phone: 676-3013).

WALTONS MUSICAL INSTRUMENT GALLERIES Stocks Scottish bagpipes, *uilleann* pipes, harps, tin whistles, old violins, and *bodhráns.* Recordings are also available. 2-5 N. Frederick St. (phone: 747805).

WATERSTONE & CO. Another great bookshop, a branch of the British firm of the same name, with an array of volumes on international topics, as well as ceiling-high shelves on Irish history, literature, language, politics, cookery, and crafts. Open daily. 7 Dawson St. (phone: 679-1415).

WEIR & SONS A tradition in Dublin, this classy shop offers the best in jewelry, gold, silver, antiques, glass, china, and leather goods. 96-97 Grafton St. (phone: 677-9678).

SPORTS AND FITNESS

BICYCLING Irish Raleigh Industries operates *Rent-a-Bike* at a number of city locations (phone: 626-1333). Two downtown shops offering bicycle rentals are *USIT Rent-A-Bike* (58 Lower Gardiner's Row; phone: 872-5349) and *McDonald's* (38 Wexford St.; phone: 475-2586). Charges are per day or per week with a deposit required.

GAELIC GAMES Football and hurling are two fast, enthralling field sports; important matches are played at *Croke Park* (Jones Rd; phone: 363222). For details, consult local newspapers or the tourist board.

GOLF More than 30 golf courses are within easy reach of Dublin; visitors are welcome at all clubs on weekdays, but gaining admission can be more difficult on weekends.

TOP TEE-OFF SPOTS

Portmarnock This fabled layout, just outside Dublin, is perhaps the best single course in the Republic. The short flag sticks, which are set on springs to let them swing freely in the breeze, indicate something about the wind hazards here, and the last 5 holes are diabolically difficult. However, the quality of the course, especially the greens, is superb. Be prepared for the strong prevailing northeasterly wind, soaring scores — and a bracing outing. Portmarnock (phone: 846-2968).

Royal Dublin The "other" Dublin-area golfing magnet, though second to *Portmarnock,* still deserves a place among Europe's best. The winds blow here as well, and the rough grows to a size not normally known in the New World. Founded in 1885, the course is famous for its four short holes — the 4th, 6th, 9th, and 12th — all of which call for a keen eye and precision play; the demanding 5th hole, with its narrow valley of a fairway, once prompted the late comedian Danny Kaye to ask his caddie for a rifle. Dollymount (phone: 336346).

GREYHOUND RACING You can go to the dogs regularly at two tracks, *Shelbourne Park Stadium* and *Harold's Cross Stadium,* each an 8-minute ride from the city center. Details in local newspapers or at the tourist board.

HORSE RACING Six miles south of the city in Foxrock is the *Leopardstown* racecourse (phone: 289-3607), a modern track with glass-enclosed viewing areas. The best-known course in the Dublin vicinity is *Curragh* (phone: 45-41025), about a mile or so outside the town of Kildare in County Kildare, about an hour's drive from Dublin. This modern complex hosts the *Irish Derby* in June and other high-stakes races throughout the year. The Irish Racing Board at *Leopardstown* (phone: 289-7277) can provide information about all local racing events. For additional details, see *Horsing Around* in DIVERSIONS.

HORSEBACK RIDING A list of riding establishments close to Dublin is available at the tourist board.

TENNIS Dublin is close to a first-rate international facility, one of the best in the country. During the second week of July, it hosts the *Irish Open.* For information contact *Tennis Ireland* (54 Wellington Rd.; phone: 668-1841).

Kilternan Country Club Set on 2 acres in the sylvan Dublin Mountains, about 15 minutes south of the city, this leisure hotel complex adjoins a multimillion-dollar national tennis center, whose 8 courts (4 indoor, 4 outdoor) are open from early in the morning until midnight. Equipment may be rented at *Pro Shop Kilternan.* In addition, the complex includes an 18-hole golf course, an indoor heated swimming pool, a gym, saunas, and an artificial ski slope. Horseback riding also is available. Kilternan (phone: 295-3742).

There are a few public courts, generally outdoors, in and around Dublin, where visitors can play for a small fee. The most central is Herbert Park. Ballsbridge (phone: 668-4364).

THEATER

There are at least ten main theaters in the city center; smaller theater troupes perform at universities, suburban theaters, and occasionally pubs and hotels. Some theaters reliably turn out productions and concerts that are more interesting or wonderful than others, and some theaters are worth a visit in their own right, because they are either particularly beautiful or unusually historic. For complete program listings, see the publications listed in *Tourist Information,* above.

Abbey Theatre Alas, the original *Abbey Theatre,* founded by Yeats and Lady Gregory on the site of the old city morgue, is no more. In 1951, at the close of a performance of O'Casey's *Plough and the Stars* — a play that ends with Dublin blazing in the aftermath of rebellion — the theater itself caught fire and burned to the ground. The new *Abbey,* designed by Michael Scott, one of the country's foremost architects, opened in 1966 on the site of the original building. The lobby, which can be seen daily except Sundays, contains portraits of those connected with the theater's early successes. The *Abbey* still presents the best of contemporary Irish playwriting, including productions of works by Brian Friel, Hugh Leonard, and Thomas Murphy, among others, as well as revivals of the classics that made the 85-year-old *Abbey Players* famous. Work of a more experimental nature is presented downstairs, in the *Peacock;* the opportunity to visit this wonderfully intimate auditorium should not be missed. Lower Abbey St. (phone: 878-7222).

Andrews Lane Theatre Tucked in an alley off Dame Street and not far from Trinity College, this is one of Dublin's newest venues, making its mark with performances of contemporary plays. In addition to the main theater, there is a small studio that serves as a stage for avant-garde productions, including occasional lunchtime shows and performances by all-female acting troupes. 9-17 Andrews La. (phone: 679-5720).

Focus Theatre Dublin's smallest theater is also one of its most exciting. In 1963, when Deirdre O'Connell returned to Ireland after studying in New York at Lee Strasberg's Actors' Studio, she began to train some Dublin actors in Stanislavskian technique. By 1967 she had formed the nucleus of a company, which she moved into a converted garage in a lane off Pembroke Street. An evening in this tiny, 72-seat auditorium is never disappointing, whether the play is a classic by Chekhov or the latest offering of a young Irish writer. Besides the resident *Focus Company,* there is a *Studio Company* of young actors-in-training who occasionally present their own improvised and very original adaptations of Irish legends and literature. It is no exaggeration to say that, along with some of the finest actors in Dublin (including O'Connell herself), *Focus* theatergoers glimpse the stars of tomorrow. 6 Pembroke Pl. (phone: 676-3071).

Gaiety Theatre Here is where many a Dublin child, brought for a special occasion to a pantomime perhaps or a Gilbert and Sullivan musical, gets a first taste of the magic of theater. It was founded in 1871 by Michael Gunn and his brother John (a bust of whom can be seen on the staircase that leads to the circle), and although the original gallery, or "gods," was removed when the theater was renovated in 1955, the theater remains a very fine example of the typical late-Victorian playhouse: marvelously opulent, with red carpets, dark pillars, golden draperies, and ornate pink cream plasterwork. The orchestra pit's brass surround enhances the total effect. In a private box, patrons feel like no less than visiting royalty. The list of those who have played at the *Gaiety* is formidable, including Lily Langtry, the *D'Oyly Carte Opera Company,* Burgess Meredith, Siobhán McKenna, the *Bolshoi Ballet,* Peter O'Toole — and Dublin's own Jimmy O'Dea, who for nearly 30 years appeared in pantomime and musical performances and, in the character of Biddy Mulligan, captured the true spirit of the city. In April and September the *Dublin Grand Opera Society* holds its spring and winter seasons here. S. King St. (phone: 677-1717).

Gate Theatre The name of the theater is synonymous with those of the late Michael MacLiammoir and Hilton Edwards, who organized the company in 1928 to present plays of unusual interest, regardless of nationality or period, at a time when the *Abbey* (above) devoted itself entirely to Irish work. The founders' tradition continues under the direction of Michael Colgan, and theatergoers here are as likely to find a play by Tennessee Williams or a young unknown as one by native Brian Friel. The visual emphasis is strong, and the theater has received awards for its stage designs. The auditorium is quite small and, as might be expected from the

Gate's reputation for stage design, beautifully decorated, so that it feels less like a modern playhouse than an 18th-century aristocrat's court theater. 1 Cavendish Row (phone: 874-4045).

Olympia Theatre This stage occupies a special place in the hearts of Dubliners, perhaps because of its connection with the music hall, always the most popular form of theater here. On the 1879 opening night of Dan Lowrey's *Star of Erin* (as the playhouse was then called), patrons enjoyed such spectacles as Mademoiselle Miaco, the Boneless Wonder; and Signor Zula, who swung from a high trapeze by his feet. The only theater in Dublin that still retains its gallery — from whose dizzying heights one can see the tops of the performers' heads far below — it is also notable for the Waterford cut-glass chandeliers and the two huge mirrors on either side of the circle in which the spectators can monitor their own reactions while watching the performance. Though television has meant the end of theatrical variety shows, the *Olympia* still presents concerts (including rock concerts) and pantomimes as well as plays, both Irish and foreign, and hosts visiting performers. 72 Dame St. (phone: 677-7744).

Other noteworthy theaters include the avant-garde *Project Arts Centre* (39 E. Essex St.; phone: 671-2321); the *Tivoli* (135-138 Francis St.; phone: 544472), which features controversial Irish plays and imports from London; and the *New Eblana* (Store St.; phone: 679-8404), a revived "pocket" theater in the basement of Busáras, the central bus station, that's a venue for contemporary plays. The *Lambert Mews Puppet Theatre* in the suburb of Monkstown (Clifden La.; phone: 280-0974) proves irresistible to children.

It is always advisable to make reservations for theater performances in Dublin. You can make bookings at theaters, major department stores, and some record shops, such as *HMV Golden Discs* (65 Grafton St.; phone: 677-1025). Most theaters accept telephone reservations and credit cards.

MUSIC

Settling on an evening's entertainment (or an afternoon's, for that matter) can pose some problems in Dublin, as there are so many choices.

HIGH NOTES

National Concert Hall Situated just off St. Stephen's Green, this historic 1,200-seat hall is the center of Dublin's active musical life and the home stage of the *Radio Telefis Eireann (RTE) Symphony Orchestra* and the *New Ireland Chamber Orchestra*. Originally built as a concert and entertainment venue for the *Great Exhibition* of 1865, it eventually became the Examination Hall for University College in 1908. However, when the college moved to its present location, it was decided (amid public controversy) that the hall be converted into a music locale. The programs are mostly classical, but there also is an ever-changing program of jazz, Gilbert and Sullivan, and solo performances by top artists from Ireland and abroad. Earlsfort Ter. (phone: 671-1888).

The Point Also known as the "Point Depot" because it was formerly a depot building, this new theater–cum–concert hall with state-of-the-art acoustics presents everything from *U2* concerts to Broadway hits. Ticket prices are heftier here than at any other performing arts venue in Dublin, and most events are booked well in advance. E. Link Bridge (phone: 363633).

Royal Dublin Society Concert Hall While most people think of traditional Irish music when they envision Dublin, it's also true that quality classical music can be found here. This is at least in part thanks to the Royal Dublin Society (RDS), which stages recitals from November to March in its 1,206-seat *Members' Hall,* also known as the *RDS Concert Hall.* Although the acoustics are not all that one might desire for small chamber ensembles and soloists, the attractive book-lined walls add a touch of intimacy that is not often encountered in concert halls nowadays, and many distinguished musicians have played here in recent years — among them the *Smetana String Quartet* and Isaac Stern. Ballsbridge (phone: 668-0645).

In addition, traditional Irish music is a must in Dublin. *Seisiún* (sessions) are held at many places around the city by an organization called *Comhaltas Ceoltóirí Eireann* (phone: 280-0295); informal sessions are held on Friday and Saturday nights at its headquarters (32 Belgrave Sq., in Monkstown; take *DART* to Seapoint station; admission charge); ballad sessions are held nightly except Sundays in the *Barn* on the ground floor of the *Abbey Tavern* (Howth, 10 miles north of the city on the coast; phone: 322006 or 390307). Many pubs offer music informally; see *Sharing a Pint* for a list of the best.

NIGHTCLUBS AND NIGHTLIFE

There is little in the way of large-scale cabaret-cum-dancing in Dublin; swinging Dublin tends to congregate in the discotheques. Premises range from big, bustling places where an escort is not necessarily required to small, intimate clubs. Most discotheques have only wine licenses. Among the more established discotheques on a rapidly changing scene are the large and lively *Annabel's* in the *Burlington* hotel (Leeson St.; phone: 660-5222), *Raffles* in the *Sachs* (Northampton Rd.; phone: 668-0995), *Blinkers* at *Leopardstown* racecourse (phone: 896307), the *Night Train* (7 Lower Mount St.; phone: 676-1717), and the *Waterfront* (14-15 Sir John Roger's Quay; phone: 679-9258). Smaller, cozier clubs are mainly to be found in the Leeson Street area: *Styx* (phone: 676-1560) and *Cats* (phone: 661-6151) are two. The most famous traditional cabaret in Dublin is the established *Jurys Cabaret,* performed nightly except Mondays from April through October at *Jurys* hotel (see *Checking In*). Also good are the *Braemor Rooms* (Churchtown; phone: 298-1016); *Doyle's Irish Cabaret,* presented from April through October at the *Burlington* hotel (Leeson St.; phone: 660-5222); and the *Clontarf Castle* dinner show (Castle Ave.; phone: 332271).

Best in Town

CHECKING IN

With the opening of several hotels in recent years, along with the refurbishment of still others, Dublin's accommodations have risen significantly in quality, but they still tend to fall short of world class standards. Most of Dublin's major hotels have complete facilities for the business traveler. Those hotels listed below as having "business services" usually offer such conveniences as a concierge, meeting rooms, photocopiers, computers, translation services, foreign currency exchange, and express checkout, among others. Call the hotel for additional information. Expect to pay $225 or more for a double room at hotels classified as very expensive; $165 to $225 at those classified as expensive; $75 to $165 at places listed as moderate; and less than $75 at those in the inexpensive category. A room with Irish breakfast for two in a private home in a residential neighborhood will cost $60 or less.

> **NOTE** The tourist board offers a list of hotels it has inspected and graded; it also offers a computerized reservation service for lodging all over Ireland (see *Tourist Information,* above). Reservations for many of the hotels may be made through international reservations services; the applicable numbers are listed in individual hotel entries below. All telephone numbers are in the 1 city code unless otherwise indicated.

VERY EXPENSIVE

Berkeley Court The flagship of the Doyle group and the first Irish member of the Leading Hotels of the World. Close to the city in the leafy suburb of Ballsbridge, it combines graciousness with modern efficiency. Contemporary and antique furnishings harmonize, and the service is exceptionally warm and friendly. There are 210 rooms and 6 suites (all with Jacuzzis), including a 6-room, $2,000-a-night penthouse. There also is an excellent dining room, the *Berkeley Room* (see *Eating Out*), a conservatory-style coffee shop, 24-hour room service, a health center with indoor pool and saunas, a shopping arcade. Business services. Lansdowne Rd. (phone: 660-1711; 800-223-6800 or 800-44-UTELL from the US; fax: 661-7238).

Conrad Opened in 1990 by the US Hilton hotel chain, it is in the heart of the city, opposite the *National Concert Hall* and across from St. Stephen's Green.

The hotel has 192 bright and airy guestrooms (including 10 suites), all with bay windows. Each room has an executive desk, 2 or 3 telephones, mini-bar, color TV set, and a large marble bathroom. One floor is reserved for nonsmokers. Other facilities include a hair salon and a garage. The *Alexandra* (see *Eating Out*) is the hotel's most elegant restaurant; there also is an informal brasserie, a lively pub, and 24-hour room service. Business services. Earlsfort Ter. (phone: 676-5555; 800-HILTONS from the US; fax: 676-5076).

Jurys In Ballsbridge opposite the American Embassy, this modern complex has a multistory, skylit lobby area and a dome-shaped central atrium. The main hotel offers 290 rooms. In addition, 100 extra-large rooms and suites are located in a newer, separate but connected 8-story wing known as the *Towers*. Each of the computer-key-accessible rooms has a bay window, mini-bar, 3 telephone lines, work area, satellite TV, marble bathroom, and either king- or queen-size bed. Two floors are designated as nonsmoking. There are 2 restaurants, including the noteworthy *Kish* (see *Eating Out*); a 24-hour coffee shop; 2 bars; indoor/outdoor swimming pool; a health center; and 24-hour room service. For entertainment, there is *Jurys Cabaret,* Ireland's longest running variety show. Business services. Pembroke Rd. (phone: 660-5000; 800-44-UTELL or 800-THE-OMNI from the US; fax: 660-5540).

Shelbourne This venerable establishment, a nice mixture of the dignified and the lively, now is more polished than ever after a $5-million face-lift. Some of the 164 rooms are truly splendid, particularly the front rooms on the second floor. The *Horseshoe Bar* is one of the livelier fixtures of Dublin pub life, while the main restaurant, with its 1826 plasterwork and trio of Waterford crystal chandeliers, is a showcase for modern Irish cuisine. There's also 24-hour room service. Business services. 27 St. Stephen's Green (phone: 676-6471; 800-223-5672 from the continental US or Canada; fax: 661-6006).

Westbury The fashionable centerpiece of a chic mall of shops and restaurants, this hotel is a member of the Doyle group. The management emphasizes elegance, and the 206 rooms and suites have canopied beds and an abundance of mahogany and brass furnishings. Executive suites with Jacuzzis and balconies also are available. Public facilities include a restaurant, coffee shop, seafood pub, and a lobby lounge with pianist. There's also 24-hour room service. Business services. Grafton St. (phone: 679-1122; 800-223-6800 or 800-44-UTELL from the US; fax: 679-7078).

EXPENSIVE

Gresham Once considered one of the grandest of Dublin hotels, it has changed ownership a number of times and recently came to rest in the Ryan Holdings group. Though you hardly could call it grand these days, this

200-room hostelry once attracted lots of luminaries. The restaurant features a good selection of seafood dishes; there's also 24-hour room service. Business services. Upper O'Connell St. (phone: 874-6881; 800-223-0888 or 800-44-UTELL from the US; fax: 878-7175).

Mont Clare One of the city's oldest hotels, this 6-story Georgian-style property was totally revamped and refurbished in 1990. It sits in the heart of the business district, at the corner of Clare Street overlooking Merrion Square, close to Trinity College, the Irish government buildings, and museums. There are 80 air conditioned rooms, each with bath, phone, TV set, radio, hair dryer, mini-bar/refrigerator, tea/coffee-maker, and trouser press. A restaurant, lounge, 24-hour room service, and enclosed parking lot are on the premises. Business services. Merrion Sq. (phone: 661-6799; 800-44-UTELL from the US; fax: 661-5663).

Stephen's Hall An alternative to the traditional hotel or guesthouse, this property offers apartment-style accommodations on a short-term basis — ideal for travelers who want to entertain or do business in Dublin or for those who want to save money by cooking for themselves. The exterior is a replica of a Georgian building that formerly stood on the site, and the interior is modern and functional. Each of the 37 suites consists of a sitting room, dining area, well-equipped kitchen, bathroom, and 1 or 2 bedrooms with phone. Services include daily housekeeping and underground parking. 14-17 Lower Leeson St., Earlsford Ter. (phone: 661-0585; 800-223-6510 from the US; fax: 661-0606).

MODERATE

Anglesea Townhouse Near the American Embassy, this Edwardian residence is the home of Helen Kirrane, who spoils her guests with hearty breakfasts of fresh fish, homemade breads and scones, fresh-squeezed juices, baked fruits, and warm cereals. Heirlooms and family antiques add to the ambience of this jewel of a bed and breakfast guesthouse. All 7 rooms have private baths/showers, TV sets, and direct-dial telephones. 63 Anglesea Rd., Ballsbridge (phone: 668-3877; fax: 668-3461).

Ariel House Best described as a country home in the city, this historic Victorian guesthouse (built in 1850) is situated in the residential area of Ballsbridge (it's 1 block from the *DART* station, providing easy access to downtown). Operated by the O'Brien family, it has 27 rooms decorated with period furniture and original oil paintings and watercolors; each room has a private bath, TV set, phone, and hair dryer. There's also a restaurant and wine bar on the premises. 52 Lansdowne Rd., opposite the *Berkeley Court* hotel (phone: 668-5512; fax: 668-5845).

Fitzwilliam Situated at the corner of Fitzwilliam and Baggot Streets in the heart of Georgian Dublin within walking distance of St. Stephen's Green, this spacious townhouse dates back to the mid-1700s. Originally a private residence, it has been restored and converted into a 12-room guesthouse, owned and operated by the Reddin family. Each room is comfortably furnished and equipped with a phone, TV set, and modern bathroom. Facilities include a restaurant and a cozy parlor with a marble fireplace. 41 Upper Fitzwilliam St. (phone: 660-0448; fax: 676-7488).

Georgian House Recently renovated, this centrally located guesthouse is less than 2 blocks south of St. Stephen's Green. It offers 18 bedrooms with private baths/showers, phone, and TV set, but no elevator. There also is a basement-level seafood restaurant featuring Irish music at night and an enclosed parking area. 20 Lower Baggot St. (phone: 661-8832; fax: 661-8834).

Longfields Located on one of the city's most fashionable streets, this small hostelry offers all the charm of a Georgian home with modern comforts. It is composed of two 18th-century Georgian townhouses, originally owned by Richard Longfield, also known as Viscount Longueville, a member of the Irish Parliament more than 200 years ago. Completely restored and refurbished over the last 5 years, it now has 26 rooms, each with private bath, and a decor that reflects both the Georgian period and more modern influences. Each room has a phone, color TV set, mini-bar, and hair dryer. The *Number Ten* restaurant offers a fine menu of French cuisine. Business services. 10 Lower Fitzwilliam St. (phone: 676-1367; fax: 676-1542).

Montrose Near the National Radio and Television studios, across the road from the Belfield campus of University College, the 190 bedrooms here are inviting and comfortable. There is a good restaurant as well as a grill, a bar, a hairdressing salon, a souvenir shop, and 24-hour room service. Business services. About 10 minutes from the center of Dublin on Stillorgan Rd. (phone: 269-3311; 800-223-0888 from the US; fax: 269-1164).

Russell Court Two former Georgian houses have been transformed into this convenient lodging place less than a block from St. Stephen's Green. The decor in the public areas is Art Deco, and the 22 modern bedrooms, all with baths, are decorated in light woods and pastel tones. Facilities include a restaurant, lounge, and nightclub. 21-23 Harcourt St. (phone: 478-4066; 800-521-0643 from the US; fax: 478-1576).

St. Aidan's Managed by the O'Dwyer family, this Victorian house offers 9 warm, comfortable rooms with private baths. A traditional Irish breakfast is served each morning. Situated in quiet Rathgar, close to the center of Dublin. 32 Brighton Rd. (phone: 902011 or 906178; fax: 920234).

INEXPENSIVE

Egan's House Another comfortable guesthouse, offering 23 rooms, all with private baths, TV sets, phones, and hair dryers. There is also a small restaurant. 7 Iona Park (phone: 303611; fax: 303312).

Iona House A guesthouse with 11 rooms, all with private baths, TV sets, direct-dial telephones, and a traditional breakfast. 5 Iona Park (phone: 306217; fax: 306732).

Mount Herbert Close to the city center in a quaint neighborhood, this well-run, family-owned Georgian mansion has 110 rooms (100 with private baths), a health facility, a good restaurant, and 24-hour room service. No bar (wine license only) but a pleasant atmosphere. Business service. 7 Herbert Rd. (phone: 668-4321; fax: 660-7077; telex: 92173).

Northumberland Lodge This gracious Georgian family home features 6 comfortable rooms with private baths. Near the US Embassy, it's just 5 minutes from the city center. Ballsbridge (phone: 660-5270; fax: 668-8679).

EATING OUT

Although traditional dishes such as Irish stew, Dublin coddle, and bacon and cabbage are rarely served in better restaurants, when it comes to meals prepared with the finest produce, Ireland's top restaurants can compare with the best anywhere. Dublin offers a wide range of first class restaurants, a somewhat more restricted range of moderately priced establishments, and a number of fast-service, inexpensive eating places.

Dinner for two (excluding wine, drinks, and tip) will cost $90 or more in expensive restaurants; $45 to $90 in moderate places; and under $45 in inexpensive spots. All telephone numbers are in the 1 city code unless otherwise indicated.

For an unforgettable dining experience, we begin with our culinary favorites, followed by our cost and quality choices, listed by price category.

DELIGHTFUL DINING

Old Dublin This cozy eatery has rose-colored linen and walls, in addition to roaring fireplaces. Specialties on the menu include Scandinavian-style fish, which owner Eamonn Walsh learned to love while in Finland. Venalainen smokies — filets of hake, halibut, sea trout, or other fish smoked on the premises and served as an appetizer in a white wine, cream, and dill sauce — are a study in varying tastes and textures. For a main course, try salmon coulibiac. For meat eaters, there's filet à la Novgorod — a chateaubriand sliced and served Russian-style on sauerkraut alongside fried kasha, spicy mushrooms, caviar, and sour cream. The atmosphere is clubby, with all the patrons on a first-name basis. There also is a good wine list. Open weekdays for lunch and dinner; Saturdays for dinner only; closed holidays. Reservations advised. Major credit cards accepted. 91 Francis St. (phone: 542028 or 542346; fax: 541406).

Patrick Guilbaud A trendy place for classic French cuisine that draws a stylish crowd. The atmosphere is hushed as local devotees enjoy nouvelle concoctions served in bird-size portions. Freshwater pike, which choke up the lakes, is seldom found on Irish tables, but when Guilbaud and his chef Guillaume Lebrun strike it lucky on a fishing expedition in Wicklow, pike is on the menu. Pride of the chef's heart is the sea bass, pan-fried in saffron butter and served with herbs and an onion *confit,* but there are other delightful dishes as well, including the noteworthy filets of hare sautéed in walnut oil and doused with a red wine and juniper sauce. Open for lunch and dinner; closed Sundays and Mondays. Reservations essential. Major credit cards accepted. 46 James Pl., off Baggot St. (phone: 676-4192).

EXPENSIVE

Alexandra Small and intimate, this dining spot in the *Conrad* hotel is somewhat like a private club, with open fireplaces, paneled walls, crystal chandeliers, brass fittings, and oil paintings. The imaginative menu includes such dishes as salmon paupiettes in cabbage and spinach leaves, loin of lamb with truffle and caper juice, and medallions of veal in ginger. Open for dinner only; closed Sundays. Reservations advised. Major credit cards accepted. Earlsfort Ter. (phone: 676-5555).

Berkeley Room One of Dublin's best hotel dining rooms, it is elegant and lavishly appointed; its prize-winning chef produces highly satisfactory fare, including rack of lamb, roast duckling, and prime ribs carved at tableside. Open daily for lunch and dinner. Reservations advised. Major credit cards accepted. *Berkeley Court Hotel,* Lansdowne Rd. (phone: 660-1711).

The Commons Situated in the basement of 18th-century Newman House, the historic seat of the University of Ireland, this eatery is set in the original commons room. Totally restored in recent years, the interior has a spacious feeling, with high ceilings and contemporary artwork — much of it featuring James Joyce. In the summer, guests can sit outdoors in a charming terraced garden at the rear of the building. The menu, international with some Oriental influences, includes minted prawns, grilled black sole with a mussel and chive ragout, steamed *paupiettes* of brill in champagne sauce, and medallions of veal with lime and ginger sauce. Open for lunch and dinner; closed Sundays. Reservations advised. Major credit cards accepted. 85-86 St. Stephen's Green (phone: 872-5597).

Le Coq Hardi This gracious Georgian establishment is run by owner/chef John Howard, twice gold-medal winner in the prestigious *Hotelympia/Salon Culinaire* contest. Its extensive à la carte menu offers many house specialties, including Howard's renowned ducking *à l'orange.* Open for lunch and dinner daily. Reservations necessary. Major credit cards accepted. 35 Pembroke Rd., Ballsbridge (phone: 668-9070).

Dobbins A wine-cellar atmosphere prevails at this relaxed bistro with a sawdust-strewn floor, wooden benches, and checkered linen. On warm days there is additional seating on a tropical patio with a sliding-glass roof. The varied international menu includes salmon and sole with prawn tails and spinach soufflé, beef teriyaki, and breast of chicken with garlic and vodka butter. There often is live Irish harp music on weekends. Open for lunch and dinner; closed Sundays. Reservations advised. Major credit cards accepted. Stephen's La. (phone: 676-4679, 676-4670, or 661-3321).

Ernie's This place earned its far-reaching reputation under the direction of master seafood chef Ernie Evans. Though Ernie has passed away, his family carries on the restaurant's fine tradition. The menu still features *fruits de mer,* including Valentia scallops, garlic prawns, and fresh salmon. Open for lunch and dinner; closed Sundays and Mondays. Reservations necessary. Major credit cards accepted. Mulberry Gardens, Donnybrook (phone: 269-3300 or 269-3260).

Les Frères Jacques Centrally situated downtown beside the *Olympia Theatre* and close to Trinity College, this busy second-floor eatery melds creative French fare with a relaxed Dublin atmosphere and live piano music. The menu includes such choices as filet of turbot with salmon ravioli, roast suckling pig with caramelized apple and cider sauce, and roast breast of free-range duck marinated with spices and soy sauce with ginger root. Open for lunch and dinner; closed Sundays. Reservations necessary. Major credit cards accepted. 74 Dame St. (phone: 679-4555).

Grey Door This restaurant has achieved an enviable reputation for fine Russian and Finnish cuisine. The wine list is good and the more adventurous imbiber can sample such rarities as Russian champagne. The setting behind this elegant doorway in the heart of Georgian Dublin is intimate, rather like dining in a private home. There's also a small guesthouse on the premises. Open for lunch and dinner; closed Sundays. Reservations advised. Major credit cards accepted. 23 Upper Pembroke St. (phone: 676-3286).

Kish Seafood is the unmistakable star of the menu here. The chef's specialties include baked sole filled with oysters, prawns, and lobster in anise sauce; Dublin Bay prawns wrapped in smoked salmon on cider butter; and filet of salmon in phyllo pastry on a yellow pepper and scallop sauce. Open for dinner; closed Sundays. Reservations necessary. Major credit cards accepted. At *Jurys Hotel,* Pembroke Rd., Ballsbridge (phone: 660-5000).

Locks A French provincial eatery on the banks of the Grand Canal near Portobello Bridge. Only the freshest produce is used for such dishes as wild salmon and breast of pigeon. Open for lunch and dinner; closed Sundays. Reservations necessary. Major credit cards accepted. 1 Windsor Ter., Portobello (phone: 538352 or 543391).

Lord Edward Dublin's oldest seafood restaurant is set in a tall Victorian building opposite historic Christ Church Cathedral in the older part of the city. The daily selection of fish and shellfish is prepared and served in the classic French manner, and there's always a meat or chicken dish for those who don't eat seafood. Open for lunch and dinner; closed Sundays. Reservations advised. Major credit cards accepted. 23 Christ Church Pl. (phone: 542420 or 542158).

The Soup Bowl In the late 1960s, when non-hotel restaurants were scarce, an establishment bearing this name was one of the "in" spots in Dublin. Now, more than 25 years later, the eatery has been revived in a location near the original by a leading Dublin socialite and recharged with similar culinary popularity. The menu changes daily but always emphasizes fresh seafood and game, with an extensive wine list. Open for lunch and dinner; closed Saturdays and Sundays. Reservations necessary. Major credit cards accepted. 2 Molesworth Pl. (phone: 661-8918).

MODERATE

Chapter One Given its location in the *Dublin Writers' Museum,* it is not surprising that this place exudes a literary ambience. The menu, enlivened with appropriate quotes on food and dining by Irish writers, features a mix of traditional Irish dishes and creative new recipes, with choices such as Irish stew, and cockles and mussels, as well as breast of duckling with peppered pineapple, filet of beef wrapped in bacon with brandy butter sauce, and oysters and prawns in pastry. Open daily for lunch and dinner. Reservations advised, especially for dinner. Major credit cards accepted. 18-19 Parnell Sq. (phone: 217766).

Coffers This small, comfortable eatery specializes in wild Atlantic salmon in season and steaks — varying from a plain filet to a pork steak cooked in fresh apples and Pernod. It features a special pre-theater dinner daily except Sundays. Open for dinner daily; weekdays for lunch. Reservations advised. Major credit cards accepted. 6 Cope St. (phone: 671-5740).

Gallagher's Boxty House Casual and unpretentious, this spot is a haven for traditional Irish cooking, from lamb stew to boiled cabbage and bacon. As its name implies, it also is a good place to try the traditional dish called "boxty," a potato pancake rolled like a burrito around a variety of fillings such as chicken, ham, or vegetables. Open daily for lunch and dinner. No reservations. Major credit cards accepted. 20-21 Temple Bar (phone: 677-2762; fax: 676-8567).

Gallery 22 A pleasant, garden-like atmosphere pervades this dining spot near the *Shelbourne* hotel. The innovative menu includes seafood pancakes, rack of lamb, sea trout, and filet steaks with vermouth sauce. Vegetarian dishes also are served. A pre-theater dinner is offered. Open for lunch and dinner; closed Sundays. Reservations necessary. Major credit cards accepted. 22 St. Stephen's Green (phone: 661-6669).

La Grenouille A French-style bistro next to the *Powerscourt Town House Centre.* Each dish on the limited menu is cooked to order. Choices include rack of lamb, chicken in blue cheese sauce, steaks, and duck. Open daily for dinner year-round; lunch on weekdays. Reservations advised. Diners Club, MasterCard, and Visa accepted. 64 S. William St. (phone: 677-9157).

Kilmartin's Originally owned by a turf accountant (a bookie), this eatery retains its old atmosphere, thanks to an antiques-filled decor. Now run by a husband and wife team, it specializes in poached salmon and crispy duck. The house wine is particularly good. Open for lunch and dinner weekdays; dinner only on Saturdays and Sundays. Reservations advised. Major credit cards accepted. 19 Upper Baggot St. (phone: 668-6674).

McGrattans' in the Lane An elegant Georgian door is the entrance to this restaurant, tucked in an alley between Lower Baggot Street and Merrion Square. The interior is equally inviting, with a cozy living room–like cocktail area and a skylit and plant-filled dining room. The menu melds French recipes and Irish ingredients: poached salmon Florentine, *canard aux noix* (crispy duck with walnuts and honey sauce), *poulet* William (breast of chicken in pastry with citrus sauce), and noisettes of lamb diable (roast lamb with mustard and tarragon sauce). Open daily for lunch and dinner. Reservations advised. Major credit cards accepted. 76 Fitzwilliam La. (phone: 661-8808).

Mitchell's Set in the cellar of *Mitchell's Wine Merchants,* this is where swinging Dubliners come for lunch. The menu is somewhat limited, but the helpings are large, the cooking quite good, and the desserts mouth-watering. Alas, it's not open in the evenings. Get here before 12:30 PM, or you'll find yourself in for a long wait (which you can while away by sampling some of their splendid wines). Closed Sundays year-round; closed Saturdays June through August. No reservations. Major credit cards accepted. 21 Kildare St. (phone: 668-0362).

Osprey's Around the corner from *Jurys* and the American Embassy, this cozy candlelit restaurant has two small dining rooms, each with a fireplace. Flambé cooking is a specialty here, as are such international dishes as beef Wellington, salmon *en croûte,* chicken Madeira, Wiener schnitzel, and Dover sole. Closed Sundays. Reservations advised. Major credit cards accepted. 41-43 Shelbourne Rd. (phone: 660-8087).

Polo One Less than a block from St. Stephen's Green and tucked between Kildare and Dawson Streets, this dining place is close to all the major sights and shops. The white-and-blue modern decor is enhanced by a fine collection of paintings by local artists. The menu, a hybrid of Italian, Spanish, and American influences, emphasizes fresh Irish ingredients, local cheeses, seafood, and fruit. Open for lunch and dinner; closed Sundays. Reservations advised. Major credit cards accepted. 5-6 Molesworth Pl. (phone: 676-6442).

Unicorn Established in 1939, this small Italian spot is a favorite with Irish politicians and literati. All pasta and sauces are freshly prepared daily. Open for lunch and dinner; closed Sundays. Reservations advised. Master-Card and Visa accepted. Merrion Ct., off Merrion Row (phone: 676-2182 or 668-8552).

INEXPENSIVE

Bad Ass Café One of the brightest and liveliest eating spots to hit town in some time. It's famed as much for its (loud) rock music and videos as for its great pizza. Steaks are another specialty. Open daily for lunch and dinner. Reservations unnecessary. Major credit cards accepted. 9-11 Crown Alley, behind the Central Bank on Dame St. (phone: 671-2596).

Beshoff Owned by a family long known as purveyors of fresh fish, this is a classy version of the traditional Dublin fish-and-chips shop, with a black-and-white marble decor. The menu features chips (French fries) with salmon, shark, squid, turbot, or prawns, as well as the humble cod. Open daily, noon to midnight. Reservations unnecessary. No credit cards accepted. 14 Westmoreland St. (phone: 677-8781).

Captain America's Specializes in "genuine American hamburgers," Tex-Mex, and barbecue dishes, served with American beer and rock music. Open daily for lunch and dinner. Reservations unnecessary. No credit cards accepted. Grafton Ct., 1st floor, Grafton St. (phone: 671-5266).

SHARING A PINT

Until you have been in a pub, you have not experienced Dublin. Here Dubliners come to pursue two serious occupations: drinking and conversation. Many pubs are ugly and modern, complete with Muzak and plastic, but plenty of traditional pubs remain — noisy, companionable places for the pursuit of friendly ghosts of bygone Dublin in an unhurried atmosphere.

HIGH SPIRITS

Bailey The watering place for generations of Dublin's writers and artists, this pub has been preempted by ubiquitous youth, and the clientele is now what can only be described as androgynous. At night, it's jammed with the young and pretty. At other times, there is peace and time enough to admire the handsome iron and marble tables, and many young artists, some writers, and some musicians are still among the crowd. The best way to experience the pub is to come for drinks at noon and, at about 1 PM (having reserved a table), climb the stairs to the restaurant overhead, where the food is good and the service faultless. On the way up or down, don't miss the pub's unique feature — the original door of Leopold Bloom's house at 7 Eccles

Street, lovingly preserved by the *Bailey*'s former owner, artist, and patron John Ryan. 2 Duke St. (phone: 679-3734).

Brazen Head Here, legend has it, the winsome Robert Emmet plotted the ragged and abortive little rebellion of 1803. Although only a few hundred yards from the Guinness brewery, this establishment hubristically disdains to serve draft stout. It is a dark and intimate place, with hallways leading off in all directions, one of them into a little room where poetry and music sessions are held. The poetry readings have a charmingly inverted nature: One gets the impression that the people are listening to poetry while drinking, rather than the opposite. 20 Lower Bridge St. (phone: 679-5186).

Davy Byrne's This, the "moral pub" in which Leopold Bloom had gorgonzola cheese and his glass of burgundy on June 16, 1904, today bears little resemblance to the place Joyce was evoking when he wrote of Bloom's visit in *Ulysses*. The pub has undergone much updating, but still features murals by Cecil Salkeld (father-in-law of Brendan Behan) that depict famous Irish literary and artistic personalities of the early 20th century, and one of the three bars still bears the name of the novel in which it was immortalized. At the hub of the main shopping and business district of Dublin, it attracts a predictably varied clientele. Food is served all day, the specialties being salads and sandwiches made with fresh or smoked salmon — except on June 16, when gorgonzola and burgundy may take precedence for some. 21 Duke St. (phone: 711298).

Doheny & Nesbitt Owned and run by Ned Doheny and Tom Nesbitt, this establishment is very small, and at times, it's almost impossible to breathe for the heaving mass of trainee architects, students, and tired political pundits taking time off from reporting the proceedings in the Dáil (Parliament) around the corner. So come early, or, better still, sidle in at noontime, when there is breathing space as well as an opportunity to munch on hot beef sandwiches, medium, well done, or (unusual in Ireland) rare. 5 Lower Baggot St. (phone: 676-2945).

Mulligans This pub, which has been in existence since the 1750s, serves nothing but plain drink. But what it does, it does well, and the Guinness draft offered here is probably the most consistently good, if not the best, in the country. (A constant flow throughout the day is one of the secrets, they say.) Three rooms are in constant use, and since the pub is situated between the harbor, the *Irish Press,* and Trinity College, the patrons include journalists, dock workers, and students. Part of the fun of drinking here is guessing whether that long-haired melancholic in the corner is a music critic, a longshoreman, or an aspiring Lionel Trilling. 8 Poolbeg St. (phone: 677-5582).

Neary's The back door of this pub opens directly opposite the stage door of the *Gaiety,* the capital's principal variety theater, so the noises here are made mostly by actors, musicians, and the sorts of pallid cohorts that these two professions attract. Visiting celebrities from both professions drop in here from time to time, so visitors may find themselves rubbing shoulders with the great. When this happens, the place is full, and there is little comfort; but at lunchtime, it's easy to find consolation in the sandwiches or, in season, fresh oysters. Four beautiful gas lamps stand on the marble counter, the seating is plush and bouncy, and there is usually a young "lounge boy" running his feet off trying to serve everybody at once. 1 Chatham St. (phone: 677-8596).

Stag's Head Nowadays, this classic pub, gorgeously turned out right down to its stained glass windows, generally draws a clientele from all strata of society, but at lunchtime on weekdays the observant will note a preponderance of pinstripe vests, fob watches, and cold noses of members of the legal profession as they dig into their hot-meat-and-two-veg meals. Unfortunately, the pub is awkward to get to, even though it's in the heart of the city. 1 Dame Ct. (phone: 679-3701).

Among the Dublin pubs known for their traditional music, *O'Donoghue's* (15 Merrion Row; phone: 661-4303) is one of the most famous (and least comfortable). Others to try: *An Béal Bocht* (Charlemont St.; phone: 475-5614); *Slattery's* (Capel St.; phone: 872-7971); the *Baggot Inn* (Lower Baggot St.; phone: 676-1430); *Kitty O'Shea's* (23-25 Upper Grand Canal St.; phone: 660-9965); and *Foley's* (1 Merrion Row; phone: 661-0115). Other favorites — where drinking and talking are the primary amusements — include *Toner's* (Lower Baggot St.; phone: 676-3090); the *Horseshoe Bar* in the *Shelbourne* hotel, favored by the uppity, horsey set; the *Palace Bar* (21 Fleet St.; phone: 677-9290), a traditional haunt of journalists and literati; the award-winning *Dubliner* in *Jurys* hotel, which offers an airy atmosphere with a fireplace and a section called the "Press Room," serving (lethal) seasonal drinks; and last, but certainly not least, the delightful *Ryans* (28 Parkgate St.; phone: 677-6097), with its shining mirrors, courteous barmen, and snugs where guests can drink quietly and enjoy first-rate pub grub.

Galway City

The ancient port of Galway is rich with historic ambience. The past lingers quite literally in the city's narrow streets, in its carved stone windows and low-arched doorways, and in the massive walls of historic merchants' warehouses. The surrounding landscape — a beautiful and wild expanse of wide bay, stony hills, and unspoiled bog — has long supplied the city with song and story. A lively respect for lore and legend keeps an ancient presence alive in the imaginations of natives and visitors alike.

This ancient city's most famous legend is of the mayor who hanged his own son. This archetype of the stern father was one James Lynch Fitzstephen, who in 1493 condemned his son Walter as a murderer. Apparently, Walter had killed a visiting Spaniard for stealing his girlfriend. So popular was Walter throughout Galway that no one could be found to hang him, so the father had to do it himself. A stone memorial window marks the execution spot. Even though historians have debunked this story in modern times, most Galwegians are loyal to the legend.

There's a stronger ring of truth to another oft-told tale, one that has Christopher Columbus visiting Galway before he ever clapped a weather eye on America. It is believed that he called here and prayed in St. Nicholas's Church en route to the uncharted western seas. Whatever the truth of the Columbus story, it is hard to shake the faith of Galway natives in their own notable explorer and saint, Brendan. They and many other Irish people believe that St. Brendan discovered the New World centuries before the Italian upstart. Naturally, it's said that Brendan sailed from Galway.

Galway's origins go back long before the 6th-century St. Brendan and Christian times. There were settlements on its river in pagan days. The Irish for Galway is *Gaillimh* (pronounced *Goll*-iv), and legend has it that the name comes from a princess, Gaillimh, who was drowned in the river. Nowadays, the river is called the Corrib, and its surging waters rushing into Galway Bay are the pulsing soul and spirit of the city. In summertime, silver salmon swarm in from the Atlantic feeding grounds in response to the immemorial spawning call and fight their way upriver to the place where they were born. This natural phenomenon used to be one of the more uplifting sights in Galway, and it still is in a way, though the salmon have been thinned out by pollution and the nets of factory ships.

Although its character is unmistakably Irish, Galway has a proud international heritage. It was the Normans who developed Galway into a thriving mercantile city. During the 13th century, they hopscotched from Britain to Ireland with the help of a pope and a traitorous Irish prince. When their armies reached Galway, they quickly subdued the native tribes, taking over the city. They built stout walls around it to keep out the wild Irish — and then, in a matter of decades, became more Irish than the Irish themselves. In the 15th and 16th centuries, their trade relations with Spain kept the port bustling and their coffers full.

Galway became known as the City of the Tribes because of the 14 dynastic merchant families that controlled its wealth and fortune for several centuries. Outside the walls, across the river, the relics of the ancient Irish civilization survived in the fishing village called Claddagh, which spreads out from Nimmo's Pier at the estuary of Galway Bay. Its thatch-roofed cottages have been torn down and replaced by drab, utilitarian homes, but it still manages to retain its identity and remain independent of Galway City.

From the middle of the 19th century until quite recently, Galway was a port for passenger liners plying the Atlantic between the United States and Europe. The passage was not always comfortable. During the potato famine of the 1840s, thousands of starving Irish peasants sailed from Galway to the New World aboard vessels whose abysmal conditions won them the chilling name "coffin ships."

Only in recent years has Galway expanded and become industrialized. In 1985, an extension of the city's borders by a half-mile in all directions increased Galway's population overnight, from 30,000 to its present 50,000, and a massive urban-renewal program begun in the late 1980s continues to transform the downtown area. Galway, however, learned from other Irish cities and has carefully preserved its old charm while expanding. Pieces of the Old City walls have been incorporated into the *Eyre Square Centre,* an attractive shopping center cleverly tucked into formerly derelict space. Wooden shopfronts have been restored or reinstated where plastic once defaced the old buildings, and most new buildings use the native gray limestone, blending beautifully in color as well as scale with the old.

Galway may be rich in history, but its heart is young. The presence of a university and technical college fills the streets with young people. Most are Irish, but the town becomes more and more cosmopolitan each year. French, German, and Italian can be heard on the streets and women dressed in saris no longer draw stares. The arts thrive in Galway, in yearly festivals and in year-round offerings in local theaters and galleries. As the locals put it, "There's a great buzz" here.

Galway At-a-Glance

SEEING THE CITY

There are no really great vantage points from which to get an overall view of Galway City. For a bird's-eye reconnaissance, try the top of the parking lot of the *Eyre Square Centre.* It's open 8 AM to 10 PM Mondays through Saturdays and is right in the middle of town. From this somewhat unusual vantage point, the busy docks can be seen just below, the church steeples punctuate the sky, and on a clear day the hills of Clare are visible to the south.

SPECIAL PLACES

Galway is a small town, so just about everything worth seeing can be covered in a single day on foot. A walk through the city streets (be sure not to miss those history-haunted back lanes) is highly recommended.

Visitors should be aware that Galway weather is infuriatingly temperamental, and rain clouds are never far off. Still, even in the gentle drizzle of the Irish "soft day," it's fun to set off with a mac and cover the whole town. Consider walking out to Salthill, the seaside resort about 1½ miles from downtown, which offers one of the best sunset views over Galway Bay.

EYRE SQUARE This is the heart of the city and the place visitors usually see first. It once was the Fair Green, where livestock and produce were sold, and is now named after one of the ruling merchant tribes, the Eyres. (Charlotte Brontë got the title of her famous novel when she saw the name Jane Eyre on a gravestone during a visit to Galway.) The park within the square is named after John F. Kennedy, in memory of his Galway visit. There's a fascinating statue of a quirky gnome of an Irish writer named Pádraic O Conaire at the northern end. A splendid cut-stone doorway, of a type seen in the better homes of long ago, also stands in the park, this one from the home of another tribe, the Brownes.

EYRE SQUARE CENTRE This inner-city shopping and strolling development incorporates parts of the Old City walls. An assortment of attractive shops sell everything from sweaters to groceries and a lively café fills part of the enclosed courtyard. Enter from Eyre Sq. or *Corbettcourt* on William St.

ST. NICHOLAS'S CHURCH According to the Irish, this is the place where Columbus prayed before sailing off to discover America. Originally built by the Anglo-Normans in 1320, it has been greatly altered through the ensuing centuries. It retains its original chancel, however, and is a repository for some striking medieval stone carvings and relics. The three-gabled west front is unparalleled in Ireland. After the Reformation, the church became the prize in a tug-of-war between Protestants and Catholics and changed hands a number of times before Cromwell's forces finally secured it for the Protestants. The marks of that struggle and the subsequent occupation by disrespectful troops are still visible. Market St.

LYNCH MEMORIAL WINDOW Just up the street from the church, this stone window marks the spot where the mayor of the city, James Lynch Fitzstephen, is said to have hanged his son Walter for murder in 1493. But it isn't the actual window through which the luckless lad exited to the next world — this one was carved some 200 years later. Market St.

LYNCH'S CASTLE The ubiquitous Lynch tribe that gave so many mayors to the city originally lived in this 16th-century building. It has been lovingly restored and is now the Allied Irish Bank. Shop St. at the Four Corners (phone: 67041).

SALMON WEIR The centuries-old salmon fishery is below the Salmon Weir Bridge, opposite the Cathedral of Our Lady (see below). This is a pleasant place to pass an hour in summer watching the salmon (sadly, in much depleted numbers) on their way up the weir to the spawning grounds.

CATHEDRAL OF OUR LADY On the site of a former jailhouse opposite the Salmon Weir Bridge, this structure, built in the early 1960s, was inspired by Renaissance and other church architecture of the past. It is a large and impressive building, beloved by its congregation but with an ungraceful presence.

SPANISH ARCH The best-known landmark in Galway, the arch was built in 1594 as an addition to the Old Town wall and to provide protection for the docked Spanish ships unloading their wines nearby. Attached to the arch is the *Galway City Museum* (see *Museums*). From here it's possible to climb to the top of the arch and look across the Corrib to Claddagh. At press time, the Spanish Arch was undergoing restoration with plans for completion by the end of this year. Beside Wolfe Tone Bridge, where the river enters the bay.

CLADDAGH This district was originally a fishing village where the native Irish clung to their old culture in defiance of the usurping Anglo-Normans within the walls. Claddagh people no longer fish, nor do they speak Irish, but they still proudly maintain a sense of separateness from the city. The famous Claddagh ring — two hands clasping a heart surmounted by a crown — was fashioned by local goldsmiths as the traditional wedding band. Cross the Corrib at Wolfe Tone Bridge to reach Claddagh.

SALTHILL Galway's seaside resort is really part of the city, a mere 1½ miles from downtown. Salthill has three sandy beaches on Galway Bay, but invariably the weather is too chilly for Americans to sunbathe or swim. The *Leisureland* complex that dominates the seafront has a newly revamped, heated indoor swimming pool and water amusements for children. Southwest of Galway, reachable on foot or by frequent buses from Eyre Square.

FRANCISCAN ABBEY Built in 1836, the abbey is on the site of a 13th-century friary that was founded by the De Burgos (Burkes), the first Norman Lords of Galway. St. Francis St.

UNIVERSITY COLLEGE The original building, completed in 1849, was modeled on some of the neo-Gothic-style colleges at Oxford. Built as a nondenominational institution, it was once condemned as godless by the Catholic bishops, who forbade Catholics to attend, but the ban was ignored. The main entrance to the campus is off University Rd. (phone: 24411).

Sources and Resources

TOURIST INFORMATION

For comprehensive information and advice, first go to the tourist board, Aras Fáilte, just south of the western side of Eyre Square. During the summer, another office is open on the Promenade in Salthill (phone for either office: 63081). Pick up all of the free literature and maps, as well as the *County Galway Tourist Guide* (about $1.50) and, when available, the Galway Junior Chamber of Commerce listing of summer events in Galway and Salthill. A small booklet, *Tourist Trail of Old Galway,* is also available at the tourist office.

Hardiman's *History of Galway* is the definitive work on the city's past and can be bought at the *Connacht Tribune* newspaper office (Market St.; phone: 67251) or at *Kenny's Bookshop* (High St.; phone: 62739 or 61014). For additional sources, try the County Library in the Hynes Building (St. Augustine St.; phone: 61666).

LOCAL COVERAGE Two weeklies, the *Connacht Tribune* and the *Connacht Sentinel,* and two giveaways, the *Galway Advertiser* and the *Galway Observer,* provide strictly local news.

TELEPHONE The area code for Galway City and the immediate vicinity is 91. When calling from within the Republic of Ireland, dial 091 before the local number.

GETTING AROUND

If the weather allows, it's easy to walk throughout the city without undue exertion.

AIRPORT Regularly scheduled *Aer Lingus* flights connect Galway with Dublin. For information, call 55569.

BICYCLE Many of Galway's streets are better suited to bicycles than they are to cars; the surrounding countryside also provides gentle cycling terrain. Bikes are available for rent at *Cycle World* (Tuam Rd.; phone: 53455), *Richard Walsh & Sons Ltd.* (Headford Rd. and Wood Quay; phone: 65710), and *Station Rent-A-Bike* (Eyre Sq.; phone: 66219).

BUS The central departure point for all city buses is the west side of Eyre Square. City bus service stops at 11:30 PM. Buses for points outside the city leave from the railway station on Eyre Square, behind the *Great Southern* hotel. (The only trains leaving the station are for Dublin and intervening stops.) All buses, trains, and touring coaches are run by *Bus Eireann* and *Iarnrod Eireann* (phone: 62000 for both). Two private bus companies offer service between Galway and Dublin, with stops in Oranmore, Craughwell, Loughrea, Ballinasloe, and Athlone: *Nestor's* (phone: 97144), with departures from Eyre Square, and *Burke's Coaches* (phone: 93-55416 for reservations Mondays through Saturdays from 9:30 AM to 6 PM), with departures from Forster Street near Eyre Square.

CAR RENTAL It's best to pick up a car at the port of arrival in Ireland, usually Shannon or Dublin, where all the major international and local rental companies operate. Rental companies in Galway include *Budget* (12 Eyre Sq.; phone: 66376), *Johnson & Perrott* at *Higgins Garage* (Headford Rd.; phone: 68886), and *Murray's/Europcar* (Headford Rd.; phone: 62222).

TAXI Plenty of cabs are available, and they're not too costly. The central cabstand is on the north side of Eyre Sq. (phone: 61111).

SPECIAL EVENTS

Generally, Galway is a quiet place, but it does have its moments. September is the city's liveliest month.

FAVORITE FETES

Galway Oyster Festival The bays surrounding Galway have always been famous for their oysters and scallops. It's only appropriate, then, that the big annual wingding here is devoted to the succulent creatures. The festivities are traditionally held during the last weekend in September, just as the bivalves come back into season after a succession of r-less months (oyster season is from September through December). Unlike some of the cultural festivals, the aim here is simply to relax and have fun. The festival begins with the *Irish Oyster-Opening Championship,* followed the next day by the *World Oyster-Opening Championship,* which draws participants from around the globe. Throughout the festival, yacht races, golf competitions, and other festivities take place. The organized events of the festival are rather expensive and must be booked in advance. It's also advisable to reserve a hotel room, especially if you're planning on staying at the *Great Southern* (see *Checking In*) — the center of the festival — or at any of the other better hotels. A full ticket, which covers all the events of the festival, from Friday night to Sunday morning, including a reception and dinner, festival banquet, lunch, oyster tasting, and recuperative Irish coffee "morning after," costs about $250 per sore head. For details, contact Ann Flanagan (20 Oaklands, Salthill, Galway, Irish Republic; phone: 22066; fax: 27282) or the tourist board (phone: 63081).

Clarenbridge Oyster Festival An offshoot of the Galway celebration, this festival is held in early September in the pubs and streets of the bayside village of Clarenbridge. This is a family fete, with a less frenetic atmosphere than its Galway counterpart. For information, contact Ann Walsh (phone: 96155; fax: 96001).

In addition, don't miss *Galway Race Week,* beginning on the last Monday of July, 6 days of heavy gambling on the ponies running at *Ballybrit* racecourse, about 2 miles from the city center. It also entails heroic, round-the-clock drinking and heavy poker sessions in hotel bedrooms, all earthy and great fun even if you don't like horses or cards. The *Salthill Festival,* featuring a free concert series, pony jumping, fishing competitions, yacht races, and more, is held in early July in the bayside area of Salthill. The *Irish Show Jumping Championship* is held later in the month at Salthill Park. The *Galway Arts Festival,* held for 10 days in July, has developed into a prime cultural event, attracting hosts of young people from all over Ireland and abroad. It features a brilliant array of Irish and international plays, musical events, and art exhibitions, as well as a week-long carnival and all sorts of fringe events. Details can be obtained from the tourist board or the *Arts Centre,* Nun's Island (phone: 65886).

MUSEUMS

Galway's only notable museum is the *Galway City Museum,* located at the bottom of Quay St. near the Spanish Arch. Though tiny, it houses a range of exhibitions that highlight the city's past. A spiral staircase leads from the museum to the top of the Spanish Arch, which offers a fine view across the Corrib to Claddagh. At press time, both the museum and the Spanish Arch were undergoing reconstruction with plans to reopen by the end of this year (phone: 68151).

SHOPPING

Good values are found in native knitwear and homespun tweeds, as well as Irish glass, bone china, Connemara marble, and other ornamental items. Shops are generally closed on Sundays.

ARCH TACK ROOMS Everything for the rider and a few items even non-horsey types might want to own, such as handsome riding gloves and Aigle rubber riding boots that perform beautifully on rainy city streets. Spanish Parade, facing the Spanish Arch (phone: 64247).

ARCHWAY ANTIQUES Pricey but good old china, jewelry, and furniture. Victoria Pl. (phone: 62041).

AULDE STOCK For good, old pine furniture, and the odd silver spoon. Kirwans La., at the bottom of Quay St. (no phone).

BRIDGE MILLS A selection of shops (pottery, art, antiques) in a renovated old mill. A pleasant coffee shop is on the lower level (see *Eating Out*). Mill St., on O'Brien's Bridge (phone: 66231).

COBWEBS A quaint, old-fashioned shop specializing in antique and estate jewelry, small antiques, and upstairs, a selection of nostalgic toys. 7 Quay La., opposite the Spanish Arch (phone: 64388).

DESIGN IRISH PLUS All things Irish and beautifully designed, from pottery to sweaters to jewelry. *The Cornstore,* Middle St. (phone: 67716).

GALWAY IRISH CRYSTAL Glass cutting demonstrations are offered in the summer at this factory shop, which sells top-quality items, discontinued patterns, and seconds. They will happily pack your purchases for shipment back home. Merlin Pk., on the Dublin road (phone: 57311).

HOUSE OF JAMES A wide array of handmade Irish items is sold here, including pottery, handwoven rugs, wooden bowls, knitwear, and silver jewelry. An eatery on the premises serves natural homemade Irish food, from farm-house cheese to ice cream. Castle St. (phone: 67776).

JUDY GREENE POTTERY Handsome pottery decorated with the wildflowers that grow in the nearby Connemara countryside fill this traditional shop in one of Galway's 17th-century buildings. 11 Cross St. (phone: 61753).

KENNY'S BOOKSHOP AND ART GALLERY Housed in two old Galway buildings, the floors may slope but the selections are terrific: from Yeats to Edna O'Brien. The art gallery hosts changing exhibitions of works by Irish artists and others. High St. (phone: 62739 or 61014; fax: 68544).

O'MAILLE'S Aran sweaters and Donegal tweeds, including tweed sold by the yard. The merchandise is pricey but of good quality, and the staff is friendly. Dominick St. (phone: 62696).

POWELLS FOUR CORNERS *The* place for a wide selection of Irish music on tape and CD. William St. (phone: 68667 or 62295).

RIVERRUN GALLERY An old warehouse converted to a bright space devoted to contemporary Irish artists. There's also a self-service restaurant. Lower Abbeygate St. (phone: 66620).

ROYAL TARA CHINA A factory in what was once an elegant mansion. Visitors are welcome to watch china decoration, as well as purchase seconds at 30–60% discounts or perfect pieces at full price. Open daily; the restaurant on the premises is open weekdays from 9 AM to 5 PM. Tara Hall, Mervue (phone: 51301).

STEPHEN FALLER LTD. Claddagh rings are the specialty, plus Waterford crystal. Williamsgate St. (phone: 61227).

T. DILLON & SONS A Galway institution, this jewelry shop has been selling Claddagh rings since 1750. 1 William St. (phone: 61317).

TOLCO ANTIQUES A short, easy 3-mile drive out of town leads to a large ware-house full of furniture and bric-a-brac. An unpretentious place, but some treasures lurk. Headford Rd. (phone: 51146).

TREASURE CHEST Housed in a building painted Wedgwood blue is a broad display of Irish crystal, pottery, woolens and tweeds, craftwork, and most notably, classic crocheted garments. William St. (phone: 63862 or 67237).

TWICE AS NICE The place to buy a bit of old lace or linen, or maybe an old-fashioned slip like the ones that caused the *Abbey Theatre* riots in 1907. 5 Quay St. (phone: 66332).

SPORTS AND FITNESS

BOATING AND SAILING Rowboats of various sizes can be hired for trips up the River Corrib and into Lough Corrib, the big lake upstream. Contact Frank Dolan (13 Riverside, Wood Quay, Galway City; phone: 65841). Frank rents boats from April through September for about $20 per day. For all types of sailing on Galway Bay, contact Pearse Purcell of the *Galway Bay Sailing Club* (Rinville, Oranmore; phone: 93610 or 63522).

FISHING A license must be bought and a fee paid to fish for salmon at the salmon weir (an enclosure in a waterway for trapping fish), near the Salmon Weir Bridge, which has an international reputation among anglers. Fishing at the salmon weir must be booked well in advance. For fee information and reservations for the season, write to the *Galway Fishery,* Nun Island, Republic of Ireland, and state the dates desired. April, May, and June are peak times and the most difficult to book. Fishing on Lough Corrib is free for brown trout; a state license is required for salmon and sea trout. For information on hiring a boat or obtaining a fishing license, contact Des Moran at the *Knockferry Lodge* (Knockferry, Rosscahill; phone: 80122; fax: 80328), or the tourist board (phone: 63081). To go sea angling for shark, contact Tom Curran (Spiddal; phone: 83535). For more details, see *Gone Fishing* in DIVERSIONS.

GOLF There's a bayside, 18-hole course in Salthill, where visitors are welcome (phone: 22169 or 21827). The *Galway Bay Golf and Country Club* (Renville, Oranmore; phone: 25711) boasts a championship course designed by Cristy O'Connor, Jr. It has a restaurant (open in summer) and a hotel is being planned. The *Rosscahill Golf Club* (phone: 53930) offers 18 gentler holes. The 9-hole course at *Glenlo Abbey* (phone: 26666) opened in March 1993 on a rolling hillside overlooking Lough Corrib. The *Athenry Golf Club* (phone: 94466), about 14 miles east of Galway, has been expanded to 18 holes.

HORSE RACING The highlight of Galway's equestrian competitions is *Galway Race Week,* held beginning the last Monday in July (see *Special Events*). Flat racing, hurdles, and a steeplechase are among the featured events. For more information, contact the Galway Race Committee (phone: 53870).

SWIMMING The beaches at Salthill are superb, with good bay bathing when the weather cooperates. The indoor pool at *Leisureland,* on the seafront in Salthill, is open daily (phone: 21455 or 22562).

THEATER

The performing arts are a way of life in Ireland, and Galway is no exception. The city has several theaters, including one of our Irish favorites.

Druid Lane Theatre Installed in a former grocery warehouse in the oldest part of the city, near the Spanish Arch, the quays, and the Old Town walls, the home of the *Druid Theatre Company* is perhaps the most attractive small theater in Ireland, its intimacy enhanced by the seating, which surrounds the stage on three sides. Currently under the direction of Maelíosa Stafford, the company was founded in 1975 by Garry Hynes (now the artistic director of the *Abbey Theatre* in Dublin), and in a short time has become renowned for its productions of Irish classics such as Boucicault's *The Colleen Bawn* and Molloy's *Wood of Whispering,* as well as contemporary Irish plays. It's widely believed that the lane on which the theater is built is haunted by the ghost of a nun who walks slowly through the street at night. But don't let this specter scare you away from an evening with this exciting young group. Druid La., also known as Chapel La. (phone: 68617).

There's also an Irish-language theater — *An Taibhdhearc* (pronounced An *Thigh*-vark) — that has been producing plays in Irish for more than 50 years. During the summer tourist season, the emphasis is on traditional Irish music and dance, interspersed with short plays in Irish so heavily mimed that no knowledge of the language is needed. The theater is on Middle Street (phone: 62024). Contact the tourist office for performance schedules and ticket information.

MUSIC

Traditional Irish music is heard in many pubs in Galway and Salthill; consult the local papers for details (also see *Sharing a Pint*). Be prepared for a smoke-filled atmosphere and late hours — music usually begins after 9 PM.

NIGHTCLUBS AND NIGHTLIFE

Although there are no true nightclubs in Galway, life does not cease at dusk. Most hotels have drinking places that function until near dawn. Some bars, too, continue serving (illegally) after closing time (11:30 PM in summer, 11 PM in winter), and discreet inquiry will gain information about them. There are a number of late-night dance clubs; check local newspapers for details. *Bentley* (Eyre Sq.; phone: 64105) is a restaurant by day, a nightclub frequented by the thirty-something crowd in the evenings. In summer, most Salthill hotels have cabarets and discos. One of the livelier Salthill dance clubs is *CJ's Night Club* (in the *Monterey* hotel; phone: 24017), which attracts Irish tourists on holiday. *Central Park* (36 Upper Abbeygate St.; phone: 65974), *Oasis* (*Warwick* hotel; phone: 21244), and *Kno-Kno's* (Eglinton St.; no phone) are popular with local folks in their 20s and 30s. In summer, the *Hangar* (Dalysfort Rd., Salthill; phone: 21009) features live music. A number of local pubs offer fine Irish music (see *Sharing a Pint*).

Best in Town

CHECKING IN

The better hotels in Galway have become expensive, though it's still possible to find some good ones in the moderate price range. A few have adopted the so-called European plan and no longer include breakfast in the room rate. Where breakfast *is* included, it's the ample Irish meal of bacon, eggs, and sausages — usually very good — and guests pay for it whether they eat it or not. In the following listings, a private bath is included unless otherwise specified. Expect to pay more than $150 a night for a double room in places listed as expensive; about $100 at hotels in the moderate category; and under $85 at the place described as inexpensive. All telephone numbers are in the 91 area code unless otherwise indicated.

EXPENSIVE

Ardilaun House Once the stately home of an aristocratic family, the grounds of this 89-room establishment still retain a quiet, almost country air. It's a 25-minute walk from town; many rooms boast a view over the gardens to Galway center and bay. The staff is friendly and *Blazers* bar is a popular spot. There are conference facilities in addition to a gym, a sauna, a steamroom, a snooker room, and a tennis court. A golf course is nearby. The award-winning *Camilaun Room* restaurant is first-rate (see *Eating Out*). Taylor's Hill (phone: 21433 or 22927; fax: 21546).

Connemara Coast Six miles from Galway and perched on the edge of the bay, this 112-room property is a scenic and comfortable place. A recently opened leisure center includes an indoor swimming pool that lets guests laugh at the Irish weather and a tennis court. There's also a restaurant and a pub featuring traditional music. Furbo (phone: 92108; fax: 92065).

Corrib Great Southern Recent renovations have greatly enlarged this modern, 180-room hotel overlooking Galway Bay. Try to get one of the bay-windowed rooms, very aptly named here. The *Curragh* restaurant also shares the magnificent view, and in summer there is nightly entertainment in *O'Malley's* bar. There's also a heated indoor swimming pool, a Jacuzzi, a steamroom, snooker, and supervised activities for children. Dublin Rd. (phone: 55281; fax: 51390).

Galway Ryan Each of the 96 rooms in this modern hotel has a TV set and direct-dial phone. There is also a gameroom and playroom for both adults and children. A restaurant serves conventional Irish fare, and during the summer, musical entertainment and dancing are featured nightly. Dublin Rd. (phone: 53181; fax: 53187).

Glenlo Abbey This hostelry is in a renovated old estate on the shores of Lough Corrib, just outside the city. The name of the place refers to the family chapel in the old manor home, which has been preserved. Public rooms recall the Georgian era, and the 24 guestrooms and 6 suites are comfortably furnished. There is also an elegant dining room, cellar bar, and 9-hole golf course overlooking the lake. Bushy Park, 7 miles from the center of town (phone: 26666; fax: 27800).

Great Southern A superior establishment, with 120 of the most comfortable rooms and suites in Galway. Accommodations are large and lovely, although those in the old part of the house have high ceilings and a bit more ambience. The newly refurbished grand foyer is the center of social life in the city. The food in the elegant *Oyster Room* restaurant is superb (see *Eating Out*). There's also the *Cocktail Bar,* a sedate and Victorian room off the lobby, and *O'Flaherty's,* a cozy cellar pub that features a carvery lunch during the day (a good value) and lively music later in the evening. The leisure center on the top floor includes a heated indoor swimming pool and sauna. 15 Eyre Sq. (phone: 64041; fax: 66704).

Salthill A modern, family hostelry with a conservatory overlooking the famous Salthill promenade and views of Galway Bay from many of its 53 rooms (family suites are available). All rooms have TV sets, direct-dial phones, and tea/coffee-making facilities. A restaurant offers an extensive seafood menu and the bar provides piano music nightly. The Promenade, Salthill (phone: 22711; fax: 21855).

MODERATE

Adare House An outstanding guesthouse if bed and breakfast is all that's required (they don't serve other meals). The 9 comfortable rooms are tastefully decorated. A good value. Father Griffin Pl. (phone: 62638).

Brennan's Yard A new 24-room hotel in an old stone building adjacent to the Spanish Arch. Simple, comfortable rooms with touches of Irish pine furniture. There is a restaurant and the attractive atrium bar seems bright even on rainy afternoons. Lower Merchants Rd. (phone: 68166; fax: 68262).

INEXPENSIVE

Roncalli House This pleasant bed and breakfast establishment overlooking the bay has 6 simple but comfortable rooms, all with baths or shower. 24 Whitestrand Ave., Lower Salthill (phone: 64159).

EATING OUT

The city has some exceptionally good eating places. The native beef and lamb are among the world's best, so it's hard to go wrong with steaks or chops. During the summer, Galway salmon from the River Corrib is superlative, and during the "r" months (September and October, and so on), the oysters from the bay are possibly the best on the entire globe. Expect to pay $80 or more (sometimes considerably more) for dinner for two (without wine, drinks, and tips) at restaurants in the expensive category; $50 to $80 in the moderate bracket; and $50 or less in places described as inexpensive. A service charge is included in all meal bills, but a tip (about 5%) is expected all the same. Note that most of the restaurants listed open briefly for lunch, then close and reopen for a 2- or 3-hour dinner period, usually from 7 PM on. Since several are out of town, it's a good idea to check on their serving hours before venturing forth. All telephone numbers are in the 91 area code unless otherwise indicated.

For an unforgettable dining experience, we begin with our culinary favorite, followed by our cost and quality choices, listed by price category.

DELIGHTFUL DINING

Drimcong House A lovely 17th-century mansion serves as the backdrop for one of Ireland's best restaurants. Owner Gerard Galvin's inventive menu changes weekly according to what's best in the garden, the lake, and Galway Bay. Specialties include baked ham in two sauces, one of the wild garlic known as ramson, the other of pink melon; medallions of squab served with pear; hot fish mousse with tomato and strawberry sauces; and a dessert sauce flavored with sweet geranium and tasting of rose and lemon simultaneously. The chef also caters to vegetarians and children. *Drimcong,* an 8-mile drive from Galway City, seems half that distance after dinner, due, no doubt, to overwhelming contentment. Open Tuesdays through Saturdays for dinner only, Sundays for lunch; closed from *Christmas* through the end of February. Reservations necessary. Major credit cards accepted. One mile past Moycullen village on N59 (phone: 85115 or 85585)

EXPENSIVE

Camilaun Room With its warm coloring and crystal chandeliers, this dining room retains an old-fashioned ambience. The food is conventional but of high quality, and it's a popular dining place for families. Fresh meat and fish are the specialties. Open daily for lunch and dinner year-round. Reservations necessary. Major credit cards accepted. At the *Ardilaun House Hotel,* Taylor's Hill (phone: 21433).

Casey's Westwood This is a friendly, family place serving French and Irish fare made with the freshest ingredients. Tasty "pub grub" is available in the *Elm Bar* all day. There's a convenient parking lot. Open daily for lunch and dinner. Reservations necessary for dinner. Major credit cards accepted. On the edge of town on the Oughterard road, Newcastle (phone: 21442 or 21645).

De Burgo's Walk down the stairs to this cozy "in" spot where fresh fish is always the specialty; the grilled salmon just can't be beat. Open daily for lunch and dinner. Reservations necessary. Major credit cards accepted. Augustine St. (phone: 62188).

Eyre House and Park House Two Galway institutions are housed in one large, comfortable establishment. Both dining rooms are the same at lunch, but in the evening the Park House becomes more formal, with linen napery and a slightly more expensive menu. Lamb and Galway Bay seafood are specialties here; the lunchtime carvery in the bar is popular and an excellent value. Open daily. Reservations advised. Major credit cards accepted. Forster St. (phone: 64924, 62396, 68293, or 63766).

Malt House This fine restaurant — sometimes called "J.J.'s" after the proprietor — is tucked down one of Galway's tiny alleys. The food is well prepared and the fish is first-rate. Light meals are served in the bar, perfect for a pre-theater dinner. Open for lunch and dinner; closed Sundays. Reservations advised. Major credit cards accepted. Old Malte Mall, High St. (phone: 67866 or 63993).

McDonagh's Fish Shop Practically every kind of fish caught in the Atlantic off the Galway coast finds its way to this dining spot, where it is served up in myriad ways. Bring your own wine. Open daily for lunch and dinner. Reservations advised. Major credit cards accepted. 22 Quay St. (phone: 65001).

Moran's Oyster Cottage The perfect light lunch in a perfect setting, that rare treat, can be found on the road to Shannon from Galway at this establishment, providing delicious native oysters, mouth-watering brown bread, and the best draft stout. Those who crave something other than the foregoing should order with care; taste the crab first, ask about the soup's ingredients, and sample it. If the weather is fine, there are tables in the sunshine at the front of the pub. Open daily for lunch and dinner; closed on *Good Friday* and *Christmas Day*. Reservations advised. Major credit cards accepted. Kilcolgan (phone: 96113).

Oyster Room In the *Great Southern* hotel, this is one of the finest all-round restaurants in the city. It boasts a new, elegant decor and serves fine fare. Try the lamb from Connemara or the Corrib salmon. The continental dishes are good, too. Open daily for dinner. Reservations necessary. Major credit cards accepted. 15 Eyre Sq. (phone: 64041).

MODERATE

Aideen's A bright and cheerful spot for pizza and pasta or just a glass of wine. Open daily for lunch and dinner. Reservations advised. MasterCard and Visa accepted. 3 Buttermilk La. (phone: 64831).

Bentley Possibly the best value in town for lunch; indulge yourself at the buffet. After dark, the eatery becomes a nightclub for people in their thirties. Open daily for lunch. Reservations unnecessary. Major credit cards accepted. Eyre Sq. (phone: 64105).

Branagans Everything from pizza to curry; all served in a lively yet cozy Victorian setting. Open Mondays through Saturdays for lunch and dinner; dinner only on Sundays. Reservations advised. MasterCard and Visa accepted. 36 Upper Abbeygate St. (phone: 65974).

Brasserie Tacos, steaks, pizza, and such served in a nice setting with an open fireplace. Open for lunch and dinner; closed Sundays. Reservations advised. Major credit cards accepted. 19 Middle St. (phone: 61610).

Bridge Mills Café and Wine Bar A warren of rooms and a popular spot downstairs in a beautifuliy converted old mill. A nice place to stop for a light meal, a drink, or just a cup of tea. Open daily from 9 AM to 5:30 PM; to 10:30 PM in summer. Reservations unnecessary. MasterCard and Visa accepted. Mill St., on O'Brien's Bridge (phone: 66231).

Chesters Tiny and atmospheric, this place serves everything from snacks to full meals. Fresh fish is a specialty. Open for lunch and dinner; closed Sundays. Reservations necessary. MasterCard and Visa accepted. 19 Upper Abbeygate St. (phone: 66441).

Cooke's A popular wine bar with an eclectic menu: pasta, steaks, and fresh fish. Last orders at 11 PM make it a handy after-theater spot. Open daily for lunch and dinner. Reservations advised. MasterCard and Visa accepted. 28 Upper Abbeygate St. (phone: 68203).

Galway Baking Company Known locally as *GBC,* this is a good place to enjoy a cup of tea and a currant-studded scone. Meals and snacks are served all day. Self-service on the ground floor; restaurant upstairs. Open daily for lunch and dinner; the downstairs section also serves breakfast. No reservations. Major credit cards accepted. Williamsgate (phone: 63087).

Lydon House Downstairs is a good, stand-up, fast-food eatery; upstairs is a more formal, sit-down restaurant that serves conventional, but tasty, meals. Open daily for lunch, dinner, and tea. Reservations advised. Major credit cards accepted. 5 Shop St. (phone: 64051 or 66586).

McSwiggan's With an upstairs restaurant and a downstairs pub, this lively spot covers all the bases. The pub attracts a young crowd with live music featured nightly. Open daily for lunch and dinner. Reservations necessary. Major credit cards accepted. 3 Eyre St. at Wood Quay (phone: 68917).

Paddy Burke's Smack in the center of Clarenbridge, less than 10 miles from Galway on the Limerick road, this place specializes in Galway Bay oysters harvested not far from the door. The seafood chowder and brown bread make a perfect lunch. Sit in one of the snugs inside the door (watch your head on the low ceiling!). Open daily from 10:30 AM to 10:30 PM. Reservations advised. Major credit cards accepted. Clarenbridge (phone: 96226).

Pasta Mista One whiff of this tiny Italian dining spot and you'll be hooked. Try the tasty pasta and excellent cappuccino. Open daily for lunch and dinner,

May through September; closed Sundays the rest of the year. Reservations advised. MasterCard and Visa accepted. Cross St. (phone: 65550).

Rabbitt's Oysters and other succulent sea dishes are the specialties of the house in this 100-year-old bar/restaurant. The bartenders are considered by some to "pull the best pint" in town. There's often live music in the evenings. Open daily for lunch and dinner. Reservations advised. Major credit cards accepted. 23-25 Forster St. (phone: 66490; fax: 61873).

Raftery's Rest Not far from town, this warm and welcoming restaurant serves good soups and fish specialties. Open daily for dinner. About 10 miles from Galway on the N18 in Kilcogan (phone: 96175).

Sev'nth Heav'n You'll find everything from steaks to vegetarian dishes in this bustling restaurant and wine bar that also offers entertainment; check the local papers to see who's playing. Open daily from noon to midnight. Reservations advised. Courthouse La., Quay St. (phone: 63838).

INEXPENSIVE

Bewley's of Galway The Galway outpost of a venerable Dublin institution. The tea and coffee are superb; so are the scones and porter cake. Hot meals are served all day; there's also a shop that sells items to take out. Self-service. Open daily. Reservations unnecessary. Major credit cards accepted. *The Cornstore,* Middle St. (phone: 65789).

Fat Freddy's Pizzeria This spot serves the city's best pizza. Open daily (late hours in summer). No reservations. Major credit cards accepted. Quay St. (phone: 67279).

SHARING A PINT

The bars in the hotels listed above are uniformly good, but don't be afraid to let instinct guide you into unfamiliar pubs. The nicest places are often discovered that way.

HIGH SPIRITS

Seagan Ua Neachtain Tabharneoir Ireland's western capital has a number of comfortable and well-run pubs, none as authentic and little changed as this house at the corner of Cross and Quay Streets, which also has a cozy upstairs restaurant. In the old days, the main door of the pub (above which the name of the original owner is still written out in Irish) would not open, and visitors had to go around to the side door on Quay Street and give a knock. The pub is the antithesis of *Durty Nelly's* that tourists' favorite in Bunratty: Voices are never raised, Irish is often spoken, and visiting patrons must endure the stares of regulars. 17 Cross St. (phone: 66172).

Still other pubs have their own attractions. *McDonagh's Thatched Pub* (Main St.; no phone) in the village of Oranmore (6 miles from downtown on the Dublin road) is old-fashioned and friendly, with plenty of atmosphere and an open fire on cold days. *Freeney's* (High St.; phone: 62609) is another old-style pub where, while standing at the bar, there's plenty of chatting with the writers and artists who are its main patrons. *Hogan's* (86 Bohermore; phone: 64584) is a friendly, atmospheric old pub with a blazing fire, tasty food, and occasional traditional music sessions. Numerous pubs offer good Irish music, including *An Pucan* (11 Forster St.; phone: 61528), the *Tribesman Bar* (19 Shop St.; phone: 62417), and the *Galway Shawl* (William St. West; phone: 62239). *Flanagan's* (William St. West; phone: 63220) and the *Crane* (Sea Rd.; phone: 67419) offer frequent performances; the latter has established itself as the city's leading traditional music pub over the past few years and offers sessions not only every night but also on Sunday mornings, with some of the finest musicians in the country. There's also *King's Head* (High St.; phone: 66630), with its wooden counters and intimate atmosphere; and the *Hole in the Wall* (Eyre St.; no phone) has a thatch roof and authentic atmosphere. *O'Flaherty's*, a cozy cellar pub at the *Great Southern* hotel (see *Checking In*), features a carvery lunch during the day and lively music in the evening (15 Eyre St.; phone: 64041). *McSwiggans* (3 Eyre St.; phone: 61972), with its wooden counters and tables, has music, but it's not always traditional. *O'Malley's* (Prospect Hill; phone: 64595) and *Paddy's* (Prospect Hill; no phone) both have music every night and on Sundays beginning at noon. In Salthill, within walking distance of the city center, the *Cottage Bar* (Lower Salthill Rd., around the corner from Devon Park; phone: 26754) and the next-door pub, *Flaherty's* (phone: 22672), occasionally resound to a few fiddles and banjos (the former on almost any night of the week).

Kilkenny Town

Ireland's best-preserved medieval town is the minute inland city of Kilkenny, 75 miles southwest of Dublin. Originally a tiny Gaelic settlement around the Monastery of St. Canice (hence its Irish name, *Cill Chainnigh,* "the cell of Canice"), it came to prominence under the Normans when Strongbow, their leader, seized it in 1170 and built a fortification on the hill over the River Nore. Between the Gothic cathedral at one end of town and the strong castle at the other, houses, inns, shops, friaries, and the merchants' parish church soon crowded inside the city walls on the high bank of the river.

Its reputation as a stable and industrious market town thus established, Kilkenny went on to achieve some notoriety. In the early 14th century, a formidable Norman woman named Dame Alice Kyteler, daughter of a banker, prosperous survivor of four husbands, and wealthy herself through moneylending (a practice, not incidentally, frowned upon by the church), was accused of witchcraft by the local bishop, Richard le Drede. Dame Alice was supported by Arnold le Poer, the seneschal (majordomo), and many powerful friends; the bishop was supported by the law and by the commission he had from the pope to extirpate heresy. Though her powerful friends resisted and even imprisoned the bishop, he and the authority of the church won out. Dame Alice fled to Scotland, her maid Petronilla was burned at the stake in her stead, and le Poer died in prison. The bishop did not get off scot-free, however. He was accused of heresy and had to flee to the papal court in Avignon.

Several decades later, the name Kilkenny became associated with infamy. As elsewhere in Ireland, the Normans had been intermarrying with the Irish and adopting some Irish customs as well. Such fraternization was perceived as a threat by the English king, who by now feared being left with too few trustworthy settlers to rule the island on his behalf. Consequently, a parliament held in Kilkenny in 1366 (the city was important enough to be a regular meeting place, along with Dublin, of the Irish Parliament the Normans had instituted) passed the Statutes of Kilkenny. These forbade the Normans to marry the Irish; prohibited them from adopting the Irish language, customs, or dress; and required that native Irish stay outside of the town walls.

At the end of the 14th century and for centuries thereafter, the castle of Kilkenny was occupied by the Butlers, Earls of Ormond, the most powerful family in medieval Ireland and long in the forefront of Irish history. They lived peaceably with the Gaelic chieftains but at the same time were rich from royal favor. They married into the royal family, hosted royal visits, and acted frequently as the king's deputy in Ireland. Under their protection, Kilkenny was spared the worst horrors of Henry VIII's Reformation and the devastating cycle of rebellion and repression that ensued during the reign of Elizabeth I; however, the Butlers conformed to Protestantism and quietly suppressed the city monasteries, which became civic property.

The city could not totally escape the racial and religious conflict of the times. When the Ulster Rebellion broke out in 1641, Kilkenny became the seat of the independent Irish Parliament set up by Anglo-Irish and Old Irish Catholics united in common defense. It met from 1642 to 1648, presided over by Lord Mountgarrett, a member of a minor Catholic branch of the Butlers (in the meantime the earl, the king's man, sat on the fence). Though the Confederation went so far as to establish a mint, manufacture weapons, raise an army, and receive ambassadors, conflict between its Norman and Irish factions eventually caused it to fall apart. In 1660, Cromwell arrived to take Kilkenny for the English Parliament.

After the ritual window breaking and statue smashing in St. Canice's Cathedral, Cromwell's rule in Kilkenny was less bloody than elsewhere. Families involved in the independent Irish Parliament were banished west of the Shannon, along with the rest of the propertied Catholics who had opposed Cromwell. Those from Kilkenny never went, however; they secretly stayed around the city until the Restoration brought back the king, with a Butler again, now Duke of Ormonde, as his viceroy. The duke managed to orchestrate a return of some of the lands confiscated from Kilkenny's leading citizens, but they and the city never quite recovered from the events of the century and never regained their former influence.

Perhaps because of the long, dark years of decline that followed, much of Kilkenny's early architecture remains intact — the city was simply not prosperous enough to tear things down and rebuild them on a grand scale, nor was there any need to do so. The gloom began to lift with a cultural revival in the 19th century and dispersed completely in recent years, leaving only a lingering air of quaintness to temper the character of a city now in expansion. The Butlers have been gone from the castle since the 1930s but they characteristically and munificently presented it to the people. Its beautiful gardens and park are intact, the art gallery has a notable collection of portraits, and the dukes' fine stables are now the *Kilkenny Design Workshops,* a wellspring of modern design talent. Some of the town's 16th-century Tudor buildings have been similarly reborn: The *Rothe House,* once a merchant's home, is now a museum and library; the *Shee Almshouse* is currently the home of the tourist board. The ancient castle and cathedral are also still important elements in the community; they resound with music each year during *Kilkenny Arts Week.* The little medieval city (pop. 8,951) that witnessed so much Irish history is still the integral core of a busy, modern, yet still traditional community.

Kilkenny At-a-Glance

SEEING THE CITY

Kilkenny lies in two neat crescents on either side of a river valley basin and does not afford heights for a sweeping panoramic view. From the terraced rose garden in front of Kilkenny Castle (at the Parade plaza), you can survey the city's limits from the castle behind you to the compact, gray St. Canice's Cathedral in the distance, while the river below offers drama and movement. From here, though, the view is *through* the town, level with the many church spires and the Tholsel clock tower. The reverse view is from the top of the round tower at the cathedral, but it is so high up that the city becomes a gray mass.

SPECIAL PLACES

The street that straggles from the castle to the cathedral is Kilkenny's Royal Mile. It starts at the castle gates as the Parade, an oblong plaza with the castle's classical stables and a decorous row of Georgian houses on one side and a tree-lined promenade, the Mayor's Walk, along the garden wall on the other side. It then turns into High Street, Kilkenny's main commercial street, with the medieval just under the surface of its respectable Georgian face. The Tholsel, "the house of taxes," is the midpoint of High Street. Beyond it on the right, the "slips" — a unique Kilkenny feature — appear at intervals. The slips are arched, stepped alleyways offering access to the street at river level. Dashing down slips and side alleys is very much a part of sightseeing and shopping in Kilkenny. After High Street, the thoroughfare widens again as Parliament Street, and the restored Rothe House and the classical courthouse come into view. Then the road narrows to medieval size as it leads through Irishtown to St. Canice's Steps at the foot of the cathedral.

KILKENNY CASTLE Kilkenny's most imposing monument looms grandly through trees over the river at the southeastern end of town. Strongbow, the Norman conqueror, had put up earthen fortifications here, and his successor in the early 13th century, William the Earl Marshall, replaced them with an irregular quadrangle of curtain walls reinforced by a fat round tower at each of the four corners. The Butler family, Norman Earls of Ormonde, bought the castle in 1391, after which they dominated the city. Though the family in residence remained the same for over 5 centuries, the castle itself underwent many changes. When the earls became dukes in the 17th century, the castle was rebuilt as a French château; it took on Gothic elements in another major reconstruction in the 19th century. The castle houses an art gallery with a fine collection of Butler family portraits. The gardens and park are open to the public in daylight hours, but at press time the interior was closed for restoration with plans to reopen in 1995. No admission charge for the grounds. The Parade (phone: 21450).

DESIGN CENTRE This cupola-crowned classical group of buildings, with a semi-circular courtyard, once formed the castle's stables. The horses' stalls originally had decorated plaster ceilings, and the grooms occupied plainer and more cramped quarters upstairs. In 1965 the buildings became the home of the government-sponsored *Kilkenny Design Workshops,* where everything from traditional craft products to electronic hardware was designed for Irish manufacturers, and young Irish designers gained initial work experience.

Since 1989, however, the complex has shifted from a single government-funded project to a mix of independent enterprises. The Kilkenny Civic Trust now operates the *Design Centre* shop, while the Crafts Council of Ireland has set up a dozen crafts workshops in the courtyard. Visitors can tour the courtyard and watch the craftspeople ply their trade and then enter the shop to purchase items (see *Shopping*). Open daily. No admission charge. The Parade (phone: 22118).

SHEE ALMSHOUSE One of the few surviving Tudor almshouses in Ireland, this was founded in 1582 by Sir Richard Shee "for the accommodation of 12 poor persons." The charity thus begun by one of Kilkenny's leading families endured for 3 centuries. After the adjoining St. Mary's Church became Protestant during the Reformation, a chapel in the almshouse was used for Catholic services. In the present century, the house has served as a storehouse, but it was refurbished and now holds the city's tourist board. Upstairs is a model of Kilkenny as it was in 1642, when the Confederation Parliament made it the capital of Ireland (a status that lasted just a few years). Admission charge for exhibits. Rose Inn St. (phone: 21755).

ST. MARY'S CATHEDRAL Parts of this church are believed to date from the 13th century. A fine display of Tudor and Stuart grave monuments is housed in the north transept. Open daily. St. Mary's La. (phone: 21253).

HIGH STREET Kilkenny's main street has undergone considerable change through the centuries, but a pause here and there still helps visitors to recall its earlier days. The Tudor house that stretches across Nos. 17, 18, and 19 High Street was built in 1582 and once belonged to the Archers, one of the town's ten original leading families (their crest is visible above the door). Behind it are the remains of the "Hole in the Wall," a supper house famous enough in the late 18th and early 19th centuries to have merited a verse: "If you ever go to Kilkenny /Ask for the Hole in the Wall / You may there get blind drunk for a penny / And tipsy for nothing at all." Above the shopfronts on the north side of High Street, about 100 yards from the main cross street, is a Tudor gable with the joined coats of arms of Henry Shee and his wife, Frances. He was a Mayor of Kilkenny in the early 17th century and this was their townhouse.

THOLSEL The Saxon word for "the house of taxes" is another name for Kilkenny's Town Hall. Built in the mid-18th century, it has open arcades that form a marketplace below and support a fine Georgian council chamber above. No admission charge. High St. (phone: 21076).

ROTHE HOUSE John Rothe built this solid Tudor merchant's house — actually three houses around two courtyards, with room for a shop, storage, and living quarters — in 1594. Rothe was a member of one of Kilkenny's important families, and his wife, Rose, was a member of another prominent clan, the Archers. The Rothes lost the house in the 17th century because of their association with the Confederation of Kilkenny, and it later became a school. It now houses a library and a museum of local history operated by the Kilkenny Archaeological Society. Open Mondays through Saturdays from 10:30 AM to 5 PM; Sundays from 3 to 5 PM. Admission charge. Parliament St. (phone: 22893).

ST. FRANCIS ABBEY The remains of this onetime Franciscan friary are on the premises of the 18th-century Smithwicks Brewery, desolate among beer casks and empty crates but still worth seeing. The abbey was founded in the 13th century by Richard the Marshall and suppressed, along with the rest of the Irish monasteries, in the 16th century. The east window and the bell tower with its unusual supporting figures are from the 14th century. Off Parliament St.

BLACK ABBEY The church of the Dominicans, or Black Friars, is on high-walled Abbey Street just beyond Black Freren Gate, the last remaining gate in the city walls. Its history is similar to that of the Franciscan abbey; both were founded and suppressed at approximately the same time. Immediately after suppression, however, townspeople built thatch-roofed huts within the Black Abbey's walls, and it was for a time used as a courthouse before being reclaimed by the Dominicans and restored. It survives today as an active Dominican priory. No admission charge. Abbey St. (phone: 21274).

ST. CANICE'S CATHEDRAL This building, raised in the 13th century by the first Norman bishop, Hugh de Rous, occupies the site of the early Irish Monastery of St. Canice and a later Romanesque church. A plain cruciform structure, it is nevertheless impressive for its size — it's the second largest medieval cathedral in Ireland — and its simplicity. The Master of Gowran (a mason who also worked on a neighboring church at Gowran) contributed some vigorous stone carving, in the west doorway particularly, but the renowned stained glass of the east window survived the Reformation only to be smashed to bits by Cromwell's troops, who also left the cathedral roofless and did considerable damage to its many monuments. The church's collection of 16th- and 17th-century tomb sculptures, many by the O'Tunneys, a local family of sculptors, is still remarkably rich, and its hammer-beam roof (a product of a later restoration) is notable. Outside, the round tower predates the cathedral, though its roof is not the original one. St. Canice's Library, established 300 years ago, has 3,000 old volumes. Open Mondays through Saturdays from 9 AM to 1 PM and 2 to 6 PM; Sundays from 2 to 6 PM. Admission charge to climb to the top of the round tower. Reached via St. Canice's Steps, which are linked to St. Canice's Pl. by Velvet La. (phone: 21516).

Sources and Resources

TOURIST INFORMATION

In Kilkenny, the tourist board (Shee Almshouse, Rose Inn St.; phone: 21755) has information, maps, and leaflets. The city map is free; the *Kilkenny Guide* costs under $2. A Kilkenny crafts guide is free.

LOCAL COVERAGE The *Kilkenny People* is published on Wednesdays. The three Dublin morning dailies also are available. Local events are posted weekly in the Tholsel arcade on High Street; details on daily happenings are available at the tourist board.

TELEPHONE The area code for Kilkenny and the immediate vicinity is 56. When calling from within the Republic of Ireland, dial 056.

GETTING AROUND

Kilkenny is a walkable city, and there is no city bus service. From castle to cathedral is just over a mile. The railway station, which is a little farther away, can be reached by taxi.

BUS AND TRAIN *Bus Eireann* and *Irish Rail*, divisions of *CIE (Córas Iompair Eireann, National Transport Company)*, serve McDonagh Station, John St. Upper (phone: 22024).

CAR RENTAL The nearest rental agencies are *South East Budget* (College Rd., New Ross, County Wexford; phone: 51-21550), *Auto Rentals* (Ferrybank, County Wexford; phone: 53-23917), and *Budget* (41 The Quay, Waterford; phone: 51-21670), but they will pick up and drop off at the Kilkenny Tourist Board, where bookings can be made.

TAXI Cabs are available from *Delaney* (phone: 22457), *Howe* (phone: 65874), *K&M* (phone: 61333), *Larkin* (phone: 62622), and *Nagle* (phone: 63300).

WALKING TOURS Guided historical walking tours leave from the tourist office March through October at 9:15 and 10:30 AM, and 12:15, 1:30, 3, and 4:30 PM on Mondays through Saturdays; and at 11 AM, and 12:15, 3, and 4:30 PM on Sundays. For more information, contact *Tynan Tours* (Shee Almshouse, Rose Inn St.; phone: 61348), which operates out of the tourist office. The cost is about $4.

SPECIAL EVENTS

Kilkenny hosts several celebrations throughout the year, including one that's worth a special trip.

Kilkenny Arts Week Held at the end of August or the beginning of September, this is basically a music festival, with lunchtime recitals and grand evening concerts in the castle and cathedral, the classical music interspersed with programs of traditional music and folk song. There are also art exhibitions, street theater performances, and poetry readings, but although some noted writers — poets Robert Lowell and Ted Hughes among them — have read their work here, music is the main thing, and many of the performers are internationally known. This is a friendly, participatory event that actually lasts for 9 days, each day ending at the *Arts Week Club,* where the social side of the festival goes on until the wee hours. For additional details, contact the Kilkenny Tourist Board (see above).

In addition, this year the *Mount Juliet Golf Club* at Thomastown, County Kilkenny (phone: 24725) is the site of the *Irish Open Golf Tournament* in mid-June. The *Thomas Moore Literary Weekend,* a festival of poetry and story reading, music, and literary gatherings, is held annually in October (phone: 65063 or 28307 for information).

MUSEUMS

In addition to those listed in *Special Places,* Kilkenny has two notable art galleries. The *Kilkenny People Gallery* (High St., phone: 21015) features illustrations and other local art, and the *Canice Gallery* (4 Lower Patrick St.; phone: 51122) is a setting for works by 19th- and 20th-century Irish painters.

SHOPPING

Synonymous with fine craftsmanship, Kilkenny has a glassware factory and an assortment of interesting crafts shops. Most shops remain open until 9 PM on Thursdays and Fridays, and are closed Sundays.

ALLEN & SONS A good selection of Waterford glass, which they will pack safely and dispatch to overseas addresses duty-free. 94 High St. (phone: 22258).

BOOK CENTRE A great source of maps and books on the Kilkenny area, as well as local newspapers and magazines. There's also a fine selection of books on Irish literature and history. A coffee shop on the second floor is open during the day. 10 High St. (phone: 63070).

DESIGN CENTRE An Aladdin's cave of modern Irish design in silver, glass, pottery, wood, and textiles, many items crafted on the premises (see *Special Places*). Good bargains in household items. There's also a self-service restaurant. Open daily April through December; closed Sundays, January through March. The Parade (phone: 22118).

KILKENNY CRYSTAL Established in 1969, this glassware shop stocks a variety of hand-cut crystal items. Visitors are welcome to tour the factory at Callan, 10 miles south of town. 19 Rose Inn St. (phone: 21090).

LIAM COSTIGAN Modern jewelry by a *Kilkenny Design Workshops* graduate. Colliers La. (phone: 62408).

MARCHIONESS BOUTIQUE Women's clothing with a wide selection of designer fashions, Irish-made ready-to-wear, tweeds, and hand-knits. 6 The Parade (phone: 65921).

NICHOLAS MOSSE POTTERY Distinctive hand-thrown pottery, decorated with the rich colors of the Irish countryside, draws many visitors to this old mill/ workshop 4 miles south of Kilkenny. The factory outlet on the premises sells seconds at bargain prices. Bennettsbridge (phone: 27126).

PADMORE & BARNES LTD. This shop offers hand-crafted shoes for men and women at factory outlet prices. In addition to more traditional products, shoes made of elkhide are produced here. Wolfe Tone St. (phone: 21037).

P. T. MURPHY Just the spot to find a Claddagh ring, Tara brooch, or Celtic cross, as well as Irish silver, jewelry, Waterford crystal, and Royal Tara china. 84-85 High St. (phone: 21127).

RUDOLF HELTZEL Exquisite modern jewelry by a pioneer *Kilkenny Design Workshops* teacher. 10 Patrick St. (phone: 21497).

YESTERDAYS This eclectic midtown shop offers a variety of antique and modern collectibles, including locally produced scent and soap, vintage brass, bottles, jewelry, toy animals, and dolls. 30 Patrick St. (phone: 65557).

SPORTS AND FITNESS

BICYCLING Bikes can be rented from *J. J. Wall,* 88 Maudlin St. (phone: 21236).

FISHING There is good trout fishing in the rivers Nore and Dinan north of Kilkenny. Consult J. J. Carrigan at the *Sport Shop,* 82 High St. (phone: 21517).

GOLF There are two courses in the area, one truly outstanding.

TOP TEE-OFF SPOT

Mount Juliet Designed by Jack Nicklaus, this 18-hole championship parkland course is one of Ireland's newest (opened in 1991). Set on the 180-acre grounds of the *Mount Juliet* hotel, close to the River Nore, it has a 7,083-yard layout. Water comes into play on 6 holes, and the woodland is ever present, with some 80 vigilant bunkers, strategically placed throughout the course, to place a premium on accuracy from tee to green. Nicklaus designed the course with an elaborate drainage and tee-through-green watering system, to keep it in top playing condition year-round. Site of this year's *Irish Open, Mount Juliet* offers a first for Ireland, the *Jack Nicklaus Golf Teaching Academy,* which encompasses a separate mini-course, designed to help both novice and experienced players fine-tune their game. Thomastown (phone: 24725).

In addition, the *Kilkenny Golf Club,* with its pleasant 18-hole course, is about a mile from town (phone: 61730 or 22125).

GREYHOUND RACING Races are held at *St. James's Park* every Wednesday and Friday evening (phone: 21214).

HILL WALKING Join the local group that meets Sunday mornings, and wear sturdy hiking boots. Check local paper for time and venue.

HORSEBACK RIDING Among the best of the nearby stables are *Millett's* (Castlecomer Rd.; phone: 22872) and the *Thomastown Equitation Centre* (Thomastown; phone: 24112), both of which offer year-round indoor and outdoor riding, plus cross-country runs and training. Another good riding establishment is the *Mount Juliet* hotel's *Equestrian Centre,* also in Thomastown (phone: 24522), which has a year-round program of riding, trekking, hunting, and cross-country activities. For additional details, see *Horsing Around* in DIVERSIONS.

HORSE RACING The racecourse at lovely *Gowran Park,* 10 miles from the city, is the site of eight meets a year (phone: 26126).

HURLING Ireland's ancient stick-and-ball game is played most stylishly in Kilkenny. There is usually a game on Sunday afternoons at *Nowlan Park,* located northeast of Kilkenny, off the Dublin road. Contact the tourist office for schedules.

THEATER

The *Galloglass Theatre* company, a traveling troupe, and other local groups perform contemporary and traditional plays regularly at *Cleere's Theatre* (28 Parliament St.; phone: 62573). During the summer months, local groups present plays at various venues, including the *Club House* hotel (Patrick St.; phone: 21994). Other events occur in association with *Kilkenny Arts Week.* The new *Watergate Theatre* (West End; phone: 61674), slated to open this year, provides another venue for the dramatic arts. Check at the tourist office for performance schedules.

MUSIC

For traditional Irish music, try the *seisiún* presented by *Comhaltas Ceoiltóirí Eireann* once a week in July and August in Kilkenny Castle (phone: 21450). In the summer months, the *Newpark* hotel (see *Checking In*) also stages an Irish Night cabaret, usually on Wednesdays. Traditional music can be enjoyed throughout the year on Tuesdays at *P.V.'s Lounge* in the *Kilford Arms* (John St.; phone: 61018). *Kilkenny Arts Week* features a wide range of musical events (see *Special Events*). Check the local newspaper for information on concerts and performances throughout the year. For additional traditional Irish music venues, see *Sharing a Pint*.

NIGHTCLUBS AND NIGHTLIFE

Pubs are the center of Kilkenny nightlife, as in most Irish towns, but recent years have spawned a few nightclubs offering a variety of music and dancing, including *Bentley's* (John St.; phone: 21969), *The Cellar* at the *Kilkenny* hotel (see *Checking In*), *DaVinci's* at the *Springhill Court* hotel (Waterford Rd.; phone: 21122), and *Nero's* at *Kyteler's Inn* (see *Eating Out*).

Best in Town

CHECKING IN

Despite its obvious attractions, Kilkenny has not been much of a hotel town until recently. The tourist circuit of Ireland tends to go clockwise around the coast, ignoring the interior, and only lately have hotels in midland towns roused themselves from a rather dull state of commercial plainness. Although you'll pay $125 or more (possibly much more) for a night at the *Mount Juliet,* most Kilkenny hotels are in the moderate bracket, charging $75 to $125 per double room per night; double rooms in places listed as inexpensive cost $75 or less per night. The tourist board is happy to help tourists who can't find rooms. The alternative may be a town or country home or farmhouse. All telephone numbers are in the 56 area code unless otherwise indicated.

For an unforgettable experience, we begin with our favorite local spot, followed by our cost and quality choices, listed by price category.

SPECIAL HAVEN

Mount Juliet A 2-mile-long driveway provides a scenic introduction to this secluded property; the drive passes neatly fenced green pastures (home of the Ballylinch Stud Farm) dotted with thoroughbreds, strutting pheasants, and lambs grazing beside the banks of the River Nore. The manor house is set high on a hill overlooking the 1,500-acre estate. An elegant Georgian-style structure built in the 1760s, it is the last of the great homes built by Somerset Hamilton Butler, the eighth Viscount Ikerrin, first Earl of Carrick, who named the property after his wife Juliana. There are 23 rooms and 9 suites, each with a private bath, direct-dial phones, and a TV set. Rooms are individually decorated with antiques, original paintings, fresh flowers, and books. The *Lady Helen McCalmont* restaurant offers distinctive formal dining, while the *Old Kitchen* is a more casual, country-style eatery (see *Eating Out* for details on both). Other public areas include a bar and a library. Guests have full run of the estate's formal gardens, woodlands, and parklands, as well their choice of sporting activities — horseback riding, fishing for salmon and trout, pheasant shooting, and fox hunting with the *Kilkenny Hunt,* which is headquartered on the estate. In addition, there's a Jack Nicklaus–designed championship golf course (see

Golf, above), and outdoor tennis courts. The estate is also the home of Ireland's oldest cricket club. Located just over a mile from Thomastown, County Kilkenny, in the heart of central Ireland; about 10 miles south of Kilkenny; 75 miles southwest of Dublin; and 100 miles southeast of Shannon (phone: 24455; 800-447-7462 from the US; fax: 24522).

MODERATE

Butler House Situated in the heart of downtown behind the former stables of Kilkenny Castle, this 3-story guesthouse was once the dower house of the castle, built by the Earls of Ormond in the 18th century. Each of the 13 spacious rooms and suites has been restored and outfitted with up-to-date amenities including private baths, TV sets, direct-dial telephones, and tea/coffee-makers. The grounds include a delightful walled garden and an off-street parking lot. 16 Patrick St. (phone: 65707; fax: 65626).

Kilkenny This Regency gem was designed by and was the residence of William Robertson, the architect who gave Kilkenny Castle its final Gothic trim. Here Robertson produced a fanciful structure, and the hotel's public rooms have retained some of their former domestic charm. The 60 bedrooms — ultramodern and spacious — are in a separate building. There's also a restaurant with a continental/Irish menu, an indoor swimming pool, a sauna, a hot tub, a gym, and tennis courts. College Rd. (phone: 62000; fax: 65984).

Newpark On the north edge of the city, this Victorian country house has been skillfully combined with modern additions and converted into a comfortable hotel with 60 rooms (each with private bath and phone) in a peaceful garden setting. Facilities include *Damask,* a first-rate dining room (see *Eating Out*), a noon-to-midnight grillroom, and a health center with an indoor pool, saunas, a Jacuzzi, a fully equipped gym, and tennis courts. Evening entertainment includes Irish music and a twice-weekly disco. The staff is efficient and enthusiastic. Castlecomer Rd. (phone: 22122; fax: 61111).

INEXPENSIVE

Lacken House An old Georgian residence about a half-mile east of Kilkenny, this lovely guesthouse has been renovated and updated by the McSweeney family to include 8 rooms, each with private bath, as well as a first class restaurant in the basement (see *Eating Out*). Open year-round. Dublin Rd. (phone: 61085 or 65611; fax: 62435).

EATING OUT

In the past few years, Kilkenny and its environs have earned a reputation for fine food. Hotel dining rooms often rival local restaurants. For those traveling by car, some worthwhile places in attractive spots at a distance have been included here. Expect dinner for two (without wine, drinks, or tips) to cost $100 or more at the restaurant listed as very expensive; $75 to $100 at dining spots in the expensive category; $40 to $75 at places in the moderate bracket; and under $40 at the one listed as inexpensive. All telephone numbers are in the 56 area code unless otherwise indicated.

VERY EXPENSIVE

Lady Helen McCalmont An aura of grandeur prevails at this lovely country-house dining place at the *Mount Juliet* hotel. The setting is enhanced by views of the River Nore. The menu offers such dishes as salmon with black currant leaf sauce, breast of chicken with cheese mousse and red pepper butter, wrapped rack of lamb, and stir-fried rabbit with leeks. Open nightly. Reservations necessary. Major credit cards accepted. Thomastown, 10 miles southeast of Kilkenny (phone: 24455).

EXPENSIVE

Damask The elegant dining room of the *Newpark* hotel features piano music 6 nights a week. The bill of fare ranges from *coquilles St.-Jacques* to chateaubriand, with some imaginative veal and chicken dishes, too. Open daily. Reservations necessary. Major credit cards accepted. Castlecomer Rd. (phone: 22122).

Lacken House Chef Eugene McSweeney, formerly of the *Berkeley Court* in Dublin, is making his bid for haute cuisine laurels with this family operation. Fresh fish that comes daily from Dunmore East is the specialty. Dishes range from baked crab au gratin to *paupiettes* of plaice with salmon stuffing, as well as filet of pork and medallions of beef. Open for dinner only; closed Sundays and Mondays. Reservations advised. MasterCard and Visa accepted. Dublin Rd. (phone: 61085 or 65611).

Ristorante Rinuccini Chef-owner Antonio Cavaliere has brought a little bit of Italy to town with this stylish candlelit restaurant opposite Kilkenny Castle. The menu includes a fine selection of pasta as well as grilled scampi, lobster *dello* chef (with Dijon mustard, cream, and cognac), chicken cacciatore, saltimbocca, salmon *cardinale* (with prawns and cream), and vegetarian dishes. Open for lunch and dinner; closed Sundays. Reservations necessary. Major credit cards accepted. 1 The Parade (phone: 61575).

MODERATE

Kyteler's Inn Once the home of Dame Alice Kyteler, who was convicted of witchcraft and forced to flee to Scotland for her life, this old tavern has been in operation since 1324. While it may not be a spot for deluxe dining, it is rich in atmosphere. Burgers, steaks, spareribs, and other simple fare are served downstairs in a medieval setting. There are several bars and lounges on the upper level. Open daily. Reservations unnecessary. MasterCard and Visa accepted. St. Kieran St. (phone: 21064).

Lautrec's This bistro/wine bar has a French café atmosphere. The menu ranges from the healthy — freshly made soups, salads, and vegetarian dishes — to the trendy — curries and burritos. There are also spareribs and steaks. Open for lunch and dinner; closed Sundays. Reservations advised. Diners Club, MasterCard, and Visa accepted. 9 St. Kieran St. (phone: 62720).

Old Kitchen An informal alternative at the *Mount Juliet* hotel, this eatery is situated in the basement of the manor house, where the original kitchens were. Cozy and wood-trimmed, it offers hearty fare such as "soup from the cauldron"; chicken and ham pie; beef, Guinness, and mushroom pie; vegetable and herb lasagna; deep-fried prawns; and steaks. There's also salmon from the River Nore, which passes through the grounds. Open daily for breakfast, lunch, and dinner. Reservations necessary for dinner. Major credit cards accepted. Thomastown, 10 miles southeast of Kilkenny (phone: 24455).

INEXPENSIVE

Molloy's An Old World ambience prevails at this centrally located spot, where baking is done on the premises. Breakfast and lunch are served, and light snacks are available throughout the day, with a menu ranging from soups, salads, steaks, and sausage rolls, to a tempting array of cakes, breads, and pastries. Closed Sundays. No reservations needed. No credit cards accepted. 2 Rose Inn St. (phone: 21449).

SHARING A PINT

Smithwick's, a medium-tart ale-type beer, has been the local brew for well over 200 years. Free samples are offered on the guided brewery tour (Parliament St.; phone: 21014) at 3 PM daily, May through September. To try it elsewhere, pick a pub.

HIGH SPIRITS

Edward Langton's This is a superb spot for food and drink as well as for atmosphere. The hand-painted murals make the façade remarkable even in a city renowned for its shopfronts. The low-ceilinged bar inside, conducive to whispering and gossip, leads out to a conservatory full of light and air from Gothic-style beveled-glass windows, through which remnants of Kilkenny's walls, complete with gun slits, are visible. Owner Eamonn Langton has built a reputation for food of a high standard, including pub grub consisting of five hot dishes daily. Have a drink and admire the slightly gloomy atmosphere, the old prints, the stained glass, the mirrors, and the polished granite tables. 69 John St. (phone: 65133).

Also try *Tynan's Bar* (2 Horseleap Slip; phone: 21291), a turn-of-the-century pub that has survived with its fittings — brass scales, grocery drawers, beer pumps, gilt mirrors — miraculously intact. Locals and cosmopolitans share its great atmosphere and honest drink. The exterior of the *Marble City Bar* (66 High St.; phone: 62366) is a museum piece; the interior is less authentic, but its character has not been overwhelmed by modernization. *Kyteler's Inn* (St. Kieran St.; phone: 21064) was once the house of the redoubtable Dame Alice. It now has a friendly nest of bars. The *Club House Bar* (Patrick St.; phone: 21994), in the hotel of the same name, is a quiet oasis with sporting prints, cartoons, and cast-iron bar tables. Other pubs known for their food and convivial atmosphere are the *Court Arms* (9 Parliament St.; no phone); *Jim Holland* (60 St. Kieran St.; phone: 62273); *Jim Langton's* (23-24 John St.; phone: 21917); and *Caisléan Ui Cuan* (*Castle Inn;* Patrick St., facing Kilkenny Castle; no phone).

Killarney

Just off the Atlantic in County Kerry, not far from Ireland's southwest coast, Killarney is a sheltered Camelot-like town, surrounded by 23 square miles of idyllic lakes, mountains, islands, castles, waterfalls, and parklands. Unlike Camelot, however, the rains and mists come often to Killarney, but the natives say the moisture is what keeps it such a naturally verdant paradise.

The place name of Killarney is believed to have come from the Irish or Gaelic name *Cill Airne,* meaning "church of the sloe." There are many sloe (*airne*), or blackthorn, woods in the area.

Killarney is the best known of Ireland's tourism centers. But visitors come not just for the town itself but also for its surroundings. The lakes of Killarney and the mountains that hold them reside in a boulder- and rock-strewn land of unrivaled natural beauty, sculpted by the Ice Age and trimmed with gentle woodlands. Ireland's highest range of mountains, MacGillicuddy's Reeks, are a part of this panoramic tableau. To tell the truth, the scenery surrounding Killarney is by far the most compelling reason to visit; tourism's assault on the city proper has turned it into the most commercial (and occasionally tacky) town in the Republic.

Unlike most areas in Ireland, not a great deal is known about Killarney's early days, although some links to a Bronze Age civilization have been found. Earliest historical accounts go back to various monastic sites founded around the lakes during the 7th century and to the rule of early Irish chieftains called McCarthy, O'Donoghue, and O'Sullivan — surnames that predominate still. It was not until the mid-18th century, however, that Killarney began to make an impact and to draw visitors to its beautiful scenery. Thanks to Lord Kenmare, a local landowner, major roads were built from Killarney Town to Tralee, Limerick, Cork, Kenmare, and beyond.

The mid-19th century brought the railroad to Killarney and the subsequent building of the *Great Southern* hotel. The Lord Kenmare of that time, following his predecessor's lead, gave Killarney another boost in 1861, when he invited Queen Victoria and members of the royal family to visit his lakeland paradise. The people of Killarney spruced up the town in a big way and prepared suitable accommodations for all who were expected to come to see the queen. Following the queen's visit, Victorians became the most enthusiastic travelers to Killarney. The area's purple glens, silent glades, ruined castles, and fairy-tale isles on misty lakes appealed to the Victorian imagination, and the journals of their travels are breathless with wonderment at what they saw. Twentieth-century visitors will find that the enthralling scenery hasn't changed at all.

There are three major Killarney lakes. Nearest the town is the Lower Lake (also known as Lough Leane, "lake of learning"). This is the largest lake (5,000 acres), with about 30 islands, including Innisfallen, site of a medieval monastery and an early seat of learning. On the eastern shore of the Lower Lake are two other popular Killarney historic sites, Muckross Abbey and Ross Castle.

The wooded peninsula of Muckross separates the Lower Lake from the Middle Lake (680 acres), sometimes called Muckross Lake. On the eastern shore of this body of water is the manor home and folk museum called *Muckross House,* and close by is the 60-foot natural cascade known as Torc Waterfall.

A narrow strait called the Long Range leads to the slender, finger-like Upper Lake (430 acres), which is almost embedded in mountains. The Upper Lake is the smallest but, in the opinion of many, the most beautiful of the lakes, with MacGillicuddy's Reeks rising to the west. Added to the spectacle of the three main lakes are many other, smaller lakes in the folds of the mountains as well as numerous picturesque cascades and waterfalls.

Plant and animal life are also an important part of Killarney's landscape. The woodlands thrive with a luxuriant medley of oak, birch, yew, ash, cedar, and juniper. The smaller native flora include holly, fern, rhododendron, and arbutus (the strawberry tree), the special botanic glory of the area, recognizable by its small, glossy, dark leaves, white flowers in the spring, and brilliant red berries in autumn and winter. All of this is natural habitat for the unique Killarney red deer, the only deer herd of native stock in the country. There are many other animals as well, from Japanese sika deer to black Kerry cattle, and no less than 114 species of birds.

It is not surprising that Killarney is smack on the beaten tourist track and takes advantage of it. Although Killarney is relatively small (pop. 7,859), the town is fiercely commercialized, with an abundance of souvenir and gift shops and visitor services. The local folk scramble to woo visitors to see the sights by motorcoach, minibus, private taxi, boat, bicycle, horseback, and, most of all, by jaunting car, the traditional Killarney mode of transport. This is a one-horse-drawn sidecart on which riders sit facing the scenery while the driver (known as a "jarvey") tries to beguile them with commentary laced with a story or song.

To be sure, the town has its detractors who point out that Killarney is more of a tourist center than a representative Irish city — and none the prettier for this transformation. Its fans will answer that this spot has long been a tourist attraction and that there is no denying the beauty of the surroundings. Quite simply, you just haven't seen all of Ireland until you feast your eyes on Killarney.

Killarney At-a-Glance

SEEING THE CITY

The entire Killarney vista — from the spire of the cathedral to MacGillicuddy's Reeks and the Iveragh Mountains — can be seen on a clear day in one sweeping panorama from Aghadoe Hill (400 ft.). This lookout is about 2 miles north of the town, just off N22, the main Killarney–Tralee road. Another perspective is from a spot 12 miles south of Killarney on the Kenmare road, N71, from which the broad valley of the three lakes can be seen. This vantage point, known locally as "Ladies View," is said to have been named for Queen Victoria's ladies-in-waiting, who visited the site more than a century ago.

SPECIAL PLACES

Although the ancient abbeys, stately buildings, manor homes, and castles of Killarney are well worth seeing, the real attraction of this lakeside paradise is the natural beauty of its surrounding parklands and lakeshore countryside. To appreciate the town at its best, allow enough time to see a blend of indoor and outdoor sights.

IN THE TOWN

KERRY POETS MONUMENT Located at the east end of town in a section known as Fair Hill, this statue, which depicts Ireland as a *speir bhean* (beautiful woman), was sculpted by Seamus Murphy. It was erected in 1940 as a tribute to County Kerry's four best-known poets — Pierce Ferriter, Geoffrey O'Donoghue, Egan O'Rahilly, and Owen Roe O'Sullivan. East Avenue Rd. at Fair Hill.

KNOCKREER ESTATE Once the home of the Kenmare family, this splendid parkland stretches from Killarney Town to the shores of the Lower Lake. Visitors may wander through the gardens, which feature a mix of ancient trees plus flowering cherries, magnolias, camellias, rhododendrons, and azaleas. Open daily in summer; weekends at other times. Entrance on New St.

ST. MARY'S CATHEDRAL Built between 1842 and 1855, the Catholic Church of St. Mary of the Assumption, as it is officially named, was designed in the Gothic Revival style by the celebrated 19th-century architect Augustus W. Pugin. This fine limestone structure is cruciform in shape, with a massive square central tower capped by a spire. Open daily. New St.

ST. MARY'S CHURCH This neo-Gothic style structure was built in 1870 and belongs to the Church of Ireland. More interesting, however, is the fact that a succession of churches can be traced to this spot. It has been a place of worship for at least 7 or 8 centuries — perhaps even longer. According to one theory, this was once the site of the original *Cill Airne,* the medieval church from which Killarney takes its name. Open Sundays. Main St.

NATIONAL MUSEUM OF IRISH TRANSPORT Housed in a huge hall near the heart of town is a permanent exhibit of antique and veteran cars. The collection includes the world's rarest car (a one-of-a-kind 1907 Silver Stream, built in Kildare), the car of the century (a 1904 Germain), and the world's first bicycle (designed by James Starley in England in 1884), as well as pennyfarthing bicycles and tricycles, vintage carriages, and more than 2,000 other transport-related items. There's also a reference library. Open daily year-round. Admission charge. East Avenue Rd. (phone: 32638 or 32639).

ENVIRONS

MUCKROSS HOUSE AND GARDENS This splendid Elizabethan-style house, built in 1843 by the Herbert family, is a showcase of 19th-century architecture, adorned with mullioned and stepped windows, 62 chimneys, and decorated with locally made period furniture and needlework. It's also a folk museum, with exhibits about County Kerry life, history, cartography, geography, geology, flora, and fauna. The emphasis at this museum, among the Republic's most forward-looking, is as much on displaying the objects in an interesting way as on preserving them, and a great deal of thought and effort has been put into every exhibit. In addition, there are a number of basement workshops, where visitors can watch artisans practicing the crafts of earlier days — weaving, pottery making, bookbinding, spinning, basket making, blacksmithing — and creating the kinds of items displayed in the museum proper. When sated with art and history, visitors can go out for a stroll in the manicured gardens or on one of the nature trails that meander across the vast grounds, which were presented, along with the house, to the nation in 1932 and now comprise the 25,000-acre Killarney National Park (see below). Open year-round. Admission charge. Kenmare Rd. (phone: 31440).

KILLARNEY NATIONAL PARK The heart of Killarney's legendary beauty, this 25,000-acre natural expanse encompasses three lakes, various nature trails, valleys, islands, rivers, waterfalls, bogs, mountains, and woods. The grounds include the most extensive area of natural oak woodland remaining in Ireland as well as characteristic plants, such as the arbutus, and a rare herd of native red deer that are said to have been here since the end of the last Ice Age. Access is available from several points around Killarney, particularly along the Killarney–Kenmare road. The park is best explored on foot, by bicycle, or in a jaunting car. Open year-round. Several entrances off Kenmara Rd.

MUCKROSS ABBEY Founded in the 1440s by the Franciscan friars, this abbey flourished on the edge of the Lower Lake for more than 300 years, until it was suppressed by the Penal Laws. The present well-preserved remains include a church with a wide belfry tower and beautifully vaulted cloisters, with an arched arcade surrounding a square courtyard whose centerpiece is an imposing and ancient yew tree, said to be as old as the abbey. Through the years, the abbey grounds served as a burial place for local chieftains and, during the 17th and 18th centuries, for the famous Kerry poets. Now a part of the Muckross estate, it's located 3 miles from Killarney on the Kenmare road (it's a favorite route for jaunting car drivers).

KERRY COUNTRY LIFE EXPERIENCE Opened in 1993, this $1.2 million attraction aims to depict life in a County Kerry agricultural community in the 1930s before electricity. Situated on a 70-acre site close to *Muckross House* and overlooking the lakes, it features a series of walk-in exhibits including farmers' houses of various sizes and levels of prosperity, a laborer's cottage, a lime kiln, a carpenter's workshop, and a blacksmith's forge, as well as a real working farm. The organic produce raised on the land is served at the adjoining restaurant. Admission charge. Muckross Rd. (phone: 31440 or 31335).

KERRY GLASS This is Killarney's own glassware factory, where distinctive colored glass designs in vases, bowls, paperweights, and figurines are produced. Visitors are welcome to watch and photograph the craftsmen firing, blowing, shaping, and coloring the glass. Open weekdays from 8 AM to 1 PM and 2 to 4 PM year-round. No admission charge. Killalee, Fossa (phone: 32587).

ROSS CASTLE Now a ruin, this 15th-century structure was one of the finest examples of castle-building in County Kerry. The remains include a 16th-century tower surrounded by a *bawn* (rampart) with rounded turrets. As a stronghold of the O'Donoghue chieftains, the building's main claim to fame is as the last castle in Ireland to fall to Cromwell's army (it was taken in 1652). Standing on a peninsula jutting into the Lower Lake, about 2 miles from the center of Killarney off the Kenmare road, the castle today is the ideal gateway to the lakes and serves as a rendezvous point for rental boats and boatmen.

INNISFALLEN ISLAND A 21-acre island floating in the northern end of the Lower Lake, this was once the site of a flourishing abbey, founded about AD 600 by St. Fallen. The *Annals of Innisfallen,* a chronicle of world and Irish history, written in Gaelic and Latin, was compiled here at intervals from the 10th to the 14th century by a succession of 39 monastic scribes (the manuscript is now housed at the Bodleian Library, Oxford). Although the monastery lasted until the 17th century, all that remains today are the ruins of 11th- and 12th-century structures and a remarkably varied terrain of heights and hollows, headlands and bays, woods and open spaces. Boats and boatmen can be hired at Ross Castle.

TORC WATERFALL A footpath winds its way up beside 60 feet of cascading waters, affording magnificent views of the lake district. This impressive waterfall, in its sylvan setting, is about 4 miles from Killarney. The area is well signposted and has its own parking lot. Off the main road to Kenmare.

GAP OF DUNLOE A winding and rocky gorge of Ice Age origin, it winds between MacGillicuddy's Reeks and the Purple and Tomies mountains, 9 miles southwest of Killarney. The best way to experience the Gap is to take one of the full-day tours, which usually depart each morning by bus or jaunting car from the various hotels. Disembarkation is at *Kate Kearney's Cottage,* a former coaching inn turned snack bar, pub, and souvenir shop at the entrance to the Gap. From here, the energetic can walk the 7 miles through the Gap to the shore of the Upper Lake; those less ambitious can opt to ride the route on horseback or with several other passengers via traditional pony and trap. For the first 4 miles, the scene turns extraordinarily remote and gloomy, with massive rocks on either side and an accompanying narrow stream widening here and there into a sullen lake. One of these — Lough Black, or Serpent Lake — is where St. Patrick is said to have drowned the last snake in Ireland. Emerging from the Gap, the wooded Upper Lake, still 3 miles away, comes into view, and Black Valley stretches off in the distance to the right. A popular stop for a picnic lunch (sometimes included in the price of the day's trip) is *Lord Brandon's Cottage,* near the lakeshore, after which everyone boards open boats for the return trip via the Killarney lakes. From the Upper Lake, the boats turn into the Long Range, which grows progressively swifter until the boatmen "shoot the rapids" at the Old Weir Bridge into a beautiful calm spot called the Meeting of the Waters. Next is the Middle Lake, in the shadow of Torc Mountain, and then under Brickeen Bridge into the Lower Lake. The tour ends at 15th-century Ross Castle, where jaunting cars are lined up to take passengers back to Killarney Town. The total price of this day-long, multi-conveyance excursion (about $35 to $40) is set and regulated by the Urban District Council, so be sure to check with the tourist office for the current rate.

CRAG CAVE Fifteen miles north of Killarney, this underground wonder is believed to be over 1 million years old, although it has been open officially to visitors only since late 1989. One of Ireland's largest cave systems (it has a total surveyed length of 12,510 feet and a depth of over 60 feet), its passageways are spiked with the largest stalactites in Europe, and there are many unique rock formations. Special lighting produces a haunting effect, showing off dark caverns and obscure crevices that would otherwise go unnoticed. Guided tours are available, and there are exhibit areas, a craft shop, and a restaurant. Open daily, March through November. Admission charge. Castleisland (phone: 66-41244).

Sources and Resources

TOURIST INFORMATION

The Killarney Tourist Board is in the Town Hall (Main St.; phone: 31633). A large facility, it is divided into two sections, one for processing room reservations, the other for information and the sale of pamphlets, guides, and maps. Summer hours are 9 AM to 8 PM Mondays through Saturdays, 10 AM to 6 PM Sundays. The rest of the year, it is open 9:15 AM to 5:30 PM

Mondays through Fridays, 9:15 AM to 1 PM Saturdays. Useful publications include the inexpensive *Killarney Area Guide* and the *Kerry Guide,* and *The Cork & Kerry Visitor Guide* (issued free and updated annually).

LOCAL COVERAGE County Kerry's weekly newspaper, the *Kerryman,* is published every Thursday and contains current information on Killarney area entertainment, sports, and events. Two other publications, the *Kingdom* (issued biweekly on Tuesdays) and the *Kerry People* (published every Friday), are also full of helpful listings and news.

TELEPHONE The area code for Killarney and the immediate vicinity is 64. When calling from within the Republic of Ireland, dial 064 before the local number.

GETTING AROUND

There is no local public transport within Killarney because the downtown area is relatively small and can easily be explored on foot. A good way to get oriented is to purchase *The Killarney Tourist Trail* at the tourist board or at a local shop and then follow the route outlined. The disc parking system is in effect on local streets; discs can be obtained at hotels, shops, or the tourist office.

BICYCLES A particularly enjoyable way to savor the Killarney sights. Most bike rental dealers are open daily 9 AM to 9 PM May to September, with shorter hours during the rest of the year. Full-day rentals are inexpensive. The following shops have large rental fleets: *Laurel's Lane Bike Hire* (Old Market La., off Main St.; phone: 32771); *O'Callaghan Bros.* (College St.; phone: 31175); *O'Neill's Cycles* (6 Plunkett St.; phone: 31970); and *O'Sullivan's* (Pawn Office La., off High St.; phone: 31282).

CAR RENTAL The following companies maintain car rental operations in Killarney: *Budget* (*International Hotel,* Kenmare Pl.; phone: 34341); *Hertz* (Plunkett St.; phone: 34126); *Avis* (Cork Rd.; phone: 31555); and *Randles Europcar* (Muckross Rd.; phone: 31237).

JAUNTING CARS Since many of Killarney's most scenic lake and parkland areas are not open to automobile traffic, the jaunting car is undoubtedly one of the best ways to get around, especially for those who don't enjoy walking or biking. In many ways, jaunting cars have become synonymous with Killarney, although the experience may not always be idyllic — the jarveys can be a bit aggressive in pestering visitors to take a ride. The cars usually are lined up along Main Street and Kenmare Place, near the major hotels in town (the *Killarney Great Southern* and the *International*), or at the entrance to major sights (such as *Muckross House and Gardens* or *Ross Castle*). Rates are reasonable and depend on the duration and distance of the trip. Rates are set and carefully monitored by the Urban District Council, so there is no need to be suspicious of being overcharged.

TAXI There are taxi stands on College Square and at the *Killarney Great Southern* hotel. Taxis also line up to meet arriving trains and buses at the Killarney railway station. To order a taxi by phone, contact *Deros* (phone: 31251), *O'Connor's* (phone: 31052), or *Cronin's* (phone: 31521).

TOURS During July and August, *Bus Eireann,* a division of *CIE* (*Córas Iompair Eireann, National Transport Company;* phone: 31067) operates full-day sightseeing bus trips around the Ring of Kerry and the Dingle Peninsula, with regular departures from the Killarney railway station, adjacent to the *Great Southern* hotel. Half-day tours of the Killarney lake district and full-day excursions to the Gap of Dunloe or the Ring of Kerry are also available from *Castlelough Tours* (7 High St.; phone: 32496 or 31115), *Cronin's Tours* (College St.; phone: 31521), *Deros Tours* (22 Main St.; phone: 31251), *Killarney Express Tours* (Park Rd.; phone: 34018), and *O'Connor's Tours* (Ardross, Ross Rd.; phone: 31052).

TRAINS AND BUSES *Irish Rail* and *Bus Eireann,* divisions of *CIE,* connect Killarney to all major Irish cities and towns, such as Dublin, Limerick, Tralee, and Cork. All trains and buses arrive and depart from the Killarney railway station next to the *Great Southern* hotel. For schedules and fare information, call *CIE* (see *Tours,* above).

WATER EXCURSIONS The ideal way to see the lakes is via an enclosed motorized cruise boat, such as the *Lily of Killarney,* operated by *Killarney Watercoach Cruises* (3 High St.; phone: 31068) or the *Pride of the Lakes,* operated by *Destination Killarney* (East Ave. Rd.; phone: 32638). These tours last approximately 1 hour.

SPECIAL EVENTS

The *International Motor Rally of the Lakes,* which tours around the lake district, is held in early December. For information, check with the tourist office.

MUSEUMS

Besides those mentioned in *Special Places,* a particularly pleasant place to visit on a rainy day is the *Killarney Art Gallery* (47 High St.; phone: 34628). This permanent exhibit contains an impressive selection of Irish landscapes and local scenes. Killarney's other showcase for the arts is the *Frank Lewis Gallery* (Bridewell La.; phone: 31108), which has changing exhibits of works by both local and international artists.

SHOPPING

As a town that basks in tourism, Killarney has more than its share of souvenir and gift shops. The selection and variety of goods are great, quality is high, and the prices usually are competitive. The range of goods is not particularly native to the area but includes all the visitor favorites —

Aran hand-knits, Donegal tweed, cashmere, Waterford crystal, and Belleek china. Some local handicrafts, such as hand-thrown pottery, handwoven clothing, artwork, and Kerry glass, are also sold at many outlets. Official shopping hours are 9 AM to 6 PM, Mondays through Saturdays, with an early closing on Monday afternoons. In high season, however, many of the busier stores remain open until 10 or 11 PM 7 days a week.

CELTIC SHOP An all-purpose store that offers a wide selection of knitwear and tweeds as well as traditional Irish dolls, road signs, crystal, china, and pewter. 33 College St. (phone: 31126).

KILKENNY SHOP Synonymous with fine design, this is an offshoot of the famous Dublin shop of the same name, now owned by the Blarney Woollen Mills of Cork. Like its sister shops, this place sells a wide variety of Irish-made goods, from tweeds and knitwear to crystal, china, pottery, and souvenir items — all at competitive prices. 10-11 Main St. (phone: 33222).

KILLARNEY BOOKSHOP A great source of local maps and travel guides as well as books on Irish history, folklore, and fiction. 32 Main St. (phone: 34108).

O'LEARY'S ANTIQUE STORE A treasure-trove of old silver, brass, glass, and china, as well as antique prints and vintage postcards. 33 Main St. (no phone).

QUILLS WOOLLEN MARKET For hand-knit sweaters of all colors, sizes, textures, and styles. 1 High St. (phone: 32277). In May through September, a branch store operates at 1 Fair Hill, opposite the *Killarney Great Southern* hotel (phone: 325577).

SERENDIPITY This shop features a wealth of knitwear in alpaca, mohair, and cashmere, as well as hand-thrown pottery, studio glass, linen, handwoven bedspreads, antique prints, paintings, copper, and hand-crafted silver and gold. 15 College St. (phone: 31056).

VIKING CRAFTS The shelves here are stocked with tweed, china, silver, and lace, as well as fishing flies, shamrock seeds, heraldic crests, rugby shirts, Irish ballad books, local shell crafts, Irish coffee mugs, and leprechauns of various sizes and shapes. 3-5 Kenmare Pl. (phone: 33820).

WHITE HEATHER HOME CRAFTS Handmade Irish lace and antique lace are specialties here, as are collectors' character dolls, framed dried Kerry flowers, handmade jewelry, crochet work, and glassware. Two locations: 48 New St. (phone: 31145) and Plunkett St. (phone: 32160).

SPORTS AND FITNESS

BOATING Rowboats can be hired for trips on the Killarney lakes at Ross Castle; contact the Killarney Tourist Board for a list of operators.

FISHING On the River Laune and the River Flesk, anglers can enjoy salmon fishing (using spinning gear of any type) and trout fishing (using flies only).

Daily permits are required for both types of fishing, and salmon fishermen must also obtain a state license. All of this documentation can easily be obtained from the Fishery Office (c/o Park Superintendent, Knockreer Estate Office, New St., Killarney; phone: 31246), which also will reserve beats (stretches of water) in advance by mail. The salmon season extends from mid-January to mid-October, trout season from mid-February to early October. For more details, see *Gone Fishing* in DIVERSIONS.

GAELIC GAMES The Irish national games of hurling and Gaelic football are played most Sunday afternoons during the summer by local teams at *Fitzgerald Stadium* (Lewis Rd.; phone: 31700). Check the *Kerryman* newspaper or call the stadium for the latest schedule. Admission charge.

GOLF Killarney boasts a world class golf club.

TOP TEE-OFF SPOT

Killarney Golf and Fishing Club The scenery is lovely and dramatic in this fabled spot, and it may take an act of will to keep your head down while playing on one of the two championship courses, *Killeen* or *Mahoney's Point,* though it may not be worth the effort. The sight of the lakes framing the purple mountains is a once-in-a-lifetime experience. Among the most scenic in Ireland, both courses are lakeside, 18 holes, par 72. The greens fee entitles players to try both courses in the same day. Site of several *Irish Open* events, the older *Killeen* course presents the more taxing challenge. Mahoney's Pt., 3 miles from town (phone: 31034).

HORSE RACING Since 1936, the *Killarney* racecourse (Ross Rd.; phone: 31125) has been drawing people from all parts of Ireland to its annual May and July meets. Check for details in any national or local newspaper, or call the track.

HORSEBACK RIDING Horses and ponies are available from the *Killarney Riding Stables* (Ballydowney, Killarney; phone: 31686) and *Rocklands Stables* (Tralee Rd.; phone: 32592). Hourly rates are available; extended trail riding can also be arranged.

SWIMMING The best swimming is available at some of the Atlantic coastal beaches along the Ring of Kerry, such as Castlecove, Rosebeigh, and Waterville, as well as at Inch Strand on the Dingle Peninsula.

JOGGING The Killarney National Park offers four fully developed and signposted nature trails, ideal for jogging or walking.

TENNIS Many Killarney hotels, such as the *Gleneagle* (Muckross Rd.; phone: 31870), *Cahernane, Dunloe Castle, Europe,* and the *Killarney Great Southern* (see *Checking In*), have tennis courts for guests.

WALKING With its wide open lakelands and national parklands, Killarney is a walker's paradise. Although visitors are free to follow trails and paths individually, there are also a number of organized guided walks, priced from $20 a day per person, operated by *Kerry Country Rambles* (53 High St.; phone: 35277). This outdoor sports firm also offers rafting, boating, biking, fishing, horseback riding, and mountain-climbing programs varying in duration from one day to a weekend or a full week (see also *Great Walks and Mountains Rambles* in DIVERSIONS).

THEATER

Evenings from May to October, the *Gleneagle* hotel presents a varied program of entertainment. Reservations are recommended. At the *Arus Pádraig Hall* (Lewis Rd.; phone: 33516) the local *Dóchas Drama Group* presents plays during the winter, and a traditional Irish dance show is performed here during the summer. The tourist board has times and schedules.

MUSIC

Irish cabaret music sessions are held throughout the summer at a number of Killarney hotels, including *Gleneagle* (see *Tennis,* above), *Killarney Ryan* (Cork Rd.; phone: 31555), *Dunloe Castle, Europe, Killarney Great Southern, Aghadoe Heights,* and the *International* (see *Checking In*). For additional details on traditional Irish music in local pubs see *Sharing a Pint.*

NIGHTCLUBS AND NIGHTLIFE

Most of Killarney's nightlife is in its pubs. In addition to Irish music, *Danny Mann Inn* (97 New St.; phone: 31640) operates the *Scoundrels Night Club.* Other discos include *Wings Night Club,* at the *Gleneagle* (see *Tennis,* above), *Revelles,* at the *East Avenue* hotel (Kenmare Pl.; phone: 32522), and *Molly's Loft,* at the *Muckross Park* hotel (see *Checking In). Killarney Manor* (Loreto Rd.; phone: 31551) offers 19th-century–style banquets complete with traditional music.

Best in Town

CHECKING IN

As Ireland's most popular pure resort area, Killarney has hundreds of places to stay — from luxurious Old World hotels and modern motels to simple farmhouses and private homes. During the summer, prices are higher than in most other parts of the country, but off-season rates (October/November through April) can provide substantial savings (up to 35%). In summer, expect to pay $150 a night or more for a double in hotels designated as very expensive, $100 to $145 in the expensive category, $50 to $100 in a hotel or motel listed as moderate, and under $50 at places described as inexpensive. Modest accommodations in private homes and farmhouses, usually without private bath, run less than $40 a night for a double room with a full Irish breakfast. The Killarney Tourist Board operates a reservation service to assist visitors in finding accommodations. All telephone numbers are in the 64 area code unless otherwise indicated.

VERY EXPENSIVE

Aghadoe Heights Set amid 8½ acres on a hillside 2 miles west of town, this modern hostelry enjoys panoramic vistas of Killarney, the lake district, and the surrounding mountain ranges. To match the spectacular views, the British-based owners have renovated the 60 guestrooms and public areas with new furnishings, brass fittings, and other fine touches. The rooftop restaurant also has been redone with plush decor and new kitchens. Salmon fishing is available on a private stretch of the River Laune, and special arrangements can be made at Killarney's two golf courses. A new fitness center with an indoor swimming pool is to be completed next year. Aghadoe, off N22 (phone: 31766; 800-44-UTELL from the US; fax: 31345).

Killarney Park With a handsome neo-Georgian façade, this 4-story property is located on the eastern edge of town. It offers posh and spacious public rooms including a lobby and lounges with crackling fireplaces, brass fixtures, oil paintings, wainscot paneling, and comfortable seating, as well as a handsome sunlit conservatory-style lounge overlooking the gardens. It has 55 rooms and suites, all with private marble-finished bathroom and modern furnishings of dark and light woods and quilted designer fabrics. Facilities include a restaurant, a piano bar, a patio, a swimming pool, a gym, a steamroom, and ample parking. Kenmare Pl. (phone: 35555; fax: 35266).

EXPENSIVE

Cahernane Built in 1877 as the manor home of the Herbert family (the Earls of Pembroke), this gracious country inn offers a bucolic parkland setting, complete with rose gardens, on the shores of Killarney's Lower Lake, less than a mile from town. An Old World atmosphere prevails in all the public rooms, including the elegant à la carte restaurant, but the 52 bedrooms offer all the 20th-century comforts, including private baths/showers. Guest facilities include outdoor tennis courts, pitch and putt golf, croquet, and reserved fishing privileges. Closed January and February. Muckross Rd. (phone: 31895, 33936, or 33937; 800-447-7462 from the US; fax: 34340).

Dunloe Castle This is not an old Irish fortress, but a modern German-owned château-style hotel near the Gap of Dunloe and adjacent to the ruins of the original 15th-century Dunloe Castle. All 140 rooms have private baths. Other amenities include an excellent restaurant, a heated indoor pool, saunas, tennis courts, horseback riding, fishing, croquet, a putting green, a fitness track, tropical gardens, and nightly entertainment. Open April through September. Beaufort, west of Killarney off the Killorglin road (phone: 44111; 800-221-1074 from the US; fax: 44583).

Europe Hugging the Lower Lake's shoreline, surrounded by tropical gardens, and next to Killarney's two golf courses, it is a favorite with European and American visitors. The 200 rooms all have private bathrooms, TV sets, and phones; most also have balconies with spectacular views. The main restaurant has panoramic views and offers an international menu, while the coffee shop offers faster service and simpler fare in a skylit, alpine setting. Other amenities include an indoor heated swimming pool, a health center, indoor tennis courts, and facilities for horseback riding, boating, and fishing. There's also evening entertainment. Open March through October. Fossa, west of Killarney off the Killorglin road (phone: 31900; 800-221-1074 from the US; fax: 32118).

Killarney Great Southern On the eastern edge of the town, set on 36 acres of rolling fields and manicured gardens, this 135-year-old, ivy-covered landmark is the grande dame of Killarney hotels. The 180 bedrooms (all with private baths) have been recently refurbished, and 10 deluxe suites have been added. The public areas have been revitalized with classic sofas and armchairs and plush carpeting, but there is still a roaring fire glowing in the lobby, and the Waterford crystal chandeliers, ornate plasterwork, and high ceilings proudly remain. The main dining room is elegant, and is as large as a ballroom; for an excellent meal, try the adjoining *Malton Room* (see *Eating Out*). There is an indoor heated swimming pool, Jacuzzi, steamroom, plunge pool, gymnasium, saunas, tennis courts, and a fashionable boutique. During the summer, evening entertainment is provided by various cabaret groups. Open March to December. Station Rd., off East Avenue Rd. (phone: 31262; 800-44-UTELL, or 800-243-7687 from the US; fax: 31262).

Muckross Park Situated across the street from *Muckross House* and the *Killarney National Park,* this 2-story roadside inn is the result of a recent total refurbishment of the oldest hotel in Killarney, dating back to 1795. It has 27 rooms and suites, each with bath and TV set. The rooms vary in size and decor, but most have half-canopy beds, period furniture, and Victorian-style ruffled drapes and ceiling fixtures. Facilities include a restaurant; a traditional, thatch-roofed pub; and a nightclub. Closed November through mid-March. Muckross Rd. (phone: 31938; fax: 31965).

MODERATE

Castlerosse Set on the beautiful Kenmare estate, overlooking lakes and mountains, near Killarney's golf courses, it has 65 motel-style bedrooms, each with private bath/shower. Facilities include a restaurant, gym, sauna, outdoor tennis court, putting green, and jogging trails. Closed from the end of October to early March. Killorglin Rd. (phone: 31114; 800-528-1234 from the US; fax: 31031).

International Although situated right in the middle of town, the front rooms of this landmark hotel, a Best Western affiliate, offer sweeping views of the mountains. The interior harks back to the grand old days, with a hand-carved central staircase (there's an elevator for those who prefer) and antiques and memorabilia. Each of the 88 rooms has a modern, private bath. Other facilities include a formal dining room, the *Whaler* seafood restaurant, a coffee shop, a sun deck, and a lounge bar with Irish entertainment nightly during the summer. The hotel supplies complimentary parking discs. Open March through October. Kenmare Pl. (phone: 31816; 800-528-1234 from the US; fax: 31837).

Kathleen's Country House A family residence that has been extended to include 17 modern bedrooms with private baths/showers, color TV sets, direct-dial phones, hair dryers, and orthopedic beds. This delightful guest home is on spacious grounds, complete with landscaped gardens and a private parking lot. Open March through December. Madam's Height, 2 miles north on the Tralee road, N22 (phone: 32810; fax: 32340).

Killarney Towers Situated in the heart of town, this refurbished building's façade has retained its original Georgian charm, but the 102 guestrooms (all with private baths) are comfortably furnished with light woods and pastel-toned fabrics, and in-room amenities — coffee/tea-makers, hair dryers, and remote control TV sets — have been added. Facilities include a dining room, an informal pub-style bar, a piano bar, and a private parking lot. College Sq., College St. (phone: 31038; fax: 31755).

Killeen House Opened as a hotel in 1992, this rambling country manor is a perfect retreat for those who seek a homey ambience with hotel comforts. There are 15 bedrooms, each with private bath, phone, and TV set. The public areas include a restaurant, a fireside lounge, a golf-themed bar, and a conversation-piece wall displaying over 800 golf balls from all over the world. Aghadoe (phone: 31711; 800-833-4373 from the US; fax: 31811).

Linden House On the edge of town in a quiet neighborhood near the cathedral, this popular inn is run by the Knoblauch family, known for their German-Irish hospitality. There are 20 rooms, each with a private bath/shower, TV set and phone; a full-service restaurant with a liquor license; and a private parking lot. Open February through November. New Rd. (phone: 31379).

INEXPENSIVE

Killarney Town House This new 4-story guesthouse is situated on one of the town's busiest commercial streets and within walking distance of most major attractions and shops. The 12 bedrooms are small and simple but offer all basic amenities including private baths, direct-dial phones, and TV sets. Rates include full Irish breakfast. 31 New St. (phone: 35388; fax: 35382).

Park Lodge Within walking distance of town, this is an enlarged 2-story home set on spacious grounds in a residential area. It offers 20 comfortable rooms, each with private bath, radio or TV set, and phone. Owner Mary Fleming cooks a hearty breakfast for guests each morning as part of the rate. Closed December to February. Cork Rd. (phone: 31539).

EATING OUT

Killarney's restaurants are concentrated within a few blocks in town. For dinner for two (without wine, drinks, or tip), expect to pay $75 and up at places in the expensive category, $35 to $70 at restaurants listed as moderate, and $30 or less at places in the inexpensive category. All telephone numbers are in the 64 area code unless otherwise indicated.

EXPENSIVE

Gaby's The atmosphere is bright and nautical, with light knotty pine, colored tablecloths, and a lobster tank at the entrance where diners may choose their own. Other entrées include rainbow trout, scallops mornay, turbot, haddock, and seafood combination platters. Open March through January for lunch and dinner except Sunday dinner and Monday lunch. Reservations necessary. Major credit cards accepted. 27 High St. (phone: 32519).

Killarney Manor Set high in the hills overlooking the lakes and countryside, this former abbey/school has been transformed into a 19th-century banquet hall. Guests assemble in the "Gallery," a former chapel with richly colored stained glass windows. Here a welcome drink is provided by the "lord" of the manor, an entertainer/host who orchestrates the evening's music and song. Dinner is served in the adjacent "Great Hall." The menu includes an appetizer of traditional Irish spiced beef, soup, a choice of roast Kerry lamb or fresh salmon, vegetables, and oat cake for dessert. The evening's entertainment ends with a reenactment of a Killarney stag hunt, with rousing ballads and dancing. Open daily for dinner April through October. Reservations necessary. Major credit cards accepted. Loreto Rd., off Muckross Rd. (phone: 31551).

Malton Room Small and intimate, this is the Georgian-style, à la carte restaurant of the *Killarney Great Southern* hotel. It is named for 18th-century Irish artist James Malton, whose watercolors line the walls. The menu, printed in both English and Irish, includes rack of lamb, beef Wellington, pan-fried veal, and sea scallops in port wine and brandy sauce. Dishes prepared at tableside, such as steak Diane and lamb kidney flambé, are also a specialty. The atmosphere, enhanced by candlelight, and Irish silver and linen, is elegant, and the service excellent. Open daily for dinner. Reservations necessary. Major credit cards accepted. Station Rd., off East Avenue Rd. (phone: 31262).

Strawberry Tree A shopfront eatery, it has a surprisingly romantic atmosphere, with a decor of subtle pink and gray tones, an open fireplace, and classical music playing in the background. The fare features local ingredients, with such dishes as a trio of gamebirds with wild mushrooms, wild rabbit pie, pan-fried beef in Guinness sauce, and white crab cakes in shallot and wine sauce. Closed Sundays and during December and January. Reservations necessary. Major credit cards accepted. 24 Plunkett St. (phone: 32688).

MODERATE

Bricín With a decor of original stone walls, pine furniture, and turf fireplaces, this eatery is housed in a building dating back to the 1830s. By day it is a café and by night a full-service restaurant. The menu features fresh seafood and beef as well as traditional Irish dishes, such as boxty (potato pancakes with meat or vegetable fillings) and Irish lamb stew. There are also a bookstore, a gallery, and a craft shop on the premises. Open daily. Reservations advised for dinner. MasterCard and Visa accepted. 26 High St. (phone: 34902).

Dingles The decor of this basement bistro is a blend of oak panels, cathedral choir stalls, arched ceilings, and cozy alcoves. The eclectic menu, prepared by owner/chef Gerry Cunningham, includes chicken curry, chili con carne, beef Stroganoff, and Irish stew as well as some exceptional seafood dishes such as monkfish casserole, giant prawns in garlic, and crab and shrimp au gratin. Open nightly for dinner in summer; closed from the end of November through February. Reservations necessary. Major credit cards accepted. 40 New St. (phone: 31079).

Foley's A delightful Georgian place, decked out with flowers and candlelight, it offers seafood specialties — mussel soup, Dingle Bay scallops, and local salmon — as well as steaks. The brown bread scones are home-baked. On weekends a tuxedo-clad pianist plays traditional Irish tunes as well as classical and contemporary music. Open for lunch and dinner year-round. Reservations necessary. Major credit cards accepted. 23 High St. (phone: 31217).

West End House Set in a 19th-century structure, which was built by the Earls of Kenmare and over the years served as a school, presbytery, local army headquarters, and private residence, this cozy eatery specializes in charcoal-grilled steaks, spareribs, and chicken. Other dishes include chicken breast in raspberry sauce, pork medallions in brandy cream, rack of lamb, and a variety of local seafood dishes. Open for dinner only; closed Sundays and during February. Reservations advised. Major credit cards accepted. Lower New St. (phone: 32271).

Picasso's This informal shopfront wine bar adds an international ambience to the town. The menu ranges from light snacks including muffins, crumpets, and scones to traditional Irish fare. A resident pianist plays in the evenings. Open 10 AM to 10 PM; closed Sundays. Reservations advised for dinner. MasterCard and Visa accepted. 10 College St. (phone: 31329).

SHARING A PINT

Many of Killarney's pubs are the focus of evening entertainment, particularly in the busy summer season. The most popular places for Irish ballads are the *Laurels* (Main St.; phone: 31149) and *Danny Mann Inn* (97 New St.; phone: 31640). Spontaneous and informal music sessions are often on tap at *Dunloe Lodge* (Punkett St.; phone: 32502), *Tatler Jack's* (Plunkett St.; phone: 32361), and *Scruffy's* (College St.; phone: 31038). For a quiet drink and an insight into the Kerry football tradition, try *Buckley's Bar* (2 College St.; phone: 31037) — the walls are lined with photos and mementos of this favorite Killarney sport. For a drink in a traditional setting, try *Molly Darcy's* (Muckross Rd.; phone: 31938), a cozy thatch-roofed pub with stone walls, oak beams, open fireplaces, alcoves, nooks and crannies, and snugs. On long summer evenings, an ideal gathering place is *Scott's Beer Garden* (off College St.; phone: 31870), the town's only bar with an outdoor setting and *Oktoberfest* atmosphere. Seven miles outside of Killarney, at the entrance to the Gap of Dunloe, it's fun to raise a toast in the rustic setting of *Kate Kearney's Cottage* (phone: 31060), a former inn and now a cozy watering hole for all those about to embark on the 7-mile trek through the mountainous Gap.

Limerick City

The fourth-largest city (pop. 76,000) on the Irish island, Belfast included, Limerick (in Irish, *Luimneach*) is a city of narrow streets, handsome Georgian houses, and impressive public buildings such as the Custom House and the Town Hall. It is also a major port, an inevitable product of its enviable position on the River Shannon, and while the city has a reputation for industry, those industries it is most famous for are all amiably light: traditional Limerick lace, still produced here; wonderful cured hams and bacon; salmon fishing; and flour milling.

Invaded by the Danes in the early 10th century, the Limerick area suffered many long years of skirmishing, which ended only when the Vikings were finally crushed by the Irish chieftain Brian Ború, who made Limerick the capital of Munster. In the 12th century, the Anglo-Normans conquered the town, and, settling on the island formed by the River Shannon and its tributary, the Abbey, they built stout walls to keep the natives at bay. This area became known as English Town, and the section across the river as Irish Town.

Undeterred by walls, the Irish continued to make sallies into English Town, led by the King of Munster, Donal Mor O'Brien. Upon his death in 1194, however, the Normans consolidated their position, and in 1210 King John ordered a strong castle and fortified bridge built to control the crossing point of the River Shannon. In later years the city walls were extended for added security.

During the 17th century the city was torn between revolts by the Irish, who seized the city, and sieges by the English under King William III and his followers, the Williamites. The Treaty of Limerick, signed in 1691, was to end hostilities and grant political and religious liberty to the Irish Catholics, but repeated violations of the treaty forced thousands into exile. Many of Limerick's most important landmarks — Thomond Bridge, the city walls, and St. Mary's Cathedral — have associations with these turbulent times.

In recent years the 1,000-year-old city has experienced a minor renaissance. Thanks to an urban renewal program that has cleaned up slums, refurbished the City Hall area, and built an industrial park that has attracted new companies and jobs, Limerick's image and quality of life have improved. In an effort to increase tourism, the city also has refurbished King John's Castle, a medieval structure that is now a major cultural center.

In fact, contemporary Limerick, as the major western gateway to Ireland (it's a half-hour drive from Shannon Airport), has a great deal to offer today's travelers. In addition to visiting its historic sites, a roster of possible activities includes fishing, horseback riding, horse racing, golfing, and swimming and boating on the Shannon. The medieval banquets held at the nearby Bunratty and Knappogue castles, as well as the *céilis* at the Folk Park, offer a delightful sampling of traditional Irish hospitality. The countryside surrounding Limerick has a quiet beauty, perfect for a peaceful day's rambling: Low hill ranges ruffle the plains, and small towns rise here and there, each with its ruined castle, abbey, or bridge.

Limerick has a somewhat unusual literary heritage. Its most famous native writer is Kate O'Brien (1897-1974), whose best-known work is the novel *Without My Cloak* (a *Kate O'Brien Literary Weekend* is held each February). The city's most acclaimed literary association, however, is as the home of the limerick, that famous five-line rhyme derived from a round game in which an individual extemporized a nonsense verse, followed by a chorus that included the words "Will you come up to Limerick?" Over the years the term *limerick* became associated with the rhyme scheme *aabba*, devised by the 19th-century nonsense poet Edward Lear. A typical limerick might go like this:

> *There once was a fair Irish city,*
> *That lent its good name to a ditty;*
> *Though of dubious worth*
> *The verse caused great mirth,*
> *Now the limerick outshines Limerick City.*

Limerick At-a-Glance

SEEING THE CITY

The best views of this rather flat city are from the top of King John's Castle and from the spire of St. Mary's Cathedral (see *Special Places* for details on both).

SPECIAL PLACES

Limerick is very compact and most of the important sights are located in one area. As traffic is sometimes congested, the city is best seen on foot.

CITY CENTER

THOMOND BRIDGE The present bridge, dating from 1840, was designed by Irish architect James Pain to replace the 13th-century structure erected by King John to defend the city. The original had a guardhouse and gate at the west end, and a drawbridge at the east end near the castle. The Treaty Stone, on which the famous Treaty of Limerick reputedly was signed in 1691, is on the west side of the new bridge.

KING JOHN'S CASTLE This fortification at the east foot of Thomond Bridge was built in 1210 by King John to guard the city against invaders. Located in the medieval section of the city, it is one of the oldest examples of Norman architecture in Ireland, with rounded gate towers standing sentry over the curtain walls. After a $7-million restoration, completed in 1991, the castle is evolving into a major international heritage and tourist center, with the added attraction of an authentic archaeological excavation of a site dating back to Hiberno/Norse times. The exhibits include two galleries of historical displays and authentic artifacts from the castle. In addition, there is a 100-seat theater offering continuous showings of an audiovisual program that provides an overview of Limerick's history. Recent archaeological remains are also exhibited on a subterranean level, with supporting interpretive displays. Open daily April through October; weekends during the off-season. Admission charge. Nicholas St. (phone: 411210).

ST. MARY'S CATHEDRAL Established in 1172 by Donal Mor O'Brien, the last King of Munster, this cathedral in the city's medieval section has been restored and extended a number of times and combines features from many different centuries. Note especially the unusual (and unique in Ireland) 15th-century choir stalls. The misericords (small projections on the bottom of the seats that offer support to standing worshipers) are carved with many medieval emblems, including those of Richard III. The cathedral is open year-round Mondays through Saturdays from 9:30 AM to 12:45 PM and from 2:15 to 5 PM. Nicholas and Bridge Sts. (phone: 416238).

BALL'S BRIDGE The structure that originally stood at this site linked the turf of the conquerors — English Town — with that of the natives — Irish Town. The bridge had no battlements, but rather supported a row of houses. These disappeared in 1830 when the present bridge was constructed.

LIMERICK WALLS Forming a rough diamond shape, the Limerick walls run east and southeast from Ball's Bridge, along Old Clare and Lelia Streets to the grounds of St. John's Hospital. There were four main gates: East Watergate, John's Gate, Mungret Gate, and West Watergate. The largest remaining portion of the walls is behind Lelia Street. Traces of the Black Battery (where a small band of defenders successfully resisted the Williamites) are found on the hospital grounds, while a badly deteriorated bit can be seen from Pike's Row near High Street. There are two other sections of wall remaining — one forms part of the building housing *Sinnott's Joinery Works* and the other stands in the Charlotte Quay parking lot.

ST. JOHN'S CATHEDRAL Originally intended as a parish church, this Gothic Revival cathedral built in the 19th century eventually became the see of the Catholic diocese. It houses two of Ireland's most remarkable ecclesiastical treasures, the magnificently carved miter and crozier made by Cornelius O'Dea, who was one of Limerick's bishops in the 15th century. At 280 feet, St. John's spire is the highest in Ireland; it's more ornate than the rest of the structure. At Cathedral Pl. (phone: 414624).

ST. JOHN'S SQUARE A few steps from the cathedral, this square — constructed around 1751 — once was lined with fashionable stone houses owned by the local gentry. The square declined slowly over the years until the 20th century, when the houses were used less glamorously as offices, tenements, barracks, and a butcher shop. Eventually they fell into neglect and were abandoned, but the square has undergone restoration and the area is being revived.

NEWTOWN PERY Just 200 years old, this is the "new" part of Limerick — a grid of streets roughly extending between Sarsfield Street on the north and the Crescent on the south. Named after Edward Sexton Pery, a speaker of the Irish House of Commons, under whose patronage the renovation was begun, the development is distinctly Georgian in character, with townhouses constructed of red brick. In the Crescent is a memorial to Daniel O'Connell, "the Liberator" — founder of the movement for Catholic emancipation — created by Irish sculptor John Hogan in 1857.

GRANARY Originally opened as a Georgian grain store in 1787, this old building has become the commercial hub of Limerick. Set among the quays near the River Shannon, it includes offices, the city library, ancestral research archives, and a tavern. Open daily year-round. Charlotte Quay, Michael St.

ENVIRONS

BUNRATTY CASTLE AND FOLK PARK The original castle on this site was built in the 15th century by the McNamara family but was appropriated around 1500 by Conor O'Brien, Earl of Thomond. Refurbished in the 1950s, it is now famous for the colorful medieval banquets presented in the great hall every evening (also see *Mead and Meat Pies: Historical Banquets* in DIVERSIONS), but the castle also houses an incredible collection of European paintings, furniture, and tapestries dating from the 14th to the 17th century. Together with the adjoining folk park, whose several acres abound with replicas of Irish rural and town dwellings as they would have appeared at the turn of the century, it provides a charming glimpse of how the Irish have lived during the last few centuries. In addition to touring the castle, visitors can explore a typical landowner's *bothán* (hut), whitewashed or limestone farmhouses, cottages, hovels, and other domiciles from different regions of Ireland, as well as a blacksmith's forge, a weaver's shed, and a village street. Bunratty House, a substantial late-Georgian dwelling of the type once occupied by minor gentry, rounds out Bunratty's fine depiction of Irish social history. A small, well-illustrated guidebook to the castle, available on the spot, is worth purchasing. The castle is open daily from 9:30 AM to 4:30 PM; the park, from 9:30 AM to 5:30 PM. Admission charge. The castle and folk park are both on the main Ennis road (phone: 361511 or 360788).

QUIN ABBEY Although the Franciscan friary, from 1402, is now roofless and in ruins, the tombs of the founding McNamara clan are still intact. No admission charge. About 22 miles northwest of Limerick in Quin.

CRAGGAUNOWEN This project, like Bunratty, was developed to document life-styles in Ireland long ago. Craggaunowen Castle, built by the McNamaras around 1550 and furnished with many items of historical and artistic importance from the John Hunt collection, is only the centerpiece of this unique outdoor museum, which includes a number of other structures that reach deep into the past to convey a sense of local life in prehistoric times. On an island in the lake, a stone dwelling known as a *crannóg* has been reconstructed on the foundations of an original; it is approached by a causeway that may have been used as early as the Bronze Age. There is also a reconstructed ring fort, the farmstead of Ireland's early history, which has an underground passageway for storage and refuge. Displays also include the *Brendan,* the leather boat in which the writer and amateur sailor Tim Severin crossed the Atlantic more than a decade ago in an attempt to prove that the 5th-century St. Brendan *could* have discovered America as he sailed the seas in search of paradise, as Irish legend says he did. There's also a program aimed at training young people in the traditional art of thatching. Open daily March to October. Admission charge. On the Ennis road (N18) in Quin (phone: 367178).

BALLYCASEY CRAFT COURTYARD AND DESIGN CENTRE The crafts workshops here produce everything from jewelry and knitwear to pottery. Adjacent to the center stands Balleycaseymore House, a Georgian-style building (not open to the public). The workshops are open daily year-round. No admission charge. Shannon, 10 miles west of Limerick, about 3 miles from Shannon Airport (phone: 362105).

LOUGH GUR Around this lake are found a number of ancient ruins, including stone circles, cairns, dolmens, and *crannógs.* Human bones, weapons, and pottery have all been unearthed here, and experts estimate that the site was inhabited as early as 2000 BC. A guide to the area ($1.75) and a self-guided walking tour booklet (75¢) can be obtained from the Limerick Tourist Information Office. Open daily May to September. Admission charge. 12 miles south of Limerick on the Bruff road (phone: 85186).

HUNT MUSEUM The museum's large collection of artifacts dating from the Bronze and Early Iron ages, found in Ireland and throughout the world, was donated by Celtic historian John Hunt, who also sponsored the Craggaunowen project in Quin (see above). Note: Plans were under way to move the Hunt Collection to the Old Customs House in Limerick City for the 1994 season. Call ahead to check. Open daily 10 AM to 6 PM, May through September. Admission charge. University of Limerick, Plassey House, 3 miles east of Limerick, off the Dublin road (phone: 333644).

FLYING BOAT MUSEUM An aviation and maritime center at Foynes (a small town southwest of Limerick City on the Shannon estuary), this museum focuses on the important role played by Ireland in the development of air travel from the US. In the early days of transatlantic flights, from the 1930s to the mid-1940s, Foynes was a principal landing, takeoff, and berthing port in Europe for flying boats and seaplanes. The museum houses a variety of memorabilia and equipment including an original terminal; a working version of the Short brothers' *Sunderland Flying Boat;* radio, navigation, and meteorological devices; and film footage from the flying boat era. There is also a tearoom with 1940s-style decor. Open daily, April through October. Admission charge. About 25 miles from Limerick in Foynes (phone: 69-65416).

EXTRA SPECIAL Built in 1467 by the McNamara family, Knappogue Castle was bought in 1966 by an American and restored to its original 15th-century elegance. Surrounded by lush green pastures and grazing cattle, Knappogue presents an imposing front. The interior is no less impressive, with its soaring ceilings and handsome antique furnishings. Ask to see the owners' magnificent private dining room. Open daily, May to October. Admission charge. About 12 miles northwest of Limerick, near Quin (phone: 368103; or *Shannon Castle Banquets,* phone: 360788). Also see *Mead and Meat Pies: Historical Banquets* in DIVERSIONS.

Sources and Resources

TOURIST INFORMATION

For information, brochures, and maps, visit the Limerick Tourist Information Office (Arthur's Quay; phone: 317522). The staff can answer questions and make hotel reservations anywhere in Ireland. Guides to Limerick, as well as Clare and Tipperary ($1.70 to $2.50), are also available.

LOCAL COVERAGE The city has three newspapers: the *Limerick Chronicle,* Ireland's oldest newspaper, is published on Tuesdays; the *Limerick Post* comes out on Thursdays; and the *Limerick Leader* is published every weekday. The tourist board's annual *Shannon Region Visitors' Guide* carries entertainment schedules.

TELEPHONE The area code for Limerick and the immediate vicinity is 61. When calling from within the Republic of Ireland, dial 061 before the local number.

GETTING AROUND

BUS Service between Dublin, Limerick, and Shannon Airport is frequent and convenient. The terminal, Colbert Station, is on Parnell Street. For departure and arrival schedules, call 313333.

CAR RENTAL All the major Irish and international firms are represented at Shannon Airport. Car rental companies in the Limerick area include *Payless*

Bunratty Car Hire (Coonagh Motors, Coonagh Cross, Caherdavin; phone: 451741); *Dan Dooley Rent-a-Car* (Knocklong; phone: 62-53103); *Thrifty Irish Car Rentals* (Ennis Rd.; phone: 453049); and *Treaty Car Rental* (37 William St.; phone: 416512). The disc parking system is in effect. Discs can be purchased at shops and at the tourist office.

SIGHTSEEING Day tours by bus are operated by *Bus Eireann*, a division of *CIE (Córas Iompair Eireann, National Transport Company)*, from the railway stations at Limerick (phone: 313333) and Ennis (phone: 65-24177), and from the tourist office during the summer; and by *Gray Line Sightseeing*, at the tourist office (*Arthur's Quay*, phone: 413088).

TAXI There are cabstands on Thomas Street, Cecil Street, and Bedford Row, and at Colbert Station. Or call *Economy Cabs* (phone: 411422), *Top Cabs* (phone: 417417), *Fast Cabs* (phone: 419994), or *SpeediTaxis* (phone: 318844).

WALKING TOURS Inexpensive walking tours of Old Limerick are conducted from early June to mid-September; they leave at 3:30 PM from the tourist office. Further information is available from the tourist office.

WATER CRUISES From June through August, afternoon sightseeing cruises along the River Shannon are offered on the 48-passenger boat, the *Derg Princess*, based at Killaloe, about 20 miles northeast of Limerick. For information and schedules, call 376364.

SPECIAL EVENTS

The most important annual event in the Limerick area is the annual *Limerick Civic Week* in mid-March, which features a *St. Patrick's Day* parade, a choral competition, a crafts exhibit, an international band competition, and a charity ball hosted by the mayor. Since 1990, the 2-week *Adare Festival,* a musical event of international stature, has been held in mid- to late July. The *New Jersey Symphony* (from the US) and the *Irish National Symphony Orchestra* have been the featured performers; the festival also draws a host of noted soloists from around the world. The program is usually a blend of classical works, opera favorites, traditional Irish music, Broadway show tunes, and big band jazz. For information on this year's lineup, call 800-262-7390 or 201-379-6286 in New Jersey; 1-676-8333 in Dublin; or 86150 in Adare. Other notable events include the *Limerick Summer Festival* in early July, which features the *Limerick Lady Contest,* country music, horse racing, water events, and a big fireworks display; and the *Limerick Flower Festival* in August. Check with the tourist office for details.

MUSEUMS

The *Limerick City Gallery of Art* (in People's Park, Pery Sq.; phone: 310633) exhibits modern Irish works; the *Limerick City Museum* (1 St.

John's Sq.; phone: 417826) documents local history, and features displays on local crafts and archaeology. There's no admission charge for either museum.

SHOPPING

The latest trend in Limerick is the mid-city shopping mall, such as *Arthur's Quay,* a giant 4-story skylit complex, built in Georgian style to meld with the surrounding architecture on Patrick Street. It boasts a variety of big department stores and boutiques, as well as a food court and covered parking. Other large shopping complexes include *Williams Court* (William St.), *Cruise's Street Shopping Centre* (Cruise's St.), and *Spaight's* (Henry St.). For shops with traditional Irish crafts, O'Connell Street is still the best bet, although Patrick Street is also worth browsing.

ANN SULLIVAN ANTIQUES AND CRAFTS Formerly *The Stables Antiques* of Ellen Street, this shop is now located in the heart of the city's historic district, between St. Mary's Cathedral and King John's Castle. The selection of antique lace, tapestries, brass, silver, curios, and crafts makes a detour from the main shopping strip worthwhile. 20 Nicholas St. (phone: 419140).

BILLY HIGGINS For a full selection of Burberry coats, hats, and accessories, this shop is a must. It also offers specially tailored Donegal tweed and cashmere jackets for both men and women, and an assortment of cashmere sweaters. 8 Sarsfield St. (phone: 414996).

BUNRATTY COTTAGE Northwest of the city, across the street from Bunratty Castle, this shop is a treasure trove of Irish haute couture — from Limerick lace blouses to Donegal tweed capes and hand-crocheted gowns, as well as Celtic designer jewelry, linen, crystal, and more. Bunratty (phone: 364188).

CARLTON VARNEY'S ROSE COTTAGE The internationally acclaimed interior decorator from the US has set up shop here, selling wallpaper, fabric, and tableware of his own design as well as jewelry and antiques. Ennis Rd., Newmarket-on-Fergus (phone: 368071).

GOOD SHEPHERD CONVENT Offering the famous Limerick lace. Clare St. (phone: 415183).

HONAN'S A treasure trove of antique grandfather clocks, candlesticks, stained glass, brass lighting fixtures, and other home furnishings. 14 Abbey St. (phone: 28137)

IRISH HANDCRAFTS This spacious midtown shop offers a wide variety of traditional crafts — tweeds, knitwear, crystal, linen, and souvenirs. 26 Patrick St. (phone: 415504).

LEONARD'S A good source for Limerick lace, as well as tweeds, cashmeres, and riding wear. 23 O'Connell St. (phone: 415721).

MICHELINA & GEORGE STACPOOLE Located about 10 miles south of Limerick in Adare, this exquisite shop, operated by a husband-wife team, offers an array of antiques and antiquarian books, as well as crafts and high-fashion knitwear. Main St., Adare (phone: 396409); there's a branch shop in the *Dunraven Arms* hotel down the street (phone: 396209).

ORIGINAL DESIGNER LACE, LTD. Beautiful handmade Irish lace in a multitude of delicate designs. Dominick St. (phone: 419477).

WHITE AND GOLD Fine china, porcelain, and crystal. 34 O'Connell St. (phone: 419977).

WOOL SHOP Slightly off the beaten track, this small one-woman shop is a leading source for hand-knit Irish sweaters made with 100% pure new wool. A variety of yarns is for sale, too. Closed Thursday afternoons and daily from 1 to 2 PM. 3A Lower Cecil St. (no phone).

SPORTS AND FITNESS

BICYCLING Bikes can be rented from *The Bike Shop* (O'Connell Ave.; phone: 315900) or *Emerald Cycles* (1 Patrick St.; phone: 416983).

BOATING In Killaloe, about 12 miles north of Limerick, cabin boats for cruising the River Shannon and neighboring lakes can be rented from *Derg Line Cruisers* (phone: 376364).

FISHING To fish for salmon in the Shannon or for trout and grilse in the rivers in and near Limerick, you must obtain a permit or a license. The best source is *Nestor's Sports Shop* (28 O'Connell St.; phone: 414096). For additional details, see *Gone Fishing* in DIVERSIONS.

GOLF The *Limerick Golf Club* (at Ballyclough; phone: 414083), the *Shannon Golf Club* (at the airport; phone: 61020), and the *Castletroy Golf Club* (on the Dublin road; phone: 335261) are open to the public. All three rent equipment and have a clubhouse.

GREYHOUND RACING Races take place Mondays and Thursdays at 8 PM and Saturdays at 8:15 PM at *Market's Field* (Mulgrave St.; phone: 316788). Check local papers for details.

HORSEBACK RIDING AND HUNTING Horses can be hired at *Clonshire Equestrian Centre* (Adare; phone: 396770), *Smithtown Riding Centre* (Ennis Rd., Newmarket-on-Fergus; phone: 361494), and *Clarina Riding Centre* (Clarina; phone: 353087). For hunters, the cost of hiring a horse for a day will run about $60, the cap fee about $80. To make arrangements to join a hunt, contact Bryan Murphy, *Foxhunting Centre of Ireland,* c/o *Dunraven Arms Hotel,* Adare (phone: 396209).

HORSE RACING In this part of horse-crazy Ireland, playing the ponies is a most fitting sin. Place your bet at one of Limerick City's many turf accountant (bookie) offices or at the racetrack. Although the two main events, the *Irish Derby* and the *Irish Grand National,* are both held in County Kildare, the excitement runs as high at the smaller races held at *Greenpark* (phone: 229377), in the city's southwestern suburbs, and at *Limerick Junction* (phone: 62-51357 or 62-51000), about an hour's drive on the Tipperary road. At both courses there will be 10 or 12 colorful turf accountants; lists of runners and the odds being offered are written on blackboards. "Punters" (gamblers) simply walk up to a turf accountant, hand him the money, name their choice of horse, and receive a betting slip with the man's name on it. Winners return their slips to the turf accountant for their payoff — first allowing another race to lapse so that he can make up his cash.

TENNIS Visitors are always welcome at *Limerick Lawn Tennis Club* (Ennis Rd.; phone: 452316), one of Ireland's oldest tennis centers, which has squash courts and a convivial bar as well.

THEATER

The *Theatre Royal* (Upper Cecil St.; phone: 414224) offers a varied year-round program of drama, music, and concerts. The *Belltable Arts Centre* (69 O'Connell St.; phone: 319866) has lunchtime and evening performances by local and touring companies, as well as concerts, exhibits, and other year-round cultural events.

MUSIC

In Limerick, the venues of choice are *Nancy Blake's* (Upper Denmark St.; phone: 416443) and the *Vintage Club* (9 Ellen St.; phone: 410694). For additional venues near Limerick City, see *Traditional Irish Music* in DIVERSIONS.

NIGHTCLUBS AND NIGHTLIFE

Son et Lumière, a sound-and-light show portraying the history of Limerick, takes place inside 800-year-old St. Mary's Cathedral (Nicholas and Bridge Sts.) at 9:15 nightly from mid-June to mid-September. For more information, contact the Limerick Tourist Information Office (see above). The *céilí* offered at Bunratty Folk Park is a program of singing, dancing, and storytelling accompanied by an Irish meal. In a similar vein are the banquets held at Bunratty and Knappogue castles — medieval feasts enlivened by traditional music and historical sketches. Both are on or near the main Limerick–Ennis road; for reservations, call *Shannon Castle Banquets* (phone: 360788). Traditional music concerts, followed by *céilí* dancing with audience participation, are held on various nights year-round (check for information on special weekend concerts) at *Cois na hAbhna* (pronounced Cush-na-*how*-na), the Irish Traditional Cultural Centre (Gort Rd., Ennis; phone: 368166). Irish cabaret, a dinner-plus-variety show, is offered by several hotels in the area, including *Jurys* (see *Checking*

In) and the *West County* (Limerick Rd., Ennis; phone: 065-28421); check with the tourist office for details. Finally, Limerick has many sing-along pubs, and local papers provide information on these.

Best in Town

CHECKING IN

Because of its proximity to Shannon Airport, the Limerick City hotel scene embraces part of County Clare (in which the airport is located). Hence, many of the hotels listed here are actually west of the city, between the environs of Shannon and downtown Limerick. Expect to pay $200 or more for a double room in our *Special Havens,* between $100 and $150 at places in the expensive category, between $50 and $100 for a double in a moderate hotel, and under $50 at places described as inexpensive. In addition to the large hotels, there are accommodations at numerous small guesthouses and private homes; reservations for these places can be made at the tourist board. All telephone numbers are in the 61 area code unless otherwise indicated.

For an unforgettable experience, we begin with our favorites, followed by our cost and quality choices, listed by price category.

SPECIAL HAVENS

Adare Manor About 10 miles south of Limerick, this 19th-century Tudor-Gothic mansion is set on the banks of the River Maigue, amid formal gardens on an 840-acre estate. Built in the early 19th century, this multi-towered and turreted château was the country home of the Earls of Dunraven. It was acquired by American owners who spent about $10 million to restore, refurbish, and open it as a hotel in 1988. The interior features barrel-vaulted ceilings, 15th-century Flemish doors, more than 50 individually carved fireplaces, and a banquet hall with a 2-story gallery. There are 64 antiques-filled bedrooms, each with a private bath. The restaurant offers a fine menu with a romantic setting. A complete resort, the *Manor* has a health center with an indoor swimming pool, and also offers a variety of daytime activities, such as salmon and trout fishing, horseback riding, fox hunting, clay pigeon shooting, and golfing on a new 18-hole championship course designed by Robert Trent Jones, Sr. Adare (phone: 396566; 800-462-3273 from the US; fax: 396124).

Dromoland Castle This castle sits in the heart of a 450-acre park some 20 miles northwest of Limerick where green velvet lawns roll away into dark green woods, and Ireland's banner flies from the battlements mirrored in the small lake. If *Dromoland* looks like a fantasy come true, it's because it is — for guests who roam its garden, golf on its 18-hole course, fish and boat on its lake and streams, ride horseback over neighboring hills, and call this member of the Relais & Châteaux group their temporary home. Inside, antique portraits line halls that glow with rich wood paneling and silken fabrics. Through the tall dining room windows, guests can watch deer while they try to restrain themselves at the breakfast buffet; at night the dining room's damask walls and polished silver gleam in the chandelier light — a proper setting for the carefully prepared food served therein (see *Eating Out*). The 73 rooms are airy and bright, and each has a private bath. The occasional Irish purist harrumphs and finds it "all a bit too grand." But its many repeat guests wouldn't have it any other way. Open year-round. Newmarket-on-Fergus (phone: 368144; 800-346-7007 from the US; fax: 363355).

EXPENSIVE

Castletroy Park Located on a grassy hill off the main road 2 miles east of downtown near the University of Limerick, this property (opened in 1991) has a rich, Old World decor, its lobby all mahogany and Oriental rugs, and its 110 luxurious guestrooms and suites decorated in coral and green floral prints. Each room has a remote control TV set, two telephones, and a computer card access system. The restaurant has the feel of a cozy manor library, and the menu features the freshest of fare. There's also a conservatory lounge, and a fitness center with an indoor pool, sauna, steamroom, Jacuzzi, gym, aerobics area, and massage room. The 16-acre gardens offer a number of jogging trails. The 18-hole *Castletroy Park* golf course is adjacent. Dublin Rd. (phone: 335566; 800-44-UTELL from the US; fax: 331117).

Clare Inn With wide-windowed views of the Shannon estuary, this contemporary property is particularly appealing to golf enthusiasts, since it is surrounded by the 18-hole golf course of neighboring *Dromoland Castle*. There also is a health and fitness center with a heated indoor pool, Jacuzzi, sauna, steamroom, and gym. The 121 modern rooms offer lovely views of the surrounding County Clare countryside. Other facilities include a restaurant, a lounge featuring weekend entertainment, and a coffee shop. Newmarket-on-Fergus (phone: 368161; 800-473-8954 from the US; fax: 368622).

Fitzpatrick's Bunratty Shamrock A modern, ranch-style property, owned and managed by two generations of the Fitzpatrick family, who also have major hotels in Dublin and Cork. This hostelry, next to Bunratty Castle, is set back from the main Limerick road amid extensive gardens and grounds. The 115 rooms are decorated with designer fabrics, many have half-canopy beds, and each room has a remote control TV set. There is a heated pool, a sauna and steamroom, plus a lively bar, and a shop. The restaurant serves French and Irish fare. There is ample parking, and a courtesy minibus shuttles guests to and from Shannon Airport. Bunratty (phone: 361177; 800-367-7701 from the US; fax: 471252).

Great Southern For those with early morning flight departures or late-night arrivals, this hotel (formerly the *Shannon International*) is ideal. Located opposite the main terminal at Shannon Airport, it was taken over by the Great Southern group and totally revamped in 1991. It offers 101 totally refurbished rooms, each with private bath, telephone, TV set, hair dryer, and tea/coffee maker. Public areas include a business center for executives, a terraced restaurant with views of the River Shannon, and a lounge with traditional entertainment on summer evenings. Guests also enjoy reduced rates at the adjacent 18-hole *Shannon Golf Club*. For those in transit, day rooms are available. Airport Rd., Shannon Airport (phone: 471122; 800-44-UTELL or 800-243-7687 from the US; fax: 61982).

Jurys Situated in a quiet garden setting across the river from downtown, this hotel is just a 5-minute walk from the heart of the city. Refurbished and expanded in 1991, it offers 100 well-appointed rooms decorated with dark wood, brass fixtures, and marble and tile bathrooms. Added in-room conveniences include an extra phone in the bathroom and good reading lamps over the bed. There is a bright and airy lobby and reception area, plus a fitness center with an indoor heated swimming pool, saunas, a steamroom, a Jacuzzi, and a tennis court. Other pluses include the highly acclaimed *Copper Room* restaurant (see *Eating Out*), a coffee shop, a Limerick-themed pub, a piano bar, and plenty of parking. Ennis Rd. (phone: 327777; 800-44-UTELL from the US; fax: 326400).

MODERATE

Dunraven Arms Dating back to the 19th century, this family-run inn is the centerpiece of the picturesque little town of Adare, 10 miles south of Limerick. The 45 guestrooms vary in size and decor, but all have private baths, cable TV, and direct-dial phones. There is also a restaurant, a cozy Old World bar, and lovely gardens. Horseback riding or fox hunting can easily be arranged for guests. Adare (phone: 396209; 800-447-7462 from the US; fax: 396541).

INEXPENSIVE

Bunratty Lodge Located just a mile from the celebrated castle of the same name, this neo-Georgian–style guest home is an exceptional value in the area. Owner Mary Browne offers 6 well-kept rooms, all with color TV sets, and private baths/showers with heated towel racks. There's no restaurant, but guests are served a hearty breakfast. Closed mid-December to mid-January. Bunratty (phone: 369402).

LIVE LIKE A LORD (OR LADY) For an extra-special treat, spend the night in a fully staffed, Georgian-style manor house on the grounds of *Dromoland Castle. Thomond House* is the private residence and seat of the

Right Honorable Lord Inchiquin, Conor Myles John O'Brien, head of the O'-Brien clan and the only man in Ireland to hold a British peerage and an Irish chieftaincy. He now welcomes visitors into his home as "private house-guests." There are 5 deluxe bedrooms, each with private bath and views of the 900-acre estate. Lord Inchiquin, in grand fashion, presides over nightly dinners in the candlelit dining room. Rates are approximately $250 per day per room, double or single, including breakfast. Dinner is extra at $60 per person. Rooms are available April through October or mid-November. For further information, contact Lord or Lady Inchiquin, Thomond House, New-market-on-Fergus (phone: 368304).

EATING OUT

Although it's never been known for its wealth of restaurants, the Limerick-Shannon area has added some distinguished eateries, and you won't be disappointed with a meal at any of the places recommended below. Expect to pay $125 or more for dinner for two (excluding wine, drinks, and tips) in places listed as very expensive; from $100 to $125 at restaurants described as expensive; from $50 to $100 at places in the moderate category; and less than $50 in those spots listed as inexpensive. All telephone numbers are in the 61 area code unless otherwise indicated.

For an unforgettable dining experience, we begin with our culinary favorite, followed by our cost and quality choices, listed by price category.

DELIGHTFUL DINING

MacCloskeys A stone's throw up the hill from the fabled Bunratty Castle, the location of this restaurant undoubtedly helped to launch it more than a decade ago, but it is the food, impeccably prepared and presented by chef Gerry MacCloskey, that brings customers back time after time. Specialties include veal with sweet and sour sauces, *noisettes* of lamb with minted béarnaise sauce, River Fergus salmon, and West Cork lobster. Desserts are equally tempting — strawberry soufflé, chocolate mousse with brandy, and baked pear puffs. The Old World setting is charming, with four cozy candlelit dining areas in the former mews and a 19th-century Georgian wine cellar, with the original whitewashed walls, carved archways, and polished slate floors. The chef's wife and partner, Marie MacCloskey, greets every customer individually and offers an aperitif by the fireside. The service is deft. Open for dinner only; closed Sundays and Mondays. Reservations essential. Major credit cards accepted. Bunratty Folk Park, Bunratty (phone: 364082).

VERY EXPENSIVE

Dromoland Castle Presided over by a French chef who has garnered top culinary awards, the main dining room of this fairy tale–style castle melds the best of French cooking with Irish ingredients in a romantic lakeside setting. Menu highlights might include braised salmon in a sorrel-flavored champagne sauce, roasted tournedos of monkfish with pepper sauce and braised lettuce, and lamb laced with foie gras. The dessert cart is equally creative. Open daily for lunch and dinner. Reservations necessary. Major credit cards accepted. Newmarket-on-Fergus (phone: 368144).

EXPENSIVE

Copper Room The best in the downtown area, this small but attractive place is often completely booked several nights in advance. The menu offers excellently prepared French dishes such as *coquilles St-Jacques,* prawns in garlic butter, veal steak stuffed with dressed spinach, filets of beef *en croûte,* and chateaubriand. Open for dinner only; closed Sundays. Reservations essential. Major credit cards accepted. *Jurys Hotel,* Ennis Rd. (phone: 327777).

The Loft As the name implies, this restaurant is on an upper level — of *Durty Nelly's* pub, a landmark in the Limerick-Shannon area. With a sloping ceiling of rafters and beams, this cozy, lantern-lit eatery is a quiet retreat from the boisterous pub below. The international menu includes *coquille* of crab mornay, scampi flambéed in brandy, chicken in a white wine and ginger sauce, and veal escallops stuffed with pork and herbs. Open for dinner only; closed Sundays. Reservations advised. Diners Club, MasterCard, and Visa accepted. At *Durty Nelly's,* Bunratty exit off N18, Bunratty (phone: 364861).

The Mustard Seed In a historic Old World village setting, this thatch-roofed cottage dining spot is known for its beef Wellington as well as such innovative dishes as scallops and stir-fried vegetables, mushroom ravioli with thyme butter, wild Irish salmon with a leek and tomato fondue, apple sorbet, and Baileys- and hazelnut-flavored ice cream. Open for dinner only; closed Sundays and Mondays and in February. Reservations advised. Major credit cards accepted. At the *Rose Cottage,* Main St., Adare (phone: 396451).

Restaurant de la Fontaine Located on the second floor of a downtown storefront building, this charming bistro and wine bar features *cuisine moderne.* Choices include beef flambé with peppercorns and foie gras; breast of chicken stuffed with smoked salmon and topped with a whiskey and hazelnut cream sauce; and "symphony of the sea," an assortment of fresh seafood presented in a watercress and lime sauce. Closed Sundays. Reservations necessary. MasterCard and Visa accepted. 12 Upper Gerald Griffin St. (phone: 414461).

Silver Plate Occupying the lower level of a Georgian townhouse, this downtown restaurant is known for its elegant pastel-toned decor and its French fare. The menu changes nightly, but often includes sea trout, salmon *en papil-*

lote, filet of beef, sole stuffed with shellfish, medallions of venison, and lobsters from the tank. Open for dinner only; closed Sundays. Reservations necessary. Major credit cards accepted. 74 O'Connell St. (phone: 316311).

MODERATE

The Oyster Located on the ground floor of the famous 17th-century *Durty Nelly's* pub, this informal eatery hasn't changed much with the years — mounted elk heads and old lanterns on the walls, sawdust on the floor, and glowing fires crackling in open turf fireplaces. This is a good spot for soup, steaks, seafood, and lighter fare, as well as hearty Irish stew or boiled cabbage and bacon. Spontaneous traditional music is usually on tap in the evenings. Open daily for lunch and dinner. Reservations advised for dinner. Diners Club, MasterCard, and Visa accepted. At *Durty Nelly's,* Bunratty exit off N18, Bunratty (phone: 364861).

Piccola Italia With an Italian decor and menu, this *ristorante* adds a Mediterranean ambience to the heart of Limerick. The menu includes a variety of freshly made pasta, as well as salmon *alla griglia,* shrimp scampi, sole parmesan, beefsteak *alla pepperoni,* and veal *pizzaiola.* Open daily for dinner. Reservations necessary. Major credit cards accepted. 55 O'Connell St. (phone: 315844).

Players' Club This bi-level eatery, decorated with theatrical memorabilia and musical instruments, is attached to *Patrick Punch's Pub,* a lively watering hole on the south end of town. The menu offers such choices as filet of salmon, *paupiettes* of lemon sole, chicken Kiev, rack of lamb, prime ribs, and steaks, as well as "lite bites" — sandwiches, burgers, pasta, and vegetarian salads. On warm days, food and drink are served on an outdoor patio. Open for lunch and dinner daily. Reservations advised. Major credit cards accepted. O'Connell Ave. (N20), Punch's Cross (phone: 229588).

INEXPENSIVE

Rowan Berry Part of the Ballycasey craft complex near Shannon Airport, this popular eatery is ideal for lunch or a light evening meal. The offerings include shepherd's pie, homemade scones and pastries, garden vegetable soup, salads, and seafood platters, as well as more predictable fare like pizza, lasagna, and quiche. Closed Sundays. No reservations. Major credit cards accepted. Ballycasey Craft Centre, Shannon (phone: 360590).

SHARING A PINT

There's always a welcome at *Hogan's* (72 Catherine St.; phone: 414138). Known for its cozy snug, chiming antique clock, and small nooks that surround the classic old bar, this pub has been in the same family (named Ryan, not Hogan) for nearly 100 years. A literary atmosphere prevails at the *James Joyce* (4 Ellen St.; phone: 416711), where a bust of the author dominates the modern decor, which also includes Joycean photos, sketches, and quotes. *Nancy Blake's* (19 Denmark St.; phone: 416443) is a quiet, friendly little pub where local working people drink. The oak-beamed *Vintage Club* (9 Ellen St.; phone: 410694) used to be a wine store, so the wines available range from the pedestrian to the extraordinary. The place also serves bar snacks — salads, soup, sandwiches — and attracts a youngish crowd in the late evening, when it can become crowded. The *Olde Tom* (19 Thomas St.; phone: 417091) is a family-run place known for its pub meals and fresh salads during the day; in the evenings for impromptu music sessions, dancing, and poetry readings. *Durty Nelly's* (phone: 364861), which may be the best-known pub in Ireland, is about 10 miles from Limerick City, right next door to Bunratty Castle. Although often jammed with both tourists and locals, the place is quite attractive and has two restaurants (see *Eating Out*). If you're lucky, you might also catch some music. About 15 miles northeast of Limerick at Birdhill, on the main Dublin road (N7), is a replica of a 19th-century farmer's pub called *Matt the Thresher* (phone: 379219). The cottage-like surroundings are replete with open fireplaces, antique furnishings, traditional snugs, and agricultural memorabilia. There's also a full-service restaurant and a wide spectrum of pub grub.

Londonderry

Londonderry — more popularly known by its original name, Derry — is Northern Ireland's second most important city. Although only 75 miles from Belfast, its position in the northwest corner of the country has rendered it remote from Northern Ireland's other population centers. This condition, a disadvantage in some ways, has served to slow the rate of change and preserve the city's historic character and appearance.

A friendly place, with quiet Georgian corners, and just the right size for strolling, Londonderry has the feeling of a village, its warmhearted citizens still good-natured in spite of "the troubles," both recent and historic. It's a cohesive city, even though its very name causes confusion — and rankles Nationalists in both the North and the Republic. Some still consider the prefix *London* — added to Derry in the early 17th century during the controversial Plantation period — an unwelcome intrusion.

Progress is catching up with Londonderry, which is becoming increasingly modernized. The worst of the bombings in the latest round of internecine battles occurred more than a decade ago, and relative calm has returned. The 1980s were accompanied by citywide restoration and the construction of new buildings and attractions. Despite occasional recent violence, the vast majority of the people of Derry are committed to the basic economics of business as usual, with everybody interested in keeping the city on its course of commercial invigoration. Firms are encouraged to relocate to the area to create jobs in a city that has one of the worst unemployment rates in Western Europe. Strong civic pride has surfaced in response to extensive redevelopment in the past 15 years, which has resulted in a city that looks — and feels — attractive from most angles. Londonderry also has acquired a university town atmosphere, thanks to the city's Magee College, now a part of the University of Ulster. The University's College of Tourism, in particular, attracts many students from abroad.

Derry — derived from the Gaelic word *doire* (oak grove) — was a densely wooded hilltop when St. Columba (Colmcille), fleeing a plague in Donegal, arrived in AD 546 to establish his first abbey. During ensuing centuries, the religious settlement became known as Derry Colmcille. The abbey was burned by piratical Danes in 812 — the first of a succession of invasions Derry was to endure. Neither the Vikings, who marauded the area for several hundred years from the 9th century onward, nor Normans, who crossed the River Bann and headed west in the 12th century, left much behind. Nevertheless, the city grew in size and importance, and its magnificent medieval church Templemore was built in about 1164.

Like other Irish cities, Derry came under English control when King Henry II claimed Ireland in the 12th century. The skirmishes that followed did not seriously damage the city until the 1566 rebellion led by Ulster chieftain Shane O'Neill, during which Templemore was destroyed. Queen Elizabeth I sent a small army to fortify Derry, but it failed and withdrew. In 1600, an English army led by Sir Henry Docwra besieged and took possession of the city. Docwra called for the erection of huge earthen bulwarks to protect Derry against further invasions, but in 1608 the Irish chieftain Cahir O'Doherty sacked the city.

With the accession of James I to the English throne in 1603, Derry was made a satellite of the city of London, with the resulting name change to Londonderry. The city fell subject to the policy of Plantation, whereby lands forfeited by vanquished Irish leaders — such as Cahir O'Doherty, who was killed — were distributed among English and Scottish colonists. Estates went for a nickel an acre, and a newly created hereditary title *baronet* sold for the equivalent of $2,500. Londonderry and the surrounding district were subsequently sold to the Livery Companies (tradesmen associations) of the city of London, at that time the wealthiest corporation on earth. With varying degrees of enthusiasm, clothmakers, tailors, ironmongers, mercers, vintners, salters, drapers, haberdashers, fishmongers, grocers, goldsmiths, and skinners began to settle the area near the River Foyle, the Sperrin Mountains, and the lower River Bann. From 1614 to 1617, the Society of the Governors and Assistants of London of the New Plantation in Ulster within the Realm of Ireland or, more simply, the Irish Society — which still is the ground landlord in Londonderry — built the famous 1-mile-long, 18-foot-thick (on average) city walls, made of earth faced with stone. Today, the fortifications are the only complete city walls left in the United Kingdom. The Plantation of Ulster, of which Derry was such a significant part, strained the resources of the city of London and its Livery Companies to the limit. This financial drain played a major role in the catastrophic rift that gradually grew between the commoners and the crown, which paved the way for civil war in England.

During the 17th century Londonderry successfully withstood three more sieges, living up to her centuries-old sobriquet "Maiden City," given in recognition of the fact that she never succumbed to any would-be conqueror. The first of the three came in 1641, when the Irish rose yet again against the English; the second in 1648, during the English Civil War, when Derry faced a 4-month attack by Royalist forces. But it was the third siege that was most memorable.

On December 7, 1688, troops loyal to England's deposed Roman Catholic King James II advanced to the walled city of Londonderry to claim it. (James needed a foothold in Ireland with which to attempt to reclaim the English crown.) However, their demand for admission at the city's Ferryquay Gate was met with hesitation by the city fathers who, although not wanting to oppose James openly — he was still their lawful monarch — favored the Protestant William, husband of James's daughter Mary and prince of Holland's House of Orange. Deliberation on the entry issue ended abruptly when a group of 13 apprentice boys took the decision into their own hands, yanking up the drawbridge at Ferryquay and slamming the doors, shutting out James and his men, who were forced to turn back.

In April 1689, James II resumed in earnest his siege of Londonderry, which was to last an additional 105 days. Jacobite troops shelled the city and blockaded the River Foyle, throwing a boom across it — where the new Foyle Bridge now spans — to prevent the passage of provision ships. The strategy was to starve the inhabitants into submission. The only person who deserted the city during its difficulties was the governor, Colonel Lundy. (Since then, Lundy has been hanged in effigy annually.) Lundy was succeeded by the Reverend George Walker, under whose leadership the city's 30,000 citizens held firm.

But provisions for Londonderry's population soon ran short. More than 7,000 perished, all within sight of a fleet of food-filled ships lying at anchor just beyond the blockade. Nevertheless, when James's troops fired a hollowed out cannonball at St. Columb's Cathedral that carried a message with terms for an armistice, Derry's citizens staunchly replied, "No surrender" — which ever since has been the watchword of the city and Ulster's Loyal Orange lodges.

Finally, on July 30, 1689, the relief ship *Mountjoy* burst the barrier across the Foyle. That day, the siege was broken, and each year the event is recalled by special celebrations in the city. Not quite a year later, in 1690, on July 1 — which became July 12 when the calendar was changed in the 18th century — James II finally lost his throne to William III at the Battle of the Boyne, fought near Drogheda in the Irish Republic.

From early in the 18th century into the 19th, Londonderry served as the principal port for the wave of emigrants who left Ulster for New World opportunities across the Atlantic. Ulster men and women became the second most numerous group in the colonial population (the English being the most numerous at that time). Ulster immigrants played a prominent part in the American Revolution as well as in the settlement of the new country's western frontier. Londonderry also served as a major port of embarkation for the mass migrations from all over Ireland that resulted from the potato crop failures and famines of the mid- to late-19th century.

During World War II, as the closest port across the Atlantic for US and Canadian supply convoys, Derry was tremendously important to the Allies. (The Republic of Ireland declared neutrality during the war, so its ports were closed to the Allies.) Many North American troops received training in the area for the *D-Day* invasion of Normandy.

Derry's more recent history has been less noble. In 1966, in what can be seen as a classic case of gerrymandering, two new electoral constituencies were created in Derry, serving to exacerbate the conflicts between Unionists (largely Protestants who to this day want Northern Ireland to remain part of the United Kingdom) and Nationalists (mostly Catholics who insist that Ulster be reunited with the Irish Republic). On October 5,

1968, the first confrontation in the city's current round of "troubles" occurred between civil rights demonstrators and the police. A period of conflict ensued, which, by August 12, 1969, resulted in a state of siege in the Catholic neighborhood of Bogside. Violence was a sadly familiar presence in the community during the 1970s. Bombings resulted in the destruction of some buildings and monuments. The remains of some of these — such as Walker's Monument, erected on Royal Bastion of the city walls in 1828 — have been left as memorials to this period. However, visitors to today's Derry generally find the city cleared of the rubble of the past and its citizens enthusiastically focusing on the present and looking to the future.

Londonderry At-a-Glance

SEEING THE CITY

The best vantage point for views within the city is the roof of the *Tower Museum* (see *Special Places,* below), which rises well above the city walls. From here, one can see Derry's distinctive, sturdy houses with their brightly colored façades steeply terraced on the hillsides; several steeples that seem to spear clouds from the sky; and the long brick buildings that formerly were linen-shirt factories, a legacy of the mid-19th century. From paths atop the surrounding walls themselves are splendid perspectives of sights both within the city and over the peaceful landscape well beyond. Other fine views of Derry are available from Brook Park, from along the Waterside district on the opposite banks of the Foyle, and from Foyle Bridge.

SPECIAL PLACES

The city within the walls — which are roughly rectangular in shape and which reach about a mile in total length — retains its original 17th-century layout, with four main streets radiating from a center square (called the Diamond) to the original gates: Shipquay, Ferryquay (the gate closed against James II by the 13 apprentices in 1688), Butcher's, and Bishop's. These have all been rebuilt over the centuries, and three newer gates have been added. The main street of the compact city within the walls begins at Shipquay Gate. As Shipquay Street — arguably the steepest street in Ireland — rises to the Diamond, it exudes a decidedly Georgian flavor, although most of the buildings date from Victorian times. Continuing straight across the Diamond, the road becomes Bishop Street. Along its several blocks before the street reaches Bishop's Gate at the top of the town are many of the city's finest buildings: the Northern Counties Club; the 1830 Deanery, with its fine classical Georgian doorway; The Honourable Irish Society headquarters, inscribed with the date 1764; and the Courthouse. Derry has several good Georgian residential rowhouse terraces, in particular those on Clarendon, Queen, and Bishop Streets.

THE WALLS Londonderry's most notable physical feature, the walls, form a mile-long terrace walk around the inner city. Each of the wall's bastions has its own name and story. Coward's Bastion, near the *Tower Museum*, is so named because it was the safest sector of the city during the 1689 siege. On Double Bastion, between Butcher's and Bishop's gates, is Roaring Meg, a circa-1642 brass cannon that is a veteran of the siege. The cannon, which got its name from the violent bang that accompanied its use, overlooks the area from which Jacobite troops attacked the city. For current information about access to Derry's walls and walking tours of them, inquire at the tourist board; see *Tourist Information,* below.

WITHIN THE WALLS

ST. COLUMB'S CATHEDRAL The Church of Ireland Cathedral is the most historic building in Londonderry. Begun in 1628 and finished in 1633, it has undergone much restoration and alteration, although its façade remains basically the simple, austere, well-proportioned Planter's Gothic. The nearby city walls rise higher in this picturesque precinct to protect the cathedral, which fired cannons from its bastions during the 1689 siege. Just inside the door is the hollowed cannonball that was shot into the church-yard with the proposed terms of surrender; elsewhere in the cathedral and in the chapterhouse other city artifacts are displayed, including locks and keys from the four original gates. A 20-minute video describes the city's history and the role of the cathedral in it. Open from 9 AM to 1 PM and from 2 to 5 PM; closed Sundays. Admission charge. London St. (phone: 262746).

TOWER MUSEUM Mellowed stones were used to construct this modern castle, which serves as the interpretive center for visitors to the city. The high-tech "Story of Derry" exhibition, which recounts the history of the area from its geological formation to its development as a modern city, is an excellent point of introduction. Of particular interest are sections that illustrate the spread of Irish monasticism, the famous 1689 Siege of Derry, and the road to the partition of Ireland. There's also an exhibit of artifacts recovered from a ship of the 1588 Spanish Armada wrecked off the nearby Donegal coast. The view from the roof is exceptional. Open year-round, Tuesdays through Saturdays from 10 AM to 1 PM and 2 to 5 PM. Admission charge. Union Hall Pl. (phone: 372411).

COURTHOUSE Designed by John Bowden and constructed of white sandstone in 1813, the Courthouse is one of Ireland's best examples of Greek Revival architecture. The portico is modeled after the Temple of Erechtheus in Athens. Bishop St.

BISHOP'S GATE The most memorable of the city's four original gates, Bishop's was extended upward into a triumphal arch in 1789, the centenary of Derry's great siege. Sculptured faces on either side of the arch are river gods of the Foyle and the Boyne. At the top of Bishop St.

GUILDHALL The Guildhall was built in Tudor Gothic style of red sandstone from Antrim in 1890. Its richly decorated façade has mullioned and transomed windows and a four-faced chiming spire clock that is one of the largest in Britain. Striking stained glass windows throughout the building illustrate almost every episode of note in the city's compelling history. The assembly hall, where concerts and other special events are held, has a decorated timber ceiling and one of the finest organs in Europe. Open year-round on weekdays from 9 AM to 4 PM. From mid-June to mid-September reservations are not required for free guided tours of the building; during the rest of the year make advance arrangements by contacting Catherine O'Connor (phone: 365151). No admission charge. At the foot of Shipquay St.

DERRY QUAY Memorialized in song and story, often sadly, Derry Quay (the popular name for the Foyle Quay), behind the Guildhall, was the embarkation point for hundreds of thousands of Irish emigrants — including the ancestors of several US presidents — who crossed the Atlantic in the 18th and 19th centuries. A small monument recalls the mass emigrations. Foyle Embankment.

ST. EUGENE'S CATHEDRAL The Roman Catholic cathedral, with its lofty granite spire, was finished in 1873. Built in Gothic Revival style, it is tall and airy, with exceptional stained glass windows depicting the Crucifixion. In the Catholic district called Bogside; reached from Strand Rd. along Great James St.

LONG TOWER CHURCH (ST. COLUMBA'S) Just outside the city walls to the southwest, this church was built in 1784 on the site of the former 12th-century Templemore Church. Long Tower, which seats 2,000, features attractive hand-carved woodwork, an unusual sloping balcony, and beautiful stained glass. The splendid altarpiece of contrasting marbles incorporates ancient Corinthian column heads that were the gift of the colorful and eccentric Bishop Frederick Augustus Hervey, who cut a wide swath in Derry in the late 18th century (see "Downhill" in *Antrim Coast,* DIRECTIONS). The edifice is surrounded by a complex of church schools; the view from the churchyard across grassy slopes to the city walls is lovely. Long Tower St.

ENVIRONS

STRABANE Americans find the town of Strabane of interest principally because of *Gray's Printing Shop* (49 Main St.; phone: 884094), which dates from the 18th century and is still in operation. In the room where some 19th-century presses remain, John Dunlap and James Wilson served as apprentices. Dunlap was the first of the two men to emigrate to Philadelphia, where he founded America's first daily newspaper, *The Pennsylvania*

Packet. In 1776 he printed the Declaration of Independence from Thomas Jefferson's original manuscript. Dunlap was also a captain in General George Washington's bodyguard. By 1807, Wilson too had emigrated to Philadelphia, where he became a judge, a newspaper editor, and, eventually, the grandfather of Woodrow Wilson, the 28th President of the United States. The 19th-century hand printing presses can be seen daily except Thursdays, Sundays, and bank holidays from 2 to 5:30 PM in April through September. Admission charge. John Dunlap was born at 21 Meetinghouse Street, which is marked by a plaque.

Strabane is reached on A5 south from Londonderry, along the River Foyle. Take the pretty, unclassified road eastward from Strabane to Plumbridge to enter the wild and lovely landscape of the Sperrin Mountains. At Plumbridge, follow B47 for the scenic splendors of the Glenelly Valley. Continue to Draperstown, then swing north and west on B40, B74, and A6 to return to Londonderry.

Sources and Resources

TOURIST INFORMATION

The Derry Tourist Board (8 Bishop St.; phone: 267284) is opposite the bus station, near the colorfully painted Craigavon Bridge. Information, maps, and pamphlets on the area are free; the *Derry City Council Official Guide* is inexpensive. Open weekdays from 9 AM to 5:15 PM year-round; in July and August hours are extended and the office is also open on weekends. As Londonderry is the doorway to County Donegal in the Republic, the tourist center also is staffed by Bord Fáilte, the Irish Tourist Board, during peak travel periods (phone: 369501).

LOCAL COVERAGE In addition to the daily *Belfast Telegraph,* the *Derry Journal* is published on Tuesdays and Fridays and the *Sentinel* on Wednesdays.

TELEPHONE The area code for Londonderry and the immediate vicinity is 504. When calling from within Northern Ireland, dial 0504 before the local number.

GETTING AROUND

Walking is the best way to discover the charms of this friendly city. Within the walls, Londonderry is very compact, although it is steep in spots. Flights of stone stairs lead to the tops of the walls.

AIRPORT Derry is served by Eglinton Airport, 8 miles from the city, which has regular flights to and from Glasgow and Dublin (phone: 810784). Belfast International Airport can be reached by train; disembark at the Antrim stop, 3 miles from the airport.

BUS The bus station is on Foyle Street. There is regular bus service to surrounding towns and to coastal resorts in County Donegal, as well as daily coach and express service to Belfast and Dublin and weekend service to London and Glasgow. For detailed information, contact *Ulsterbus* (phone: 262261, 262262, 262263, or 262264) and the *Londonderry and Lough Swilly Railway Co.* (phone: 262017).

CAR RENTAL Derry has three car rental firms: *Eakin Brothers* (Maydown; phone: 860601), *Hertz* (173 Strand Rd.; phone: 260420), and *Vehicle Services* (Campsie; phone: 810832).

TAXI There usually are a few taxis waiting at the railway station. In addition, there are several radio taxi services: *Blue Star* (phone: 648888), *Central Taxi* (phone: 61911), *Foyle Car Service and Taxi* (phone: 63905), and *Quick Cabs* (phone: 260515).

TRAIN *Northern Ireland Rail* operates six trains between Londonderry and Belfast Mondays through Saturdays, and two trains on Sundays. Waterside Station is on Duke Street (phone: 42228).

SPECIAL EVENTS

Londonderry both preserves and celebrates its important cultural heritage. The *Londonderry Feis* (festival), held for a week during February or March, features music, drama, ballet, and speeches. *Feis Dhoire Cholmcille,* with Irish songs, dancing, and instrumental music, is held during *Easter Week* at various venues, such as the Guildhall and St. Columb's Hall. Programs may include works by city natives, poet Seamus Heaney, and playwright Brian Friel. For information, contact the tourist board.

MUSEUMS

EARHART CENTRE/BALLYARNET FIELD This is the farm field where Amelia Earhart, the first woman to fly across the Atlantic Ocean solo, landed her plane on May 21, 1932. The field, part of a 150-acre wildlife sanctuary, offers a sculptured memorial and a reconstructed cottage where photographs and other memorabilia are on display. The cottage is open Mondays through Thursdays from 9 AM to 4:30 PM, Fridays until 1 PM, and weekends in June through September from 9 AM to 6 PM. The wildlife sanctuary is open daily from 10 AM to dusk. No admission charge. At Culmore, 1½ miles beyond Foyle Bridge, off Muff Rd., B194 (phone: 354040).

FOYLE VALLEY RAILWAY CENTRE Derry once had four railway lines emanating from it, two standard and two narrow-gauge. This museum houses railroad memorabilia, including steam engines and historic railway displays. Visitors may take a short picturesque ride on one of the old trains, departing from Craigavon Bridge. Open Tuesdays through Saturdays from 10 AM to 5 PM, and on Sundays from 2 to 6 PM in May to September. Admission charge. Foyle Rd., near Craigavon Bridge (phone: 265234).

ORCHARD GALLERY Contemporary and traditional artwork and crafts by local, national, and international artists are exhibited here. The gallery also hosts small theater events, films, concerts, and lectures. Closed Sundays. No admission charge. Orchard St. (phone: 269675).

SHOPPING

There are two shopping centers in town: the *Richmond Shopping Complex* (on the Diamond), which houses a variety of stores; and *Craft Village* (entrances at Shipquay and Magazine Sts.), a collection of shops selling handmade Irish gifts, clothes, and quilts. Most shops are open Mondays through Saturdays; store hours are 9 AM to 5:30 PM; to 9 PM on Thursdays and Fridays.

AUSTIN'S Derry's main department store, it has a restaurant. The Diamond (phone: 261817).

BOOKWORM Traditional Irish literature and recordings. Bishop St. (phone: 261616).

DONEGAL SHOP A good place to purchase the area's famous tweeds. 8 Shipquay St. (phone: 266928).

GORDON GALLERY The work of established Irish artists is for sale here. Ferryquay St. (phone: 266261).

ULSTER CERAMICS Pottery, kitchenware, tableware, Irish crystal, and table linen — all at factory shop prices. Springtown Industrial Estate, Buncrana Rd. (phone: 265742).

SPORTS AND FITNESS

BOATING Sailboats, rowboats, and power boats are available for hire along the East Bank 2 miles upstream from Craigavon Bridge. Contact *Prehen Boat Hires* (phone: 43405).

FISHING The fishing in the Foyle and its tributaries is legendary. Coarse fishing requires no license; a game rod license for salmon and trout (sea, brown, and rainbow) can be obtained from the *Foyle Fisheries Commission* (8 Victoria Rd.; phone: 42100). Sea fishing is possible from piers or boats. For more information, contact the fisheries commission; also see *Gone Fishing* in DIVERSIONS.

FITNESS CENTERS The Derry area has several public fitness centers offering swimming pools, squash courts, saunas, weight rooms, and other facilities. For information, contact the tourist board.

GOLF The 18-hole *City of Derry Golf Club,* which also has a 9-hole practice course, is sprawled scenically along the shores of the River Foyle. Open to the public, the course is in Prehen, 2 miles south of the city on the Strabane road (phone: 311496).

SOCCER *Brandywell Stadium* is home to the *Derry City Football Club,* which has won its way into the premier division of the League of Ireland. On Sundays when the team plays at home, the event attracts whole families and those of both religious persuasions to what is a highly popular outlet for civic pride. The stadium is in the Brandywell district. For ticket information, contact the *Derry City Football Club,* Crawford Sq. (phone: 262276).

THEATER

There is no established theater in Derry, but productions are mounted in St. Columb's Hall (seating 1,000) which serves several thriving amateur theater groups (Bishop St.; box office phone: 262880). The Guildhall (at the foot of Shipquay St.) periodically hosts full-scale dramatic productions, including premieres by Derry playwright Brian Friel. North of the city center, Magee College of the University of Ulster also stages theater productions (phone: 265621). Visitors can reserve tickets for most city events at the *Rialto Entertainment Centre* (Market St.; phone: 260516).

MUSIC

The city has an especially strong musical tradition, and there are still many families in which every member plays an instrument. In his song "The Town I Love So Well," Derryman Phil Coulter, composer and pianist, writes: "There was music there in the Derry air / Like a language that we all could understand. . . ." The Guildhall (at the foot of Shipquay St.) is the major city entertainment venue. Its lovely, acoustically superb assembly hall, which seats 700, is the site of performances by the *Ulster Orchestra,* as well as jazz concerts, organ recitals, cabaret, and other events. For schedule and ticket information contact the Derry City Council Marketing and Tourism Department (phone: 365151). The *Orchard Gallery* (Orchard St.; phone: 269675) also hosts varied musical events at St. Columb's Hall. For information on traditional Irish music venues, see *Sharing a Pint.*

Best in Town

CHECKING IN

Although there are no luxurious accommodations within Londonderry, there are several commendable properties in the immediate vicinity, some with restaurants. The ones listed as expensive will cost $100 or more per night for a double room with a traditional Irish breakfast; those rated as moderate range from $65 to $100 a night; and places described as inexpensive will cost under $65. Bed and breakfast accommodations in the area range from $30 to $50. The tourist board has information on availability. All telephone numbers are in the 504 area code unless otherwise indicated.

Beech Hill Country House This modern, upscale property with 12 rooms, all with private baths, is in a country setting, several miles from the city. There's a small, but fine, restaurant on the premises. About 3 miles north on the road to Ardmore. 32 Ardmore Rd. (phone: 49279; fax: 45366).

Everglades Set amid landscaped gardens and facing the Foyle, 2 miles south of the city, this modern, 2-story, 52-room property is the best place to stay near Londonderry. It offers 24-hour room service; elegant, moderately priced dining; a bar lounge; and other amenities. Prehen Rd., across the Foyle (phone: 46722; fax: 49200).

MODERATE

Broomhill House A former country house, it is refurbished inside and out with a modern addition; and is located not far from the Foyle Bridge, in a rural setting in the Waterside section of the city. All 42 rooms have private baths, central heating, TV sets, and telephones. Nonsmoking rooms are available. There's a restaurant on the premises. Limavady Rd. (phone: 47995).

Glen House This cozy place is on the tree-lined main street of a pretty village that was founded by the Grocers' Company during the Plantation era and retains an English appearance. It is a full-service, 16-room hotel with a fine, moderately priced restaurant. Nine miles northeast of Londonderry, on the road to Limavady. 9 Main St., Eglinton (phone: 810527).

INEXPENSIVE

White Horse Inn Recently renovated, this modern 43-room hotel is built around an old pub. Its *Grille Bar* restaurant is a local favorite. Northeast of Derry on the road to Limavady. 68 Clooney Rd., Campsie (phone: 860606; fax: 860371).

EATING OUT

Regional food specialties include Foyle salmon, Donegal lobster, locally cured Londonderry ham and bacon, and Ballarena smoked fish. A three-course meal for two, including service and VAT but not beverages, costs $35 to $50 in the moderate range, and $20 to $35 is inexpensive. All telephone numbers are in the 504 area code unless otherwise indicated.

MODERATE

Brown's This historic, renovated railway station, with old beams and an all-glass roof, houses a formal restaurant as well as an informal bistro; both serve European and vegetarian dishes. Open daily; closed Mondays and Saturdays for lunch. Reservations unnecessary. MasterCard and Visa accepted. At the far side of the Craigavon Bridge. 1 Victoria Rd. (phone: 45180).

Waterfoot Though unprepossessing outside, this hotel-restaurant is popular with friendly Derry folk, who come here for the good food, good value, and a good time. Set in the Waterside district near the Foyle Bridge, the inn overlooks the river and the city. Open Mondays through Saturdays for lunch; Sundays for dinner. Reservations unnecessary. Major credit cards accepted. Caw Roundabout, 14 Clooney Rd. (phone: 45500).

Bells An attractive 3-floor restaurant that offers panoramic views of the River Foyle and has a broad menu featuring fresh seafood and rack of lamb. Also on the premises is *Johnny B's,* an informal wine bar in the cellar that serves inexpensive lunches and dinners. Open daily for lunch and dinner. Reservations advised. Major credit cards accepted. Just past the *City of Derry Golf Club.* 59 Victoria Rd. (phone: 311500).

India House This local favorite features modern Indian decor replete with brass and other artifacts, and a menu that includes traditional curry dishes as well as tandoori barbecue. Open daily for dinner. Reservations unnecessary. MasterCard and Visa accepted. 51 Carlisle Rd. (phone: 260532).

SHARING A PINT

Derry offers limited nightlife, but a pub crawl along pedestrians-only Waterloo Street is a popular activity. Many pubs either have scheduled performances or informal sessions of traditional Irish music. *Gweedore Bar* (59 Waterloo St.; phone: 263513) has the best Irish music in town. Also try *Castle Bar* (26 Waterloo St.; phone: 263118), which features live traditional Irish music several evenings a week. The *Phoenix Bar* (10 Park Ave.; phone: 268978) and *Dungloe Bar* (41 Waterloo St.; phone: 267716) offer Irish airs. For a quiet atmosphere, stop in *Cole's Bar* (Strand Rd.; phone: 265308), with a wood and stained glass decor. The *Metro* (3 Bank Pl.; phone: 267401) offers drinks and pub grub (served daily for lunch) in a relaxed setting. The *Linenhall Bar* (Market St.; phone: 371665) is another quiet, comfortable place for a good pub lunch. Many of the city's pubs are renowned for their lively quiz evenings, during which local teams pit their wits against each other. Pubs serve drinks until 11 PM, with a half hour's "drinking up" time; they are now allowed to open on Sundays from 12:30 to 2:30 PM and 7 to 10 PM.

Sligo City

Set on a verdant, wooded plain, Sligo City sprawls across the banks of a river that rushes from Lough Gill to the Atlantic Ocean. On all but its ocean side, timeless mountains rise up to form majestic ramparts against the ever-changing western sky. Here, amid these pleasantly watered woodlands and mighty-shouldered mountains, William Butler Yeats, Ireland's greatest poet, spent childhood summers. Long before he won the Nobel Prize for Literature in 1923, Yeats discovered the poetic soul of Ireland's Celtic past. That past, with its mystical legends and sagas of heroic deeds, haunts the enchanted countryside and crowds the pavements of Sligo City itself. The country dominates the town: While walking the city streets, it's impossible to ignore its brooding presence. On a clear day, the mountain called Ben Bulben stands like a guardian over the town and looks across the bay to Knocknarea, the hill where Queen Maeve is said to be buried. The surrounding hills seem to link these two odd-shaped mountains.

Unlike some other Irish cities, Sligo has no abundance of relics and monuments to chronicle the march of its history, but there is a truly astonishing record of its prehistoric past nearby. Just 2 miles south of the city, at Carrowmore, lies a sprawling megalithic burial ground dating from before the Bronze Age. Its primitive rock monuments provide dramatic evidence that here, long ago, there lived a race of people capable of transporting massive boulders and raising enormous slabs of stone to mark the resting place of their dead. Rising straight up from this prehistoric home of the dead is the noble, flat-topped mountain of Knocknarea (pronounced Knock-na-*ray*), "the hill of the monarchs," surmounted by a rock cairn reputed to be the tomb of Queen Maeve, or Medb, of Connacht, the province in which Sligo is located. According to Celtic myth, Maeve was the powerful queen who sent her warriors into the province of Ulster to capture a prized bull in the celebrated Cattle Raid of Cooley. She is mentioned as Queen Mab in Shakespeare's *Romeo and Juliet,* and, for all the exotic and fanciful legends that surround her, she probably really did exist.

Inishmurray, the only true island off the coast of Sligo, has been inhabited from prehistoric to modern times. It was the site of a monastic community that was founded in the 6th century and that flourished until Elizabethan times.

One of the first mentions of Sligo in old records tells of a raid by Vikings in the 9th century. It is probable, however, that the settlement on the banks of, and named after, the River Sligeach (now called the Garavogue) had been functioning for many years before it came to the attention of the Norse pirates who were constant visitors to all the coasts of Ireland.

In the 13th century, an Anglo-Norman named Maurice Fitzgerald built a castle at the eastern end of what now is called Castle Street. The De Burgo clan, who wielded great power along the western coast, also built a castle in Sligo in 1301. No trace of either fortress can be found today.

The most solid relic of Sligo's medieval past is the Dominican abbey, constructed in 1252. The abbey was severely damaged in a fire in 1414, but that was nothing compared to what happened when Cromwell's soldiers, on their rampage of terror across Ireland, arrived in 1641. They not only set fire to the abbey but killed all the friars and then ran amok through the city streets.

Throughout the 19th century, Sligo was one of the busiest ports in Ireland, with as many as 600 ships steaming in and out of the harbor every year. During the famine in the 1840s, thousands of Irish emigrants bound for North America sailed from Sligo, many risking their lives on the notorious "coffin ships," so named because of the appalling conditions on board. Nowadays, Sligo's sea traffic has dwindled to a few small freighters that irregularly call at the port.

From the end of the 17th century to the present, the course of events in Sligo has, for the most part, been remarkably harmonious and trouble-free. Even during the War of Independence, which led to the British departure from the southern part of Ireland in the 1920s, the city managed to avoid much of the violence that convulsed the island.

Today Sligo is a prosperous and thriving city with a progressive vision of its future as well as a keen appreciation of the colorful richness of its past. In recent years, the leaders and residents of the city have been involved in an all-out effort to improve its appearance. This effort is reflected in ways large and small — from the increase in the number of flowerpots placed in windows to the preservation and restoration of many original 19th-century shopfronts. And thanks to the Hughes Bridge over the Garavogue, traffic congestion has eased in town and it is a pleasant place to stroll once again.

Sligo At-a-Glance

SEEING THE CITY

Sligo City lies at the bottom of a bowl formed by spectacular and oddly shaped mountains — some bearing a striking resemblance to the mesas of America's West. The view when approaching the town on Pearse Road is quite beautiful. Another excellent panorama may be seen from the top of Knocknarea, not a difficult climb if approached from the inland side. From on high, Sligo's setting, with its lakes and woodlands and the great bay opening out into the Atlantic, is unforgettable. For the fastest way into the hills, take N16 for 3 or 4 miles northeast and turn right into any of the three side roads encountered. The reward for this expedition is mountainous country of surpassing loveliness.

SPECIAL PLACES

With a population of 20,000, Sligo is one of Ireland's smallest cities, so it's not difficult to cover the whole place on foot in 2 to 3 hours. A printed guide and map, plotting out a tourist trail through the city, can be obtained at the Donegal-Leitrim-Sligo Regional Tourist Board (see *Tourist Information,* below). There is also a signposted 105-mile driving tour of the area that begins in the town. The tour covers the historic, literary, and scenic spots in the lovely countryside. In addition, minibus tours of Yeats Country depart daily in July and August from the tourist office. For additional information, contact guide John Houze (phone: 42747).

CITY CENTER

DOMINICAN ABBEY The ruins of the abbey, built in 1252, consist of choir, nave, and central tower. Much of the original cloisters also are still intact, as are several medieval windows, including the beautiful east window. Damage inflicted by Cromwell's Roundheads in 1641 has never been fully repaired, although the Irish government has carried out some restoration work in modern times. Abbey St. (ask at 6 Abbey St. for a key to the gate).

TOWN HALL An imposing edifice, designed in a graceful Italian Renaissance style, it was built in 1864 on a hill on Quay Street overlooking the once-busy harbor. It is thought that a Cromwellian fortress may have occupied the site originally. Inside, the Italian palatial theme is maintained with a broad sweeping stone stairway, tall pillars, and a high, arched ceiling. Quay St. (phone: 42141).

COURTHOUSE This handsome building of Donegal sandstone was built in 1878 to replace an older courthouse, part of which was incorporated into the new structure. At the height of the ravaging cholera plague that broke out in Sligo in 1832, the old courthouse was turned into a carpenter's shop for the manufacture of coffins. Teeling St. (phone: 42228 or 42429).

ST. JOHN'S CATHEDRAL (CHURCH OF IRELAND) This is the creation of a noted German architect, Richard Cassels, who designed many of Ireland's most distinguished buildings. Much of the original 1730 design has been distorted or wiped away altogether by renovation work carried out some 100 years later, but it is still a building of compelling interest. John Butler Yeats, the poet's father, was wed here in 1863, and the adjoining graveyard contains the remains of the poet's grandfather William Pollexfen. John St. (phone: 62263).

CATHEDRAL OF THE IMMACULATE CONCEPTION (ROMAN CATHOLIC) Another eminent architect, George Goldie of London, designed this fine Norman-style edifice built in 1875. The peal of its bells are to Sligo what the Bow Bells are to London; they chime on the quarter hour. Temple St. (phone: 61261).

YEATS STATUE Unveiled in May 1990 by the poet's son, Michael Yeats, this is a long overdue monument to Ireland's famous son. The whimsical bronze statue of Yeats poised mid-stride stands before the Bank of Ulster and looks across the river toward the Yeats Memorial Building. Sculptor Rowan Gillespie portrayed the poet wrapped in his words — lines from his poems cover the figure's billowing cape. Across Douglas Hyde Bridge, opposite the *Silver Swan* hotel.

YEATS MEMORIAL BUILDING This Victorian confection, formerly a bank, was given to the Yeats Society by the Allied Irish Bank in 1973. It now houses the offices of the society, which runs the *Yeats International Summer School* (see *Special Events*), and the *Sligo Art Gallery* (see *Museums*). There is an interesting library, and an audiovisual program on the life and times of W. B. Yeats is scheduled to debut this year. At Douglas Hyde Bridge (phone: 42693).

RIVERSIDE WALK This is a pleasant path around the center of town. It starts at the Douglas Hyde Bridge, which joins Wine Street to Stephen Street, and continues upstream along the waters of the Garavogue, crossing Thomas Street into Kennedy Parade (named after John F. Kennedy). The walk ends close to the Dominican abbey.

DOORLY PARK Continue upstream alongside the Garavogue on Riverside Walk to reach this spacious and tranquil woodland retreat close to Lough Gill. It offers splendid views of the surrounding mountains.

ENVIRONS

DRUMCLIFFE The parish of Drumcliffe, 4 miles north of Sligo on N15, is the most important shrine in Yeats country. The poet is buried here in what is one of the most visited cemeteries in Ireland. Yeats's great-grandfather had been rector in this church, set amidst magnificent scenery at the foot of Ben Bulben mountain. The church is on the right, just before the river, and Yeats's grave is just inside the main gate to the left. His epitaph is the final three lines of his poem, "Under Ben Bulben." Addressed to the Dananns, spectral riders said to haunt the valley between Knocknarea and Ben Bulben, it reads:

Cast a cold eye
On life, on death.
Horseman, pass by!

The fine Celtic cross in the churchyard dates from the 11th century. Across the road from the church lies the base of an unfinished round tower thought to have been started in the 6th century. Around the same time, St. Columba founded a monastery here that attracted scholars from many lands.

INISHMURRAY An excursion to this island, 4 miles off the northwest Sligo coast and about 12 miles from Sligo City, makes for a worthwhile day trip. Inishmurray, which was inhabited until 1947 (when it still had its own "king"), was the site of a monastic settlement established by St. Molaise in the 6th century. The ruins of the monastery are still there, along with a stone church and the "beehive" cells where the monks lived. Numerous ancient crosses and tombstones are found throughout the island. There is also a collection of *Clocha Breaca* (pronounced *Kluh*-ha *Brah*-ka), "cursing stones," which were used by the island's earlier pagan inhabitants to invoke misfortune on enemies. The embarkation point for Inishmurray is the tiny and lovely seaport of Mullaghmore. Take N15 north from Sligo to the village of Cliffoney, then turn left at the sign upon entering the village. In summer, boats make occasional trips to the island, weather permitting. Contact Mr. Lomax (phone: 66124) or Mr. McCallion (phone: 42391). Mullaghmore village itself is a charming old port. It has a splendid stretch of beach hugging the Atlantic, a popular gathering place in the hot days of summer.

CARROWMORE This is the oldest archaeological site in Ireland; it predates the pyramids of Egypt. The location of one of the largest megalithic graveyards in Europe, the site covers a square mile at the foot of Knocknarea Mountain. There are more than 40 tombs here, some dating from the neolithic or late Stone Age (4500–2300 BC), many undisturbed since they received the dead. There is an information center in a restored stone cottage nearby, where a slide show and guides bring the old stones to life. Open daily from 9:30 AM to 6:30 PM, mid-June to mid-September. Admission charge. Carrowmore is 2 miles southwest of Sligo on L132 at the foot Knocknarea Mountain; it is signposted from the town (phone: 61534).

Atop Knocknarea Mountain is a cairn that legend holds is the burial place of Queen Maeve of Connacht, although this story has never been tested by excavation. Local custom demands that climbers carry a stone up Knocknarea to leave on the massive cairn, and many climbers comply. To take a stone away is to invite the queen's wrath. For easiest access to and parking at Knocknarea, watch for signposts on L132.

LISSADELL HOUSE Set amid rolling wooded hills overlooking the Bay of Drumcliffe, this 19th-century Georgian structure is the childhood home of one of Ireland's greatest woman rebels, Countess Constance Markievicz of the Gore-Booth family. The countess took part in the 1916 insurrection, was imprisoned, and later became the first woman member of Dáil Eireann (the Irish Parliament). Yeats, an intimate friend of the Gore-Booths, often stayed at Lissadell. Members of the Gore-Booth family still live here, though it's getting a bit shabby around the edges. Open June 1 to September 1 from 10:30 AM to noon and 2 to 4:30 PM; closed Sundays. Admission charge. To reach Lissadell, travel north on N15, take the first left turn past

Drumcliffe, and drive through and beyond Carney for another 6 miles (phone: 63150).

HAZELWOOD A lushly wooded area on the northwest shore of Lough Gill, Hazelwood perches on a promontory that juts into the lake and is crisscrossed with shaded paths for walking. There are a number of picnic areas along the water's edge and in the woods, and an interesting display of sculpture among the trees. Take L16 east from Sligo for 3 miles and follow the signposts to the wood.

ROSSES POINT With two superb beaches and miles of sand dunes, this peninsula is Sligo's premier seaside resort. Much of Yeats's time in Sligo was spent at Rosses Point in Elsinore Lodge, the residence of his cousins, the Middletons, a wealthy merchant family. Just offshore on a stone pedestal in the sea stands the famous statue of the Metal Man, a 12-foot-high sailor forever pointing to the deepest part of the channel to guide ships into Sligo harbor. In olden days, the area was notorious as a haunt of smugglers. L16 northwest from Sligo leads to Rosses Point.

CREEVYKEEL COURT TOMB A magnificent 3,000-year-old court tomb excavated in 1935 by a Harvard archaeologist, it contains several chambers and a gallery, all surrounded by a courtyard. Drive north on N15 to the village of Cliffoney and travel another 1½ miles on the same road to the tomb site, indicated by a signpost.

DOONEY ROCK This is a massive outcrop of rock, smothered in trees and rising dramatically above the southern shore of Lough Gill. A nature walk through the woods leads to the top of the rock and a spectacular view over the island-studded lake. 4 miles east of Sligo on L117.

STRANDHILL Because of the shifting sands and strong undertow, swimming is hazardous at Strandhill, a seaside resort famous for the towering Atlantic waves that crash on its long, curved beach. However, some people are willing to take the chance. Culleenamore Beach at Strandhill is a safe place to swim and a great place to surf. It's okay to gather and eat the cockles, too. Located 5 miles west of Sligo on L132.

GLENCAR One of the loveliest valleys in Ireland, and the setting of Yeats's "Stolen Child," Glencar has massive mountains crowding in on all sides, waterfalls spilling over precipices, and, at the bottom of the glen, a lake so clear that it reflects the tall trees growing in profusion around its banks. A small path leads up the mountain to the principal Glencar waterfall, which plunges 50 feet into a pool at the bottom of a cliff. Small, unpaved roads, splendid for hiking, run up into the mountains. Glencar Lake and the river that runs through are home to good-size salmon and sea trout in summer. Take N16 from Sligo; 8 miles out, turn left at the "Waterfall" signpost.

LOUGH GILL The lake immortalized in one of Yeats's most famous poems, "The Lake Isle of Innisfree," lies just east of Sligo City, linked to it by the River

Garavogue. The poetic Innisfree is only one of many wooded islands decorating its waters. Steep rocky cliffs carpeted in greenery rise from the south shore. To the north and west are the peaks of Ben Bulben and the Cuilcagh Mountains. For a land trip around the lake, travel 2 miles south of Sligo on N4, and turn left at the "Lough Gill" signpost onto L117. Watch for signposts to a *tobernault,* an ancient "holy well" where religious ceremonies were often conducted. Make another left at Dromahair onto L112, and 4 miles beyond, turn left again onto L16 back to Sligo. The best way to enjoy the lake is to rent a rowboat and spend the day exploring its inlets and islands. Contact Mr. O'Connor (phone: 64079). For another perspective, a water bus leaves twice daily in summer from Doorly Park in Sligo City and goes up the River Garavogue and across Lough Gill to Parke's Castle. The trip takes about 2 hours; contact George McGolderick (phone: 64266).

PARKE'S CASTLE This well-restored castle home was built as a "plantation" under the system used by the English to subdue Ireland for the crown. English settlers were "planted" in strategic locations and given the land in return for service to the English monarch. Originally built in the early 1600s right on the edge of Lough Gill, the castle offers a glimpse into the good life of the age, which was in fact pretty rough by modern standards. Tours are given, and an enlightening audiovisual program describes the castle and other points of historical interest in the area. There's also a tearoom. Open the weekend nearest *St. Patrick's Day, Easter* weekend, and Tuesdays through Sundays in June through August from 9:30 AM to 6:30 PM. Admission charge. In County Leitrim, about 7 miles from Sligo on the road to Dromahair. Signposted from the center of town. The castle is on the Lough Gill drive (phone: 64149).

Sources and Resources

TOURIST INFORMATION

The prime source for all information on Sligo City and the surrounding area is the headquarters of the Donegal-Leitrim-Sligo Regional Tourist Board (Aras Reddin, Temple St.; phone: 61201). A handbook describing a signposted walking tour of the city is for sale here, along with a good selection of local maps. In July and August, guided walking tours of the city start from Aras Reddin at 11 AM Mondays through Saturdays. Guided tours at other times also can be arranged. *Keohane's Bookshop* (Castle St.; phone: 42597) stocks the most books about Sligo, its lore, and history. For in-depth background on the area, ask for *O'Rorke's History of Sligo* in the County Library (Stephen St.; phone: 42212).

Sligo is part of the National Genealogical Project, a major initiative in the process of being developed in the Republic and Northern Ireland to create a network of research centers throughout the island to assist visitors in tracing their Irish roots. The project will feature a computer database of Irish family records. Contact the *Sligo Family Research Society* via the tourist office for details.

LOCAL COVERAGE The *Sligo Champion* is the definitive local newspaper, and an essential source of information about musical events. *Sligo Weekender,* a free paper consisting mainly of advertising, can be picked up at most newsstands and hotel reception desks.

TELEPHONE The area code for Sligo City and the immediate vicinity is 71. When calling from within the Republic of Ireland, dial 071 before the local number.

GETTING AROUND

Walking is the recommended method of seeing the city and that employed by most of its inhabitants. Other modes of transportation, however, are available.

AIRPORT There are flights to and from Dublin Airport every day. In summer, pleasure and sightseeing trips in small craft are offered. The airport is in Strandhill, 5 miles west of Sligo on L132 (phone: 68280).

BICYCLE In good weather, biking is a marvelous way to see the city and countryside. Bikes can be hired for any length of time from *Conway Bros.* (High St.; phone: 61370), *Eden Hill Hostel* (Pearse Rd.; phone: 43204), or *Gary's Cycles* (Quay St.; phone: 45418).

BUS Excellent bus service runs to all parts of Sligo. Buses leave regularly from the bus depot at the railway station (Lord Edward St.; phone: 60066). This is also the terminal for provincial bus services, with service to all parts of the Republic and Northern Ireland.

CAR RENTAL It is best to book a car upon arriving in Ireland, either at Shannon Airport or in Dublin. In Sligo, cars can be hired from *Avis/Johnson & Perrott* (at the airport; phone: 68280), *O'Mara* (1 Teeling St.; phone: 44068), and *Murray's/Europcar* (at the airport; phone: 68400).

TAXI There are no cruising taxis or cabstands in Sligo, but it is possible to call a taxi from *City Cabs* (phone: 45577), *Feehily Executive Cabs* (phone: 43000), *Terry McTiernan* (phone: 45725), and *Ace Cabs* (phone: 44444).

TRAIN The only passenger rail service operating in Sligo is to and from Dublin, with stops along the line. There are three trains each way (morning, early afternoon, and early evening) Mondays through Sundays. The train station is on Lord Edward Street (phone: 69888).

SPECIAL EVENTS

The poet W. B. Yeats spent a great deal of his childhood in County Sligo, and his feelings for the extraordinarily beautiful scenery that surrounded him here infuse his work, to which an annual event devotes itself fairly seriously.

HEAD OF THE CLASS

Yeats International Summer School Considering the Yeatsian influence that permeates Sligo, it's not surprising that the major annual event is the *Yeats International Summer School* and its attendant cultural festival. Started in 1958, the summer school now attracts Yeatsian scholars from all over the world, with Americans predominating. For 2 weeks every August, students who enroll in the school immerse themselves in a wide range of activities and happenings, from the lighthearted to the heavily studious, all having some connection to the poet. Patrick Sheeran of University College, Galway, is the current director of the summer school, and classes and discussions are led by veteran faculty members from Harvard, University College (Dublin), as well as an annual crop of new lecturers. Performances of Yeats's plays, tours of the countryside, and relaxed evenings in the hospitable pubs of Sligo City provide relaxing diversions from the lively intellectual stimulation. Surprise visits by Ireland's leading literary types are not uncommon. Contact the Secretary, *Yeats Society,* Yeats Memorial Building, Douglas Hyde Bridge (phone: 42693 or 60097).

Another noteworthy summer event is the *Warriors' Run,* a footrace from Strandhill to the cairn at the top of Knocknarea. There's also a triathalon. Contact the tourist office for dates. The *Sligo Arts Festival* is held for 10 days in late summer. All of the performing arts are showcased: theater, music (classical, jazz, and traditional Irish), and dance. In addition, street festivals and buskers (wandering minstrels) liven up the town. For information, call 69802.

MUSEUMS

The *Sligo County Museum* and the *Municipal Art Gallery* share the same buildings attached to the County Library (Stephen St.; phone: 42212). The *County Museum* contains an informative array of objects and artifacts dating from Sligo's richly endowed prehistoric period. The *Municipal Art Gallery* has a fairly comprehensive collection of works by many of Ireland's major artists, including Jack Yeats (the poet's brother), John B. Yeats (their father), Paul Henry, Sean Keating, Charles Lamb, and Evie Hone. In addition, throughout the year various traveling exhibitions by local, national, and international artists are held at the *Sligo Art Gallery,* located in the Yeats Memorial Building (phone: 45847).

SHOPPING

Although the shopping in Sligo is not as varied as it is in Galway, the city has a number of fine shops that sell Irish-made products. Stores are generally closed on Sundays.

BRODERICK'S ON THE CORNER A small shop filled with crystal, china, and other beautiful breakables for the home. O'Connell St., on the corner opposite the post office (phone: 42509).

CARRAIG DONN This place offers a wonderful selection of Irish sweaters and knitwear; some of the merchandise is hand-knit. 41 O'Connell St. (phone: 44158)

COSGROVE'S An old-fashioned food emporium behind an original 19th-century façade. This is the perfect place to pick up picnic fixings — wild Irish salmon, baked ham, roast lamb, Irish cheeses, salads, and handmade Irish chocolates. 32 Market St. (phone: 42809).

THE GOURMET SHOP Tasty take-away from a chef trained by Darina Allen, Ireland's food guru and the daughter-in-law of Myrtle Allen, the doyenne of Irish cooking. 10 John St. (phone: 44617).

HENRY LYONS & CO. An old-fashioned "draper" (purveyor of fabric, linen, and home furnishings), with a good selection of Irish crafts and souvenirs and a pleasant café upstairs. Wine St. (phone: 42616, store; 42969, café).

JOSEPH MARTIN & SON An internationally known tailor shop where traditional hand-sewn methods are still used. Many prominent Americans are among its clientele. Wine St. (phone: 62257).

KATE'S KITCHEN At the front of this shop is a well-stocked *Crabtree & Evelyn* boutique. In the rear is a counter where delicious salads and casseroles can be purchased to take away for a beach picnic. 24 Market St. (phone: 43022).

KEOHANE'S BOOKSHOP A solid collection of Irish literature and a good source for works written by the lecturers at the *Yeats International Summer School*. Castle St. (phone: 42597).

MARKET YARD This attractive shopping center stands where once there were only derelict buildings. The crafts shop is particularly interesting. At the top of Harmony Hill, which is a continuation of O'Connell St.

MIKE QUIRKE Once a butcher with a yen for carving, Mr. Quirke has given up meat for wood. The butcher's counter is still here, but now it's covered with haunting carvings of legendary and historical local characters. Wine St. (phone: 42624).

MULLANEY BROS. A large clothing store with a superior line of Irish tweeds and woolens. 9 O'Connell St. (phone: 43278).

MY LADY ART GALLERY AND BOOKSHOP With this many dusty old tomes to browse among, there's always a chance of finding something valuable. A nice collection of paintings is at the rear of the shop. Castle St. (phone: 42723).

P.J. DOONEY & SON Mr. Dooney's sweaters and tweed hats are top quality. 36 O'Connell St. (phone: 42274).

W.A. & A.F. WOODS A vast, old-fashioned store that stocks about everything, from nail files to original paintings. 7 Castle St. (phone: 42021).

WEHRLY BROS. Beautifully designed gold and silver objects and elegant glassware are found in this high-quality jewelry shop with a vintage Edwardian storefront. 3 O'Connell St. (phone: 42252).

SPORTS AND FITNESS

BOATING AND SAILING The *Sligo Yacht Club* (Rosses Point, at Deadman's Point just beyond the pier; phone: 77168) is the center for sailing and other seafaring activities on the bay. Visitors are always welcome. For information on cruising and rowboating on Lough Gill, see *Special Places*.

FALCONRY Learn the ancient skill of hunting with birds of prey with Michael and Linsey Devlin at their lovely 18th-century house. Two-day introductory lessons and 5-day sporting courses are offered. Quarryfield House, Ballymote (phone: 83211).

FISHING Lough Gill is a picturesque setting in which to fish for salmon, most plentiful during May. In late June and July, sea trout also run up into the lake. The River Garavogue, which runs through Lough Gill and into Sligo City, also has good fishing beats. A license is required to fish for salmon and all other sea trout. For fishing on Lough Gill, contact Cristy Hynes, Treasurer, *The Sligo Anglers* (phone: 60834). For information on fishing elsewhere, contact *Barton Smith's Sport Shop* (Hyde Bridge; phone: 42356). For fishing boats, contact Peter Henny at the *Blue Lagoon* (phone: 45407 or 45230). For additional details, see *Gone Fishing* in DIVERSIONS.

FITNESS The *Sligo Sports Centre* (phone: 60539) has a fully equipped gym for workouts, and badminton courts. It's at Cleveragh, southeast of the city beside the racecourse; travel south on Pearse Road for a half-mile and bear left at the junction.

GOLF Sligo has several places to set your spikes, including one extraordinary layout.

TOP TEE-OFF SPOT

County Sligo Golf Club Popularly known as *Rosses Point,* this is one of Ireland's premier 18-hole golf courses. Every *Easter* it hosts the *West of Ireland Amateur Open Championship.* How one plays here depends a lot on which way the prevailing hurricane happens to be blowing. *Rosses Point* is not quite as tight a course as the other Irish monsters, and some of its greens are even reachable by mere mortals in regulation figures. Chances are that this is the Irish golf course where spirits (not scores) will soar.

Visitors are welcome. Take L16 northwest from the city. Beside the sea at Rosses Point (phone: 77186; fax: 77134).

Other courses in the area include the *Enniscrone Golf Club* (phone: 96-36297), a championship 18-hole links course on Killala Bay, about 35 miles from Sligo along a scenic drive. It's a bit out of the way, but definitely worth the trip. A less exacting 18-hole course, ideal for duffers, is at the *Strandhill Golf Club* (12 miles west on L132; phone: 68188). Easier still is *Bertie's Pitch-and-Putt* — 18 holes with a driving range (about a mile from Sligo on N15; phone: 43869).

HORSEBACK RIDING Riding and trekking at all levels, and instruction if necessary, are available at the *Moneygold Riding Centre* (Grange; phone: 63337) and the *Sligo Equitation Company* (Carrowmore, 2 miles southwest on L132; phone: 62758 or 61353). *Horse Holiday Farm Ltd.* offers residential riding programs or trail riding for experienced riders. Contact Colette and Tilman Anhold, Grange, County Sligo (phone: 66152; fax: 66400). Also see *Horsing Around* in DIVERSIONS.

TENNIS The *Sligo Tennis Club* has 6 outdoor, floodlit courts as well as 4 badminton courts and 4 squash courts. Visitors are welcome; reservations are advised. One mile from Sligo on N15 (phone: 62580).

THEATER

Named after an enchanted well from a Yeats poem, the *Hawk's Well Theatre* (Temple St., adjoining the tourist board headquarters; phone: 61526) hosts productions by the local *Sligo Drama Circle* and by visiting companies throughout the year. The *Factory* presents plays in an old warehouse on Quay St. (phone: 70431). Contact the tourist office for schedules.

MUSIC

Most musical events, except during the *Sligo Arts Festival* (see *Special Events*), are confined to singing pubs, which bring in various folk and pop groups (see *Sharing a Pint*). *McLynn's* (Old Market St.; phone: 42088) and the *Yeats Tavern* (Drumcliffe; no phone) are two popular venues. Consult the local newspapers for details. Visits by classical performers are infrequent.

The *South Sligo Summer School,* which is held in mid-July, offers a week of lessons in traditional Irish instruments, dancing, and singing. The school will arrange for accommodations upon request. Contact Rita Flannery, Tubbercurry, County Sligo (phone: 85010).

The new *Irish Music Cultural Center* (no phone) in the village of Ballintogher offers exhibits on Sligo's musical heritage, and traditional entertainment. Take the Lough Gill drive, southeast of Sligo City.

NIGHTCLUBS AND NIGHTLIFE

Except for the city's dance clubs and after-hours pubs, Sligo packs up early. *Xanadu's* (Teeling St.; no phone), a disco, pulls in mostly a young crowd. Members of the thirty-something set should feel at home in the *Oasis* nightclub at the *Blue Lagoon Saloon* (Riverside; phone: 42530), which often augments the dance beat with big-time acts. A popular spot that attracts a lively mix of people is *Toff's* nightclub at the *Embassy* (Kennedy Parade; phone: 61250). *Do Da's* in the *Southern* hotel has country music on Saturday nights year-round.

Best in Town

CHECKING IN

While there are only a few hotels in and around the city, most are very comfortable and offer good value for the money. Most also include the traditional Irish breakfast in their rate. A double room at a place listed as expensive will charge from $100 to $150; a hotel described as moderate will charge $60 to $100; and an inexpensive place, less than $60. All telephone numbers are in the 71 area code unless otherwise indicated.

For an unforgettable experience, we begin with our favorites, followed by our cost and quality choices, listed by price category.

SPECIAL HAVENS

Coopershill You'll feel like a lord (or lady) in this beautiful Georgian house set on 500 acres just 11 miles south of Sligo. Peacocks roam the lawn, lambs gambol across the fields, and a resident dog and either Brian or Lindy O'Hara come out to greet you at the sound of your wheels on the gravel. The 7 beautifully furnished guestrooms all have private baths, and beds come equipped with electric blankets, very welcome on chilly nights. The dining room, with it 14-foot-high ceilings, manages to feel elegant and cozy at the same time. Guests usually dine "at home," enjoying the set menu dinners prepared by Lindy. The estate includes a river, and the O'Haras can outfit guests for a bit of fishing if they arrive unprepared. Opportunities for golf (four 18-hole courses are within an hour's drive) and horseback riding are also nearby. Open March 15 to mid-November. Major credit cards accepted. Take N17 (the Dublin road) south to Collooney, head south on N4 to Drumfin, then follow the signposts. Rivertown (phone: 65108; 800-223-6510 from the US; fax: 65466).

Cromleach Lodge Country House This chalet-like house sits on a ridge overlooking Lough Arrow and rolling hills filled with ancient sites (a dolmen stands directly behind the grounds). Now in its fifth season, this place manages to be both luxurious (and pricey) and homey. Owners Moira and Christy

Tighe provide guests with a guidebook of local sights, as well as other thoughtful personal services. The 10 large bedrooms all have lovely views, as well as huge and comfortable beds, mini-bars, coffee/tea makers, and other welcome amenities. Half of the rooms are reserved for nonsmokers, and there are separate smoking and nonsmoking lounges as well. Sligo residents think nothing of driving the 20 miles from town for one of Moira's delicious dinners (see *Eating Out*). Open year-round. Major credit cards accepted. Take N17 (the Dublin road) south to Collooney, head south on N4 to Castlebaldwin, then follow the signposts. Ballindoon, Castlebaldwin, Boyle (phone: 65155; fax: 65455).

EXPENSIVE

Ballincar House Originally an old country house, this establishment is set in a wooded demesne, with 6 acres of magnificent gardens and views of the Atlantic. The 25 rooms each have a TV set, telephone, and private bath. The property also has a tennis court, a sauna, a snooker room, a solarium, and a good restaurant (see *Eating Out*). Fishing, golf, and shooting excursions can be arranged in season. Open year-round. Rosses Point Rd. (phone: 45361; fax: 44198).

Markree Castle A Gothic gateway leads to this stately 17th-century residence, which has been converted into a luxurious 14-room hostelry. The Cooper family has lived here since 1640. Recent renovations have preserved luster and comfort without sacrificing character; the dining room, for example, has been restored to its original gilt. Horseback riding and golf at two 18-hole courses nearby can be arranged. The hotel is the site of the celebrated *Knockmuldowney* restaurant (see *Eating Out*). Collooney, 7 miles south of Sligo City on N17 (phone: 67800; 800-223-6510 from the US; fax: 67840).

Silver Swan In the city center and perched above the rapids of the River Garavogue, this is a convenient place to stay. Recent renovations and an expansion have added 6 new guestrooms, bringing the total to 30. All have TV sets and telephones; 6 have Jacuzzis. The food served in the *Cygnet Room* restaurant is good (see *Eating Out*). Open year-round. Hyde Bridge (phone: 43231; fax: 43232).

Sligo Park Pleasantly set on the edge of town, this competently run, modern hostelry has 117 comfortable rooms, each with a phone, TV set, bath, and shower. The leisure center has an indoor pool, a whirlpool, a steamroom, a sauna, a gym, and 2 outdoor tennis courts. The *Hazelwood Room* serves good chicken and fish dishes and fresh vegetables. Restaurant reservations advised. Open year-round. Pearse Rd. (phone: 60291; fax: 69556).

Southern This refurbished gracious old hotel was once part of the railway chain of hotels that encircled Ireland. The 65 rooms are comfortable, the lobby fireplaces are usually cheerfully aglow, and the gardens are lovely. Guests also enjoy delicious meals at *The Garden* restaurant. The leisure center includes an indoor heated pool, squash courts, and a gym. Open year-round. Lord Edward St. (phone: 62101; fax: 60328).

Temple House A dream of a Georgian mansion complete with original furnishings, lots of family portraits, an authentic "water closet," and 1,000 acres of rolling land studded with lakes and streams. There are only 5 rooms (all with private baths) and they vary in size from enormous to simply large. Members of the Perceval family have lived here since 1665. The current occupants run an organic farm on the estate and serve the bounty of it at their table. They will happily escort guests to traditional music sessions in the area. Open April through November. In Ballymote, 9 miles south of Sligo, signposted from N19 (phone: 83329; fax: 83808).

Yeats Country Hotel On a mile-long stretch of beach and sand dunes, this 79-room property has tennis courts and is near a fabled local golf course. In summer, this place is a favorite of families with children. Open mid-March through December. Rosses Point; take L16 northwest from Sligo (phone: 77211; fax: 77203).

MODERATE

Ocean View Adjacent to the *Strandhill Golf Club,* this family-run establishment is a convenient lodging place for golfers. The 20 refurbished rooms are simple and straightforward. The food served in the dining room is quite good. Open March to December. Strandhill (phone: 68009).

INEXPENSIVE

Diamond's Bed and Breakfast This comfortable establishment, run by Mrs. Lily Diamond, has 5 rooms, all with private baths. It's just over a mile from town on N15, the Donegal road. Lisadorn, Lisnalurg (phone: 43417).

EATING OUT

The better restaurants in and around Sligo are included here. One or two are outstanding in any context. Expect to pay over $70 for dinner for two (excluding wine, drinks, and tips) at places listed as expensive; from $45 to $65 at places described as moderate; and less than $45 at an inexpensive place. All telephone numbers are in the 71 area code unless otherwise indicated.

EXPENSIVE

Ballincar House Overlooking the hotel's gardens, this restaurant specializes in seafood, especially lobster and salmon. Open daily for lunch and dinner. Reservations necessary. Major credit cards accepted. Rosses Point Rd. (phone: 45361).

Cromleach Lodge Country House It's well worth the 20-mile drive from Sligo to sample the culinary delights served here. Among chef Moira Tighe's specialties are wild Lough Gill salmon, veal with red and yellow pepper sauce, homemade ice cream, and chocolate terrine. The atmosphere is welcoming and elegant and the view over Lough Arrow is beautiful. Open daily for dinner. Reservations necessary. Major credit cards accepted. Take N17 (the Dublin road) south to Collooney, head south on N4 to Castlebaldwin, then follow the signposts. Ballindoon, Castlebaldwin, Boyle (phone: 65155; fax: 65455).

Cygnet Room Offering panoramic views of the River Garavogue, the *Silver Swan* hotel's dining room offers seafood, as well as US steaks and chops. Open daily for breakfast, lunch, and dinner. Reservations advised. Major credit cards accepted. Hyde Bridge (phone: 43232).

Knockmuldowney Originally in Culleenamore, this wonderful dining establishment is now located in the *Markree Castle* hotel. The food continues to be outstanding; highlights on the menu are fresh game and fish. Vegetables and fruit are homegrown. Open daily for lunch and dinner. Reservations necessary. Major credit cards accepted. Collooney, 7 miles south of Sligo City on N17 (phone: 67800).

Moorings Old timbers and ships' lanterns give a salty tang of the sea to this inn specializing in seafood served with flair. The lobster is particularly good. Open for dinner Tuesdays through Sundays; lunch is also served on Sundays. Reservations necessary. Major credit cards accepted. Rosses Point; take L16 northwest of the city (phone: 77112).

MODERATE

Eithne's This place was once the church curate's house. Seafood is a specialty, which is not surprising given that this eatery faces the seafront in the hamlet of Mullachmore. Open daily for lunch and dinner in summer; closed the rest of the year. Reservations necessary. MasterCard and Visa accepted. Sixteen miles from Sligo on the Donegal road, in Mullachmore (phone: 66407).

Gulliver's A popular, noisy eatery that serves a variety of food from pizza and burgers to curry and seafood dishes. It gets very crowded in summer. Open 10 AM to midnight Mondays through Saturdays; 12:30 to 2 PM Sundays. Reservations advised. MasterCard and Visa accepted. Grattan St. (phone: 42030).

Laura's This pub in Carney, on the way to Lissadell, serves tasty seafood. A restaurant is open daily for dinner in the summer, but the pub is open year-round. Reservations advised. No credit cards accepted. Five miles north of Sligo on N16 (phone: 63056).

Truffles Esoteric pizza is the big attraction at this eatery, a series of cozy rooms painted in sunny tones. The smoked salmon "pie" is especially popular. The menu also features fresh salads and Irish cheeses. Open 5 to 10:30 PM; Sundays to 10 PM; closed Mondays. There is a wine bar upstairs. It's open from 5 PM to midnight; closed Sundays. Reservations unnecessary. Major credit cards accepted. The Mall (phone: 44226).

INEXPENSIVE

The Cottage Tasty hot lunches and a salad bar are featured at this upstairs restaurant. Open for lunch only; closed Sundays. No reservations. No credit cards accepted. 4 Castle St. (phone: 45319).

SHARING A PINT

The most famous pub in Sligo is *Hargadon's* (4 O'Connell St.; 70933), more than a century old, with ancient mahogany counters, drawers, snugs, and whiskey mirrors. The pub lunch is popular and visitors should be sure to stop here. For good Irish music, try *McLynn's* (Old Market St.; phone: 42088) or *Yeats Tavern* (Drumcliffe; phone: 63117), which also serves especially good lunches. The *Leitrim Bar* (The Mall; phone: 43721) has music on Thursday nights; and the *Trades' Club* (Castle St.; no phone) has an Irish night on Tuesdays year-round. The *Thatch* (phone: 67288) in Ballisodare, 5 miles south of Sligo, jumps on Tuesday and Thursday nights. A bit farther away, about 20 miles south on N17, *Killoran's Pub* (phone: 85111) in Tubbercurry puts on wingdings of traditional Irish nights on Thursdays from June to September. Besides lots of music, the evening includes singing, dancing, butter churning, boxty (a traditional potato pancake that's rolled around a variety of fillings) making, displays of traditional clothing and cooking implements, and storytelling. Everyone participates in all the activities. It's corny, but lots of fun. The *May Queen,* also in Tubbercurry (phone: 85075), frequently has set dancing and music.

Waterford City

Waterford is a gentle city of Georgian doorways and back streets with lilting names like Lady Lane. It stretches for a bit more than half a mile along the southern bank of the River Suir, well up a long inlet from the sea, and during the 17th century its harbor was one of the busiest in the country.

The city's most famous landmark is a remnant of Viking times. Sitric the Dane is credited with fortifying the site of the city in the ninth century, and Reginald the Dane, a descendant of Sitric, is believed to have strengthened the fortifications in 1003 by erecting what has since become known as Reginald's Tower. Along with the city walls and two other towers, Reginald's Tower protected the city first from invasion by the Celts and later, when the Norsemen and Celts put aside their differences to join forces against a common enemy, from the Normans.

The Normans finally did take Waterford in 1170, in the person of Richard de Clare, an emissary of Henry II of England. De Clare was better known as Strongbow, for the sureness of his weapons and tactics, and his victory over the city's defenders was both an easy and a far-reaching one. The capture of Waterford was the beginning of the Anglo-Norman domination of Ireland. Strongbow's marriage shortly thereafter to Eva, the daughter of Dermot MacMurrough, the Irish King of Leinster, consolidated the position of the conquering Normans. This fateful event, too, took place in Waterford, reputedly in Reginald's Tower (though the original Viking cathedral, predecessor of Christ Church Cathedral, may have been the actual site).

King John granted the city its first charter in 1205, and for the next several centuries Waterford was intensely loyal to the English Crown. Henry VII gave it its motto, "Unconquered City," in the 15th century, in gratitude for its successful efforts in fighting off attacks by two pretenders to his throne. But loyalty to the English king in temporal matters did not extend to recognition of the crown's supremacy in the area of religious belief. The city remained Catholic in the 16th century, and because of this, its charter was eventually withdrawn and its Catholic citizens suffered greatly during the Cromwellian sieges of the mid-17th century. The city's churches and extensive abbeys were closed and confiscated, and many Catholics were sent as slaves to the West Indies.

In the 18th century, thanks to its bustling harbor, Waterford experienced a burst of development and began to outgrow its medieval dimensions. The old Waterford Glass Factory was founded in 1783, and the beautiful cut lead crystal it produced quickly gained renown. Graceful Georgian homes belonging to the merchant class began to appear along the Mall, and John Roberts, an architect responsible for many of the city's elegant structures, was at work designing the public buildings and churches — including City Hall and the Catholic and Protestant cathedrals — that are among the city's most prominent landmarks. The Protestant cathedral, which was erected between 1773 and 1779 on the site of a much earlier church, is a stately monument to Waterford's rich Protestant families, some of whom were carried up the slight incline into Cathedral Square in sedan chairs.

Today, most visitors come to Waterford to tour the glass factory and to browse through the gift shops around the quays. But there are revealing detours from the beaten path, such as a walk out to Ballybricken Green, one of the city's oldest sections. At one time located outside the city walls, this was were the Irish lived when Waterford was under Norman rule. The side streets and back lanes of this city of almost 39,500 people also are worth discovering for their quaint houses, historic churches, and unexpected finds, such as the ancient carvings on the friary wall in Lady Lane. Not much of the great abbeys may remain, but in these narrow passageways, Waterford's medieval atmosphere seems preserved forever.

Waterford At-a-Glance

SEEING THE CITY

Ignatius Rice Bridge (formerly Redmond Bridge) spans the River Suir at the western end of the city. It can be a quiet spot for viewing the town, which looks not unlike an 18th-century New England coastal village with its large buildings and many church spires. From its hilltop location across the river, *Jurys* hotel (see *Checking In*) also offers a panoramic view of Waterford.

SPECIAL PLACES

With the exception of the Waterford Glass Factory, about 1½ miles from the center, most of the city's major points of interest are conveniently located in a central area between Ignatius Rice Bridge and Reginald's Tower, either along the quays or just a few blocks from them. The glass factory is best reached by car, taxi, or bus. The rest of the sights can be seen on a walking tour; most of the city's shops, restaurants, pubs, and hotels are in the same vicinity.

WATERFORD GLASS FACTORY Nearly 3,000 people a week visit the Waterford Glass Factory to watch Ireland's most famous crystal being mixed, blown, and cut by hand from the raw ingredients of silica sand, potash, and red lead. The original plant opened in 1783 and continued operating until 1851, when English law imposed heavy duties on the exported glass and made the operation unprofitable. With the help of the Irish government, Waterford reopened on a small scale in 1947 and has since outgrown its buildings several times. The company now employs 1,700 people, who cannot keep up with orders for their product. The factory is closed on weekends and usually during the first 3 weeks of August. Tours are given on weekdays at 10:15, 11, and 11:45 AM and at 1:45 and 2:30 PM. Be sure to call ahead to check on the times and reserve a place on a tour — reservations are necessary year-round (phone 73311); arrangements also can be made through the tourist board. Showrooms are open weekdays from 9 AM to 5 PM and on Saturdays from 9 AM to 12:30 PM. No admission charge. About 1½ miles from the center of Waterford on the Cork road.

WATERFORD HERITAGE CENTRE Housed in a former church, this interpretative center focuses on Waterford's early days of Viking and Norman settlements. Open weekdays from 10 AM to 3 PM in May through September. Admission charge. Greyfriar's St. (phone: 71227).

ST. SAVIOUR'S DOMINICAN CHURCH This handsome church was built in 1874. The solemn interior features Corinthian columns and lovely frescoes over the altar. Corner of Bridge and O'Connell Sts. (phone: 76581).

CHAMBER OF COMMERCE Architect John Roberts designed this aristocratic building in 1795 as a home for the Morris family, who were prominent in the shipping trade. The house was purchased by the Chamber of Commerce in 1815. A large fanlight graces the entrance, and it is worth a look inside to see the beautiful plasterwork and splendid oval staircase. Open weekdays. No admission charge. George's St. (phone: 72639).

CLOCK TOWER Nineteenth-century sea captains relied on this landmark along the quays to keep their ships on schedule. It once had troughs of water at its base from which horses could drink, and was thus known as the Fountain Clock. Built in 1861, the original clock was replaced in 1954. The Quay.

CATHEDRAL OF THE MOST HOLY TRINITY After the confiscation of their churches in the mid-17th century, the Catholics of Waterford did not receive permission from the city's Protestant-controlled government to build another until 1792. Architect John Roberts designed this one; it was completed in 1796. The cathedral has a beautifully carved oak pulpit. Barronstrand St. (phone: 74757).

LADY LANE This little passage has been described as the best surviving example of a medieval street in Waterford. It is a charming byway with Georgian doorways on one side and two old stone carvings (one dated 1613) visible on the wall of the Franciscan friary on the other side. On Broad St., off Upper Barronstrand St.

CHRIST CHURCH CATHEDRAL John Roberts also designed this Protestant church, which was completed in 1779 on the site of an earlier Norse church. The Norsemen had made Waterford a diocese of its own, and the old church, erected in 1050, grew in size and property through several centuries until Henry VIII's Dissolution of the Monasteries. Later, Cromwell's troops occupied the original church for a time. The present cathedral incorporates some monuments from the old church and a number of interesting tombs. Cathedral Sq. (phone: 74119).

FRENCH CHURCH Founded as a Franciscan abbey in 1240, this once included six chambers, a kitchen with four cellars, and stables in addition to the church whose ruined nave, choir, and Lady Chapel still remain. After it was dissolved by Henry VIII, the friary saw use as a hospital, a burial place for some of Waterford's prominent families, and a parish church for French Huguenot refugees. Architect John Roberts is among those buried here. Obtain the key to visit the church from the house across the road; a notice on the door gives the address. Bailey's New St.

REGINALD'S TOWER This 70-foot stone tower on the quays was built for defense by Reginald the Dane in 1003. It was captured by Strongbow in 1170, and in the centuries since has been used as a mint, a military storehouse, and an air-raid shelter. It now houses a historical museum containing some of the city's original charters, swords (including one of King John's), and municipal muniments. Open weekdays from 11 AM to 1 PM and 2 to 7 PM, Saturdays from 11 AM to 2 PM, April through September; closed in winter. Admission charge. Corner of the Quay and the Mall (phone: 73501).

FATHER LUKE WADDING STATUE AND THE MALL This statue just across the street from Reginald's Tower commemorates the birth in 1588 of one of Waterford's most distinguished sons. Although the famed Franciscan scholar spent most of his life in Rome, he helped his Catholic countrymen both morally and financially in their attempts to establish their own constitution and government. The *Tower* hotel (see *Checking In*) on the left is on the site of the old bowling green. City Hall, completed in 1788 for the merchants of Waterford, now houses a museum (see *Museums*) and the *Theatre Royal* as well as administrative offices. Behind City Hall is the Bishop's Palace, now used by the city engineering staff.

CELTWORLD Situated a mile south of Waterford in a seaside setting, this indoor attraction is devoted to life in Ireland during Celtic times, over 1,500 years ago. A variety of exhibits and animated displays are devoted to Irish myths and folklore, telling the stories of such legendary figures as Finn MacCool, Cuchulainn, Oisin, and Lir. Open daily from 10 AM to 6 PM in March through October; weekends only the rest of the year. Admission charge. Tramore (phone: 86166).

Sources and Resources

TOURIST INFORMATION

The tourist board (41 the Quay; phone: 75788) is open year-round. Hours are usually 9 AM to 6 PM Mondays through Saturdays, April through

October; 9 AM to 5:15 PM weekdays and 10 AM to 1 PM on Saturdays in winter. In July through August, the office is also open from 10 AM to 5 PM on Sundays. One of the most helpful pamphlets for sale is the *Waterford Guide*. The tourist board in nearby Tramore (Railway Sq.; phone: 81572), the large seaside resort about 8 miles southwest of Waterford, is open from late June to early September.

LOCAL COVERAGE The *Munster Express,* published Thursdays and Fridays, and the *Waterford News and Star,* published every Friday, give specific information on entertainment and special events in the city and vicinity.

TELEPHONE The area code for Waterford and the immediate vicinity is 51. When calling from within the Republic of Ireland, dial 051 before the local number.

GETTING AROUND

Waterford can be a busy turnstile for traffic. Both the Dublin–Cork and Wexford–Tipperary roads pass through the city, but much of the traffic avoids the narrow streets of the Old City, traveling instead along the quays and then out along the Mall. Inexpensive disc parking spaces are plentiful along the Quay; discs can be purchased at the tourist board and most shops. The city is easily explored on foot, but an afternoon cruise on the River Suir — with tea served en route — makes for a nice supplementary excursion (see *Tours* below).

BUS AND TRAIN Local buses board beside the Clock Tower along the Quay, and some buses also leave from Plunkett Station, as do trains for Dublin, Limerick, and Rosslare Harbour (and intervening points); the station is near Ignatius Rice Bridge on the north side of the River Suir (phone: 73401).

CAR RENTAL Among the car rental agencies in Waterford are *Murray's/Europcar* (Cork Rd.; phone: 73144), *Practical Car Rental* (Catherine St.; phone: 78982), and *Budget* (41 the Quay; phone: 21670).

FERRY Save an hour's driving time to Wexford via N25 by taking the 10-minute car ferry from Passage East, south of Waterford, and then picking up L159. The fare per car is inexpensive, whether round trip or one way. No reservations necessary (phone: 82488).

TAXI Cabs wait at Plunkett Station and along Barronstrand Street. Otherwise, a radio cab can be called from *A. B. Cabs* (phone: 79100), *Concorde Cabs* (phone: 32333), *Five O Cars* (phone: 50000), or *Sevens Taxi* (phone: 77777). The tourist board will also call cabs as a service to visitors.

TOURS Bus tours of Waterford and the surrounding area are operated by *Bus Eireann,* a subsidiary of *CIE* (*Córas Iompair Eireann, National Transport Company*), departing from Plunkett Station in June through August (phone: 73401). The *Galley* cruise boats, enclosed barges that provide lunch and dinner sailings from New Ross, also offer 2-hour afternoon sightseeing cruises from Waterford City during July and August. The cost of a cruise is very reasonable, and afternoon tea is served on board. Boats depart daily at 3 PM from the Quay (opposite *Shaw's* department store). For information and reservations call the *Galley* dock (New Ross; phone: 21723). Two-hour narrated sightseeing tours on the River Suir are also offered by *Waterford Viking Cruises* daily from May through September at noon and 3:30 and 8 PM. The boats leave Waterford Harbour from the Quay (opposite Reginald's Tower) and travel downriver to Passage East, the Island, Cheekpoint, Ballyhack, and Arthurstown. For more information and reservations, call 72800.

From June through August, walking tours of the city commence at the tourist office (41 the Quay) and end at Reginald's Tower, taking in ten historic sites en route. Tours depart at 11 AM and 3 PM Mondays through Saturdays; cost is approximately $3.30 per person (phone: 94577).

SPECIAL EVENTS

The *Waterford International Festival of Light Opera* has been held every September for over 20 years. For 2 weeks, amateur companies from England, Wales, Scotland, Northern Ireland, and the Republic try to outdo each other with performances of operettas or musicals. Fringe events include a ball, band concerts, bridge tournaments, sports competitions, and singing competitions in the pubs, which, as usual during a festival in Ireland, are open late. Tickets are reasonably priced and can be obtained along with specific information on programs and dates from Sean Dower, Secretary of the Waterford Festival, New St., Waterford (phone: 75911 or 75437).

MUSEUMS

In addition to those described in *Special Places,* Waterford has a museum in its City Hall. During normal business hours, the Council Chamber of this spacious building is open to the public. Especially noteworthy is the beautiful glass chandelier, made at the original Waterford factory (a replica of the chandelier hangs in Philadelphia's Independence Hall). There is also a complete dinner service of old Waterford glass, and a flag from the Irish Brigade that fought on the Union side in the American Civil War. The Mall (phone: 73501).

SHOPPING

While Waterford is known for its crystal products, the city is also a source for a wide range of Irish-made gifts and souvenirs. You'll find most of the best shops along the Quay and on the long street that begins at Barronstrand. In recent years, several shopping malls have opened, including *George's Court* (between George's and Barronstrand Sts.), *Broad Street*

Centre (Broad and Patrick Sts.), and *City Square* (off the Mall). Smaller shops close on Thursdays and some shops stay open late on Friday evenings. All stores are closed Sundays unless otherwise noted.

AISLING Bearing a name that means "dream" in the Irish language, this quality crafts shop features the best of Irish-made products — from local crystal and pottery to patchwork quilts, knitwear, and linen. 7 Barronstrand St. (phone: 73262).

BOOK CENTRE Large, with a good selection of works by Irish authors. 9 Michael St. (phone: 73823).

THE CRYSTAL GALLERY Located at the Waterford crystal factory, this shop sells mouth-blown, hand-cut pieces. Wedgwood china (now owned by Waterford) also is available. On Cork Rd., Kilbarry (phone: 73311).

HENNEBRY CAMERA All the basics and accessories plus kindly proprietors who will try to help when your shutter won't or the flash doesn't. 109 the Quay (phone: 75049).

JOANN'S A good place to buy brass, silver, crystal, and china. 30 Michael St. (phone: 73138).

JOSEPH KNOX This lovely store behind a Victorian shopfront is a major distributor of Waterford crystal and English bone china, and it's often crowded. If you do more than browse — there are many handsome pieces of porcelain and cut glass on display — you can arrange for your booty to be mailed. 3-4 Barronstrand St. (phone: 75307).

MIDGET, LTD. Stocked with stacks of appealing hand-crafted baskets, crocks, stoneware, Kilkenny pottery, homespuns, and such. 85 the Quay (phone: 74127).

PENROSE Although its manufacture was revived only in 1978, this locally made glassware dates from 1786 and is well worth a look. Visitors are welcome to watch the craftsmen as they hand-cut the floral motifs into the glass. Open daily. 32 John St. (phone: 76537).

QUAY ANTIQUES Near Reginald's Tower is a treasure trove of collectibles, posters, brass, and the like. 128 the Quay (phone: 77789).

WOOLCRAFT Established in 1887, this place specializes in Aran knit, mohair, Icelandic, and lamb's wool sweaters. Also tapestry jackets, gloves, tams, and scarves. 11 Michael St. (phone: 74082).

SPORTS AND FITNESS
Waterford has a variety of sports facilities both within and just outside the city, and the seaside resort of Tramore, about 8 miles southwest of

Waterford, has a 50-acre amusement complex and a 3-mile-long beach. In summer, buses to Tramore leave on the half hour from the Quay.

GOLF The 18-hole course of the *Waterford Golf Club* (phone: 76748) is open to the public. It's in a scenic setting about 1½ miles outside the city. Visitors are also welcome at the 18-hole course of the *Tramore Golf Club,* a mile from Tramore (phone: 86170).

GREYHOUND RACING The dogs race at *Kilcohan Park* on Tuesdays and Saturdays in June, and daily for a week in August. For specific information, call the *Waterford Greyhound Track* (phone: 74531).

HORSEBACK RIDING Horses can be hired at *Melody's Riding Stables* (Ballmacarberry, near Clonmel, about 15 miles northwest of Waterford (phone: 52-36147) and *Kilotteran Equitation Centre* (Kilotteran, about 3 miles southwest of Waterford; phone: 84158).

JOGGING Visitors are welcome to use the all-weather athletic track and other indoor/outdoor facilities at the *Waterford Regional Sports Centre,* Tramore Rd. (phone: 77566).

POLO Europe's only residential polo vacation school is at *Whitfield Court,* with 2 polo grounds, wooden horses, an enclosed riding school, video equipment, and 20 polo ponies. For information contact Major Hugh Dawnay, *Whitfield Court,* Waterford (phone: 84216). For additional details, see *Horsing Around* in DIVERSIONS.

SAILING Details are available from the *Waterford Sailing Club* in Dunmore East, 9 miles southeast of the city (phone: 83230).

SQUASH *Henry Downe's Pub* (10 Thomas St.; phone: 74118) has 2 courts. Other facilities are at the *Celtic Squash Club* (71 Barrack St.; phone: 76541).

SWIMMING The *Waterford Glass Swimming Pool* on the Cork road is open to the public. Admission is on the hour for a 45-minute session. Hours vary, so it's probably a good idea to check in advance by calling the pool manager, Waterford Glass Ltd. (phone: 73311, ext. 266). Tramore has a 3-mile beach, with lifeguards on duty in summer. Surfboards and deck chairs can be rented at the beach.

TENNIS *Waterford Tennis Club* (St. John's Hill; phone: 74350) has both grass and hard courts.

THEATER

Special productions take place in summer at the *Theatre Royal* (housed in City Hall, the Mall; phone: 74402). Contemporary plays, films, and concerts are presented year-round at the *Garter Lane Arts Centre and Theatre* (22A O'Connell St.; phone: 77133); the innovative and award-winning *Red Kettle Theatre Company* regularly performs here.

MUSIC

Concerts on a large scale, featuring such internationally known artists as the *Chieftains* and Frank Patterson, take place periodically at the *Forum* (at the Glen; phone: 71111). The high point of the city's musical season is the 2-week *Waterford International Festival of Light Opera* in September. In addition to the light opera, the program includes singing competitions in local pubs (see *Special Events*). For traditional and folk music sessions, try *T. & H. Doolan's* pub (32 George's St.; phone: 72764); traditional Irish music is featured at any number of other pubs, including *Mullane's* (15 Newgate St.; phone: 73854). There is jazz every Sunday at *Reginald's* (on the Mall; phone: 55087).

NIGHTCLUBS AND NIGHTLIFE

Nightclubs include *Preachers* (10 John St.; phone: 79184), *Snage's* (36-37 Barronstrand St.; phone: 75619), *Excalibur* (the Mall; phone: 55087), and *Olympus* (in the *Bridge Hotel,* 1 The Quay; phone: 77222). *Cheers* (18 O'Connell St.; phone: 55089) features an ever-changing agenda of cabaret, dancing, ballad, folk, and disco music Tuesdays through Sundays. Some pubs feature special appearances by singing groups, both popular and traditional. *Egan's Bar* (36-37 Barronstrand St.; phone: 75619) offers laser *karaoke* (background music to which patrons sing the lyrics) on Thursday and Sunday evenings. The best way to keep abreast of all evening festivities is to consult the tourist board and the local papers.

Best in Town

CHECKING IN

Waterford's hotels are convenient to the city center, and they offer travelers a nice choice between the old and the new. There are also a number of bed and breakfast establishments in the area. The tourist board will help find a vacancy in a house that meets its approval. Expect to pay from $125 to $200 for a double room at hotels in the expensive category, and under $75 at a hostelry in the inexpensive category. All telephone numbers are in the 51 area code unless otherwise indicated.

For an unforgettable experience, we begin with our favorite Waterford lodging, followed by our cost and quality choices, listed by price category.

SPECIAL HAVEN

Waterford Castle Completely secluded on a 310-acre island in the River Suir, this castle was built circa 1160 for the FitzGeralds, one of Ireland's most famous ruling families, and remained in their hands for over 800 years. Its current owner, Edward Kearns, has invested millions on masterful restoration and refurbishment. Consisting of two wings, it is built entirely of stone with a lead roof, mullioned windows, graceful archways, ancient gargoyles, turrets, towers, and battlements. There are 20 bedrooms and suites of varying sizes, each with antique furnishings and fixtures, a four-poster or canopied bed, and private bath. The public rooms have spacious sitting areas and huge, stone fireplaces, handwoven Connemara carpets, oil paintings, oak-paneled walls, and ornate plaster ceilings. Dining by candlelight in the restaurant is appropriately regal — from the Waterford crystal stemware to the Wedgwood place settings and Irish linen. Guests enjoy full access to the island's outdoor facilities — tennis, horseback riding, salmon and trout fishing, fox hunting, pheasant and duck shooting, and a variety of water sports. There also is a heated indoor swimming pool with a health and fitness center, and a new 18-hole championship golf course. The hotel is very pricey, and only overnight guests or visitors with lunch or dinner reservations are given ferry access to the island. About 2½ miles from Waterford City in Ballinakill (phone: 78203; 800-221-1074 from the US; fax: 79316).

EXPENSIVE

Granville This Georgian mansion, once the home of Irish patriot Thomas Meagher, is Waterford's classiest hotel in the downtown business area. It exudes an air of graciousness and respectability, with 66 appealing rooms, an attractive paneled lounge bar, the elegant *Bells* restaurant (see *Eating Out*), and a grill on the premises. The Quay (phone: 55111; 800-528-1234 from the US; fax: 70307).

Jurys Set on 38 acres on a hillside along the north banks of the River Suir, this modern 6-story establishment, originally known as the *Ardree* (the name means "High King" in Gaelic), offers panoramic views of Waterford City and the river from each of its 100 rooms. The interior is equally eye-catching, with artful moldings and trim, dark wood furnishings, and well-lit marble and tile bathrooms. The restaurant offers unbeatable vistas (especially at night when the city lights shine). Other facilities include a fitness center with a heated indoor swimming pool, a whirlpool, a steam-room, a plunge pool, a gymnasium, saunas, and solariums; 2 lighted outdoor tennis courts; and ample parking. The *Waterford Golf Club* is adjacent to the property. Ferrybank (phone: 32111; 800-THE-OMNI from the US; fax: 32863).

Tower Centrally located on the Mall opposite the landmark Reginald's Tower, this veteran establishment was enlarged and totally renovated in 1991. The decor is bright and airy with Art Deco overtones and picture windows with wide views of the River Suir. Each of the 125 guestrooms has a modern tiled bathroom, a TV set, a telephone, and a hair dryer. Facilities include a restaurant, a lounge with river views, and a fitness center with an indoor pool, whirlpool, plunge pool, steamroom, saunas, sunbed, and exercise room. The Mall (phone: 75801; fax: 70129).

Blenheim House About 3 miles southeast of Waterford, overlooking the city and the River Suir, this gracious home was built in 1763. The current owners have restored it fully and have furnished it with their own antiques and dazzling collection of Waterford crystal. Each of the 6 guest bedrooms has a private bath. Blenheim Heights, off the Passage East road (phone: 74115).

Three Rivers Situated 7 miles east of Waterford on the harbor where the rivers Suir, Nore, and Barrow meet, this lovely guesthouse has 15 rooms, each with private bath and telephone, and bright modern furnishings. The Fitzgerald family provides a warm welcome and excellent breakfast. Cheekpoint (phone: 82520; fax: 82542).

EATING OUT

Waterford does not have a large selection of restaurants, but with the inclusion of a few hotel dining rooms, there are enough good ones to keep visitors well fed. For anyone in a hurry or homesick for the US, there is *Chapman's Delicatessen* (61 the Quay; phone: 74938). Most pubs serve a lunch of soup and a sandwich or a special of the day for about $3 to $5. Dinner for two (wine, drinks, and tips not included) will cost over $75 in an expensive restaurant, and between $40 and $75 in a moderate place. All telephone numbers are in the 51 area code unless otherwise indicated.

EXPENSIVE

Bells With gilt-edged mirrors, brass sconces, floral drapes, original artwork, fine linen, and candlelight, this small 36-seat à la carte restaurant is an elegant feature of the *Granville* hotel. The nouvelle cuisine menu offers such choices as salmon trout with shellfish sauce, prawns with orange and grapes, and lamb Sugarloaf (a filet of lamb with vegetable purée and fresh herb sauce). Open for dinner only; closed Sundays. Reservations essential. Major credit cards accepted. The Quay (phone: 55111).

Dwyer's With a homey pastel-toned decor and orchestral music in the background, this family-run establishment offers a creative menu including choices such as monkfish with smoked salmon sauce; filet mignon cooked with tomatoes, mushrooms, and cream; and roast pheasant in a walnut, orange, and grape sauce. A reduced-price early bird menu is available on most evenings at 6 PM. Open for dinner only; closed Sundays. Reservations advised. Major credit cards accepted. 8 Mary St. (phone: 77478 or 71183).

MODERATE

La Dolce Vita The sights and sounds of Italy prevail at this little eatery, with prints of Rome on the walls, red and white linen, hanging wine bottles, and the strains of opera playing in the background. The menu includes homemade pasta and entrées named for famous Italians, such as veal Sophia Loren (with cheese and ham, in a cream sauce with mushrooms, red peppers, white wine, and brandy), as well as veal parmesan, saltimbocca, and scallops Florentine. Open daily for dinner. Reservations advised. Major credit cards accepted. 8 the Mall (phone: 78102).

Loughman's On the second floor of the *George's Court Shopping Mall,* this is a bright and airy restaurant filled with hanging plants. The menu is eclectic, ranging from steaks and mixed grills to pizza, pasta, salads, and casseroles, with self-service for breakfast and lunch and table-service at dinner. Open Mondays through Saturdays from 8:30 AM to 9:30 PM; Sundays from 12:30 to 5:30 PM. No reservations. No credit cards accepted. George's Court and Barronstrand Sts. (phone: 78407).

Prendiville's Just south of town, this place is housed in a 19th-century Gothic-style stone gate lodge that appears on Ireland's National Trust list of historic buildings. New owners have enhanced the decor with light woods and modern Irish art, and broadened the menu to include such dishes as roast duck breast with honey and rosemary glaze, free-range chicken cooked with bacon and served on pasta with wild mushroom sauce, and brill filets with salmon and fennel in ginger butter. Open for lunch and dinner; closed Sundays. Reservations advised. MasterCard and Visa accepted. Cork Rd. (phone: 78851).

The Reginald The original grillroom/bar, tucked beside Reginald's Tower, is better known for its buffet lunches, and creative cocktails (see *Sharing a Pint*). The newer section, in an adjacent house overlooking the Mall, has a more formal atmosphere with fine linen and candlelight dining, plus a bill of fare that includes baked pink trout *en papillote,* sweet and sour monkfish, filet mignon stuffed with mushrooms, and chicken Kiev. Open daily for lunch and dinner. Reservations advised for dinner. Major credit cards accepted. The Mall (phone: 55087).

SHARING A PINT

We begin with our favorite Waterford watering hole.

HIGH SPIRITS

Reginald This establishment on the Mall is just behind and adjacent to Reginald's Tower. The pub incorporates part of the old walls of the tower and the Old City, and patrons drink in niches that have been burrowed into the walls. On display in the pub are old weapons, a full suit of armor, and other remembrances of Waterford's history. A peat fire usually burns on the hearth, and on Sunday afternoons Waterford musicians often play some good jazz. The Mall (phone: 55087).

Also stop in at *Egan's* (36-37 Barronstrand St.; phone: 75619), a Tudor-style bar with plenty of room to stretch. It's a convenient place to pause from shopping. *T. & H. Doolan's* (32 George's St.; phone: 72764) is a small, old-fashioned gem. A good pub for bar food is the Victorian-themed *Old Stand* (Michael St.; phone: 79488). Finally, whatever you do, don't leave town without looking in at the *Munster* (on the Mall; phone: 74656), a 300-year-old inn revived and expanded by the Fitzgerald family. The entrance to the mellowed-though-modern lounge, a favorite meeting and greeting spot for young Waterforders, is on the Mall, but walk around to the original Bailey's New Street door to see the men's bar (one of a few remaining such male enclaves in Ireland; women still are not welcome) on the right.

Wexford Town

The main attraction in Wexford Town is the people. Spend a pleasant day browsing among the narrow streets of this hilly town, then head for the nearest bar stool (an easy assignment, as one local claims there are more than 50 pubs in Wexford). A friendly comment or two from a visitor is likely to get a native monologue going, be it a recitation of the local history or a soliloquy on the praiseworthy local weather. An Irish American can expect a lively debate on the political fortunes of the Kennedy family, whose ancestors came from nearby Dunganstown in County Wexford.

But the Wexford folks' spirit is more than just a gift for gab. It has produced such illustrious native sons as John Barry, regarded as the founder of the US Navy, born 10 miles from Wexford at Ballysampson, and Sir Robert J. McClure, discoverer of the Northwest Passage. The boldest and proudest Wexford men of days gone by, however, were those who took part in the Rebellion of 1798. In that year, the United Irishmen were unsuccessful in planning a general uprising against the British, so Father John Murphy, a County Wexford priest, independently led his parishioners, armed with pitchforks and pikes, in revolt. The rebellion lasted a month before it was suppressed, but it has remained alive in folk memory through Irish ballads such as "The Wearing of the Green" and "The Boys of Wexford."

Wexford has a population of more than 10,300, with another several thousand living in the nearby countryside. Located where the River Slaney flows into the shallow Wexford Harbour, the town has an impossibly narrow main street, a legacy of its Viking past. It is said that a Gaelic settlement existed here as early as AD 150, but it was the Vikings who developed it, calling it *Waesfjord,* meaning "harbor of mud flats." Initially, the Vikings used this as a base from which to plunder the countryside and later turned it into a major trading post.

The Anglo-Norman invasion led by Richard de Clare, Earl of Pembroke, known as Strongbow, ousted the Vikings in 1169 and launched a new era of domination. The face of the town also changed. Selskar Abbey rose at its northwestern edge, and Wexford soon became a walled town, with five fortified gateways and four castles. The only remains of these defenses are the Westgate, built in the 14th century and used until the end of the 16th century, and a portion of wall nearby.

Norman nobles used one of the town's squares for the bloody sport of bull-baiting. To this day the square is called the Bull Ring, despite the fact that the worst of a much bloodier slaughter, the massacre of Wexford's citizenry by Oliver Cromwell in 1649, occurred in the same place. The townspeople erected no monument to remind them of this deed, but in 1905, when they got around to commemorating the insurgency of 1798, they placed their statue of an Irish pikeman here. More of the same independent spirit lies behind the confusion of Wexford's street names. Many have two names, one dating from the days of British rule, the other from the founding of the Irish Republic in 1922, the latter likely to be the name of a rebel.

In recent years, the establishment of an industrial estate with German and American firms has brought needed jobs into the area. Lett & Company, which transplants small seed mussels into Wexford Harbour from less nourishing areas, is located in Wexford Town and is the biggest single employer in the Irish fishing industry.

Then there's the tourist industry, which Wexford comes by almost effortlessly, given its location in the sunniest part of Ireland, near the 6-mile beach of Rosslare. Tourism is not *entirely* effortless, however, because the energy that goes into the yearly *Wexford Opera Festival* and all its accompanying fringe events cannot be discounted.

But whether during the lively opera festival, the sunny summer months, or any other time of year, the friendly folk of Wexford make the ancient town a welcome stop on any traveler's tour.

Wexford At-a-Glance

SEEING THE CITY

The best way to see Wexford is on foot. To enjoy the harbor and the sea air, begin at the tourist board on Crescent Quay and head north. Any street off the quays leads to Main Street, which runs parallel to the harbor and is the central shopping area, but a left turn at the Bank of Ireland onto Common Quay Street (also known as O'Hanlon Walsh Street) brings you to the Bull Ring. Follow Bull Ring, which winds around to the right into the Cornmarket and George Street, where *White's* hotel is situated.

SPECIAL PLACES

The town's memorials, churches, and abbey are all within a 5-minute walk of Main Street.

JOHN BARRY MEMORIAL In 1956, the US presented Ireland with this handsome statue of the founder of the US Navy, who was born in County Wexford in 1745. Commodore Barry stands on Crescent Quay where two former American presidents, Dwight D. Eisenhower and John F. Kennedy, laid wreaths on separate occasions. The inscriptions on the monument list a few of Barry's accomplishments during the American Revolution. Walk up the street behind the monument for a lifelike view of the commodore looking out to sea with his mighty cape blowing in the wind. Crescent Quay.

WEXFORD HERITAGE CENTRE Westgate, a 13th-century gate tower that was originally part of the Viking/Norman walls of the town, has been fully restored and was reopened in 1992 as a museum focusing on Wexford's past. In addition to artifacts and displays, there is an audiovisual presentation depicting the varied history of the town from its origins as a Gaelic and Viking settlement to the present day. Open daily, year-round. Admission charge. Westgate St. (phone: 42611).

MARITIME MUSEUM A retired lighthouse ship, the *Guillemot* — moored about 15 miles southwest of town at Kilmore Quay — is home to a museum devoted to Wexford's seafaring days. Open in summer only, usually from 2 to 8 PM on weekdays and noon to 6 PM on weekends. When the ship's flag is flying, the museum is open. Admission charge. Kilmore Quay.

BULL RING The medieval practice of bull-baiting — killing bulls for sport — once took place in this small, historic square. This is also the place where on October 1, 1649, Oliver Cromwell had 2,000 Irish men, women, and children slaughtered. A statue to a pikeman, done by Oliver Sheppard and erected in 1905, now dominates the square in tribute to the peasants who took part in what came to be known as the Rebellion of 1798. At the east side of the ring a market is held on Fridays from 9:30 AM to 12:30 PM. Here Wexford women sell their vegetables, baked goods, jams, jellies, honey, and sometimes crafts in buildings dating from 1871.

ST. IBERIUS CHURCH This Georgian masterpiece (Church of Ireland) was built in 1760 on land occupied by other houses of worship dating from earliest Norse days. The handsome interior and superb acoustics make it a favorite concert hall during the *Wexford Opera Festival*. South of the Bull Ring on Main St. (phone: 43013).

WEXFORD ARTS CENTRE Once the Market House, then Town Hall, this 18th-century building was restored as a cultural headquarters and special-events site. Its now-elegant second story boasts five Waterford crystal chandeliers. Around the corner from the Bull Ring, Cornmarket (phone: 23764).

TWIN CHURCHES The Roman Catholic churches of the Immaculate Conception on Rowe Street and of the Assumption on Bride Street, both designed by Robert Pierce, were inaugurated on the same day in 1858 when Wexford's original nine parishes were consolidated into two. Rowe and Bride Sts. (phone: 22055).

SELSKAR ABBEY The 12th-century abbey was once quite extensive, although all that can be seen today are a 14th-century battlement tower and church. A long, covered passage runs underground to the far side of town. Tradition says that Henry II did penance here for ordering the murder of Thomas à Becket, but historians now think St. Mary's, protected within the town walls, a more likely site for his acts of contrition. To explore the ruins, visitors must obtain a key from a nearby house (a notice on the gate explains where). Behind the abbey remains the old Westgate, the only one of Wexford's five original gateways still standing, which now houses the

Wexford Heritage Centre (see above). Entrance at the intersection of Temperance Row, Westgate, and Slaney St.

FRANCISCAN FRIARY Built in the 17th century on the site of an earlier church destroyed during Cromwellian times, this was the parish church for Wexford Town until the twin churches of the Assumption and the Immaculate Conception were completed in 1858. The Franciscan friary was extensively redecorated in the 19th century, when the vaulted ceiling, marble columns, and organ were added. School St. (phone: 22758).

IRISH NATIONAL HERITAGE PARK Located on the banks of the River Slaney, this outdoor museum reflects 9 centuries of Ireland's history. Among the structures are a *crannóg* (an early lake dwelling), ring forts, *souterrains* (underground escape passages), a *fulacht fiagh* (an ancient cooking place that used hot stones to heat food), burial sites, dolmens, early Christian churches, round towers, and the buildings found in the first Viking and Norman communities. Open daily March through October. Admission charge. Ferrycarrig, about 2 miles north of Wexford Town (phone: 22211 or 47133).

IRISH AGRICULTURAL MUSEUM In the restored 19th-century farm buildings of Victorian Gothic Johnstown Castle, this museum provides an excellent picture of just how much Irish farming has changed in the last 50 years. Its display of old farming and rural craft items, the country's largest, includes the hand flails, pitchers, turnip pulpers, ploughs, harrows, sowers, mowing machines, and carts and traps that were once among every Irish farmer's most important tools. The castle's 50-acre gardens are also a delight. The castle and surrounding farm are used for soil research by the Agricultural Institute. Open daily, April through mid-November; weekdays only the rest of the year. Admission charge. The gardens are open to the public without charge from 10 AM to 6 PM daily — take a picnic basket. A tearoom at the museum is open from June through August. Off the Rosslare Harbour road, 2½ miles southwest of Wexford (phone: 42888).

BALLYLANE FARM This 200-acre property, owned by the Hickey family, enables visitors to get a firsthand look at farm life in general, as well as the particular specialty of deer and pheasant raising. Open daily from 10 AM to 4 PM, May through September. Admission charge. New Ross, about 22 miles from Wexford Town (phone: 51-21315).

EXTRA SPECIAL The Saltee Islands, Ireland's largest and most famous bird sanctuary, are an excellent place for an outdoor excursion. During spring and early summer, Great Saltee (which is 1 mile long) and Little Saltee are home to more than 3 million gulls, puffins, and other feathered creatures that delight bird watchers. The islands are a 45-minute boat trip off the coast of Kilmore Quay, about 20 miles southwest of Wexford. To arrange a trip, call **Willie Bates** (phone: 29644) or **Tom O'Brien** (phone: 29727). Also see *Southeast Ireland: Dublin to New Ross* in DIRECTIONS.

Sources and Resources

TOURIST INFORMATION

Wexford's large tourist board on Crescent Quay is open all year, 9 AM to 6 PM Mondays through Saturdays, and on Sundays from 10 AM to 5 PM in July and August (phone: 23111); winter hours may differ slightly. The board offers extensive information on hotels and sights in the area. In summer the Junior Chamber of Commerce puts out an excellent monthly guide that is available free from the tourist board and from most hotels. It contains names and phone numbers of doctors, dentists, and pharmacists as well as the timetable for buses and trains to Dublin and ferries operating out of Rosslare Harbour. It also has two good maps of the town with a suggested walking tour. The Chamber of Commerce publishes a small brochure with some of the same information in a more condensed form along with a map.

LOCAL COVERAGE The *Wexford People* and the *Wexford Echo*, the town's two weekly newspapers, both come out on Thursdays with news and an entertainment listing for the area.

TELEPHONE The area code for Wexford and the immediate vicinity is 53. When calling from within the Republic of Ireland, dial 053 before the local number.

GETTING AROUND

Plan to park your car and see Wexford on foot. The disc parking system is in effect for all street parking spaces; discs are sold at the tourist office. Among the dozen or so parking lots, there's a convenient one near the tourist board — turn left onto Custom House Quay from the bridge, the lot is on the right just before the statue of John Barry. (For other lots, see the detailed town map in the Junior Chamber of Commerce guide.) Consider tagging along on an Old Wexford Society walking tour. Its members conduct them throughout the year at hours set to suit visitor demand. Check starting times and places at hotels or the tourist board.

BICYCLE *Hayes Cycle Shop* (108 S. Main St.; phone: 22462) and *The Bike Shop* (9 Selskar St.; phone: 22514) have bikes for rent.

BUS AND TRAIN There is no in-town bus service — it's not necessary. The bus and railway terminals for trips beyond the town are in Redmond Place, near the quays just north of the bridge. *Bus Eireann* and *Irish Rail*, divisions of *CIE (Córas Iompair Eireann, National Transport Company)*, operate buses and trains between Wexford and Dublin and between Wexford and Rosslare Harbour, 13 miles southeast (not to be confused with Rosslare or Rosslare Strand, the seaside resort between Wexford and Rosslare Harbour). Ferries leave Rosslare Harbour regularly for Wales and for Le Havre and Cherbourg, France. Irish trains and buses are not known for their strict adherence to timetables, so check with *CIE* for information about delays (phone: 22522 from 6:30 AM to 6 PM). For information on ferries to Wales, call *British Rail* (phone: 33115). For information on ferries to France, call *Irish Ferries* (phone: 33158).

CAR RENTAL A number of car rental companies operate in Wexford and in nearby Rosslare Harbour, and some have dropping-off stations for their vehicles rented elsewhere. They include *Auto Rentals* (Ferrybank, Wexford; phone: 23917); *Budget* (Rosslare Harbour; phone: 33318); and *Murray's* (Redmond Pl., Wexford; phone: 22122).

TAXI Cabs do not cruise or congregate in Wexford, so it is best to call. For fast service, ask a hotel or the tourist office to arrange for a cab, or call one of the radio-dispatched local companies such as *Andrew's Taxi* (phone: 45933), *Ryan's Taxi* (phone: 24056), or *Wexford Taxi* (phone: 41608).

TOURS *Bus Eireann,* a division of *CIE,* operates afternoon bus tours of nearby scenic areas during July and August from Redmond Place (phone: 22522). From April though November, *Westgate Mini Tours* (phone: 24655) operates daily morning and afternoon tours to nearby attractions such as the Irish National Heritage Park and Johnstown Castle. Prices, which include entrance fees, are very reasonable for a 2-hour trip. All tours leave from the tourist office.

SPECIAL EVENTS

Ushering in the autumn season is a 12-day celebration known worldwide. This year the *Wexford Opera Festival* marks its 43rd anniversary.

FAVORITE FETE

Wexford Opera Festival In the latter half of October, when the nights get long and cold, this harbor town comes alive with an event that, from a social point of view alone, is probably one of the most enjoyable in Ireland, filling the town's narrow winding streets with opera lovers from all over the world. The festival's long drawing card is the opera — usually two seldom-performed works by well-known composers and one contemporary opus. Ticket prices are low, even by European standards, and performance quality is high, as it has been since the festival's inception in 1951. What makes it really special, though, is the setting — a tiny opera house that seats only 446, crouched on a capillary of a side street — and a general feeling of style and opulence. Among the broad range of corollary events are concerts, recitals, and exhibitions and readings at the local arts center. There are also singing competitions in pubs and a window display competition that gets butchers, bakers, grocers, and others into the act. Rounding out the roster are theater performances, lectures, walking tours, flower shows, art exhibits, and other cultural events. To add to the glamour, several of Wexford's public buildings, including a few designed by Pugin, are floodlit for the duration. For information, contact the *Theatre Royal,* High St., Wexford (phone: 22244 or 22240).

At nearby Enniscorthy the popular *Wexford Strawberry Festival* is held in late June and early July, featuring a week of music and strawberry tasting.

SHOPPING

The best method of shopping in Wexford is to walk along Main Street and browse the storefronts. Most stores are open 9 AM to 5:30 PM, slightly later on Fridays and Saturdays. Most are closed on Sundays and often on Thursdays in fall and winter as well.

BARKERS Established in 1848, this dependable shop offers Waterford crystal, Belleek and Royal Tara china, linen, and other gift items. 36-40 S. Main St. (phone: 23159).

BOOK CENTRE A wide selection of books on Wexford and Ireland, as well as cards, stationery, and music cassettes, with a literary-themed coffee shop upstairs. 5 S. Main St. (phone: 23543).

DIANA DONNELLY For locally designed Irish fashions, this shop has a chic array of women's knitwear, jackets, coats, skirts, trousers, blouses, and accessories. Bull Ring (phone: 22175).

FALLER'S SWEATER SHOP An enormous emporium of modern Irish-made knitwear. 4 N. Main St. (phone: 24659).

FERRYCARRIG CRYSTAL This enterprise is both a shop and a studio, offering delicately mouth-blown and hand-cut glassware fashioned on site by former Waterford crystal craftsmen. The range of items for sale includes bridal gifts, trophies, decanters, jars, vases, ring holders, and perfume bottles. Open daily May through October. 20 Henrietta St. (phone: 23211).

HORE'S A good place for Irish linen. 31-37 S. Main St. (phone: 22200).

JOYCE'S CHINA SHOP For more than 40 years this spot has been known for Irish crystal, Belleek china, Wedgwood, Lladró, and other fine European products. 3 N. Main St. (phone: 22212).

LAURENCE'S A jewelry shop with attractive rings at reasonable prices, as well as crystal, china, and silver. 83 N. Main St. (phone: 24319).

LOWNEY'S SHOPPING MALL An enclave of ten little shops under one roof, it offers glassware, ceramics, framed prints, brassware, shell ornaments, and more. 61 S. Main St. (phone: 23140).

MARTIN DOYLE Fine hand-wrought gold and silver jewelry. Lower Rowe St. (phone: 41167).

OYSTER CRAFTS Situated just a block from the tourist office, this attractive shop offers a wide variety of locally made crafts: pottery, woodwork, ceramics, crystal, and candles, as well as knitwear, note cards, miniatures, dried flowers, and woolly lamb souvenirs. Paul Quay (phone: 24130).

WEXFORD GALLERY A showcase for local crafts, this shop sells paintings, pottery, knitwear, crochetwork, hand-cut glass, enamel, and woodwork. Open daily. Crescent Quay (phone: 23630).

WOOL SHOP For a large selection of Aran sweaters, woven belts, and local sheepskin and goatskin rugs. 39-41 S. Main St. (phone: 22247).

SPORTS AND FITNESS

The monthly guide published by the Junior Chamber of Commerce has detailed information on recreational activities. The leisure center in the *Talbot* hotel on the quays is open to non-registered guests and has a number of facilities including a heated indoor swimming pool, squash courts, and saunas.

GOLF The *Wexford Golf Club* (phone: 42238) has an 18-hole course just one-quarter mile from downtown. The *Rosslare Golf Club* (phone: 32203) has an 18-hole course at Rosslare, 11 miles southeast of Wexford.

HORSEBACK RIDING At *Horetown House* (12 miles west on L160 at Foulksmills; phone: 63633, manor house; 63786, stables), the Young family offers daily rides, all levels of instruction, an indoor ring, and a cross-country course for experienced riders (also see *Horsing Around* in DIVERSIONS). Horses also can be hired at *Laraheen Pony Trekking* (Laraheen House, Gorey; phone: 55-28289) and *Boro Hill Equestrian Centre* (Clonroche, Enniscorthy; phone: 54-44117).

HORSE RACING Flat racing is held five times a year in the small-town atmosphere of Wexford's racecourse at Bettyville, west of downtown, on the main Waterford road, N25 (phone: 21681).

SWIMMING Southeast Ireland is known for its comparative abundance of sunshine, which can be enjoyed at a number of beaches around Wexford, including Curracloe, Rosslare, Carne, and Kilmore Quay. Some hotels, such as the *Great Southern* and *Kelly's Strand,* also have indoor swimming pools for guests; the pool at the *Talbot* is open to non-registered guests (see *Checking In*).

TENNIS *Kelly's Strand,* a family-run hotel since 1845, has 2 tennis outdoor and 2 indoor courts, and is usually booked well in advance. This property also features a squash court, indoor/outdoor pools, a sauna, and the nearby beach (Rosslare; phone: 32114). In addition, visitors are welcome to use the all-weather courts at the *Wexford Harbour Boat Club,* Redmond Rd. (phone: 22039).

THEATER

In summer an Irish cabaret is held several nights a week at the *Talbot* hotel (see *Checking In*). Special programs take place at the *Wexford Arts Centre* (see *Special Places*) and at the *Theatre Royal* (High St.; phone: 22144). The *Razor's Edge Arts Theatre Co.* (Paul Quay, phone: 22948) offers contemporary plays, plus summertime street and beach entertainment.

MUSIC

Wexford is a lively town at night, with plenty of good singing pubs, cabaret, and ballroom dancing at most of the larger hotels. If you're lucky, *Sonas,* a popular group of five young musicians, will be singing Irish ballads as well as a few humorous, modern tunes. There is Irish music most nights in the *Shelmalier Bar* of *White's* hotel and in the *Tavern* of the *Talbot* hotel. There also is jazz on Sundays at the *Talbot.* Look for a *seisiún,* an evening — or session — of song and dance, sponsored by *Comhaltas Ceoltóirí Eireann,* a national organization for the promotion of traditional Irish folk music. These very authentic sessions are held in some 30 cities and towns during the summer. In Wexford, they usually take place once a week at *White's* and the *Talbot.* South of Wexford, traditional *ceili* dances are held on Thursday and Saturday evenings at the *Yola Farmstead,* and reservations are necessary (Tagoat; phone: 31177). For information on music festivals, see *Special Events.*

NIGHTCLUBS AND NIGHTLIFE

The *Park's Nite Club* disco swings into action on Thursday, Friday, and Saturday nights at *White's* hotel (see *Checking In*), as does *Speaker's Music Bar,* which is also in the hotel. *Kelly's Strand* hotel, in Rosslare (phone: 32114), also has dancing and entertainment most evenings.

Best in Town

CHECKING IN

Wexford is a very hospitable town, offering several fine hotels and plenty of bed and breakfast establishments. Most hotels include breakfast in their rates. In summer, an expensive hotel room will cost about $100 and up for a double, and a moderate room will run from $65 to $95. A single room in a bed and breakfast establishment will cost about $20 a night, a double about $40. Rates are lower from December through March, but about $10 higher per room on bank holidays and during the opera festival. All telephone numbers are in the 53 area code unless otherwise indicated.

EXPENSIVE

Ferrycarrig The top choice in this town is actually out of town, about 2 miles north. Ideally situated, it overlooks the River Slaney estuary, near Ferrycarrig Bridge and opposite the Irish National Heritage Park. Each of the stylishly furnished 40 bedrooms offers a lovely view of the water and surrounding countryside. Facilities include 2 outdoor tennis courts and walking trails, as well as a first-rate restaurant (see *Eating Out*). Enniscorthy Rd. (phone: 22999; fax: 41982).

Talbot Overlooking Wexford Harbour along the quays, it has 104 rooms, all with baths/showers; and 2 fine restaurants, the *Guillemont* and the *Pike Room* (see *Eating Out*). Its leisure center has a heated indoor pool, gym, squash courts, saunas, and a solarium. The *Tavern* offers live music, from traditional to jazz, and there's a weekly Irish cabaret in summer. Trinity St. (phone: 22566; 800-223-6510 from the US; fax: 23377).

White's Originally opened in 1779, it is now also known as the "new" *White's*, with 82 rooms of varying size and quality but all with baths. There are 2 restaurants; *Captain White's* is especially good (see *Eating Out*). The hotel's 2 taverns — the *Speaker's Music Bar* and the *Shelmalier* — are popular for sing-along sessions. George St. (phone: 22311; 800-528-1234 from the US; fax: 45000).

MODERATE

Great Southern On a cliff overlooking Rosslare Harbour, it has 100 rooms, all with private baths, plus an indoor heated swimming pool, a tennis court, saunas, and evening entertainment on summer weekends. Open April through December. Rosslare Harbour (phone: 33233; 800-44-UTELL or 800-243-7687 from the US; fax: 33543).

Wexford Lodge This modern 2-story hostelry has 20 rooms, all with baths. There's also a spacious restaurant. Situated north of town overlooking the River Slaney, adjacent to Wexford Bridge. Dublin Rd. (phone: 23611; 800-365-3346 from the US; fax: 23342).

Whitford House Follow the signposts 2 miles south of town to find this modern guesthouse with countryside views from its wide windows. There are 25 cheery bedrooms, each with private bath, color TV set, and telephone; guests also enjoy a restaurant, lounge bar, reading room, and use of a heated indoor pool and tennis court. New Line Rd. (phone: 43444 or 43845).

EATING OUT

Whether a candlelight dinner or a tasty salad in relaxed surroundings is desired, visitors can find a restaurant to suit both appetite and billfold in

Wexford. Dinner for two (excluding wine, drinks, and tips) in an expensive restaurant will cost $75 or more; in a moderate one, between $40 and $75; and in an inexpensive one, under $40. All telephone numbers are in the 53 area code unless otherwise indicated.

EXPENSIVE

Captain White's Comfortable and stylish with pink linen and dark wood, this place has an international menu, offering choices such as Cajun/creole chicken and prawns, Kilmore Quay seafood pancake, lamb couscous Casablanca with fruits and spices, and New Zealand rack of lamb with pineapple pilaf and cashews. Open daily for lunch and dinner. Reservations necessary. Major credit cards accepted. In *White's Hotel,* George St. (phone: 22311).

Ferrycarrig With panoramic views of the River Slaney estuary and the surrounding gardens, this conservatory-style restaurant in the hotel of the same name offers an idyllic setting and good food. The menu, which changes daily, includes such dishes as sautéed Kilmore Quay king scallops in a dill and white wine sauce; breast of duck in a strawberry and vinaigrette sauce; and Wicklow lamb. Save room for the homemade ice cream and pastries. Open daily for lunch and dinner year-round . Reservations advised. Major credit cards accepted. Enniscorthy Rd. (phone: 22999).

Guillemot The main dining room of the *Talbot* hotel, this innovative place has introduced a dual-menu concept to serve both expensive tastes and more moderate budgets. Seafood (especially local lobster, mussels, and pink trout) is a specialty on each menu, and there is an extensive wine list. Open daily for lunch and dinner. Reservations necessary. Major credit cards accepted. Trinity St. (phone: 22566).

MODERATE

Bohemian Girl Homemade soup, salads, and appetizing seafood specials such as mussels in garlic butter make this a particularly good place to stop for lunch or a moderately priced evening meal. Eugene and Lorraine Gillen run this colorful pub/bistro named after the opera by William Balfe, who lived in the corner building. Open daily for lunch and dinner. Reservations advised for dinner. MasterCard and Visa accepted. 2-4 N. Main and Monck Sts. (phone: 24419).

Cellar Set in the former wine cellar of a 300-year-old Georgian country house, this dining place is known for its Wexford mussels in garlic, wild venison, and flaming pepper steaks. Open year-round for dinner Tuesdays through Saturdays and for lunch on Sundays. Reservations necessary. MasterCard and Visa accepted. *Horetown House,* Foulksmills, about 20 minutes west of Wexford Town (phone: 51-63771 or 51-63706).

Granary Seating is in booths in this quiet, rustic place with a beamed ceiling, wooden pillars, hanging plants, and copper kettles. Its reputation for good food is well established and the menu ranges from local lobster and mussels to free-range duck, chicken, lamb, and beef. Open Mondays through Saturdays for dinner only; reduced early bird prices are offered from 5 to 7 PM. Reservations advised. Major credit cards accepted. Westgate (phone: 23935).

Neptune This award-winner is set in a fishing village on the River Barrow estuary, about a half hour from Wexford Town. Crab claws, prawns, mussels, and lobster are among the menu's bounty of seafood; other specialties include Hungarian goulash, T-bone steaks, parsnip soup, vegetarian salads, and homemade ice cream. When weather permits, there's outdoor dining on the patio. Open daily for lunch and dinner. Closed Sundays from November through April. Reservations necessary. Diners Club, MasterCard, and Visa accepted. Ballyhack Harbour (phone: 51-89284).

Pike Room The grillroom of the *Talbot* hotel is a good spot for steaks, chops, and seafood, all served in a setting full of historical mementos. Open daily for breakfast, lunch, and dinner. Reservations unnecessary. Major credit cards accepted. Trinity St. (phone: 22566).

INEXPENSIVE

Kate's Kitchen In the heart of town, just off Main Street, this cheery little café presents fresh and homemade soups, salads, and meat pies, as well as quiches, crêpes, and pasta. It's also a great spot for a snack, or a cup of tea or coffee. Open daily for breakfast, lunch, and dinner. No credit cards accepted. Reservations unnecessary. Henrietta St. (phone: 22456).

SHARING A PINT

The *Crown Bar* (Monck St.; no phone) is one of the oldest pubs in Ireland and has been held by the same family since 1841. Fiona Kelly and her mother, Mrs. Annie Kelly, open for business in the late afternoon and they'll tell you all about the days when the *Crown* was a stagecoach inn popular with traveling judges and their assistants. The cozy back rooms are filled with antique prints, military gear, swords, and other arms that the proprietor's father collected from all over the world. Another good place to stop for a drink and a chat is the *Thomas Moore Tavern* (in the Cornmarket; phone: 24348); the poet's mother was born here. *Tim's Tavern* (51 S. Main St.; phone: 23861) has thatching over the bar and good snacks, and the *Wren's Nest* (Custom House Quay; phone: 22359) has a seafaring atmosphere. The *Westgate Bar* (Enniscorthy Rd.; phone: 22086), near the Old City walls, is also worth a visit. If you're looking for an unusual photo opportunity, the "Bar and Undertaker" sign at *Con Macken's* (near Bull Ring; phone: 22949) is a classic. Have a drink while enjoying a view of the River Slaney at the *Oak Tavern* (about 2 miles north of town on Enniscorthy Rd. in Ferrycarrig; phone: 24922).

Diversions
Unexpected Pleasures and Treasures

For the Experience

Quintessential Ireland

Ireland's small size tempts visitors to try to see the entire country in a single trip. The distances look short on a map and the miles seem quite modest, but don't be deceived.

Trying to get from Killarney to Galway between lunch and dinner means not only rushing through Counties Limerick and Clare, but also missing the essence of Ireland. True, even at this speed, it is impossible to miss the rainbow of greens, the rainbows themselves, and the otherwise gorgeous skies and scenery. But the whole point of Ireland is her people — ancient or living, silent or talkative — their histories and connections. Everything in Ireland seems built to human scale. Every nook and cranny has its own name, usually linking it with real or imagined former inhabitants. Scenery, however grand, never intimidates visitors, and otherwise forbidding mountains have names that are musical and wonderfully personal — Ben Lettery, Ben Bulben, and Errigal. Cities and towns are more hospitable to pedestrians than to drivers, and can be walked thoroughly with little strain. Even cosmopolitan Dublin feels cozy for a city of a million souls.

The Irish concept of time is unique and elastic; it often feels imprecise to Americans. In every transaction, there is always time for a chat. Anything after noon can be "evening"; revels of all types start late and go long into the night — making a night of it means the *whole* night. Take your time in Ireland and pretty soon you'll think you have far more of it. Here is just a sampling of the unique experiences that make a visit to Ireland pure magic:

TREADING THE IRISH BOARDS When the *Abbey,* Dublin's most famous theater, offers productions of plays by early Irish playwrights like John Millington Synge, Sean O'Casey, or co-founder William Butler Yeats, these classics open the Irish heart and mind to a visitor. The *Abbey* is not the sole keeper of the keys to the kingdom, however. Check local theaters around the country like the *Druid Theatre* and *An Taibhdhearc* in Galway, the *Hawk's Well* in Sligo, and the *Guildhall* in Derry for renditions of Irish drama from Oscar Wilde and Synge to Brian Friel and Tom Murphy. The level of talent — both professional and amateur — is exemplary, the theaters intimate, and the sound of Irish voices absolutely magical.

SHORTENING THE ROAD It is not uncommon for Irish vacationers traveling, say, from Dublin to Clifden, a nonstop drive of about 5 hours, to "shorten the road" with a few stops at favorite pubs along the way. They pause as much for spiritual as for liquid refreshment, to take the local conversational temperature as it varies from County Meath to County Roscommon to County Galway. Behind the wheel, all is speed, dash, and more than a little daring. Be assured, however, Irish travelers know how to take their time, pausing to savor a chat more than the scenery. For American visitors, the English language in the mouth of an Irish man, woman, or child sounds like a marvelous new tongue. Few words are rarely used when more will do; color rather than precision is the rule. A pub stop for directions may not clarify the way, but it will illuminate the country.

SHARING A "JAR" AT A COUNTRY PUB You may park next to a petrol pump, squeeze past bundles of peat and bags of feed and fertilizer, and be distracted by shelves of groceries, but be assured there is a bar in there somewhere. Country pubs are rural Ireland's answer to the mini-mall, invented before the question was even asked, and usually crammed into a space too small to swing a cat. Locals arrive by foot or on bikes, buy milk, bread, and bacon, and have a sociable sip before heading back down their own *boreen* (a tiny, unpaved lane). A wonderfully workable Irish solution to after-hours shopping is the family-owned pub attached to a grocery store. No matter that the shop is dark and long closed, nor that it appears to be a separate entity. A polite inquiry to the barman (and the patience to wait while he attends to the more important business of dispensing pints) will yield the milk or bread or other necessity. If he's very busy, he might just open the door to the shop, tell you to get what you want, and pay at the bar on the way out.

WHEN OYSTERS (AND MORE) "R" IN SEASON Let there be oysters under the sea — or in this case, Galway Bay — and there will always be love. Smallish and tasting like a sweet smack of the sea, these exquisitely fresh oysters deserve frequent sampling, and are best washed down with a tall jar of Guinness stout. When September heralds the "r" months once again, the folks in Galway celebrate with an *Oyster Festival:* 2 days of partying that leave visitors feeling they have been celebrating for a month. (Oyster lovers beware: The large, rough Japanese oysters are beginning to creep into the menus of some establishments. These don't have a "closed" season, so are available year-round, but connoisseurs insist they are mediocre mollusks.) Happily, another Irish delectable, smoked salmon, *is* available year-round. Aficionados ask for wild rather than farmed salmon, but when it's well smoked, it is often hard to tell the difference. Enamored visitors have been known to eat smoked salmon scrambled into their breakfast eggs, on slabs of brown bread and butter at lunch, and then again as a "starter" before dinner — all in the same day. Interrupt the seaborne goodies with liberal doses of native cheeses, most of them handmade, all creamy rich and fresh-air infused. Known as farmhouse cheeses, they are made in small batches, usually on the same farm as the goats and cows that produced the raw ingredients. In good restaurants and small grocery stores, look for names like Cashel Blue from County Tipperary, Ireland's answer to Stilton; Lough Caum, a creamy goat cheese from County Clare; or Milleens, a soft cow's milk cheese from County Cork. When in doubt, be sure to try anything made nearby.

A SOFT DAY It's not exactly raining, but the wipers are on; you don't need an umbrella, but your feet are getting wet. The Irish have many onomatopoeic expressions for precipitation — it may be showering, lashing, belting, or even pissing — but none so apt as "soft." A soft day magically lights up the landscape, for the wet veil over the sun casts a special glow. You may not see the distant mountains standing atop the garden steps of Powerscourt, but the flower borders bloom incandescently and the shadowy ruin of the house comes alive again. Soft days fur the trees and rock walls with mosses, stud the hedgerows with tiny ferns, and transform a country lane into a glade full of magical life. A soft day makes travelers slow down, look about for a rainbow, and understand the genesis of Irish tweed.

TAILORING THE TWEEDS Irish tweeds perfectly capture the myriad greens and hazy blues of the country's fields and sky, the luminous grays of the cliffs, the splashes of bright fuchsia blossoms, and the golden flicker of gorse and lichen on the rocks. Anything made from this sturdy, appealing fabric stands up well however soft the weather, and keeps the wearer dry and cozy (but not burdened). County Donegal is practically a synonym for tweed, and while all manner of tweed items are sold throughout the country, a special cachet lingers over a jacket or skirt purchased on its home ground. Companies like *Magee's* and *John Molloy* still employ home weavers throughout the county, and include the craftsperson's name in the garment label. Other counties have their own claims to tweed fame: *Millar's* in Clifden, County Galway, weaves tweed blankets as distinctive as the Connemara landscape; *Avoca Weavers,* whose home is in County Wicklow, capture the soft rainbow colors of Ireland's garden; nontraditional weavers like *Helena Ruuth* in Bray near Dublin combine silks and linens in a misty Irish palette. Best get one of each.

SING AN IRISH SONG Ireland's music, laden with the country's heartbreaking history, ironically inspires the most extraordinarily cheerful evenings. Each part of Ireland has its song: "The Rose of Tralee," "The Fields of Athenry," "Dublin in the Rare Old Times," "The Mountains of Mourne," and "The West's Awake" are just a few of the best-known. Pubs like the *King's Head* in Galway City, the *Corner Stone* in Lahinch, County Clare, *O'Connor's* in Doolin, County Clare, or *Mannion's* in Clifden, County Galway, post signs announcing "Traditional Music Tonight." Informal playing, however — called a *seisún* (session) — is common at these and countless other pubs. Impromptu songfests are the Irish version of a digestif at private parties, as well as at country hotels like the *Rock Glen,* near Clifden, County Galway. Every Irish man, woman, and child has a party piece, and everyone participates, entertaining each other with a gusto that makes one forget that television was ever invented. Sessions go late into the night, kept afloat with lashings of spirits and pints. Resist the impulse to retire at a sensible hour, be sure to take a turn buying a round of drinks, and don't worry about being in good voice. Participation counts much more than talent, and the hospitable Irish will likely break into "New York, New York" or "I Left My Heart in San Francisco" in reciprocal delight at your contribution.

THE KINGDOM OF CONNEMARA, COUNTY GALWAY You can drive round it in a day and not see it all in a year. This marvelously diverse western shoulder of County Galway has no official boundaries, but Galway Bay on one side and the Atlantic Ocean on another are generally accepted. There are only rough approximations for the rest.

Just beyond the wooded outskirts of Oughterard, the road bends and rises, the trees disappear, and the looming Maamturk Mountains appear ahead. For travelers from Galway, Connemara begins here with this small taste of astonishing geographical diversity. Farther on, the landscape stretches over bog and lake, one minute wooded and shadowy, the next wild and beautifully stark. The coast is rocky and forbidding, but liberally studded with wide, sandy beaches and hidden, pebbled coves. To make it really your own, ride a Connemara pony along the broad beach at Dog's Bay near Roundstone or on the cliffside fields of Errislannen peninsula. Or see Connemara from one of its high places, like the Sky Road in Clifden, so called because there's more sky than road. A walk along the rolling trails in the Connemara National Park will make you feel master of every bog, island, and inlet spread out at your feet.

POETIC PERFECTION, COUNTIES SLIGO AND GALWAY County Sligo's landscape, draped with song and story, inspired the young William Butler Yeats's poetic imagination. His own legend now clings to those favorite spots, and Glencar Waterfall, the Lake Isle of Inishfree, and the Hazelwood are part of the landscape of great English literature — as lovely as the poems they inspired. Yeats's grave, at the foot of Ben Bulben Mountain, is as dramatic a landmark as he intended and an authentic goose-bump experience — even for non-English majors. Farther south there is another Yeats landscape, the gentler one surrounding his ancient tower home, Thoor Ballylee in County Galway. Here, where he wrote the mature poems that are the bedrock of his genius, the poet's spirit lingers in the murmur of the little river flowing under the "ancient bridge" by the tower.

ON BLOOM'S TRAIL Ireland was the country James Joyce loved to hate, but Dublin he simply loved. Never mind that many of the hallowed halls and houses of the hero of his *Ulysses* no longer stand; devoted Joyceans follow Leopold Bloom's minutely described footsteps each *Bloomsday,* June 16.

For those who never get past page 23, a visit to the Martello tower overlooking Dublin Bay at Sandycove near Dún Laoghaire, site of stately, plump Buck Mulligan's blasphemous revels, evokes images of the irreverent master.

A WEEK AT THE RACES The city of Galway is a frenzy during *July Race Week,* for generations a fixture of this horse-mad country. Though crawling with serious fans, this meet has a holiday air and you need only know the front of a horse from the back to be part of it all. Sit in the stands to get a good view of both the flat and steeplechase racing. Galwegians, however, find the real *craic* (meaning "fun" and pronounced *crack*) in the popular enclosure, where betting, hawking, and all manner of amusements vie with the horses for attention.

THE BURREN, COUNTY CLARE It means "rocky place" in Irish, which is an understatement. Hills and fields formed by slabs of limestone in a rainbow of grays conceal a wealth of tiny wildflowers in their crannies. Rivers flow underground, salt spray mists the stony coast, and tiny pastures form astonishingly fertile grassy oases in the rock. The Burren's unique and fragile ecosystem fascinates serious botanists and naturalists, and captivates the rest of us with its haunting, desolate beauty. Ireland's earliest people lived here and left rings of stones that look full of hidden messages. To walk in the ancient silence, broken by the hum and moan of the wind in the rocks, is to feel them trying to speak.

LAND OF SAINTS Christianity came to Ireland in the 5th century and took the country by storm. Tempest-tossed relics of this fervent hurricane litter the country; it is impossible to go very far without seeing a roofless church, usually with a companion round tower, both embraced by a crumbling stone wall. Some, like Clonmacnoise on the River Shannon, restored and carefully labeled, are nearly as busy with visitors and the faithful as they were in their heyday. Others, like Jerpoint Abbey near Thomastown, County Kilkenny, and Kilmacdaugh near Gort, County Galway, stand wrapped in silence. At small ruins like these, get the key from the caretaker as directed by the sign on the gate, and take a few minutes to find the old, worn small faces carved in the walls. Their simple ancient lines speak of the particular, idiosyncratic kind of faith that still endures in Ireland as nowhere else. Less formal and likely more ancient sacred spots like holy wells and hilltop shrines are known in many country places. A climb up steep, pyramid-shaped Croagh Patrick in County Mayo combines a devout pilgrimage with that spirit of jovial outing the Irish bring to their religious observances.

BY THE BOOK Monks in Ireland's monasteries kept the lamp of learning flickering through Europe's Dark Ages, laboring over manuscripts in their dimly lit towers. Another bookish explosion, which began with the Literary Renaissance in the early part of this century and is still going strong, keeps

Irish bookshops well stocked with collectible first editions. Almost any Irish bookstore provides a diverting haven on a rainy day. A gem like *Kenny's* on High Street in Galway combines a browser's heaven of old and collectible books and another of prints and maps with an excellent stock of Ireland's contemporary poets and writers. The shop rambles over 5 floors of two back-to-back old Galway houses, and includes a gallery featuring Ireland's best contemporary artists. Each member of the affable Kenny family will happily share his or her expertise or opinion, and while away an afternoon, rainy or otherwise.

Pub Crawling

There are more than 10,000 pubs in the Republic of Ireland and another 2,000 in the North — which means there's a pub for every 360 people. There are high class bars in expensive luxury hotels, with modern, tiled WCs, and there are age-darkened country pubs with outside toilets (the state of the toilet being a fair indication of the pub's standard). A Roscommon establishment, *James J. Harlow's Funeral Requisites and Furniture Stores,* is at once pub, hardware shop, and gallery of old advertising; Richard MacDonnell's pub in Dingle sells shoes, boots, and leather belts hand-fashioned by the octogenarian proprietor opposite the bar, where he pulls a wonderful pint of Guinness. At *Joe McHugh's Bar* in the lobster-fishing town of Liscannor, County Clare (and at many others like it), it's possible to buy barley sugar, freshly sliced bacon, or a pair of rubber boots along with stout; the *Humbert Inn* in Castlebar, County Mayo, is crammed with musty memorabilia — whips and cudgels from an old English jail, Victorian bottle corkers, and other curiosities. There are sailors' and fishermen's pubs, expatriates' pubs, pubs with gallows and pubs with gardens, pubs with 90-foot bars, country pubs where the dart board is well used and the tables are marked with the rings of a thousand nights of wet-bottomed glasses, city pubs with stained glass and elaborately paneled snugs that have witnessed all manner of clandestine meetings and revolutionary conspiracies. And that's just the beginning. But no matter what its type, the Irish pub — and not the private party — is where weddings, christenings, and funerals invariably end.

The center of pub life, besides the talk, is the distinctive, robust black beer with a creamy white head known as stout. Rich and full-bodied in taste, it was brewed for the first time in Dublin in 1759 and is now consumed in Ireland to the tune of some 2 million pints a day. Three different brands of stout are available: Guinness, which is Dublin's brew, made in Europe's biggest brewery, and two stouts from Cork, Beamish & Crawford and Murphy's. Each brand has a distinctive flavor, but even the same make varies from one pub to the next, depending on how the pints are pulled. Pulling is considered a high art in Ireland: The method by which the brew is put into the glass is paramount; the stout must be left to rest a minute while the glass is partly filled before being topped off, and the excess foam must be wiped off with a ruler or other straight edge, then topped off again so that the drink can be consumed through the creamy foam. Other factors are equally important, however: the temperature in the cellar where the casks are kept (it must be constant and just so), the distance between cask and tap, and the frequency with which the stout is drawn. It all makes a difference.

But stout is not the only drink. There is also Harp, which is brewed in Dundalk, and Smithwick's — a bit darker than Harp, but not as dark as stout — which has been made in Kilkenny since 1710 in a brewery on the site of a 12th-century Franciscan monastery whose Romanesque tower still stands.

Whiskey is also a traditional drink, the word itself deriving from the Irish *uisge beatha,* meaning "water of life." (Note that it is spelled with an *e,* in contrast to Scotch *whisky.*) Russia's Peter the Great called Irish whiskey "the best of all the wines." The top brands are Jameson, Power, Paddy, and Bushmills — the last made at a distillery dating from 1608, the world's oldest.

Another local liquor, with roots deep in Ireland's liquid past, is the fiery white distilled spirit known as *poitín* (also known as *poteen* and pronounced put-*cheen*). Many Irish-Americans involved in bootlegging during Prohibition had learned how to distill spirits from making this liquid fire at home in Ireland by boiling together barley, sugar, yeast, and water over a constant flame with the steam running through copper pipe in a barrel of icy water. It was illegal then and continues to be so, though it is still widely manufactured around Connemara and is sold at about half the price of legal liquor. But if it isn't made with scrupulous care — or if it's unscrupulously adulterated with pure alcohol — it can be dangerous, so it's wise to avoid it.

Pub hours vary. In the Republic, pubs are open Mondays through Saturdays from 11:30 AM to 11 PM in winter, a half hour later in summer; Sunday hours are noon to 11 PM with some places closing from 2 to 4 PM. In Northern Ireland, pubs are open Mondays through Saturdays from 11:30 AM to 11 PM, with an additional half-hour "drink up" time. Licensing laws now permit pubs in Northern Ireland to open Sundays from 12:30 to 2:30 PM and 7 to 10 PM; some publicans, however, choose to remain closed. In both the Republic and Northern Ireland, hotel guests are entitled to drink in their hotel outside the legal hours, though availability depends on individual circumstances and staffing. Check with the hotel management about their policy regarding legal closing time.

Bars are generally quiet in the daytime, since most people don't usually come out to drink until about 9 in the evening. So to meet a few locals and swap some yarns, late evening is the time to start. But while enjoying the convivial drinking scene until the very moment that the publican's "Time, gentlemen, time" sounds serious, remember the saying of the wise old seer:

"The first cup for thirst, the second for pleasure, the third for intemperance, and the rest for madness." Consider, too, that the *gardaí* (police), traditionally indulgent toward "a drop too much," have changed their tune in recent years. Nowadays the rule is: If you indulge, let someone else do the driving.

For a list of the best pubs in Ireland's major cities and towns, see *Sharing a Pint* in the individual chapters in THE CITIES. The following is a representative selection of some of the most interesting Irish pubs found off the beaten path, listed alphabetically by county and town, beginning with the Irish Republic. See *Traditional Irish Music* for still other ideas. But be prepared to explore — there are plenty of other pubs to choose from and that memorable spot may be just around the corner. *Sláinte!*

DERRAGARRA INN, Butlersbridge, County Cavan, Irish Republic Nobody could miss this pub, probably the best in the midlands and certainly the one with the most character: On the roof stands a life-size replica of a donkey and cart. Inside, turf and log fires in the two large open hearths ward off the chill when the weather demands. Since present owner John Clancy took over, the place has won 19 awards for its food and its homey decor. Food, all homemade and freshly prepared, is served every day during licensed hours. The steaks are famous throughout the midlands, and none of the meat ever sees a deep freeze, a fact that Clancy relays to visitors in a tone that conveys his horror at the very thought. Details: *Derragarra Inn,* Butlersbridge, County Cavan, Irish Republic (phone: 49-31003).

DURTY NELLY'S, Bunratty, County Clare, Irish Republic Stationed on the main road within 10 miles of Limerick City and Shannon Airport, this pub is next door to Bunratty Castle, where the buses disgorge great clumps of tourists bound for the medieval banquets (see *Mead and Meat Pies: Historical Banquets*); and so the pub is never without its share of rubberneckers, mostly American. Nonetheless, most of the people in the vast and almost always crowded premises are Irish — and intent on enjoying themselves in the lounge, where the tourists go; in the local bar, where they do not; or in the piano room, which separates the other two rooms and from which the highest volume of music comes. Upstairs is what the management terms the "quiet bar"; and sure enough, it's an oasis of stillness, where the murmuring of the 2 dozen white doves kept by owner Humphrey O'Connor is about the only sound. The *Oyster,* one of two restaurants on the premises, which has a small stand-up bar, is also pleasant; visitors are permitted to sit at the tables only when ordering a meal. The fare is good, the prices are reasonable, and the restaurant is popular with locals on a night out. A second restaurant, the *Loft,* is more formal, with a continental menu. Hearty sandwiches and soup also are available in the bars. Music and song may erupt at any time; it's welcomed and even encouraged by the enlightened management. Details: *Durty Nelly's,* Bunratty, County Clare, Irish Republic (phone: 61-364861).

FANNY O'DEA'S, Lissycasey, County Clare, Irish Republic This west Clare pub, about halfway between Ennis and Kilrush, is noteworthy for both its unique history and a unique potable. The story of the pub's founding goes something like this: On a winter's night in 1790, a judge named Robert Vere O'Brien was traveling by horse-drawn coach from Ennis to Kilrush, when a snowstorm forced him to seek shelter in Lissycasey from Fanny O'Dea, who catered to his needs and served him a drink known as an egg flip. In appreciation for her hospitality, the judge granted O'Dea a license to sell intoxicating drinks. Today, the egg flip — which tastes something like *advocaat* (a Dutch eggnog) and is made using an ancient recipe that its custodians will not divulge — is the specialty of the house. Apart from this and other alcoholic beverages (including an excellent Irish coffee), the pub serves only tea, coffee, and sandwiches. Details: *Fanny O'Dea's,* Lissycasey, County Clare, Irish Republic (phone: 65-26304).

AHERNE'S, Youghal, County Cork, Irish Republic Located in an attractive Victorian seaside resort, this establishment, owned and managed by John and David Fitzgibbon and their families, is perhaps the best and most unpretentious pub restaurant in the south. The bar dispenses delectable smoked mackerel, smoked salmon, oysters, and dressed crab in addition to chicken liver pâté, vegetarian salad, and all kinds of succulent sandwiches; the restaurant offers lobster, scallops, prawns, mussels, black sole, fresh trout, and salmon from the River Blackwater, which enters the sea here, as well as a number of non-piscine dishes. The bar food is available all day, but dinner reservations are advised. Details: *Aherne's Pub & Seafood Bar,* 162-163 N. Main St., Youghal, County Cork, Irish Republic (phone: 24-92424).

TOWERS, Glenbeigh, County Kerry, Irish Republic Hotel bars tend to feel as if they've been cut from one cloth — there's a certain sameness about them. There are a few notable exceptions to this rule, however, among them the bar of Dublin's *Shelbourne* and this one, which is really an annex to a good seafood restaurant. The *Towers* is famous for being famous, and dozens of international celebrities have stayed here — understandably, since Glenbeigh is the perfect base for exploring the Ring of Kerry. There is music here every night during July and August, much of it of the inspired amateur variety and some of it even very enjoyable. Details: *Towers,* Glenbeigh, County Kerry, Irish Republic (phone: 66-68212).

MORRISEY'S, Abbeyleix, County Laois, Irish Republic This is the sort of pub that a true drinking man would stop into on a cold Monday morning and then not want to leave for a week. With its pot-bellied stove almost as rotund as some of the locals, it looks as if it hasn't changed since the time of our forebears. No meals or snacks are served, as the smell might interfere with the patrons' enjoyment of the marvelous pints of Guinness served here. An ideal R&R stop on the trip between Dublin and Cork. Details: *Morrisey's,* Abbeyleix, County Laois, Irish Republic (phone: 502-31233).

STANFORD'S PUB, Dromahair, County Leitrim, Irish Republic Structurally, this Main Street bar has endured none of the graftings and remodelings of most Irish pubs in the last century. In fact, even the family who owns it is the same: Proprietor Della McGowan is among the fourth generation of Stanfords to run the pub. Behind the bar are a couple of fiddles, a pair of guitars, a melodeon, a mandolin, a tin whistle, and a Jew's harp — not surprising considering the musical heritage of the area and the melodic inclinations of Tom McGowan. You may even get to hear an impromptu session one summer evening. Pub grub ranges from smoked salmon to Irish stew, and lunches and evening meals are served in the restaurant beside the bar. Details: *Stanford's Pub,* Dromahair, County Leitrim, Irish Republic (phone: 71-64140).

ANTRIM ARMS, Ballycastle, County Antrim, Northern Ireland One of the oldest hotels in Ireland, built as a coaching inn in 1745, this establishment retains its basic structure and antique appearance, right down to the windows, which are original. Novelist William Makepeace Thackeray's complimentary comments about its comforts in his *Travels Around Ireland* are still entirely relevant. From a drinker's point of view, however, what stands out are the bar's 100 or so malt whiskeys meant for display as well as for drinking, including the locally distilled Bushmills. Pub grub and more extensive meals are served year-round. Details: *Antrim Arms,* Castle St., Ballycastle, County Antrim, Northern Ireland (phone: 265-762284).

LONDONDERRY ARMS, Carnlough, County Antrim, Northern Ireland A horseshoe worn by Ireland's most famous horse, Arkle, when he won one of his three *Cheltenham Gold Cups* in the 1960s, is the proudest possession of Frank O'Neill, whose family has owned the *Londonderry Arms* hotel since 1947. It's not surprising, then, that this equine memento occupies the place of honor in its *Oak Panel* bar, along with a painting of the horse and Pat Taaffe, the jockey who rode him to victory. Other adornments include a scattering of driftwood carvings by local artist John Henshaw and a portrait of Lady Londonderry, who had the hotel built in 1848 and whose grandson, none other than Winston Churchill, inherited it in 1921. There's pub grub at lunchtime, and excellent dinners are served in the hotel dining room in the evenings. Details: *Londonderry Arms,* 20 Harbour Rd., Carnlough, County Antrim, Northern Ireland (phone: 574-885255).

DOBBINS INN, Carrickfergus, County Antrim, Northern Ireland The bar at this 16th-century former coaching inn is called the *John Paul Jones* because the American hero achieved the nascent United States' first naval victory in the bay that the inn overlooks. The decor takes a definitely nautical cue from this circumstance: A ship's wheel is at center stage, prints and pictures of ships hang on the walls, and bands from sailors' hats indicating the ships on which they served are on display. Only Maud, the pub's resident ghost, has nothing to do with the sea, but manifests herself by banging doors and knocking glasses off tables, but never too early in the morning, when people are "curing" themselves — in Ireland even a ghost knows that would be too much of a shock. Pub grub is served weekdays year-round, and the restaurant specializes in steaks. Details: *Dobbins Inn,* 6 High St., Carrickfergus, County Antrim, Northern Ireland (phone: 960-351905).

BAYVIEW, Portballintrae, County Antrim, Northern Ireland This is the only hotel ever to come under naval fire in Ireland, and the *Porthole Bar* displays proof of the attack: a piece of a shell fired by a German U-boat in 1918 at a ship that happened to be facing the hotel. (The shell overshot its target and came through the roof.) The pub grub is of a high standard; the specialty of the house is a steak flambéed with Bushmills and served with a red wine and cream sauce. Details: *Bayview,* 2 Bayhead Rd., Portballintrae, County Antrim, Northern Ireland (phone: 265-731453).

BLAKE'S OF THE HOLLOW, Enniskillen, County Fermanagh, Northern Ireland This handsome old pub is tucked away in a rabbit's warren of streets and alleys not far from St. MacCartan's Cathedral. Lamentably, the stock of rare Old Dublin Potstill whiskey, an Irishman's collector's item that was once among the alcoholic specialties of the house, has been depleted. But otherwise things are much the same as they were when the premises were last refurbished in 1887. (Note the long, marble-topped mahogany bar and the pine snugs, attractive enough to warrant praise from Ulster Heritage Societies publications and a government preservation listing). The exterior is still emblazoned with the great stripes of black and red that were originally painted for the benefit of the illiterate among its patrons, the Guinness is well pulled, and the faces of the patrons well creased. As for the mood, it is always subdued, and television intrudes on the drinkers' solitude only during major sporting events. The entrance on Church Street is the easiest to find. Details: *Blake's of the Hollow,* 6 Church St., Enniskillen, County Fermanagh, Northern Ireland (phone: 365-322143).

MELLON COUNTRY INN, Omagh, near Newtownstewart, County Tyrone, Northern Ireland Almost every American touring Northern Ireland visits the *Ulster-American Folk Park,* which illustrates some of the ties that have been forged down the centuries between Ulster and the US (see *Marvelous Museums*). This modern pub, a mile north of the folk park, provides relaxation, food, and drink for travelers. The menu offers steak sandwiches, surf-and-turf, and the like. A locally bred, hormone-free beef known as Tyrone black — which its producers consider to be Ireland's best — is the house specialty, along with whiskey: There are more than 150 different malt whiskeys in stock, including some from Wales, Japan, and the Isle of Man. Details: *Mellon Country Inn,* 134 Beltany Rd., Omagh, near Newtownstewart, County Tyrone, Northern Ireland (phone: 662-661224).

DIVERSIONS PUB CRAWLING

Rural Retreats

To travelers from abroad, one of the most striking features of the Irish countryside is the absence of billboards, the almost total lack of motels, and the abundance of homey inns, guesthouses, and country manors–turned–hotels. The tradition of hospitality goes back centuries, to the year 438, when the law of the land bade all who had the means to do so to entertain visitors, no questions asked. Even then there were guesthouses, where a fire continuously blazed on the hearth and meats were kept hot in vast cauldrons. In the 16th century, the Mayor of Dublin, Patrick Sarsfield, held open house every evening, dispensing libations freely. In today's hostelries, wooden stair treads worn to concavity by the footsteps of travelers through the ages, half-timbered walls, and beamed ceilings impart the same old-time feeling of hospitality.

Here is an assortment of some of Ireland's best rural retreats (listed alphabetically by county and town, beginning with the Irish Republic), including castle-hotels, inns, and country houses. Some warrant a stop if they're not too far afield; a handful of others, perhaps a shade more wonderful on one or more counts, are worth planning a whole holiday around. (For descriptions of special havens in and near Ireland's major cities and towns, see the *Checking In* sections in the individual chapters of THE CITIES; also see *Gone Fishing* in this section for a list of fishing hotels.)

Visitors should note that Irish hotel owners are usually a bit casual about when their establishments open and close. So if you are making a special trip — or if there is a specific establishment said to close in October that you want to visit in November — it's a good idea to check in advance before setting your plans in stone.

WORTH A LONG DETOUR

GREGANS CASTLE, near Ballyvaughan, County Clare, Irish Republic This sprawling country house is eminently comfortable, homey, and atmospheric, with traditional turf fires burning in the handsome fireplaces in the public rooms when the weather is chilly, a marble-floored entrance foyer, and antiques scattered throughout. But what really sets the place apart from other hostelries is its location, just an hour from Shannon Airport, in the center of the Burren, an area of enormous interest to serious botanists, amateur plant lovers, and inveterate admirers of magnificent scenery. The whole area is austere, mile upon mile of all-but-bare rock, riven by slashes of green, although in May and June it's dotted with colorful alpine flowers. Most of the comfortable bedrooms have magnificent views over this fabulous land and nearby Galway Bay. The restaurant has won awards for its food, and if the selection is not vast, the offerings are good and carefully prepared. As expected at an establishment just 4 miles from the harbor, seafood is a specialty. It also serves a good selection of local Burren cheeses, as well as vegetables fresh from the garden. A golf course is a half hour away, fishing can be arranged, and the area abounds in antiquities. Botanists who sally forth at odd hours should note that snacks and other viands are available all day in the *Corkscrew Bar,* named not for the oenophilic instrument but for the adjacent road, a narrow, tortuous lane that clings to the Burren slopes. Open *Easter* through October; 18 rooms and 4 suites, all with baths. Details: *Gregans Castle Hotel,* near Bally-vaughan, County Clare, Irish Republic (phone: 65-77005).

SEA VIEW HOUSE, Ballylickey, Bantry, County Cork, Irish Republic Not the least of this establishment's assets is its location, just 400 yards from a winding inlet of beautiful Bantry Bay in the tiny town of Ballylickey. The house itself, a tall, white structure built in 1890, has been masterfully doubled in size, without altering the lines or charm of the original façade. The 17 guestrooms have been enlarged into mini-suites, all with spacious, modern, private bathrooms. Each room, enhanced by panoramic views of the bay or gardens, is tastefully furnished with antiques and local period pieces. Although there are some ground-level accommodations (one room is equipped for disabled guests), most rooms are on the second or third floors. The food, prepared by proprietor Kathleen O'Sullivan, rates among the best in County Cork and the southwest. The traditional country-style fare includes fresh seafood, homemade soup and baked goods, local fruits, and vegetables from nearby and European markets. Horseback riding, fishing, boating, and other sports can be arranged. Open April through October. Details: *Sea View House Hotel,* Ballylickey, Bantry, County Cork, Irish Republic (phone: 27-50073).

CASHEL HOUSE, Cashel, County Galway, Irish Republic This Cashel — the other is in County Tipperary — is in Connemara, on the extreme west coast, a magical place of indigo mountains, winding inlets, and violet bog land where sheep sun themselves on the narrow roads. It is also the home of Dermot and Kay McEvilly's gracious mansion-turned-hotel, a Relais & Châteaux establishment where discreet informality is the watchword. The kitchen emphasizes seafood: Wild mussels, picked from the ocean just 20 yards across the road, make the world's fastest transit from sea to steamer. Dinners are not overly formal, and lunches are packed in picnic baskets or served unfussily in the little bar; plaice stuffed with smoked salmon mousse is a typical offering. Between meals, spend a few hours at the tiny private beach, glistening white and washed with icy Atlantic water. Horseback riding is a specialty; Connemara ponies are bred here and the house has several that are available to guests. There's angling in the nearby lakes, rivers, and ocean, and guests also can borrow a small sailing dinghy or rowboat to cruise the quiet waters of the bay not far away. Open March through November; 17 bedrooms and 13 mini-suites, all with private baths. Details: *Cashel House Hotel,* Cashel, County Galway, Irish Republic (phone: 95-31001; fax: 95-31077).

CURRAREVAGH HOUSE, Oughterard, County Galway, Irish Republic All the trappings of the old Anglo-Irish gentry adorn this Victorian-era house set on 150 beautiful acres at the edge of Lough Corrib. A tiger skin hangs on one wall, other furred and feathered trophies sit on mantles and bookshelves, and the garden is full of rhododendrons — kinder and gentler souvenirs of the family's Indian sojourns. There's even the requisite family legend, which holds that the original property, all 28,000 acres of it, was won from one of the wild O'Flaherty's in a game of cards. These days the family seat is a homey retreat for travelers. There are 15 guestrooms, all with private baths; and Harry and June Hodgson serve a six-course set dinner at 8 PM sharp. Lough Corrib and surrounding waters beckon fishermen with a yen for hooking brown trout, salmon, pike, and perch. Non-fishing guests can take a boat to the little island of Inchagoill to visit the ruined churches and enjoy the quiet. Others play tennis or explore the Connemara countryside. Open April to October (the dining room is open to non-guests by prior arrangement only). Details: *Currarevagh House,* Oughterard, County Galway, Irish Republic (phone: 91-82312 or 91-82313; fax: 91-82731).

PARK, Kenmare, County Kerry, Irish Republic The words "beautiful," "sumptuous," and "exquisitely tasteful" describe this late-Victorian establishment. Museum pieces are scattered throughout the hotel, beginning in the lobby, where guests register at an antique stockbroker's desk not far from a magnificent Italian water tank standing on dolphins and sea horses. Some bedrooms are furnished in the plain Georgian style, with cheval mirrors and four-poster beds; others are massively Victorian, done up with touches of William Morris; still others are contemporary in style. Everywhere, the standard of comfort is superb, and the views are heart-stopping. This alone makes the hotel worth visiting, but the restaurant here is a seminal influence on modern Irish cuisine. The food has earned a Michelin star, among other awards. Lobster and salmon are worth close attention, but game is served in season as well. The clientele includes the Irish who love luxury and the international set; the owner, Francis Brennan, actually manages to combine family warmth and sophisticated ambience. Open April to January 1; 50 guestrooms (of which 37 are suites with separate sitting rooms), all with private baths. Details: *Park Hotel Kenmare,* Kenmare, County Kerry, Irish Republic (phone: 64-41200; fax: 64-41402).

SHEEN FALLS LODGE, Kenmare, County Kerry, Irish Republic The 300-acre site was originally chosen as a home for the Earl of Kerry in the 18th century and was later used as a fishing lodge and a commercial fishery before it was purchased in 1988 by the present Danish owners, who have turned it into one of Ireland's finest hotels. The furnishings and decor are bright and airy, but an Old World charm is retained, thanks to open fireplaces, antiques, polished-brass fixtures, high ceilings, and original art. The 40 rooms and 8 suites are spacious and have king-size beds and every modern amenity, as well as wide-windowed views of the ever-flowing falls. This is an especially good spot for the sports-minded, with private salmon fishing on a 15-mile stretch of the River Sheen. (The hotel staff will clean and smoke salmon caught by guests and vacuum-pack it for transport home.) The grounds also include stables, with horses available for riding or trekking; miles of walking trails; extensive Victorian-style gardens; tennis courts; and croquet lawns. There also is an indoor leisure center with a Jacuzzi, sauna, steamroom, and sun deck, with aerobics classes and a masseuse available. A 9-hole golf course (slated to expand to 18 holes this year) is nearby. A fine restaurant, *La Cascade,* is aptly named after the falls that splash continuously beneath its windows. The restaurant, which is particularly romantic at night when the waters are floodlit, offers creative Irish cuisine for dinner; light lunches are served in the adjacent lounge. Other amenities include a billiard room, library, hair salon, wine cellar, and an outdoor barbecue area. The hotel also maintains a vintage 1922 Buick to provide local excursions for guests. Open mid-March through December. Details: *Sheen Falls Lodge,* Kenmare, County Kerry, Irish Republic (phone: 64-41600; fax: 64-48386).

GREAT SOUTHERN, Parknasilla, County Kerry, Irish Republic George Bernard Shaw, who came here twice annually for 15 years, wrote most of *Saint Joan* here, though how he managed to stay awake long enough to complete the first act is a mystery: The sheer soothing greenness and the soft air of the place are the world's greatest cures for insomnia. Although this hotel is state-run, without an especially gracious (or dotty) owner presiding, it does have a very distinguished ghost — the Protestant Bishop of Limerick Charles Graves, grandfather of poet and author Robert Graves, manifests himself occasionally in the west wing. But the place is exceptional for other reasons as well. The property itself is handsome, the gardens lush, and the dining room has distinguished itself for its French-accented menu. Among the specialties of the house are quenelles of seafood in basil sauce, breast of roast duck sauced with port, and chateaubriand carved at the table, as well as the finny dishes to be expected at a seaside location, and sweet endings ranging from flambéed puddings to sorbets and homemade ice creams. The selection of recreational opportunities is extremely wide: riding, a 9-hole golf course, a heated indoor pool, and more. Two small trawlers can be hired by the day to fish offshore for skate and shark, and freshwater anglers can go after trout in Long Lake in Tahilla. Open April through December; 84 guestrooms (including 3 suites) in several grades of comfort and cost, all with baths. Details: *Great Southern Hotel,* Parknasilla, County Kerry, Irish Republic (phone: 64-45122; fax: 64-45323).

KILKEA CASTLE, Castledermot, County Kildare, Irish Republic Tucked amid flat farmlands of the Kildare countryside, this imposing stone structure is the oldest inhabited castle in Ireland, dating back to 1180. Over the centuries, the castle changed hands many times until it opened as a hotel in the 1970s, but insufficient funding brought it to a close within a decade. It took a new owner, American-born and Hong Kong-based, to invest over $8 million and bring the castle up to international hotel standards. The guestrooms are located in both the original castle building (11 rooms), and a newer courtyard building (34 rooms). All are outfitted with half-canopied beds, chandeliers, remote control TV sets, and modern bathrooms. The main dining room, *de Lacy's,* emphasizes innovative Irish cuisine, with such dishes as smoked pheasant and juniper berries glazed with a black cherry sauce; breast of chicken filled with potato and leek soufflé on a mango and orange essence; and filet of lemon sole with nutmeg and ginger in a light shrimp sauce. The *Geraldine Room* is an atmospheric bar with original stone walls, stained glass windows, and a huge fireplace. There also is a health and fitness club with an indoor heated pool, an exercise room, saunas, a spa pool, steamrooms, a sunbed, and more. The grounds offer formal gardens, fishing for brown trout on the adjacent River Greese, 2 lighted hard-surface tennis courts, clay pigeon shooting, and an archery range. In addition, a new 18-hole golf course is scheduled to be completed this year. The castle is approximately 2½ miles from Castledermot and is well signposted from the town. Although slightly off the beaten track, it makes a good touring base since it is within an hour's drive of Kilkenny, Dublin, Waterford, and Wexford. Details: *Kilkea Castle Hotel,* Castledermot, County Kildare, Irish Republic (phone: 503-45156 or 503-45100; fax: 503-45187).

MOYGLARE MANOR, Molygare, Maynooth, County Kildare, Irish Republic Tall, gaunt, gray, and highly regarded by architects, this former residence of the Dukes of Leinster and retreat of superannuated duchesses is more warm and inhabitable than grand, despite its fine plaster ceilings and stately Georgian façade. The 17 bedrooms (16 doubles and a garden suite) are enchanting, furnished in Victorian style; some are ballroom-size with matching bathrooms, while others have half-tester beds or four-posters. The grounds are attractively landscaped, and the views leave no doubt as to the primary business of the area: This is horse country. The Curragh (see *Horsing Around*) is nearby; young horses gambol in the fields of the adjacent stud farm; and fellow guests include breeders, trainers, and buyers. Arrangements can be made for horseback riding at local stables and, in season and for experienced riders, for hunting with the *Kildare Foxhounds* or the *Ward Union.* The kitchen here is Franco-Irish-international, and food runs to the hearty rather than haute. On-the-spot, non-equine recreation is provided by a hard-surface tennis court and a pitch-and-putt golf course. All in all, this is a good base for seeing Dublin and its environs.

Open year-round, except for a few days at *Christmas*. Details: *Moyglare Manor,* Moyglare, Maynooth, County Kildare, Irish Republic (phone: 1-628-6351; fax: 1-628-5405).

KILDARE HOTEL AND COUNTRY CLUB, Straffan, County Kildare, Irish Republic
Opened in 1991, this property is already taking its place among the most luxurious accommodations in Ireland. The complex, set on 330 acres 30 miles from Dublin, consists of Straffan House, a 19th-century mansion that now serves as the main hotel building; a new hotel wing, which is actually a replica of the original mansion; several courtyard apartment units adjacent to the hotel; a 3-bedroom lodge; and a country club — popularly known as the *"K Club"* — which includes an 18-hole golf course, a clubhouse, and a large fitness center. The *Kildare* already has been awarded Five Diamonds by *AAA,* the only Irish hotel to receive that designation. The place exudes an air of elegance, tranquillity, and comfort. The 45 rooms and suites — decorated with antique furniture — feature all the extras, including color satellite TV, VCRs, mini-bars, direct-dial phones, hair dryers, and bathrobes. There's also 24-hour room service and maid service, a hair salon, shops, and ample parking. The elegant *Bryerley Turk* dining room features French fare, and afternoon tea is served in the lovely *Gallery.* Around the hotel buildings stretch the rolling green fairways of an 18-hole, 7,150-yard Arnold Palmer–designed golf course, the centerpiece of the *K Club.* The grounds also feature a mile-long stretch of the River Liffey where guests may fish for salmon and wild brown trout, and five lakes that are stocked with brown and rainbow trout, bream, carp, tench, and rudd. Horseback riding and hunting excursions also can be arranged. The clubhouse features the *Legends* restaurant and bar overlooking the golf course; the fitness center includes 2 indoor and 2 outdoor tennis courts and a tennis pro, squash courts, a large gym, a swimming pool, a sauna, a solarium, a spa, shops, and a snack bar. The country club facilities are open to visitors as well as hotel guests and club members; a smaller leisure center in the hotel, with a pool, small gym, sauna, steamroom, and spa, is reserved for registered guests. Details: *Kildare Hotel and Country Club,* Straffan, County Kildare, Irish Republic (phone: 1-627-3111; fax: 1-627-1008).

ASHFORD CASTLE, Cong, County Mayo, Irish Republic At first glance this establishment looks like a cross between the last of the dinosaurs and the castle inhabited by Snow White's stepmother. The shape is long, low, and gray, with the battlements ridged like the scales down a dragon's back. The original hefty 13th-century section housed the Norman family known as the De Burgos, who conquered the surrounding land. The 18th-century French château section in the middle was home to the Oranmore and Browne families, and the most recent residents were kin of the stoutbrewing Guinnesses, in the persons of Lord and Lady Ardilaun. A hotel since 1939, unstintingly refurbished in recent years by a consortium of

Irish-American owners, the place is luxury incarnate, from the thick Oriental-toned carpeting to the Waterford chandeliers. Fine paintings, sculpture, and uninhabited antique armor are artfully deployed around the public rooms. The recreation is of the outdoor kind. Angling for trout, pike, perch, char, rudd, and bream is in adjacent Lough Corrib (the hotel kitchen will prepare the catch). Shooting rights over 25,000 acres — 2,000 of which are a controlled area — provide the chance of bagging pheasant, teal duck, snipe, and woodcock (see *Stalking and Shooting*); the lakeside chalet where Lord and Lady Ardilaun spent their wedding night is now in less romantic use as a site for shooters' lunches. Golf, tennis, and hunting are also part of the picture. The sedentary can ramble around the estate in jaunting cars and cruise up the lake in a boat that holds 50. The restaurant, which seats 40, has begun to win accolades. But despite the scope and the grandeur of it all, the castle is a delightful place, friendly and hospitable. Open year-round; 83 bedrooms and 6 suites, all with baths. A member of the Relais & Châteaux group. Details: *Ashford Castle Hotel,* Cong, County Mayo, Irish Republic (phone: 92-46003; fax: 92-46260).

HILTON PARK, near Clones, County Monaghan, Irish Republic Johnny and Lucy Madden, whose ancestors moved into the house in 1730, now live here in conditions that are at once shabby and grand. On the one hand is the worn carpet on the stairs; on the other are the giant interconnecting salons, kitchens the size of most houses, and the breast-high four-poster beds equipped with a ladder and covered with slippery, hand-embroidered linen counterpanes. Some bathrooms are the size of parks, but others — among them one with a fine view toward one of the nearby lakes — are minimal, consisting of pitchers and bowls on washstands. The dining room is a gallery of portraits, including clerical and military figures as well as a fellow who looks like a descendant of Count Dracula. Dinners and breakfasts are included, along with snack lunches on request, most of the raw materials for which come from the 550-acre farm and the fine kitchen garden. The cooking is generally inventive, and Lucy Madden even makes her own cream cheese. There's fishing for pike and trout on the property's two lakes and on others nearby, where guests can also go swimming and canoeing. Horseback riding and shooting are available by special arrangement nearby, and on the property are a 9-hole golf course and a lawn for croquet — which is a blood sport here. Open April through September by reservation only and at other times by arrangement (dining room for residents only); 5 double bedrooms, 3 with baths. Details: *Hilton Park,* Scotshouse, Clones, County Monaghan, Irish Republic (phone: 47-56007).

MARLFIELD HOUSE, Gorey, County Wexford, Irish Republic This handsome Regency mansion in the southeastern part of the country was a dower house for the Earls of Courtown, where their widows lived after their husbands' demise. This was life on a grand scale, among marble fireplaces and magnificent staircases, surrounded by views of the beautiful grounds seen through tall, elegant windows. As for the Relais & Châteaux hotel that now occupies the beautifully restored premises, there are almost not enough walls in the house to hold the awards that have been heaped on it, the only constant complaint being that the crows in the gardens caw too loudly in the morning. Bedrooms are charmingly furnished with four-poster or canopied beds, and other handsome pieces. The meals are positively sumptuous — as much for their settings as for the food — with breakfasts that include trout as well as porridge and cream; lunches served in the bar, where a mighty log fire blazes continuously; and dinners laid out in an elegant dining room that looks into a romantic curvilinear Victorian cast-iron conservatory. There's a private tennis court on the premises, and a golf course and long silvery strands of beach about a mile away. A pack of hounds is within striking distance, and bird watching, shooting, and fishing are all possible. Booking in advance is essential, especially during the tourist season. Open year-round, except for a week or so at *Christmas;* 13 bedrooms and 6 suites, all with baths. Details: *Marlfield House,* Gorey, County Wexford, Irish Republic (phone: 55-21124; fax: 55-21572).

TINAKILLY HOUSE, Rathnew, County Wicklow, Irish Republic An enormous gray Victorian mansion, this property stands out among the rolling green and purple hills of Wicklow. The building was originally erected in the 1870s for Captain Robert Halpin of the Great Eastern, the company that laid the first telegraph cable between Europe and America, and as far as possible, the furnishings are of that period. The 29 guestrooms, each with bath and up-to-date amenities, have a strongly masculine character befitting the old salt who built them. They are furnished with antiques, needlepoint chairs, and wood paneling; a number also have marble fireplaces, and four-poster or half tester beds, all very comfortable. Many look over the sea or the nearby bird sanctuary. The food has varied in quality over the years as chefs have come and gone; the present chef is highly regarded. One thing guests can always count on is proprietor Bea Power's superb brown bread. The house is an hour from Dublin along good roads, close to Glendalough and other attractions of County Wicklow, including the famous Mount Usher Gardens (see *Stately Homes and Great Gardens*). There is a tennis court on the grounds, riding can be arranged, and there is access to golf courses. This mansion is popular with BBC film crews and with actors. Open year-round except in late December. Details: *Tinakilly House Hotel,* Rathnew, County Wicklow, Irish Republic (phone: 404-69274; fax: 404-67806).

IF YOU'RE NEARBY

BALLYLICKEY MANOR HOUSE, Ballylickey, County Cork, Irish Republic The management of this property stresses personal service and aims to offer only the best. The hunting lodge that originally stood on this site burned in 1983, and the present main house was rebuilt according to the plans of the original. With two wings of suites, it provides true seclusion. There are also a number of cottages. The handsome lawns, gardens, and parkland bordering the River Ouvane, as well as the heated outdoor swimming pool, make this Relais & Châteaux establishment a lovely base for tours of Cork and Kerry. Closed November to March; 11 rooms, each with bath. Details: *Ballylickey Manor House,* Ballylickey, County Cork, Irish Republic (phone: 27-50071; fax: 27-50124).

BANTRY HOUSE AND GARDENS, Bantry, County Cork, Irish Republic Housed in the east and west wings of this 18th-century brick and stone mansion is an elegant bed and breakfast establishment with 9 rooms (8 with private baths). During a stay, guests can enjoy the fine gardens, as well as many pieces collected by the second Earl of Bantry during his travels in Europe from 1820 to 1840 (for more information on the collection, see *Stately Homes and Great Gardens*). Details: *Bantry House and Gardens,* Bantry, County Cork, Irish Republic (phone: 27-50047; fax: 27-50795).

ASSOLAS COUNTRY HOUSE, Kanturk, County Cork, Irish Republic This fine 17th-century manor is an idyll inside and out, with its riverside gardens, and public spaces and bedrooms full of comfortable chairs and attractive period furnishings. There's a flagstone-floored dining room inside and a grass tennis court outside — well maintained and ready for use. Open mid-March through October; 9 rooms, all with baths. Details: *Assolas Country House,* Kanturk, County Cork, Irish Republic (phone: 29-50015; fax: 29-50795).

ARD NA GREINE INN, Schull, County Cork, Irish Republic A farmhouse until the 1970s, this establishment is now a homey country inn full of 18th-century charm, and with its secluded location and extensive gardens it makes a delightful rural retreat. Schull itself is a pretty little fishing port in the shadow of Mount Gabriel, a good departure point for fair-weather trips to the windswept Carbery's Hundred Isles. Open April through October; 7 rooms, each with bath. Details: *Ard Na Greine Inn,* Schull, County Cork, Irish Republic (phone: 28-28181).

RATHMULLAN HOUSE, Rathmullan, County Donegal, Irish Republic This late-18th-century country-house resort (a member of the well-regarded *Irish Country Houses and Restaurants* association) is as snug as can be. Log and turf fires burn in the drawing room and library; the assorted rooms are stylishly fitted with antiques; and the conservatory-style dining room, with its tented ceiling, makes guests feel that they are dining in a garden. Outside the scenery is magnificent — from the tree-lined shore of Lough Swilly (on whose banks the hostelry sits) to the wildly grand coast and mountains to the west. The gardens are stunning and have won several awards. On its 25 acres, the hotel also has 2 tennis courts, a croquet lawn, and a putting green. There's a beautiful indoor pool as well. Open March to November; 23 rooms, 20 with private baths (room No. 4 has a particularly lovely view of the lake and the gardens). Details: *Rathmullan House,* Rathmullan, County Donegal, Irish Republic (phone: 74-58188; fax: 74-58200).

ROSLEAGUE MANOR, near Letterfrack, Connemara, County Galway, Irish Republic
Civilized and comfortable, this establishment is a gracious Georgian manor overlooking a quiet bay edged with woods. The public rooms are decked with antique silver and oil paintings, and the elegant dining room overlooks Ballinakill Bay and Diamond Hill. Owner/chef Paddy Foyle does wonders with local produce. There's also a tennis court and a sauna. Open *Easter* through October; 17 rooms, all with baths. Details: *Rosleague Manor,* Letterfrack, Connemara, County Galway, Irish Republic (phone: 95-41101; fax: 95-41168).

RENVYLE HOUSE, Renvyle, Connemara, County Galway, Irish Republic This attractive hotel overlooking the sea was once the country place of Oliver St. John Gogarty, a great Irish wit whom James Joyce immortalized as Buck Mulligan in *Ulysses.* The decor is antique and the atmosphere gracious; the guestrooms have a country cottage feel. Fishing is a big deal in these parts. It's a great place for families, and there are always lots of children here in the summer. Open late March through December; 56 rooms, each with bath. Details: *Renvyle House Hotel,* Renvyle, Connemara, County Galway, Irish Republic (phone: 95-43511 or 95-43444; fax: 95-43515).

KYLEMORE HOUSE, Kylemore, County Galway, Irish Republic One of the best of a number of superior lodging places in the area. Bordered by 7 wooded acres, it offers country-house elegance as well as good food. It has 6 rooms, 5 with baths. Not to be confused with the *Kylemore Pass* hotel. Open April through October. Details: *Kylemore House Guesthouse,* near Kylemore Abbey, Kylemore, County Galway, Irish Republic (phone: 95-41143).

CAHERNANE, Killarney, County Kerry, Irish Republic A former Victorian home that occupies a peaceful 100-acre estate, with parklands, pastures, lakes, and mountains providing a backdrop. The high-ceilinged, antiques-furnished guestrooms in the original mansion are more romantic than those in the modern annex. On-site sports facilities include private river fishing, hard-court tennis, 9-hole miniature golf, and croquet. Open March to October; 52 rooms, each with bath. Details: *Cahernane Hotel,* Muckross Rd., Killarney, County Kerry, Irish Republic (phone: 64-31895, 64-33936, or 64-33937; fax: 64-34340).

NEWPORT HOUSE, Newport, County Mayo, Irish Republic From its Georgian exterior to its graciously furnished interior, this Relais & Châteaux hotel lacks nothing in atmosphere. Many of the bedrooms, which are traditionally furnished, look out onto a pretty courtyard. A highlight of any guest's stay here is dinner, which might consist of wonderful smoked salmon and brown bread for starters, a fresh salmon entrée, and berries picked from the gardens in back for dessert. Large sections of the Newport River belong exclusively to the manor, so there's all manner of fishing to be enjoyed. Open late March through early October; 19 rooms, each with bath or shower. Details: *Newport House Hotel,* Newport, County Mayo, Irish Republic (phone: 98-41222; fax: 98-41613).

LONDONDERRY ARMS, Carnlough, County Antrim, Northern Ireland An old coaching inn built in 1848 by the Marquis of Londonderry and inherited by his great-grandson Sir Winston Churchill in 1921, this family-run hostelry is full of unusual pieces of carved furniture, paintings by Ulster artists, early Irish maps, and open fires. It also boasts a fine garden that runs down to the sea. The home-cooked meals feature seasonal local produce. Open year-round; 15 comfortably furnished rooms, each with bath. Details: *Londonderry Arms,* 20 Harbour Rd., Carnlough, County Antrim, Northern Ireland (phone: 574-885255).

A SPECIAL TREAT

One of the greatest pleasures Ireland has to offer is an overnight stay at one of its fine stately homes — those symmetrical Georgian structures that preside graciously over the lush fields here and there throughout the country. Some are available only to groups, but others offer lodging for independent travelers.

To find out more, contact *Elegant Ireland* (15 Harcourt St., Dublin 2, Irish Republic; phone: 1-475-1665) or its agent in the US, *Abercrombie & Kent International* (1420 Kensington Rd., Suite 212, Oak Brook, IL 60521; phone: 708-954-2944 in Illinois; 800-323-7308 elsewhere in the US).

Stately Homes and Great Gardens

Before the mid-17th century, most Irish and Anglo-Irish gentry lived either in battle-worthy castles or in long, medieval, thatch-roofed houses. But then a rush of prosperity sparked a building boom, and great houses with gardens appeared all over the country. Many of these homes were torched during the euphemistically named "troubles," the struggle for independence from Britain. Some were spared, by accident or intent. (The kerosene had already been poured in the foyer of Glin Castle when the invalid knight came down and, holding tightly on to his wheelchair, announced that the rebels would have to burn him as well. Stopped in their tracks, they repaired to the local pub, drank until morning, and went on to the next big house.) Of those houses that remained, some were sold by impoverished owners to religious orders and schools, and some were abandoned entirely. Others remain in the hands of the descendants of their builders, but in such decrepit conditions that they are constant reminders to their owners of the need for restorations and of the perennial lack of necessary funds. Tax rebates, legislated for historic houses that are open to the public for a period each year, scarcely make a dent in the cost of maintaining such structures in their original conditions. But they do enable the rest of the world to get an idea of the scale on which the wealthy once lived — not as grandly as the wealthy across the Irish Sea, but impressively nonetheless, particularly where the gardens are concerned.

Many fine castles, stately homes, and gardens are open to the public. Those in or near Ireland's major cities and towns are described in the *Special Places* sections of the individual chapters in THE CITIES. What follows is a representative and decidedly personal selection of some of the best homes and gardens in the Irish countryside, listed alphabetically by county and town. In addition, fairly good listings can be found in the Irish Tourist Board publications *Irish Gardens, Historic Houses, Castles & Gardens,* and *Ireland's Heritage.* Other sources include *The Noble Dwellings of Ireland,* by John Fitzmaurice Mills; *In an Irish Garden,* by Sybil Connolly and Helen Dillon; and *The Gardens of Ireland,* by Michael George and Patrick Bowe, all available from booksellers. Admission fees are nonexistent to nominal; be sure to call ahead to check hours.

BANTRY HOUSE AND GARDENS, Bantry, County Cork, Irish Republic In December 1796, amid rumblings that the French were about to invade to help free the nation from English rule, Bantry House owner Richard White helped prepare the defense and was eventually made an earl for his efforts. The title is now extinct, and the house's present owner, Egerton Shelswell-White, is descended through the female line. However, the brick and stone mansion, built in 1750 as a fairly modest residence and considerably enlarged by baroque grafts in the ensuing years, is impressive. The second Earl of Bantry traveled in Europe between 1820 and 1840, buying up bits and pieces of the Continent and amassing a collection of international antiques. Though much has been dispersed over the last 100 years, it is possible to get an idea of its scope from what remains: Russian icons; Pompeiian mosaics; French period furniture; paintings from a Venetian palace; Flemish tapestries; and stained glass from Switzerland, France, Germany, and Flanders. Aubusson tapestries made for Marie Antoinette, Gobelin tapestries from another French royal connection, and fireplaces that are believed to have come from Versailles' Petit Trianon embellish one set of grandiose rooms. The gardens are small but have great charm, their Italianate formality contrasting with the wild beauty of the bay just beyond. Cannon dating from the invasion attempt are ranged along the terrace, along with white-painted nymphs up to their classical knees in shrubs. The area is especially pretty in May and June, when wisteria and rhododendrons bloom, and in autumn with the turning of the leaves. Bantry House was one of the first of Ireland's stately homes to be opened to the public after World War II. Its east and west wings have been renovated as a posh bed and breakfast establishment (9 rooms, 8 with baths), giving visitors the opportunity to play at being Earl of Bantry for a night. House and gardens are open daily from 9 AM to 6 PM year-round.

Details: *Bantry House and Gardens,* Bantry, County Cork, Irish Republic (phone: 27-50047).

ANNES GROVE GARDENS, Castletownroche, County Cork, Irish Republic The beautiful and romantic gardens at Annes Grove, a pretty, though worn, example of Georgian domestic architecture that has been the home of the Grove Annesley family since 1700, resemble a Henri Rousseau jungle. Since the soil is by turns acid and limestone, it supports an enormous mix of plants. The woodland section abounds in the progeny of seed collected in China, Tibet, and Nepal by the great plant hunter Kingdom Ward. Elsewhere, Ward's outstanding deciduous azaleas, rhododendrons, and cherries bloom in spring. June is brightened with the blossoms of many varieties of deutzias from North America and China, including both *Cornus kousa,* their bracts thick and white as waxed paper, and the exquisite little *Cornus alternifolia argentia.* In July, herbaceous borders get star billing along with the astilbes, gunnera, lysichiton, polygonum, sulphur-yellow *Primula florindae,* and superb chalices of *Eucryphia nymansay* that carpet the banks of the River Awbeg, which inspired the Elizabethan poet Edmund Spenser in his *Faerie Queene.* Also at their best in July are the wildflowers that occupy a 4-acre semiwild meadow. August brings the New Zealand hoherias, while September offers the drama of *Parrottia persica* in its autumn foliage and the pink leaves of cercidophyllums, which are of Japanese origin. The house, which is accessible from the main Fermoy–Mallow–Killarney road, a mile north of Castletownroche, can be shown to groups by prior arrangement, with lunch if desired. Open Mondays through Fridays from 10 AM to 5 PM; Saturdays and Sundays from 1 to 6 PM; closed October through *Easter.* Details: *Annes Grove Gardens,* Castletownroche, County Cork, Irish Republic (phone: 22-26145).

GLENVEAGH CASTLE AND GARDENS, Glenveagh, County Donegal, Irish Republic A battlemented Victorian fantasy of the baronial, on 24,000 wild and remote acres, Glenveagh Castle is filled with exceptional furniture, including many Georgian pieces, some of them fine 18th-century Irish creations, and a scattering of Victoriana. But the gardens, created by successive owners and now among the finest in the country, are the real reason to visit here. They are of the utmost beauty — graced with statuary, crisscrossed by secret pathways, full of discrete spaces that are really like outdoor rooms that dissolve gradually into the native heather scrub and dwarf oak of the rugged mountains all around. There are terraces, a formal pool, a statue garden, a rose garden, a Gothic orangery, and more. Rhododendrons, some of them 30 feet high, scent the air with almost overpowering fragrance when they bloom in early June. In spite of Glenveagh's position in Ireland's most northerly county, tender exotica such as palms and mimosas prosper, as do all manner of other plants, from the park's thousands of rare shrubs and trees. Peregrine falcons and red deer breed on the wild moors (there are some 800 to 900 at any given time), and Lough Veagh, a long tongue of water on the estate, is alive with game fish. The outlying lands were purchased by the government in 1975, the gardens and castle were given to the Irish people in 1981, and the whole complex is now open as a national park, together with the former home of painter Derek Hill at Gartan Lough, where some fine paintings are on exhibit in the *Glebe Gallery*. Since private cars are not permitted in the park, visitors are advised to wear stout shoes or boots and to be prepared for walking if they plan any lengthy inspection. Accessible from the Letterkenny–Gweedore road, about 10 miles from Letterkenny. Grounds open year-round; castle closed late October through late March. (Also see *Marvelous Museums*.) Details: *Glenveagh Castle and Gardens,* Glenveagh, County Donegal, Irish Republic (phone: 74-37088).

CASTLETOWN HOUSE, Celbridge, County Kildare, Irish Republic The Irish Georgian Society has done a great deal to nurture the present trend in conservation. This structure, the society's former headquarters, has become an example of what can be achieved through painstaking restoration. Georgian architecture on the most princely scale, the house was built in 1722 for William Conolly, a pubkeeper's son who became an attorney and, after making a fortune dealing in estates forfeited after the Battle of the Boyne in 1690, was elected Speaker of the House of Irish Commons. Oak, marble, and the finest Irish building materials went into Conolly's grand home. The Palladian façade is most impressive, 60 feet tall and flanked on either side by graceful colonnades. Inside, the staircase has airy, elegant, rococo plasterwork that incorporates family portraits in bas relief. The Print Room is a masterwork of panels, garlands, niches, and busts beneath a compartmented ceiling. The Red Drawing Room, with its brocade walls, and the Long Gallery, done in the Pompeiian style and hung with Venetian chandeliers, are equally impressive. The grounds are not the place of grandeur that they once were, but the Folly that the speaker's widow built in 1740, a striking pillar atop a complex of arches, and the Wonderful Barn, a corkscrew-shaped tower affair, invite exploration. Open year-round with varying seasonal admission times. Details: *Castletown House,* Celbridge, County Kildare, Irish Republic (phone: 1-628-8252).

BIRR CASTLE AND GARDENS, Birr, County Offaly, Irish Republic Originally the Black Castle of the O'Carroll clan, Birr Castle eventually passed into the hands of Laurence Parsons, whose family became the Earls of Rosse and who occupy the house today. The carriage-driving championship that the present earl mounts every year in mid-September (see *Horsing Around*) is not the only reason to visit the 1,000-acre demesne. The scenery is quite splendid, with fine foliage and a lake fed by the River Camcor. In the Robinsonian 100-acre gardens there are specimen trees and shrubs of great rarity: a *Koelreuteria bipinnata,* one of only two in Europe; 35-foot-high boxwood hedges planted in 1782 to frame the formal gardens and now the tallest in the world; and examples of the famous hybrid tree peony named for the present earl's mother, Anne Rosse. The remains of the Birr Leviathan, a famous telescope developed in 1845 by the third earl, a distinguished astronomer, are also here; its 72-inch reflector made the device the world's largest of its type until 1915. The castle, the bulk of which dates from the early 1600s, can be toured only by groups who have arranged well in advance; those fortunate enough to fall into this class will see how the premises have been changed and modified since their beginnings. Gardens, telescope, and an annual exhibition mounted by the earl on a theme of family interest are open daily year-round from 9 AM to 1 PM and from 2 to 6 PM; groups of 25 to 35 can be entertained at luncheons or champagne receptions in the castle with Lord and Lady Rosse in attendance from April to June or in September and October by special arrangement through *Elegant Ireland* (15 Harcourt St., Dublin 2, Irish Republic; phone: 1-475-1665) or its agent in the US, *Abercrombie & Kent International* (1420 Kensington Rd., Oak Brook, IL 60521; phone: 708-954-2944 or 800-323-7308). Details: *Birr Castle and Gardens,* Birr, County Offaly, Irish Republic (phone: 509-20056).

MOUNT USHER GARDENS, Ashford, County Wicklow, Irish Republic The 20 acres of gardens here, crossed by the lovely River Vartry, are a textbook explication of the theories of the famous Irish landscape architect William Robinson, who wrote *The Wild Garden* more than a century ago and liked his bulbs naturalized under trees, his trees growing where they felt happiest, and his plantings lush, wild, and untainted by formality. The gardens were planted by Edward Walpole in 1860, beginning with a single acre and then developed by successive generations of his family, who were Dublin's principal linen merchants for several decades. The land is now in the hands of an American, Madeleine Jay, who bought the place in 1980. In the woodlands, rare trees vie with each other for the horticulturist's attention. There are no less than 70 species in the eucalyptus group. Gunnera, those giant rhubarb-like plants frequently found in Irish water gardens, grow in vast clumps by the river, and there are fine groups of American and Chinese skunk cabbage. Fern enthusiasts (properly prepared with insect repellent) can creep along a disused millstream to inspect specimens. The property is famous for its eucryphias, most notable among them the original *Eucryphia x nymanensis* Mount Usher, which was first hybridized here from two Chilean species. Since the estate's soil is practically lime-free, rhododendrons and camellias also flourish. Accessible via the main Dublin–Wicklow road and open daily from 11 AM to 6 PM from mid-March through October. Details: *Mount Usher Gardens,* Ashford, County Wicklow, Irish Republic (phone: 404-40116).

KILLRUDDERY, Bray, County Wicklow, Irish Republic Home of the Earls of Meath since 1618, Killruddery as viewed today is largely a creation of the architect Sir Richard Morrison and his son, who designed it around 1820 in Tudor style for the tenth earl. While the house is well worth visiting for its impressive drawing room, a study in chilly French grandeur, the gardens are of prime interest here, and they are magic on sunny days when the blue cone of Sugarloaf Mountain shimmers in the distance. Perhaps the oldest in Ireland, dating from the mid-17th century, the gardens were planned in accordance with the priority of the day — to provide a place for large numbers of people to stroll and otherwise enjoy themselves. So there is a bowling green, and hedges of beech delineate pathways encircling a fountain and enclose heavily shaded walks. Converging and intersecting hedges of yew and hornbeam, with statues to complete the perspective, offer still other places to stroll. The *Sylvan Theatre* has a grass stage and grass banks for seating, with the appropriate deities smiling and scowling from the surrounding thickets. To the rear, behind the fine orangery, there's a pretty box parterre with a fountain. A unique feature of the garden is a pair of canals, each 550 feet long, that reflect the house and the changing sky and lead the eye toward the cool green of the trees beyond. Accessible by the Greystones road about a mile out of Bray. Open daily from 1 to 5 PM in May, June, and September, and to groups by special arrangement at other times of year. Details: *Killruddery,* Bray, County Wicklow, Irish Republic (phone: 1-286-3405).

POWERSCOURT ESTATE AND GARDENS, Enniskerry, County Wicklow, Irish Republic Powerscourt, which was home to several generations of the Wingfield family from the time of James I until 1961, when the house and its contents were sold to the Slazengers, was completely destroyed by fire in 1974. Fortunately, the gardens to which the house was a mere backdrop were unharmed, and they are on a scale so vast that the visitor can only gasp and admire. Steps lead down a set of five terraces that extend for half a mile, flanked by statues, urns, and clipped trees, to a formal lake with a magnificent collection of trees below: a 30-foot aromatic *Drimys winteri,* a cousin of the magnolia; a whole avenue of that curiosity of the Victorians, the monkey puzzle; a eucalyptus over 100 feet tall; and a Sitka spruce that is supposed to be the tallest tree in the country. The statuary is on a heroic scale; the spectacular golden entrance gates were bought in Paris in 1867, and there are many others, all glorious. The garden was constructed in so many stages, by so many hands, that no one person can take overall credit, though Richard, the sixth Lord Powerscourt, definitively influenced the shape of the gardens today, lavishing them with costly presents and adornments. In the decade beginning in 1870, he planted some 400,000 trees annually, almost completely afforesting the surrounding mountains. This estate is one of the musts of Irish tourism, though definitely not the place where visitors will pick up ideas for their patches of soil back home. Accessible via the main Dublin–Enniskerry road or the Dublin–Wexford road. Open daily from 9 AM to 5:30 PM from March 17 through October. Details: *Powerscourt Estate and Gardens,* Enniskerry, County Wicklow, Irish Republic (phone: 1-286-7676).

Mead and Meat Pies: Historical Banquets

It would be hard to find a more touristy way to pass an evening than by partaking of one of Ireland's period banquets. Yet, like a good Gothic novel, these entertainments are a painless way to absorb a bit of history, and the chance they provide to wolf down a five-course feast in the best Tom Jones fashion — that is, with a knife as the only utensil — can be a lot of fun besides. Knights and ladies in satins and velvets, jesters, minstrels, and maybe a king or queen provide entertainment as participants sup, and there are a handful of wenches and colleens to serve and sing.

The medieval evenings usually begin in a foyer where a bit of bread is served with salt "to ward away evil spirits" and everyone's health is toasted with mead — a heady fermented concoction of honey, apples, and spices — "to be drunk for virility and fertility," as the hosts inform their guests. After the mead has taken effect, the merrymakers proceed to a banqueting hall full of long oak trestle tables set with pewter plates, mugs, and the knife with which you're to shovel in your supper. (Most people find this progressively less difficult as the evening wears on — perhaps thanks to the copious quantities of wine and beer that are poured with each "remove," or course.) Serving wenches keep the food coming, and between removes, the singers and jesters and harpists try to keep folks smiling; they actually succeed with some people.

Some banquets operate nightly, and a credit card number is acceptable to secure a reservation. The cost ranges from about $38 to $48. Before leaving the US, advance reservations can be made by calling *CIE Tours International* (phone: 201-292-3438 or 800-343-8687). For listings of other feasts, some of them from periods other than the medieval, contact the Irish Tourist Board.

For additional information about any of the banquets listed below alphabetically by county and town, contact *Shannon Castle Banquets*, Shannon International Airport, County Clare, Irish Republic (phone: 61-360788).

BUNRATTY CASTLE, Bunratty, County Clare, Irish Republic After climbing the narrow circular stone stairway to the dining hall and quaffing the first goblet of mead, guests can stroll around for a close look at this 15th-century castle's remarkable collection of art and antiques; traditional songs and harp music sustain a medieval mood during the banquet.

SHANNON CEILI, Bunratty Folk Park, County Clare, Irish Republic The music and song at this evening of Irish merriment are purely traditional; there are flutes and fiddles, *bodhráns* and spoons, an accordionist, and singers. The meal is equally traditional: Irish stew, soda bread, apple pie doused with fresh cream, and tea and wine. Open year-round.

KNAPPOGUE CASTLE, Quin, County Clare, Irish Republic Served in a huge stone dining hall lit by candles and hung with tapestries, the banquet here is hearty, if not especially medieval: salad, soup, chicken, vegetables, cheese, and fruit. The evening's program features snippets of Irish history and some fine music performed on the harp and sung by the "ladies of the castle." The castle itself, one of 42 massive structures built by the McNamara tribe that ruled the territory of Clancullen from the 5th to the mid-15th century, deserves a daytime visit in its own right to explore its several elegantly furnished rooms and to meander through its verdant and undulating grounds. Its excellent state of preservation is due to the cooperation of its owners, a Houston couple, with the Shannon Free Airport Development Company and the Irish Tourist Board.

DUNGUAIRE CASTLE, Kinvara, County Galway, Irish Republic On the site of the King of Connaught's 7th-century castle, this 500-year-old stone gray castle has a lovely setting overlooking Galway Bay. The menu usually features a taste of the sea (such as fried prawns or fish) as an appetizer, followed by salad or soup, beef, vegetables, pudding, and cheese. The entertainment, a program of music, poetry, and recitations, focuses on light-hearted extracts from literary greats associated with Ireland's west coast, including Synge, Yeats, and Gogarty. We think this is one of the nicest castle evenings offered. Open mid-May through September. Details: *Shannon Castle Banquets* (see above) or Aras Failte, Galway (91-63081).

Antiques and Auctions

Some people are driven to possess a chunk of the past, not content just to admire it in a museum. Those who count themselves as members of this group should be sure to bring their checkbooks when they come to Ireland. The past is everywhere, and the Irish are prepared to part with a bit of it — for a price, of course. Perhaps you'll fall for a little silver photo frame or a pinchbeck muff chain. Or maybe life would not be worth living without that fine piece of Irish Georgian silver. Before hesitating and passing that object of desire by, just remember: There's no time like the past — and no time to enjoy it like the present. Note that any purchase made in the Irish Republic or Northern Ireland that is mailed or shipped by the shop to an address outside the country is free of Value Added Tax (VAT). On purchases that overseas visitors take home in their luggage, the VAT can be refunded; the shop can supply the details on how to go about it. For advice about shipping and customs regulations, and for general information about buying antiques in Ireland, contact the *Irish Antique Dealers Association* (28 Molesworth St., Dublin 2; phone: 1-661-4986), whose members adhere to strict standards of quality and authenticity. You also might want to consult the following two publications:

The British Art and Antique Dealers Directory, available from National Magazine House (72 Broadwick St., London W1V 2BP, England; phone: 71-439-5000). Details all aspects of the antiques trade and contains comprehensive information about what is available in Ireland, cross-referenced by specialty. Revised annually.

Irish Arts Review Quarterly (Carrick-on-Suir, County Tipperary, Irish Republic; phone: 51-40524). An exceptionally beautiful periodical that keeps collectors up to date on Irish antiques.

A number of distinctly different antiques buying options exist. Though European-style flea markets are little in evidence, there are a number of stalls and secondhand and junk shops in the various arcades and covered markets that spring up here and there in cities and towns. True bargains may be found here — by those willing to sift through the not always interesting and usually rather grubby miscellanea to find them. There are other ways to go as well.

ANTIQUES SHOPS

From Belfast to Killarney antiques shops abound; they tend to have a little bit of this and that. But whether the quarry be barometers or bond certificates, stamps or steel engravings, there's a shop that stocks some rare, special item. Since ethical standards are high, don't be surprised if a dealer spontaneously divulges defects in an item you've got your eye on; members of the *Irish Antique Dealers Association* (address above) are very good in this way. If a dealer is not forthcoming with caveats about flaws, be sure to question him about what is original, what has been restored or retouched, and what has simply been replaced. By the way, a number of establishments specialize in the restoration of furniture and ceramics. Consult the Golden Pages, Ireland's commercial classified phone book, then phone the establishment to try to find out what restoration and subsequent mailing, with insurance, will cost — preferably before buying the piece under consideration. Those who plan to spend any significant sum to acquire an item that has been restored should have the dealer put the qualifications in writing. Should a whisper lure you to a little shop up a lane in a village about 40 miles away, be sure to call ahead. Shop hours outside the larger cities and towns can be erratic.

For listings of the best "olde curiosity shoppes" in Ireland's major cities and towns, see the *Shopping* sections of the individual reports in THE CITIES. Among our favorites tucked in nooks and crannies throughout the country-side are the following.

BUNRATTY, County Clare, Irish Republic *Mike McGlynn Antiques,* only about 15 minutes from Shannon Airport, deals in fine furniture, porcelain, and artwork; sold from a traditional Irish cottage. Ennis Rd. (phone: 61-364294).

ENNIS, County Clare, Irish Republic *Honan's* is a treasure trove of antique grandfather clocks, candlesticks, stained glass, brass lighting fixtures, and other home furnishings. 14 Abbey St. (phone: 61-28137).

ADARE, County Limerick, Irish Republic *Michelina and George Stacpoole* offer silver, treen, and objets d'art, along with a fine collection of old prints and antiquarian and secondhand books, plus high-fashion knitwear. Main St. (phone: 61-396409).

AUCTION HOUSES

Auction houses can almost always yield a treasure or two when the circumstances are right. In Ireland, there are generally two kinds of sales: those of objects acquired by the firm from several sources and held on the firm's premises, and those held in private homes to dispose of their contents. Not too many visitors turn up at the latter — it's necessary to see the newspaper notice in the first place, find the house (not always the easiest task), and then get there twice, once for the preview and again for the sale. But in a domestic auction there is the opportunity to see objects in their setting — and to see the inside of a fine house before its contents are, sadly, dispersed. Items are often sold in lots on these occasions, so if one bidder ends up with 14 brass doorknobs, he or she may be able to make a deal with the person who got all the ivory bookends.

To find out about upcoming auctions, check the papers and watch for posters. No matter what the auction, be sure to find out about viewing days and times, and go to the preview to examine the wares up close and away from the heat of bidding. Use common sense. Remember that words like "style" or "attributed" are not the same as "fine" or "important." Bearing that in mind and figuring in the taxes and commissions that will be levied, set a spending limit in advance. Then at the sale, stick to that limit. It's best not to try to outbid the dealers, but if you get carried away, well, don't worry, because it's all part of the fun.

DUBLIN, Irish Republic As the focal point for the Irish antiques trade, the auction scene can be lively, and there are salerooms for all purses. Among the best:

Hamilton, Osborne, King: Fine furniture, glass, and china dispersal auctions all over Ireland. The firm has a courteous and helpful staff. Pay a visit to the lovely Georgian building to see what's coming up. 32 Molesworth St. (phone: 1-676-0251).

James Adam & Sons: Ireland's foremost fine-art auction house. Even the window display is an education. 26 St. Stephen's Green (phone: 1-676-0261).

Thomas P. Adams & Co.: This small auction house specializes in fine furniture and objets d'art. 38 Main St. (phone: 1-288-5146).

Tormey Brothers: Weekly auctions of antiques and general household merchandise, including furniture. This is one of several houses of the same ilk, here and elsewhere in the city. Watch for newspaper advertising or consult the Golden Pages of the phone book for a list. 27 Ormond Quay (phone: 1-872-6781).

BELFAST, Northern Ireland There are plenty of auction houses here. For starters, try *Anderson's Auction Rooms,* which has viewings on Tuesdays, sales the next day. 28 Linenhall St. (phone: 232-321401).

RARE-BOOK DEALERS

Browsing among old books, their pages yellowed and brittle and their covers soft leather or beautifully marbled paper, is one of the pleasures of antiques hunting in Ireland, and there are a number of good dealers. However, since many keep their stock at suburban locations or deal out of their own homes, it is generally appropriate to make an appointment.

DUBLIN, Irish Republic There are two establishments worth visiting. *Cathach Books* (10 Duke St.; phone: 1-671-8676) specializes in Irish books and maps; *Figgis Rare Books* (53 Pembroke Rd.; phone: 1-660-9491) has a fine collection of a broader range.

CASTLECOMER, County Kilkenny, Irish Republic The remarkable rare-book auctioneer *George Mealy & Sons* (Chatsworth St.; phone: 56-41229) also has rooms here.

GALWAY, Irish Republic Old, rare, or just out-of-print books invite browsers at *Kenny's Bookshop and Art Gallery* (High St.; phone: 91-62739 or 91-61014; fax: 91-68544). One of the Kenny clan will offer eager, informed assistance.

BELFAST, Northern Ireland Of several sources here, start with *J. A. Gamble* (539 Antrim Rd., Belfast BT15 3BU; phone: 232-370798). To see his collection of rare books of Irish interest, it's definitely necessary to make an appointment in advance. Write for a free catalogue.

ANTIQUES FAIRS Fairs often bring many dealers — and many wares — together in one place and provide prospective buyers with the chance to survey many collections at once. The *Irish Antiques Fair,* held annually in Dublin during July or August, is the premier event. It offers an excellent overview of what's happening on the Irish antiques scene, plus high quality, high prices, and a selection that can't be beat. For information, contact the Dublin Tourism Office (phone: 874-7733).

Shopping Spree

SHOPPING SPREE DIVERSIONS

No matter where the dollar stands relative to the Irish pound, the lure of shopping in Ireland is irresistible. Dublin, a walker's city, can awaken the dormant consumer in even the most monastic visitor: Wonderful covered arcades and centuries-old shops, tucked away on side streets, await the curious. And Belfast, long out of the mainstream, is enjoying a resurgence, especially in the downtown shopping areas.

Quality, durability, and "value for money" are the norm throughout Ireland. A purchase made here will more than likely last for years and never go out of style, partly because it never pretended to be high style to begin with, although this is changing somewhat. Irish fashion designs have made an increasingly noticeable impact over the years.

BEST BUYS

Ireland is one of the last holdouts against synthetic materials. Some of the products and shops are of a superior quality, which may put them on the road to obsolescence, like the great ocean liners, so let yourself be tempted by classic adornments while they are still available. Ireland is the perfect place for self-indulgence. Following is an item-by-item guide to what to buy in Ireland. For listings of recommended shops in Ireland's major cities and towns, see the *Shopping* sections of the individual reports in THE CITIES. Stores in both the Irish Republic and Northern Ireland are usually closed on Sundays.

BOOKS AND MAPS Throughout Ireland's cities and towns, addicted browsers will find it difficult to escape one of the many bookstores lining the streets. A number have collections of rare books and maps, and large selections of volumes of Irish literature and history.

BRASS Solid brass articles have religious, artistic, and functional use in Ireland. Door knockers, which adorn Georgian doors in Dublin, are among the most popular items to take home.

CHINA (CERAMICS, POTTERY) World-famous Irish china — a full range of both decorative and functional items — is produced primarily in factories in Wicklow, Cork, Galway, and Fermanagh. In addition, there are scores of small studio potteries producing varied designs (see local listings). One of the best outlets is *Arklow Pottery* (Arklow, County Wicklow; phone: 402-32401), which makes heavy, functional ware of modern design. The factory shop is open daily, and several times a month crates are wheeled outside for special sales. Wafer-thin Belleek pariah china is made in the famous *Belleek Pottery* factory (Belleek, County Fermanah; phone: 365-65501), where tours are given weekdays (in winter months, it is advisable to call ahead for an appointment). The factory shop sells the complete line at retail prices — no seconds. It's open Mondays through Saturdays from 9 AM to 6 PM.

CRYSTAL AND GLASS Crystal is manufactured mainly in counties Waterford, Galway, and Cavan in the Irish Republic, and in Tyrone in Northern Ireland. *Tyrone Crystal* (Oaks Rd., Tyronne; phone: 868-725335) has rivaled Waterford's popularity in recent years. The factory store sells seconds only; first-quality items can be ordered and shipped. Factory tours are offered. Open weekdays from 9 AM to 5 PM and Saturdays from 10 AM to 4 PM.

DESIGNER CLOTHING Ireland may not share honors with the top fashion centers of the world, but its clothing industry shows signs of lively creativity. The most notable international designer in Ireland is Dublin-based Sybil Connolly.

FOODSTUFFS AND LIQUOR Jams and marmalades, blended teas, shortbread, salmon, and other edibles for sale throughout Ireland make wonderful souvenirs — to keep or to give as gifts. Irish whiskeys, which come in a wider selection than ordinarily found in the US, are also appreciated as gifts. Power, Jameson, Bushmills, Paddy, and Tullamore Dew are a few of the better-known brands. Good liqueurs are Bailey's, Emmets, and Irish Mist. Look for special offers in supermarkets and wine shops or purchase them in duty-free shops.

Northern Ireland, in particular, is famous for its bread, which comes in all flavors and shapes. Farl, a triangle shape with a rounded edge, is the most popular version of soda bread. Potato bread is also well known in both Northern Ireland and the Republic.

With so many cows in the fields, it's surprising that farmhouse cheeses didn't become popular sooner, but now they are the talk of fine Irish cooks and cheese lovers. The best known types, available in good supermarkets, are Cashel blue (the only Irish blue), cooleeney (camembert type), gubbeen (soft, surface-ripening cheese, both plain and smoked), lavistown (with natural rind, crumbly texture), ring (hard, with a nutty flavor), St. Killian (another camembert type), Burren gold (gouda type), and regatto (sharp, Italian type).

Don't miss the opportunity to pick up a side of Irish salmon, one of the world's great indulgences, before leaving for home. There are three types: "wild," the best and most expensive, which comes from the surrounding sea and streams; "farmed," which is raised in Irish fish farms; and "imported" (from Canada or California), which is only smoked in Ireland. The price of salmon, determined by type and origin, is generally lower in town than at the airports. Smoked mackerel is general available at the same places salmon is sold. It's both inexpensive and delicious. Be sure your fishy souvenir is properly packed for travel.

HANDICRAFTS Ireland has hand-thrown, handwoven, hand-spun, and hand-knit products galore. Because it escaped the worst of the Industrial Revolution, many traditional crafts never died out, and the last few years' revival in interest has caused many to flourish as never before. Emigrés from the rest of Europe have brought new ideas and increased sophistication to rural craftspeople, so that workshops and stores throughout the country now stock handmade goods in both traditional and contemporary styles.

Shillelaghs and blackthorn walking sticks are still to be found, and briar pipes are world-famous. There are hand-turned tableware and platters, salt and pepper shakers, and tables and chairs with rustic-looking seats made of twisted hay or straw. Pottery is being produced in studios all over the island in simple sculptured shapes and earthy colors. Metalsmiths produce bowls and bracelets, chains and earrings, pendants and rings, and tea and coffee sets in silver, gold, and copper. Sometimes jewelry is set with semi-precious stones or half-moons of Connemara marble; sometimes the designs are derived from the colorful *Book of Kells*. Other shopping finds are basketwork, stained glass, patchwork quilts, cut stones, St. Bridgit crosses made of straw, decorative items made of turf, candles, handmade carpets, soft toys, and quaint rag dolls. Fine cotton Irish lace, the crafting of which was introduced during the 1840 famine, has died as an industry and is difficult to find except in a few shops or private homes. Every county has its specialty item and its assortment of little shops, some of which keep company with workshops in crafts centers (or "craft clusters") where shoppers can watch artisans at work.

HATS Consistently cool, damp weather has led to a number of distinctive kinds of headgear in Ireland. The famous hat known as the "Original Irish Country Hat," the "Irish Walking Hat," or the "Fishing Hat" is made at *Millar's Connemara Tweeds, Ltd.* (Main St., Clifden, County Galway; phone: 95-21038). As they tell it, the only place it may not be worn is to bed. It's made from wool purchased from local farmers and processed in a mill that incorporates part of the town's old railway station, and it's an essential part of every sporting person's wardrobe. In addition, they make wonderful blankets (called "rugs" here) of rough wool in brilliant colors.

HERALDIC CRESTS Hand-painted heraldic crests immortalizing Irish family names make unique souvenirs.

JEWELRY Perhaps the best-known Irish ornament is the Claddagh ring, dating from the 16th century. It is exchanged as a token of friendship, love, and betrothal of marriage. Its design, two hands holding a crown, symbolizes friendship, love, and loyalty. Authentic rings are worked in gold or silver and bear an assay as well as a Made-in-Ireland mark. They are sold by fine jewelers throughout the country. (Also see "Silver.")

LACE Handmade Irish lace is more difficult to find these days — and expensive — as the craft dies out, but it is available. The best outlets are in Limerick and Carrickmacross, where lacemaking is still taught.

LINEN Authentic Irish linen is expensive. To be sure the linen is made in Ireland, not merely packaged here or bearing an Irish linen design, read the labels carefully.

MADE-TO-MEASURE (BESPOKE) CLOTHING Although London is well known for its bespoke shirtmakers and tailors, many Londoners travel to Dublin to have their suits made. Quality in the Irish capital is excellent, the price considerably less. In addition, *William J. Frazer* in the town of Hospital in County Limerick (Main St.; phone: 61-83118) is reputed to be the best hunting attire tailor in the world. He also makes men's and women's suits as fine as any from Saville Row.

MUSICAL INSTRUMENTS Traditional Irish musical instruments are made and sold in both Northern Ireland and the Republic. Flutes are the specialty of *Samuel Murray* (3 Fairyknowe Pk., Whitewell Rd., Newtownabbey, County Antrim; phone: 232-771406). For a fiddle, see *Jim McKillop* (55 Ballymena Rd., Carnlough, County Antrim; phone: 574-85424). *Uilleann* pipes are made by *Robbie Hughes* (100 Ballyduggan Rd., Downpatrick, County Down; phone: 396-4989).

SHEEPSKINS The country that manufactures superb woolens also produces skins. Shannon and Dublin airports in the Irish Republic have small sheepskin rugs that are easily rolled and carried on board.

SILVER Silver ornamentation, which has been made in Ireland for 4,000 years, is available from numerous individual artisans as well as from fine shops.

TWEEDS Wool is a way of life in Ireland as well as an attraction for tourists. Superlative tweeds, plaids, and knits are to be found in nearly every shop and department store. Although Irish weavers no longer give the world the kind of homespun, handwoven tweeds that differed from one part of the country to the next (because of regional variations in the wool and dyes), tweed from Donegal on the northwest coast is still one of the country's best buys, as are the items made from it.

Donegal is the birthplace of Irish tweeds, woven in wonderful herringbones, houndstooth checks, and other patterns. Though synthetic dyes are sometimes substituted, vegetable matter is still the coloring material that yields the distinctively subtle, luscious hues. In addition to Donegal Town, Adara is a good place for a tweed-hunting excursion. Stop by the *John Molloy Ltd.* factory store (Killybegs Rd.; phone: 75-41133) for good buys. A handweaver works on the premises in summer. Two shops on the main street of Adara are also worth checking out: *Kennedy's of Ardara* (phone: 75-41106) features Donegal tweed jackets and has good buys on locally knit Aran sweaters; *Bonner's* (phone: 75-41303; fax: 75-41270) sells Donegal tweed by the yard.

Beside a stream in the lovely village of Kilmacanogue in County Wicklow, *Avoca Handweavers* (phone: 1-286-7482) is known for its soft tweeds in muted colors. A full range of mohair products includes throws and sweaters. Other shops that carry the brand are in Avoca (phone: 402-35105), in Bunratty (County Clare; phone: 61-364029), and at *Connemara Handicrafts* in Letterfrack (County Galway; phone: 95-41058).

WOOL SWEATERS Ireland is known for its fishermen's sweaters, hand-knit from heavily oiled or scoured off-white wool in traditional stitches — tree of life, crooked road, tobacco, carrageen moss, castle, and popcorn-like bobaleen — combined in almost sculptural patterns that sometimes resemble the carvings on Celtic crosses. There's a special meaning to each pattern. Originally, they were made on the Aran Islands, but cottage knitters throughout the west and north now produce them for sale across the nation and around the world. Since no two are quite alike, it's best to shop where the selection is largest — nowadays in Dublin and Galway — and keep looking until you find one you can't resist.

Busloads of shoppers line up outside the mammoth *Blarney Woollen Mills* (County Cork; phone: 21-385280) to buy Aran sweaters, woolens, and every imaginable kind of Irish souvenir. There's also a branch in Dublin.

Quills Woollen Market (Main St., Ballingeary; phone: 26-47008), run by the Quill family, offers knitwear, particularly sweaters, of all colors and types, with emphasis on hand-knits made locally in the homes of this Irish-speaking area, 50 miles west of Cork City. Branches are located in Cork City (phone: 21-271717), Killarney (phone: 64-32277), Kenmare (phone: 64-41078), and Sneem (phone: 64-45277).

For the Mind

Marvelous Museums

Ireland's antiquities, impressive by any standards, are mostly concentrated in the *National Museum* in Dublin, which should not be missed under any circumstances. Descriptions of this and other major Irish museums located in the larger cities and towns can be found in the individual reports in THE CITIES. But numerous small museums in the countryside and off the beaten path offer local collections and eccentric private collections of varying quality. Ireland also boasts a number of fine open-air facilities that explain the lifestyles of earlier people in vivid detail through restored or reconstructed dwellings and workplaces. Most of these are in settings of great beauty. The selections below, listed alphabetically by county, will provide many days of enlightenment and entertainment. All charge nominal admission fees, if any, and are open year-round unless otherwise indicated; be sure to call for current hours before making a special trip.

PIGHOUSE COLLECTION, Cornafean, County Cavan, Irish Republic Housed in Mrs. Phyllis Faris's former piggery and several other outbuildings on her picturesque farm, this collection of folk items is an odd and idiosyncratic hodgepodge of dishes, tools, implements, pictures, bicycles, carriages, parasols, lace, 19th-century costumes, bric-a-brac, and even a few rare treasures. Though out of the way, it is worth a visit — perhaps as a detour on the way to Killykeen Forest Park — not only for the collection itself but also for the trip through the pleasant and little-traveled countryside. From the midland town of Cavan, take the road west toward Killeshandra, then watch for the signpost. The gallery is about 8 miles from Cavan. Mrs. Faris has no staff, so call ahead to make sure she'll be available. Details: *Pighouse Collection,* Corr House, Cornafean, County Cavan, Irish Republic (phone: 49-37248).

CLARE HERITAGE CENTRE, Corofin, County Clare, Irish Republic This enterprising project is located in an attractive small town at the edge of the Burren, a desolately beautiful semidesert of limestone rock that is transformed in May and June by the brilliant blossoms of rare and varied flowering plants. Housed in the converted early 19th-century Church of St. Catherine, the center's collection, which has won several awards for its creator, Naoise Cleary, includes artifacts and documents from all over the county, attractively displayed alongside texts that are lively, readable, and informative. The center is also the source of extraordinarily complete documentation on Clare families during the years 1800 to 1860. Open from 10 AM to 6 PM daily April through October, and weekends only November through

March. Details: *Clare Heritage Centre,* Corofin, County Clare, Irish Republic (phone: 65-27955).

GLENVEAGH CASTLE AND GLEBE GALLERY, Glenveagh, County Donegal, Irish Republic Glenveagh Castle, with its towers and battlements, is one of the more romantic creations of 19th-century Ireland. Located in Glenveagh National Park, the castle and its grounds are now open to the public, along with the former home of painter Derek Hill at Gartan Lough, near the edge of the estate. The castle is filled with rare furniture — mostly Georgian, some Irish, all of it very fine — and the *Glebe Gallery,* on the grounds of Hill's home, displays the painter's extensive art collection, which includes ceramics by Picasso, lithographs by Kokoschka, paintings and sketches by Annigoni, and wallpapers by William Morris, as well as works by distinguished Irish artists. A visitors' center, restaurant, and café are on the premises, and a free minibus takes travelers around the grounds. Closed from mid-October through April. Also see *Stately Homes and Great Gardens.* Details: *Glenveagh National Park and Castle,* Glenveagh, County Donegal, Irish Republic (phone: 74-37088 for the castle and 74-37071 for the gallery).

IRISH HORSE MUSEUM, Tully, County Kildare, Irish Republic Ireland, which has produced some of the world's greatest thoroughbreds, is still turning them out at the Irish National Stud, on whose grounds this museum is located; a few of these animals — and their progeny — may be seen before and after viewing the museum collections. Small but interesting, the exhibits trace the history of the horse from the Bronze Age to modern times. Occupying center stage is the skeleton of the late Arkle (1957–66), one of the nation's greatest and best-loved steeplechasers, who made a place for himself in equine history when he won the *Cheltenham Gold Cup* 3 years in a row — much to the consternation of British trainers and the glee of every Irishman — plus some 27 other victories in only 35 starts. For achievement-oriented visitors, there's an automated quiz and nearby are beautiful Japanese gardens laid out by a turn-of-the-century Japanese landscape architect named Eida. Open daily from *Easter* through October. Details: *Irish Horse Museum,* Tully, County Kildare, Irish Republic (phone: 45-21251).

MONAGHAN COUNTY MUSEUM, Monaghan, County Monaghan, Irish Republic One of the Republic's first county museums, this institution has a stunning and eclectic collection that ranges from Neolithic relics to folk items. Stuffed with china dinner sets, lace made in nearby Carrickmacross, and the cotton crochet known as Clones lace, the museum also contains such artifacts as the *Cross of Clogher,* which dates from the early 15th century; a cauldron (ca. 800 BC) found in a bog in 1854; old photographs; and, in an open-access exhibition area, a collection of querns (hand mills), milk churns, and milestones from the now-unused Ulster Canal. Closed Sundays in September through May. Details: *Monaghan County Museum,* 1-2 Hill St., Monaghan, County Monaghan, Irish Republic (phone: 47-88109).

COUNTY CASTLE MUSEUM, Enniscorthy, County Wexford, Irish Republic The museum, housed in a 13th-century Norman castle on which the Elizabethan poet Edmund Spenser once held a lease, contains muskets, pikes, and other relics of the battle in which the Irish rebels were defeated at Vinegar Hill in 1798, as well as objects from the 1916 Rising (this town was the last in the country to surrender). But the museum's contents are not restricted to military impedimenta: A kitchen at the back of the castle and a dairy showcase traditional cooking utensils and tools, including churns used in the old days for making butter and cheese. There are also striking displays of figureheads salvaged from ships wrecked off the coast, a stone covered with *ogham* script (an Old Irish alphabet used in the 5th and 6th centuries), ships' anchors, stone crosses, and chalices dating from the 17th century. A recently added feature is a sports collection, housed in a hitherto unused tower of the castle. If all this is not sufficient enticement, there's a fantastic view from the castle roof that alone is worth the visit. Open daily February through November; open Sundays only in December and January. Details: *County Castle Museum,* Castle Hill, Enniscorthy, County Wexford, Irish Republic (phone: 54-35926).

ULSTER–AMERICAN FOLK PARK, near Omagh, County Tyrone, Northern Ireland Born in 1813 in a thatch-roofed cottage near here, Thomas Mellon emigrated to the New World at the age of 5 and then traveled overland by wagon to western Pennsylvania, where he grew up as the son of struggling small farmers to found the banking empire that bears his name. Now, more than 150 years later, the original Mellon cottage is restored, and it serves as the centerpiece of a 26-acre folk park that commemorates Ulster emigration to America, relating the history of hundreds of thousands of nameless settlers as well as that of the Ulster natives who, like Mellon, went on to become well-known figures in America.

The folk park opened in July 1976 to coincide with the bicentennial of American independence, in which immigrants from Ulster played a prominent part (five signed the Declaration of Independence, a sixth was secretary to the Congress that adopted it, and a seventh printed it). It is difficult to overstate the influence Ulster people had on the developing American nation. One-quarter of US presidents have had Ulster roots, and three presidents (first-generation Americans) were sons of immigrants from Ulster.

The Old World and the New stand side by side in this park, which re-creates the lives on both sides of the Atlantic of participants in the two great waves of emigration from Ulster to America, the first during the 18th and early 19th centuries and the second in the mid-19th century. Among the structures are the Mellon cottage, a meeting house, a schoolhouse, a weaver's cottage, a blacksmith forge, log cabins, bars, and a replica of the larger house the Mellons built in America. A recently added exhibit is a reconstructed early 19th-century emigrant ship — with costumed guides and realistic sounds, smells, and other details of the difficult Atlantic crossings. Another addition, a replica of an American city street, is expected to be completed by 1995. It features a re-creation of the Mellon family's earliest bank in Philadelphia and a wheelery for Conestoga wagons. Great attention to detail makes it all feel remarkably real. Closed weekends October through February. Details: *Ulster–American Folk Park,* Camphill, Omagh, County Tyrone, Northern Ireland (phone: 662-243292).

Traditional Irish Music

Though there are more concerts, folk festivals, folk clubs, and informal sessions of music making in Ireland than ever before, those magical nights of wild, sweet music and hilarity can be as elusive as the rainbow's end. So before setting out to fill your ears with the sounds of concertinas and flutes, it's useful to have a pretty good idea about where they might be found.

To track down the best places for an evening of music in Ireland's major cities and towns, check the *Music* and *Sharing a Pint* sections in individual chapters of THE CITIES. Dublin and Galway in particular are noted for their music venues. For additional information about concerts, folk clubs, and festivals around the country, see the folk column in Friday's Dublin *Evening Press*. Also, before leaving Dublin, stop in at the elegant Belgrave Square, Monkstown, headquarters of the *Comhaltas Ceoltóirí Eireann* (phone: 1-280-0295). The *CCE* stages traditional music concerts, shows, and informal sessions nightly year-round; it also sponsors the *All-Ireland Festival,* or *Fleadh Cheoil na hÉireann* (see *Feis and Fleadh: The Best Festivals*), every year on the fourth weekend in August, a carnival of Irish traditional music that attracts up to 100,000 people. In addition, there are more than 30 provincial and county *fleadhanna,* which often produce music of an equivalent standard, but are cozier, more informal, more redolent of regional flavors, and consequently potentially even more interesting. The *CCE* office can provide the particulars, and can tell you where to find traditional music "down the country." The following rural and small-town spots are among the best places to experience Ireland's lilting airs.

COUNTY CLARE, Irish Republic Locals deem Clare the home of the best Irish music. The town of Miltown Malbay hosts the week-long *Scoil Samraidh Willie Clancy,* a traditional music school that draws the county's finest musicians for nonstop music sessions — in the pubs and hotels, on street corners, in tents, and under open skies all day and all night during the first week in July (see *Feis and Fleadh: The Best Festivals*).

In Ennis, often regarded as the center of Irish traditional music, *Kelly's* pub (5 Carmody St.; phone: 65-28155) has good weekend sessions. The *Cois na hAbhna,* the cultural auditorium out on the Galway road (phone: 61-368166), has programs from Wednesdays through Saturdays in winter for those who want to learn the steps of Irish set dancing. Mondays, Thursdays, and Saturdays in July and August are also lively, with tea and scones served to visitors along with a show, songs, dances, and chat. The *Fleadh Nua,* a late-May weekend of music and dancing in Ennis (see *Feis and Fleadh: The Best Festivals*), is definitely worth attending. Kilmihil, Mullagh, Feakle, Scariff, and Tulla (home of the *Tulla Céilí Band,* still going strong after 4 decades) are good bets throughout the year. At *Gus O'Connor's* (phone: 65-74168), a homey pub in Doolin, with lobster pots hanging from the ceiling and photos of local musicians on the walls, Micho Russell can often be found playing his tin whistle in the simple, centuries-old style he learned over 60 years ago. The place itself was established in 1832 and has been owned by the same family for six generations. Other Clare towns that are favorites with traditional musicians are Kilrush, home of *Crotty's Pub* (phone: 65-51590), and Ballyvaughan, home of the *Ballyvaughan Inn* (phone: 65-77003) and *Monk's Pub* (phone: 65-77059).

COUNTIES CORK AND KERRY, Irish Republic The mountainous area of County Kerry known as *Sliabh Luachra,* with its bordering county of north Cork, is one of the few places in Ireland where people still dance to the music. For as long as anyone can remember, traditional music and dancing have thrived here in the land of melodeons, polkas, and slides. In tiny Knocknagree, in northwest Cork, the locals — including more than one sprightly octogenarian — have been tripping it out every Friday and Sunday night for a couple of decades at *Dan O'Connell's Music House* (phone: 64-56238). The accordion music is provided by Johnny O'Leary, widely reckoned to be among the most original masters of the squeeze-box in Britain and Ireland; he founded the sessions with the late Denis Murphy, one of the best pupils of that great fiddle master Padraig O'Keeffe. Rathmore is known for its music pubs, as are Newmarket, Kenmare, Scartlaglen, Ballydesmond, and Kanturk, birthplace of the accordionist Jackie Daly, who used to play with the group *De Danann.*

Traveling west through Kerry, there's traditional music in various pubs in Tralee and in Irish-speaking Dingle. At the *National Folk Theatre* (The Green; phone: 66-21288) in Tralee, aficionados can experience the *Siamsa Tíre,* described below (see *Feis and Fleadh: The Best Festivals*) During July and August, similar sessions take place weekly at Finuge, 3 miles from Listowel, and at Carraig, 6 miles from Dingle. *Bailey's Corner* (phone: 66-26230) in Tralee is also known for its traditional music. *Ceolann* (phone: 66-32323), in the village of Lixnaw, between Tralee and Listowel, hosts periodic concerts and *céilí* dances, including an *oíche cheoil,* or Irish night, the first Friday of the month, giving visitors a chance to enjoy and join in the music making and dancing. Venues on the Dingle Peninsula include *An Bóthar* (phone: 66-55342) at Brandon Creek, Ballydavid; *Tigh Ui Murchu* (*Murphy's Bar;* phone: 66-56224) at Ballyferriter; *Quinn's Ventry Inn* (no phone) at Ventry; *Garvey's* (phone: 66-51649), *O'Flaherty's* (phone: 66-51461), *Tabairne an Droicead Beag* (*Small Bridge;* phone: 66-51723), and *Murphy's* (phone: 66-51450) in Dingle Town; and *Kruger's* (no phone) of Dunquin, named after the Boer War leader Paul Kruger, who is described in a locally famous poem by Brendan Behan.

In neighboring County Cork, best-known spots include *O'Riada's* (phone: 26-42106) in Macroom, the *Spaniard* (phone: 21-772436) and the *Shanakee* (no phone) in Kinsale, *Craigie's* (phone: 27-70379) at Castletownbere, and the *Clock House Tavern* (phone: 22-42768) in Mallow. In northern Kerry, on the border of County Limerick, the tiny town of Glin is famous for its storybook castle and for the music sessions at *O'Shaughnessy's Pub* (phone: 68-34115) on the main square. A *bodhrán* (drum), fiddle, and accordion are a permanent part of the decor here, even when no one plays them at the regular daytime gatherings. The pub closes at 7 PM.

COUNTY DONEGAL, Irish Republic Donegal is fiddle country, and it's scarcely possible to pass through it without hearing about the Fiddler King, Johnny Doherty, born in Fintown in 1895 into a family of traveling musicians and tinsmiths. Until his death, this little town drew many musicians and listeners who came to hear him play. Now a noteworthy spot for great bowing (nightly), *Teach Hiudai Bhig* (no phone) in Bunbeg also has the traditional after-Mass get-together on Sunday mornings. *Teach Leo* (*Leo's Tavern*) in the village of Crolly (Meenaleck; phone: 75-48143), is also a good bet for music, particularly when the local group *Clannad,* now internationally known, is at home.

The island of Arranmore — only a short ferry ride from Burtonport — exists in another time and another world, and the sessions go on into the wee hours at Bernadette and Tony Cox's *Plohogue* pub (no phone), which is tucked away at the less frequented top end of the island. Musicians come from the mainland and from Belfast. In August, don't miss the *Festival of International Folk Music* in Letterkenny. For information, contact Mrs. Judie Ball (phone: 74-21754).

COUNTY GALWAY, Irish Republic County Galway is the home of rocky, desertlike, Irish-speaking Connemara, where the musical emphasis is not so much on instruments as on songs, which are sung in the *sean nós* style — solo, heavily ornamented, unaccompanied, and in Irish. Look for music at *Mannion's Bar* in Clifden, Connemara's capital (Market St.; phone: 95-21780); at the *An Droighnean Donn* (phone: 91-83279) and *Hughes* (phone: 91-83240) pubs in the town of An Spideal (Spiddal); and at the *Connemara Coast* hotel (phone: 91-92108) in Furbo, farther into the country. In tiny Cleggan, 10 miles from Clifden, there are sessions at the *Pier Bar* (phone:

95-44663) on Fridays. Some nights on Inishbofin Island, musicians blast away at *Day's* pub (phone: 95-45829) until long after licensing hours — since no *gardaí* (police) live on the island, its pubs never have to close. With any luck, visitors can also find good music in East Galway, around Woodford and Loughrea, where *Moylan's* (phone: 91-41449) has a long-standing Saturday night session.

OTHER MUSICAL SPOTS

In County Mayo, musicians gather on summer evenings at the *Asgard Tavern* (phone: 98-25319) on the Quay in Westport.

The area of south Sligo and north Roscommon is great flute and fiddle country. The local newspapers will note who is playing and where — usually on weekends around Ballymote, Gurteen, and Boyle. Pubs in this area known for their traditional music sessions include *Ellen's* (no phone) at Maugherow, one of the last of the old Irish thatch-roofed establishments; the *Thatch* (phone: 71-67288) at Ballisodare; and *Laura's* (phone: 71-63056) at Carney.

In Northern Ireland, Irish music is played enthusiastically in County Antrim, especially in and around the Glens; and the town of Portglenone is noted for its fine sessions. Also highly recommended is the beautiful thatch-roofed *Crosskeys Inn* (off the main Randalstown-Portglenone road, 33 Grange St., Toomebridge; phone: 648-50694) where on a Saturday night there might be four sessions at once and turf fires warming the old kitchen, one of the loveliest sections of the premises.

In County Fermanagh, *Blake's of the Hollow* (phone: 365-322143), a most handsome spot in Enniskillen, turns musical on Friday and Saturday nights (see *Pub Crawling*).

Feis and Fleadh: The Best Festivals

With such a wealth of talent in so many fields, it's hardly surprising that Ireland should be blossoming with festivals. What is surprising is that they are planned without a thought as to the possibility of warm and sunny weather; they take place virtually year-round and last anywhere from a day or a week to a month or two. Some are oddball events devoted to strawberries or the arcane mysteries of the *uilleann* (elbow) pipes. Others are rooted in the European tradition of street musicians, buskers, and parades. Lisdoonvarna, in Clare, has a matchmaking festival in September, and Belfast an agricultural exhibition in May. There are rallies and angling competitions, horse shows and country fairs, and simple celebrations that find people standing around in their town's main square chatting with neighbors and listening to bands or balladeers. There is a good reason for this abundance of festivals: During festival times, the draconian Irish licensing laws ease up a bit, and all bars are allowed to stay open later than usual (though in the cities, late-night drinking — that great source of Irish joy — is confined to a single appointed place). Consequently, the atmosphere is usually jolly, and there is generally a feeling that something is actually happening.

Music festivals are abundant, though it should be said that some kind of music — traditional or popular, jazz or rock — is part of every Irish festival worthy of the name. Since Ireland is the home of *U2,* and a host of other international contemporary musical heavies, visitors might catch the latest planetary sensation doing a gig at a sports stadium in the provinces or at *The Point* theater in the capital. Rock events, in any case, are held mainly in June and July and, if the weather is good, they can be very enjoyable. The same goes for the kind of event known in Ireland as a *fleadh cheoil* (festival of music), one of which convenes almost every summer weekend somewhere in Ireland. The festivals manage to combine 1960s bonhomie with the long-standing Irish tradition of playing music at fairs. Whether it be the biggest of the breed, the *Fleadh Cheoil na hÉireann* (All-Ireland Festival), which generally takes place the fourth weekend in August, or one of the smaller affairs, the experience is fairly unbelievable. Thousands of people, young and old, take over the host town. Guesthouses and hotels don't have a bed to spare, ordinary homes are transformed into lodging places, and the young put up tents. People drink in the streets, and day and night the music goes on and on. Many of the best interpreters of Irish traditional music and dance show up for performances and competitions alike. The size of the throngs who come to listen and take part demonstrates once again how Irish traditional music has grown in importance and popularity over the last decade. For dates, contact the central organizers in Dublin: *Comhaltas Ceoltóirí Eireann,* 32 Belgrave Sq., Monkstown, County Dublin, Irish Republic (phone: 1-280-0295). When attending an Irish festival, or *fleadh,* it is sensible to buy a program. But look upon it as a souvenir, a reminder of the event attended, an aid to identifying some featured celebrity, or even a place to take notes; don't view it as a timetable, even in the loosest sense of the word. Timetables are for trains — the festival program is a guide to possibilities. In certain circumstances, the greater part of the festival crowd may decamp to another town in pursuit of more music or, simply, as they say in Ireland, "for the craic," which means "for the fun of it."

For information on festivals that take place in Ireland's major cities and towns, see the *Special Events* sections of the individual chapters of THE CITIES. The following are noteworthy celebrations (listed alphabetically) that take place in smaller towns and in the countryside. Tourist boards of the Irish Republic and Northern Ireland can supply complete listings of events as well as the current dates.

WORTH A LONG DETOUR

FLEADH CHEOIL NA hÉIREANN, varying venues, Irish Republic The *All-Ireland Festival,* which takes place the fourth weekend in August, is the culmination of the traditional music year in Ireland. Staged in a different town each year, it brings great numbers of Ireland's musicians and singers together for 3 days to compete, to judge, to listen, and above all, to play and sing in concert halls, pubs, parking lots, squares, and streets, to audiences numbering in the tens of thousands. Total informality and sheer physical stamina are the order of the day. Visitors are likely to find themselves footing out a handy polka on the macadam surface of some remote main street to fiddle music provided by a local doctor seated on an upturned beer keg. Don't worry — they'll never believe it back home anyway! Details: *Comhaltas Ceoltóirí Eireann,* 32 Belgrave Sq., Monkstown, County Dublin, Irish Republic (phone: 1-280-0295).

FLEADH NUA, Ennis, County Clare, Irish Republic A little more formal than the clamorous jollifications of the *All-Ireland Festival,* from which it sprang, this late May event showcases Irish musicians, dancers, and singers in a pretty little inland town just a few miles down the road from Shannon Airport. Details: *Comhaltas Ceoltóirí Eireann* (see above).

KINSALE GOURMET FESTIVAL, Kinsale, County Cork, Irish Republic This brightly painted and beflowered 18th-century town a few miles south of Cork City is like one huge restaurant, with streets instead of stairs; it's the best place for a food lover to be almost any time, but especially during the *Kinsale Gourmet Festival* in early October, when the grub crawling is as furious as the pub crawling. Then, as during the rest of the year, seafood is the specialty, a fact that is not surprising since the town is the hilly backdrop to the picturesque little harbor. Sitting on a dock post with a Guinness in one hand and a fistful of oysters (or periwinkles or crab claws) in the other is one way to go, but all matter of sea creatures also appear on the menus of restaurants like Michael Reise's cozy and romantic *Vintage* (Main St.; phone: 21-77250); Brian and Anne Cronin's *Blue Haven* (Pearse St.; phone: 21-772209); or any of a number of other restaurants and uncounted pubs occupying buildings 2 centuries old or more. At the 12 restaurants of the *Kinsale Good Food Circle,* the organization that has contributed so greatly to the current culinary state of things, the style ranges from Irish country to French provincial to nouvelle. Details: *Kinsale Chamber of Tourism,* Kinsale, County Cork, Irish Republic (phone: 21-774026).

LISTOWEL WRITERS' WEEK, Listowel, County Kerry, Irish Republic Listowel is the chief town and center of an area distinguished by its writers, among them playwright John B. Keane, who runs a pub here, the short-story writer Brian MacMahon, and the poets Brendan Kennally and Gabriel Fitzmaurice, who are the presiding spirits of this increasingly popular and enjoyable festival usually held during late May or early June. The local scribes hold workshops in drama, poetry, and fiction writing for the interested and aspiring, plays are produced by authors new and old, books are launched, and writers give lectures on and readings from their own works and those of others. Yet the atmosphere is anything but academic. Among the musical concerts, art exhibitions, book fairs, and poster showings is the *John Jameson Humorous Essay Open Competition* (first prize: a cut-glass decanter full of James Joyce's favorite whiskey). At this event, the main purpose is enjoyment — and people have been known to engage in the pursuit thereof all night. The pubs are friendly, and there's also an official club where a band plays dance music, and the assembled writers, aspiring writers, and other attendant festive spirits — when not drinking — leap about the floor. Details: *Listowel Writers' Week,* c/o The Secretary, PO Box 147, Listowel, County Kerry, Irish Republic (phone: 68-21074 or 68-21454).

ROSE OF TRALEE INTERNATIONAL FESTIVAL, Tralee, County Kerry, Irish Republic

Nowadays, nobody takes the competitive element of this beauty-contest-with-a-difference too seriously, but young women still come from all over the world at the end of August or early September to vie for a Waterford crystal trophy and the title Rose of Tralee. This 6-day event is also a sort of Irish *Mardi Gras,* providing an extraordinary range of entertainment, from donkey and greyhound races and tugs-of-war to fireworks, brass band concerts, performances of traditional music, cabarets, and much more. At any given moment, it might be possible to find four or five acts going on in different parts of the town. People roam the streets from early morning until late at night, and the Guinness flows like a flood. There's always something happening, and most of it is free. Nearly 100,000 attend. Details: *Rose of Tralee International Festival,* 5 Lower Castle St., Tralee, County Kerry, Irish Republic (phone: 66-21322).

SIAMSA TÍRE, THE NATIONAL FOLK THEATRE OF IRELAND, Tralee, County Kerry, Irish Republic

In the evenings before television, the country people of Ireland would gather around a turf fire to play music, sing songs, tell stories, and recount the day's activities. Such an occasion was called a *siamsa* (pronounced shee-*am*-sah) and down in The Kingdom, as Kerry is called, *Siamsa Tíre* has taken the spirit of those days of neighborly entertainment and translated it into a stage show that has been received with delight not only abroad but, proof of its faithfulness to tradition, in Ireland itself. The show *Siamsa,* which theater critic Clive Barnes acclaimed as "absolutely superb," is a whirlwind of song, dance, and music in three acts that re-creates a time when life was simpler, certainly harder, but perhaps more rewarding in its closeness to nature. To watch the performance in *Siamsa Tíre*'s fine new theater in Tralee is to be transported to a country kitchen of long ago. The production is not only a re-creation of the past, but also proof of the continuing vitality of Irish traditions. Presented from June through September. Details: *Siamsa Tire Theatre,* The Green, Tralee, County Kerry, Irish Republic (phone: 66-23055).

ST. PATRICK'S WEEK, Irish Republic The Irish by birth, ancestry, or natural conviction descend on the Emerald Isle to celebrate the 17th of March with a week of holiday fun. In Dublin, there are performances of music and dance in St. Stephen's Green, Gaelic football and hurling matches, an annual dog show hoary with tradition, and the biggest parade the capital can muster — with foreign and local brass bands, silver bands, fife and drum bands, pipe bands, and accordion bands, competitive exhibits on foot and on huge floats, Irish dancers in battalions, Irish and American majorettes, antique cars, and 18th-century ceremonial coaches bearing lord mayors dripping with gold chains and driven by solemn fellows in tricorn hats, not to mention legions of happy visitors, almost every one of them green-hatted and beflagged. All of Ireland's other villages and towns do as much as they can of the same program — and many have their parades on the Sunday after the big day to give the citizenry the chance to do the whole thing not once but twice. It's March — often wet, cold, and windy. But most of the time visitors don't notice the weather, even if they forget their waterproofs. Details: *Irish Tourist Board/Bord Fáilte* in Dublin, Irish Republic (phone: 1-676-5871).

IF YOU'RE NEARBY

AN TOSTAL, Drumshanbo, County Leitrim, Irish Republic Over 3 decades ago, when the Irish Tourist Board dreamed of a nationwide festival to launch a new era in the tourist industry, the locals of little Drumshanbo responded with this festival, whose name means "gathering" or "muster," and they've been having it every year ever since. A ballad-singing competition, road races, and an art exhibition are among the goings-on — not especially unusual but a lot of fun. The shindig — held in June or July — always kicks off with a parade and the hoisting of the *Tóstal* flag on Main Street. Details: *Ms. Aoife Mooney,* Drumshanbo, County Leitrim, Irish Republic (phone: 78-41013 or 78-41120).

CASTLEBAR INTERNATIONAL FOUR DAYS' WALKS, Castlebar, County Mayo, Irish Republic A friendly get-together for dedicated trampers, this event also has room for those who enjoy a not overly strenuous stroll in good company in the quiet countryside. The non-competitive, well-supervised walks are held in June or July. There are treks for every age and fitness level, and a certificate is awarded to everyone who completes one. There's an entry fee for those 18 and over. Details: *Castlebar International Four Days' Walks,* Castlebar, County Mayo, Irish Republic (phone: 94-24102); or call Brighid O'Connor (phone: 94-21339) or Robert Kilkelly (phone: 94-21264 or 94-22798; fax: 94-24569).

CLIFDEN COMMUNITY ARTS WEEK, Clifden, County Galway, Irish Republic All things artistic, from painting and photography to theater and classical music, are celebrated in the town of Clifden during the last week in September. Concerts, lectures, and exhibits are held in schools, hotels, pubs — even in the seldom-used Church of Ireland. The whole town turns out and sometimes that feels like half the country. Well-known artists such as poet Seamus Heaney and actress Siobhán McKenna have graced the festival in years past; organizer Brendan Flynn always seems to entice the country's best to this tiny town nestled in the gorgeous Connemara countryside. Details: *Brendan Flynn,* Clifden Community School, Clifden, County Galway, Irish Republic (phone: 95-21184 or 95-21295).

DÚN LAOGHAIRE SUMMER FESTIVAL, Dún Laoghaire, County Dublin, Irish Republic During the last week in June, this prosperous and well-kept old borough 6 miles from Dublin expresses its essentially Victorian style with art exhibits and musical soirées in the Maritime Institute (High St.), local tours and trips to nearby Dalkey Island, a ball, a regatta, and everything from sea chantey concerts to Punch and Judy shows. Dún Laoghaire's popular harbor is jammed with boats and yachts during festival week. Details: *Mrs. Rita Hughes,* Festival Director, Marine Rd., Dún Laoghaire, County Dublin, Irish Republic (phone: 1-284-1888 or 1-285-2345).

OULD LAMMAS FAIR, Ballycastle, County Antrim, Northern Ireland A glass or two or three of Bushmills enlivens the conversation at this genuine folk event, the North's most popular traditional fair, and the accents fly thick and fast. For the duration, the otherwise fairly placid little town throbs with activity. Farmers cart in their livestock and stalls sell souvenirs of all imaginable variety, the local specialties being the dried, edible seaweed known as dulse and a sweet known as yellow man. The festivities take place the last Monday and Tuesday in August. Details: *Northern Ireland Tourist Board* (phone: 232-231221).

STRADBALLY STEAM RALLY, Stradbally, County Laois, Irish Republic A gathering of steam engines and those who love them, this event associated with the *Irish Steam Museum* (the home of a fine collection of cars, tricycles, fire engines, and other manifestations of the power of steam) swells an otherwise quiet little village with thousands of steam engine enthusiasts. Owners and attendants are proud, hospitable, and very patient. The rally take place over 2 days in early August. Details: *Ette Kennedy,* Main St., Stradbally, County Laois, Irish Republic (phone: 502-25444).

SUMMER SCHOOLS

Summer schools, an important fixture of the Irish summer season, are not so much over-serious academic gatherings redolent with credits and credentials as they are special-interest festivals that feature, as their entertainment, members of the Irish intelligentsia devoting themselves without restraint to that most venerable of Irish recreations — talk. Some of the best talkers in the country are in attendance, happily moving from one seat of learning to another as the summer advances, so visitors are bound to learn a lot on, and off, the "campus."

MACGILL SUMMER SCHOOL, Glenties, County Donegal, Irish Republic This school, which convenes on the rugged northwest coast, honors the novelist and poet Patrick MacGill, whose first book sold 120,000 copies within 2 weeks of publication and who, like France's Emile Zola, is the voice of the repressed and neglected of his people: the traveling building and agricultural workers of the first half of the century. Accordingly, topics with modern social and political themes are chosen. As at other summer schools, the living creators of modern Irish literature are much in evidence; visitors with literary talent might well find room for their latest short stories or epic poems on the elastic program. Details: *Inishkeel Co-op*, c/o Mary Claire O'Donnell, Main St., Glenties, County Donegal, Irish Republic (phone: 75-51103).

MERRIMAN SUMMER SCHOOL, County Clare, Irish Republic Held during the last week in August in a different Clare town every year, this event is affectionately known as "the lark in the Clare air." It fondly recalls its namesake, the 18th-century schoolteacher Brian Merriman, popular for his elegant, racy, and dream-like satire on ancient bardic epics, "Cúirt an Mheán Oíche" ("The Midnight Court"), in which Ireland's women indict their menfolk for contempt of matrimony in the court of the Fairy Queen, and win. Too strong for public taste of the day, the poem was suppressed for many years. The primary topic of the school varies wildly from one season to the next. Matriculants might find themselves considering the O'Brien family and its 30-foot-long pedigree dating back to 1200 BC, Ireland's maritime history, or the state of the Irish legal profession. The lecture roll includes politicians, scientists, poets, novelists, and university professors, and all of them are expected to dance a reel or jig, to quaff the odd libation, and to entertain the assembled company with a song or two at the *Merriman Club* each night. (Thus one learns that there are some fine singers in Irish academe and on the Front Bench in Government and Opposition.) They are also supposed to pull themselves together each morning for their day's lectures — and to their credit, they do. Details: *Mary Murphy*, 6 Aravan Court, Bray, County Wicklow, Irish Republic (phone: 1-286-9305).

WILLIE CLANCY SUMMER SCHOOL, Miltown Malbay, County Clare, Irish Republic Following the early death of the great piper Willie Clancy, a delightful man, his friends decided that musicians — particularly pipers — should come together every year in July in his memory to play, teach, and learn the pipes — not hearty warpipes but the cunning, sweetly toned little *uilleann*, traditional and unique to Ireland. There's a saying in these parts that the Irish exported bagpipes to Scotland — and the Scots haven't yet caught on to the joke. But the Irish version of the instrument lacks the shrillness of Scottish warpipes and has a wide melodic variation. Old and young, American and Irish, novices and experts who can pipe their listeners into a trance, and a wildly diverse host of others jam the pubs, and the music goes on and on. Come official closing time, the doors are locked so that no new merrymakers may enter, but those present remain as long as they can stay awake. Details: *Muiris O'Rochain,* Miltown Malbay, County Clare, Irish Republic (phone: 65-84148).

Ancient Monuments and Ruins

A land of 10,000 tales and a 100,000 memories, Ireland is littered with cairns and forts, dolmens and abbeys, standing stones and high crosses, monastic hermitages and feudal castles, with the oldest dating back thousands of years. But though the earliest traces of human life here date from about 6000 BC, it was not until about 3000 BC that humans built on a scale large enough to leave memorials to themselves. Those that survive are tombs of a type known as court cairns — long chambers divided into compartments. The earliest structure that grips the visitor's imagination is the passage grave. Found in groups, each under a huge mound, these typically consist of a long passage leading to a central space, with a roof of large stones, onto which other chambers open on three sides. The graves usually have one or more stone basins inside, and, on all the stones, are great numbers of incised geometric motifs and even stylized human faces. The group in the Boyne Valley of County Meath, which includes the magnificent Newgrange, is the most striking.

Equally arresting are Ireland's great standing stones, or dolmens. Outlined against the sky, crowned by enormous capstones, they were built in about 2000 BC, probably as tombs. Men in pubs call them "beds of Diarmuid and Grainne," referring to the Irish king's daughter who, betrothed to the venerable giant Finn MacCool, eloped with the younger Diarmuid on the night before her wedding and slept in prehistoric tombs during a furious years-long chase that ended with Diarmuid's death at the snout of an enchanted boar and the wayward lady's marriage. During the Bronze Age, at about the time the Celts arrived here, stone circles such as the piper's stones of County Wicklow were erected. There, it was believed, the "little people" played the bagpipes for dancers. Hill forts like Tara, the legendary dwelling of the high king of Ireland, came later, in the Iron Age, around 500 BC. A hill fort's outer fortifications enclosed a large area, so the owner was certainly an important figure. Ring forts, of which there are some 3,000 scattered around the country, are smaller, ranging in scale from the Grianán of Aileach in County Donegal to the occasional odd shape in a field. They generally date from the Iron Age to early Christian times.

Christianity came to Ireland in the 5th century, and with it the nation embarked on an era of great building. Monasteries sprang up all over Ireland. Bearing little resemblance to their more modern counterparts, they consisted of simple clusters of stone huts and a sheltering wall, like those on the Dingle Peninsula in County Kerry and at Glendalough in County Wicklow. Round towers, also seen at Glendalough, were put up as refuges from Viking raids. The devout also built crosses which at first were just cross-shaped slabs or slabs incised with a cross motif. Later came the increasingly more ornate high crosses, which had geometric designs and even scenes from the Bible, with a circle around the intersection of the horizontal and vertical arms. In the 12th century, Irish Romanesque architecture made its debut on the ecclesiastical scene. Examples like the Chapel of Cormac at Cashel, in County Tipperary, and Ballintubber Abbey, in County Mayo, show the distinctive signs: round-headed doorways, fantastic animal and human masks in stone, with intertwining beards and tails, chevrons, and foliage decorating arches, doorways, capitals, and sometimes church windows.

In the 13th century, Franciscans and Dominicans arrived with Gothic ideas in their saddle bags. In cathedral towns like Kilkenny, Kildare, and Limerick, many of the older parish church buildings still in use abound in lancet windows and other distinctive marks of the style. By the 15th century, the Cistercians' cathedral-making talents had risen to the glories of Holy Cross in County Tipperary.

Meanwhile, a more durable class of fortress, the castle, was developing. The Norman invasion sparked the creation of fortresses like Carrickfergus Castle, in County Antrim, and the round keep at Nenagh, in County Tipperary. There was no stopping the masons and their masters of this period. Between 1450 and 1650 every family of any importance built a castle. Few of these structures disappeared entirely from the landscape, and some — most notably Bunratty Castle in County Clare — are in splendid shape.

Christian Ireland is a pamphlet published by the Irish Tourist Board. It is available for about $2.50.

National Monuments in the Republic of Ireland, by Peter Harbison, covers monuments in both the Republic and Northern Ireland. It can be ordered for about $12.50 from Gill and Macmillan, Goldenbridge, Inchicore, Dublin 8, Irish Republic.

Whether ecclesiastical or secular, each type of building has its saga and its place in Irish history, and with a little imagination, they spring vividly to life when you visit them. Those listed below, in roughly the order in which they were constructed, include some of the most important and most compelling. In addition, for descriptions of noteworthy monuments and ruins in Ireland's major cities and towns, see the individual chapters of THE CITIES.

NEWGRANGE, Newgrange, County Meath, Irish Republic Few relics of the daily life of the people of the Neolithic Age (ca. 3700–2000 BC) survive in Ireland today; it seems as if all the creative energies of the communities of this period were directed toward the construction not of homes for the living but of monumental repositories for the remains of the dead, and the whole valley of the River Boyne, about 30 miles north of Dublin, is scattered with cairns, standing stones, and earthworks both large and small. Of these, Newgrange is the most impressive by far. In fact, this passage grave ranks among the most important of its type in Europe, and scholars have spent centuries studying it. Literature of the ancient Irish links it to a mysterious personage who is sometimes called Oengus an Brogha (Oengus of the Palace) and other times referred to as Oengus mac an Dagda (Oengus Son of the Good God); some archaeologists have suggested that Newgrange and similar tombs on the Continent were constructed for the important personages in groups of traders and prospectors who first migrated from Spain or Portugal around 4000 BC.

The earth mound that is the most immediately obvious feature of Newgrange, entirely manmade, using alternate layers of turf and stones, is unusually large — 40 feet high and 300 feet in diameter; estimates put the quantity of stones required for the whole undertaking at 180,000 tons. The mound was originally paved with white quartz pebbles so that it glistened brightly enough in the sun to be seen from afar. Today the top of the mound is covered with grass, and the sides with large white stones. Inside, leading into the depth of the hill from the entrance on the southeastern frontage, is a 62-foot-long, yard-wide passage. High enough to let a person walk upright and lined with a series of orthostats (upright stones) 5 to 8 feet high, it ends at a generally circular burial chamber with a beehive-shaped ceiling paved with overlapping stones (following a method of construction found over and over again at Irish ruins of this period). Adjoining the main chamber — and giving the tomb's interior a roughly cruciform shape — are three recesses containing stone troughs or basins probably once used to contain the ashes of the dead. On the morning of the shortest day of the year, rays of sun shine directly up the passageway to the center of the burial chamber — a design that required some sort of calendar to calculate. The decoration throughout further confirms that sophisticated minds were at work. The ceiling of the north recess, covered with carved spirals, lozenges, triangles, zigzags, diamonds, and other shapes, is particularly noteworthy, as are the gigantic threshold stone, at the entrance to the tomb, and many of the orthostats. A museum and tourist information office at Newgrange can provide details about Newgrange as well as about nearby Dowth and Knowth, the two other major monuments in this area, which is often called Brugh na Boinne (Palace of the Boyne). Note that access to the Newgrange monument is allowed only as part of the excellent guided tours at the site. Details: *Midlands-East Tourism Office,* Dublin Rd., Mullingar, County Westmeath, Irish Republic (phone: 44-48761).

HILL OF TARA, near Navan, County Meath, Irish Republic Little but legend and a handful of earthworks and stones remain of the glories of Tara — but of legend and conjecture there is plenty, and this 512-foot hill about 25 miles from Dublin, commanding a fine view of a vast expanse of lush meadows, is well worth a visit. Already a significant burial place 2 millennia before Christ (as revealed by the excavation of one of the site's most notable monuments, Dúnha na nGiall — the Mound of the Hostages), it ranked among Ireland's most important political and religious sites for almost 2,000 years. It became the center of priestly rulers even before St. Patrick came to Ireland in the 5th century and long served as a residence for anyone strong enough to make himself at least nominally High King of Ireland. Tara enjoyed one of its most glorious periods in the first centuries after Christ, when the celebrated Cormac the Wise constructed the wooden palaces that are mentioned in some of Ireland's early literature. However, Tara's importance declined until its abandonment in 1022. Relics of all of these eras can be seen today. The Mound of the Hostages, an early passage grave (ca. 1800 BC) which has a 17-foot-long corridor and is covered by a mound that measures 72 feet in diameter, is at one edge of the large, circular Iron Age ring fort called the Rath na Ríogh (Royal Enclosure), at whose center are two other earthworks — the Forradh (Royal Seat) and Teach Cormaic (Cormac's House), where visitors will see a modern statue of St. Patrick and the 5-foot-long chunk of granite known as Lia Fail (the Stone of Destiny). The latter, according to popular legend, would roar if the king being crowned upon it was acceptable. Just south of the Royal Enclosure is Rath Laoghaire, which is said to be near King Loaghaire's burial place. To the north stand the Rath na Seanad (Rath of the Synods), an erstwhile fortress and burial place; the Teach Miodchuarta (Banquet Hall), where each stratum of society had its own compartment and whose festivities are reported in the 12th-century *Book of Leinster;* the circular Rath Gráinne; and the odd-shaped Claoin Fhearta (Sloping Trenches), which probably had a ceremonial function of some sort. Also interesting is Adamnán's Stone, a 6-foot-high chunk of sandstone bearing the incised likeness of a human figure — perhaps the horned Celtic Cernunnos or a type of fertility figure known as a *sheila-na-gig* ("sheila of the breasts" — paradoxically a figure that is mostly face and thighs). Details: *Midlands-East Tourism Office,* Dublin Rd., Mullingar, County Westmeath, Irish Republic (phone: 44-48761).

GRIANÁN OF AILEACH, Burt, County Donegal, Irish Republic Ulster cannot boast megalithic monuments of the scope of Leinster's Boyne Valley cemeteries, although standing stones, stone circles, and dolmens do exist, as well as several structures with elaborate entranceways that have earned them the name court graves. Here, however, the most characteristic and striking ruins are those of circle-shaped ring forts, which protected farmhouses until AD 1000, and which are found today by the thousands, scattered throughout Ulster's fields. Even more striking are the stone cashels, circular walls enclosing groups of domestic or ecclesiastical buildings. The Grianán of Aileach (the sunny place in the territory of Aileach), one of the most important antiquities in the northern part of the country, is among the most noteworthy of these. Perched atop 800-foot Grianán Mountain, not far from Londonderry, this fortification measures about 77 feet across; the 13-foot-thick walls, restored in the 1870s by the bishop of Derry to their original height of 17 feet, contain galleries and guard chambers and enclose a series of stairway-connected terraces. Already badly battered in 676 during an attack by the southern O'Neills, under Finechta the Festive, the structure was finally destroyed by Murtogh O'Brien, the King of Munster, who, avenging the pillaging of his own residence, instructed each of his men to carry away a single stone of the fort. The exact date of construction is unknown, since no excavations have been made here; in their *Annals of the Kingdom of Ireland,* the Four Masters put its origins back in the Iron Age, while other scholars suggest that it was probably built within a few centuries before St. Patrick (who lived in the 5th century AD). Similar and equally impressive fortifications include Dun Aengus in the Aran Islands and Staigue Fort in County Kerry. Details: *Donegal/ Leitrim/Sligo Region Tourist Information Office,* Temple St., Sligo, County Sligo, Irish Republic (phone: 71-61201).

GLENDALOUGH, County Wicklow, Irish Republic Nestled deep in the Wicklow Mountains, about 30 miles south of Dublin, this "valley of the two lakes" is the beautiful setting for one of Ireland's important early Christian monasteries, particularly striking in May when the gorse is in full bloom. Built on the site where St. Kevin settled to renounce human love and to live as a hermit during the 6th century, Glendalough, like many other Irish monasteries, was pillaged and sacked many times by the Vikings and assorted other marauders. Famous as a seat of learning, like Clonmacnois (see below), it was particularly vulnerable and, as at Clonmacnois, the ruins are extensive: more than half a dozen churches, crosses, grave slabs, a priest's house, a round tower, and old wells. The stone of which most of these are constructed, granite and mica-schist, has chipped and crumbled over the centuries, giving the walls a rough texture and providing a fine medium for the growth of the pale, soft local lichen, so that the buildings at Glendalough have that particularly aged look that many folks imagine all ruins have until they find out otherwise. Especially noteworthy are the 7th-century cathedral, Ireland's largest pre-Romanesque church; St. Kevin's Church (popularly known as St. Kevin's Kitchen), with its round tower-like belfry rising up above a stone roof; the small, 12th-century Priest's House, perhaps originally a mortuary chapel or even the saint's shrine; the Reefert Church, around whose walls sleep many Leinster kings; and, farther down the valley, accessible via a narrow sylvan path, St. Saviour's Monastery, a 12th-century church probably built by Laurence

O'Toole, former abbot of Glendalough, archbishop of Dublin, and Ireland's first canonized saint. There are especially fine walks around the upper lake, which is picturesquely backed by the steep cliffs of 2,296-foot Camaderry and 2,154-foot Lugduff Mountains, ribboned by the rushing Glenealo Stream and a waterfall. Details: *Midlands-East Tourism Office, Dublin Rd., Mullinger, County Westmeath, Irish Republic* (phone: 44-48761).

CLONMACNOIS, Shannonbridge, County Offaly, Irish Republic Founded by St. Ciaran in the mid-6th century on a large, serenely beautiful site on a reed-edged curve of the River Shannon between loughs Derg and Ree, Clonmacnois has been plundered and burned by Vikings, desecrated by Danes, harassed by the Normans, and, much later, during the Dissolution of the Monasteries, carried away, piece by piece. But until this consummate act of vandalism, it grew strong, flourished, and became the Oxford of medieval Ireland. Fine manuscripts were created here, and some of the country's greatest scholars and intellects came here to live, pray, work, and be buried. What remains are the most extensive monastic ruins in Ireland: eight churches, two round towers, a cathedral, and a castle, as well as three high crosses, parts of two others, and more than 200 6th- through 12th-century gravestones vividly illustrating the many types of graves used in early Ireland. Of all the structures here, the celebrated Flann's High Cross, carved with scenes of the Last Judgment and the Crucifixion, is exceptionally beautiful, and the Nun's Church, whose doorways have capitals crawling with fierce-looking beasts, has the most interesting story: This was where the pathetic Dervorgilla retired in penance after eloping with Dermot MacMurrough, the King of Leinster — thereby setting off the Norman invasion. Rising in lonely tranquillity above the lush green landscape, the ruins possess an air of peace and dignity, as befits a national treasure. Details: *Midlands-East Tourism Office,* Dublin Rd., Mullingar, County Westmeath, Irish Republic (phone: 44-48761).

BALLINTUBBER ABBEY, Ballintubber, County Mayo, Irish Republic The site of this Augustinian community has long been important; tradition tells us that St. Patrick baptized local peasants with water from its well. Later, the monastery became the departure point for pilgrimages to Croagh Patrick. Now it is noteworthy because mass has been said in its church regularly ever since the community was founded in 1216 — despite the suppression of the abbey under Henry VIII and the depredations of the Cromwellians in 1653. In addition to its special history, the structure is also exceptionally handsome. Thanks to sensitive restoration work finished in 1966, a new wooden roof was constructed for the nave and the interior walls whitewashed in the traditional fashion, so that the church looks much as it must have upon its completion. The abbey includes a cruciform church with nave transepts and a choir. Three blocked windows of Norman design with double dog's-tooth molding are over the altar. In a chapel to the south of the choir is an elaborate altar tomb with a row of figures on the pediment. The carving around the three lancet windows in the gable and on the capitals of the chancel exemplifies the best work of a school of talented late-Romanesque carvers who worked in the province of Connacht in the early 13th century after the rest of the country had adopted the Gothic style. The wonderfully monstrous snakes twined around each other on the capitals between the triple round-headed window in the front of the church (to see them in those distant gloomy recesses requires field glasses) and the grotesque creatures creeping along the corbels that uphold the chancel's ribbed vaulting are just two examples of the unique designs. Nearby is the well where St. Patrick administered baptism, as well as the attractive cloisters reconstructed from the ruins of the 15th-century originals with the aid of fragments uncovered in the course of archaeological excavations in the 1960s. Details: *Westport Tourist Information Office,* The Mall, Westport, County Mayo, Irish Republic (phone: 98-25711).

MELLIFONT ABBEY, Drogheda, County Louth, Irish Republic Near the banks of the narrow River Mattock, 6 miles west of Drogheda, are the meager, but moving and exceedingly graceful, remains of this abbey, Ireland's first of the Cistercian order. There are ruins of rounded chapels in the transepts of a church of continental European design, a fine 2-storied chapter house with a handsomely groined roof in the Norman style, a massive gate house, and other interesting elements, including a crypt under the abbey church, unusual for a structure built in 12th-century Ireland. The whole complex, reputedly commissioned by St. Bernard of Clairvaux and consecrated with great pomp and circumstance in the presence of a papal legate in 1157, initiated a program of reform that quickly took hold and sprouted daughter establishments all over Ireland. At the time of the Dissolution, the abbey was acquired by Edward Moore, and from him it was passed on to the Balfours of Townley Hall, who never lived here. A century ago it was used as a piggery. Details: *Tourist Information Office,* Market Sq., Dundalk, County Louth, Irish Republic (phone: 42-35484).

CARRICKFERGUS CASTLE, County Antrim, Northern Ireland Along with Trim Castle in County Meath, Carrickfergus Castle remains the mightiest symbol of the Norman presence in Ireland after the invasion of 1169. Situated strategically on the shores of Belfast Lough, it is one of Ireland's strongest castles, and its name repeatedly crops up at a number of important junctures in Irish history. Founded in 1180 by John de Courcy, the first Norman Lord of Ulster, it was besieged in 1210 by King John of England, who feared the rising independence of his Norman barons. A century and a considerable amount of construction later, it fell to Robert the Bruce, whose brother Edward had invaded Ireland from Scotland in 1315, but it was returned to the Crown with the defeat of the Bruces a few years later. For nearly 3 centuries, it existed in comparative quiet and increasing decay. Then in 1690, William of Orange landed here during his campaign to defeat the Stuart kings for the possession of Ireland; some 70 years after that, it was taken temporarily by a French expeditionary force. In 1778, the American John Paul Jones, captain of the *Ranger,* defeated the HMS *Drake,* which was moored beneath the castle. In the 18th century, the castle was used as a prison for United Irishmen and others. Visitors enter the impressive structure through a gate flanked by two rounded towers and then proceed through the outer ward past a handful of 16th-century storehouses into the middle ward. Adjacent to the middle ward, the inner ward is dominated by the squarish keep — 5 stories, about 90 feet high, 56 feet across, and 58 feet deep. Inside the 8-foot-thick walls is a stairway that climbs from the ground level (where there is an early-20th-century steam engine and an antique wooden dugout canoe) to a group of military exhibits on the floor above and into the great chamber, a spacious room with large windows. The castle is open daily (phone: 960-351273). Details: For information on the medieval fairs and banquets held at the castle during June and July, call 960-351604; for other information, contact the *Northern Ireland Tourist Board* (phone: 232-246609; fax: 232-240960).

For the Body

Great Golf

True golf devotees contend that some of the finest — and most authentic — golf courses in the world are found in Ireland. This is hardly surprising since the sandy land along its coasts is much the same sort of terrain on which the game was spawned in Scotland. It's hard to believe that less than a century ago golf was virtually unknown anywhere outside Scotland, though the Scots proved great apostles, spreading the word from Perth (where the first recognizable 6-hole course is thought to have been constructed on the city's North Inch), St. Andrews, Prestwick, and Dornoch — sacred shrines to a game that has gripped the attention of an entire planet.

At about the time golf leaped the Atlantic in the late 19th century, it also settled into Ireland. Even now the courses found in Scotland, England, Northern Ireland, and the Irish Republic provide a different sense of the game than can be acquired anywhere else on earth. Nature was the architect of these courses, providing more challenges than the craftiest landscapers could imagine.

But it's more than history that lures generations of modern golfers to the game's breeding grounds. Particularly in Ireland, where there are more golf courses per capita than in any other country in the world — more than 200 courses at last count — there's a friendliness to the sport; it's a community game, not cloistered and clubby. The intensity of the challenge found on these courses remains as vital as ever, and the chance to pit one's skill against the achievements of golf's greatest historic figures is nearly irresistible. Not to play these courses at least once in a lifetime is not to know the real heritage of the game.

A word about particulars: Greens fees average approximately $16 to $27, but soar up to $90 for some of the top championship courses. The charge usually is per day, not per round. It is wise to book tee times in advance by calling the club secretary. Golf clubs are not generally available to rent, but some clubs do carry a limited number of sets. Caddies, where available, generally must be booked in advance. Caddie carts (usually pullcarts only — there are few motorized carts in Ireland) are available at most clubs for about $2.25 per round. It is best, therefore, to bring only a light "Sunday" bag, as it may be necessary to carry it yourself. Also bring clothing to protect against wind and rain, even on the apparently sunniest days, particularly on coastal courses (Irish golfers rarely pause for weather). For information about the best courses in or near Ireland's major cities and towns, see the *Golf* entries in the individual chapters in THE CITIES. In addition, we recommend the following courses, listed alphabetically by county and town, beginning with the Irish Republic.

LAHINCH, Lahinch, County Clare, Irish Republic Created a century ago by some Irish merchants and a group of Scottish Black Watch regiment members stationed nearby, the extraordinary *Old Course* has been known to inflict players with every conceivable plague, save famine and flood. The *St. Andrews* of Ireland — once famous for its grazing goats (they've died off in recent years) — has one short par 5 that has been toughened a bit by putting something that looks like the Great Wall of China in the middle of the fairway. To add a little extra spice, there's a 145-yard par 3 that's completely blind. The second 18-hole course is less demanding, but of championship standard nonetheless. Our pick for the best fun in the west of Ireland. Details: *Lahinch Golf Club,* Lahinch, County Clare, Irish Republic (phone: 65-81003).

BALLYBUNION, Ballybunion, County Kerry, Irish Republic The original course here is one of the two Irish tracks that Tom Watson plays every year or two (*Lahinch* is the other), and no less an authority than Herbert Warren Wind considers the *Old Course* (as it's called) one of the ten toughest in the world. Visiting golfers will have no reason to disagree. The course is laid out at the point where the River Shannon estuary meets the Atlantic Ocean. Its 14th, 17th, and 18th holes are all roaring winds, and the out-of-bounds area beside the 1st hole is a graveyard. Welcome to Ireland. A second Robert Trent Jones, Sr. 18-holer is also on the club grounds. Details: *Ballybunion Golf Club,* County Kerry, Irish Republic (phone: 68-27146).

TRALEE GOLF CLUB, Barrow, Ardfert, Tralee, County Kerry, Irish Republic Reaching into Tralee Bay off the Atlantic about 7 miles west of Tralee Town on the Barrow Peninsula, this new 18-hole links course is Arnold Palmer's first European creation. His assessment proudly says it all, "I have never come across a piece of land so ideally suited for the building of a golf course. . .we have one of the world's great links here." Perhaps the strongest hole is the par-4 17th, which plays from a high tee, across a deep gorge, to a green perched high against a backdrop of blue mountain. The *Tralee* links measure 6,521 yards and play to a par 71. Details: *Tralee Golf Club,* Barrow, Ardfert, Tralee, County Kerry, Irish Republic (phone: 66-36379).

WATERVILLE GOLF LINKS, Waterville, County Kerry, Irish Republic A modern resort hotel adjoins this championship course, but don't get the idea that this is an easy resort track; the layout is nearly as rugged as the surrounding countryside. This longest of Irish tracks (7,234 yards from the championship tees) plays between the Atlantic coast and an inland lake that's best known to trout and salmon fishermen. Though long teeing areas allow the course to be shortened to 6,024 yards (society tees), the brave playing from the back are in for an exhilarating and challenging afternoon. One of the few Irish courses to offer electric golf carts. Details: *Waterville Golf Links,* Waterville, County Kerry, Irish Republic (phone: 667-4102).

ROYAL PORTRUSH, Portrush, County Antrim, Northern Ireland Of the two 18-hole layouts here, the *Dunluce* course — the only club in Ireland ever to host the *British Open* and site of last year's *British Amateur Open* — is the championship track. It is named after the striking old castle perched on the white cliffs to its east. The wind off the North Sea is usually intense and constant, and no less an authority than Pete Dye estimated that the course should be ranked eighth best in the world. Details: *Royal Portrush Golf Club,* Dunluce Rd., Portrush, County Antrim BT56 8JQ, Northern Ireland (phone: 265-822311).

ROYAL COUNTY DOWN, Newcastle, County Down, Northern Ireland This is "where the mountains of Mourne sweep down to the sea." The *British Amateur* championship was played here in 1970, and Gene Sarazen, the noted golf professional, voted it the number one course in the world. So no one should be too surprised to find that some of the hazards can prove rather startling to weak-kneed players. The minutes of the founding club meeting in 1889 reported that "the Secretaries were empowered to employ Tom Morris to lay out the course at a cost not to exceed £4." God alone only knows how Old Tom hacked these holes out of the rough sandhills for that price, but he did make a beauty. Details: *Royal County Down Golf Club,* Newcastle, County Down BT33 0AN, Northern Ireland (phone: 396-723314)

Tennis

Although tennis has a long way to go before it becomes as popular in Ireland as it is in the US, there are now thousands of players, and courts are seldom hard to find. While real buffs still wouldn't come to Ireland just to play tennis, those who do play should be sure to pack racquet and tennis whites, since a tennis match is a fine and quick way to get off the standard tourist circuit and into local life. In these circles, playing well is considered important — but playing as if you mean to win at all costs isn't the Irish style. If you pass muster, you may end the match with at least an invitation to the nearest pub.

WHERE TO PLAY

Municipal courts abound in both the Republic and Northern Ireland; tourist literature lists their locations. In addition, many of the more luxurious hotels have their own courts (see listings in THE CITIES and in DIRECTIONS). Otherwise, the following organizations are the best sources of information:

> ***Fitzwilliam Lawn and Tennis Club*** (Appian Way, Dublin 6, Irish Republic; phone: 1-660-3988). The major tennis venue for Dublin tennis events.
>
> ***Tennis Ireland*** (54 Wellington Rd., Dublin 4, Irish Republic; phone: 1-668-1841). Provides information about the sport throughout the Republic.

For more than just a casual hour a day on the courts, plan your trip around stops at a handful of resorts. For information about tennis centers in or near Ireland's major cities and towns, see the *Tennis* entries in the individual chapters in THE CITIES. The following are two other top spots.

RIVERVIEW CLUB, Beech Hill, Clonskeagh, County Dublin, Irish Republic Although a private club, it accepts visitors who are staying at any of the seven Doyle hotels of Dublin. It has 12 indoor and 6 outdoor courts (phone: 1-283-0322).

SLIEVE DONARD, Newcastle, County Down, Northern Ireland A fully restored, 19th-century, landmark railway hotel with a recreation center, including 2 all-weather courts set on a lawn facing the Irish Sea and the Mourne Mountains (phone: 396-723681; fax: 396-724830).

WHERE TO WATCH

The *Irish Open* is the major event of the season. Although it's not now a world class tournament, a number of up-and-coming players from the international circuit try to make the scene. The open usually is held during the second week of July, just after *Wimbledon*. For advance information on this and other tourneys, contact *Tennis Ireland* (address above).

Horsing Around

An old Irish saying has it that there are three glories to any gathering — a beautiful wife, a good horse, and a swift hound. In Ireland, it is the horse that provides the excuse to hold the gathering in the first place. (This is, after all, a country that almost unanimously voted a horse as Personality of the Year — the legendary steeplechaser Arkle, the quadruped folk hero who won the *Cheltenham Gold Cup* 3 years running, thereby humiliating, to the immense satisfaction of the Irish, every one of the champion's British counterparts.) Irish horses and their "connections" — trainers, riders, and breeders — are legendary. Hundreds of mares are brought to Ireland to be mated with celebrated stallions now retired to Irish farms; thanks to a governmental ruling that gives stud fees tax-exempt status, the business is flourishing.

Irish horse gatherings come in all shapes and descriptions. There are events in which horses are ridden, raced, hunted, bought, sold, jumped, driven, backed, cursed, argued over, and immortalized. All offer visitors plenty of opportunities to get in on the act.

RACES, SHOWS, MEETS, AND SALES

The Irish are on their favorite turf at these events. There are nearly 300 race days, on the flat and over the jumps, on 2 dozen racecourses each year, all wonderfully entertaining, with the brouhaha of punters placing their bets on named horses and on-course bookies shouting the odds, which are posted on the boards, wiped out, and reposted as wagers are placed. At some festival meetings, all the inhabitants for miles around stop work to go to the races — and a great portion of the rest of the population plans holidays around a favorite meeting.

Since Norman and Elizabethan days, the focal point of Irish racing has been the *Curragh,* the great plain of Kildare, southwest of Dublin — 6,000 wide-open acres that are home to many of the best stables; at any given time, a few million pounds' worth of bloodstock can be seen trotting over its windswept expanses of short grass. The *Curragh* is the venue for the five Irish classic races — the *One Thousand Guineas* and *Two Thousand Guineas* in May, the *Irish Derby* in June, the *Irish Oaks* in July, and the *Irish St. Leger* in October. (Each of these is also referred to by the name of its sponsor, which changes periodically.) Adjacent to the racecourse, whose grandstands brood silently over the plain through most of the year, is the fascinating *Irish National Stud* (Tully, County Kildare, Irish Republic; phone: 45-21251). Each aristocratic stallion has a brass nameplate on his stable door, and the grassy meadows beyond are full of mares and skipping foals. On the grounds is the *Irish Horse Museum* (phone: 45-21251), full of objects and information on matters equine, with good coverage of draft horses as well as racing, hunting, show jumping, and steeplechasing; the center of attraction, lovingly admired by all, is the standing skeleton of the steeplechaser Arkle.

Steeplechasing, a pell-mell charge through the fields with no particular end in sight, said to be descended from the Tudor-era wild-goose chase, was born in Ireland in 1752, when two riders in County Cork raced each other from one church to another a few miles away, leaping walls, ditches, hedges, and other impediments en route. Soon it became the height of fashion among Irish horse folk and is still popular today; the greatest steeplechasers on earth are trained here.

One of the best places to watch the Irish and their great horses is *Leopardstown,* 6 miles south of Dublin, a flat course modeled on England's *Sandown,* with a modern glass-enclosed, all-weather facility. In addition, there are the following jumping, or national hunt, courses: *Galway,* which hosts the *Guinness Hurdle* and the *Galway Plate* on its jumping course in August; *Punchestown,* in Naas, County Kildare, 20 miles from Dublin, steeplechasing's headquarters since 1850, which has a festival meeting in late April or early May; *Gowran,* County Kilkenny, where feature races are run in January, May, and September; *Fairyhouse,* in County Meath, 14 miles from Dublin, the venue for the *Irish Grand National* each *Easter*

Monday; and *Navan,* County Meath, where there are feature events in January and November.

In Northern Ireland, the races at *Downpatrick* (phone: 396-612054), which has a somewhat undulating track, and at *Down Royal* in Lisburn (phone: 846-621256), a good galloping track, enjoy an enthusiastic year-round following. The *Ulster Harp National,* the country's most important steeplechase, is held annually in February at *Downpatrick.*

In addition, there are literally hundreds of well-supported horse shows, or gymkhanas, held all over Ireland from February to October — events that last from 1 to 3 days, give neighbors the chance to mingle, visitors the chance to soak up some local color, and participants a crack at qualifying for the *Dublin Horse Show.* Some of the best show jumpers in the country can often be seen at these local events. The rivalries are as heated, and the audiences as enthusiastic, as at the *Dublin Horse Show* itself.

Admission to all courses for all kinds of races is about $10 per adult, a bit more for the bigger races, with an extra charge for the reserved enclosure. There is plenty to eat and drink, and binoculars are for rent at about $4.50 plus a deposit. Don't fail to take in the bumper races — usually the last on the day's card; these events for amateur riders often provide the best sport and the greatest excitement. And since no day at the races is complete without "taking an interest" (putting precious pounds on a nag), those so inclined will want to "study form" in the daily papers — the weekly *Irish Field,* or the *Irish Racing Form* — which can be purchased at the course for about $3.50. Bets can be placed with the government-run Tote (minimum IR£1) or with the bookmaker (minimum IR£5).

Flat races take place from summer through fall, overlapping the commencement of the jumping season, which is in full swing between late December and *Easter,* ending with the late April meeting at *Punchestown.*

The races and equine events listed alphabetically below by county and town are among the best of their types. For their dates, along with a calendar of all races, contact the *Irish Racing Board, Leopardstown Racecourse,* Foxrock, Dublin 18, Irish Republic (phone: 1-289-2888).

DUBLIN HORSE SHOW, County Dublin, Irish Republic First held in 1868, this is one of the best shows of its kind in the world. Held annually in July through early August, with its hunt balls and social and diplomatic parties, it is certainly the high point of the year for Dublin society. For *Ladies' Day,* the Thursday of *Horse Show Week,* citizens don their best bib and tucker, and a glittering automobile is presented to the most attractively dressed and suitably groomed lady at the show. The main show jumping events, held on Friday and Saturday, are the *Nations Cup* for the Aga Khan Trophy and the *Grand Prix of Ireland* — the richest jumping competitions in the world. Grandstand tickets for these competitions, as well as for others held during the week, are quite difficult to come by, but standing room is always available. Details: *Royal Dublin Society,* PO Box 121, Ballsbridge, Dublin 4, Irish Republic (phone: 1-668-0645); for housing details, *Dublin Tourism Office,* 13-14 Upper O'Connell St., Dublin 1, Irish Republic (phone: 1-874-7733).

BALLINASLOE HORSE FAIR, Ballinasloe, County Galway, Irish Republic With Irish horses such valuable exports, traditional sales held at various times in Dublin under the auspices of the *Royal Dublin Society* and at the renowned *Goffs' Sales Paddocks* at Kill, County Kildare, bring scores of American and European millionaires and Middle Eastern potentates humming in and out in helicopters and wearing costly silks and cashmeres along with their tweeds. The famous October horse and cattle fair in Ballinasloe is different. For this venerable event, the country's largest livestock market and the largest horse fair in Europe in the days of horse-drawn transport, the big, cheerful country town of Ballinasloe leaps out of its usual drowse. The excitement that characterizes the buying and selling of horses anywhere is crazily mixed up here with the color of a traditional fair in high Irish spirits. Details: *Irish Tourist Board,* 757 Third Ave., New York, NY 10017 (phone: 212-418-0800).

CONNEMARA PONY SHOW, Clifden, County Galway, Irish Republic These deep-chested, versatile, even-tempered, intelligent native ponies — said to be descended from horses that managed to swim to shore from the wrecks of the Spanish Armada — have been the focus of increasing attention in recent years, but have been showcased at this professionally run country show held annually on the third Thursday in August for more than 60 years. The animals make fine pets and excellent jumpers, and this fair, at which some 300 of the best are judged, bought, and traded, is a grand one indeed. The breeders are a lively, mixed group — simple farmers and aristocrats alike — and the town goes all out, with Guinness flowing freely. Details: *Connemara Pony Breeders Society,* Marion Turley, Hospital Rd., Clifden, County Galway, Irish Republic (phone: 95-21863).

GALWAY RACES, near Galway City, County Galway, Irish Republic These hilarious, exhilarating late July races at Ballybrit, a few miles from city center with a fine view of Galway Bay, are an Irish legend; the whole city practically closes down every afternoon so that the citizenry can make the scene. Racing takes place over a course that is a fair test of stamina for any horse, just as race week's side show of fast-talking hawkers, itinerant musicians, soothsayers, and assorted others of perhaps less than sterling character tries the endurance of visitors and residents. If you make a few dollars while "taking an interest," as most people do (some IR£1 million is put on the line every day), take care that you don't lose it — and more — in a *Galway Race Week* poker game. Details: *Irish Racing Board* (see above).

IRISH DERBY, Kildare, County Kildare, Irish Republic Irish racing is world famous, and Irish-bred horses regularly win the Continent's classic competitions; this event, a 1½-miler for 3-year-olds held at the *Curragh* annually in late June or early July, is Ireland's star race. Among the other classic races that make this track so important are the *Irish One Thousand Guineas* (1 mile for 3-year-old fillies, in May), the *Irish Two Thousand Guineas* (1 mile for 3-year-olds, in May), the *Irish Oaks* (1½ miles for 3-year-old fillies, in July), and the *Irish St. Leger* (1¾ miles for 3-year-olds and up, in October). Details: *Irish Racing Board* (see above).

HORSE TRIALS, Punchestown, County Kildare, Irish Republic This annual 3-day competition in late May offers visitors the chance to join Irish equestrians in "full fig" (fully outfitted) from the tips of their hard hats to the toes of their close-fitting boots. Horse lovers, some bringing caravans and mobile homes, come from Bermuda, Canada, Spain, and even New Zealand to enjoy the goings-on: dressage the first day, cross-country steeplechasing the second, show jumping the third. International stars are invariably on hand to show their stuff, but — this being the country of the horse — the hit of the day is just as apt to be the 58-year-old sportsman who gets himself and his half-breed, still together, around the course. Details: *Irish Racing Board* (see above).

IRISH GRAND NATIONAL, Fairyhouse, County Meath, Irish Republic The whole nation knows who is going to win this famous fixture of the jumping season — so the whole nation "takes an interest." Seeing the line of horses taking the first fence on a sunny *Easter Monday* is a sight worth waiting for. Details: *Irish Racing Board* (see above).

LAYTOWN STRAND RACES, Laytown, County Meath, Irish Republic This small resort town at the mouth of the River Nanny, some 30 miles north of Dublin, holds just one meet a year, usually in mid-August. It is not the sort of event that draws the top horses or the top jockeys. What makes it exceptional, however, is its venue — the town's long, broad, gently sloping strand. For just this one day a year, the beach is all horse. Details: *Irish Racing Board* (see above).

LIMERICK JUNCTION RACECOURSE, Limerick Junction, County Tipperary, Irish Republic For those who are jaded by big meetings, this small racecourse named after the nearby railway station (and not the distant town) is ideal. In the heart of racing Ireland, 115 miles from Dublin — not far from the home of Vincent O'Brien, one of the world's leading buyers, breeders, and trainers of racehorses — this racecourse hosts events regularly from March through November and draws a crowd that is at least as interesting as the horses. In its own small way, the *Limerick Junction* shows offer everything that is delightful about Irish racing — and Irish character. Details: *Irish Racing Board* (see above).

TRAMORE RACES, Tramore, County Waterford, Irish Republic Down in the sunny southeast, by the sea, this mid-August race has a flavor all its own. Nobody takes anything too seriously — except the horses. Those who manage to save something from the bookies can spend it on a piece of crystal from the famous Waterford manufacturer, just down the road. Details: *Irish Racing Board* (see above).

RIDING HOLIDAYS, TREKKING, AND TRAIL RIDING

The Irish flock to horse holidays with exactly the same enthusiasm that Americans flock to dude ranches — except that they are more likely to wear jodhpurs than jeans, swing into saddles without horns as well as with, and do their riding at a stable that doesn't have anything more than a casual arrangement with their lodging place. Topnotch horses, delightful scenery, and the chance to join the natives in one of their favorite pastimes are the main attractions.

Literature describing equestrian holidays often contains bewildering lingo. The term *riding holiday,* for instance, refers to not just any vacation spent on horseback but specifically to one where participants trot, canter, occasionally even take small jumps, and get basic instruction by a full-fledged instructor registered with the Association of Irish Riding Establishments (AIRE), one currently accredited by the British Horse Society (BHSI or BHSAI) or, in smaller establishments, horse folk who instruct as a summer job. The organizations that provide these activities, which are available year-round, may also arrange for their guests to compete in local shows, or gymkhanas, where they can get to know the local horsey set (and in Ireland that's practically everybody). Some riding holiday centers are residential, with accommodations on the premises; others arrange for participants to lodge nearby in small hotels or guesthouses, or even with local families. Rank beginners and advanced equestrians are both welcome. Visitors are advised to check their insurance before going and to look into any limitations on the insurance available through the chosen riding establishment.

Many horsey establishments offer ponies or horses for trekking in nearby mountains or woods. To accommodate novice riders and the less fit, travel is at a walking pace. These rides combine the leisurely enjoyment of the open air and great sweeps of scenery with the pleasures of traveling astride a walking horse. Children under 14 may find it a bit tedious, but it is the rare experienced day trekker who remains unmotivated to go on to the next level — post trekking, also known as trail riding.

Trail riding is a more ambitious sort of holiday that lasts several days and takes riders from one post to the next, 20 to 25 miles a day. Participants — in the company of an experienced guide — ride over rugged hills, through leafy lanes, or across deserted sandy beaches. Picnics, cookouts, and barbecues offer diversion en route, and overnight stops provide for plenty of hot water, huge quantities of food, and good company. Luggage usually is transported separately.

The following, listed alphabetically by county and town, beginning with the Irish Republic, include some of the best Irish establishments offering riding, trekking, and trail riding. Also note that the Irish Tourist Board publication *Equestrian Ireland* is helpful.

WILLIAM LEAHY, the Connemara Trail, Aille Cross, Loughrea, County Galway, Irish Republic The particular attractions of this establishment's ride along the Connemara Trail, aside from the wonderful landscape that unfolds en route along pretty hill roads and tracks, are the lodgings in places such as Galway's *Great Southern* hotel, where the trip begins and ends, climaxing with a glorious romp down a long and windswept beach. The mounts are hunters or half-breed horses. Trips are offered year-round. Details: *The Connemara Trail,* c/o William Leahy, Aille Cross, Loughrea, County Galway, Irish Republic (phone: 91-41216; fax: 91-42363).

MILCHEM EQUESTIAN CENTRE, Tynagh, Loughrea, County Galway, Irish Republic Trail rides along the "Galway to Tipperary" trail take in myriad mountains, rivers, forest, bog, farmland, and lake shore around Lough Derg — but few roads and little traffic. There is special emphasis on fine food on these 6-night treks, based at a selection of inns in the Shannon region. Open May through October. Details: *Milchem Equestrian Centre,* Tynagh, Loughrea, County Galway, Irish Republic (phone: 905-76388).

EL RANCHO HORSE HOLIDAYS, Ballyard, Tralee, County Kerry, Irish Republic This establishment offers, among other things, an adventurous 80-mile, week-long circle trip along out-of-the-way bridle paths through mountain defiles and lovely stretches of sand in the breezy, sea-washed area of rugged hills where the film *Ryan's Daughter* was made. Accommodations en route are in farmhouses and hotels, where the food is both tasty and plentiful. May to October. Details: *El Rancho Horse Holidays,* c/o William J. O'Connor, Ballyard, Tralee, County Kerry, Irish Republic (phone: 66-21840).

MOUNT JULIET, Thomastown, County Kilkenny, Irish Republic Home to the Ballylinch Stud Farm, this expansive 1,500-acre estate is a haven for equestrian enthusiasts. There are 10 miles of professionally planned bridle paths and qualified instructors, including internationally renowned rider/trainer Iris Kellet. Equipment and riding gear also are available. Overnight packages include accommodations, breakfast, and dinner at the manor house. Open year-round. Details: *Mount Juliet,* Thomastown, County Kilkenny, Irish Republic (phone: 56-24455).

GREYSTONES EQUESTRIAN CENTRE, Castle Leslie, Glaslough, County Monaghan, Irish Republic Riding lessons, with five separate cross-country courses full of prepared fences and all sorts of natural obstacles — rivers, ditches, fallen trees, log piles, stone walls, hedges, drops, and the like — are featured here; the area was once called "the St. Moritz of equestrianism." Lodging is in a Victorian country house, and meals are typical Irish country fare. Open year-round. Details: *Greystones Equestrian Centre,* Castle Leslie, Glaslough, County Monaghan, Irish Republic (phone: 47-88100).

HORSE HOLIDAY FARM, Grange, County Sligo, Irish Republic Riding vacations (including overnight accommodations) as well as day trail rides for non-registered guests are offered here. The trails along the beaches and glens of County Sligo are truly memorable — this is the place to come if you like your riding accompanied by poetic landscape. Details: Colette and Tilman Anhold, *Horse Holiday Farm,* Grange, County Sligo, Irish Republic (phone: 71-66152; fax: 71-66400).

WHITFIELD COURT POLO SCHOOL, Waterford, County Waterford, Irish Republic It's not surprising that horse-loving Ireland is home to Europe's only residential polo school. Though the game was first played in India over 2,000 years ago and was brought to the West by Her Majesty's Ninth Lancers, the Irish picked it up as if they had been born playing. *Whitfield Court* has had beginners and advanced players alike from more than 25 countries; some call their polo vacation the most memorable of their lives. There's also a heated swimming pool, and a tennis court. One-week sessions are offered from May to August; advance reservations are essential. Instruction is by Major Hugh Dawnay. (Those who would rather watch than play can catch the polo matches in Dublin's Phoenix Park during *Horse Show Week* — or observe the practice at *Whitfield Court* every Saturday and Sunday afternoon, May through September.) Details: *Whitfield Court Polo School,* Waterford, County Waterford, Irish Republic (phone: 51-84216).

HORETOWN HOUSE, Foulksmills, County Wexford, Irish Republic Offers week-long packages, including trekking or riding lessons in dressage, show jumping, and cross-country, with lodging in a 17th-century Georgian manor house. More than one guest has gone home applauding and agreeing with the Americans who called *Horetown House* "an authentic Irish country experience, with warm people, a cozy environment, and nourishing fires, food, and talk." Details: *Horetown House,* Foulksmills, County Wexford, Irish Republic (phone: 51-63633).

MOUNT PLEASANT PONY TREKKING CENTRE, Castlewellan, County Down, Northern Ireland Escorted trekking is available through the 15,000-acre Castlewellan Forest Park and the foothills of the fabled Mournes. Details: *Mount Pleasant Pony Trekking Centre,* 15 Bannanstown Rd., Castlewellan, County Down BT31 9BG, Northern Ireland (phone: 396-778651).

ASHBROOKE RIDING SCHOOL, Brookeborough, County Fermanagh, Northern Ireland Instruction for riders of all levels; training includes dressage, show jumping, and cross-country events. Restored housekeeping cottages are available or guests can stay with a family on Viscount Brookeborough's estate. Details: *Ashbrooke Riding School,* Brookeborough, County Fermanagh, Northern Ireland (phone: 396-553242).

EDERGOLE RIDING CENTRE, Cookstown, County Tyrone, Northern Ireland Escorted and unescorted trekking through the Sperrin Mountains, plus British Horse Society–approved instruction at all levels and post trail rides (tours using a succession of farm guesthouses for overnight stays). The riding center also has accommodations. Details: *Edergole Riding Centre,* 70 Moneymore Rd., Cookstown, County Tyrone, Northern Ireland BT80 8PY (phone: 648-762924).

HORSE-DRAWN CARAVANNING

Meandering along a narrow lane in a horse-drawn wagon, flanked by billowing meadows and fields, with grand vistas stretching off toward a purple-haze horizon, is one of the most relaxing ways to spend a week — and Ireland is one of the few countries in the world where it's possible. Agencies in a number of regions rent old-style Gypsy wagons, brightly painted outside and fitted with berths and cooking facilities inside (but without toilets), and the roads of the surrounding countryside are small and traffic-free — perfect for this kind of caravanning. Agents can suggest the most scenic routes; direct their guests to the beaches, overlooks, quaint old pubs, interesting restaurants, and historic sites in the areas through which they'll be passing; and name the best overnight spots, usually about 10 miles apart. The weekly cost for a caravan that will accommodate four is about $390 to $600, depending on the operator and the season.

Principal operators of horse-drawn caravans include the following:

Dieter Clissmann Horse-Drawn Caravans (Carrigmore Farm, County Wicklow, Irish Republic; phone: 404-48188).
Slattery's Horse-Drawn Caravans (1 Russell St., Tralee, County Kerry, Irish Republic; phone: 66-21722).

HUNTING ON HORSEBACK

With just a little effort, riders so inclined can hunt 7 days a week in Ireland during the fall and winter months, in their pick of locations, since riding to hounds — as distinct from shooting, as the Irish call going after game with firearms — is extremely popular here. There are dozens of hunts, including many that welcome guests. The scenery is stupendous, so that a rider may be forgiven for taking a tumble when distracted by the view. And since hunting is very democratic, it provides an opportunity to meet all sorts of people — not only the gentry, but also priests and diplomats, business executives and farmers, secretaries and students. Non-riders often follow the action on foot, by bicycle, or in their cars, standing by to catch a glimpse of the passing hounds and riders as they charge through the fields. From the stirrup cup that almost invariably precedes each meet, to the rendezvous afterward in some favored hostelry, the atmosphere is at once orderly, friendly, and convivial; and the hunter is judged not only on his skill with the horse but also on his ability to hold his own in the best of company. A number of types of hunting while on horseback are popular in Ireland.

FOX HUNTING

Chasing a pack of hounds on horseback, in hot pursuit of the wily fox, is the favorite sport of some of the most fascinating characters in a country full of memorable personalities; fox hunting in Ireland has history, folklore, gossip, and a social flavor all its own. What really counts is your seat on the horse — and whether you keep it!

Hunt secretaries can advise on hiring a mount — usually an Irish-bred horse with fence-taking ability in his blood. Expect to spend $130 to $180 per day.

COUNTY GALWAY, Irish Republic Dedicated hunting folk say that if you can hunt in only one place in Ireland, it should be in County Galway, where miles of loose gray limestone walls give gritty character to the landscape and local interest supports no less than three hunts, all of which welcome visitors. The season runs roughly from October to March:

County Galway Hunt (*The Blazers,* c/o Mrs. J. Coveney, Caherdevane, Craughwell, County Galway, Irish Republic; phone: 91-46387). This celebrated hunt is more informally known as the *Galway Blazers.*

East Galway Hunt (c/o Mr. Joe McEvoy, Lawrencetown, County Galway, Irish Republic; phone: 905-76138).

North Galway Hunt (c/o Ms. Patricia Cunningham, Bridge House, Tuam, County Galway, Irish Republic; phone: 93-24155).

Visiting hunters will also find a warm welcome and an understanding and knowledgeable host at the *Great Southern* hotel (Eyre Sq., Galway; phone: 91-64041).

COUNTIES CLARE, CORK, AND LIMERICK, Irish Republic Second to Galway, this is Ireland's favorite hunt country, notable for great bank ditches of clay and stone that test the mettle of the bravest. A handful of hunts here are of interest because of the variety of terrain and the availability of associated guesthouses and hotels.

County Clare Hunt (c/o Ms. Margaret Meehan, Ballycar Rd., Newmarket-on-Fergus, County Clare, Irish Republic; phone: 61-368329). The Georgian-style *Ballykilty Manor* hotel in Quin (phone: 65-25627), surrounded by a handsome 50-acre park, and the luxurious *Old Ground* hotel in Ennis (Station Rd.; phone: 65-28127) cater to hunters and organize enjoyable hunting parties themselves.

> *County Limerick Hunt* (c/o Mrs. F. Ward, Adelaide House, Bruff, County Limerick, Irish Republic; phone: 61-82114).
>
> *Duhallow Hunt* (c/o Capt. P. Coleman, Dromore, Dromahane, Mallow, County Cork, Irish Republic; phone: 22-29350).

OTHER FOX HUNTS IN THE REPUBLIC The *Dunraven Arms* hotel (Adare, County Limerick; phone: 61-396209) specializes in fox hunting arrangements and is affiliated with eight different hunt clubs in Limerick, Clare, Galway, and Tipperary. A tiny guesthouse known as *Ballycormac Cottage* (Aglish, near Roscrea, County Tipperary, Irish Republic; phone: 67-21129) can arrange for visitors to hunt with some of the most famous packs of hounds in the country, including the *Ormond* (the country's oldest), the *Westmeath,* and the *Roscommon Harriers.* The centrally located *Mount Juliet* estate (Thomastown, County Kilkenny; phone: 56-24455), home to the *Kilkenny Hunt,* can arrange for guests to participate in eight additional nearby hunts in Tipperary, Killinick, Waterford, Wexford, Ormond, Carlow, Kilmoganny, and Bree. Packages include equipment and riding gear (if needed), and accommodations in the manor house.

NORTHERN IRELAND Fox hunting is no less popular here, and there are a number of clubs. The best-known is *East Down Foxhounds,* c/o Mrs. Johnston, *White Lodge,* 89 Whiterock Rd., Killinchy, County Down, Northern Ireland (phone: 238-541561).

CUBBING

Most hunts hold cub meets in September, October, and November. Workman-like affairs whose purpose is to train the hounds, break up litters of young foxes and thin their population, and otherwise get things in order, they are held in early mornings and are open to proficient riders by arrangement with individual hunt secretaries.

HARRIER HUNTING

Less glamorous, with a hare rather than fox as quarry, harrier hunting is done by about 30 Irish hunts. Two near Dublin welcome visitors by appointment:

> *Bray Harriers* (c/o C. J. Warren, 11 Whitethorn Rd., Dublin 14, Irish Republic; phone: 1-269-4403).
>
> *Fingal Harriers* (c/o Miss Patricia Murtagh, The Grange, Skerries, County Dublin, Irish Republic; phone: 1-849-1467).

OTHER EQUINE EXPERIENCES

Anyone in search of still other ways to enjoy Ireland's favorite quadruped need not want for opportunities.

HARNESS RACING This sport is variously known as harness racing, sulky racing, and "Ben Hur with bucket seats." There are tracks at *Portmarnock* in

County Dublin and at *Whitehouse* in County Antrim. But nowhere else do the locals get into the cut and thrust of sulky racing with the zest of West Cork. The 2-day event at *Leap,* which takes place in a 25-acre field every May or early June, is the biggest of dozens of races all around the country; there are about a thousand spectators and three bookies, and the last few yards of the *Kentucky Derby* won't beat it for heart-stopping tension. Details: *Irish Trotting and Harness Racing Federation,* c/o James Connolly, Maugh House, Dunmanway, County Cork, Irish Republic (phone: 23-45360).

CARRIAGE DRIVING It would be easy to jump to the conclusion that this is a sport befitting only well-heeled nincompoops, but there's a lot more to it. This can be seen clearly by a visit to the Irish championships, a 2-day all-Ireland event that takes place at the end of August or early September on the splendidly scenic, 1,000-acre demesne of 17th-century Birr Castle, under the auspices of its owner, the Earl of Rosse and his wife, the Countess of Rosse. The 18-mile-long marathon course along the roads, through the fields, and even in and across streams is ferocious; some of the riverbanks appear to deviate little from the vertical. The little Shetland ponies that draw the carriages (unprepossessing conveyances that are really more like traps) at times have to turn into hairy submarines, moving virtually underwater, with only nostrils and ear tips showing, along the bed of the fast-flowing Camcor and Little Brosna rivers. The grounds alone would be worth the trip: The trees are in fine color, and the tall boxwood hedges — the world's tallest, according to *The Guinness Book of World Records* — are wonderfully fragrant. Details: *Cloonanagh, Silvermines,* c/o Mr. and Mrs. Charles H. Powell, Nenagh, County Tipperary, Irish Republic (phone: 67-25256).

Wonderful Waterways and Coastal Cruises

Ireland is a watery place in the pleasantest possible way. No point is more than 70 miles from the nearest seashore, and the entire country is crisscrossed by rivers and canals and dotted with lakes. As a result, boats play an important role in the lives of many Irish families. Often, they're simply the most convenient way to fish the clear waters, whether fresh or salt. But the calm waters of ancient canals and the challenging seas of the rugged Atlantic seaboard alike also provide access to a whole world of recreation.

The national sailing and boating magazine, *Afloat* (Shamrock House, Upper Kilmacud Rd., Dundrum, Dublin 14, Irish Republic; phone: 1-298-8696), provides information on what's going on in every corner of the Irish boating world, at all levels of interest and experience.

SAILING

Thanks to good breezes, excellent waters, a 2,000-mile shoreline, and an almost infinite choice of possible anchorages, sailing has long been a popular Irish sport. For instance, on the most popular cruising coastline, the handsome southwestern seaboard between sheltered Cork Harbour and the impressive Blasket Islands (known informally as "the last parish before America"), it's reckoned that there are 143 different places to tie up, no two alike — and that stretch is just a quarter of the country's coastline. Other areas can offer as much variety, and each section of the seas can range from millpond-calm to rough, hard, and roiling; the variety is part of the challenge.

GETTING INFORMATION

The national sailing and boating authority in the Irish Republic is the *Irish Yachting Association* (3 Park Rd., Dún Laoghaire, County Dublin; phone: 1-280-0239). It provides the first point of contact to the 120 yacht and sailing clubs that play a pivotal role in the country's life afloat. In Northern Ireland, the same function is served by the *Royal Yachting Association* (House of Sport, Upper Malone Rd., Belfast BT9, Northern Ireland; phone: 232-381222). The organizations maintain close ties with each other, as sailing and boating here is essentially an all-Ireland affair, carried on in the friendliest style.

CLUBS

Clubs have played a paramount role in the Irish sailing scene ever since the days of the *Water Club,* the world's oldest sailing organization. All the clubs, from the smallest to the grandest, maintain a busy annual program in addition to the active social schedule that has made the Irish après-sailing atmosphere famous among European yachtsmen. Even the *Royal Cork Yacht Club* (Crosshaven, County Cork, Irish Republic; phone: 21-831440), a direct descendant of the old *Water Club,* wears its years lightly and is most hospitable and entertaining.

For visitors, one of the fascinations of sailing in Ireland lies in savoring the different characters of the many clubs. On the south coast, there's the modern *Royal Cork Yacht Club* (address above) and the nearby *Kinsale Yacht Club* (Lower O'Connell St., Kinsale, County Cork; phone: 21-772196). In Northern Ireland are the up-to-date harbors at Carrickfergus and Belfast Lough at Bangor in County Down. On the east coast is Dún Laoghaire, on Dublin Bay, where a huge artificial harbor is home to hundreds of boats, and stately yacht clubs with imposing façades line the waterfront with style. Also at Dublin Bay, on its northern arm, is the strikingly contemporary club at Howth.

EVENTS

In the early part of the season, during May and June, activity rapidly develops around the main clubs with a hectic program of regional championships, offshore races, and local regattas. Then, during July, the pace quickens with race weeks involving large fleets of cruiser-racers from both Ireland and abroad. Events of this period include the following, beginning with the Irish Republic.

ROUND IRELAND RACE Takes place in June under the auspices of the *Wicklow Sailing Club* (The Quay, Wicklow, County Wicklow, Irish Republic; phone: 404-68104) and covers 704 nautical miles around the nation's coast.

CORK WEEK Staged by the *Royal Cork Yacht Club* (address above) in July in even-numbered years, this includes the *European Offshore Team Championship,* a colorful affair that attracts teams from every continent.

ISORA WEEK Alternates between England and Ireland, taking place in the Irish Sea in July in odd-numbered years. It's administered by the *Irish Sea Offshore Racing Association* (119 Chelwood Ave., Liverpool L16 2LL, England).

BANGOR OFFSHORE WEEK The premier regatta series in Northern Ireland, run by the North's senior club, the *Royal Ulster Yacht Club* (Clifton Rd., Bangor, County Down, Northern Ireland; phone: 247-270568). It takes place in July in odd-numbered years.

Later in the summer, the emphasis turns from sailing centers near large urban areas to more remote coasts, and the first week of August brings with it a highly entertaining program of rural regattas along the incomparable West Cork seaboard. Dinghy championships are staged at attractive venues such as Sligo, Dunmore East, and Baltimore, and an extensive boardsailing calendar makes a colorful contribution.

At summer's end, though many boats head for home, autumn leagues begin attracting huge fleets to centers such as Cork Harbour, Howth, Belfast Lough, and Strangford Lough.

SAILING SCHOOLS

More fun than watching is doing it yourself — and, unbeknown to most, Ireland is an excellent place to learn. Week-long sailing courses in dinghies and cruisers, for novices and more advanced sailors alike, are available at dozens of sailing schools and clubs. Administering many of these in the Republic is the *Irish Association for Sail Training* (c/o Confederation House, Kildare St., Dublin 2; phone: 1-677-9801). For Northern Ireland, the same service is provided by the *Royal Yachting Association* (House of Sport, Upper Malone Rd., Belfast BT9 5LA, Northern Ireland; phone: 232-381222). Sailing schools such as the following (listed alphabetically by county and town, beginning with the Irish Republic) mirror the variety of the clubs.

BALTIMORE SAILING SCHOOL, Baltimore, County Cork, Irish Republic Sailing instruction here uses traditional craft and modern dinghies among Carbery's

Hundred Isles and around Baltimore, Crookhaven, and Cork. Details: *Baltimore Sailing School,* The Pier, Baltimore, County Cork, Irish Republic (phone: 28-20141).

INTERNATIONAL SAILING CENTRE, Cobh, County Cork, Irish Republic The ancestors of many Americans bade farewell to the Emerald Isle from Cobh, whose seafaring tradition goes back centuries. Nowadays, *International Sailing Centre* excursions visit hidden creeks and wooden coves once frequented by topsail schooners. Sailing, windsurfing, and cruising holidays are available, and lodgings range from simple bunkhouses to comfortable hotels. Details: *International Sailing Centre,* 5 East Beach, Cobh, County Cork, Irish Republic (phone: 21-811237).

GLENANS IRISH SAILING CENTRE, Dublin, County Dublin, Irish Republic Though associated with the famous French sail training group of the same name, this organization has a uniquely Irish character. Bases are located at Baltimore and Bere Island in the south, and in island-studded Clew Bay on the west coast, and the range of courses for everyone, from absolute beginners through the most experienced offshore sailors, is remarkably comprehensive. Details: *Glenans Irish Sailing Centre,* 28 Merrion Sq., Dublin 2, Irish Republic (phone: 1-661-1481).

IRISH NATIONAL SAILING SCHOOL, Dún Laoghaire, County Dublin, Irish Republic This school's extensive course offerings range from 3-hour dinghy instruction to cruises in the Irish Sea and to the Isle of Man. Details: *Irish National Sailing School,* 115 Lower Georges St., Dún Laoghaire, County Dublin, Irish Republic (phone: 1-280-6654).

FINGALL SAILING SCHOOL, Malahide, County Dublin, Irish Republic Sailing and windsurfing instruction is available on the safe Broadmeadow Estuary, as well as in Malahide Inlet and along the coast from Howth to Skerries. Details: *Fingall Sailing School,* Upper Strand Rd., Malahide, County Dublin, Irish Republic (phone: 1-845-1979).

DOLPHIN OFFSHORE SAILING GROUP, Sutton, County Dublin, Irish Republic For those who are experienced sailors and wish to broaden their knowledge of navigation, seamanship, and meteorology, this school offers a 5-day practical course in yacht mastering (off-shore). Details: *Dolphin Offshore Sailing Group,* St. Domhnach's Well, Baldoyle Rd., Sutton, County Dublin, Irish Republic (phone: 1-323938).

GALWAY SAILING CENTRE, Galway, County Galway, Irish Republic This facility provides instruction in dinghy sailing and boardsailing on the sheltered waters of Rinville Harbour, a safe inlet of Galway Bay, and canoeing on the Connemara lakes. Details: *Galway Sailing Centre,* 8 Father Griffin Rd., Galway, County Galway, Irish Republic (phone: 91-63522).

SHANNON SAILING, Nenagh, County Tipperary, Irish Republic This family-run sailing school is based on one of Ireland's largest and most attractive lakes,

Lough Derg (described in more detail below in the entry on the River Shannon). Fully equipped sailing cruisers can be hired for holidays afloat. Details: *Shannon Sailing,* New Harbour, Dromineer, Nenagh, County Tipperary, Irish Republic; phone: 67-24295).

ULSTER CRUISING SCHOOL, Carrickfergus, County Antrim, Northern Ireland This organization offers special pre-flotilla cruise training, offshore sailing in the Irish Sea and the Scottish Hebrides, and other active holidays. Details: *Ulster Cruising School,* Carrickfergus Marina, Carrickfergus, County Antrim, Northern Ireland (phone: 960-368818).

CRAIGAVON WATER SPORTS CENTRE SAILING SCHOOL, Craigavon, County Armagh, Northern Ireland Activities here in season (April through October) take place on 170-acre Craigavon Lake, not far from several bird sanctuaries and 153-square-mile Lough Neagh, the largest lake in Britain and Ireland. Details: *Craigavon Water Sports Centre Sailing School,* Craigavon Lakes, Portadown, Craigavon, County Armagh, Northern Ireland (phone: 762-342669).

BANGOR SAILING SCHOOL, Bangor, County Down, Northern Ireland Skippered sails around Lough Belfast, and instruction in cruising. Cruisers, dinghies, canoes, and pedal boats for hire. Details: *Bangor Sailing School,* John Irwin, 13 Gray's Hill Rd., Bangor, County Down, Northern Ireland (phone: 247-455967).

ON YOUR OWN

Crews who wish to make their own way to the many harbors and anchorages around Ireland's coast will find the venerable *Irish Cruising Club*'s two-volume *Sailing Directions* indispensable. The books are available from good nautical booksellers in Ireland or the United Kingdom. For information on charters, contact the Irish Tourist Board, 757 Third Ave., New York, NY 10017 (phone: 212-418-0800).

CRUISING THE INLAND WATERWAYS

Complementing the salty waters of Ireland's coast is one of the most fascinating systems of inland waterways in Europe; its fresh, clear, unpolluted waters are one of Ireland's secret attractions. These can be explored gently by charter boats, widely available for hire on the main waterways. Cruising is simple, idyllic, and restorative, featuring fishing, floating, and feasting while on the water as well as stops at restaurants and pubs en route. It reveals a quieter, more private facet of Ireland's character, and it provides a most unusual way to get to know the people, especially at cruises-in-company, such as the week-long *Shannon Boat Rally* organized by the *Inland Waterways Association of Ireland (AWAI)* every July.

The *AWAI* is responsible for coordinating all inland waterway activities. It is active in the promotion, preservation, and restoration of the canal and river system, and can be contacted in care of its secretary at Stone Cottage, Claremount Rd., Killiney, County Dublin (phone: 1-852258). For more on companies cruising Irish waterways, see GETTING READY TO GO.

THE RIVER SHANNON, Irish Republic Although the longest river in Ireland, this ancient waterway may seem small by worldwide standards since its navigable sector, which curves westward to the sea from the center of the country, comprises only 140 miles. Nevertheless, the Shannon's quiet majesty as it flows with the tranquillity of a canal between low-lying shores and then swells into vast lakes as temperamental as the ocean itself makes the traditional sobriquet "the lordly Shannon" seem not at all inappropriate. In fact, the system is so extensive that overcrowding is well-nigh impossible. In addition to the riverine portions, the Shannon includes three lakes — the large Lough Key, Loughs Ree and Derg — which themselves are practically inland seas. Measuring some 25 miles long and an average 2 to 3 miles across, Derg in particular is a world unto itself, its lovely coastline dotted with delightful miniature ports, each with its own little harbor built to shelter cargo barges in times past and now home to fleets of power and sailing cruisers. Just beyond the banks, soft hills rise green and cool. Nearby there is access to the placid 80-mile-long Grand Canal, a once-bustling commercial link between Dublin and the River Shannon and the even quieter River Barrow. The canal winds between grassy banks speckled with the blossoms of yellow irises, orchids, and daisies in season; sometimes great vistas open up onto the rolling pastureland or wide bogs, sometimes the vegetation closes in like an emerald tunnel. The Barrow, for its part, meanders southward through the southeastern corner of the country, a hidden area of lush farmland, gentle woods, and ancient castles, and ends at the sea near Waterford. Amateur botanists, ornithologists, and peripatetic archaeologists alike should have a field day; there are wildflowers here that do not grow anywhere else in Ireland, as well as herons, swans, curlew, grebes, cormorants, and dozens of other birds.

For particulars, consult the *Inland Waterways Association of Ireland Guide to the Grand Canal and Barrow River* (about $7.50), the *Shell Guide to the Shannon* (about $20), and other books available in leading bookstores throughout Ireland. Self-skippered charter boats can be rented through several organizations; the Irish Tourist Board can provide a complete list.

LOUGH ERNE, Northern Ireland Unlike the Shannon and the Barrow, the two huge island-studded lakes that make up the Erne system provide no direct access to the sea, but they are full of character nonetheless — the upper lake a hidden place of winding channels and dense mazes of islands (a few with lakes of their own), the lower lake a majestic place of open water, wide skyscapes, and spectacular scenery. A cruise that takes in the pair is an idyll for anglers, bird watchers, and lovers of wildflowers and churches, castles, caves, ruined monasteries, round towers, and mysterious pagan statues — all of which can be found here, along with dozens of coves and inlets, good hotels, tackle shops, and charter boat operators.

The free booklet *Holidays Afloat and Ashore on the Erne Waterway* will sketch the possibilities. To get a copy, contact the *Erne Charter Boat Association,* Lakeland Visitor Centre, Shore Rd., Enniskillen, County Fermanagh, Northern Ireland (phone: 365-323110).

RIVER BANN, Northern Ireland In itself, the River Bann would make for a pleasant cruise, with its flourishing bird and plant life, its sedgy shoreline, its uninhabited islets, the thatched shoreside villages where old-fashioned customs have maintained their hold just a bit longer than they have elsewhere. But the available cruising grounds multiply, encompassing some 150 square miles, if they include the lake from which the river emerges, Lough Neagh. The largest lake in the British Isles, Neagh supposedly was created when Finn MacCool scooped out a giant-size clod of earth and tossed it into the Irish Sea. According to the same mythology, its depths are the home of Eochu, lord of the underworld, but if that be the case, the sunny beauties of the scenery on a fine day give no hint of it. The wide-open spaces, making up with windswept grandeur what is lost in charming intimacy, are full of the special peace that gentle travel over calm waters can bring. For more information, contact the Northern Ireland Tourist Board.

Gone Fishing

Travelers to Ireland can appreciate what outdoor writers really mean when they talk about a "watery kingdom." In this island's 32,000 square miles, there are 9,000 miles of river and over 600,000 acres of lakes (or loughs, as the Irish call the better ones to distinguish them from the English lakes, which they deem inferior), for a total of about an acre of water for every 35 of land. Visitors who cannot find somewhere to wet their lines have only themselves to blame.

Almost all of this water holds fish, and very good fish they are. The limestone bedrock that lies inland from the mostly granite mountains of the Irish coast not only enriches the grass with the bone-building calcium on which the nation's horses thrive but also creates just the right acid balance in the waters that gurgle down from the undulating hills and through the pastures. Under such conditions, the wild brown trout, as well as pike and coarse, are the best in Europe.

Irish mountain freshets bear little in the way of food when they make their way to the coastal waters downstream, so the brown trout do not get fat. But what they lack in size, they make up for in heart. The bigger ones, weighing half a pound, create such a fuss at the business end of the tackle and fight so hard for their freedom that the discerning, experienced angler will agree with the novice as to the marvels of Irish sport. The salmon and sea trout angler awaits the return of these migratory species to the scenic fresh waters with the eagerness of a child at *Christmas.*

Fishing is considered an important tourist activity in the Irish Republic, and the Irish Tourist Board has worked with regional fishery boards to develop the nation's angling to a very high standard, giving attention not only to water management but also to access, parking, bankside facilities such as stiles, footbridges, and platforms, and, on loughs, good moorings, convenient slipways for put-in, and a reasonable supply of rental boats and "ghillies," as guides are generally known here. In addition, the board has given its stamp of approval to a number of salmon, trout, pike, and coarse fishing waters that offer visitors good facilities and reliably good sport. These fisheries are indicated by a special Angling Tourism logo in tourist board literature.

In recent years, fishing has been going through some changes in the Republic of Ireland, and there have been a number of disputes concerning licensing and regulation. Although things seem to have been resolved, visitors should check with the *Central Fisheries Board* (Mobhi Boreen, Glasnevin, Dublin 9; phone: 1-837-9206) to make sure that they get the proper licenses and pay the current fees. The board also can provide a vast amount of information about the Irish fishing scene. The Northern Ireland Tourist Board provides comparable services for the six counties in the North in conjunction with the *Department of Agriculture* (Fisheries Division, Stormont, Belfast BT4 3TA, Northern Ireland; phone: 232-520100), the ultimate authority on the nation's fisheries.

GAME ANGLING

The typical game fisherperson has catholic tastes when it comes to the different species. He or she goes for salmon and brown trout, sea trout, and stocked rainbows alike, and finds them all in Ireland within a remarkably small area. Moreover, since even the heartland of the island is less than 70 miles from the sea, it's possible to salt a game fishing vacation with a day of angling offshore.

BROWN AND SEA TROUT

These fish abound in both rivers and loughs. Sea trout fisheries are all along the coastline, with counties Kerry, Galway, Mayo, Sligo, and Donegal the standouts of those along the Atlantic (and Waterford and Cork also provide reasonable sport). The rivers Fane in County Louth, Boyne in County Meath, and Slaney in County Wexford are the most notable of those along the Irish Sea coastline, but there is heavy local club demand.

In Northern Ireland, there is acceptable sea trout fishing near the mouth of the Upper Bann and plenty of brown trout action on the Lower

Bann, the Ballinderry, the Moyola, the Maine, and the Blackwater — all rivers that feed 150-square-mile Lough Neagh, the largest lake in Ireland, itself seldom fished with rod and line since most anglers stick to feeder streams. The rivers in the narrow, picturesque valleys known as the Glens of Antrim have good runs of sea trout in July and August. Lough Melvin, in the west, is worth a special visit since it also contains three unique trout species — the sonaghan, the gillaroo, and the ferox — as well as an Ice Age predecessor of trout known as the char.

Throughout the area, Irish sea trout weigh in at a pound on the average — less than those in, say, Scottish waters, but they're tremendous fighters nonetheless. At the end of June and into the first week of July, when they start returning to the fresh waters (with the bigger ones leading the way), 3- and 4-pounders are pretty common on fly. For the rest of the season, sea trout offer excellent sport; the fact that they can be taken the day long on Irish rivers and loughs gives the Emerald Isle a special allure. When to go? Never before the final week in June or early July, except perhaps to the Waterville Fishery in County Kerry, which experiences an early run, and never after the close of the season, which is October 12 in most locations.

Brown trout are found almost everywhere. On the better brown trout rivers, the angler will come across enough fish in the 3/4-pound range to satisfy, while 2- and 3-pounders are always a possibility to the fly and spinner, and even bigger ones make their presence felt to those fishing the depths with heavy metal or worms. Meanwhile, in loughs, fish of a pound are about average to the fly and spinner, and 2- to 4-pounders are not uncommon. Dapping natural flies brings bigger trout to the surface, especially at mayfly time. A number of fish weighing in at above 10 pounds are taken on the deep troll — but this method is not popular with the Irish. The season opens on February 15 in many fisheries (though it may be wise to delay visiting until April). Sport is available in one place or another through October 12.

STREAM TROUTING There is a whole world awaiting the visiting brook, stream, and river angler, much of it to be enjoyed in undisturbed peace. (Ireland has a small population and, particularly on weekdays, the native angler will be at the office.)

Fly life on Irish rivers is not widely found until April, except for some large dark olives (adults), which anglers endeavor to simulate with dark olive quill, rough olive, and Greenwells glory patterns. There are also plentiful shrimp, and the March brown and Wickhams fancy are popular artificials. Natural fly becomes more abundant in April, the month of the medium black olive dun, the rough olive, and especially the iron blue dun and jenny spinner. The black duck fly chironimid and a variety of midges and buzzers also appear at this time.

Of the May olives, the iron blue is the most common. It shares the water surface with gray flag, brown flag, and gray Wulff silver sedges, and green drake, gray drake, and spent gnat mayflies in some rivers. Fish feed throughout the day in May, especially on warm evenings.

In June, sedges produce the most exciting sport, with the best fishing in the evening. Spent mayflies, olives, and midges will also be attracting the brown trout's notice. Conditions are never very good on Irish rivers in July and August. A combination of low water, heavy weed, and occasional sultry weather affects the sport. Olives, sedges, midges, and terrestrials, such as daddy longlegs, grasshoppers, and white moths, are always evident, but it may take the blue-winged olive and its spent fly (the sherry spinner) to do the trick at dusk. Artificial patterns of the pale watery are also worth trying where there is an August hatch, and some rivers will offer an opportunity for those who can tie a nice brown or red ant pattern.

Weather conditions in September are more favorable, and wet-fly sedge patterns nearly always score.

All legal methods are allowed on most waters, though some places, particularly those that are also sea trout rivers, may be confined to fly.

LOUGH TROUTING All legal methods are allowed on the Republic's loughs, but at certain times some may be limited to fly only. Check with the relevant fishery board. Wet-fly fishing is the norm, but it is different from that practiced in Europe, the US, and many parts of Britain. Anglers fishing on British waters, for instance, must fish deep because of poor water quality, among other reasons, and use all kinds of streamers, dog-hobblers, and weighted nymphs on sinking lines to tease the deep-lying trout. On Irish loughs, by contrast, floating line and three wet flies, size 10 to 12, are generally used. The fly nearest the rod tip is bobbed along to attract attention and is fished partly dry and partly in the surface film. This is traditional lough wet-fly fishing — and it's a league apart from streamer and lure fishing which, if everyone were honest, would not be termed fly fishing at all.

Dry-fly anglers also have success on the loughs, though fishing the dry artificial is the exception rather than the rule. A most interesting form of angling known as dapping — one born among the Irish, extremely popular here, and not used to any great extent elsewhere — often outscores other techniques. Brown trout, sea trout, and salmon all take the dapped insect, and both brown and sea trout that come to the dapped mayfly tend to be larger than those that take wet flies.

Although the lough fishing season opens in February, visitors would be wise to stay home until April. Given mild weather, April can be a great fishing month, especially on Lough Corrib, where duck fly hatches generate great sport. There are generous hatches of other buzzers also, and lake olives become more numerous during April. May and June can be marvelous if conditions are suitable. Good hatches of brighter olives, sedges, buzzers, and the eagerly awaited mayfly provide the best fishing of the year.

Beginning in June, terrestrials find their way onto the water surface, and dapping them — or imitating them with wet- and dry-fly patterns — can provide good creels. Brown trout loughs tend to be a bit less productive during July and early August, except in evenings and early mornings; but fishing can be lively from the second half of August to the end of the season.

Lough sea trouting offers special sport from July onward. While a number of sea trout fisheries close on October 1, some stay open through October 12. They are worth a visit, if only because of the scenery (though it would be an unlucky visiting angler who took home nothing more than memories of pretty landscapes).

Exclusivity again is the name of the game on the Republic's sea trout loughs. The number of boats is limited and, in some cases, the loughs are actually divided into boat beats. Visitors should check with the *North Western Regional Fisheries Board* to make sure that they get the proper licenses and pay the current fees. The board distributes a 50-minute video that demonstrates the game, sea, and coarse angling opportunities available in the region. The video may be ordered through the *North Western Regional Fisheries Board* (Ardnaree House, Abbey St., Ballina, County Mayo; phone: 96-22788). For Northern Ireland particulars, contact the *Department of Agriculture* (Fisheries Division, Stormont, Belfast BT4 3TA, Northern Ireland; phone: 232-520100).

TROUTING REGULATIONS In the Republic, state fishing licenses are necessary to fish for sea trout (an annual license, which also covers salmon fishing, costs about $43; a 21-day license costs about $10; and a 1-day license about $14). Brown trout permits (or tickets) are sometimes required by local fishery boards; they usually cost $5 to $8 per day. Many of the better brown trout rivers and most sea trout rivers are controlled by clubs, and a bag limit may apply. In both instances, visitors are generally welcome, especially on commercially run fisheries, and permission to fish is granted by day or week for about $5 to $8.50 a day on club brown trout streams, slightly more on club sea trout stretches (though on the better sea trout rivers the cost to tourists runs from about $30 to $45 a day — a tremendous value compared with the costs of such exclusivity elsewhere). Many sea trouting streams in the Republic are divided into beats, so the angler has a stretch of possibly a mile or more to oneself. Alternatively, the number of rods on the river is strictly measured and controlled.

In Northern Ireland, rod licenses are required for brown trout fishing. Many of the waters, including some of the best, are owned and managed by the *Department of Agriculture* (address above), and the permits that are required to fish them (separate from and in addition to rod licenses, which cost about $20) are relatively inexpensive — about $13 for a daily permit to $22 for an annual coarse fishing permit. The only other expense the angler will incur to fish on a lough is for the hire of a boat — a must — which runs about $25, with an additional $10 charge for an outboard engine, or $50 for a package that includes boat, engine, and guide-boat-man, the preferred situation. For sea trout fishing, permits are necessary for some waters but not for others. To find out what's required, contact the *Department of Agriculture* (address above); the *Foyle Fisheries Commission* (8 Victoria Rd., Londonderry, County Derry, Northern Ireland; phone: 504-42100), which controls many waters drained by the Foyle-Mourne-Camowen system, in the northwest of the country; or the *Fisheries Conservancy Board* (1 Mahon Rd., Portadown, County Armagh BT62 3EE, Northern Ireland; phone: 762-334666), which covers the rest of the country.

SALMON

The failure on the part of successive governments in the Republic to introduce a program to ensure a reasonable stock of freshwater fish has taken its toll on wild salmon stocks in the Irish Republic, and spring runs have dwindled to almost nothing. This is sad, since Ireland is responsible for maintaining a considerable percentage of the world's wild Atlantic salmon. Between 1964 and 1975, its contribution to the overall international catch averaged 20% — twice what it is today. Still, angling for summer salmon and grilse can be good at times, even by international standards. The fish put up a fierce fight, and the cost is a fraction of what anglers would pay in Scotland for the same sport.

Due to the moderating influence of the nearby Gulf Stream, among other factors, the Irish salmon angling season opens as early as the first of January. And since rivers are hardly ever covered with ice here, angling is possible as early as *New Year's Day*. In fact, there usually is some national interest in the season's first salmon from the three rivers that open then — the Liffey (which gives Dublin the distinction of being the only capital city where salmon can be caught within the city limits), the Garavogue in Sligo, and the Bundrowes, just 20 miles north of Garavogue, near Bundoran.

Angling opens on a number of other rivers in February and March — most notably the Slaney, Nore, Barrow, the big Munster or Cork Blackwater, Laune, Caragh (Upper and Lower), Waterville system (including the River Inny), Lower Shannon, Corrib, the Bundowragha (part of Connemara's Delphi Fishery), and the Owenmore in County Mayo. These are later joined by two other noteworthy Mayo rivers, the Newport and the Moy, which open in late March or April.

Spinning is most popular with Irish anglers on these spring fisheries, where salmon average around 12 pounds and occasionally come in at 15 and 30 pounds. Prawning and worming are also common. Fly fishing with sunken line, with large flies in sizes 2 and 4, and with tube flies will get results whenever conditions are suitable, but the number of early season fly anglers, like the spring salmon, has shown a dramatic decline.

Beginning in late May, certainly by June, the grilse arrive; mature, undersized fish coming inland to spawn for the first time, they dominate the catches for the rest of the season. There is a good supply of summer salmon from as early as April.

Most of the spring fisheries also offer summer angling, but spate fisheries, their waters entirely dependent on flood to provide sufficient water for fish to travel upstream and take freely, account for a considerable portion of the sport. They are unpredictable, but when conditions are right, even the wildest of angling dreams can be realized, and six or seven salmon to a rod is far from unusual; double those numbers are achieved by locals who know how best to tease or coax a take.

The Connemara and Mayo fisheries, where salmon and sea trout generally share, are the big attractions in summer. The *Ballynahinch Castle* hotel fishery (Ballynahinch; phone: 95-31006), the River Erriff, the River Corrib's *Galway Weir Fishery,* and Ballycroy and Burrishoole from July onward are the prime salmon waters that also turn up thousands of sea trout. Add to these the aforementioned spring fisheries and throw in the famed Costelloe, Inver, Gowla, Kylemore, and a few Upper Ballynahinch sea trout gems, where occasional salmon also show, to assemble a truly marvelous selection.

There is also some spring and summer lough salmon angling to be enjoyed — a considerable amount of it on the systems and fisheries mentioned above.

In Northern Ireland, open seasons are April to October 20 for rivers in the Foyle area (from March 1 on loughs), February 1 to September 30 in *Fisheries Conservancy Board* waters such as Lough Melvin (from March 1 for the Erne system), and March through October for the rest, with exceptions here and there.

REGULATIONS AND METHODS Required at all times when fishing for salmon in the Republic is a state salmon license (which also covers sea trout and can be purchased in tackle shops or through the fisheries' boards). An annual license, covering the entire country, costs $43; a 21-day license is $17; and a 1-day license to fish anywhere is about $14. In addition, a ticket/permit is generally required on privately owned or club-controlled salmon waters; costs average $34 to $120 per rod. This price may include a boat ghillie (guide) on the loughs, but not a river guide. Guide services cost another $25 to $34 for two or more rods.

In Northern Ireland, rod licenses are necessary for salmon, and permits may also be required. Contact the *Department of Agriculture* (address above) and the Northern Ireland Tourist Board for details.

From March through June and in July and September, the best months for salmon angling, bring a single-handed rod that can cast an 8-to-10 line and 11-pound leader. A double-handed 13-to-15-foot rod can be a godsend on some waters in summer and is always required in spring. The leader to the sunken line for the springers should be at least 15 pounds.

Good spring fly patterns, mostly size 4, include the thunder and lightning, spring blue, Jock Scott, fiery brown, hairy Mary, butcher, black doctor fenian, and the various shrimp. The silver doctor, hairy Mary, blue charm, gray dog, black goldfinch, and shrimp patterns in small sizes, 4 to 9, according to water conditions, score most in summer — nearly always on a floating line. Favorite low-water patterns are the black widow, blue charm, March brown, fiery brown, Lady Caroline, and shrimps in sizes 7 to 10. Dry flies are little used for salmon, but tube flies are popular.

Wading is always necessary in spring, seldom in summer. However, quite a number of fisheries have casting platforms or other improvements that make it nearly possible to fish in shoes. However, short rubber boots, hip waders, or Wellingtons are the norm. And since the better-presented fly often means wading, chest waders are helpful.

COARSE FISHING

All the fish in freshwater rivers and lakes that are not trout or salmon are lumped into the class of coarse fish. These include bream, carp, chub, dace, perch, roach, rudd, eel, and tench. Some pike anglers, especially Europeans, would include this great predator among the list of game fish. In Ireland, however, the pike must put up with being coarse, though it fights with unbridled ferocity.

All of these breed with wild abandon, feed furiously, and grow fatter practically by the minute. Although recently more and more anglers have discovered the joys of Ireland's slow, deep rivers, its half-dozen great lakes, and its thousands of lesser lakes, many waters are still greatly underfished. The fact that these waters also are freer from pollution than those found almost anywhere else in Europe makes for some truly exceptional angling. Not many Irish fish are as heavy as the 42-pound pike caught in the River Barrow or the 38-pounder caught in Lough Corrib a few years back, but most Irish believe that plenty of far bigger fish, particularly pike, lurk in the rivers' depths. Some people say that these giants haven't been caught simply because most fishermen aren't equipped to land them.

In the Irish Republic, the River Erne, which runs into Northern Ireland, offers great coarse fishing, with the major centers to be found at lovely Lough Gowna, the source of the Erne, and the area near Belturbet, County Cavan, between the two lakes. At nearby Foley's Bridge and Drumlane Lake, the action is so lively that some locals swear that everyone catches a fish. The River Barrow, flanked by the kind of supremely pastoral countryside that visitors expect when they go to Ireland, has its best fishing at Graiguenamanagh, County Kilkenny, an attractive village in the shadow of Mount Leinster, once a great monastic center. Best of all is the lordly River Shannon, with its three great lakes — lovely 25-mile Lough Derg, 17-mile Lough Ree, and 7-mile Lough Allen. Some of the best centers are at Mohill, County Leitrim, well-organized Carrick-on-Shannon, and Lanesborough, County Longford, in a famous "hot water" stretch, where catches of bream, rudd, and hybrids running into the hundreds of pounds have been made.

Northern Ireland, though still best known for its game fishing, offers some of Europe's finest coarse fishing as well. On the Upper Bann, the section above Lough Neagh is a standout, and individual anglers regularly catch more than 100 pounds of bream and roach in 5-hour matches. The Lower Bann, north of Lough Neagh, also has fine coarse angling, especially for perch. Also superb is Lough Erne, with its two gigantic loughs: The area around Enniskillen, where the world 5-hour match record is regularly broken, still holds the record of 258 pounds, 9½ ounces — which exceeded the previous record by more than 50 pounds. The Fairy Water, a tributary of the Foyle via the Strule, was the first of Northern Ireland's coarse fisheries to come into the public eye, and it still yields roach in immense quantities. Lough Creeve has proved to have a perch growth rate exceeding that of all other Irish waters. And the Quoile, which flows south from its source not far from Ballynahinch, has made a big splash with its rudd production. Pike fishing, another of the province's attractions, is found at its best in both Loughs Erne and in the two Loughs Macnean and Lough Beg, at the mouth of Lough Neagh.

INFORMATION AND REGULATIONS No license payment is required. However, voluntary payments to local fishing boards are encouraged and it is expected that local Fishery Cooperative Societies will eventually phase in voluntary share certificates to help maintain fisheries. There is no closed season. For detailed information about these streams and others, consult the Irish Tourist Board's *Coarse Angling* pamphlet or contact the *Central Fisheries Board* (address above). Bait is available for purchase. Note: Those who wish to bring their own bait should not pack it in soil or vegetable materials, neither of which can be brought into the country.

In Northern Ireland, anglers usually need a rod license and may also need a permit, depending on the waters to be fished. There is no closed season. *An Informative Guide to Coarse Fishing*, published by the Northern Ireland Tourist Board, gives details.

SEA ANGLING

Ireland has hundreds of miles of ragged coastline where anglers reel in anything from half-pound flounders off a sandy bottom to giant mako sharks in deep waters, or wrasse, pollock, and mackerel from the rocks. No license is necessary, and few advance arrangements are required; tackle can usually be hired; and the chefs in most hotels will cook a guest's prize on request. For trips out over the wrecks and sunken reefs where some of the bigger fish lurk, boats and professional skippers are readily available, and a day's outing with a local who can rendezvous with fish on request can be a most rewarding (and reasonably priced) experience. All that's required is a stomach strong enough for a day on the short, choppy seas. Shore fishing for sea bass with a powerful rod and reel requires a little more equipment — namely good oilskins — since these delicious creatures favor "storm beaches," and the best fishing is done when there's a strong onshore wind that will drench an angler to the skin with salt spray. In the Republic, though sea angling has been organized only for the last quarter century, about 150 clubs sponsor dozens of fishing competitions throughout the year. The big quarry include shark and skate — blue shark, which can weigh in at over 200 pounds and come around the south and west coasts from mid-June to mid-October; porbeagle shark, the Irish record for which was a 365-pound specimen caught off the Mayo coast; the tough-fighting, hard-to-catch mako shark, which visits the south coast in summer; the common skate, a worthy adversary growing to over 200 pounds, which is at its most plentiful around the south and west coasts in deep water from April to early October; and the somewhat smaller white skate, which favors the western seaboard. Flatfish, halibut, conger, monkfish, mackerel, ling, cod, red sea bream, pollock, ray, turbot, plaice, brill, and flounder can be found around the coast. (Note that there is a conservation order on the common skate, and to preserve the species anglers are asked to return to the water any skate caught alive.) Porbeagle shark, in particular, provide the kind of stomach-tightening fight most anglers expect to experience only vicariously.

Centers like Youghal, Kinsale, Crosshaven, Baltimore, and Courtmacsherry rank among the best places to fish in the country. In Kinsale, particularly, the angling is well organized, the town is pretty, and there are numerous good lodging places and fine restaurants. Blue shark, skate, and conger are the quarry.

Another good fishing location is Fenit, in County Kerry, where monkfish, ray, conger, and skate can be caught right from the ocean pier; boats take anglers out into the even more productive waters of Tralee Bay for larger specimens. Green Island at the south of Liscannor Bay in Clare is renowned for its rock fishing; porbeagle shark of around 150 pounds have been landed here. Ballyvaughan and Liscannor, farther up the coast, have boats and tackle for hire.

County Mayo has many major sea angling centers. Clew Bay, with its 365 islands in the shadow of Ireland's holy Croagh Patrick, has fast tides that offer splendid shore fishing, while Westport boasts a number of excellent charter boats that go out for the renowned shark and skate fishing, as well as good angling-oriented hostelries, features that attract many Europeans. Lovely Achill Island, once so favored by English anglers that the coastline resounded with their clipped accents, still has superb deep-sea fishing, and past creels have included a number of record-size shark; the main centers are Purteen Harbour and Darby's Point. Belmullet, the peninsula on the northwest coast, is also famous for its deep-sea action and shore fishing, as are Newport and Killala.

In Northern Ireland, the entire coast offers an abundance of rocky points, piers, estuaries, and storm beaches where the action doesn't get nearly the attention it deserves as some of Ireland's best. An Irish record hake was caught in Belfast Lough, and Lough Carlingford in County

Antrim has produced a national record tope (66 pounds, 8 ounces). Off Ballintoy, also in County Antrim, is the very unusual fishing for herring on rods with feathered lures, done at dusk and dawn in May and June. Wreck fishing from Portaferry, at the mouth of Strangford Lough, always guarantees good cod, ling, and conger.

INFORMATION AND REGULATIONS No licenses or permits are required for sea angling in the waters of the Republic or Northern Ireland. *Sea Angling,* published by the Irish Tourist Board, provides details about what can be caught where, when, and with what in the Republic. The *Irish Federation of Sea Anglers* (c/o Mr. Hugh O'Rourke, 67 Windsor Dr., Monkstown, County Dublin, Irish Republic; phone: 1-280-6873) administers local competitions and can provide details. The *Central Fisheries Board* (address above) can also be helpful.

For Northern Ireland, consult the Tourist Board's *Sea Fishing from Boats,* a good guide to the possibilities.

FISHING SCHOOLS

Those interested in acquiring or polishing their game fishing techniques have several alternatives in Ireland. A number of salmon and trout ghillies (guides) on the Dempster Fishery and the Blackwater Lodge Fishery (both on the Munster Blackwater) can instruct in casting and advise on techniques if requested. In spring, quite a few angling clubs offer courses to members covering the same topics, along with fly tying and entomology. In addition, a number of establishments offer formal angling schools.

BALLYNAHINCH CASTLE, Ballinafad, County Galway, Irish Republic Casting, fly presentation, and fishing the two-handed rod for salmon are a few of the issues addressed in this school held in May. The course includes lodging, meals, and instruction. Fly-tying weekends are held in March. At any time, ghillies (guides) are available for $43 a day. Practice and instruction are on the River Owenmore, the outlet for the Ballynahinch system. Lodging is available on the premises. Details: *Ballynahinch Castle Hotel,* Ballinafad, County Galway, Irish Republic (phone: 95-31006; fax: 95-31085).

MOUNT JULIET FISHING ACADEMY, Thomastown, County Kilkenny, Irish Republic This relatively new salmon angling center offers professional instruction to beginning and experienced fishermen alike. Three lakes are maintained and fully stocked for students. In addition, two rivers — the Nore and its tributary, the King's — run through the estate, providing over 4 miles of riverside fishing, including 3 pools and 16 beats that have produced record catches in recent years. Packages include overnight accommodations and meals at the manor house on the estate. Details: *Mount Juliet Fishing Academy,* Thomastown, County Kilkenny, Irish Republic (phone: 56-24522).

PONTOON BRIDGE, Pontoon, near Foxford, County Mayo, Irish Republic Held weekly from May to October, courses here cover all areas of casting with fly and spinner for salmon and trout, as well as instruction in float fishing if requested. Students also attend slide-illustrated lectures, receive an introduction to fly tying and entomology, and are instructed in boat and bank angling by Allan Pierson, member of the Freshwater Biological Association. Details: *Pontoon Bridge Hotel,* Pontoon, near Foxford, County Mayo, Irish Republic (phone: 94-56120 or 94-56156; fax: 94-56120).

FISHING HOTELS

A fishing vacation can be even more pleasant if it includes accommodation in an establishment whose management knows how to meet an angler's needs. One of the beauties of the Irish angling scene is that such hostelries are numerous. They often control rights to stretches of nearby streams; when they don't, they can help make the necessary arrangements. They can also provide fishing maps, information on fishing conditions, and facilities for storing gear or for drying wet clothes overnight. They may even time meals to suit anglers' habits. Information about town and country houses and guest farms that offer such facilities is available from two sources:

> *Irish Farm Holidays Association* (Ashton Grove, Knockraha, County Cork, Irish Republic; phone: 21-821537).
> *Town and Country Homes Association* (Donegal Rd., Ballyshannon, County Donegal, Irish Republic; phone: 72-51377 or 72-51653).

The following hotels and guesthouses with facilities for anglers make a good beginning. Below, we list them alphabetically by county and town, beginning with the Irish Republic.

DROMOLAND CASTLE, Newmarket-on-Fergus, County Clare, Irish Republic In a 400-acre park, only 8 miles from Shannon Airport, this luxuriously appointed hotel (a member of the Relais & Châteaux group) offers coarse fishing on a lake and trout and late salmon fishing in a small river. It also makes a good base for fishing Lough Derg when the mayfly is up. Details: *Dromoland Castle,* Newmarket-on-Fergus, County Clare, Irish Republic (phone: 61-368144).

BALLYNAHINCH CASTLE, Ballinafad, County Galway, Irish Republic This is a superb base for the serious salmon, grilse, and sea trout angler. Surrounded by woods crisscrossed by footpaths, the expertly managed fishery is on the Owenmore River. Its salmon pools are well defined, and the sea trout record is one of Ireland's best. Shooting is also offered. Details: *Ballynahinch Castle Hotel,* Ballinafad, Connemara, County Galway, Irish Republic (phone: 95-31006).

ZETLAND, Cashel Bay, County Galway, Irish Republic This panoramic hotel overlooking Cashel Bay ranks among the country's most comfortable fishing hotels. Anglers go for its sea trout fishery, one of the best in the country, on the Gowla fishery's several lakes and rivers. Details: *Zetland Hotel,* Cashel Bay, County Galway, Irish Republic (phone: 95-31111 fax: 65-31117).

RENVYLE HOUSE, Renvyle, Connemara, County Galway, Irish Republic This hotel-by-the-sea, an excellent choice for the all-around sportsman on holiday with a family, offers trouting on the grounds' Rushduff Lake, as well as shore-fishing, deep-water ocean angling, and, nearby, plenty of action on some fine Connemara sea trout fisheries. Other amenities — on the premises or nearby include golf, tennis, bowling, horseback riding, snooker, and a sauna. Also see *Rural Retreats.* Details: *Renvyle House Hotel,* Renvyle, Connemara, County Galway, Irish Republic (phone: 95-43444 or 95-43511; fax: 95-43515).

ANGLERS REST, Headford, County Galway, Irish Republic This owner-operated hotel, a few miles from Lough Corrib, boasts a simple, relaxed atmosphere and a long tradition in the care and feeding of anglers. Details: *Anglers Rest Hotel,* Headford, County Galway, Irish Republic (phone: 93-35528; fax: 93-35749).

DOONMORE, Inishbofin Island, County Galway, Irish Republic A unique site on a beautiful offshore island is only one of the features that has made the *Doonmore* a favored refuge of deep-sea divers, nature lovers, bird watchers, and artists — not to mention sea anglers, who avail themselves of the hotel's oceangoing boat. Other features include good, unpretentious fare and simple accommodations. Details: *Doonmore Hotel,* Inishbofin Island, County Galway, Irish Republic (phone: 95-45804; fax: 91-45814).

KYLEMORE PASS, Kylemore, County Galway, Irish Republic In addition to a magnificent view from its perch atop one of the Twelve Bens, overlooking Kylemore Lake, guests enjoy the traditional music regularly performed in the hotel bar, the friendly atmosphere, and, above all, the fishing (for sea, river, and lake trout as well as salmon — and for the free brown trout in the hotel's lake). Also see *Rural Retreats.* Details: *Kylemore Pass Inn,* Kylemore, County Galway, Irish Republic (phone: 95-41141).

CORRIB, Oughterard, County Galway, Irish Republic This 26-room hotel is popular with fisherfolk because of its proximity to Lough Corrib and the Connemara fisheries — good sources for salmon, sea trout, brook trout, brown trout, and pike. May and June (the dapping period) are regarded by most local anglers as the best brown trout fishing months. Details: *Corrib Hotel,* Oughterard, County Galway, Irish Republic (phone: 91-82329 or 91-82204; fax: 91-82522).

CURRAREVAGH HOUSE, Oughterard, County Galway, Irish Republic This guesthouse, a 19th-century country manor surrounded by woodlands, has long catered to anglers who come to fish for brown trout and grilse when they run in June and July. They have their own boats and ghillies and will freeze your catch to take home or cook it for you that evening. Also see *Rural Retreats*. Details: *Currarevagh House Hotel*, Oughterard, County Galway, Irish Republic (phone: 91-82313 or 91-82312; 91-82731).

LAL FAHERTY'S LAKELAND, Oughterard, County Galway, Irish Republic This country home on the shores of Lough Corrib is dedicated to fishing enthusiasts. Lal is an experienced angler and dispenses advice along with boats, tackle, and flies. His wife, Mary, cooks up tasty dinners. Accommodations are simple and comfortable; the Fahertys are known for looking after their guests well. Details: *Lal Faherty's Lakeland*, Oughterard, County Galway, Irish Republic (phone: 91-82121 or 91-82146).

ROSS LAKE HOUSE, Oughterard, County Galway, Irish Republic The old Killaguille estate house, this Georgian hotel has taken its name from nearby Ross Lake, which offers coarse fishing. Golf and pony trekking also are available locally. Details: *Ross Lake House Hotel*, Rosscahill, Oughterard, County Galway, Irish Republic (phone: 91-80109; fax: 91-43515).

SWEENEY'S OUGHTERARD HOUSE, Oughterard, County Galway, Irish Republic Owned by the same family since 1913 and occupying a structure dating (in part) from the 18th century, this establishment boasts extensive gardens and a knot of ancient beeches facing the wooded banks of the Owenriff River. Many guests come to angle for trout, salmon, pike, and perch in Connemara's huge Lough Corrib. Details: *Sweeney's Oughterard House Hotel*, Oughterard, County Galway, Irish Republic (phone: 91-82207).

KNOCKFERRY LODGE, Rosscahill, County Galway, Irish Republic Owner Des Moran welcomes guests to this small, cozy establishment overlooking Lough Corrib and encourages them to stay at least a few days. Fishing enthusiasts need no persuading. Turf fires and home cooking await returning fisherfolk and sightseers. There are 10 simple rooms (8 with private baths). Seven miles from Galway on N59, turn right at the signpost, then 6 miles down the lake shore road. Details: *Knockferry Lodge*, Rosscahill, County Galway, Irish Republic (phone: 91-80122; fax: 91-80328).

DUNLOE CASTLE, Gap of Dunloe, County Kerry, Irish Republic On the grounds of a castle that, along with its historic park and gardens, dates from the 15th century, this luxurious hotel offers elegant decor with splendid period furnishings and amenities such as a heated swimming pool, sauna, tennis courts, and restaurants. To anglers, the prime interest is the River Laune, which flows across the grounds. Salmon season is from mid-January to mid-October, the best periods being from mid-February to the end of July and from mid-August to the close of the season. Trout may be taken from mid-February to mid-October, with the best months from March to July and September and October. The hotel is open from April through September. Details: *Dunloe Castle Hotel*, Gap of Dunloe, County Kerry, Irish Republic (phone: 64-44111).

BUTLER ARMS, Waterville, County Kerry, Irish Republic Considered one of the country's best fishing hotels almost since it opened more than a century ago, this homey 29-room hotel was a favorite of Charlie Chaplin. The free salmon and sea trout fishing on Lough Currane — the main attraction — is among Western Europe's best, with optimal periods from the beginning of the season until July. There is sea trout from early May until mid-October, as well as salmon fishing on the Inny, a spate river, when conditions are right. Details: *Butler Arms,* Waterville, County Kerry, Irish Republic (phone: 667-4144).

MOUNT JULIET, Thomastown, County Kilkenny, Irish Republic This 1,500-acre estate boasts two significant rivers, the Nore and its tributary, the King's, with over 2 miles of riverside fishing with 3 pools and 16 beats. The average annual catch of salmon in recent years stands at 257 pounds; the heaviest individual salmon weighed 22 pounds; the average, 9 pounds. Countless trout have been caught, too. Facilities include a fishing academy offering professional instruction at all levels. Packages include equipment and instruction, if needed, and overnight accommodations and meals. Salmon season runs from February to September; trout, March to September. Details: *Mount Juliet,* Thomastown, County Kilkenny, Irish Republic (phone: 56-24455; fax: 56-24522).

DOWNHILL, Ballina, County Mayo, Irish Republic Anglers can make arrangements to go for salmon in the pools on the River Moy and for saltwater fish in the ocean, while other family members enjoy a heated pool, squash, a sauna, a Jacuzzi, and golf on three 18-hole courses. Details: *Downhill Hotel,* Ballina, County Mayo, Irish Republic (phone: 96-21033; fax: 96-21338).

IMPERIAL, Ballina, County Mayo, Irish Republic Guests at this comfortable family-owned hotel are only a walk away from some of the River Moy's best salmon fishing pools. In addition to salmon and trout fishing on loughs Conn and Cullin, a half-hour distant, there is also sea angling in the estuary in the hotel's boat. Accustomed to making anglers feel welcome, the management is friendly and professional. Details: *Imperial Hotel,* Pearse St., Ballina, County Mayo, Irish Republic (phone: 96-22200; fax: 96-21005).

MOUNT FALCON CASTLE, Ballina, County Mayo, Irish Republic An impressive parkland setting near the River Moy, Ireland's most prolific salmon river, is only one of the features here. This establishment also owns and leases four beats on 7½ miles of the river, famous for its massive run of grilse (averaging 5 pounds), from May until mid-August, peaking from early June to mid-July. Spring salmon averaging 10 pounds can be taken in April and May. However, there are runs throughout the season since the loughs Conn and Cullin, of whose system the Moy is a part, provide a good supply of water most of the time. Good creels of wild brown trout are also taken, particularly during the mayfly hatch around the first week of June. There's a hefty fee for fishing. Details: *Mount Falcon Castle Hotel,* Ballina, County Mayo, Irish Republic (phone: 96-21172; fax: 96-21172).

ASHFORD CASTLE, Cong, County Mayo, Irish Republic This ultra-luxurious hotel (a member of the Relais & Châteaux group) has a field sports manager to help guests make the most of its extensive resources for angling — the Cong River, right on the grounds, which has a good run of grilse in June and July, and Lough Corrib, which laps at the edge of its splendid lawns. Also see *Rural Retreats.* Details: *Ashford Castle Hotel,* Cong, County Mayo, Irish Republic (phone: 92-46003; fax: 92-46260).

RYAN'S, Cong, County Mayo, Irish Republic Anglers have long patronized this family-run hotel in scenic Cong village for the simple but good food and for its accommodations, which are comfortable, if considerably less luxurious than those at the *Ashford Castle.* Details: *Ryan's Hotel,* Cong, County Mayo, Irish Republic (phone: 92-46004 or 92-46243).

PONTOON BRIDGE, Foxford, County Mayo, Irish Republic Salmon and trout fishing in Lough Conn (famous for its mayfly, grasshopper, and daddy longlegs dapping periods) and in Lough Cullen, home cooking, peace and quiet, and fantastic scenery are the attractions of this comfortable establishment. Details: *Pontoon Bridge Hotel,* Foxford, County Mayo, Irish Republic (phone: 94-56120 or 94-56156; fax: 94-56120).

NEWPORT HOUSE, Newport, County Mayo, Irish Republic This handsome country house, the home of the historic O'Donnells, offers good fishing on private waters on the Newport River and Lough Beltra, and sea fishing on the tidal river from the quay facing the estate. A member of the Relais & Châteaux group. Also see *Rural Retreats.* Details: *Newport House Hotel,* Newport, County Mayo, Irish Republic (phone: 98-41222; fax: 98-41613).

HEALY'S, Pontoon, County Mayo, Irish Republic Repeat business is the rule at the Healy family hostelry, a favorite of anglers since it was founded in 1892. The pub conversation alone can make a visit special. Details: *Healy's Hotel,* Pontoon, County Mayo, Irish Republic (phone: 94-56443; fax: 94-56572).

DUNDRUM HOUSE, Cashel, County Tipperary, Irish Republic A tributary of the River Suir flows through the grounds of this 18th-century Georgian mansion and offers private brown trout fishing that is exceptionally appealing to dry-fly purists. It also offers horseback riding and a commendable restaurant. Details: *Dundrum House Hotel,* Dundrum, near Cashel, County Tipperary, Irish Republic (phone: 62-71116; fax: 62-71366).

KNOCKLOFTY HOUSE, near Clonmel, County Tipperary, Irish Republic The former family home of the Earls of Donoughmore, this luxury hotel and time-share complex comprises 105 acres of gardens and pastureland crossed by the River Suir. Features include 1½ miles of bank fishing on the river as well as access to club trout waters nearby. Sea trouting is available on the Blackwater, 24 miles distant, from July onward. Details: *Knocklofty House Hotel,* near Clonmel, County Tipperary, Irish Republic (phone: 52-38222).

BLACKWATER LODGE, Upper Ballyduff, County Waterford, Irish Republic Owned by an avid Welsh angler, the lodge caters to the game angler. It controls 20 of the best beats on the 30-odd miles of high-record salmon waters between Lismore and Mallow on the celebrated River Blackwater; guests usually take a total of 350 to 400 salmon per season (February to September). In 1992, a record year, a total of 1,511 salmon were brought in. There is also reasonable fishing for grilse, backend, and sea trout (as well as for wild brown trout, which can range up to 3 pounds, from March 1 to September 30). Details: *Blackwater Lodge Hotel,* Upper Ballyduff, County Waterford, Irish Republic (phone: 58-60235).

BEACH HOUSE, Portballintrae, County Antrim, Northern Ireland With fishing on the River Bush, this establishment is now run by the third generation of Maclaines, whose forebears bought it more than 6 decades ago. Details: *Beach House Hotel,* Portballintrae, County Antrim BT57 8RT, Northern Ireland (phone: 265-731214).

MANVILLE HOUSE, Aughnablaney, near Kesh, County Fermanagh, Northern Ireland Close by are loughs Melvin and Erne and the River Bundrawes, where the best fishing is from March through May and in August and September. Private instruction is available, and accommodations are in a house about 100 yards from shore, with lovely views from every window. There are 5 rooms — none with private bath. Details: *Manville House,* Aughnablaney, Letter, County Fermanagh, Northern Ireland (phone: 365-631668).

CORRALEA FOREST LODGE, Belcoo, County Fermanagh, Northern Ireland Anglers who come for the action in Upper Lough McNean and nearby Lough Erne — many of them German and French — stay in the luxurious guesthouse with 4 rooms or in one of the 6 self-catering chalets. The fishing is mainly for pike, though there are also perch, bream, roach, and trout. Open April through October. Details: *Corralea Forest Lodge,* Belcoo, County Fermanagh BT93 50Z, Northern Ireland (phone: 365-86325).

ELY ISLAND CHALETS, Enniskillen, County Fermanagh, Northern Ireland When the level of the Lough Erne fell some 80 years ago, a peninsula formed that now connects Ely Island to the mainland. Set on a lovely 277-acre landscaped parkland estate, the 10 log cabins opened here in 1989 are carpeted and finished in pine. Each sleeps 5 to 6, and has a microwave oven, color TV set, private verandah, and jetty. Boats are available for hire. Open year-round. On Lower Lough Erne; 5 miles from Enniskillen. Details: *Ely Island Chalets,* Enniskillen, County Fermanagh BT74, Northern Ireland (phone: 365-89328).

MAHON'S, Irvinestown, County Fermanagh, Northern Ireland Fishing on Lough Erne, known for some of the best coarse fishing in Europe, has been a prime drawing card of this antiques-filled, family-owned establishment since it was founded in 1883. There are 18 rooms, all with private baths. Open year-round. Details: *Mahon's Hotel,* Irvinestown, County Fermanagh BT74 9XX, Northern Ireland (phone: 365-621656).

Freewheeling by Two-Wheeler

The landscapes of Ireland unfold so quickly and with such endless diversity at every bend and turn of the road that traveling through the country quickly by car seems a real shame. The villages full of charming cottages, the rolling hills, the quaint seacoast towns, and the brooding mountains all beg to be explored at bike speed — fast enough to cover a fair amount of terrain, but slow enough to stop to inspect a wildflower or admire a view.

Ireland offers not only great scenic variety in a relatively compact area but also an abundance of surfaced, little-trafficked secondary roads. That it also has many facilities for rental and repair and numerous small restaurants, bed and breakfast establishments, guesthouses, and hotels that are no less than delighted to welcome bedraggled pedalers, makes the country a well-nigh perfect candidate for cycling vacations — for beginning tourers and experts alike. Even those who are not particularly experienced and postpone their planning until the last minute can still enjoy a two-wheeling vacation here: Just travel light, start out slowly, don't be too ambitious, and don't give up just because of tender muscles or a little saddle-soreness.

BEST CYCLING AREAS

The touring possibilities in Ireland are extensive. Nearly all the roads in both the Republic and Northern Ireland, except for trunk routes between the larger cities, offer cyclists tarred surfaces and light traffic; those in the west and northwest may be somewhat rougher, since local authorities have been cutting back on upkeep in recent years. There are also back roads and unsurfaced mountain tracks — the latter only for the brave and bold.

DUBLIN ENVIRONS, Irish Republic The wonderful thing about Ireland is that only about 20 miles outside Dublin — or 10 miles from Cork, Derry, Galway, Limerick, or Waterford — the roads are virtually traffic-free. In County Meath, the doorstep of Dublin Airport is the departure point for nearly ideal runs through villages like Ballyboghil and Naul, on to Duleek, and to the remarkable Boyne Valley and the Hill of Tara (whose sites are described in *Ancient Monuments and Ruins*). Don't miss the monastic remains at Slane and Navan. South of Dublin, those who like hill climbing can take the road from suburban Rathfarnham to Sally Gap and Devil's Glen and, within a half hour, find themselves out of sight of human habitation in lovely countryside. The small but lovely Wicklow Mountains, which extend from around Dublin in the north to as far south as Arklow and inland for about 25 miles from the sandy shores of the Irish Sea, make for excellent cycling: The wide, long, dune-backed strand at Brittas Bay is one of the best places for a swim here, and Glendalough (described in *Ancient Monuments and Ruins*) is a sightseeing must. Details: *Dublin Tourism Office,* 13-14 Upper O'Connell St., Dublin 1, Irish Republic (phone: 1-874-7733).

MIDWEST, Irish Republic The 700-foot Cliffs of Moher, which plunge into the foaming sea near the fishing village of Liscannor, the spa town of Lisdoonvarna, the village of Doolin (a home of traditional Irish music), and the Burren — bare and almost lunar in appearance — are some of the notable sites in County Clare, while in more-frequented County Galway, the place to explore is rocky, boggy, lake-studded, and partially Gaelic-speaking Connemara, with the Twelve Bens presiding over flatlands speckled with ruined rock-walled cottages. There are good beaches, seldom busy, and loughs Corrib and Mask (see *Gone Fishing*) are not too distant. Still farther north, small roads meander through pretty, quiet villages scattered around the tranquil heather and rhododendron country of less-populated Mayo or hug a coastline as wild and lonesome as anyone tired of city life could ever desire. The routes from Newport and Mulrany by Lough Furnace, over the bridge at Achill Sound to Achill Island, and then around Achill Island are pleasant. Details: *Shannon Development — Tourism Division,* Shannon Town Centre, Shannon, County Clare, Irish Republic (phone: 61-361555); and *Ireland-West Tourism,* Aras Fáilte, Victoria Pl., Galway, Irish Republic (phone: 91-63081).

SOUTHWEST, Irish Republic Outside busy Cork City, counties Cork, Kerry, and Limerick are quite rural. There are mountains and steep gradients, but gently rolling hills and flat valleys are part of the cycling picture as well. The most dramatic scenery is along the coast, where lovely deep bays are interspersed with cave-pocked cliffs and promontories. Blarney Castle is here, along with the Fota House near Cork City, the fishing town of Youghal, the pretty ports of Kinsale and Cobh on Cork Harbour, the remote district around the Allihies on the coast, Georgian-era Bantry House, Killarney, *Durty Nelly's Inn* (see *Pub Crawling*), Ross Castle and the ruined remains of Muckross and Innisfallen Abbey, and the spectacular Gap of Dunloe, which slashes through the countryside between MacGillicuddy's Reeks and the Purple Mountains. The Ring of Kerry and the Dingle Peninsula are particular standouts. Details: *Cork/Kerry Region Tourism Organization,* PO Box 44, Tourist House, Grand Parade, Cork City, County Cork, Irish Republic (phone: 21-273251).

NORTHWEST, Irish Republic Head southwest from Sligo and follow an impressive scenic route that passes through Ballina and the Ox Mountains. Loop back east through Bunniconlon and by lovely Lough Tait, and continue northeast to Cloonacool. Pedal through Coolaney Gap (about 15 miles), and then by the Bronze Age tombs at Carrowmore, within sight of Knocknarea. Then return to Sligo, Yeats country, and picturesque Lough Gill. On another day, travel east from here to Manorhamilton, an erstwhile strategic center on a high plateau and a scenic spot surrounded by still other prehistoric sites of note. Then head through the country of Breffny and continue northwest to breezy Bundoran by the sea, with its fine shore views, and up to the ancient town of Donegal, once the seat of the O'Donnell family. Here is another moment of decision: to head into the wild and lovely Blue Stack Mountains or to take the relatively easy run north to Ballybofey and Letterkenny, traveling roads by Lough Swilly and Lough Foyle. Let your legs be the judge. Depending on your state of fitness, the above may be covered in about a week or more. Details: *Northwest Tourism Organization,* Aras Reddan, Temple St., Sligo, County Sligo, Irish Republic (phone: 71-61201; fax: 71-60360).

NORTHERN IRELAND Northern Ireland's 5,500 square miles encompass some of the most spectacular and varied scenery that one can imagine. Blue mountains and sandy beaches, open moorlands and clear lakes, small towns hidden away in the green places of the countryside, and fishing villages strung out along the rocky shores — and none of this splendor is ever more than an hour from the sea. The only heavy traffic on the excellent network of small, well-signposted roads is the occasional tractor, and the only traffic jams are caused by sheep and cattle changing fields. Perhaps the most rewarding outing for the cyclist is to take the 60-mile coast road from Larne up around the northeast corner of County Antrim to the resort of Portrush. The celebrated Antrim coast road, which passes pretty villages, ruined castles, and the nine green Glens of Antrim, is reminiscent of California Highway 1 south of Carmel. Ancient rocks jut out as cliffs in all their brilliant colors — bright red sandstone, white chalk, black basalt, and blue clay. Stop off at Ballycastle and take a boat across to Rathlin Island, where Robert the Bruce once found sanctuary. If you wish to stay overnight, the *Rathlin Guesthouse* (phone: 265-763917) has 4 rooms. It is possible to walk or cycle across to the bird sanctuary on the west side and explore the cliffs and caves. Once back on the mainland, pedal on to the strange and remarkable rock formation called the Giant's Causeway. Details: *Northern Ireland Tourist Board,* St. Anne's Ct., 59 North St., Belfast BT1 1NB, Northern Ireland (phone: 232-246609; fax: 232-240960).

Stalking and Shooting

Humans have been making sport of their search for game, both large and small, since the time of the pharaohs (who were so enamored of the activity that they looked forward to continuing it in the afterlife) — and the sport's devotees in Ireland are no less enthusiastic. There is immense variety of both game and terrain. Hare, cock pheasant, red grouse, woodcock, snipe, golden plover, gray partridge, pigeon, and flighting mallard, widgeon, teal, and other ducks are all shot, along with red, fallow, and sika deer. Irish gun dogs, setters and spaniels, are a pleasure, and sportsmen are supportive, offering a variety of schemes to accommodate visitors.

All shooting is done on private land, with strict controls, and it is forbidden to shoot over or into, or to carry firearms on, any lands without the permission of the owner and occupier. Some estates are managed specifically with shooting in mind, and their managers pay careful attention to the development of game stocks, with patrols to guard against poachers and to control pests. The easiest way to plan a shooting holiday on one of these estates is to contact an associated hotel or booking agency.

In addition, a number of organizations offer rough shooting for various bird species, which might include woodcock, snipe, plover, and some pheasant and flighting duck. Pigeon shooting is also available, as are driven pheasant shoots. Bags are mixed and sizes vary, depending on the sportsman's skill, game levels, weather conditions, and terrain, which can be difficult in some areas.

RULES, REGULATIONS, AND OTHER ESSENTIALS

Season opening and closing dates are published in advance, along with the species that may be shot, and the duration of the season varies from year to year. Geese are often excluded because of concern about their stock levels. (Ireland is an important wintering ground for white-fronted geese.)

FIREARMS AND FIREARM CERTIFICATES Any sportsman who wishes to shoot game in the Republic must, for each shotgun he is carrying, have a current Irish firearms certificate, which are available only to visitors who have access to shooting arrangements or who have advance bookings with a recognized shoot. The number of certificates per shoot is controlled. Good for a year from the date of issue, they are available from the Secretary, *Wildlife Service* (51 St. Stephen's Green, Dublin 2, Irish Republic; phone: 1-661-3111). The fee, about $25, must be enclosed with the application. Rifles may not be more than 22 inches or 5.6 mm. Up to 500 cartridges may accompany the weapon — but check airline limitations in advance. Shells of any bore can be purchased in the bigger Irish towns; cartridges of less than 12 bore may be difficult to find in smaller villages.

In Northern Ireland, current firearm certificates are also necessary. Write in advance for application forms to the Chief Constable, R.U.C., Firearms Branch, Lisnasharragh, Montgomery Rd., Belfast BT6 9JD, Northern Ireland (phone: 232-650222).

HUNTING LICENSES Sportsmen intending to go for anything but rabbit, pigeon, and pest species in the Republic must carry an Irish hunting license in addition to the appropriate firearms certificate. Applications must be made on special forms (available from the *Wildlife Service,* see above, or from booking agencies) and must include a formal written declaration that the visitor has proper access to shooting in the Irish Republic as the paying or invited guest of a person who controls sporting rights on the land where he will be shooting. Licenses, which expire on July 31 after the date of issue, are free.

Note that applications for both firearms certificate and hunting licenses must be made by post *well in advance* of the trip because certificates and licenses are returned only by mail. Applications in person, upon arrival in the Irish Republic, are not accepted, nor can the necessary documentation be picked up after arrival.

In Northern Ireland, hunting licenses are necessary to go for pheasant, woodcock, grouse, wild duck, pigeon, and snipe in *Department of Agriculture* forests at Fardross in County Tyrone, Drunkeeragh in County Down, and Cam and Iniscarn in County Derry. These are available from the *Forest Service* (Dundonald House, Belfast BT4 3SB, Northern Ireland; phone: 232-650111, ext. 268). For details on walking-up shoots at seven other state forests, contact the Chief Wildlife Officer, *Department of Agriculture,* Forestry Division (Seskinore, County Tyrone, Northern Ireland; phone: 662-841243).

INSURANCE Wherever you go and whatever you shoot or stalk, check before leaving home to make sure your insurance is in order. Third-party civil liability is a minimum coverage that you should carry.

BOOKING AGENCIES

These organizations can send the particulars describing several estates, including details on the shooting and fairly complete descriptions of accommodations. Most shoots are organized for groups of four to eight, and it's common for friends to get together to form a shooting party. If a visitor so desires, the agent can try to fit him into someone else's party — though naturally most groups are wary of having an inexperienced sportsman in their midst because of the risk of injury. The organizers will advise visiting hunters as to seasonal and bag limits and any local peculiarities and will help them get through the paperwork.

Shooting in the whole of the Emerald Isle is available through two organizations:

Fieldsports Ireland (25 Suffolk St., Dublin 2, Irish Republic; phone: 1-679-8576).

Irish Fieldsports Agency (174 Castlereagh Rd., Belfast BT5 5GX, Northern Ireland; phone: 232-459248).

For shooting specifically in the Republic, you also can contact the following:

Abbey Tours (50 Garville Ave., Rathgar, Dublin 6, Irish Republic; phone: 1-967314; fax: 1-967022).

Des Wallace Travel (8 Main St., Finglas, Dublin 11, Irish Republic; phone: 1-385700; fax: 1-347908).

Fáilte Travel Ltd. (McKee Ave., Finglas, Dublin 11, Irish Republic; phone: 1-344464; fax: 1-3344011).

Joe O'Reilly Travel (Blarney, County Cork, Irish Republic; phone: 21-385700; fax: 21-385257).

Shooting in Northern Ireland is offered by several booking agencies:

Forest Service (Dundonald House, Belfast BT4 3SB, Northern Ireland; phone: 232-650111, ext. 268).

McBride Sports (13 Haslem's La., Lisburn, County Antrim, Northern Ireland; phone: 846-671322).

Sperrin Sports (112 Seskinore Rd., Omagh, County Tyrone, Northern Ireland; phone: 662-840149, evenings only).

SHOOTS AND ESTATES

There are a number of shoots and estates in the Republic and Northern Ireland that like to deal directly with visitors — they want to know nearly as much about the sportsman who is planning to shoot with them as he wants to know about them. A few of these, including private estates and the bigger well-run gun clubs, are:

Ashbrooke Demesne (Brookeborough, County Fermanagh, Northern Ireland; phone: 365-53242). Deer stalking for Japanese sika deer provided by Viscount Brookeborough.

Ballywillan Gun Club (3 Orwell Park, Rathgar, Dublin 6, Irish Republic; phone: 1-975121). Rough shooting, duck, snipe, pigeon, woodcock, and hare on 30,000 acres in County Longford.

Baronscourt Estate (Baronscourt, Newtownstewart, County Tyrone, Northern Ireland; phone: 662-661638). Deer stalking courtesy of the Duke of Abercorn.

Birr Castle Game Syndicate (Croghan, Birr, County Offaly, Irish Republic; phone: 509-20056). Stalking for fallow deer on the estate of the Earl of Rosse.

Clonalis Shoot (Clonalis, Castlerea, County Roscommon, Irish Republic; phone: 907-20014). Snipe, woodcock, pheasant, hare, and duck rough shooting on the 10,000-acre estate of Mr. Pyers O'Conor–Nash.

Clonanav Shoot (Clonanav Farm, Ballymacarberry, County Waterford, Irish Republic; phone: 52-36141). Shooting for woodcock, snipe, pheasant, and duck on over 2,500 acres.

Forest Service (Dundonald House, Belfast BT4 3SB, Northern Ireland; phone: 232-650111). Pheasant, woodcock, grouse, duck, pigeon, and snipe at three forests, plus walk-up shooting in seven other forests.

Joe O'Keeffe Shoot (Portland House, Portland, Lorrha, County Tipperary, Irish Republic; phone: 509-47141). Shooting for snipe, woodcock, duck, mallard, pigeon, golden plover, curlew, wigeon, teal, hare, and rabbit on over 32,000 acres.

Luggala Estate (Roundwood, County Wicklow, Irish Republic; phone: 1-281-8102). Deer stalking, sika deer stalking, and driven pheasant for parties of ten guns on a number of Irish estates.

Suir Valley Pigeon Shoot (Kilsheelan, Clonmel, County Tipperary, Irish Republic; phone: 52-25234). Pigeon shooting on over 3,000 acres; available from July to September.

Templehouse Gun Club (Templehouse, Ballymote, County Sligo, Irish Republic; phone: 71-83329). Shooting for snipe, woodcock, and at least 5 varieties of duck on over 2,500 acres.

Tubber Game and Gun Club (County Clare, Irish Republic; phone: 91-31101). Shooting for snipe, woodcock, mallard, teal, wigeon, hare, rabbit, pigeon, and plover on over 64,000 acres.

Tubbercurry & District Gun Club (c/o Mr. Jerrard Lundy, Rhue, Tubbercurry, County Sligo, Irish Republic; phone: 71-85140; fax: 71-85768). Snipe, woodcock, duck, pigeon, and rabbit walk-up and rough shooting on over 130,000 acres of exciting terrain.

HOTELS FOR SHOOTING HOLIDAYS

A couple of hotels located in good shooting areas also organize shooting holidays for guests. Among them are the following establishments listed alphabetically by county and town:

DROMOLAND CASTLE, Newmarket-on-Fergus, County Clare, Irish Republic Rough and driven pheasant shooting and fallow deer stalking over 2,000 acres. Details: *Dromoland Castle,* Newmarket-on-Fergus, County Clare, Irish Republic (phone: 61-368144).

ZETLAND HOUSE, Cashel Bay, County Galway, Irish Republic Rough shooting of woodcock and snipe on 12,000 acres. Details: *Zetland House,* Cashel Bay, County Galway, Irish Republic (phone: 95-31011).

MOUNT JULIET, Thomastown, County Kilkenny, Irish Republic Driven shoots for pheasants are offered on this 1,500-acre estate. The pheasant population is at an optimum level of 7,000 birds, and each shoot is confined to a limit of 8 guns, with a bag limit of one brace per gun. Details: *Mount Juliet,* Thomastown, County Kilkenny, Irish Republic (phone: 56-24455).

ASHFORD CASTLE, Cong, County Mayo, Irish Republic Driven pheasant shooting and rough shooting for pheasant, woodcock, snipe, and duck over 2,000 acres, offered by the nation's most luxurious hotel, a sportsman's paradise. Also see *Rural Retreats.* Details: *Ashford Castle,* Cong, County Mayo, Irish Republic (phone: 92-46003; fax: 92-46260).

GAME AND COUNTRY FAIRS

These splendid get-togethers for huntin', shootin', fishin', and farmin' folk and all their friends and relations are a must for the traveler of a sporting turn of mind. Exhibits put on by groups ranging from gun and angling shops to specialists in game development and conservation are only the beginning; there are also displays about racing pigeons, ferrets, taxidermy, game keeping, falconry, and bookkeeping, not to mention competitions for gun dogs, archers, riflemen, wildlife photographers, pastry makers, bonnie babies, Wellington boot throwers, tug-of-war teams, and a good deal more. The grandest of the breed include the following beginning with the Irish Republic.

DUNMANWAY ANNUAL AGRICULTRUAL SHOW, Dunmanway, County Cork, Irish Republic This small 1-day fair takes place each year in July at the *Droumleener Lawn* racecourse. For details, call 23-45418.

LIMERICK SHOW, Limerick City, County Limerick, Irish Republic A 3-day event held in late August at Greenpark. It includes show jumping, horticultural exhibits, crafts, and Ireland's largest cattle show. For details, call 61-311991.

GAME AND COUNTRY FAIR, Randalstown, County Antrim, Northern Ireland Takes place on Shane's Castle estate for 3 days, usually at the end of June or the first week in July. This is the biggest fair of its kind in the North. For details, call 849-479671.

Great Walks and Mountain Rambles

Almost any walker will tell you that it is the footpaths of a country — not its roadways — that show off the landscape to best advantage. A walker is closer to earth than a person driving or even biking, and details that might otherwise be overlooked are more noticeable: incredibly tiny wildflowers blossoming in a crack between limestone boulders, or a fox lurking in the shadows of the woods at dawn. And the scenery moves by at a slow speed, so that hedgerows, fences, and the green velvet pastures can be contemplated at leisure. Churches and barns, old mills and lichen-crusted stone walls, and farms and villages are seldom far out of sight. Many paths were literally walked into existence by generations of country folk traveling to work, market, mass, or the pub. It is possible to walk more or less freely on all of these paths, provided that roads that are obviously off limits are respected.

Though some 100-odd forest parks exist throughout Ireland, the walks are mainly short and relatively easy. For longer tramps, it's necessary to head into the wild high country, mainly along the coast, where tracks are so rare and ill defined that walkers generally cross pathless hills and where map and compass are essential companions.

Spirits need not be dampened even when the weather turns rainy — as it may well do even at the height of summer — providing the visitor has come prepared. Stout walking shoes or boots are essential, as is a good rain parka, with leggings. And in addition to the usual walker's gear, a spare sweater is a necessity, even on a day hike — especially in the Irish hills, where conditions can turn arctic within a matter of hours. Hiking and backpacking equipment is best bought in the US, where the selection is greater and prices lower.

Some leading walking events which welcome visitors include the *Hill Walking Weekend* (in Glencolumbkille, County Donegal; phone: 73-30123 or 73-30116), which lasts 3 days in mid-May; the *Dublin International Two Day Walks* (in Dublin, phone: 1-847-4578) in June; the *Kenmare Walking Festival* (in Kenmare, County Kerry; phone: 64-41034 or 64-41333), held 3 days in early June; and the *Castlebar International Four Days' Walks* (in County Mayo; phone: 94-24102), held in late June or early July.

WHERE TO WALK

Ireland is a rich agricultural nation, and all the low country that is not boggy is checkered with fields separated by hedges and, with the exception of byways and the towpaths of waterways like the Grand Canal, is not particularly good for walking. This situation is not likely to change until the state's scheme to create waymarked lowland trails to historic castles, forts, and churches around the countryside is more fully developed. For now, the walker and rambler in Ireland will generally choose to go to the hill areas near the coasts, where the scenery ranges from the limestone karst of County Clare's Burren to the bare, rocky quartzite peaks of Connemara, from the dark, vegetation-rich sandstone cliffs of Kerry to the rounded granite domes of Wicklow.

NOTE Keep in mind that Ireland's mountain areas are lonely places, generally *not* equipped with marked trails or signposts. So don't stray too far unless you are an experienced map and compass reader. In addition, expert hikers and novices alike should be sure to tell someone where they are going and when they expect to return.

The following are some of the most interesting areas in alphabetical order by county and town, beginning with the Irish Republic.

THE BURREN, County Clare, Irish Republic The unforgettable karst plateau known as the Burren is mile upon mile of all-but-bare rock, almost desert-like and making no concession to prettiness. But there is magnificence here nonetheless. Distances are short, views across Galway Bay to Connemara and the Aran Islands are magnificent, and in May and June the grikes (cracks) that seam the limestone sprout a stunning and eclectic collection of rare flowering plants unique in Europe. Sheltered from the Atlantic winds, their blossoms transform the landscape. The mighty Cliffs of Moher, a few miles to the south, offer a fine cliff-top walk, and the largest cave system in Ireland lies beneath. Most of these underground marvels are dangerous for the inexperienced or improperly equipped, but the Aillwee Cave, which is open to all, conveys the feeling. Discovered and explored by a local shepherd in the 1940s and opened to the public in 1978, it has won the Europea Nostra prize, among other awards, for the completeness with which it blends into the landscape. Refer to ½-inch Map Sheet 14, the Folding Landscapes Map of the Burren, and *Irish Walk Guide: West.* (See also "Star Treks," below.)

DONEGAL HILLS, County Donegal, Irish Republic Here in Ireland's northwest there are plenty of hills to walk and plenty of variety. Close to Donegal Town are the Blue Stack Mountains, granite domes rising from remote boggy valleys, with several attractive walks, most notably that from Lough Eske on the southeast up to crag-bound Lough Belshade and the 2,218-foot summit of Croagh Gorm. At the western extremity of the county, around Glencolumbkille, named for the famous Celtic patron saint of Derry and Donegal, stand 1,972-foot Slieve League and 1,458-foot Slieve Tooey. Though the altitudes are minor, the hills themselves are spectacular, since their cliffs fall directly from summit to sea. Scary tales are told about One Man's Path on the ridge of Slieve League, with a drop of some 1,800 feet into the roiling surf on one side and a near-vertical escarpment on the other; for the inexperienced, it is certainly not a walk for a less than perfectly clear day, nor the place to be when it's windy. But tyros can avoid it by keeping on the inshore side of the ridge for about 100 yards, and the view out over a vast expanse of briny deep and into some five counties makes every skipped heartbeat worthwhile.

In the north of Donegal, the 2,466-foot quartzite cone of Errigal, rising above Dunlewy Lake, is a dominant feature; it is quite easily climbed up the ridge from the road on the east. An isolated summit, it has fine, expansive views across Altan Lough and Muckish to the north coast and southeast over the stark ruin of Dunlewy Church to the huge, gloomy cirque of the Poisoned Glen, so named because of the toxic plants that grow there. Nearby is Glenveagh, a national park that is notable for the fine herd of red deer it shelters and the superb gardens attached to Glenveagh Castle. Refer to ½-inch Map Sheets 1 and 3 and *Irish Walk Guide: North West.*

WICKLOW MOUNTAINS, Counties Dublin and Wicklow, Irish Republic Stretching southward from Dublin City, these 1,000-odd square miles of granite domes and the deep valleys between them — including Glencree, Glendalough, and Glenmalure — offer some pleasant day hikes. The 1,654-foot summit of Sugar Loaf Mountain, which is easily accessible by bus, stands out as just one example: In the center of an area where the mountains close in on small patches of rolling farmland, it offers fine views out over the sea not far away and, beyond that, on a clear day, all the way to the Welsh mountains. The ascent begins near Rocky Valley, off the main Dublin-Glendalough road; the descent passes through the wooded Glen of the Downs — a steep-banked, 600-foot-deep ravine that the novelist Sir Walter Scott once termed "the most beautiful view" he had ever seen. From Luggala, on the road from Roundwood to Sally Gap, there is a delightful walk down the valley between loughs Tay and Dan, descending through fields on the west of the river, which is crossed via stepping stones, and returning up through the woods on the east. The going is easy, and the views are superb, especially the reflections of the huge Luggala crag in the waters of Lough Tay. Refer to ½-inch Map Sheet 16, the 1:50,000 *Wicklow Way Map, Irish Walk Guide: East,* and *Dublin and the Wicklow Mountains* by members of the *Irish Ramblers Club* (about $3.25).

CONNEMARA, County Galway, Irish Republic One of Ireland's most scenic and unspoiled regions, Connemara offers its share of the country's best walking. The quartzite pyramids known as the Twelve Bens, which are the most widely known of the peaks here and look like nothing more than minor hills, provide the quality of experience afforded by real mountains because of their cliffbound ridges and slopes of bare rock and scree. (In fact, the north face of 2,336-foot Bencorr offers some of the country's longest rock climbs.) There are several excellent walks in the Bens, but the going is tough, so allow plenty of time. For instance, the circuit of Glencoaghan, encompassing six fine summits, is only 10 miles long, but it will take a strong walker at least 6 hours. To the east of the Bens is the long chain of the Maumturks, another quartzite range, whose long traverse is one of the greatest walking challenges of Ireland. The less ambitious walker should not be put off, however; shorter walks like the one through Connemara National Park, will provide vivid insight into the nature of this wonderful wilderness. Refer to ½-inch Map Sheet 10, *Irish Walk Guide: West,* and *The Twelve Bens* by Joss Lynam (about $2.25).

BEARA PENINSULA, Counties Kerry and Cork, Irish Republic The Caha Mountains, which form the backbone of the lovely Beara Peninsula and divide Cork from Kerry, are well off the beaten tourist path, and once a bit removed from the popular 1,887-foot Sugarloaf and 2,251-foot Hungry Hill, the highest points in the range, walkers are unlikely to be crowded by fellow enthusiasts. The whole ridge makes a fine 2- or 3-day outing, with overnights at well-placed youth hostels; the less energetic can penetrate easily into the area's distinctive and beautiful cirques. The village of Lauragh is a good point of departure. Refer to ½-inch Map Sheet 24, 1-inch Killarney District Map, and the *Irish Walk Guide: South West.*

IVERAGH AND DINGLE PENINSULA MOUNTAINS, County Kerry, Irish Republic Ireland's choice offering for walkers and scramblers, this region of relatively unexplored red sandstone country is known first and foremost for the MacGillicuddy Reeks, the high peaks that roof this part of Ireland. The main peak, 3,414-foot Carrantuohill, can provide a good day's workout with fine views as the reward; local guides are available. Strong walkers can tackle the area's finest walk, the ridge line of the reeks, running from the Gap of Dunloe in the east over ten summits to Lough Acoose on the west. But the whole of the Iveragh Peninsula, the largest of Kerry's trio of peninsulas, whose eastern end the reeks occupy, boasts enough equally good walking to keep an intrepid tramper occupied for more than one vacation. The 2,739-foot Purple Mountain is to the east of the Gap of Dunloe and 2,796-foot Mangerton to the south, its summit accessible via the deep lake known as the Devil's Punchbowl, whose waters foam and plummet 60 feet over a series of sandstone crags in one of the country's prettiest waterfalls. Between these two peaks, around Killarney Lakes, is Muckross National Park, where the walks are shorter and easier, but no less beautiful. West of the reeks lies a whole wilderness of mountains — lower (not much exceeding the 2,000-foot mark) but notable for their remote, craggy, lake-filled valleys and bare summits that would be severe but for the warm brown of the stone. (See also "Star Treks," below.)

To the north of Iveragh is the long, narrow, and somewhat grander Dingle Peninsula, with a backbone of interesting summits, such as 2,623-foot Stradbally Mountain and 2,713-foot Caherconree, rising to 3,127-foot Mount Brandon, named for St. Brendan the Navigator, a 5th-century monk who is said to have discovered America when sailing the seas in search of an earthly paradise. The mountain, with its fine conical summit and its long, high wall of crag on the east, dropping almost perpendicularly into a chain of small lakes, has been acclaimed as the finest in Britain and Ireland. The summit, where the remains of the saint's oratory, cell, and well can still be seen, offers superb views to the Blasket Islands in the west. For the less adventurous, there is an easy way up from the west. Refer to ½-inch Map Sheets 20 and 21, 1:50,000 Map Sheet 78, and *Irish Walk Guide: South West.*

MAYO MOUNTAINS, County Mayo, Irish Republic From the north shore of the deep Killary Harbour fjord that separates County Mayo from Galway rises 2,688-foot Mweelrea. The highest mountain in the province of Connacht, it offers a truly spectacular circuit from Delphi in the east, a remote and beautiful spot on the Aasleagh–Louisburgh road, named by a 19th-century landowner for its resemblance to the Greek original. Farther north, not too distant from the southern shore of Clew Bay, Ireland's holy mountain, 2,510-foot Croagh Patrick, offers yet another good climb. Farther north again are the lonely Nephin Beg mountains and, to the west, two fine quartzite summits of Achill Island, 2,204-foot Slievemore and 2,194-foot Croaghaun, the latter standing at the westernmost tip of Achill; there is nothing between its summit and America. Refer to ½-inch Map Sheets 7 and 10 and *Irish Walk Guide: West.*

For information on guided hill walks in the Mayo area, contact *Skerdagh Outdoor Recreation Centre* (Glenhest, Newport, County Mayo; phone: 98-41647). Center owner/operators Joe and Pauline McDermott know the area well and can handle any level of stamina and expertise. Joe, a former history teacher, also offers 2-week guided historical and archaeological trips throughout Mayo, in conjunction with the *Irish Youth Hostels Association.*

SOUTHEAST'S SANDSTONE MOUNTAINS, Counties Tipperary and Waterford, Irish Republic South of Tipperary Town and the rich farmland of the Vale of Aherlow are the Galtee Mountains, a long ridge of peaks that provide pleasant walking, mostly dry-shod, with fine views, especially over the northern edge. To the south is the Mitchelstown Valley, with its well-known caves, and beyond, the Knockmealdown Mountains, another pleasant ridge of rounded summits 20 to 25 miles long. Farther to the east is the Comeragh Plateau, flat and boggy with huge hummocks of peat that would make walking very tiring but for the scenery — the lake-filled coums, steep-sided cirques carved out in the Ice Age, that fringe the plateau, and the dramatic Coumshingaun headwall that rises almost sheer to 2,500 feet. Refer to ½-inch Map Sheets 18 and 22 and *Irish Walk Guide: South East.*

ANTRIM COAST, County Antrim, Northern Ireland This coast offers a whole range of attractions: the basalt columns of the Giant's Causeway; the high, clean, vertical line of cliffs at Fair Head; the chalk ramparts at Garron Point; the peaceful wooded glens of Glendun and Glenariff; and historic Dunluce Castle, perched on the edge of the cliffs. There is much fenced-off private land, but all of the sites mentioned here can be reached by public footpath. Refer to 1:50,000 Map Sheet 5 and *Irish Walk Guide: North East.*

MOURNE MOUNTAINS, County Down, Northern Ireland This granite range in the northeastern section of the island south of Belfast is not very large, but the scenery is especially lovely, with good views, sapphire lakes, and rugged gray rocks. The principal peak of the group, 2,796-foot Slieve Donard, stands out as a particularly good climb, both for its relative ease and its attractiveness, especially when approached from the town of Newcastle. On fine clear days, it's possible to see the Isle of Man, the peaks of the English Lake District, the mountains of Wales, and Scotland's islands. Those with a full day to spare should walk along the ridge to 2,448-foot Slieve Binnian, to see the aptly named Silent Valley and its reservoir, the source of Belfast's water supply, and, beyond it, lonely little Lough Shannagh. Other good hikes include the ascents of 2,394-foot Slieve Bearnagh and of 2,512-foot Slieve Commedagh. The big challenge in the Mournes is to walk the wall that delineates the Belfast Water Supply catchment area, which in fact takes in all the major summits. Refer to the Mourne Country Outdoor Pursuits Map (2½ inches to the mile); J. S. Doran's *Hill Walks in the Mournes,* which describes 21 good hikes (about $1.50 from Mourne

Observer Press, Castlewellan Rd., Newcastle, County Down BT33 0JX, Northern Ireland); and *Irish Walk Guide: North East.* On the spot, the personnel at the various mountaineering club huts can be helpful; for hut locations, inquire locally before heading out, or contact the *Heart of Down Accommodations Association* (Down District Council, Strangford Rd., Downpatrick, County Down, Northern Ireland; phone: 396-614331).

STAR TREKS

The creation of a Round-Ireland Trail, with a number of sections and spur paths, is a plank in the development platform of the Republic's National Sports Council, which has set up a *Long Distance Walking Routes Committee (LDWRC)* to promote development of long-distance footpaths. While there are still many gaps, a dozen or more paths have been opened. Each of these walking trails is described in a brochure, *Walking Ireland,* available free from the Irish Tourist Board in New York (see GETTING READY TO GO). It is possible to take 1-day hikes along any of these (though it may be difficult to get a bus back to the starting point), but the more ambitious can also plan a multi-day walk, with overnight stays in hostels, bed and breakfast establishments, and guesthouses not far from the trail, or camping on local farms *(be sure to ask in advance).* Note that many of the trails run for considerable distances through state forests, where camping and fires are strictly forbidden.

The most interesting treks are listed below in the order they are encountered along the Round-Ireland Trail. Descriptive leaflets on each of those in the Republic as well as more general information can be obtained from the *LDWRC* (c/o National Sports Council, Hawkins House, 11th Floor, Dublin 2, Irish Republic; phone: 1-873-4700), or from the Irish Tourist Board. And before hitting the trail, be sure to get the relevant *Ordnance Survey Map.*

WICKLOW WAY, Marlay Park, County Dublin, to Clonegal, County Carlow, Irish Republic This 80-mile trek contours the east side of the Wicklow Mountains, then wanders among the smaller hills in the south part of County Dublin, passing through many beautiful valleys, most notably Luggala; Powerscourt, known for its waterfall; and Glendalough, whose monastic ruins are described in *Ancient Monuments and Ruins.* The route then proceeds through lush mature forests over the spurs of the mountains, with fine panoramas of hills and the Irish Sea. The Dublin Way, which crosses the Dublin mountains from east to west and joins the Wicklow Way, offers another diversion. Because both of these run close to Dublin, they are the most frequented of the Irish trails, and good accommodations, including several youth hostels, are within easy reach.

SOUTH LEINSTER WAY, Kildavin, County Carlow, to Carrick-On-Suir, County Tipperary, Irish Republic Beginning just 4 miles from the end of the Wicklow Way, this 58-mile footpath climbs via forest tracks over the shoulder of

Mount Leinster, at the 1,500-foot level, to expose vistas over Wexford to the east and the beautiful River Barrow Valley straight ahead. The trail then descends to the river and follows the riverside towpath for a few miles to Graiguenamanagh, a picturesque market town that is the site of a 13th-century Cistercian abbey. At Graiguenamanagh, it begins climbing again, over the shoulder of Brandon Hill, and thence proceeds over by-roads and forest footpaths to the River Nore, at Inistioge, and on to Carrick-on-Suir.

BURREN WAY, Ballinalacken to Ballyvaughan, County Clare, Irish Republic Covering a distance of 14 miles around the rugged, almost lunar, landscape of County Clare, this is the newest of Ireland's signposted walking trails. The route starts near the Atlantic coast, north of Doolin and slightly west of Lisdoonvarna, and stretches by the valley of Oughtdarra and Ballyryan. It then gently climbs to the uplands of Ballynahown, joining the Green Road through the highlands of the Burren, with its sheets of limestone and shale-covered hills. Next comes the contrasts of the Caher Valley, the Feenagh Valley, and the Rathborney River, ending at Ballyvaughan on the southern slopes of Galway Bay. The path takes in many sights that are indigenous to the Burren: vast stretches of limestone, massive beds of granite, rock pavements, karst land, clints (horizontal slabs), grikes (vertical fissures), caverns and caves, ruined castles, and cliff forts, as well as wildlife, birds, and flora representing a mix of Arctic, Alpine, and Mediterranean species.

MUNSTER WAY, Carrick-On-Suir, County Tipperary, to the Vee, near Clogheen, Irish Republic This is the first stage of a trail that eventually will stretch across the province of Munster in an east-to-west direction, to link up near Kenmare with the Kerry Way, County Kerry (see below), and the projected Beara Way, County Cork. The completed section starts along the towpath of the River Suir and follows a 36-mile trail, first climbing into hills, and then descending to the town of Clonmel. From there it goes south over the western fringe of the Comeragh Mountains into the pleasant farmland of the Nire Valley. The final section winds around the north-facing spurs of the Knockmealdown Mountains, with fine views across the valley to the conical summits of the Galtee Mountains to the north, and ends up in the dramatic Vee, where a main road snakes through a narrow gap between the hills, ending near Clogheen.

KERRY WAY, Killarney, County Kerry, around the Ring of Kerry, and back to Killarney, Irish Republic Following the route of the entire Iveragh Peninsula, this is the Republic's longest low-level long-distance path, set out in 2 stages. The first stage (35 miles) follows a trail from Killarney National Park to Glenbeigh, inland through wild and spectacular countryside. The second stage (90 miles) provides a coastal trail, via Cahirciveen, Waterville, Caherdaniel, Sneem, Kenmare, and back to Killarney. The total circuit is in excess of 125 miles, but can be done in one or more of nine different segments, allowing walkers to join The Way easily from main-road car parks. The route presents some of Ireland's most heralded scenery, a subtle blend of rocky peaks, rich vegetation, open boglands, and Atlantic coastline. It generally follows old green roads; these are often a little higher up along a hillside than modern roads, and command better views across Dingle Bay to the north and the River Kenmare to the south. The western sections of the route are less frequented, and provide a haven to those who seek solitude among the hills.

DINGLE WAY, Tralee, County Kerry, around the Dingle Peninsula, and back to Tralee, Irish Republic This 95-mile route is most often referred to as "Sli Chorca Dhuibhne" (Corkaguiney), one of the nine baronies of County Kerry, stretching west from Tralee to the tip of the Dingle Peninsula. From Tralee, the trail overlooks Tralee Bay en route to Blennerville and Camp, and then swings across a bog road over the peninsula to Inch, a sandy spit of land on Dingle Bay, famed as a backdrop for the movie *Ryan's Daughter*. The circuit wends its way through the towns of Annascaul and Dingle, westward around Slea Head to Dunquin, revealing wide vistas of the offshore Blasket Islands. The trail then turns back along the north coast, past Smerwick Harbour, and then below the massive Brandon Mountain. A high pass leads to Cloghane, east of Brandon, and thence The Way follows the coast along a beachfront route back toward Camp and Tralee.

ULSTER WAY (DONEGAL), Pettigo to Falcarragh, County Donegal, Irish Republic Connecting to the Ulster Way (described below) at the border town and famous pilgrimage center of Pettigo, this 62-mile trail traverses countryside that is significantly more remote than that of other trails — definitely not for the inexperienced. It begins by skirting holy Lough Derg, where anglers reel in bountiful creels and thousands of pilgrims fast and pray in a cavern on Station Island every summer, then passes beautiful Lough Eske, and steers a careful course over the eastern side of the Blue Stack Mountains. Passing through the Glendowan Mountains, it descends to Glenveagh, crosses by the Poisoned Glen to Dunlewy, and climbs over the shoulder of Errigal before descending past Altan Lough to Falcarragh on the north coast. Accommodations are not plentiful, so take a tent.

SLIEVE BLOOM WAY, Counties Laois and Offaly, Irish Republic This 32-mile-long route makes a circuit of the Slieve Bloom Mountains, which rise out of the Central Plain between Portlaoise and Tullamore, on the border of County Laois. It can be joined at any one of seven starting points and can be followed in whole or in part through the beautiful wooded valleys and glens of this range, which seems quite grand, despite its rather insignificant height (about 1,700 feet), because of the flat terrain all around. It is also possible to link up with the Kildare Trails, which largely follow the tow-paths of the Grand Canal and its branches.

ULSTER WAY, around Northern Ireland This 500-mile circle of Northern Ireland takes in some of Ireland's finest scenery, including the coast and glens of County Antrim, with the magnificent Atlantic coast cliffs and bays, the Giant's Causeway, the Sperrin Mountains, the Fermanagh Lakeland, the Mourne Mountains, and St. Patrick country, rich in legend and antiquities. From Belfast, the route winds through the quiet wooded valley of the river Lagan. In addition, the trail connects with several in the Republic: the wild and remote 62-mile-long Ulster Way in Donegal (with a junction at Pettigo); the 16-mile-long Cavan Way, short but varied and beautiful (intersecting at Blacklion, County Fermanagh); and the circular Táin Trail, a 19-mile circle through the historic Carlingford Peninsula (with an unmarked link to the Ulster Trail at Newry, County Down). Details: *Sports Council of Northern Ireland,* House of Sport, Upper Malone Rd., Belfast BT9 5LA, Northern Ireland (phone: 232-381222).

Directions

Introduction

The very nature of Ireland — primarily rural, unfailingly friendly, and almost heartbreakingly beautiful — makes it the perfect place to explore by car. While visits to the major cities of Dublin or Belfast reveal something of this island and its people, there are aspects of Ireland that can only be experienced outside the metropolitan areas — in cozy small-town pubs and shops; at elegant country guesthouses or simple rural farmhouses; on tranquil lakes brimming with fish; at ancient castles atop misty mountains, and overlooking fields glimmering green and bright purple with heather.

Driving is a particularly pleasant and efficient way to explore Ireland — because its small, it's possible to see and experience much without traveling any great distance. But perhaps most important of all, driving tours offer visitors freedom and flexibility — they may linger as long as they like.

Described on the following pages are 12 driving trips through the counties of both Northern Ireland and the Irish Republic. The routes reflect and represent every aspect of this fascinating land: from the wild and starkly beautiful areas of Connemara and the Aran Islands, the lovely lake regions of Killarney and Fermanagh, and the wooded glens and luxurious forests of Kerry to the almost impenetrable wilderness of the Mourne Mountains, the fertile farmlands of Limerick and Tipperary, and the charming seaside resorts of the east coast. Along the routes are megalithic monuments left by ancient civilizations — stone circles, passage graves, and dolmens — as well as structures built by subsequent inhabitants, settlers, and conquerors. Here, too, are communities where traditional ways of life are still carried on: villages where people live in thatch-roofed cottages warmed by peat, where fishing and farming support families as they have for centuries, and where the old songs, stories, and dances are still beloved means of entertainment. Also included are the Gaeltachts, regions where the Irish language is still spoken daily.

There is a chapter for each of the 12 routes; each one begins with an introduction to the region, then describes a driving tour designed to take from 3 to 5 days. It is possible to string together several routes to form longer itineraries, but if you are pressed for time you'll find that by following any single itinerary you'll see most of the sites and sights (and enjoy the best restaurants and accommodations) in the area. Each route includes sightseeing highlights and suggested activities. The *Checking In* sections of the tours contain our recommendations for lodging along the way, be they restored stately mansions, country guesthouses, or homey bed and breakfast establishments. The *Eating Out* entries list the places that serve the tastiest meals in the most evocative surroundings, whether poached salmon and a vintage wine in an elegant Georgian dining room or fresh oysters and Guinness at a dim but cozy pub.

These tours are not exhaustive — there is no effort to cover absolutely everything in each region. But the places recommended and the activities described were chosen to make your trip a most memorable one.

Southeast Ireland: Dublin to New Ross

This route traverses only three Irish counties — Dublin, Wicklow, and Wexford — and it stays close to shore most of the time, yet the changing mood and character of the land along the way can be surprising. The splendid isolation of the Wicklow Mountains, for example, is a mere half-hour's drive from the center of Dublin. Here, great valleys with melodious names such as Glendalough, Clara, and Avoca wind through the hills, and uncrowded roads pass unforgettable sights. Several miles out of Glencree, the boggy terrain, flaked with granite and painted in late summer with purple heather, seems lonely and primitive, whereas the wooded glens met later are soothing in their ageless beauty.

To the south lies the friendlier, less dramatic landscape of County Wexford, where fertile farmland is served by picturesque villages and the historic town of Wexford itself. The coast is lined with inviting beaches. There are busy seaside resorts with shooting galleries, amusement rides, and golf courses, but a discerning traveler can also find the secluded and tiny fishing village of Kilmore Quay, its traditional thatch-roofed cottages all freshly painted and still very much occupied.

This route travels through the suburbs of Dublin south to the residential and resort town of Dún Laoghaire and keeps to the coast as far as Bray. It then turns inland to the village of Enniskerry and the Powerscourt estate, continues west to Glencree, and turns south again over the Military Road to Laragh, the gateway to the monastic site of Glendalough. The route next passes through the vales of Clara and Avoca and returns to the coast at Arklow, where a succession of beachside resorts and villages leads south and then west to Kilmore Quay, interrupted only by the county town of Wexford on Wexford Harbour. At Kilmore Quay, it is possible to backtrack to Rosslare Harbour (a terminus for ferries to Wales and France) or to proceed to New Ross, from which Kilkenny and Waterford are not too distant.

Along the way, a double room will cost more than $150 a night at a hotel described as very expensive; from $100 to $150 at an establishment listed as expensive; $50 to $100 at a place in the moderate category; and less than $50 at a place listed as inexpensive. Dinner for two without wine, drinks, or tips will come to $80 or more in an expensive restaurant, $40 to $80 in a moderate one, and under $40 in an inexpensive place. For each location, hotels and restaurants are listed alphabetically by price category.

DUBLIN For a full report on the city, its sights, restaurants, and hotels, see *Dublin* in THE CITIES.

En Route from Dublin Go south on O'Connell Street and turn left onto Nassau Street, just after Trinity College. Follow the signs to Ballsbridge, passing Merrion Square with its Georgian houses, the American Embassy, and the grounds of the Royal Dublin Society (where the famous horse show is held every summer), and continue until Dublin Bay is visible on the left. This coastal road passes the Booterstown Bird Sanctuary and travels through the small towns of Blackrock and Monkstown and then, 7 miles south of Dublin, into Dún Laoghaire. Crafts enthusiasts will enjoy a stop in Blackrock to see the *Dublin Crystal* shop (Carysfort Ave., about a mile off Main St.; phone: 1-288-7932). This enterprise, begun in 1968, carries on glassmaking traditions that thrived in Dublin from 1764 to 1800. Tours of the factory are available by appointment.

DÚN LAOGHAIRE As the terminus of the cross-channel ferry route from Holyhead, Wales, this busy residential town, holiday resort, and yachting center is one of the main gateways into Ireland. It has grown considerably as a suburb of Dublin in recent years and has innumerable hotels and restaurants, yet a Victorian charm lies below its modern surface. Dún Laoghaire (pronounced *Dun* Leery) was named after a 5th-century Irish king (O'-Leary in English) who established a fort, or *dún,* here to protect the lands of the High Kings of Tara from their rivals. In the 16th century, the area figured in the fighting between the English, who had their main port at neighboring Dalkey, and the Irish, who opposed the English from the nearby Wicklow Mountains. (Traces of the ditch marking the Pale, the area under English control, can still be found around nearby Booterstown.) Dún Laoghaire remained primarily a small fishing village until the present harbor was built in 1817, opening the way for mailboat and ferry services with Wales. George IV came to christen the harbor in 1821 (after which the town was renamed Kingston and was known thus for the next 99 years). The railway line from Dublin arrived in 1834, and the town rapidly became a fashionable resort for the wealthy — many of the streets with their big Victorian houses are named after English royalty.

If you are just passing through town, head down to the harbor and walk the mile-long east pier, with Howth Head stretching in the distance. In summer, band concerts are sometimes held here, and on a nice night, many townspeople come to watch the departure of the evening ferry. Nearby People's Park, which has swings and lovely flower beds beneath shady trees, is the place to see next. George's Street is the main shopping area, and at the corner of Royal Marine Road is one of the most modern shopping malls in Ireland, with 3 floors of boutiques and gift shops and a tempting delicatessen in the basement. Across the way, St. Michael's Church is worth a visit. Its striking modern design incorporates a 19th-century bell tower from an earlier church destroyed by fire. Farther down

Royal Marine Road are the post office and Town Hall, built in 1878. For fresh salads and picnic or deli fare, stop by *Relish,* 70 Upper George's St. (phone: 280-9713).

An enjoyable evening can be spent near Dún Laoghaire at Culturlann na hEireann, the headquarters of *Comhaltas Ceoltóirí Eireann,* the national organization for the promotion of traditional Irish music, song, and dance. The same group that sponsors *seisiún* — sessions of authentic music and dance — throughout the country during the summer has converted a large house into a cultural center, transforming the basement into an Irish kitchen complete with peat fire. Something is happening here most evenings year-round: either *seisiún, céilí* (dancing), *fonntrai* (a show spotlighting Irish traditions), or informal sessions of music and talk. There's an admission charge. The building (32 Belgrave Sq., Monkstown; phone: 1-280-0295) is about 20 minutes on foot from Dún Laoghaire or a short drive by car (it's off the main road, so ask for directions to Belgrave Square).

CHECKING IN

Fitzpatrick Castle Two generations of Fitzpatricks oversee the operation of County Dublin's only luxury castle-hotel. Elegantly furnished with antiques and original paintings, it has 100 rooms and suites (many with four-poster beds), a fine dining room (*Truffles,* see *Eating Out*), a grill-room, a bar, a heated indoor pool, saunas, a gym, squash and tennis courts, guest privileges at the nearby *Leopardstown Golf Club,* and 9 acres of grounds with gardens and views of Killiney Bay. Courtesy coach service to the city center and the airport is provided. Killiney Hill Rd., Killiney (phone: 1-284-0700; 800-367-7701 from the US; fax: 1-285-0207). Expensive.

Royal Marine An elegant, older hotel that's set back from the waterfront by a gracious lawn and gardens. It offers 90 renovated rooms (all with baths). Amenities include saunas, a beauty salon, and a large parking lot that's just behind the shopping mall on George's Street. The restaurant is a lovely place for a drink and dinner. Royal Marine Rd., Dún Laoghaire (phone: 1-280-1911; 800-44-UTELL from the US; fax: 1-280-1089). Expensive.

Court Set on 4 acres overlooking Killiney Bay, with a private garden walk to the beach, this converted Victorian-style residence has 86 rooms, all with baths and a view of the bay, and a fine French-Irish restaurant. Downtown Dublin is a 15-minute ride away via the adjacent *DART (Dublin Area Rapid Transport)* station. On Killiney Bay (phone: 1-285-1622; 800-221-2222 from the US; fax: 1-285-2085). Expensive to moderate.

Scarsdale Situated within walking distance of Dún Laoghaire's waterfront and main shopping district, this cheery bed and breakfast establishment is run by Doris Pittman. Three of the 4 bedrooms have sinks; the other has a full private bath. 4 Tivoli Rd., Dún Laoghaire (phone: 1-280-6258). Inexpensive.

EATING OUT

na Mara A Dublin Bay restaurant in a former train station, known for its good seafood, especially prawns flame-cooked in Pernod, smoked fish pâté, and lobster. Open for lunch and dinner; closed Sundays. Reservations necessary. Major credit cards accepted. 1 Harbour Rd., Dún Laoghaire (phone: 1-280-6767). Expensive.

Guinea Pig — The Fish Restaurant Former Dalkey Mayor Mervyn Stewart is the chef-owner, and seafood is the specialty, including scallops with crab claws and *symphonie de la mer* — monkfish, salmon, sole, and shellfish simmered in herbs, garlic, butter, and lemon. Open daily for dinner; lunch only on Sundays. The early bird menu offers a reasonably priced five-course dinner from 6 to 7 PM. Reservations necessary. Major credit cards accepted. 17 Railway Rd., Dalkey (phone: 1-285-9055). Expensive to moderate.

Salty Dog Filled with Persian rugs and wall hangings, this pleasant restaurant features such dishes as boneless stuffed duckling, while on Sundays diners can partake of the special Indonesian rijsttafel (rice table) of 18 different dishes, including deep-fried chicken and spiced lamb. Open daily for dinner. Reservations advised. Major credit cards accepted. 3A Haddington Ter., Dún Laoghaire (phone: 1-280-8015). Expensive to moderate.

Truffles Housed in an 18th-century Victorian-style castle overlooking Dublin Bay, this elegant restaurant is an attraction in itself, with plush banquette seating, ornate plasterwork, and antique-framed art. The international menu offers such choices as breast of chicken stuffed with smoked salmon in a creamy mushroom sauce, veal *rosti,* and filet mignon stuffed with fois gras and wrapped in smoked ham. Open daily for dinner. Reservations necessary. Major credit cards accepted. *Fitzpatrick Castle Hotel,* Killiney Hill Rd., Killiney (phone: 1-284-0700). Expensive to moderate.

South Bank Located on the seafront near the *James Joyce Museum,* many tables at this family-run restaurant offer good water views. The imaginative menu features such dishes as pheasant with Madeira and cognac sauce; strips of beef with mango, paprika, and ginger; and breast of turkey with bourbon and peaches. Open for dinner only; closed Sundays and Mondays. Reservations necessary. MasterCard and Visa accepted. 1 Martello Ter. at Islington Ave., Sandycove, Dún Laoghaire (phone: 1-280-8788). Moderate.

Wishbone Right over the *Eagle* pub, this place is popular for steaks, burgers, fresh fish, and crêpes. Open daily for lunch and dinner. Reservations unnecessary. MasterCard and Visa accepted. 18-20 Glasthule Rd., Sandycove, Dún Laoghaire (phone: 1-280-4943). Inexpensive.

En Route from Dún Laoghaire The coastal road southeast of town leads to a district known as Sandycove, the site of a Martello tower built as protection against a possible Napoleonic invasion and now a museum dedicated to James Joyce (phone: 1-280-9265 or 1-280-8571; admission charge). The museum is open April through October, by appointment at other times. For detailed information, see *Dublin* in THE CITIES.

A short distance down the coastal road is Bullock Castle, at one time a powerful abbey and inn run by Cistercian monks who exacted tolls from ships entering Bullock Harbour. The castle — now owned by American Carmelite nuns who staff the adjoining nursing home — has been restored, and the tiny prayer cells of the monks and the large dining hall make it an interesting stop. Note the carved head on the corner of the western wall, which dates the castle to about the year 1160. It is open May through September, by appointment at other times (phone: 280-6993). Bullock Castle is at the northern approach to the small resort village of Dalkey. A major port when Dublin was developing, it was once guarded by no fewer than seven castles, two of which remain on Castle Street (one has been rebuilt as the Town Hall). Continue to follow signs for the coast road, which goes around Sorrento Point and then, via Vico Road, high over Killiney Hill for a view of Killiney Bay. A local saying, "See Killiney Bay and die," compares the view to that of the Bay of Naples. At the end of Vico Road, follow the signs to Bray, in County Wicklow; a short 12 miles from Dublin, it's one of Ireland's most popular seaside resorts. Bray has a mile-long beach (a shingly one, compared with those farther south), with a mile-long esplanade running its length to Bray Head, a nearly 800-foot cliff that rises sheer from the sea.

After Bray, turn inland and drive the short 3 miles to Enniskerry.

ENNISKERRY Though this tiny village is quite pretty, its main attraction is the 14,000-acre Powerscourt Estate on its southern outskirts (phone: 1-286-7676; admission charge). A fire in 1974 destroyed the interior of the lovely 18th-century mansion, but the wonderful formal terraced gardens with pebble-paved ramps, statuary, and ironwork are still intact in a heady location looking out over the Wicklow hills. The 400-foot waterfall on the grounds is the highest in Great Britain and Ireland. The gardens are open March 1 through October; the waterfall area is open year-round. For detailed information, see *Stately Homes and Great Gardens* in DIVERSIONS.

En Route from Enniskerry Ten miles south of Enniskerry, via the R755, the picturesque mountain village of Roundwood is worth a slight detour before heading on to Glencree. Set 780 feet above sea level, the area usually is referred to as the "highest village in Ireland."

EATING OUT

Roundwood Inn A restaurant in a rustic old coaching inn (ca. 1750) with stone fireplaces and antique furnishings, it's known for its fresh seafood — Galway Bay oysters, Dublin Bay prawns, or locally caught salmon — as well as Irish stew, rack of Wicklow lamb, venison, and international dishes such as Hungarian goulash. For lunch, try a hearty soup, such as scallop chowder, and a sandwich. Open Tuesdays through Saturdays. Reservations advised. MasterCard and Visa accepted. Roundwood (phone: 1-281-8107 or 1-281-8125). Moderate.

En Route from Roundwood Head 2 miles back on the R755, then 8 miles west on the R759, and 4 miles north on the R115 until you reach the town of Glencree. The road climbs into the splendid Wicklow Mountains on a winding course. At Glencree, follow the signs south to Sally Gap over the Military Road, so called because it was built by the British after the Rebellion of 1798 and used to flush out Irish rebels hiding in the glens of the Wicklows. This stretch of the route is a winding one, too, passing peat bogs, glacial lakes, and a landscape somber and unyielding in its flatness until it reaches the crossroads of Sally Gap (1,631 feet) and begins to descend toward Laragh through the valley of Glenmacnass. At the northern end of the glen, where the road joins the course of the River Glenmacnass, is a parking lot. Be sure to stop and walk down to the waterfall, pristine and powerful as it tumbles over slabs of stone into the deep valley below. At the glen's southern end, where the River Glenmacnass meets the Avonmore, is the village of Laragh. Browse for a while in the *Glendalough Craft Centre* (phone: 404-45156), a transformed farmhouse where weavings and jewelry are made. Then drive the mile west to the entrance to Glendalough.

GLENDALOUGH This deep glen, set between two lakes amid the towering wooded slopes and granite hills of the Wicklow Mountains, is at once a place of great natural beauty and immense historical interest. Glendalough means "the valley of the two lakes," and in the 6th century, when St. Kevin came to Wicklow in search of tranquillity, he found it here. But the hermit's sanctity attracted so many disciples that, almost unwittingly, he founded a great monastery that eventually became one of the most renowned centers of learning in Europe. It was sacked by the Vikings in the 9th and 10th centuries, and later (1398) by the English, although some of the buildings remained in use until Henry VIII dissolved the monasteries in the 16th century. Today the ruins of the monastic city are scattered over 1 1/2 miles of the valley.

The best place to begin a visit to Glendalough is at the visitors' center (phone: 404-45325) located near the main entrance. It features an interpretive exhibition on Glendalough and St. Kevin, as well as an audiovisual program, and a model of the monastery as it was in the 11th century. For those who wish a detailed tour, guides are available. The visitors' center is closed Mondays from November through mid-March; open daily the rest of the year. There's an admission charge for the exhibit and show.

From the center, visitors may want to head for the Upper Lake area. It was in the solitude of the Upper Lake at the base of 2,296-foot Camaderry and 2,154-foot Lugduff that St. Kevin first prayed in his stone beehive hut. In the same area, with its gravestones and crosses, is Reefert Church, where the O'Tooles and other local chiefs are buried. Visitors can walk or drive to the Upper Lake, use the picnic grounds, and (for a small fee) hire a boat for an excursion that provides some splendid views of the valley and a closer look at St. Kevin's Bed, an excavation in the cliff face about 25 feet above the water level, said to have been used as a retreat by the saint. As it grew, the settlement spread toward the Lower Lake and the entrance. The ruins in the Lower Lake area include the cathedral, the largest church on the site; St. Kevin's Church, with its sturdy stone ceiling; and the much-photographed Round Tower, over 100 feet high. Built in the 9th century, this was probably a bell tower, lookout point, and place of refuge all in one; the only door is fully 10 feet above the ground. Glendalough's walks and ruins are marked by plaques for easy exploration.

CHECKING IN/EATING OUT

Glendalough This country inn offers 16 cozy rooms, all overlooking the vistas and historic sites of Glendalough, and all with private baths. There is a restaurant and a tavern on the premises. Open March through October. Glendalough–Dublin road, Glendalough (phone: 1-404-45135; 800-365-3346 from US; fax: 1-404-45142). Moderate.

En Route from Glendalough Leaving by the Arklow road, T61, the route once again parallels the course of a river, this time the Avonmore, and passes through the wooded Vale of Clara before reaching the town of Rathdrum, 8 miles south of Laragh. Here it is possible to interrupt the route for an interesting diversion at the nearby *Clara-Lara Fun Park* (Rathdrum; phone: 404-46161), an outdoor amusement center featuring rowboats, rides, rafting, nature trails, and river fishing. Admission charge to the park includes fishing pole rental, but the use of boats is extra. It's open April through October.

About 1½ miles southeast of Rathdrum is Avondale (phone 404-46111), the lovely birthplace and home of the Irish patriot Charles Stewart Parnell, a member of a Protestant landowning family who became a leader in the fight for Catholic emancipation and land reform in the 19th century. The house was built in 1777 by Parnell's cousin Samuel Hayes, who was interested in forestation and wrote the first book on tree planting in Ireland in 1794. The 530-acre estate that the Parnell family inherited from Hayes in 1795 now belongs to the Forest and Wildlife Service and is used as a forestry school. The guidebook on sale at the estate discusses the wildlife and trees found on the grounds as well as recommended walks, but for tourists budgeting time, the house, with its lovely furnishings and moldings, is the main attraction. Both house and grounds are open daily, year-round. There's an admission charge.

From Avondale, return to Rathdrum and pick up the main road, T7, south toward Woodenbridge. The stretch between the two towns, approximately 8 miles, is known as the Vale of Avoca, a beautiful spot immortalized in verse by Ireland's national poet, Thomas Moore ("There is not in this wide world a valley so sweet / As that vale in whose bosom the bright waters meet"). The Meeting of the Waters, where the rivers Avonmore and Avonbeg join to form the River Avoca, is about 3½ miles south of Rathdrum, and the tree under which Moore is supposed to have sat to contemplate the beauty he saw is marked by a plaque. *The Meetings* (phone: 402-35226), a combination pub, restaurant, nightclub, and crafts shop standing on the site of a cottage where Moore once lived, overlooks this pastoral junction. Visitors can sip an Irish coffee here and listen to the hearty publican, an amateur Moore scholar, discuss the poet's works. If time permits, visit the Motte Stone, signposted near the Meeting of the Waters. The large boulder marks the halfway point between Dublin and Wexford, and from its top the view of the countryside is quite nice. Legend has it that the boulder was the hurling stone of the giant Finn MacCool.

To reach the small, friendly village of Avoca, about 3 miles south of the Meeting of the Waters, turn left at the sign for Avoca on the main road and then left again after the bridge. Here visitors can watch the weaving process at *Avoca Handweavers* (phone: 402-35105). The operation, in a cluster of stone buildings that was once a corn mill, employs about 30 people who prepare, roll, and weave the wool, about 75% of it for export. The remainder can be bought in the mill shop. There also are several bed and breakfast houses on the road near the bridge.

About 2 miles south of Avoca, the rivers Aughrim and Avoca form a second confluence at Woodenbridge, and though no poets have sung its praises, many travelers find it more beautiful than the first. The main road then bears east toward the coast and in 5 miles arrives at Arklow.

CHECKING IN/EATING OUT

Vale View This rambling Old World inn, set on a hill overlooking the mountain and river vistas of Avoca, yet close to Dublin, is an ideal spot to get away from it all. There are 10 rooms with private baths, TV sets, and telephones. There's also a restaurant, lounge, outdoor garden deck, and 2 outdoor tennis courts. Avoca (phone: 402-35236; fax: 402-35144). Moderate.

Riverview A lovely guesthouse, with 5 lovely rooms (each with private bath), run by May Byrne, a retired schoolteacher and fluent speaker of Irish. It's open from May through October only. Avoca (phone: 402-35181). Inexpensive.

ARKLOW This busy town at the mouth of the River Avoca has long been a fishing and shipping port and a boatbuilding center: *Gipsy Moth IV,* the yacht that took Sir Francis Chichester around the world, was built in an Arklow shipyard. The town is also a popular seaside resort, with beaches to the north and south, and it is the home of *Arklow Pottery,* the largest pottery manufacturer in Ireland. Arklow was founded by the Norsemen, and when they gave way to the Normans, it became the property of the Fitzwalters, ancestors of the Butlers, one of the most powerful families in Irish history. The decisive battle of the Wexford Rebellion of 1798 was fought here; the insurgent leader, Father Michael Murphy lost his life in the battle. The 1798 Memorial, a statue of Murphy that stands in front of the Catholic parish church, commemorates his bravery.

Arklow Pottery, now part of Noritake, a Japanese china company, employs more than 200 people and has been making domestic earthenware since 1934. Though the plant is open to visitors by appointment only (S. Quay; phone: 402-32401), a shop on the premises that sells seconds at discount prices is open daily. There are plenty of places to golf, fish, boat, and play tennis in the Arklow vicinity, but the major attraction outside of town is about 10 miles north, at Brittas Bay. The 3-mile stretch of silver sand and dunes can be packed with picnickers and bathers from Dublin on sunny weekends, but normally there's only a modest crowd.

CHECKING IN

Marlfield House This 18th-century mansion was once part of the extensive Courtown estate and has been handsomely restored by owners Raymond and Mary Bowe into a 19-room hotel. Closed December to early February. For detailed information, see *Rural Retreats* in DIVERSIONS. On the Gorey–Courtown road, Gorey (phone: 55-21124; 800-223-6510 from the US; fax: 55-21572). Very expensive.

Tinakilly House Once the home of Captain Robert Halpin, who laid the first successful cable connecting Europe with America, this elegant 29-room hostelry is filled with seafaring memorabilia and paintings, family silver, and other precious heirlooms. Facilities include a restaurant and tennis courts. For detailed information, see *Rural Retreats* in DIVERSIONS. About 2 miles south of Rathnew, right off the main Dublin road (phone: 404-69274; 800-223-6510 from the US; fax: 404-67806). Expensive.

Hunters This 200-year-old, 18-room coaching inn sits along the banks of the River Vartry and is known for its fine restaurant. Newrath Bridge, Rathnew (phone: 404-40106; 800-223-6510 from the US; fax: 404-40338). Moderate.

EATING OUT

The Cottage Just 200 yards from the beach at Courtown, this small and friendly restaurant is owned and operated by Maureen and Steve Savage. Steaks of various sizes and cuts are the specialty, as is locally caught seafood. Food is served from midday to midnight. Open daily from June through September; weekends only the rest of the year. Reservations advised. Major credit cards accepted. Ardamine, Courtown, about 10 miles south of Arklow (phone: 55-25151). Moderate.

Woodenbridge Attached to one of Ireland's oldest hotels (ca. 1608), this Tudor restaurant has a warm Old World atmosphere and features local produce and freshwater trout. Open daily for morning coffee, lunch, afternoon tea, and dinner; dancing and entertainment on weekends. Reservations advised. Major credit cards accepted. Woodenbridge, near Arklow (phone: 402-35146). Moderate.

En Route from Arklow While the main road south follows the railway line to Wexford, the coastal route, a pleasant, quiet drive of about 40 miles, runs along a succession of sandy beaches in the sunniest and driest part of Ireland. Courtown is a lively resort in summer; besides its 2 miles of beach, it has an 18-hole golf course, typical seaside amusements, and evening entertainment at a variety of small hotels. In August, the nearby town of Gorey, 3½ miles inland, hosts an arts festival that includes art exhibits, films, theater, and a variety of music from traditional Irish to jazz and rock. The Church of St. Michael and Christ Church are among the sights to see at other times of the year. Farther south along the coast, the beaches continue almost uninterrupted to Wexford; especially good ones, all backed by picturesque villages, are at Cahore, Kilmuckridge, Blackwater, and Curracloe. South of Curracloe, where the River Slaney runs out to sea, the road crosses the bridge into Wexford.

WEXFORD For a full report on Wexford, its sights, restaurants, and hotels, see *Wexford Town* in THE CITIES.

En Route from Wexford To visit Johnstown Castle, a 19th-century Gothic mansion now owned by the State Agricultural College, proceed south for about 3 miles via an unnumbered country road. The castle grounds have lovely ornamental gardens, walks around artificial lakes, a picnic area, and the *Irish Agricultural Museum* (phone: 53-42888), an interesting exhibition on farming and rural life. Otherwise, start out on the road to Rosslare Harbour, N25. On a fine summer day, this area southeast of Wexford is the stuff of poetry. Turn left onto R740 at Killinick and head for Rosslare, branching left when the main road bears right for Rosslare Harbour. Rosslare, or Rosslare Strand, is a seaside resort in the middle of a wonderful 6-mile beach. There are also public tennis courts, an 18-hole golf course, a playground, fishing and boating, and *Kelly's Strand* hotel (phone: 53-32114), which is a center of activity and a popular year-round retreat for the Irish.

The road south from Rosslare leads to the village of Tagoat and two possibilities. A left turn onto N25 leads to a selection of good hotels and restaurants in Rosslare Harbour, the departure point for ferries to Fishguard, Wales, and Le Havre and Cherbourg, France (but don't follow the road to the end, since it leads directly onto the boats). Driving straight through Tagoat leads to the tiny village of Broadway, which has an enormous tavern and thatch-roofed cottages. Broadway is at the head of Lady's Island Lake, actually a sea inlet, and Lady's Island is in the lake, connected to land by a causeway. The ruins of an Augustinian priory dedicated to the Virgin Mary and a Norman castle with a curiously leaning limestone tower are on the island, which has been the object of pilgrimages for centuries and is still a popular destination for both pilgrims and tourists, especially in August and September. From Lady's Island, the two possibilities are to continue east to Carne Harbour, where there is more beach and a good seafood restaurant, the *Lobster Pot* (phone: 53-31110), which is open May through August, or to return to Broadway and drive west to Kilmore Quay, one of the most delightful villages in Ireland. Kilmore Quay is a fishing village whose main street is no more than a cozy row of thatch-roofed cottages with a fishermen's cooperative at one end. Visitors with an interest in bird watching can hire a boat to visit the great bird sanctuary of the Saltee Islands, a 45-minute trip off the south coast of County Wexford (call Willie Bates, 53-29644, or Tom O'Brien, 53-29727). About three-quarters of the total Irish bird species have been seen in this county, and most of the birds frequent either Great or Little Saltee, where they rub feathers with many rare migrant birds. Great Saltee (only a mile long) was once inhabited, and caves in its rugged, rocky cliffs were used as hideaways by insurgents after the Rebellion of 1798 was crushed. The small, modern *Saltees* hotel in Kilmore Quay (phone: 53-29601 or 53-29602) has a restaurant and pleasant accommodations.

Less than 20 miles northwest of Kilmore Quay is the town of New Ross, built on a steep hill overlooking the River Barrow. *Galley Cruising Restaurants* (phone: 51-21723) offers 3-hour dinner cruises departing from New Ross at 7 PM daily during the summer and according to demand in April, May, and September. Five miles south of New Ross, on L159, is the John Fitzgerald Kennedy Memorial Park, a splendid 480-acre arboretum commemorating President Kennedy, whose ancestors came from nearby Dunganstown. The park covers the lower slopes of Slieve Coillte, from the top of which, on a nice day, the counties of Wexford and Waterford are visible. Waterford City is 15 miles southwest of New Ross, and Kilkenny Town is 26 miles northwest.

South-Central Ireland

Despite the recent influx of industry and factories, Ireland is still very much a rural, agricultural country, and this route travels through some of the island's best farmland. Tipperary Town is in the midst of the Golden Vale, fertile acreage extending from the valley of the River Suir, east of town, across the border into County Limerick, west of town. The rich pastureland rolls down to Mitchelstown in County Cork, where the vast creamery of the Mitchelstown Cooperative Agricultural Society gathers its bounty, and on to the valley of the River Blackwater. The river, which cuts across County Cork on its way into the Celtic Sea, is popular with sporting types, especially fisherfolk.

However, this farmland region is not without its mountain scenery: South of Tipperary Town, the Glen of Aherlow is a romantic stretch through the mighty Galtee Mountains. Farther south, two other ranges, the Knockmealdowns and the Comeraghs, become a palette of greens in the afternoon light. The route goes around these two, but a detour, a hairpin scenic drive called the Vee, winds through the former. Nor is seascape missing: The route also leads along the Celtic Sea from Cobh, where the great passenger liners once docked, into Youghal, where a version of *Moby Dick* was filmed, past cliffs and miles of beach into quaint Annestown, the seaside resort of Tramore, and, finally, Waterford. The route turns inland after Waterford to enter a landscape where castles guarding riverbanks are commonplace, and then it terminates at Cashel, one of Ireland's greatest historic sites. Bad weather actually enhances explorations here. A little fog and mist add a dimension of mystery to the imposing Rock of Cashel.

This route provides a glimpse of Ireland few tourists experience. It passes through a remote Irish-speaking area — one of the few pockets of traditional Irish culture not on the west coast — and includes a castle familiar to most visitors from movies. Along the way are quiet stretches of countryside interspersed with lively villages with good pubs, restaurants, and lodgings.

In this section, hotels listed as expensive will charge from $100 to $150 a night for a double room; those described as moderate, from $50 to $95; and a double room in a place in the inexpensive category will cost $50 or less — much less in the case of bed and breakfast establishments. Dinner for two (without wine, drinks, and tips) will cost $75 or more in an expensive restaurant; from $40 to $75 in a moderate one; and less than $40 in an inexpensive place. For each location, hotels and restaurants are listed alphabetically by price category.

TIPPERARY "It's a long way to Tipperary," goes the famous World War I song, but this cozy town in the Golden Vale has developed a personality and prosperity that make the journey worth the distance. Viewed fro footpaths of the hills just outside town, Tip, as it is called by the resembles a quiet New England village bordered by the green back of the Slievenamuck Mountains. This is prime farmland, and many in the area are employed in the Tipperary Cooperative Creamery at the end of Bridge Street. The town was famous during the Land League movement of the 1880s, when residents refused to pay property rents to landlord Smith-Barry and established a "New Tipperary" just outside the town borders. The plan to start a new town eventually failed, but the shops and timber houses of Emmet and Dillon Streets, once part of New Tipperary, are still inhabited.

Tipperary has had a long history (it grew around a castle built here by King John in the late 12th century), but one that contrived to leave it with few ancient or notable buildings (it was laid waste during the course of the Desmond Wars in the late 16th century). It is a friendly place, however, and the best way to sample its hospitality is to stop at one of the town's many pubs, such as *Nellie O'Brien's* (11 Main St.; phone: 62-52707), where guests can sip a pint of beer under a thatch roof; *Tony Lowry's* (46 Main St.; phone: 62-52774), a quiet place near the tourist office at the end of James Street; or *O'Brien's Bar* (6 Bridge St.; phone: 62-51274), a traditional gem with a horse-racing ambience, which dates back to 1898.

The Tipperary Tourist Office (3 James St.; phone: 62-51457), open year-round, provides information on the town and surrounding area.

CHECKING IN/ In addition to the listings below, also consider hotels in nearby Cashel, only 20 miles to the south of Tipperary. For details, see *Cashel* in THE CITIES.

Glen An inviting 24-room hotel on the drive through the Glen of Aherlow, a few miles outside Tipperary. The restaurant serves good Irish fare. Glen of Aherlow, Tipperary (phone: 62-56146; fax: 62-56152). Moderate.

Royal Right off Main Street, this older, 3-story hotel has 16 rooms, each with private bath and TV set. In addition, the restaurant, a favorite with locals, specializes in seafood dishes. Bridge St., Tipperary (phone: 62-51204). Moderate to inexpensive.

Clonmore Many visitors return to this popular bed and breakfast house run by Mary Quinn in an attractive bungalow. There are 4 rooms with private baths. Open April through October. Cork–Galbally road, Tipperary Town (phone: 62-51637). Inexpensive.

EATING OUT

Brown Trout Long established and known for its good local fare, ranging from sole on the bone to grilled trout. It's light on atmosphere but generous with portions. Open daily. Reservations advised for dinner. Major credit cards accepted. Bridge St., Tipperary (phone: 62-51912). Moderate to inexpensive.

Kickham Lounge An informal tavern, with an Old World ambience, this place is named after Charles J. Kickham, a locally born 19th-century poet, novelist, and revolutionary. The decor reflects Kickham's times, but the pub lunches and snacks are up-to-date. Open daily. No reservations. No credit cards accepted. 50 Main St., Tipperary (phone: 62-51716). Inexpensive.

En Route from Tipperary Leave by Bridge Street and follow the signs south for the Glen of Aherlow, a valley between the Slievenamuck and the Galtee Mountains that provides a lovely backdrop to a wending, scenic drive. From the parking lot before the statue of Christ the King, there is a vast view of the valley, which seems untouched by time. Two-story farmhouses are more common than modern bungalows, and donkey carts pulling containers of milk still travel the roads. Follow the signs to Galbally and then on to Mitchelstown, just over the County Cork border.

MITCHELSTOWN This butter and cheese producing town is an interesting mixture of the old and the new. The Catholic Church of the Blessed Virgin Mary, with its window-slashed brick interior, was completed in 1980. In contrast, Kingston College was erected in 1761 by the Earl of Kingston, whose family laid out much of the town. This institution is actually a collection of attached Georgian stone houses that open onto College Square. The buildings were originally built as almshouses for "decayed gentlefolk" and as residences for some of the families who worked for the Kingstons. They are now the homes of about 30 retired couples. The extensive creamery run by the Mitchelstown Cooperative Agricultural Society can be toured (stop in at the communications office in New Square; phone: 25-24211 or 25-24411). The society, which began in 1917 and grew as small cooperatives merged with it, employs about 2,300 people and has 4,500 shareholders, all of whom are farmers. Before leaving Mitchelstown, try the pastries at the *Torten* (42 Cork St.; phone: 25-24132); or the scrumptious soups, salads, and savories at *O'Callaghan's Deli & Café* (19 Cork St.; phone: 25-24657); or stop for a pint at one of the pubs on Main Street. Mitchelstown Caves, two long underground complexes with large halls and interesting formations, are 6 miles northeast, off the Cahir road. They are open daily from 10 AM to 6 PM and may be visited with a guide; admission charge (phone: 52-67246).

En Route from Mitchelstown Drive due south 10 miles to Fermoy, a fairly large, busy town that was once prosperous as a garrison for the British army and is now popular with sport fisherfolk.

FERMOY This town straddles the River Blackwater, one of the better-known salmon fishing rivers in Ireland. The Blackwater rises on the Cork-Kerry border and flows 85 miles out to sea at Youghal; the stretch around Fermoy is the part of the river that is best for salmon. *Castle Hyde House,* the beautiful Georgian home of Douglas Hyde, the first President of Ireland, is just outside town; the 6-bedroom house is available for rent

(2-week minimum). For details contact *Elegant Ireland* (15 Harcourt St., Dublin 2; phone: 1-751665). About 3 miles northwest of town, off the Glanworth road, is Labbacallee, or the Hag's Bed, one of the largest wedge-shaped gallery graves in the country. (Gallery graves are those in which the chambers are not distinct from the entrance passages.) It looks like a pile of stones from the roadside, but closer inspection (achieved by climbing over the steps in the stone wall at the side) reveals the massive shape of the two burial chambers covered by three immense capstones. It is guarded by several standing stones and dates from about 1500 BC.

En Route from Fermoy Head south to Midleton and turn west onto N25, dropping down to T12A at the turnoff for Cobh (pronounced *Cove*). The route leads across a strip of water to Great Island (approximately 17 miles by 2 miles) and curves down and around its southern side to where Cobh stands facing the greater part of Cork Harbour.

COBH One of the nicest times of year to enjoy this former port of call for the great transatlantic passenger liners is during the annual *International Folk Dance Festival,* a week of dancing, concerts, fireworks, and parades each July. The blue haze of a summer's evening settles over the harbor and the graceful tower of St. Colman's Cathedral high on the hill above gives the scene a medieval air. The cathedral, though not medieval (it was built between 1868 and 1915), is Cobh's most striking feature. It tops off the hill of old houses built shoulder to shoulder in ascending height and, from the harbor, looks like a guardian angel hovering over so many members of a family posing for a picture. During the famine years, the harbor at Cobh was the last image of Ireland impressed on the minds of many thousands of Irish emigrants. The view at that time was without the cathedral, but those who survived the coffin ships to do well in the New World sent back money to help build this crowning touch to the town's skyline. Its exterior of Dublin granite is covered with statues and gargoyles, its interior features stained glass windows and a 43-foot-high marble altar alive with carvings. There are weekly concerts on the 47-bell carillon.

Until the 18th century, Cobh was a small fishing village accessible only by ferry and known simply as the Cove of Cork. In medieval times, it belonged to an Irish chieftain whose son fought with Brian Ború against the Danes in the Battle of Clontarf (1014). Later, it became the home of Anglo-Irish families such as the Barrys, the Hodnetts, and the Roches. The British began to develop the fishing village as a strategic naval base during the American Revolution. They erected a military barracks on the site of an ancient monastery across from Cobh on Spike Island (later used as a prison for Irish rebels and now an Irish army coastal defense station) and a naval station west of Spike Island on Haulbowline Island (now the site of a huge steel complex and headquarters of the Irish navy). Many of the town's streets were laid out during the 1800s, as Georgian and Victorian homes for British officers rose along Harbour Row.

In 1838, the first transatlantic steamship sailed from Cobh, initiating an era of prominence for the town as an international passenger port, and in 1849 the Cove of Cork became Queenstown, renamed in commemoration of a visit by Queen Victoria. During World War I, both the British and the Americans used Queenstown's port facilities; when a German submarine sank the *Lusitania* off Kinsale in May 1915, it was from here that ships sailed to rescue the survivors. In recent years, *Cunard's QE 2* has called on Cobh during several of its transatlantic crossings, usually westbound sailings from Southampton, England, to New York. A new *Queenstown/Cobh Heritage Centre* features exhibits and audiovisual programs that tell the story of the town and its port. The center also includes an immigration museum with genealogical information and passenger manifests from ships that called at Cobh over the years. Open daily. There's an admission charge. For details, contact the *Cobh Heritage Trust Ltd.*, County Hall, Cork (phone: 21-813591).

Today Cobh is a holiday resort focused on its attractive harbor. The *International Sailing Centre* (5 East Beach St.; phone: 21-811237), based near the Town Hall, offers courses in sailing. Sea angling can be arranged through the *Cobh Sea Angling Club* (phone: 21-812167). The *Royal Cork Yacht Club* (phone: 21-831440), across the harbor at Crosshaven, dates from 1720 and is the oldest in the world. The *Lusitania* Memorial (Roger Casement Sq.) includes several restored Italianate shops.

In addition to Cobh, the rest of Great Island is also worth exploring. Victims of the *Lusitania* disaster are buried in the Old Church Cemetery, about a mile north. Nearby at Carrigtwohill is Fota Island, an estate once owned by the Smith-Barry family and now in the care of University College Cork. The family home, built in the 1820s, is a splendid example of Regency architecture. It is presently closed for major restoration work (for information, call 21-812678). Also on the grounds are a wildlife center and an arboretum open to the public.

CHECKING IN/EATING OUT

Commodore This veteran hotel overlooks the waterfront. It has an Old World atmosphere, modern facilities (all 36 rooms have private baths), a lovely dining room serving excellent meals, and a heated indoor swimming pool, a squash court, and a sauna. Deep-sea fishing trips can be arranged here. Cobh (phone: 21-811277; fax: 21-811672). Moderate.

Rinn Ronain Picturesquely set on landscaped grounds, with beach access on Cork Harbour, this cozy hotel was once the home of J. P. Ronayne, a 19th-century Irish patriot. It has 21 rooms with private baths, and a restaurant with a panoramic view. Open year-round. Rushbrooke, Cobh (phone: 21-812242 or 21-811407). Moderate.

En Route from Cobh The main Cork–Waterford road, N25, leads east to Youghal. But there are several reasons to turn off the road at Castlemartyr and follow the signs to Ballycotton, stopping 3 miles short of the coast at the tiny village of Shanagarry. One is a meal or an overnight stay at *Ballymaloe House,* a small hotel and family-run restaurant (see *Checking In/Eating Out*) that is one of Ireland's most delightful country properties. Another is a stop at the woodland pottery workshop of Stephen Pearce (Kilmahon; phone: 21-646807), who creates brown pottery with a distinctive frosty white glaze. Visitors also can buy the pottery at a shop in *Ballymaloe House.* Before leaving the area, drive down to the cliffs at Ballycotton for a breath of sea air, then return to the main road for the drive east into Youghal.

CHECKING IN/EATING OUT

Ballymaloe House Travelers from all over the world stay at this 30-room hotel on a 400-acre rural retreat, which is known for its award-winning restaurant and its cooking school. Other pluses include a heated swimming pool, outdoor tennis courts, 5 holes of golf, deep-sea fishing (at nearby Ballycotton), and a crafts shop. For detailed information, see *Cork City* in THE CITIES. About 20 miles from Cork City, Shanagarry, Midleton (phone: 21-652531; 800-223-6510 from the US; fax: 21-65021). Expensive.

YOUGHAL Pronounced *Yawl,* this pleasant resort town on a hill has an old section and a 5-mile beach where the River Blackwater pours into Youghal Bay. The tourist board (South Main St.; phone: 24-92390) is located in the 18th-century Clock Gate, which once served as a prison where inmates were flogged and often were hung from the windows. Stop in to pick up the *Tourist Trail* booklet, which describes a signposted walking tour of the town. The trail leads up and around the Old Town walls, which date from the 15th century and are among the best preserved in Ireland. St. Mary's Collegiate Church, dating from the 13th century, was damaged in 1579 when the town was sacked during the Desmond Rebellion, but it has been restored and is still in use. Nearby Myrtle Grove, an Elizabethan mansion, belonged to Sir Walter Raleigh. It is here that Raleigh, fresh from Virginia, is supposed to have planted Ireland's first potatoes on the property, but he probably never lived in the house. He was the Mayor, or Warden, of Youghal for a time in 1588 and 1589. He sold the estate to Sir Richard Boyle, who rose from poverty to great wealth during Elizabeth's reign and became the first Earl of Cork; a monument to him and his family is in St. Mary's. Myrtle Grove (phone: 24-92274) is open to the public for guided tours on Tuesdays, Thursdays, and Saturdays at 3 and 4 PM in June, and at 11:45 AM, 3 and 4 PM in July and August; there's an admission charge. The tourist trail leads past the remains of Tynte's Castle, a tower house built by the English in the 15th century, and past the Benedictine priory, which was Oliver Cromwell's headquarters during his Munster campaign of 1649 and is now partly converted into a tea shop. Stop for a rest here or have a drink in the *Moby Dick* lounge (Market Sq.; phone: 24-92756) around the corner from the Clock Gate. The lounge gets its name from the film starring Gregory Peck that was made in Youghal. Other pubs worth a visit are the *Clock Tavern* (56 S. Main St.; phone: 24-93003), the *Yawl Inn* (Main St.; phone: 24-93076), *The Nook* (20 N. Main St.; phone: 24-93260), and *Harbour Lights* (Market Sq.; no phone).

CHECKING IN

Aherne's An extension of the town's most acclaimed restaurant (see *Eating Out*), run by the Fitzgibbon family, this new guesthouse has 10 spacious bedrooms, each with private bath, telephone, TV set and hair dryer. The rates include full Irish breakfast. Open year-round. 163 N. Main St., Youghal (phone: 24-92424; 800-223-6510 from the US; fax: 24-93633). Moderate.

Devonshire Arms This is a friendly, older hotel convenient to town; all 10 rooms have private baths, TV sets, telephones, and hair dryers. The restaurant, *Molana,* draws rave reviews (see *Eating Out*). Open year-round. Pearse Sq., Youghal (phone: 24-92827; fax: 24-92900). Moderate.

Hilltop Just a mile west of town, this modern property has a stone icehouse from the 1800s on its grounds, as well as an outdoor swimming pool and a nightclub. All 50 rooms have private baths; many have wonderful views of the sea. The cozy restaurant features fresh salmon dishes, Irish stew, and delicious desserts. Closed November through March. Youghal (phone: 24-92911; fax: 24-93503). Moderate.

EATING OUT

Aherne's The best of the local catch is always on the menu here, including lobsters and oysters from the tank as well as succulent crab claws and giant prawns. Closed Monday evenings in off-season; open daily for lunch and dinner the rest of the year (also see *Pub Crawling* in DIVERSIONS). Reservations advised. MasterCard and Visa accepted. 162-163 N. Main St., Youghal (phone: 24-92424). Expensive to moderate.

Molana Housed in the *Devonshire Arms* hotel, this Old World–style dining room has brought au courant French-Irish fare to this historic walled seaport town. Specialties include breast of duck with honey and blackberry sauces, filet of brill with cider and green apple sauce, and sea trout with Riesling and burgundy sauces. Open daily for dinner. Reservations advised. Major credit cards accepted. Pearse Sq., Youghal (phone: 24-92018 or 24-92827). Expensive to moderate.

En Route from Youghal Waterford is 48 miles away via the main route, N25, but, time permitting, some of the side roads along the way are worth exploring. Just north of Youghal, the road crosses into County Waterford, and a few miles farther along is a turnoff for Ardmore, a quaint village with impressive cliffs on Ardmore Bay (Ardmore means "the great height") and the site of many a shipwreck. There was an Irish college here whose students included Irish patriots Eamon de Valera and Maud Gonne MacBride. Ardmore is famous for the ruins of a monastery founded by St. Declan in the 7th century. The 12th-century round tower is one of the tallest and best-preserved examples of this type of structure in Ireland. Near it is St. Declan's Church (or Cathedral), Romanesque in style, also of the 12th century. St. Declan's Oratory (or Tomb) is a small church traditionally held to be the saint's grave.

Return to the main route and continue north toward Dungarvan, but take the turnoff before Dungarvan and drive down to Ring, near Helvick Head. This is an especially beautiful spot in the evening: Travelers and locals alike sit on benches in the tall grass along the elevated waterfront and watch the sun set slowly behind the mountains as golden washes of light linger on Dungarvan Bay. Ring is a fishing village in the midst of the Waterford Gaeltacht, one of the few — and scattered — Irish-speaking areas left in Ireland. The Irish college here is half a century old and in summer it is full of students learning the language and studying traditional music and dance. All signs in the area are in Irish, including the stop signs, which read "Stad." Pause for a drink at *Mooney's* (phone: 58-46204), a flagstone bar with a front deck overlooking the water, at the turn in the road leading toward Helvick Head.

Ring, a town 5 miles south of Dungarvan, comes alive with a market on Thursdays. North of Dungarvan, leave the main route again and take the coastal route, following signs for Stradbally. The road goes inland for a distance and then follows the seacoast through a somewhat isolated region where the wind sweeps over grassy cliffs. Just before Annestown, stop at *Waterford Woodcraft,* a woodworking studio turning out functional and ornamental pieces in native woods. Annestown has a small beach and the distinction of being just about the only village in Ireland without a pub. It is named for Anna De La Pore, a Catholic relation of Lord Waterford, who is said to have given Cromwell only buttermilk to drink when he sought accommodations for the night. The coastal route leads next to Tramore, a lively seaside resort whose population nearly doubles in July and August. Tramore has a 3-mile-long beach, a 50-acre amusement park, an 18-hole golf course, horse racing (the most important meet is in August), and many hotels. The tourist board (Railway Sq.; phone: 51-81572), open in July and August, is well stocked with literature about sports, entertainment, and restaurants in town. From Tramore, it is only 8 miles north on T63 to Waterford.

EATING OUT

Seanachie The name of this thatch-roofed cottage pub-restaurant is Irish for "storyteller." Brother and sister Michael and Laurann Casey have converted old farm buildings into an intimate dining room and rustic bar. The menu is varied, featuring wholesome Irish country cooking. The barnyard is now a courtyard for dancing. Open daily for lunch; dinner served daily except Tuesdays. Reservations advised for dinner. Major credit cards accepted. Five miles south of Dungarvan on the main road (phone: 58-46285). Moderate to inexpensive.

WATERFORD For information on sights, accommodations, restaurants, and entertainment, see *Waterford City* in THE CITIES.

En Route from Waterford The town of Carrick-on-Suir is 17 miles northwest via T13 (N24). Straddling the river, part in County Waterford and part in County Tipperary, the town was another seat of the Butler family of Kilkenny Castle. The Elizabethan manor house built around 1600 by Black Tom Butler, the 10th Earl of Ormonde, is in a style uncommon in Ireland, probably because Black Tom had spent time in England and built it hoping to entice his cousin, Queen Elizabeth I, to visit (she never did). What remains of an older, 15th-century Butler castle, much damaged by Cromwell, is behind the manor house. Be sure to stop at *Shanahan Willow Crafts* (Chapel St.; phone: 51-40307). John Shanahan learned to make baskets from his father, who learned it from his father, who opened the shop in 1886. The nimble fingers of John and his brother, Michael, have woven some most unusual things — 10-foot goal posts for polo games and passenger baskets for hot-air balloons — but their most popular items are shopping baskets and baby cradles, and the prices are quite low for such skillfully crafted, handmade goods. The area's other leading crafts enterprise is *Tipperary Crystal* (phone: 51-41188), located about 3 miles west of Carrick-on-Suir at Ballynoran. Staffed by former Waterford Glass craftsmen, this small factory produces fine quality, full-lead, mouth-blown crystal stemware, at prices considerably below the more famous competition. Visitors are welcome at the factory and the adjacent shop. Open daily from May through September and on weekdays during the rest of the year. After Carrick-on-Suir, continue on T13 (N24) to Clonmel, another 13 miles.

CLONMEL According to legend, ancient settlers were led to this town — "meadow of honey" in Irish — by a swarm of bees. It is the chief town of County Tipperary, an administrative, horse-breeding, and cider-making center. St. Patrick is said to have visited the area, which eventually passed into the hands of the powerful Anglo-Norman Butler family. In 1650, the town fell to Cromwell, but only after a stiff resistance led by Hugh Dubh O'Neill. Clonmel runs along the River Suir, with wide O'Connell Street as its major thoroughfare. The Main Guard, a 17th-century building at the eastern end of the street, is said to have been designed by Christopher Wren and has been used as a courthouse, prison, and military headquarters. At the other end of O'Connell Street is West Gate, a 19th-century reconstruction of one of the town's original gates (a portion of the old 14th-century town wall still stands in the graveyard of St. Mary's Church of Ireland on Mary Street). A plaque on one side of West Gate commemorates Laurence Sterne, author of *Tristram Shandy* and a native of Clonmel. Be sure to stop by the 19th-century St. Mary's Catholic Church on O'Connell Street to see the ceiling and the ornate altar; the altar is supposed to have been made for a church in Rome but mysteriously ended up here. The Franciscan friary on Abbey Street has a 13th-century choir wall, a 15th-century tower, and a tiny chapel to St. Francis that contains a Butler family tomb. The library on Parnell Street houses a museum of local interest. Also on Parnell Street is *Hearn's* hotel (see *Checking In*), which at one time was the base of operations for the first Irish passenger transport system. In 1815, Charles Bianconi, an Italian-born resident of Clonmel, sent a horse-drawn carriage to Cahir. The number of vehicles and his network grew, and until the coming of the railways, Bianconi cars carried people all over the south of Ireland.

Clonmel has regular horse-racing meetings, weekly greyhound racing, good fishing in the Suir, and pony trekking into the Comeragh Mountains from Ballmacarberry (about 9 miles south of Clonmel). If time permits a detour, there is a magnificently scenic drive through the Knockmealdown Mountains southwest of town. Take the road to Ardfinnan and then on to Clogheen, where a left turn leads to a height of 1,700 feet and the hairpin curve known as the Vee. The descent travels into Lismore, a town on the River Blackwater and the site of Lismore Castle. Built in the 12th century and remodeled in the 19th century, it is not open to the public, though its gardens are. (The castle itself can be rented by the week; for reservations call 58-54424 several months in advance.) The village of Cappoquin is 4 miles east of Lismore, also on the river, and the stretch of valley between the two is especially beautiful. From Cappoquin, return to the route by following the main Dungarvan road, T30, east as far as the turnoff to T27, and then drive the 20 miles north to Clonmel. Slievenamon, the "mountain of the women," rises to a height of 2,368 feet northeast of Clonmel; it is said that the legendary giant Finn MacCool watched while girls raced up to its summit to win him as a husband.

CHECKING IN

Knocklofty House Set beside the River Suir on 105 acres of grounds about 4 miles east of Clonmel, this 3-story Georgian manor is the former home of the Earls of Donoughmore. Operating as both a hotel and time-share complex, it offers 15 comfortably furnished rooms, all with private baths; a restaurant with views of the river; a cozy lounge; and a galleried library that dates back to 1650. There's also a modern fitness center with an indoor swimming pool, Jacuzzi, sunbed, gym, and squash and tennis courts. Guests can also fish for salmon or trout on a private stretch of river and use the on-site equestrian center for horseback riding and hunting.

Ardfinnan Rd. (R655), Clonmel (phone: 52-38222; fax: 52-38289). Expensive.

Clonmel Arms This comfortable hotel has an elegant dining room and 35 nicely furnished rooms, most with private baths. Sarsfield St., Clonmel (phone: 52-21233; 800-221-2222 from the US; fax: 52-21526). Expensive to moderate.

Hearn's The starting point of Charles Bianconi's transport system still has the clock he used to keep the cars on schedule. This pleasant establishment has 19 rooms, 16 of them with private baths. Dining is a pleasure with a menu featuring fresh seafood, steaks, and creamy rum cheesecake. Parnell St., Clonmel (phone: 52-21611; 800-243-9111 from the US). Moderate.

EATING OUT

La Scala Housed in an old limestone building with original rustic log wood and red brick decor, this dining spot serves beef fondue, chicken in pastry, seafood crêpes, and flambé desserts. Open for dinner; closed Sundays. Reservations necessary. Major credit cards accepted. Market St., Clonmel (phone: 52-24147). Moderate.

En Route from Clonmel Take N24 west for 10 miles to Cahir. The lands of the Butlers also extended to Cahir (meaning "stone fort," and pronounced *Care*), where the family served as the Earls of Glengall. Richard, the second Earl of Glengall, helped plan much of the town, to his financial ruin. He commissioned John Nash to design the local Church of Ireland (1817) and also the *Swiss Cottage Fishing Lodge* (in Cahir Park; phone: 52-41144). Restored in 1989, the fanciful cottage was redecorated by noted Irish designer Sybil Connolly, and it's now open to the public Tuesdays through Sundays in March through November (admission charge). The town is small but pleasant and it prospers from what seems to be an annual influx of filmmakers to Cahir Castle (phone: 52-41011), one of the largest and most splendid medieval castles in Ireland. Built on a rocky inlet in the River Suir where an ancient ring fort may once have stood, the castle dates mainly from the 15th century. It was thought to be impregnable, but it was captured by Robert Devereux, Earl of Essex and Queen Elizabeth's favorite, in 1599, and by Cromwell in 1650, though each time it returned to the hands of the Butlers. It is now restored and open to the public year-round; there's an admission charge. Cashel is 11 miles north of Cahir via N8.

CHECKING IN

Kilcoran Lodge A few miles outside Cahir, on the right side of the Mitchelstown road, this former shooting lodge is a charming country hotel on a slope of the Galtee Mountains. The 25 spacious rooms all have private baths. Facilities include a health and leisure center with an indoor pool, steamroom, sauna, and gym. The food served in the airy dining room is good. Cahir (phone: 52-41288; fax: 52-41994). Expensive.

Carrigeen Castle For unusual but comfortable accommodations, try the bed and breakfast house run by Peggy Butler on the road to Cork. The 4 cozy guestrooms are decorated with antiques; 2 rooms have private baths, the other 2 have sinks. On the Cork road, Cahir (phone: 52-41370). Inexpensive.

EATING OUT

Crock of Gold The restaurant on the upper level of this little crafts shop and bookshop serves light meals daily from 9 AM to 9 PM. No reservations. Major credit cards accepted. 1 Castle St., Cahir (phone: 52-41951). Inexpensive.

Swiss Cottage In the heart of town, opposite the castle, this Old World tavern serves snacks and sandwiches as well as hearty meals of Irish stew, shepherd's pie, or roast beef with horseradish. There is traditional Irish music on tap at night. Open daily for lunch and early dinner until 8 PM. No reservations. No credit cards accepted. 3 Castle St., Cahir (phone: 52-42232). Inexpensive.

CASHEL For more information on this historic town's sights, accommodations, restaurants, and entertainment, see *Cashel* in THE CITIES.

The Dingle Peninsula

The Dingle Peninsula is the northernmost of the mountainous promontories that stick out into the Atlantic from Ireland's southwest coast like toes extended to test the water. It is a jumble of old and varied peaks and cliffs, glacial valleys and lakes, headlands and bays, islands, strands, and great sand dunes stretching 30 miles west from the low-lying country around Tralee through mountains that turn to wild hills and meet the sea in splendid coastlines. The peninsula is blessed with a remoteness that has been an inspiration to poets and religious ascetics alike.

Dingle's dramatic rendering of nature's bare essentials never ceases to delight visitors. On a clear day it offers stunning views: great panoramic expanses of green stopped by shimmering ribbons of water in the distance, then the farther gray-blue outline of the next peninsula, island, or rocky point, itself backlit by the phosphorescence of fine, silver-edged clouds. On a less clear day when the depth of the scene diminishes, the eye is drawn to the hedgerows by the roadside, made up in spring of white hawthorn or yellow-flowering furze bushes, of languorous drapings of honeysuckle, or of purplish fuchsia just bursting into bloom. Where they part, they reveal the patchwork of fields beyond and an ample sampling of Ireland's green.

Dingle's topography is mountainous, but not in the Alpine way. The landscape rises — from the eastern Slieve Mish Mountains to the western Brandon Mountains — to rounded and treeless peaks. Dingle is also alive with legend and folklore, its remote fastnesses the stamping ground of mythological heroes such as Cu Chulainn, its ports guarded by the larger-than-life Finn MacCool and his warrior army, the Fianna.

The peninsula is particularly rich in antiquities, especially prehistoric and early Christian remains, among them *galláns* (standing stones), ogham stones (pillars inscribed with the earliest form of Irish writing), and *clocháns* (circular beehive huts). Grouped in fraternal clusters or alone as solitary cells, monks isolated themselves in the *clocháns* on Ireland's lonely western fringes in the early days of Irish Christianity. The eremitical offshoot of Irish monasticism was nowhere stronger than in Kerry. Perched on the ledge of a wave-pounded rock or on the quieter summit of a deserted hill, the hermit monks could ponder at length both the awesome and the gentle face of God in nature. Not all beehive huts are ancient, however. Farmers continue to copy the technique for modern animal shelters and sheds, one of many ways Dingle's timeless appearance endures to confound seekers of authenticity.

Time has also stood still on Dingle in the matter of language. Its western reaches are part of the Gaeltacht, the collective name for the few surviving Irish-speaking areas of Ireland where geography protected what was lost elsewhere under British rule. The native Irish tongue can be heard in villages such as Dunquin and Ballyferriter, whose people use it daily, though they also speak English.

The scenic route around the peninsula is roughly in the shape of a figure eight, with the town of Dingle at the crossing. Roads are narrow and twisting but they're easy to negotiate just the same, and there's no trouble with traffic — though an unsuspecting traveler may round a bend and come upon a traveling bank truck or a collie herding the cattle home. The drive is best on a very bright day and to be avoided, if possible, in mist or continuous rain. The entire peninsula is manageable in a long day trip of approximately 100 miles from Tralee and back, including time for lunch in Dingle Town, through which the route passes twice. Though Tralee, where our route begins, is the usual gateway to Dingle, the peninsula itself offers plenty of bed and breakfast houses and farms plus small hotels and guest homes and, in Dingle Town, two modern hotels and several good guesthouses.

A double room in a hotel described as expensive will cost $100 or more for a night; a place in the moderate category will cost from $50 to $100; and a place described as inexpensive will cost $50 or less. A meal for two in an expensive restaurant (without wine, drinks, and tips) will cost $60 or more; in a moderate place, from $35 to $55; and in an inexpensive eatery, $30 or less. For each location, hotels and restaurants are listed alphabetically by price category.

TRALEE This friendly, busy trading center of 21,000 people is the chief town of County Kerry and one of the most active in southern Ireland. It grew up around the 13th-century Desmond Castle, but was destroyed at the end of the 17th century, so the oldest parts of the town that remain today — the Georgian terraces on Denny Street and in Day Place, and St. John's Cathedral Church — are mainly from the 18th and 19th centuries. Tralee's major antiquity is the ruined Rathass Church, about a mile east, dating from the 9th and 10th centuries. Inside is a stone commemorating an 8th-century notable in ogham, the earliest form of Irish writing. Ogham consists of groups of strokes and dots related to a spinal line and it arose, probably on this peninsula, around the beginning of the Christian era.

Tralee has a racecourse and an 18-hole golf course designed by Arnold Palmer, plus salmon and trout fishing in its rivers, excellent deep-sea fishing, and a choice of beaches, sailing, skin diving, and horseback riding. The Tralee Tourist Office is located beside the Town Park at Ashe Memorial Hall (Denny St.; phone: 66-21288). This hall is also the setting for the town's main indoor attraction, the *Kerry County Museum and Medieval Experience* (phone: 66-27777). A multifaceted look at Tralee and County Kerry, it includes an introductory 10-minute multi-image video program; the museum is a series of exhibits on the county's landscape, customs, history, legends, and archaeology, including items of local origin that were previously on view at the *National Museum* in Dublin; and *Geraldine Tralee,* a theme park–style ride that glides visitors through a re-creation of Tralee's streets, houses, and abbeys during the Middle Ages. Open daily; closed in January and February; admission charge .

Tralee is also the home of *Siamsa Tíre* (pronounced Shee-*am*-sah *teer*), the *National Folk Theatre of Ireland* (on the Green, next to the tourist office; phone: 66-23055), which brings to life the customs of the Irish countryside through a program of music, singing, dancing, and mime several nights each week from June through September, with other more international shows during the rest of the year. Tralee's greatest attraction, however, is the *Rose of Tralee International Festival,* otherwise known as the *Festival of Kerry,* a week of carnival-like pageantry at the end of August or the beginning of September. This is Ireland's biggest bash and its highlight is the crowning of the Rose, the loveliest young woman of Irish descent in the world and the one who best exemplifies the qualities of the original Rose of Tralee (subject of a song by William Mulchinock, who was born and died here). For details, see *Feis and Fleadh: The Best Festivals* in DIVERSIONS.

In addition, Tralee is fast gaining a reputation as a hub for the visual arts, with at least three new galleries offering exhibits of contemporary Irish art, including the *Wellspring Gallery* (16 Denney St.; phone: 66-21218), *The Art Gallery* (Ballyard; phone: 66-21915), and *Bin Ban Gallery* (Rock St.; no phone).

CHECKING IN

Brandon One of the largest hotels in County Kerry, this centrally located lodging is standard modern in style but genial in its operation. All 154 rooms have private baths. There's also a dining room, a coffee shop, a pub, a nightclub, and a leisure center with indoor pool, sauna, solarium, steamroom, and gym. Princes St., Tralee (phone: 66-23333; 800-223-6510 or 800-44-UTELL from the US; fax: 66-25019). Expensive.

Ballygarry House This country inn with a private garden has an Old World look, complete with open fireplaces, 16 individually decorated bedrooms with private baths, and a restaurant serving mostly continental cooking. About 1½ miles from town on the Killarney road, Leebrook, Tralee (phone: 66-21233; fax: 66-27630). Moderate.

Earl of Desmond In a grassy setting 2 miles south of Tralee, this modern motor hotel has 50 rooms with private baths and wide picture windows. There is a restaurant, a lounge, tennis courts and access to a private stretch of the River Laune for fishing. Closed December through February. Killarney Rd., Tralee (phone: 66-21299; fax: 66-21976). Moderate.

EATING OUT

Duffin's Conveniently located opposite the *Siamsa Tíre* and next to the *Brandon* hotel, this restaurant is situated in the basement of a 4-story Georgian townhouse. Chef Rory Duffin offers dishes such as wild salmon on a bed of pasta, grilled Dingle sole, whole lobsters, roast loin of lamb, beef Wellington, and steak Diane. Open daily for lunch and dinner. Reservations necessary. Major credit cards accepted. 14 Princes St. (phone: 66-21300). Expensive to moderate.

Heritage For Old World ambience, try this restaurant in the heart of the town at the *Imperial* hotel. It offers a menu of traditional dishes such as roast beef with Yorkshire pudding and Irish stew, as well as seafood specialties ranging from lobster or prawn thermidor to filet of turbot in vodka butter and lobster cream. Open daily. Reservations advised. Major credit cards accepted. 27 Denny St. (phone: 66-22059). Moderate.

Tankard This restaurant with sweeping seascape views offers shellfish from Tralee Bay as well as steaks, duck, chicken, and quail. Open daily for lunch and dinner year-round. Reservations advised. Major credit cards accepted. Six miles west of Tralee. Fenit (phone: 66-36164 or 66-36349). Moderate.

Oyster Tavern Visit this pub/restaurant for seafood cooked in a straightforward manner. Favorites include seafood chowder, grilled crab claws, lobster, scallops, and Atlantic salmon. Open daily for lunch and dinner year-round. Reservations unnecessary. Diners Club, MasterCard, and Visa accepted. About 3 miles west of Tralee at Spa, site of a popular watering place in the 18th century (phone: 66-36102). Moderate to inexpensive.

Brogue Inn This big barn of a pub — strewn with agricultural instruments — is a good place for a light lunch. Open daily for lunch and pub grub dinners. Reservations unnecessary. No credit cards. Rock St., Tralee (phone: 66-22126). Inexpensive.

En Route from Tralee The road to Dingle (T68) runs along the 19th-century ship canal to Blennerville, which is unusual for its restored windmill and visitors' center with its emigration exhibit, crafts shop, and gallery. Between Blennerville and Ballyard (on the outskirts of Tralee), the *Tralee-Blennerville Steam Railway* (phone: 66-28888) now operates daily 1½-mile sightseeing runs. Founded in 1891, it was originally one of the world's most impressive narrow-gauge railways, linking Tralee with the Dingle Peninsula. It ceased operation as a commercial enterprise in 1953, but the locomotive and cars were restored in 1992 as a tourist attraction. The train runs from April through September, on the hour from Tralee and on the half hour from Blennerville.

Less than a mile from the visitors' center, where a roadway comes from the left, the 12th-to-13th-century Annagh Church is hidden on the right on a site some claim is the birthplace of Brendan the Navigator, the 6th-century saint reputed to have discovered America even before the Vikings. (Fenit, across Tralee Bay, is the more likely birthplace.) Continuing out onto the peninsula, along its northern edge, there are wonderfully scenic views. The Slieve Mish Mountains are inland to the left, and to the right a sweep of green tilts gently down to magnificent beaches on the bay, the green scattered with grazing cattle and sheep to the very edge of the pale gold sand.

The tracks of the old *Tralee and Dingle Railway* are along the route, now on one side, now on the other. Where the road divides just before Camp, going right for Castlegregory and left for Dingle, take the left fork and then turn left again under the broken arch of the old railway line and head straight across the peninsula toward Aughils. The mountain to the left of this road is Caherconree. Near its summit, the curious rock formation with cliffs on three sides and a narrow approach cut off by a substantial wall is a promontory fort dating from the Iron Age (which began in Ireland about 500 BC and lasted until the arrival of St. Patrick in the 5th century AD). It is notable not only because it is inland (most of the other promontory forts on the peninsula are on the coast) but also because it is said to have been the home of Cu Roi Mac Daire, a figure from a cycle of legends dealing with Iron Age heroes. Cu Roi was killed by Cu Chulainn, a small, fierce, brave man and a womanizer, after the former had stolen the beautiful Blathnaid, a woman for whom Cu Chulainn had set his cap. There are breathtaking views from the fort, reached via a marked hiking trail that begins some distance farther along the road, and there are equally memorable views — of Dingle Bay and the Iveragh Peninsula — as the road descends to Aughils and Inch. At the sea road at Aughils, turn right. Inch is only 4 miles away.

INCH This sheltered seaside resort is at the base of the Inch Peninsula. Contrary to its name, the peninsula provides a 4-mile strip of firm, golden sand that is excellent for bathing. The beach is backed by high dunes that have yielded evidence of mysterious sand hill dwellers who lived here in the Iron Age and perhaps earlier.

ANASCAUL The inland village of Anascaul, 4 miles west of Inch, is known as the location of the *South Pole Inn*. Now a pub where you can stop for a drink (no food served), this was once the home of Thomas Crean, a member of Robert Falcon Scott's last and fatal expedition to Antarctica (1910–12). A signposted detour north from the town leads, in about 2 miles, to the beautiful Lough Anascaul in a boulder-scattered valley. This lovely place is the setting of another Cu Chulainn story: A giant was carrying off a girl, Scál, but Cu Chulainn came to her rescue. From the mountains on either side of the lake, the giants threw great stones at each other. Cu Chulainn was wounded and Scál, thinking him dead, drowned herself in the water.

En Route from Anascaul Here the road rejoins the main Tralee–Dingle road, T68. Continuing west, it next passes through Lispole. Less than a mile farther, look left for the *gallán* (standing stone) of Ballineetig, about 100 yards from the road. This Bronze Age gravestone is the largest on the peninsula. The roughly pointed tip shows that it was a monument for a man — the tips on monuments for women were scooped out.

A bit farther along the road, there is a good view of Dingle Harbour. Still farther, turn left after the sign indicating an accident blackspot (a place with a bad record for auto accidents), then make a sharp left at a house. A third of a mile beyond this, in a field on the left, is the little burial place of Ballintaggart, an important site for the study of ogham stones — stones engraved with the earliest form of Irish writing. Inside the circular wall are nine rounded stones inscribed with an unusual form of the Old Irish, or ogham, alphabet. (Ogham consists of groups of strokes and dots related to a spinal line, but in this case the spinal line is omitted.) The inscription on one stone commemorates the "three sons of Mailagnos," the next has a long Latin cross, and two others have short Greek crosses, possibly added later as Christianity began to replace paganism. Before leaving Ballintaggart, take a moment to enjoy the splendid sight of the Skellig Rocks off the coast of the Iveragh Peninsula in the distance. Then return to the main road and drive the remaining 1½ miles into Dingle.

DINGLE The peninsula's chief town lies at the foot of a steep slope on the north side of the harbor and is bounded on three sides by hills. It was the main port of Kerry in the old Spanish trading days, and in the reign of Queen Elizabeth I it was important enough as an outpost to merit a protective wall. In the 18th century, Dingle became a smuggling center, and during the French Revolution, a local man, Colonel James Rice, was the linchpin of a plot to rescue Marie Antoinette and spirit her to "the highest house on the hill," on Main Street. She refused to go, however, when she learned that her family would not go with her. The house has since been replaced by the Catholic presbytery. Today Dingle's population of 1,400 is dependent on fishing and tourism. Deep-sea fishing facilities are excellent, bathing is good at various beaches in the vicinity, and there is pony trekking into the surrounding hills. Traditional Irish music sessions are often held at the rough-hewn, barn-like *O'Flaherty's Pub* (Bridge St.; phone: 66-51461); order a Guinness, pull up an orange crate, and sit down and listen. Also worth a visit are *Murphy's* (Strand St.; phone: 66-51450) and *Tabairne an Droicead Beag* (The Small Bridge; Lower Main St.; phone: 66-51723), which both offer Irish traditional music and a friendly atmosphere.

Dingle is also the gateway to the West Kerry Gaeltacht, the Irish-speaking district, as well as a good base for extended exploration of the archaeological antiquities of this rich area. Begin with the enormous rock called a *bullaun* on Main Street. It has holes in it and was probably used for grinding hard wheat in early Christian times.

A unique attraction in recent years has been "Fungie," a dolphin that swam solo into the waters of Dingle Harbour and has remained frolicking off the coast ever since. Some of the more enterprising local boat owners have built up a business ferrying visitors to see — or swim beside — Fungie. Inquire at the harbor office or call 66-51629 to check on sightings and schedules.

CHECKING IN

Benner's Originally a coaching inn, this 250-year-old hotel in the heart of town has been restored by American owners. Each of the 25 bedrooms has a private bathroom, and the furnishings are a blend of brass, etched glass, and local antiques. Facilities include a restaurant, a walled garden, and a pub-style lounge. Closed January to mid-March. Main St., Dingle (phone: 66-51638; fax: 66-51412). Expensive.

Skelligs Sitting on the eastern edge of town in an ideal location overlooking Dingle Bay, this contemporary 3-story establishment has been expanded and totally refurbished. The 75 rooms in this Best Western affiliate are bright and airy and feature private baths/showers, TV sets, and telephones. Public areas include a restaurant with a bay view, a lounge with musical entertainment on most summer evenings, and a leisure center with a heated pool, exercise room, saunas, and tanning beds. There's also an outdoor tennis court; local fishing and boating trips can be arranged. Closed mid-November to mid-March. Dingle (phone: 66-51144; 800-528-1234 from the US; fax: 66-51501). Expensive.

Doyle's Townhouse In the heart of town sits this little gem, an outgrowth of the successful *Doyle's Seafood Bar* next door (see *Eating Out*). The public areas are rich in Victorian and Edwardian antiques, while the 8 rooms of varying sizes all boast telephones, TV sets, adjustable beds, and modern bathrooms of Italian marble. Open mid-March to mid-November. John St., Dingle (phone: 66-51174; 800-223-6510 from the US; fax: 66-51816). Moderate.

Alpine House A modern, centrally heated guesthouse with 14 rooms, each with private bath/shower. At the entrance to Dingle Town, it offers pleasant views, a lounge, and a dining room. Open March through November. Dingle (phone: 66-51250). Inexpensive.

Greenmount House Set on a hillside overlooking Dingle Harbour and town, this wonderful, modern, bungalow-type home of John and Mary Curran has 8 guestrooms with such hotel-style comforts as private baths, telephones, and TV sets. A plant-filled conservatory is the setting for delicious and innovative breakfasts (ham and pineapple toasties, smoked salmon), and guests have access to an enclosed porch and a sitting room with picture-window views. Open year-round. No credit cards accepted. John St., Gortonora, Dingle (phone: 66-51414). Inexpensive.

EATING OUT

Beginish Named after an island off the Kerry coast, this restaurant is one of the best in the area. Situated in a Georgian townhouse, there are two small, elegant dining rooms, one with a fireplace and the other overlooking the gardens. The short but varied menu ranges from rack of lamb and filet of beef to seafood *à la nage* (a mini-tureen of scallops, prawns, mussels, monkfish, and salmon, with vegetables and herbs in Pernod sauce). Desserts are light and delicious. Open for dinner only; closed Mondays and from December through mid-March. Reservations necessary. Major credit cards accepted. Green St. (phone: 66-51588). Expensive to moderate.

Doyle's Seafood Bar In a small town known for its fine restaurants, this is the leader; its award-winning specialties include a unique nettle (spinach-like) soup, crab bisque, local lobster, and a popular seafood Mornay. Picnickers can buy homemade brown bread and smoked salmon to go. Open for dinner only; closed Sundays and from mid-November through mid-March. Reservations advised. Major credit cards accepted. John St., Dingle (phone: 66-51174). Moderate.

Lord Baker's Housed in what is believed to be the oldest pub in Dingle, this restaurant is named after a 19th-century Dingle publican, entrepreneur, orator, politician, and poet. The menu offers bar food such as crab claws or prawns in garlic butter, or dinner specialties such as fresh lobster, duck with orange sauce, or baked chicken with herb stuffing. Open daily for lunch and dinner year-round. Reservations advised for dinner. MasterCard and Visa accepted. Main St. (phone: 66-51277). Moderate.

Islandman With volumes of books lining the shelves on the walls, this restaurant/bar features an eclectic mix of bar food, as well as more substantial dishes ranging from Atlantic salmon and crab claws to baked chicken or steaks. Open daily from 9 AM to 8 PM; closed January and February. Reservations advised for dinner. MasterCard and Visa accepted. Main St. (phone: 66-51803). Moderate to inexpensive.

An Café Liteartha Serving simple fare such as salads, casseroles, and sandwiches, this place is best known for its bookshop, with an excellent section on Ireland and the Irish. Open daily year-round. No reservations. No credit cards accepted. Dykegate St., Dingle (phone: 66-51388). Inexpensive.

En Route from Dingle Head west out of town, passing the marina. To the right is Ceardlann na Coille, a craft village on a hillside, where over a half-dozen craftspeople sell their wares, from knitwear and handwoven articles to wood and leather goods, pottery, and art. Continue out of town, and at the junction take the road in the direction of Slea Head. Just beyond a modern cemetery at Milltown is an interesting set of antiquities inside a gate on the right. The site, an ancient burial ground referred to as the "gates of glory," consists of one great *gallán* (standing stone), two others that have fallen, and broken pieces of more stones. The mysterious writings on top of one of the fallen *galláns* were made by early metalworkers who came to Ireland from Spain some 4,000 years ago. The scooped-out hollows are called cup marks. Many such stones can be found in Kerry, but no one has yet offered an adequate interpretation of them.

VENTRY About 4 miles from Dingle, this little village has a delightful beach. In Irish legend, Ventry Harbour was the scene of a great battle won by the hero Finn MacCool and his warriors, the Fianna, against the forces of the "king of the world," Daire Donn, who crammed the harbor with his ships and was held off for a year and a day before his forces were wiped out to the last man. Keep an eye open for the *Ventry Inn,* a modern pub with panoramic views and a congenial place to have a drink or a cup of coffee. Beyond the harbor, the road continues to Slea Head on the lower slopes of Mt. Eagle, providing lovely coastal views of Dingle Bay. The cliff-hugging part of the route is particularly scenic and will be familiar to those who saw the film *Ryan's Daughter.* The area from Ventry to Slea Head is also rich in archaeological remains.

DUNBEG AND FAHAN Just under 4 miles from Ventry, an Iron Age promontory fort, Dunbeg, can be seen below the road to the left. In addition to the wall that cuts off the triangular promontory, there are four earthen defensive rings, an underground escape passage *(souterrain)* at the entrance, and the remains of an inner house. Dunbeg may have been the first bridgehead established by the people who built the ancient town of Fahan, site of the greatest collection of antiquities in all of Ireland. Fahan consists of more than 400 *clocháns* (circular beehive huts constructed without mortar of overlapped or corbeled stones), cave dwellings, standing and inscribed stones and crosses, *souterrains,* forts, and a church — the remains of more than 500 structures and monuments in all — strewn along an old road above the main road for about 3 miles. The best way to see this settlement, which was possibly a full-fledged community between the 6th and 10th centuries, as large then as Dingle is now, is to keep to the main road until it passes the small ford at Glenfahan, after which a sign indicates the beehive huts. These are among the most interesting and convenient *clocháns* in the country. The owners of the property expect a small payment from visitors.

SLEA HEAD The road from Dingle continues to Slea Head at the tip of the peninsula, where the view of the Blasket Islands, the westernmost point in Europe (except for Iceland), is spectacular. In September 1588, four ships of the Spanish Armada were driven by storms through Blasket Sound. Two reached shelter, but a third, the *Santa Maria de la Rosa,* came flying through the sound with its sails in tatters, crashed onto a rock, and sank, as did the fourth, the *San Juan de Ragusa.* (The remains of the *Santa Maria de la Rosa* were found at the bottom of Blasket Sound in the late 1960s.) The beach between Slea Head and the next promontory, Dunmore Head, is Coumeenole Strand, attractive but dangerous for swimming.

BLASKET ISLANDS This now-deserted group of 7 islands was inhabited from prehistoric times by an Irish-speaking community. The largest island,

Great Blasket (4 miles long and three-quarters of a mile wide), was "the next parish to America" until 1953, when the population of barely 100, no longer able to support itself after several disastrous fishing seasons, resettled on the mainland. Blasket Islanders were adept at the art of storytelling and produced a number of books. The best-selling *Twenty Years A-growing* by Maurice O'Sullivan; *The Islander,* a masterpiece by Thomas O'Crohan; and *Peig* by Peig Sayers were all written by island natives. Boats to the Blaskets sometimes can be hired in Dunquin, north of Slea Head. There is no scheduled ferry service.

En Route from Slea Head The road leaves the seacoast to cut across Dunmore Head and continues north to Dunquin along a coast where many forms of fossils can be found. At Dunquin Harbour, the colored Silurian rocks in the cliffs are 400 million years old. A new visitors'-interpretative center is under way on the hillside overlooking Dunquin Harbour. Slated to open this year, it will offer an audiovisual program and various historic and geographic exhibits focusing on life on the Dingle Peninsula. From Dunquin there are fairly regular sailings in summer to the Blaskets. After Dunquin, the route passes Clogher Head and turns inland toward the village of Ballyferriter. Watch for Liam Mulcahy's pottery workshop (known in Gaelic as *Potadóireacht na Caolóige;* phone: 66-56229) at Clogher, where travelers can see potters at work and buy some of the simple, colorful pieces they produce.

BALLYFERRITER Here is a small, mostly Irish-speaking village whose population is increased in summer by students enrolled in Irish language schools. The ruined Castle Sybil, the home of the Anglo-Norman Ferriter family, is about 2 miles northwest of the village just above Ferriter's Cove. The castle was the birthplace of Kerry poet and patriot Piaras Ferriter, an insurgent leader who was hanged by the Cromwellians in 1653. Castle Sybil is said to be named after Sybil Lynch of Galway, who eloped with a Ferriter. When her father sought her out she hid in the cave beneath the castle and was drowned by the rising tide.

Smerwick Harbour is about a mile north of Ballyferriter. The small Dún An Oir (Golden Fort) once stood on a promontory in the harbor. In 1580, an expedition of some 600 men financed by the pope — mainly Italians, but also Spanish, Irish, and English — entrenched at the fort to support the cause of the Catholic Irish against the Protestant English in what was the first significant invasion of the British Isles for many centuries. The English bombarded the fort from land and sea and soon its defenders capitulated. Once disarmed, they were slaughtered, and word of the massacre of Smerwick rang throughout Europe, a warning to anyone who might again attempt to invade the queen's territory.

CHECKING IN/EATING OUT

Dún An Oir A pleasant hotel popular with families, it features 21 rooms and 20 cottages. There's also a restaurant, featuring fresh seafood; a tennis court;

a heated outdoor pool; a sauna; and a children's playroom. Smerwick Harbour (phone: 66-56133).

En Route from Ballyferriter Follow the main road east, keeping to the left (avoid the narrow road that bears right up a hill). Turn right at a gasoline pump, cross over the bridge, then, almost immediately, turn right again. The recently excavated eremitical and monastic site of Reask is a short distance down this road (about three-quarters of a mile east of Ballyferriter). This gives visitors a good idea of the layout of an early — perhaps 7th- or 8th-century — monastery. Return by the same road, turn right, and follow the signposts for the Gallarus Oratory, about 4 miles northwest of Dingle.

GALLARUS ORATORY This small, rectangular church in the shape of an upturned boat is the best example of dry-rubble masonry in Ireland and probably the most perfect piece of early Irish architecture extant. Oratories are standard in monastic sites, but everywhere except here and on the remote Skellig Rocks, the unmortared roofs have fallen in from the great weight of their stones. Gallarus, which is still completely watertight, may date from as early as the 8th century, though the mastery of the corbel technique used in its building suggests a later date to some experts — perhaps as late as the 11th or 12th century. Aside from a cross pillar, signs of an early monastic settlement around it are yet to be found.

KILMALKEDAR At the crossroads north of Gallarus, take a sharp left to see the remains of Kilmalkedar Church, a fine example of Irish Romanesque architecture. The nave was built in the mid-12th century, the chancel a little later. Look inside the church for the "alphabet" stone, crudely carved with a Latin cross and the Latin alphabet, used for instruction in an early-7th-century school. A holed stone inside and another with ogham outside recall Indian yoni stones, through which worshipers would have to pass to achieve regeneration. Reminiscent of these practices, the east window of the medieval church is known as the "eye of the needle," through which the faithful must pass to be saved. A well-carved pre-Christian sundial and a large, crudely cut cross, one of the few in Kerry, are also outside.

Just north of the church is a roadway, and where it forks, the 15th-century St. Brendan's house is on the left. This was probably a presbytery for the church and had nothing to do with St. Brendan. The old Saints' Road, which ran through this area bisecting the fork, however, led to the top of Mt. Brandon, named after St. Brendan, who is said to have had his retreat there.

En Route from Kilmalkedar Continue on the road beyond town and, at the T-junction, turn right and follow the signposts for Brandon Creek. It was from this spot that St. Brendan is reputed to have set out on his 6th-century voyages searching for the Land of Promise and, the legend goes, discovering America. Two 9th-century manuscripts, one recounting the story of his life and the other the story of his travels, were immensely popular in early medieval Europe and provided inspiration for many voyagers, including Columbus. At least as far as his travels are concerned, however, there may have been some confusion between the saint's name and that of the hero of an Irish pagan story, *The Voyage of Bran*. Bran and his Kerry companions traveled to magical western islands and, returning from one voyage, put ashore at Brandon Point, northeast of here. By this account, it was Bran, not St. Brendan, who gave his name to the great Mt. Brandon.

From Brandon Creek, turn back toward Dingle. Just 2 miles along, after crossing the Saints' Road again, turn left and drive up as far as possible. The 3,127-foot summit of Mt. Brandon, Ireland's second-highest peak, is most accessible from this spot. It's about a 3½-mile walk to the top, and on a clear day the views are magnificent. Return to Dingle and take the Connor Pass road out of town.

CONNOR PASS Driving this road demands great care and it should be avoided in bad weather. Leave Dingle by the unclassified road marked Connor (or Conair) Pass, which climbs northeast between the Brandon and the central Dingle groups of mountains. The summit (1,500 feet) provides magnificent views in both directions, south over Dingle Town and Dingle Bay, north to the bays of Brandon and Tralee, the great beaches of north Kerry, and on to the mouth of the Shannon. The road descends between cliffs and valleys and then, below the pass, continues east running parallel to beautiful beaches on Brandon Bay. At Stradbally, take the left fork for Castlegregory.

CASTLEGREGORY The castle from which this tiny village got its name is now gone. It was built in the 16th century by a local chief, Gregory Hoare, whose daughter-in-law came to grief in 1580 when she poured out all the castle's wine rather than offer it to her country's enemies, Lord Grey and his English troops, who were lodging at the castle on their way to attack the fort at Smerwick Harbour. Her husband killed her in a fit of rage, and the next day he himself died suddenly. The village is at the neck of a sandy spit of land that separates the Tralee and Brandon bays. Beyond the limestone tip of the spit are the Magharee Islands, also known as the Seven Hogs. On one of these, Illauntannig — as on nearly every remote outcropping of rock in western Kerry — remains of an early Christian monastic settlement have been found. Arranging a boat to the island can be done only with difficulty, and the ruins are in poor condition. Most visitors are content with a drive out along the spit from Castlegregory or a visit to Lough Gill, west of the village, an attractive lake noted for its waterfowl, including a species of swan that comes all the way from Siberia to winter here.

En Route from Castlegregory Continue east, and at the town of Camp take T68 back to Tralee, which is only 20 miles north of Killarney, the gateway to the *Ring of Kerry* route.

County Clare

Clare, in the middle of the west coast of Ireland, has retained much of the past — a sturdy political and economic independence, a music livelier and more varied than that of other parts of Ireland, a tenacious grasp on folk traditions, and a speech dotted with the remnants of Irish language forms.

The landscape of Clare is varied. Heading inward from the coast, the terrain changes strikingly, from the wild rocky sea cliffs to the marshy uplands behind them to the central limestone plain dotted with lakes to the great brown hills of the east. In the north is the Burren country, a stony moonscape plateau.

History has left many interesting remains in Clare. Scattered over the northern hills are more than 150 dolmens, or Stone Age tombs, of the farmers who migrated here from France 5,000 years ago. There are nearly 3,000 circular forts in earth and stone, the fortified settlements of the farmers' Celtic successors. There are also more than 200 castles still standing, the earliest ones built by the Normans, the later by the Irish. Traces of the early Catholic church are also found in Clare. Most "churches" are of the eremitical type; there are several on Scattery Island, St. Senan's monastic retreat in the mouth of the Shannon, and they dot the islets and the hillsides up the coast. Such ruins are particularly plentiful in the Burren where the early hermits found the isolation they desired; here the stony desert is dotted with oratories, "saints' beds" or shrines, wells, and stone crosses.

The people of Clare have long been known as mature and practiced politicians, wise and pragmatic when choosing a leader. In the 10th century they picked Brian Ború, head of an obscure clan called the Dalg Cais. They fought for him until he became first King of Munster and then High King of Ireland; they died with him as he defeated the Vikings on the coast of Dublin Bay. During the great upsurge of Irish democracy in the 19th century they voted in Daniel O'Connell as Member of Parliament for Clare, and they supported Charles Stewart Parnell in the Land League Movement. In this century they elected Eamon De Valera as a representative to Parliament; he later became *Taoiseach* (head of the Irish government), and in 1959 was elected President of Ireland.

Although most Clare folk still pursue a rural lifestyle on small dairy farms, they are gradually adapting to a new world. The international airport at Shannon not only has established a duty-free zone and nurtured an industrial park with many welcome new jobs, but also has made County Clare the major western gateway to Ireland, creating opportunities in the transportation, tourism, and service industries.

Our route begins in Limerick City, which is where most people spend their first night after landing at Shannon. From here, the route travels to

Ennis, capital of Clare, then along the River Shannon through numerous little towns out to the lonely peninsula of Loop Head. From this wild Atlantic seascape, the road turns north to the resort towns of Kilkee and Lahinch and on to the great Cliffs of Moher. An eastern leg explores the wonderland of the Burren with its unusual rock formations, caves, flora, and ruins.

Except in the Limerick City area, which has many large new hotels, accommodations in County Clare tend to be small hotels or bed and breakfast houses. In this area, expect to pay $100 or more a night for a double room at those places listed as expensive; from $60 to $95 at places in the moderate category; and under $60 a night for inexpensive accommodations. A meal for two, excluding wine, tips, or drinks, will cost $75 or more in places listed as expensive; $40 to $75 in moderate restaurants; and under $40 in those restaurants listed as inexpensive. For each location, hotels and restaurants are listed alphabetically by price category.

LIMERICK CITY For a detailed report on the city, its hotels, and restaurants, see *Limerick City,* THE CITIES.

En Route from Limerick City About 20 miles down the main Limerick–Ennis road (N18) is the tiny village of Newmarket-on-Fergus, which owes its name to a track-crazy 18th-century landlord who renamed it after the great center of English horse racing. The long demesne wall beyond the town encloses Dromoland Castle, which is well worth a look. It was once the home of the O'Briens, Earls of Inchiquin, descendants of the High King Brian Ború, and is now the deluxe *Dromoland Castle* hotel (see *Limerick City,* in THE CITIES).

ENNIS Just 18½ miles northwest of Limerick lies the county seat of Clare (pop. 8,000), with a narrow, winding main street intersected by even narrower lanes, and a lively medieval charm. Off Francis Street are the ruins of a Franciscan friary founded about 1240 by Donough Mor O'Brien. A monument to Daniel O'Connell, the Liberator, who secured Catholic emancipation and sat in Parliament for Clare, is in O'Connell Square. The modern *De Valera Library and Museum* (Harmony Row; phone: 65-21616), which was ingeniously adapted from a disused church, houses mementos of Irish history. Outside of town on the Limerick road are signposts to Clare Abbey, the now undistinguished and abandoned ruins of an Augustinian monastery established in 1189 by Donal Mor O'Brien, King of Munster.

CHECKING IN

Old Ground One of the rooms in this ivy-clad, centrally located 17th-century hotel was once the Town Hall and another was the town jail. In all there are 61 rooms with private baths, some decorated with antiques and others with a more modern decor. There is a fireplace in the lobby, a restaurant, and the *Poet's Corner* bar, a great spot to meet the locals. O'Connell St., Ennis (phone: 65-28127; 800-CALL-THF or 800-FORTE-40 from the US; fax: 65-28112). Expensive.

West County Inn Situated just south of town, this is a large, modern Best Western affiliate with 109 rooms, each with private bath. Facilities include a fitness center with a sauna, Jacuzzi, plunge pool, steamroom, snooker room, and 2 hard-surface tennis courts. Other pluses are a coffee shop, a restaurant, a conservatory, and a lounge featuring traditional Irish music. Dinner dances are held every Saturday evening, and Irish cabaret shows are staged on summer evenings. Clare Rd., Ennis (phone: 65-28421; 800-528-1234 or 800-473-8954 from the US; fax: 65-28801). Moderate.

EATING OUT

Cloister Next to Ennis Abbey, this landmark houses both a homey pub and a fine dining room. The pub is noted for its inexpensive all-day lunch menu including fisherman's pie and hot crab claws; the restaurant is quite another matter, with such specialties as baked Atlantic seafood in champagne sauce, pan-fried sirloin steak with brandy and herb butter, roast loin of lamb with port and mustard crust, and grilled golden sole with prawns. Save room for Grand Marnier mousse or blackberry and apple strudel. A pianist or harpist entertains nightly. Open daily for lunch and dinner. Reservations necessary for dinner. Major credit cards accepted. Abbey St., Ennis (phone: 65-29521). Expensive.

Brogan's This atmospheric old pub serves steaks, smoked salmon, soup, and sandwiches. There is traditional Irish music on Tuesday and Thursday nights. Open daily for lunch and dinner. Reservations advised for dinner. Major credit cards accepted. 24 O'Connell St., Ennis (phone: 65-29859). Moderate.

En Route from Ennis L51 travels along the bank of the Shannon estuary 26 miles to Kilrush. The landscape is gentle and pastoral, offering fine views across the Shannon of the little wooded harbor town of Foynes, of Glin with its Regency castle, and of Tarbert with its lighthouse and electric power station. At Killimer a car ferry crosses every hour on the hour to Tarbert on the Kerry shore. For schedules and fares call 65-51060.

KILRUSH The chief market town of southwest Clare, it has a new 250-berth marina and a number of small industries, including a factory for processing seaweed. Just outside Kilrush is Cappagh Pier. From here boats go to Scattery Island, the monastic retreat founded in the 6th century by St. Senan. On the island are five early churches dating from the 9th to the 11th century and a 120-foot round tower, the tallest in Ireland.

EATING OUT

Malone's Haven Arms Ale House Restored and refurbished, this Old World pub in the middle of town is a good lunch stop. The menu includes tasty soup, sandwiches, and traditional hot dishes. Open daily for lunch and pub grub dinners. Reservations unnecessary. No credit cards accepted. 10-12 Henry St., Kilrush (phone: 65-51267). Moderate to inexpensive.

En Route from Kilrush Take T41 toward Kilkee, a stretch that passes through the rushy, windswept landscape typical of south Clare. About 6 miles along, there's a sign for a holy well; turn left and in 2½ miles the tidily kept well dedicated to St. Martin comes into view. Turning back from the well, head straight east, parallel to the estuary for some unforgettable views of this western coast.

LOOP HEAD PENINSULA The first hamlet along the road, Doonaha, is the birthplace of Eugene O'Curry, a pioneer 19th-century Irish scholar and topographer. The road hits the estuary again at Carrigaholt, a picturesque village wrapped around a crescent of beach with a tall O'Brien castle guarding the little harbor. Another 8 miles farther down the spine of the peninsula is the last village, Kilbaha, and 4½ miles beyond that is the lonely lighthouse of Loop Head. From the headland facing south, there are superb views of the mountains of Kerry — MacGillycuddy's Reeks crowned by Carrantuohill, the highest point in Ireland, and Mt. Brandon at the west end of the Dingle Peninsula. To the north are the whale-backed Aran Islands in Galway Bay and the sawtooth peaks of Connemara. Below the lighthouse are some rocks separated from the shore by a deep chasm. Legend has it that the Irish hero Cu Chulainn made a bold leap across this gap while being pursued by a persistent female admirer.

EATING OUT

The Long Dock Overlooking the Shannon estuary on the Loop Head Peninsula, this cozy seafood eatery serves pub grub throughout the day in the lounge, and dinner in the main restaurant. The menu emphasizes fresh fish (including oysters farmed by the restaurant's owners), as well as meat and chicken dishes. On most evenings, there is live traditional music by the fireplace. Open daily June through August, and on weekends only during the rest of the year. Reservations advised for dinner. Major credit cards accepted. West St., Carrigaholt (phone: 65-58106). Expensive to moderate.

En Route from Loop Head On the return journey from Loop Head, take the left branch of the road at the village of Kilbaha for a mile to the Moneen church. In a baptistery chapel on the left of the altar is a little wooden hut with a canvas roof and windows. The hut, a relic of the period of anti-Catholic discrimination, was the only church allowed in this area in the first half of the 19th century. A bigoted landlord refused to allow a church to be built, so the parish priest had this structure erected. Each Sunday it was drawn onto the beach, where the priest said Mass and his congregation knelt in the open. Known as the Little Ark, the wooden chapel is still an object of veneration, and the story is illustrated in stained glass over the church door.

A half-mile farther, beyond the village of Cross, make a right turn onto a narrow road, which after 2 miles reaches the coast and the top of Oldtown Hill, affording a view of miles of rugged cliffs ahead. The road soon begins to hug the cliff tops, and the next 5 miles into Kilkee provide a dramatic unfolding panorama of rock stacks and precipices. Occasionally, remains of castle towers and stone forts are visible in inaccessible places in the rock. The most striking phenomenon is Bishop's Island, a sheer stack of rock that's been cut off from the mainland but retains a beehive oratory and house associated with St. Senan.

KILKEE This little resort town, with its charming rows of Regency Gothic houses, has been a popular vacation spot for well-to-do people from Limerick since they came here by Shannon steamer in the early 19th century. Its powdery, horseshoe-shaped beach is protected from the full force of the Atlantic by two bold headlands and offers safe bathing and boating. Because most of Kilkee's visitors rent houses, there are few hotels. It's best to stop here for a dip, and then pull up a stool at the *Central Bar* (O'Curry St; phone: 65-56103), *Dolphin' Bar* (Erin St.; phone: 65-56584), *Marrinan's* (O'Connell St.; 65-56298), the *Hide-Out* (Erin St.; 65-56092), or the *Old Barrel* (O'Connell St.; no phone) for a drink and some good conversation.

EATING OUT

Manuel's Run by an energetic husband-and-wife team, this eatery is one of the best in town. It's in a scenic site off the main road (N67) about a mile north of the town center. The menu reflects whatever is in season, and usually includes at least ten different varieties of fresh fish. Open daily from *Easter* to mid-September for dinner only. Reservations advised. Diners Club, MasterCard, and Visa accepted. Corbally, Kilkee (phone: 65-56211). Moderate.

En Route from Kilkee The road to Lahinch (N67) runs inland for the next 20 miles, but, time permitting, take a detour to see the high cliffs of Baltard Bay, guarded by an O'Brien tower, or the white strand of beach beyond the village of Doonbeg. Along the road is the small fishing village of Quilty and the *Leon* pub, named after the Spanish Armada ship that was wrecked off nearby Mutton Island. The distinctive stone walls on the beach here are for drying seaweed, a valued crop.

MILTOWN MALBAY This village on the way to Lahinch is a strong traditional music center that hosts the Willie Clancy Summer School (named after a beloved local piper) each July. Featured here are the *uilleann* pipes — the Irish type played with a bellows under the elbow. They have a wide melodic variation and none of the shrieking shrillness of their cousins, the Scottish warpipes. On Sundays and holidays, particularly during the school term, almost all the bars in Miltown Malbay have traditional music, as do those in nearby villages such as Mullagh, the Crosses of Annagh, and Quilty. Be warned, however: Traditional music happens spontaneously rather than by schedule, and you have to stalk it.

The nearby resort of Spanish Point commemorates sailors of the Spanish Armada who drowned here in September 1588. Those whom the sea did not claim were butchered by the followers of Loyalist Sir Turlough O'Brien of Liscannor.

LAHINCH Prettily set on the shores of Liscannor Bay, Lahinch is a cubistic composition of pastel houses perched on a cliff; it has a somewhat exotic Mediterranean look. There's plenty to do: Surfboards can be rented at the beach, bicycles can be hired at the *Lahinch Camping and Caravan Park* (phone: 65-81424), boats are available for both deep-sea and freshwater fishing, and the celebrated 18-hole championship *Lahinch* seaside golf course is open to guests (phone: 65-81003; also see *Great Golf* in DIVERSIONS).

CHECKING IN/EATING OUT

Aberdeen Arms Opened in 1850, this establishment is reputed to be the oldest golf links hotel in Ireland. Now completely refurbished, it offers 55 modern rooms, each with private bath, TV set, telephone, and coffee-maker. Rooms overlook the *Lahinch* golf course (overnight guests are entitled to reduced greens fees) or the nearby beach. Public facilities include a restaurant, a grillroom and golf-themed bar, as well as a health center with a gym, Jacuzzi, and sauna. Open year-round. Lahinch (phone: 65-81100; fax: 65-81228). Expensive to moderate.

En Route from Lahinch Take the coast road past the ruined tower house of Dough set among the golf greens on the left; on the right in the sandhills are the "tiger" holes of the golf course. Legend has it that the fairy king Donn of the Sandhills rides his horse here on moonlit nights.

The ruined medieval church of Kilmacrehy is about a mile farther, to the left. Its founder, St. Mac Creiche, is said to have fought dragons and cured plagues; he was buried between high and low tides at a spot called "Mac Creiche's bed." About 3 miles northwest is Liscannor.

LISCANNOR An ancient O'Brien tower guards this fishing village, which was also the birthplace of John P. Holland, inventor of the submarine and founder of the Electric Boat Company (which became General Dynamics). There is a small museum and library of Holland memorabilia. The road climbs steadily out of Liscannor and at one point comes abreast of a tall urn-crowned column on the left. This is a good stopping point. Below is Liscannor Bay and all the billowy coast toward Miltown Malbay. The column was built to honor local hero Cornelius O'Brien, a Clare landlord and patron. Beside it is Dabhac Bhrighde, St. Bridget's Well, a local folk shrine still much visited by pilgrims. Its rushing waters, quaint white-washed courtyard surrounded by scarlet fuchsia, and ex voto offerings — pictures, rosary beads, a pair of crutches — contribute to the abiding religious feeling of this place, which has been a sacred spot since pre-Christian times, when the spring was dedicated to an ancient Celtic goddess.

EATING OUT

Captain's Deck On the upper level of an antiques shop overlooking Liscannor Bay, this nautically themed restaurant is earning a far-reaching reputation for its fresh seafood dishes, including wild salmon, stone crab, local lobster, and surf and turf. Open *Easter* through September; lunch daily, dinner Tuesdays through Sundays. Reservations advised. Major credit cards accepted. Liscannor (phone: 65-81385). Moderate.

CLIFFS OF MOHER Two miles from St. Bridget's Well, turn right into the parking lot for the majestic Cliffs of Moher, where there is a visitors' center with a restaurant and a crafts shop. Follow the path up the hillside to the little tower, built by Cornelius O'Brien, who intended it as a tea house "for the entertainment and refreshment of lady visitors." Now it's just a lookout, but the view from the top is spectacular: north to the Aran Islands and the Connemara mountains and south toward the Cliffs of Moher, a great curtain of sheer cliff face, rippling 5 miles along the coast and hanging over 600 feet above the sea.

En Route from Liscannor The main road out of Liscannor passes the Cliffs of Moher and offers some marvelous views looking toward the Aran Islands. On the nearest island, Inisheer, are an O'Brien castle, a lighthouse, and a village to the right. The inhabitants of Inisheer speak Irish, farm and fish for a living, and retain many of the customs described in the plays and essays of John M. Synge and in the novels of Liam O'Flaherty. (Also see the *Connemara and the Aran Islands* route).

The hills on the right of the road produce a slate flagstone — called Liscannor or Moher flag — that is used for roofing stables and outhouses and for decorative work in architecture. About 5 miles from the Cliffs of Moher is a detour that leads 2 miles to the left to the village and harbor of Doolin. The village is a single row of thatched fisherman's houses. Beside them is a pub, *Gus O'Connor's* (phone: 65-74168), which is famous for traditional music. Motor launches and *curraghs* cross from Doolin Harbor to Inisheer. In addition, a passenger ferry service links Doolin with the Aran Islands from April through September. The ride takes 30 minutes; round-trip fare is about $17. For more information, call 65-74189.

EATING OUT

Bruach na hAille This restaurant serves innovative dishes featuring monkfish, turbot, scallops, crab, and other seafood prepared in both the French nouvelle and Irish country cooking styles. Open daily for dinner from mid-March through late October. Reservations advised. No credit cards accepted. Doolin (phone: 65-74120). Moderate.

Ivy Cottage Also known as "Ilsa's Kitchen," this splendid little thatch-roofed, ivy- and rose-covered cottage is just a few doors down the road from *Gus O'Connor's* pub. Specializing in wholesome dishes and locally caught seafood, this candlelit health food oasis also doubles as an art gallery. Open for dinner daily from May to September. Reservations advised. Major credit cards accepted. Doolin (phone: 65-74244). Moderate.

LISDOONVARNA Beach hotels and boardinghouses have been part of this spa resort, about 27 miles east of Doolin, since the 18th century because of its curative sulfur and iron springs. The *Spa Wells Health Centre* (phone: 65-74023) is open June to October; a sulfur bath costs about $10. Lisdoonvarna also plays host to a music festival during the second weekend in July, a nonstop event featuring folk, rock, traditional, and country music. In September, the *Matchmaking Festival of Ireland,* during which the country's shy bachelors seek spouses, is held here. For festival information, contact the local tourist board (phone: 65-74062) during summer or the Limerick City Tourist Board year-round (phone: 61-317522).

CHECKING IN/EATING OUT

King Thomond Situated on 8 acres of parkland at the edge of the village, this Georgian-style hotel has 62 modern guestrooms, all with private baths, TV sets, telephones, hair dryers, and coffee/tea makers. There's also a restaurant, and a lounge that presents Irish country entertainment on summer evenings. Open April through October. Lisdoonvarna (phone: 65-74444; fax: 65-74406). Moderate.

En Route from Lisdoonvarna Two routes go to Ballyvaughan, either the scenic coastal road (R477) through Black Head or Corkscrew Road (N67) through the Burren country.

About a mile out of Lisdoonvarna on the coastal road is Ballynalacken, the 15th-century O'Brien castle, now a roofless but walled ruin. The castle's parapets offer a great view west across the bay to the Aran Islands and east over the gray hills of the Burren. Continuing north from Ballynalacken, the road runs along a shelf between the sea and overhanging limestone terraces. It's about 10 miles to the lighthouse at Black Head, from which there are fine views across Galway Bay to the mountains of Mayo and Connemara. In another 5 miles the road reaches Ballyvaughan.

Although it's only 10 miles long, the aptly named Corkscrew Road is a narrow, tortuous lane clinging to the Burren hillsides. The vistas are nothing short of breathtaking, with soft mists rising prism-like from the neighboring valleys. The Burren takes its name from the Irish word *boireann,* meaning "rocky." It is literally a rocky desert of silvery gray limestone. General Ludlow, a commander in Cromwell's forces, returned after a reconnaissance to report that the area had "not enough wood to hang a man, earth to bury a man, or water to drown a man!"

The Burren arrived at its present denuded state through the actions of ice, water, air, and frost over scores of centuries. The color of the rock ranges from a somber pewter to a light silver, and it has been rubbed and carved into marvelous shapes. The long fingers of green that reach between the crags provide summer grazing for cattle and relief for the eye.

Because of the absence of trees and heavy vegetation, the Burren is open to broad untrammeled light, which in conjunction with other natural factors produces the Burren's final glory — its wildflowers. At the end of May, this desert blooms. The sparse patches of earth and grass on the bare rock face suddenly become bejeweled with as exotic a collection of flora as can be seen anywhere in the world. Clumps of creamy gold mountain avens from the Arctic grow side by side with tall red and white orchids or the scarlet splash of bloody cranesbill from the Mediterranean. Beside these are the intense blue stars of the spring flowering gentian, which also grows in the Alps. Small wonder that the monks of nearby Corcomroe named their abbey St. Mary's of the Fertile Rock.

BALLYVAUGHAN This little coastal village is nestled in one of the green valleys that slope down from the Burren hills. Two miles southeast of the town is Aillwee Cave, the only cave in the Burren open to the public. Its remarkable stalagmites, stalactites, and mysterious bear pits draw more than 100,000 visitors a year. A tea shop, restaurant, crafts shop, and the *Burren Gold Cheesemaking* center are all at the entrance to the caves. Open daily mid-March to early November (phone: 65-77036).

Some atmospheric pubs in town include the *Ballyvaughan Inn* (phone: 65-77003), which offers folk music and talk; *MacNeill O'LocLainn's* (no phone), a tiny, traditional pub; and the *Monk's Pub* (at the pier; phone: 65-77059), offering seafood and music.

CHECKING IN

Gregans Castle Undoubtedly the best place to stay in the region, this family-run 22-room inn at the foot of Corkscrew Hill, overlooking the Burren country and Galway Bay, has a charming homey feeling as well as a highly acclaimed wine cellar and restaurant. Open *Easter* through October. For additional details, see *Rural Retreats* in DIVERSIONS. Ballyvaughan (phone: 65-77005; 800-223-6510 from the US; fax: 65-77111). Expensive.

Hyland's A clean, cheerful, small inn (12 rooms, 11 with private baths/showers), run by the seventh and eighth generations of Hylands, with a dining room featuring seafood. Open April through October. Ballyvaughan (phone: 65-77037; 800-447-7462 from the US; fax: 65-77131). Moderate.

EATING OUT

Manus Walsh's Gallery and Claire's Restaurant At this jewel of a spot, Manus sells paintings and crafts and his wife, Claire, serves up scrumptious lobster, crab, mackerel, and homemade bread and cakes. Open April through October for dinner only; closed Sundays. Reservations necessary. Major credit cards accepted. Ballyvaughan (phone: 65-77029). Moderate.

En Route from Ballyvaughan From here, you can return to Ennis, or head to Galway (see alternate route, below). To reach Ennis, take R480 south. About 3 miles from Ballyvaughan is a spectacular tomb, the Poulnabrone Portal dolmen, well worth stopping the car and walking across the field to view. A few miles farther are signposts to the right for Caherconnell, a well-preserved *caher,* or stone ring fort, which protected four Iron Age and early Christian settlements. At the next crossroad stands Leamaneh Castle, a tower house built by the O'Briens in the 15th century, enlarged and fortified in the 17th century, and abandoned in the 18th century in favor of Dromoland Castle. Some features of Leamaneh — a fireplace and gateway — were subsequently moved to the *Dromoland Castle* hotel.

A 4-mile digression west on R476 into the village of Kilfenora is recommended for a look at the remains of its 12th-century cathedral, whose chancel has some good stone carving. In the cemetery are three Irish high crosses carved with Bible scenes and Celtic and Scandinavian interlace ornamentation. At the *Kilfenora Burren Display Centre* (R476; phone: 65-88030), the unusual and fascinating flora of the Burren are reproduced in wax and silk. A tearoom and crafts shop are also on the premises. The center is open daily mid-March through October; admission charge. Return to the crossroads and turn south on R476 toward Corofin.

COROFIN Of special interest here is the *Clare Heritage Centre* (phone: 65-27955) housed in St. Catherine's Church. This museum traces the history of western Ireland from 1800 to 1860, a significant period of famine and mass emigration to the US. It's open daily April through October; weekends November through March. There's an admission charge. For additional details, see *Marvelous Museums* in DIVERSIONS.

EATING OUT

Bofey Quinn's Situated in the heart of town, this rustic pub-style eatery is ideal for a quick lunch or a casual dinner. The house specialty is lobster, taken fresh from the seawater tank and prepared in a variety of ways. Open daily. Reservations advised. MasterCard and Visa accepted. Main St., Corofin (phone: 65-27627). Moderate.

En route from Corofin From Corofin, it's 13 miles south on R476 to Ennis. Midway between Corofin and Ennis on Ennistymon Road is Dysert O'Dea Castle, a recently restored local landmark, built by Diarmuid O'Dea between 1470 and 1490. Home of the O'Dea clan until 1961, the castle is now the focus of a newly developed heritage trail that spans a 2-mile radius and includes 25 other historical sites, from Iron Age stone forts and medieval battlefields to a high cross dating from the 12th century. There is also a round tower, built between 900 and 1100, and the foundations of an 8th-century church. The castle houses a museum, archaeology center, exhibits, an audiovisual show, tearoom, and souvenir shop. The castle is open daily, May through September. There's an admission charge for the castle but not for the walking trail. For more information, call 65-27722.

Alternate route from Ballyvaughan An alternative to returning to Ennis is to travel from Ballyvaughan to Galway City by way of Gort and Thoor Ballylee and to connect with the *Connemara and the Aran Islands* tour route.

To take this alternate route, continue east along the coast road, N67, from Ballyvaughan for 9 miles and turn right at the green monument signpost for Corcomroe Abbey. The abbey is reached by a narrow lane (signposted) just beyond the post office. Corcomroe, or St. Mary of the Fertile Rock, was founded in 1196 for the Cistercians by Donal Mor O'Brien, King of Munster. The church is distinguished by some vigorous Irish Romanesque carving on its columns and the important tomb of Conor O'Brien, grandson of the founder.

About 15 miles farther on N67 is Kinvara, where the 15th-century *Dunguaire Castle* overlooks Galway Bay and offers delightful medieval banquets on summer evenings (phone: 61-360788 or 91-37108).

Take a sharp right at the road signposted for Gort, which is about 11 miles south. About a mile outside Gort, turn left onto N18, the Galway road, and follow signposts into Coole Park. This was the estate of Lady Augusta Gregory, the playwright and founder, with W. B. Yeats, of the *Abbey Theatre* and hostess to such literary lights as Yeats, George Bernard Shaw, John M. Synge, and Sean O'Casey. The house has been demolished, but the garden, with its autograph tree on which Lady Gregory's guests carved their names, survives, and a new visitors' center offers exhibits and artifacts, housed in an old stone barn structure on the property. Walk by the lake and through the woods so often described by Yeats in his verse.

After leaving Coole Park, continue north on N18 for another mile and turn right at the signpost for Thoor Ballylee; follow the narrow road for a mile or so. Thoor Ballylee, a 16th-century tower house built by the De Burgo family, was Yeats's home from 1917 to 1929 and a frequent symbol in his poetry. Open daily during the summer. Admission charge (phone: 91-31436). Stop to browse in the bookshop and pop into the tea shop for a cup and a slice of "barm brack" — raisin cake.

From here, it's just 21 miles north on N18 to Galway City, where the *Connemara and the Aran Islands* tour route begins.

County Donegal

Donegal seems forever haunted by its history, harking back to the days when it was a proud and independent enclave ruled by its own kings and chieftains. Spiritually and physically remote from the rest of Ireland, the area retains a strong individuality and a vital awareness of its former glory.

Originally, the region was known as Tirconnaill (pronounced Cheer-*kuhn*-il), meaning the Land of Conall. It was named for Conall Gulban, son of an Irish king known as Niall of the Nine Hostages because of his habit of taking prisoners when he raided foreign lands. This piratical king endowed his son with the wild territory of Donegal, and in the 5th century Conall founded his kingdom, which remained a monarchy until 1071.

The later name, Donegal, comes from the Irish *Dún na nGall,* "fort of the foreigners." It may refer to the Vikings who constantly raided the Irish coast during the 9th and 10th centuries. On the other hand, the name might have arisen from the fact that, long before the Norsemen came, this northwestern region of Ireland was inhabited by migrant races who made successive incursions into Ireland — traces of them, including crude Stone Age weapons and tools, have been found in Donegal.

The most glorious era in Donegal's history began with the emergence of the O'Donnell dynasty around AD 1200. The mighty O'Donnells held sway over the region for 4 centuries, wielding power not only in Donegal but throughout Ireland.

In 1587, one of the clan, young Red Hugh O'Donnell (the second), was kidnapped by an agent of Queen Elizabeth I and held hostage in Dublin Castle in an attempt to extort loyalty to the queen from his father. When Red Hugh escaped after 5 years, he became the hero of Gaelic Ireland. He and another great chieftain, Hugh O'Neill of Tyrone, joined forces with an invading Spanish army in a final effort to defeat the armies of Elizabeth. Instead, they were themselves crushed at the disastrous Battle of Kinsale on *Christmas Day* 1601. This was the final death rattle of the old Irish chiefs. O'Donnell fled to Spain where he died, apparently from poisoning. His brother and successor, Rory O'Donnell, along with O'Neill, sailed in exile from the Donegal port of Rathmullan in 1607, an event known as the Flight of the Earls. With their departure, all hope of a revival of Gaelic dominance was squashed forever.

These stirring historical events are a vital part of the folk memory of Donegal and have helped shape the character and personality of its people, most of whom still live off the land or the sea, or make a living weaving the famous Donegal tweeds. In some parts of the county, Irish is still spoken just as it was in the time of the first Red Hugh.

Our tour, which starts at the most natural departure point, Donegal Town, covers about 200 miles and can be driven comfortably in 4 days. It heads northeast in a huge, straggling circle, girdling the entire county and returning to Donegal Town at the end. The greater part of the tour is along the sea, following a coastline with some of the most dramatic scenery in Ireland. It also takes in Donegal's magnificent mountains and valleys and lonesome bogs. The roads are not in great shape, however, and in some stretches would unnerve a stunt driver, so ease off the gas pedal.

In the hotels along this route, expect to pay $120 or more for a double room at places in the expensive category; $75 to $120 at establishments described as moderate; and less than $75 at those listed as inexpensive. Dinner for two (excluding wine, drinks, and tips) in an expensive restaurant will cost $50 and up; in a moderate place, $30 to $50; and in an inexpensive spot, under $30. For each location, hotels and restaurants are listed alphabetically by price category.

DONEGAL TOWN For a complete report on the town, its sights, hotels, and restaurants, see *Donegal Town* in THE CITIES.

En Route from Donegal Town From Donegal Town, take N15 northeast. Seven miles out is the Barnesmore Gap, a passage through the Blue Stack Mountains joining south and north Donegal. In olden days, the gap was a lucrative hunting ground for highwaymen and assorted brigands who preyed on travelers making their way through the mountains. The road passes through the twin towns of Ballybofey and Stranorlar, which are linked by a bridge over the River Finn, where there's excellent salmon and trout fishing. At Stranorlar, turn north onto N56 and continue for 10 miles to a signposted T-junction. Turn east onto N13 and head for Manorcunningham, 4 miles away. This is the entrance to the Inishowen Peninsula.

CHECKING IN

Kee's A fine, homey hostelry serving simple but good fare. All of the 37 rooms have private baths and TV sets. There's also a fitness center with an indoor pool, Jacuzzi, and sauna. Main St., Stranorlar (phone: 74-31018; fax: 74-31917). Moderate.

Finn View House A comfortable family house with 3 rooms. Lifford Rd., Ballybofey (phone: 74-31351). Inexpensive.

EATING OUT

Biddy's O'Barnes This pub at the entrance to the Barnesmore Gap is a pleasant place to relax with good food and drink. Home-baked brown bread is the specialty of the house, along with hearty fresh soup from the kitchen tureen. Open for lunch and dinner daily. No reservations. No credit cards accepted. Barnesmore Gap, 7 miles north of Donegal Town on N15 (phone: 73-21402). Moderate.

INISHOWEN PENINSULA This wild, rugged territory juts defiantly into the Atlantic and is almost completely surrounded by the ocean. At one time, it must have been considered an island, because the name Inish Owen means "island of Owen." The Owen in question is Cinel Owen (another son of Niall of the Nine Hostages), who ruled the territory during the 5th century. Inishowen is lavishly beautiful, with towering mountains running up its central spine and vast, open lowlands where heather and bracken grow wild in the bogs. The early Christian church must have been a potent influence on the peninsula, because ecclesiastical ruins and monuments are everywhere. Much of Inishowen's turbulent spirit can perhaps be blamed on its long-standing boast that the best *poitín* (the original Irish whiskey, now illegal) was distilled here.

En Route from Manorcunningham About 5 miles north of Manorcunningham, off N13, lie the ruins of Balleeghan Friary, under a mound of ivy beside Lough Swilly. This monastery was built by the O'Donnells for the Franciscans in the 15th century.

Pick up N13 and continue through Newtowncunningham. About 5 miles past this village, the heights of Mount Grianán will come into view on the right. On top of this hill, 800 feet up, stands one of the most spectacular of Ireland's ancient monuments — the Grianán of Aileach. To reach the site, turn right (south) at the church in Speenoge. It is possible to drive to within a few yards of this imposing fortress, which is thought to have been a temple of the sun during pagan times. For a detailed description of the site, see *Monuments and Ruins* in DIVERSIONS.

Return to N13 and turn right (east). At Bridgend, which is on the border of Northern Ireland, turn left (northwest) for Burnfoot and then right (east) for the village of Muff. From here, head northeast on R238 for about 12 miles along the shores of Lough Foyle, to Moville.

MOVILLE The port of Moville was established during the 18th century by Samuel Montgomery, an ancestor of Viscount Montgomery of El Alamein, the greatest of the British World War II generals and a friendly rival of Dwight Eisenhower. Moville was once a point of departure for steamships bound for America. The town square, shaded by trees, is one of the most attractive in Ireland, and a beautiful seafront promenade leads beyond the town to a long walk that follows the coast beneath tall cliffs and stately mountains. About a mile north of the town is the Cooley Cross, a tall stone sculpture made in early Christian times. What looks like a footprint can be discerned on the rock on which the cross stands; the truly devout believe it was made by the foot of St. Patrick.

CHECKING IN/EATING OUT

McNamara's Small and friendly, this family-run hotel has 17 rooms, most with private baths. There's a snug little bar with a log fire, and the restaurant excites the palate with a daily supply of fresh lobster, turbot, crab, and mackerel brought up from the harbor. Foyle St., Moville (phone: 77-82010; fax: 77-82564). Moderate.

Redcastle This is a splendid 17th-century mansion on 22 acres of woodland on the edge of the Atlantic. The original character of the house has been preserved, though modern comforts have been worked into the 39 guest-rooms and the public spaces. Outdoor holidays featuring game fishing and horseback riding are a specialty of this establishment. There's also a 9-hole golf course, and the restaurant has won a number of awards. Three miles south of Moville on R238 (phone: 77-82073; fax: 77-82214). Moderate.

GREENCASTLE Four miles from Moville along the coast road (R241), at a point where the Lough Foyle channel narrows and the opposite shore in Northern Ireland is only a mile away, is one of the Irish Republic's major fishing ports. Greencastle takes its name from the castle that now lies in ruins above the town. It was built in 1305 by the Norman Earl Richard de Burgo (Burke) as a gesture of defiance against the two ruling clans of Inishowen, the O'Donnells and the O'Dohertys. Eventually the castle fell into the hands of the O'Donnells, but it was captured from them by Elizabethan Planters.

From here, backtrack to Moville.

En Route from Moville About 7 miles north of Moville on the Culdaff road, R238, is the village of Leckemy, where evidence supports the allegation that sauna baths originated in Ireland. At the foot of Crocknamerragh Hill is a beehive-shaped stone sweathouse, measuring almost 8 feet high. Such sweathouses are believed to have been used during pagan times to exorcise demons. Later, they were used as treatment for all types of ailments and infirmities. The houses were heated by peat fires. Two or three naked people squeezed into the tiny space and were sealed inside for several hours to sweat. Immediately afterward, in a ritual still followed in Finland today, they plunged into a river or submerged themselves in a tub of icy water.

Drive through Culdaff, and a short distance north is the lovely village of Malin, close to the northernmost tip of Ireland. Malin is a picture-postcard hamlet founded by English Planters in the 17th century. Houses of that period surround its central diamond. It's worth abandoning the car for a while in Malin to walk in the nearby Knockmany Bens (peaks). For an enjoyable hike, follow the narrow side road that goes from Malin into the heart of the hills, a heather-clad range of low mountains that command magnificent panoramic views across the Atlantic to the Mull of Kintyre in Scotland.

A reasonably good link road, R242, goes all the way to Malin Head, at the very brink of the island of Ireland, for another breathtaking ocean vista. Down below, at the foot of the cliff, the sea races furiously through a channel between needle-pointed rocks in the place known as Hell's Hole, over which clouds of spray hang perpetually like white smoke. To the east, massive cathedral cliffs rear out of the ocean and run for 12 miles down to Glengad Head.

From Malin village, take R242 south toward Carndonagh, and just outside that town bear right (northwest) onto R238 toward Ballyliffin. A graveyard on the left has a large stone cross at the gate. This is St. Patrick's Cross, probably the oldest standing cross in Ireland, dating from the 7th century.

Ballyliffin is a popular resort with a pristine beach running for 2 miles and sand dunes with rich deposits of calcified and crumbled sea shells, thousands of years old. Three miles south on R238 is Clonmany and the ruins of a church that was built on the site of a monastery established by St. Columba (also known as St. Columbkille or St. Colmcille). Downstream on the River Clonmany, at Glenview, is a 40-foot waterfall. From Clonmany, take the ring road (an unnumbered route that runs in a semicircle northwest through Straid, Kindrohid, Dunaff, and Claggan) through the Mamore Gap for some of the most majestic scenery on the entire peninsula. The road climbs high into the mountains above the sea and then cuts through the gap, a desolate glen of stunning beauty hemmed in by lofty peaks.

From the gap it's a steep downhill run all the way to Buncrana, which has two castles worth visiting and a fine sandy beach. In summer, there's an active nightlife with numerous dance clubs and singing pubs open until dawn. There are two golf courses in the area: the 18-hole *North-West* (phone: 77-61027) and the 9-hole *Buncrana Municipal* (phone: 77-61716). Both offer sea views. Also worth a look in town are the *Tullyarvan Mill* (phone: 77-61613), a restored textile mill; the *Vintage Car and Carriage Museum* (phone: 77-61130); and the *Knitting Centre* (phone: 77-62355), which demonstrates how sweaters are designed and made. There's a small admission charge at each place.

From Buncrana, rejoin R238, which runs south through Fahan to Burnfoot and Bridgend, from which it is possible to double back on N13 to Manorcunningham and from there travel 7 miles west toward Letterkenny.

CHECKING IN

White Strand Warm personal attention is a conspicuous feature of this family-owned modern motel. The 12 rooms are comfortable and well equipped, and the food is good. Railway Rd., Buncrana (phone: 77-61059 or 77-61144; fax: 77-62278). Moderate.

Strand Each of the 12 rooms in this excellent family-run property has been given an individual touch, along with modern facilities, including a TV set, radio, and phone. Everything served in the restaurant is fresh or home-produced, and there's a marvelous variety of fish dishes. An added attraction is the beautiful garden at the rear of the hotel. Ballyliffin (phone: 77-76107; fax: 77-76486). Moderate to inexpensive.

EATING OUT

St. John's Housed in a restored Georgian house overlooking Lough Swilly, this elegant restaurant has won a number of well-deserved awards for its cooking. An abundance of fresh fish is prepared with great skill, as is Donegal lamb. Open for dinner only; closed Mondays. Reservations advised. Major credit cards accepted. Fahan (phone: 77-60289). Moderate.

LETTERKENNY With a population of more than 10,000, Letterkenny, on the banks of the River Swilly, is the county's largest town and its ecclesiastical center. Its name is derived from the Gaelic *Leitir Ceannain* ("Hillside of the O'Cannons," a clan that inhabited the area before Norman times). Although the town itself is not remarkable, it is a good base from which to enjoy day trips to the northwest coastal areas. Letterkenny has received a face-lift in recent years. The town square has been spruced up to include a bandstand and seating for foot-weary shoppers. A booklet outlining a signposted walking tour of the town is available from the tourist office (just outside the town center on N56; phone: 74-21160; fax: 74-25180). The booklet leads visitors to churches and old buildings, including the spot where patriot Wolfe Tone was arrested in 1798, and is full of interesting historical and legendary stories. There also is a leisure center in Letterkenny (Port Rd.; phone: 74-25251) with a swimming pool, sauna, Jacuzzi, and steamroom. There's an admission charge.

CHECKING IN/EATING OUT

Mount Errigal This modern hostelry has 82 comfortable rooms, each with private bath and cable TV, and a restaurant serving traditional Irish fare. On the outskirts of Letterkenny on the R245 at Ballyraine (phone: 74-22700; fax: 74-25085). Expensive to moderate.

Gallagher's A small (27 rooms with private baths), old-fashioned, and comfortable place to stay, right in the center of town. The food is fresh, good, and served in gargantuan portions. Main St., Letterkenny (phone: 74-22066; fax: 74-21016). Moderate.

En Route from Letterkenny At this point it is possible to diverge from the grand tour of County Donegal and become completely immersed in the solitude and splendor of Glenveagh National Park, only 13 miles to the northwest on N56. The route goes first to Kilmacrenan, a hamlet of great charm and particular appeal to anglers because the fast-flowing River Leannan is possibly the best trout water in Donegal and an exciting challenge to the fly caster. The ruins of a 16th-century Franciscan friary, built by one of the O'Donnells, can be found in a churchyard north of the village. Just 1½ miles to the east is Doon Rock, a coronation stone used for many centuries to inaugurate successive O'Donnell chieftains. To reach Glenveagh, travel 3 miles farther along N56, turn left (west) at Termon onto L77, then right (north) at the junction of L82. The entrance to the park is 2 miles beyond on the left.

GLENVEAGH NATIONAL PARK Glenveagh is very precious — a wild domain of nature, almost untouched from the day it was fashioned, with herds of red deer grazing on the uplands, peregrine falcons circling above the lake, and a sequestered glen where civilization and its turmoils are kept at bay and great silences prevail. The privacy of this place is rooted in tragedy: John George Adair, the man who took over Glenveagh in the 19th century, drove 200 families from their homes on the estate so he could have it all to himself. It was he who built the overembellished Gothic castle above the lake. During the 1930s, Glenveagh came into the possession of a more humane landlord, Henry McIlhenny, a man of seemingly limitless wealth gained from the manufacture of gas meters in Philadelphia, where his grandfather, a Donegal man, had emigrated. McIlhenny spent his summers in the castle, living in the resplendent style of a Renaissance prince but winning the affection of the local populace through his generosity. He was a bright light in the international society of the 1930s and 1940s, and many celebrities stayed in the castle as his guests, including Greta Garbo, Cecil Beaton, and Yehudi Menuhin. Upon his death, McIlhenny left the 25,000-acre estate and its castle to the Irish nation, though his widow continued to live in the castle for 36 years. The gardens on the castle grounds are superb, but the real enchantment of Glenveagh is in the wild splendor of its mountainous landscape, where it is possible to walk for miles without seeing a house. The park is open daily *Easter* through October; closed Mondays in April and October, except on public holidays. There's an admission charge for both the park and castle (phone: 74-37088).

En Route from Glenveagh National Park Before returning to Letterkenny, it's worth traveling 7 miles south on L82 to Gartan, the birthplace of St. Columba (Colmcille). Donegal's remarkable saint evangelized parts of Scotland, where he established a renowned monastery on the island of Iona. His life wasn't entirely one of prayer, however, and in his early years his fiery temper sometimes landed him in trouble. On one notable occasion, he mustered an army to do battle with none less than the High King of Ireland — and defeated him. He died on Iona in 597 at the age of 76. The *Colmcille Heritage Centre* at Gartan relates the life and times of the irascible saint in a peaceful lakeside spot. It's open from *Easter* to mid-October, weekdays and Sunday afternoons. There's an admission charge (phone: 74-37306). Another pleasant detour after Glenveagh is the *Glebe Gallery* (signposted from Glenveagh; phone: 74-37071). The house of painter Derek Hill now is an exhibition space featuring works (from Hill's collection) by Picasso, Kokoschka, and other famous artists. The surrounding gardens feature some rare trees and shrubs. The gallery is open daily from late May through September; closed Mondays. There's an admission charge. For additional details, see *Marvelous Museums* in DI-VERSIONS. A stop might also be made at Lurgyvale Cottage (phone: 74-39216) in Kilmacrenana. This delightful 150-year-old, thatch-roofed dwelling has been preserved in its original condition, complete with period domestic furnishings and farm implements. It's a good place to experience an old lifestyle and to sample delicious hot scones and tea; open May through September. As you near Letterkenny, turn left (east) onto R245 just outside of town, then bear north for Ramelton (sometimes called Rathmelton), a tiny community that has been declared a Heritage Town by Bord Fáilte, the Irish Tourist Board. Over a third of the buildings are Georgian in this lovely riverside town with a dignified, elegant air.

RATHMULLAN This tiny seaside village is a lovely place rich in history. It was here in 1587 that the young Red Hugh O'Donnell (the second) was kidnapped at the behest of Queen Elizabeth I; the youngster was lured aboard a British ship anchored off Rathmullan, chained in the hold, and taken to Dublin, where he was held for 5 years before he escaped and made his way back to Tirconnaill to rally his warriors against Elizabeth.

It was also the scene of one of the most tragic events in Irish history: the Flight of the Earls, when the great chieftains O'Donnell and O'Neill, attended by a retinue of followers, boarded a ship to sail in exile to Europe in 1607. They were the last of the Gaelic chiefs, and their departure cleared the way for the final phase of the English conquest of Ireland. Rathmullen's *Flight of Earls Heritage Centre* (phone: 74-58131 or 74-58178) is housed in the Battery Fort. The simple but dramatic displays illustrate the town's tragic history. It's open daily June through September. Admission charge.

History was again swept up on Rathmullan's shores in 1798, when the French fleet, planning to invade Ireland and aid a native rebellion against the British, came to grief in Lough Swilly. Aboard one of the captured French ships was the leader of the insurrection, Wolfe Tone, a revered Irish patriot. Tone died, possibly by his own hand, while in prison awaiting execution.

The bay of Lough Swilly, on which Rathmullan is located, is one of the deepest sea anchorages in Europe. There's great fishing offshore, and fisherfolk from many lands gather in Rathmullan for the sea angling festival every June.

CHECKING IN

Rathmullan House This magnificent, rambling old mansion, hidden among the trees near the shores of Lough Swilly, is one of the loveliest hotels in Ireland, with a restaurant offering excellent food. There are 23 guestrooms

(21 with private baths) and a heated indoor pool. About a half mile from Rathmullan on the Portsalon road; watch for the sign on the gates at the right (phone: 74-58188; fax: 74-58200). Expensive.

Fort Royal A delightful 15-room country-house hotel, with its own beach on Lough Swilly, it has an executive (par 3) golf course, tennis courts, and fine food. About a half mile from Rathmullan on the Portsalon road, immediately beyond the gates of *Rathmullan House;* there's a sign indicating the narrow road that leads to it (phone: 74-58100; fax: 74-58103). Expensive to moderate.

EATING OUT

Water's Edge Perched on the brink of Lough Swilly, this superb restaurant makes the most of the fish readily at hand. Boned duckling in an exotic sauce is another specialty. Open daily for lunch and dinner from *Easter* through September; closed Sunday nights and Mondays the rest of the year. Reservations advised for tables with views of the lake. MasterCard and Visa accepted. Ballyboe, on L77, on the approach to Rathmullan from Rathmelton (phone: 74-58182). Moderate.

En Route from Rathmullan Visitors can walk unhindered for miles along the sandy shore of Lough Swilly or drive north toward Fanad Head, taking the Knockalla coast road. Follow the signposts (the road is unnumbered) to Portsalon, 8 miles away. It's a precipitous and thrilling drive, for the road first climbs a coastal cliff towering above the Atlantic and then dips suddenly and sweeps downward to Ballymastocker Bay, a crescent of golden sand. There is a golf course with a clubhouse at Portsalon overlooking Lough Swilly. Visitors are welcome at this pleasant course with panoramic views (phone: 74-59111). North of Portsalon, the road turns really mean, but it's worth chancing the final 3 miles to Fanad Head just to take in the view from the top of the cliffs. Then turn south and drive to the village of Tawney, continuing down along the eastern fringe of beautiful Mulroy Bay to Kerrykeel and from there to Milford, at the southern tip of Mulroy Bay.

EATING OUT

The Village Inn A small but marvelous dining place, owned by a chef who has won awards for his special way with seafood. Open daily for lunch and dinner year-round. Reservations advised for dinner. No credit cards accepted. Kerrykeel (phone: 74-50062). Moderate.

SHARING A PINT

Moore's Inn Good drinks and tasty snacks can be had at this atmospheric 19th-century pub where the welcome is warm. Main St., Milford (phone: 74-53123). Inexpensive.

CARRIGART/ROSGUILL Head north along the western edge of Mulroy Bay on R245 toward Carrigart, a typical planned estate village of the Victorian era, 10 miles away. A narrow, elongated inlet with trees edging its shore, the bay is a lovely sight, evoking the Scandinavian fjords. Three miles from Carrigart, the road winds by Cratlagh Wood, where in 1878 one of the most hated landlords in Ireland, the third Earl of Leitrim, was murdered, along with two of his servants. At Carrigart, turn west, and then just on the edge of town, turn right (north) at the signpost for Rosapenna onto R248. This leads onto the Rosguill Peninsula, one of the many Gaeltacht pockets of Donegal, where Irish is still a living language. At the headland of Rosguill, another spectacular seascape unfolds along the circular Atlantic Drive. The drive goes through an ecologically devastated "desert," where not a blade of grass grows, and around lovely Dooagh Bay. (The athletically inclined should consider walking this part of the route, which is about 15 miles — it's less nerve-racking and allows full attention to be devoted to the scenery.) Leaving the Rosguill headland on the way back to Carrigart, turn right (southwest) onto the road to Creeslough.

CHECKING IN/EATING OUT

Rosapenna Golf The great attraction at this 40-room hotel is the 18-hole golf course, but no less gratifying is the splendid fare served in its restaurant. There are also 2 tennis courts. Open daily for lunch and dinner. Reservations advised. Major credit cards accepted. Right turn at the signpost on the edge of Carrigart, 1 mile onto the Rosguill headland (phone: 74-55301; fax: 55128). Expensive.

Carrigart Noted for its conviviality and warm informality, this place serves good food and has 48 rooms, all with private baths. Open daily for breakfast, lunch, and dinner. Reservations advised for dinner. No credit cards. Top of Main St., Carrigart (phone: 74-55114; fax: 74-55250). Moderate.

DOE CASTLE/CREESLOUGH About 6 miles southwest of Carrigart, at the village of Cashel, turn right (north) at the signpost for Doe Castle; it's 1 mile down the side road. Perched on the edge of the sea, the castle is one of the finest fortresses left in Ireland; to explore it, ask for the key in the second house up from the entrance. In the early 16th century, Doe Castle was the stronghold of the MacSweeneys, a clan of "gallowglasses" (mercenaries) from Scotland who came to Donegal to fight for the O'Donnell chieftains and gained a foothold in the county themselves. Survivors of the Spanish Armada who swam from their wrecked ships to the Donegal coast found a haven in this castle. The road from Doe Castle runs into Creeslough, a pretty town overlooking the coast. Creeslough is a convenient base for expeditions to Muckish Mountain. Muckish must be climbed simply because it's there (though it's "not any easy climb," according to the locals, who understate such things). The view of the north of Ireland from its 2,000-foot peak is magnificent.

EATING OUT

Corncutters' Rest One of the few pub-cum-fast-food eateries in Donegal that can be relied on for cleanliness and efficiency. Snacks downstairs during the day and an à la carte menu upstairs in the evening. Open daily. Reservations advised. Major credit cards accepted. Main St., Creeslough (phone: 74-38067). Moderate to inexpensive.

En Route from Creeslough About 3 miles north, on N56 heading toward Port-na-Blagh and Dunfanaghy, the texture of the landscape changes suddenly and dramatically — the stark, rugged barrenness gives way to a soft, green-wooded peninsula that juts into Sheep Haven Bay. This is the Ards Forest Park, open year-round. Paths wander through woods and clearings perfect for picnicking, and at the edge of the forest, white strands run down to the sea, where, on those rare days when the sun brings the water up to a bearable temperature, the hardy can swim.

Port-na-Blagh and Dunfanaghy are delightfully unspoiled seaside resorts surrounded by beaches. Just beyond Dunfanaghy, swing right and follow the signpost to Horn Head for another drive around the cliffs above the Atlantic (a strong heart and a steady hand on the steering wheel are required). The massive cathedral cliffs provide a nesting haven for thousands of seabirds in midsummer, a phenomenon that attracts bird watchers from many countries.

Back on N56 again, head southwest to Falcarragh, 7 miles away, which is part of the Gortahork Gaeltacht. Falcarragh has much Gaelic flavor because Irish is still widely spoken, and many students come here every summer to study the native tongue. It is also another point from which to climb Muckish Mountain (see "Doe Castle/Creeslough" earlier in this section). Turn left (south) at the village crossroads and travel the side road 6 miles to the mountain.

CHECKING IN/EATING OUT

Carrig Rua This former coaching inn with 22 rooms retains its Old World flavor, and owners Valerie and Cyril Robinson provide an attentive personal touch. The food is splendid. Open May through October. Lunch in the grillroom and dinner in the dining room daily. Reservations advised for dinner. Major credit cards accepted. Dunfanaghy (phone: 74-36133). Expensive.

Arnold's Homey and hospitable, this family-run hostelry is known for indulging its guests. There are 34 rooms, including 2 family units. The excellent restaurant features vegetables from the garden and fresh fish. Open daily for breakfast, lunch, and dinner. Reservations advised for dinner. Major credit cards accepted. Dunfanaghy (phone: 74-36208; fax: 74-36142). Moderate.

Port-na-Blagh The dining room at this spacious, 45-room modern hotel, perched on a cliff overlooking Sheep Haven Bay, has particularly good fish selections. Open daily for breakfast, lunch, and dinner. Reservations advised for dinner. Major credit cards accepted. On the left along the road into Port-na-Blagh from Creeslough (phone: 74-36129). Moderate.

TORY ISLAND Just 9 miles off the coast in the Falcarragh area sits Tory Island, the subject of many legends. One dating from antiquity tells of an ancient race of giants known as the Formorians inhabiting the island. Their chief was the feared Balor of the Evil Eye, who was said to have supernatural powers; the ruins that stand on the cliffs at the eastern side of the island are said to be the remains of his castle. More civilized influences prevailed after the arrival of Christianity, and there also are some ruins of a settlement of monks once presided over by Donegal's most famous saint, Columba.

Today there are only about 150 year-round residents of the island left, and their lifestyle is much the same as that of their ancestors. They speak an Irish with undertones of Scots Gaelic because of the age-old connection between Tory and Scotland. The men still go to sea on fishing expeditions in frail *curraghs* — the tarred-canvas–covered boats used in Ireland for centuries.

Some rather fascinating compensations relieve this hard and bitter life. There are no rats whatsoever on Tory Island. The reason for this — according to the islanders — is that St. Columba banished rats from Tory and blessed the soil so they dare not return. Even better, perhaps, is the fact that islanders don't have to pay any taxes.

While on the island, try to scale the two tors (steep hills) from which Tory gets its name; the views are splendid. On top of one there's a holy stone — it is said that those who stand on it and spin around three times to the right will be granted any wish that they make.

It is possible to sail to Tory from a number of ports, and Falcarragh is as convenient as any; contact *James Ferry* (phone: 74-35177). Travelers can also take the mail boat from Bunbeg. Inquire at the pier. To avoid being marooned on the island, make sure that no bad weather is in the offing on the day of departure. Wild Atlantic storms are frequent, and Tory is often cut off from the mainland for 2 or 3 weeks at a time. But the people are extraordinarily kind and hospitable, so that even an enforced stay can be a pleasant experience.

En Route from Tory Island After returning to the mainland, get back on N56 in Falcarragh and head southwest to Gortahork. At this point take the signposted road that runs northwest to Meenaclady along the northern coast toward the promontory known as Bloody Foreland, located at the extreme northwestern tip of the Gaeltacht region known as Gweedore. It got its name from the blood-red color of the rocks as they are struck by the setting sun. The road swings around the headland and then turns south through the seaside resorts of Derrybeg and Bunbeg, where numerous modern vacation homes have been built in recent years.

Turn left (west) in Bunbeg and follow the signpost to Gweedore village, returning to N56, the main route. From Gweedore, it's 2 miles east to Dunlewy, which is just south of Errigal Mountain.

CHECKING IN/EATING OUT

Gweedore Perched vertiginously on the brink of a cliff way above a golden beach, this smart, ultramodern hostelry with 38 rooms and 3 suites offers all the creature comforts, including good food. A signpost on Bunbeg's main street points the way (phone: 75-31177; fax: 75-31726). Expensive to moderate.

McFadden's A venerable and classy family-run hotel, where friendliness and personal attention are the winning points. The food can be recommended, too. There are 18 guestrooms, all with private baths and TV sets. Main St., Gortahork (phone: 74-35267). Moderate.

ERRIGAL MOUNTAIN/DUNLEWY People unskilled in mountain climbing should not attempt Errigal unless accompanied by a local guide. From the summit of this 2,466-foot mountain it is possible to see as far away as the Scottish Highlands. While in Dunlewy, take the opportunity to walk south of the village into an exotic valley called the Poisoned Glen. Poisonous weeds known as spurge grow prolifically in the glen and have contaminated a lake, making its waters unsafe to drink. When the weather turns warm in summer, all sorts of creeping and flying insects infest the place, making it feel uncomfortably like a rain forest — but without the trees.

En Route from Dunlewy Return to the main road, N56, and head southwest for 6 miles to the area called "the Rosses" (meaning promontories or headlands, of which there are countless hereabouts). The bleakness of the large, lonely stretches of uninhabited bogland draws many tourists every summer.

About 3 miles south of Gweedore is the village of Crolly, home of the well-known traditional band, *Clannad*. When they are in town, the music in these parts is even better than usual. Check at their father's place, *Leo's Tavern* (Meenaleck; phone: 75-48143). Walk south of Crolly on the Dungloe road, but be prepared for a deafening crash as you pass by a giant glacial boulder. This is the Big Stone of the Leaping Fox, and legend says it will come tumbling down when an honest person passes it — so you've been warned. Instead of taking the main road from Crolly directly to Dungloe, the real heart of the Rosses, turn right (west) at the signposted road to Annagary, which circles the coast through Kincasslagh to Burtonport.

BURTONPORT/ARRANMORE ISLAND Turn right at the signpost for Burtonport, one of the busiest fishing ports in Ireland, which lands more salmon and lobster than anywhere else in the country. Boats to the island of Arranmore, 3 miles offshore, also leave from Burtonport. There are frequent departures starting at 10:30 AM (phone: 75-21532); the ferry can carry a small number of automobiles. Those who want to relax and fish can catch rainbow trout in Lough Shure; contact Philip Boyle (phone: 75-21508). Those who prefer more strenuous activity can try the 4-mile walk to Rinrawros Point, a lovely spot dominated by a lighthouse.

CHECKING IN/EATING OUT

Ostan Na Rosann A good, modern 48-room hotel, with an indoor pool and a dining room serving wholesome food in enormous portions. Just outside Dungloe on the road to Burtonport (phone: 75-21088; fax: 75-21365). Moderate.

En Route from Burtonport Take the signposted road from Burtonport south to Dungloe.

DUNGLOE This is considered the capital of the Rosses. Although the town itself is unremarkable, there is some good trout fishing in the lakes and rivers nearby.

En Route from Dungloe Take N56 south to Maas, 13 miles away, and turn right (west) to reach the pretty villages of Narin and Portnoo, both high above Gweebarra Bay. There is real solitude here because this area has not yet been overrun by tourists, and a number of secluded beaches and coves can be found along the coast. When the tide is out, it is possible to walk across the sands from Narin to the island of Iniskeel to see the ruins of a 6th-century church.

Travel around the circular road from Portnoo, through Rosbeg, to the junction of R261, and then turn right (south) for Ardara, which is tucked away in a deep valley where the River Owentocker races over rocks and boulders into Loughros More Bay. It is an area renowned for the weaving of Donegal tweed, and many shops in the village offer real bargains in tweed goods. *Kennedy's of Ardara* (phone: 75-41106) features Donegal tweed jackets and has good buys on locally knit Aran sweaters. *Bonner's* (phone: 75-41303; fax: 75-41270) sells Donegal tweed by the yard. Both are on the main street. Just outside town on the Killibegs road is *John Molloy's* factory and spacious tweed shop (phone: 75-41133; fax: 75-41336). A *Weavers' Fair,* usually held the first weekend of July, fills the streets of the village. The fair recalls the way the tweed was marketed in the old days, when weavers from all over the countryside brought their fabric to town to be sold. These days, however, the emphasis is on preserving the old crafts: Weavers ply the looms set up in street stalls, and farther down the street sheep are shorn and wool is carded and spun. There's plenty of music in the pubs in the evenings.

Adventurous visitors may want to look for the signposts that point the way to the Maghera sea caves, where moonshiners used to ply their illicit art. Exploring these caves is an exciting experience, but first check the tide schedules to avoid any danger. Be sure to visit the Church of the Holy Family, which contains fine stained glass by the artist Evie Hone.

Two miles south of Ardara on N56, turn right (west) at the signpost for Glencolumbkille. At Crobane, 3 miles farther, take the right fork, which runs through the Glengesh Pass, a thrilling drive. The road climbs 900 feet into the clouds and then plunges dizzily to the valley below. The landscape flattens as the road reaches Glencolumbkille.

CHECKING IN/EATING OUT

Lake House An old-fashioned hostelry offering friendly personal attention and wholesome home-cooked food. There are 10 guestrooms, 6 with private baths. Portnoo (phone: 75-45123). Inexpensive.

Nesbitt Arms A traditional inn with 27 rooms (8 with private baths), where the comfort of guests is always kept in mind. Great food and a good buy. Main St., Ardara (phone: 75-41103). Inexpensive.

GLENCOLUMBKILLE This is the lost valley where Columba, the patron saint of Donegal, lived in retreat from the world. He built a monastic prayer house here in the 6th century, and even today reminders of his presence are scattered around the glen. The whole place has a timelessness about it; there's little to remind visitors of the outside world.

On *St. Columba's Feast Day,* June 9, hundreds of people make a 3-mile pilgrimage through the glen, stopping to pray at ancient stone crosses along the way. At one of those crosses, beside the Protestant church, the pilgrims kiss the stone and then peer through an opening in the top in the belief that if they are without sin they may be given a glimpse of the next world.

But not only Christian artifacts are to be found in Glencolumbkille. There's also much evidence of an earlier presence. Nearly 50 monuments traceable to pre-Christian times are scattered throughout the glen, including underground passages and burial places.

Some years back, to provide employment and halt emigration from the glen, the local people formed a cooperative to develop craftsmanship and home industries and to attract more tourists. The result, the *Glencolumbkille Cooperative Society* (phone: 73-30015), has been one of the most encouraging success stories of rural Ireland. To see what life was like beneath the thatched roofs of Irish cottages in other eras, visit the nearby *Glencolumbkille Folk Village* (phone: 73-30017), where the past has been reconstructed in fine detail. It's open daily; admission charge.

CHECKING IN/EATING OUT

Glencolumbkille The only hotel in the valley has 19 rooms (all with private baths) and offers a reasonable degree of comfort. It has an exceptionally friendly staff and fairly good food. Malinmore, Glencolumbkille (phone: 73-30003). Moderate.

En Route from Glencolumbkille To complete the tour circuit back to Donegal Town, take R263 from Glencolumbkille for 20 miles through Carrick, Kilcar, and Killybegs. Killybegs is Ireland's most important fishing port, and the sight of its fishing fleet coming home in the evening, with thousands of sea gulls shrieking above it, is a great spectacle. Just north of Killybegs, rejoin N56. From here it's a 17-mile run into Donegal Town.

West Cork

Although often overlooked in favor of Kerry, its more famous neighbor, West Cork is a very special part of Ireland. Here the landscape is a palette of constantly changing colors, and the terrain varies from the soft shoulders of the inland Shehy Mountains to the sandy coves along the southern coast. The area around Bantry Bay — kissed by the warm, gentle Gulf Stream current — abounds with soaring palm trees and other lush, subtropical foliage.

But scenic beauty is by no means Cork's sole attraction. Its fine bathing strands, climbable peaks, excellent fishing waters, and busy marinas make the area a paradise for sports enthusiasts. In addition, there are many lively, cheerful villages where pub regulars have formed singing groups; small mountain towns where the lilt of the ancient Irish tongue is still heard; remote, lovely places where time seems to have stood still.

Our route, which begins and ends in Cork City, traces a leisurely circuit around West Cork. First stops are the towns of Macroom and Irish-speaking Ballingeary, and next is the historic, lovely lake of Gougane Barra. The route continues west to balmy Bantry Bay, with an excursion around the Beara Peninsula (which must include a bit of County Kerry), then south and east to the picturesque villages of Skibbereen, Clonakilty, and Kinsale. The entire route is about 200 miles and can be covered easily in 2 to 3 days.

Except perhaps in high season, it's fairly safe to ramble along without hotel reservations, although many places are open only from May to October. A wide selection of accommodations is available, from bed and breakfast lodging in a simple bungalow to an elegant room with a fine meal in a former mansion. Expect to pay $150 or more per night for a double room at places listed as expensive, from $75 to $100 at establishments in the moderate category, and less than $75 at inexpensive places. A meal for two (excluding wine, tips, and drinks) will cost $75 and up in a restaurant listed as expensive, between $35 and $70 in those described as moderate, and under $30 at places in the inexpensive category. For each location, hotels and restaurants are listed alphabetically by price category.

CORK For a detailed report on sights, hotels, and restaurants, see *Cork City* in THE CITIES.

En Route from Cork R618 winds 23½ miles along the north bank of the River Lee and passes through the charming village of Dripsey, with its woolen mills, and then through Coachford to Macroom.

MACROOM At the center of town stands Macroom Castle, granted to Admiral William Penn by Oliver Cromwell in 1654. (Penn, once Governor of Kinsale, was the father of William Penn, founder of Pennsylvania.) Over the years, the castle endured much strife and was burned for the final time during the Irish civil war in the early 1920s. The ruins have been declared a national monument and are partly restored. There's a 9-hole golf course nearby on a steep slope overlooking the River Sullane.

Macroom owes its existence to its location near the confluence of three rivers — the Lee, Laney, and Sullane. It's a thriving market town, with an annual agricultural show in summer. Posters for this show advertise competitions for "horses, cakes, sheep, and honey" — a compelling collage of images and flavors.

En Route from Macroom Go back 1 mile on the Cork road and turn south onto R584 for Inchigeelagh. Past Inchigeelagh, the road hugs the north bank of the long and lovely Lough Allua. But this route follows the minor road along the south bank, which is even more beautiful, for 24 miles.

BALLINGEARY This village is in the heart of the Gaeltacht — an Irish-speaking district — in West Cork, and every summer young people flock here from all over the country to study in school-sponsored Irish language programs. Villagers, however, greet visitors in perfect and often mellifluous English. *Quill's Woollen Market* on the main street (phone: 26-47008), a superb crafts and knitwear shop, produces and sells handsome garments made from the skins of sheep and goats.

Make a right turn 3¾ miles beyond Ballingeary, at the sign for Gougane Barra. The fork in the road is marked by a large crucifixion tableau and a memorial to local poet Máire Bhuí Ní Laoghaire.

GOUGANE BARRA The mountain-encircled lake of Gougane Barra, source of the River Lee, is where St. Finbarre, the founder of Cork, had his hermitage in the 6th century. It's clear why this isolated and serene valley was chosen for monastic contemplation. Joined to the lakeshore by a causeway is an island with a modern Irish Romanesque chapel. The surrounding area is a beautiful forest park with picnic areas and hiking trails. Fishing is free, but don't expect a great catch; as one local put it, "Saint Finbarre let everybody fish free, and that was about a thousand years ago, so I don't expect there's much left to catch."

Return to R584 and continue southwest as the road descends via Keimaneigh Pass and the Ouvane Valley 11 miles to Ballylickey and Bantry.

CHECKING IN/EATING OUT

Gougane Barra A family-run hotel that offers 25 rooms, each with a private bath, and a dining room with a lovely view of the lake and hills. It's an ideal base for hiking the spectacularly beautiful 400-acre forest park along the Lee. Open April to October. Gougane Barra (phone: 26-47069; 800-447-7462 from the US; fax: 26-47226). Moderate.

BANTRY This town is the site of the spectacular, mostly Georgian Bantry House (phone: 27-50047), once the seat of the Earls of Bantry. The mansion is furnished with antiques, tapestries, and paintings collected by the second Earl of Bantry during his travels in Europe in the early 19th century. Surrounded by elegant terraces and gardens, it overlooks beautiful Bantry Bay. It's open daily from 9 AM to 6 PM; admission charge.

Bantry is the perfect stop for those interested in water sports; there's a small beach and facilities for skin diving and water skiing. Check at the tourist board (New St.; phone: 27-50229). It is also a good base for excursions into the Beara Peninsula.

CHECKING IN

Ballylickey Manor House Although this lovely Georgian mansion was gutted by fire 11 years ago, its cottages and a couple of suites in the main house (a total of 11 rooms) are open to guests. Pluses include an outdoor swimming pool and a poolside restaurant. Open April through October. For additional details, see *Rural Retreats* in DIVERSIONS. Ballylickey (phone: 27-50071; 800-223-6510 from the US; fax: 27-50124). Expensive to moderate.

Sea View House Aptly named, this lovely, 17-room white manor house is perched in a sylvan setting overlooking Bantry Bay. The heirlooms-filled public rooms include an award-winning restaurant (see *Eating Out*) and an oak-trimmed lounge with an adjacent sun deck. Open mid-March through mid-November. For additional details, see *Rural Retreats* in DIVERSIONS. Ballylickey, Bantry (phone: 27-50073; 800-447-7462 from the US; fax: 27-51555). Expensive to moderate.

Westlodge Here is a modern 90-room hotel, bordered by mountains on one side and Bantry Bay on the other. There's a restaurant, a tavern, an indoor pool, a sauna, an all-weather tennis court, squash courts, and a jogging trail. About a mile outside Bantry on N71, the coastal road (phone: 27-50360; fax: 27-50438). Moderate.

Shangri-La A modern, private residence with hotel-type comforts, it offers 6 rooms (5 with private baths), a restaurant with wine license, and a parking lot. Open year-round. Overlooking Bantry Bay, just outside the village (phone: 27-50244; fax: 27-51417). Inexpensive.

EATING OUT

Blair's Cove This restaurant in a renovated stone barn with a 250-year-old Georgian courtyard is on a country lane southeast of Bantry, overlooking Dunmanus Bay. Specialties include seafood, beef, and lamb grilled in an oak fireplace. Open Tuesdays through Saturdays for dinner and Sundays for lunch, early March to mid-October; also open for dinner Mondays in

July and August. Reservations necessary. Major credit cards accepted. The Durrus–Barley Cove road, Bantry (phone: 27-61127). Expensive.

Larchwood House Situated in a quiet setting about 3 miles from Bantry, this modern restaurant overlooks a 6-acre garden and the river. The emphasis is on new Irish cuisine, with specialties such as roast smoked pheasant with red currant sauce, John Dory sole with elderflower sauce, or rack of lamb with lemon and mint. Open for dinner only, Mondays through Saturdays from May through October, Thursdays through Saturdays the rest of the year. Reservations advised. Diners Club, MasterCard, and Visa accepted. Signposted about a mile off the main Ballylickey–Bantry road. Pearsons Bridge, Bantry (phone: 27-66181). Expensive.

Shiro The secluded Sheep's Head Peninsula may seem an unlikely place to find a great restaurant, let alone one serving authentic Japanese fare. But here it is, on Dunmanus Bay, about 15 miles southwest of Bantry, in the unique country home and 12-seat dining room of Kei and Werner Pilz. The menu ranges from sashimi and tempura to *tun-katsu* pork and *gyo-za* beef. Open daily for dinner; closed January. Reservations essential. Major credit cards accepted. Ahakista (phone: 27-67030). Expensive.

Sea View House Surrounded by lush gardens and with views of Bantry Bay, the elegance of this country house dining room is enhanced by the culinary creativity of chef-owner Kathleen O'Sullivan. The menu changes nightly, but often includes appetizers such as pear and walnut salad or seafood mousse with vermouth sauce, and such main courses as scallops Parisienne served in the shell with cheese and wine sauce, chicken breast stuffed with wild herbs, or monkfish with batons of fresh vegetables. For dessert, the homemade ice creams (in such exotic flavors as plum and prune or brown bread) are extremely tempting. Open for lunch and dinner daily, April through October. Reservations advised. Major credit cards accepted. Ballylickey (phone: 27-50073). Expensive to moderate.

Tra Amici Nestled in a brook-side garden amid flowers and eucalyptus trees, this modern eatery exudes a country cottage atmosphere. The restaurant's name means "among friends" in Italian, and accordingly the chef blends Italian recipes with Irish ingredients, such as large grilled prawns in garlic, lemon, and olive oil; filet of beef stuffed with Gorgonzola cheese; and veal picatta *al limone*. Open for dinner Mondays through Saturdays, April through October; Fridays and Saturdays only from November through March. Reservations advised. MasterCard and Visa accepted. Coomhola Rd., Dromkeal, Bantry (phone: 27-50235). Moderate.

En Route from Bantry For a scenic, if curvy, drive into the village of Glengarriff from Bantry or Ballylickey, take the main road, N71, which for the next 10 miles hugs the edge of the bay.

GLENGARRIFF The name means "rough glen," a description that is only partially true of this lovely village snuggled into a deeply wooded glen at the southeastern corner of the Beara Peninsula. There is really nothing rough about it. Sheltered as it is from any harsh winds by mountains on three sides, the village has a justly famous reputation for mild weather and luxuriant vegetation. Arbutus, eucalyptus, fuchsia, rhododendron, and blue-eyed grass are among the plants and trees that flourish in the glen, and on Garinish Island in Glengarriff Harbour, the growth is subtropical. Until the early part of this century, the island was bare, but its owners began to transform it with an extraordinary richness of flowers and foliage laid out in beautiful, Italian-style formal gardens. At the highest point of the island is a Martello tower, the first of many built around Britain and Ireland in preparation for the expected Napoleonic invasion of 1804–5. The island was privately owned until 1939, when it was given to Ireland. It is open to the public (admission charge for the gardens). Boats leave Glengarriff regularly between 9:30 AM and 6 PM on Mondays through Saturdays, 1 to 6 PM on Sundays, in March through October. Contact the *Harbour Queen Ferry* (phone: 27-63081) or the *Blue Pool Ferry* (phone: 27-63170). There is excellent sea and river fishing in and around Glengarriff, and bathing is good along the nearby coves, one of which, Poulgorm ("blue pool"), is an extremely picturesque spot just a 2-minute walk from the post office. The village also has tennis courts, a golf course, and unlimited terrain for riding and walking.

CHECKING IN/EATING OUT

Eccles Overlooking Glengarriff Harbour, this traditional, but updated and expanded, hotel offers 49 rooms, all with private baths, TV sets, and phones. Guests also enjoy a restaurant, a lounge, and lovely gardens. Open year-round. Glengarriff (phone: 27-63003; fax: 27-63319). Moderate.

En Route from Glengarriff Route R572 twists west into the poor and rocky country along the south coast of the Beara Peninsula, a thinly populated, underdeveloped region that is quite beautiful and the least frequented of the three great southwestern peninsulas. The full circuit can fill at least a day, but it can be shortened by cutting across the center of the peninsula on the spectacular Healy Pass road. Upon reaching Adrigole village, 12 miles from Glengarriff, take the signposted road, R574, to the right for the Healy Pass.

HEALY PASS Work on this road began as a relief project during the famine years of the mid-19th century but stopped shortly thereafter. It was resumed in 1928 at the direction of Tim Healy, the first Governor-General of the Irish Free State (a native of Bantry), and was finished 3 years later. The road climbs to a height of 1,084 feet as it crosses the Caha Mountains (and the border between County Cork and County Kerry) and provides rewarding views over Mizen Head and Sheep's Head to the south, and Derreen, Kilmakilloge Harbour, the River Kenmare, and the mountains of the Iveragh Peninsula to the north. The road descends to Lauragh on the northern coast of the peninsula, but those who wish to explore the isolated region farther west can retrace their route along Healy Pass, admiring the splendid sight of Bantry Bay along the way to Adrigole.

En Route from Adrigole Proceed west 8 miles on R572. The route to Castletownbere is dominated by the lean, well-named Hungry Hill (a reminder of the famine of 1845 and, at 2,251 feet, the highest point on the peninsula), while Bere Island, with its two Martello towers, emerges to the left in Bantry Bay. The island was named for Beara, a Spanish princess married to Eogan, a legend-steeped historical figure who landed here during an invasion of Ireland. Eventually, the whole peninsula was named for the princess.

CASTLETOWNBERE No more than a string of houses along both sides of the street, this village grew up at the beginning of the 19th century when the copper mines at Allihies, west of town, were opened. Its sheltered natural harbor continued to earn the community a living as the site of a British naval base until 1938, and it is now becoming one of Ireland's main fishing centers, with tourism also on the rise. Note the seven dormer windows, like elegant ships' portholes, on the three houses facing the pier — this architectural feature is typical of this area. The ruins of the 15th-century Dunboy Castle, the stronghold of the branch of the O'Sullivans who were lords of this peninsula, are about 2 miles west of town.

CHECKING IN/EATING OUT

Craigie's Cametringane House Opened in 1985, this family-run inn is nestled in an idyllic setting on Bantry Bay, just outside the village. A good place to relax and enjoy some tennis, sailing, windsurfing, and fishing, it has 18 rooms (14 with private baths), a seafood restaurant, and a convivial pub. Open year-round. Castletownbere (phone: 27-70379; 800-447-7462 from the US). Moderate.

En Route from Castletownbere Continue west on R572 for about 6 miles. When the road divides, with a sign pointing each way to Allihies, take the road to the right, R575. Along the way are good views of the two Skellig Rocks and of Scariff and Deenish islands at the end of the River Kenmare. The road passes the abandoned Allihies copper mines, first worked by Iberian miners some 4,000 years ago and reopened during the Napoleonic wars by the Puxley family, who made a great fortune. The Puxleys employed no fewer than 1,200 people before the operation succumbed to competition in 1886. Writer Daphne du Maurier used Puxley family papers as part of the research for her book *Hungry Hill*.

After skirting the little village of Allihies, now a shadow of its former self, follow the signs to Eyeries, then on to Ardgroom and to Lauragh, at the head of Kilmakillage Harbour and the border of County Kerry. On a good day, this 31-mile stretch of the route provides some of the most striking scenery in all of West Cork and Kerry. The road, however, is narrow and twisting most of the way.

LAURAGH The Healy Pass road across the peninsula joins the scenic sea road, R571, at Lauragh, County Kerry. Close to the village is the estate of Derreen House (Kenmare–Castletownbere Rd.; phone: 64-83103), whose beautiful subtropical gardens are open to visitors daily from 11 AM to 6 PM from early April through September. The gardens — much less formal than those of Garinish Island or Muckross House — are remarkable for their rhododendron, camellias, tree ferns, bamboo, and eucalyptus.

En Route from Lauragh From Lauragh, R571 passes the Cloonie lakes and Lough Inchiquin — well stocked with salmon and sea and brown trout — as it continues east along the coast to Kenmare, County Kerry (see *The Ring of Kerry* route). From Kenmare, it is 17 miles back to Glengarriff and 29 miles to Bantry via N71.

Head south from Kenmare on N71, which provides fine views of the River Kenmare and of the surrounding mountains. The road follows the valley of the River Sheen for several miles, then crosses the River Baurearagh and begins to climb through a series of tunnels, the longest one passing under the border between County Cork and County Kerry. Beyond the main tunnel, far to the right, is Barley Lake, a striking glacial corrie (basin) filled with water, with an improbable road snaking up to it. The tortuous Caha Mountains are on the right, and the great stretch of Bantry Bay is visible below, with the tip of Whiddy Island barely discernible. The road then descends through a valley into Glengarriff. Return to Bantry via N71.

En Route from Bantry Just beyond Bantry, N71 leaves the sea, and the landscape becomes a great patchwork of farm fields, with colors changing every mile. This region has enjoyed an increased affluence in the past decade, and the prosperity is reflected in freshly painted farmhouses and neatly kept yards. In West Cork, as elsewhere in Ireland, cattle are the mainstay of the economy. (The human population of the entire Republic is just over 3.5 million; the livestock population often reaches three times that number.) On the road, it is often necessary to stop your car to give way to lumbering herds.

From Ballydehob, you can drive 8 miles directly to Skibbereen or try a scenic side trip westward down the peninsula. The first community on the detour is Schull, a little village popular with fisherfolk and sailors; a deep-sea angling competition is held here in July and a regatta in August.

From Schull, follow the road to Goleen, where the fine strand nearby offers prime sunbathing, then press on to Crookhaven, a pretty harbor town with some small beaches. A few miles farther are the dramatic cliffs of Mizen Head, the southernmost point in Ireland. Rather than backtrack, return to Schull and Ballydehob via the northern route across the peninsula, which passes Mt. Gabriel (1,339 feet) and the well-preserved castle of Dunmanus, one of the many 15th- and 16th-century strongholds that dot this part of the country.

CHECKING IN/EATING OUT

Ard Na Greine On secluded grounds just a mile outside the village and harbor of Schull, this 18th-century farmhouse is now a delightful country inn, with 7 rooms (each with private bath), a seafood restaurant, a pub, and extensive gardens. Open *Easter* through October. For additional details, see *Rural Retreats* in DIVERSIONS. Schull (phone: 28-28181; 800-223-6510 from the US; fax: 28-28573). Moderate.

Barley Cove Beach On a cliff overlooking the Atlantic, this complex includes 10 rooms and 23 chalets (all with private baths), a heated indoor pool, a tennis court, fishing, and a 9-hole, par 3 golf course. Barley Cove, near Goleen (phone: 28-35234; 800-447-7462 from the US; fax: 28-35100). Moderate.

SKIBBEREEN This town offers some first-rate fishing in the nearby Shepperton, Ballinlough, Lissard, and Ballyalla lakes (tackle and boats may be rented). It's also a convenient jumping-off point for exploring the shores and islands of the quaintly named Roaring Water Bay. Eight miles to the southwest, the little town of Baltimore has been one of Ireland's more popular ports of call for hundreds of years because of its sheltered harbor. There is good fishing and boating here, and a ferry goes over to the Irish-speaking Cape Clear Island, which boasts megalithic stones, an ancient church, a bird observatory, and a youth hostel. There's also a ferry to Sherkin Island, with its ruins of a Franciscan friary. (For ferry information call *Coiste Naomh Ciaran;* phone: 28-39119.) Baltimore is also the home of the *Glenans Irish Sailing Centre* (phone: 28-20154).

En Route from Skibbereen The 25-mile drive along the coast road to Kinsale is pretty and relaxing. Each small town has a particular attraction: Castletownshend's ruined castle and prehistoric stone fort are worth a look; Glandore offers good fishing; Rosscarbery is the site of a monastery established by St. Fachtna in the 6th century; Clonakilty, close to many fine beaches, is also the home of the *West Cork Regional Museum* (Western Rd.; no phone); and the Franciscan abbey in Timoleague dates from the 14th century.

CHECKING IN/EATING OUT

Ardnavaha House About 5 miles north of Clonakilty, with 40 acres of woods, meadows, and gardens, this renovated Georgian manor house has a modern addition with 36 rooms, each with a private bath and a balcony or terrace. It also has a restaurant, a heated outdoor pool, a sauna, a tennis court, and riding stables with an arena. Open year-round. Ballinascarthy (phone: 23-39135; 800-44-UTELL from the US; fax: 23-39316). Expensive to moderate.

KINSALE Clinging to a hill overlooking the Bandon River estuary, Kinsale is an appealing little town (population 2,000) whose tall, whitewashed houses huddle together along narrow, twisting lanes. A morning's stroll along the signposted walking tour takes visitors through the town's most charming streets and past St. Multose Church, an impressive stone structure dating from the 13th century; the museum/courthouse on Market Square; Desmond Castle, a 16th-century tower house on Cork Street (also known as the French Prison because Frenchmen were imprisoned there during the Napoleonic wars); and the Carmelite friary, dating from 1314, with its nearby ruins of a Holy Well.

On the outskirts of Kinsale are two magnificent old fortresses. James Fort, on the Castlepark road, is a perfect example of a 17th-century star design. It was built in 1601. Charles Fort, on the Summer Cove road, was begun around 1677 but now has many more recent additions. It's also laid out on the star plan and was in use as a major harbor fortification until 1922.

The wide, sheltered harbor at Kinsale is one of the most scenic in Ireland, and since the building of a modern marina in 1979 it has become a favorite port with British and European yachtsmen. Deep-sea fishing off the Old Head of Kinsale can be arranged — try the *Kinsale Marine Services Angling Centre* (Lower O'Connell St.; phone: 21-772611) or the *Trident Hotel Angling Centre* (World's End; phone: 21-772301) — and the swimming and sunning are wonderful on the neighboring strands at Sandy Cove and James Fort. Sailing and windsurfing can be arranged through the nearby *Oysterhaven Centre* (Belgooly; phone: 21-770738). Kinsale also has a growing reputation as the culinary capital of Ireland. For the town's size, it offers an extraordinary range of top class restaurants (see *Eating Out,* below) whose proprietors sponsor the *Kinsale Gourmet Festival* every October (for detailed information, see *Feis and Fleadh: The Best Festivals* in DIVERSIONS).

Kinsale also played an interesting role in Irish history, for it was here in 1601 that the Irish forces, led by the chieftains Hugh O'Neill and Hugh O'Donnell, suffered their final defeat at the hands of Queen Elizabeth I's army under Lord Mountjoy. This little village was also the focus of the world's attention in May 1915, when the *Lusitania* was torpedoed and sunk off the Old Head of Kinsale with a loss of more than 1,500 lives.

CHECKING IN

Acton's This member of the Forte hotel chain has a terrific location facing the harbor, extensive rose gardens, a seafood restaurant, a nautical tavern, and a leisure complex with an indoor swimming pool, saunas, sunbeds, and a gymnasium. There are 55 rooms, each with private bath. The Waterfront, Kinsale (phone: 21-772135; 800-CALL-THF or 800-FORTE-40 from the US; fax: 21-772231). Expensive.

Blue Haven In the middle of the village, this small, cozy hotel has 10 rooms (7 with private baths). Each room is individually named and decorated with furnishings and paintings by local artists and artisans. For fine dining, visit the hotel's acclaimed restaurant (see *Eating Out*). There is a homey breakfast room, a wood-paneled bar with an open fireplace, and a sunlit conservatory. Open year-round. Pearse St., Kinsale (phone: 21-772209; fax: 21-774268). Expensive.

The Moorings Overlooking the harbor and marina, this modern guesthouse has 8 rooms, all bright, cheery, and outfitted with private baths, color TV sets, direct-dial phones, and coffee/tea makers. Five rooms with balconies face the harbor; the rest overlook the garden. Rates include full Irish breakfast. Open year-round. Scilly, Kinsale (phone: 21-772376; fax: 21-772675). Moderate.

Trident A modern stone-faced structure of 54 bedrooms (each with private bath), this property is ideally situated right on the harbor, with a seafood restaurant and a Kinsale version of a Fisherman's Wharf bar. There's a fishing and scuba diving center on the premises. World's End, Kinsale (phone: 21-772301; fax: 21-774173). Moderate.

Old Bank House Located in the heart of town next to the post office, this Georgian-style guesthouse is owned by the Riese family, who also operate the long-established *Vintage* restaurant (see *Eating Out*). There are 9 guestrooms, each with a private bath or shower, TV set, telephone, and period furnishings. Open year-round. Pearse St., Kinsale (phone: 21-774075 or 21-772968). Moderate to inexpensive.

EATING OUT

Blue Haven In a town known for its fine restaurants, this is one of the best. Owners Brian and Anne Cronin have won many accolades over the years for such specialties as prawn tails with salmon mousse, wood-smoked filet of brill, duck baked in brandy, and heaping platters of the local catch of the day. The adjacent pub is known for its innovative light lunch items.

Open daily for lunch and dinner. Reservations advised. Major credit cards accepted. Pearse St., Kinsale (phone: 21-772209). Expensive to moderate.

Cottage Loft Originally on the edge of town and now in the heart of the action, this award-winning restaurant has all the warmth of an Irish hearth. The bill of fare features a range of dishes from seafood kebabs and sole on the bone to Peking pork and duck in black cherry sauce. Open for lunch and dinner; closed Mondays from late October to mid-March. Reservations advised. MasterCard and Visa accepted. 6 Main St., Kinsale (phone: 21-772803). Expensive to moderate.

Man Friday Beautifully situated in its own garden, this dining spot, another award winner, has a rustic decor and a menu that includes stuffed sole with prawns, crab, and leek; duck with nectarine and brandy sauce; and steak *au poivre.* Open for dinner only; closed Sundays. Reservations advised. MasterCard and Visa accepted. Scilly, Kinsale (phone: 21-772260). Expensive to moderate.

Vintage A small, vine-covered restaurant with beamed ceilings, it stands on a winding street near the harbor. The cooking is imaginative, with particular emphasis on local produce. Choices include rack of lamb, free-range duckling, and medallions of monkfish. Open for dinner only; closed Sundays and January and February. Reservations necessary. Major credit cards accepted. Main St., Kinsale (phone: 21-772502). Expensive to moderate.

Bernard's The emphasis is on new Irish cuisine, served in a modern bistro setting, with such entrées as wild rabbit in cider, chicken stuffed with oysters, filet of black sole, and Kinsale bouillabaisse. Open for lunch and dinner; closed Tuesdays. Reservations advised. MasterCard and Visa accepted. Main St. at Emmet Pl., Kinsale (phone: 21-772233). Moderate.

Chez Jean Marc Previously located in Tralee, this newly transplanted restaurant adds a French flair to this food-loving town. The menu presents standards such as duck a l'orange, steak *au poivre,* seafood crêpes, and *coquilles St-Jacques.* Open for dinner nightly except Sunday from June through September, with a reduced schedule in the off-season. Reservations advised. Major credit cards accepted. Lower O'Connell St., Kinsale (phone: 21-774625). Moderate.

Max's Wine Bar Tiny but busy, this bistro serves simple meals — salad, soup, oysters, and spinach pasta with fresh salmon. Open daily for lunch and dinner, March through October. Reservations advised. MasterCard and Visa accepted. Main St., Kinsale (phone: 21-772443). Moderate to inexpensive.

1601 The name of this small bistro and bar refers to the year of the historic battle of Kinsale, which is depicted here in a wall-size mural. This is the ideal spot for a light meal — the menu offers homemade soup, quiche, salad, and pâté, as well as burgers, steaks, and seafood platters. Cappuccino, espresso, and pastries also are served. Open daily for lunch, dinner, and snacks. Reservations unnecessary. MasterCard and Visa accepted. Pearse St., Kinsale (phone: 772529). Inexpensive.

SHARING A PINT Kinsale is also well known for its assortment of lively public houses. Try the *Greyhound* (Marian Ter.; phone: 21-772889) or the *Anchor* (Main St.; phone: 21-772092) for pub grub, the *Dock* (Castle Park; phone: 21-772522) for memorable views of Kinsale's inner harbor. Pubs known for their music and entertainment include the *Spaniard* (Scilly; phone: 21-772436), *Shanakee* (Pearse St.; no phone), and *Creole's* (Pearse St.; phone: 21-774109). Other pubs as intriguing as their names are the *White House* (Pearse St.; phone: 21-772125), *Hole in the Wall* (Glen St.; phone: 21-772401), *Silver Salmon* (Market St.; no phone), *Cuckoo's Nest* (Main St.; phone: 21-774065), and *Lord Kinsale* (Main St.; phone: 21-772371).

En Route from Kinsale From Kinsale, it's just 18 miles back to Cork City. Any of several routes will do; R600, the most direct, passes by Cork Airport.

The Ring of Kerry

Artists and writers have for centuries celebrated the beauty of the kingdom of Kerry, where the majesty of Ireland's highest mountains contrasts starkly with romantic glens, and the splendor of the rugged coastline gives way to glorious lakes and luxurious forests. It is a landscape of great variety, with the sea and the ever-changing patterns in the sky as much a part of the vistas as the primordial shapes of solid ground or the seasonal come-and-go of blossoming bushes, trees, and green ground cover. A good portion of this southwestern county is made up of three peninsulas that constitute Kerry at its picturesque best: Dingle, Iveragh, and Beara, the last shared largely with County Cork.

The best known of these mountainous projections into the Atlantic is the middle one, the Iveragh Peninsula, circled by a much-promoted scenic route known as the Ring of Kerry. An air of remoteness still clings to Iveragh, in tiny fishing villages where Irish is still widely spoken and in ancient stones left behind by forgotten peoples. Ascetic monks who withdrew as far as they could from the world built their retreat on Skellig Michael, today a deserted site attracting only the extremely inquisitive.

The complete circuit of the peninsula — which extends nearly 40 miles southwest of Killarney and has an average breadth of 15 miles — is an approximately 110-mile round trip that will take the greater part of a day if toured at a leisurely pace. The route may be traveled clockwise (from Killarney to Kenmare and around), but the counterclockwise approach as described here (from Killarney to Killorglin and around) is suggested because it shows the scenery to its best advantage. Do not attempt this scenic run during heavy and continuous rain or if there is so much as a sea mist, because visibility will be extremely poor. If in doubt, call the Valentia Meteorological Station (phone: 66-72176) for a weather report.

If your plans include a night's stay or two on the Ring, estimate that a double room in lodgings classified as very expensive will cost $200 or more; in the expensive category, $125 to $200; in the moderate class, $75 to $125; and in the inexpensive category, under $75. Dinner for two (excluding wine, drinks, and tips) will be more than $100 in a very expensive restaurant, $75 to $100 in an expensive place, $50 to $75 in a moderate spot, and $50 or less in an inexpensive place. For each location, hotels and restaurants are listed alphabetically by price category.

KILLARNEY For a complete report on the city, its sights, hotels, and restaurants, see *Killarney* in THE CITIES.

En Route from Killarney To begin the route, take R562 northwest to Killorglin. The jagged mountains to the left are MacGillicuddy's Reeks, reduced to stumps by 200 million years of ruthless erosion but crowned nonetheless by the highest peak in Ireland, Carrantuohill (3,414 feet). Eight miles from Killarney, make a left turn at the signpost for Ballymalis Castle, on the banks of the River Laune. This is one of a line of castles built here by the Anglo-Normans, who then overran the area in the early 13th century. The present castle — partly restored — is a typical 16th-century tower house of 4 stories: the ground floor for storage, the second for defense, the third for sleeping, and the top, a single, splendid living room. Return to R562 and continue the remaining 5 miles into Killorglin.

KILLORGLIN The presence of another Anglo-Norman castle, now almost totally ruined, gave rise to this small town on the River Laune. Killorglin is famous for its *Puck Fair,* actually a 3-day horse, sheep, and cattle sale. Held every year from August 10 to 12, it is the area's greatest festival and draws people from all over County Kerry. On the first day, called *Gathering Day,* men of the town go into the mountains and capture the "puck," or wild male goat, who is then decorated with ribbons and enthroned on a platform above the town square, from which he presides over the festivities until *Scattering Day,* the end of the fair. In the meantime, shops are open day and night. The origins of the *Puck Fair* are uncertain. It may derive from the worship of the Celtic sun god Lúg, or it may date from the 17th century, when a herd of wild goats stampeded through the town ahead of approaching Cromwellian soldiers and thereby saved many lives.

EATING OUT

Nick's Located in an old stone house in the center of town, this award-winning spot offers hearty soup, sandwiches, and light meals by day and full dinner fare at night. Specialties range from game and vegetarian dishes to local seafoods. The decor is cozy with alcoves, an open fireplace, and a resident pianist. Open daily. Reservations necessary. Major credit cards accepted. 22 Lower Bridge St., Killorglin (phone: 66-61219). Moderate.

The Fishery Situated at the east end of town overlooking the river, this restaurant/pub is known for its salmon, both fresh and smoked, and other seafood. There's also an adjacent craft shop and art gallery. Open daily for lunch and dinner. Reservations advised for dinner. Major credit cards accepted. The Bridge, Killorglin (phone: 66-61106). Moderate to inexpensive.

En Route from Killorglin Continue southwest on N70 for 9 miles to Glenbeigh. Along the way, the road passes Lough Caragh on the left. Surrounded by magnificent scenery, it is definitely worth a detour.

Midway between Killorglin and Glenbeigh is a new attraction, the *Kerry Bog Village Museum* (phone: 66-69184), at Ballycleave on the main Killarney road. It is a re-creation of an early-19th-century Irish community, with replicas of a blacksmith's forge and house, turf cutter's house, laborer's cottage, thatcher's dwelling, stable, dairy, and hen house. The interiors of each building contain authentic implements and furnishings. The museum is open daily, May through September, with a reduced schedule in the off-season. There's an admission charge.

CHECKING IN

Ard na Sidhe Elegant, quiet, and beautifully secluded in the forest at Lough Caragh, this inn was once a private home. It now has 20 rooms, each with private bath. To find *Ard na Sidhe* (Irish for "hill of the fairies"), look for the signs on N70 between Killorglin and Glenbeigh. Open May through September. Carragh Lake, Killorglin (phone: 66-69105, or 800-221-1074 from the US; fax: 66-69282). Expensive.

GLENBEIGH This tiny holiday and fishing resort is situated at the foot of Seefin Mountain (1,621 feet), not far from where the River Behy flows out into Dingle Bay. One of Ireland's oldest and best golf courses, *Dooks,* overlooks the bay (phone: 66-68205). The Glenbeigh Horseshoe, a semicircle of hills from Seefin to Drung Hill, is known to nature lovers as one of the county's most scenic mountain walks. At the end of the village are the gaunt — and burnt — ruins of Glenbeigh Towers, or "Wynne's Folly," built by the local landlord, Lord Headley Wynne, during the 1870s.

A right turn onto an unclassified road beyond Glenbeigh leads, in 1½ miles, to Rossbeigh Strand, a long spit of land reaching into Dingle Bay to nearly meet its counterpart, Inch Strand, coming across the water from the Dingle Peninsula. The 2 miles of sand beach are backed by dunes, and at the end of the spit is a 19th-century stone tower built to guide ships into Castlemaine Harbour. During the 18th century, many transatlantic ships, driven by terrifying southwest storms, met their end at Rossbeigh, sometimes helped, it is said, by shipwreckers greedy for their cargo.

This region was the site of many stories from the Fenian cycle of Irish legends. It was here that Oisín, the son of Finn MacCool (the leader of the Fianna, a sort of standing army of the Iron Age), met the beautiful, golden-haired Niamh, who persuaded him to return with her to her own kingdom. Together the pair mounted the girl's white horse and galloped out along the Rossbeigh spit into the western ocean to the paradisiacal Land of Youth. Oisín came back 300 years later, but once off the horse he immediately turned into a very old man. Another legend set in the area is that of Diarmuid and Grainne. Daughter of the King of Ireland, Grainne was betrothed to Finn, whom she found too old, so she forced Diarmuid, a handsome young Kerryman, to elope with her. With a gang of murderous desperadoes (hired by Finn) in hot pursuit, they fled — first to a cave at Glenbeigh. The chase lasted 7 years, and eventually Diarmuid was killed by a magic boar and Grainne did marry Finn. In popular speech, many Irish prehistoric tombs are still called "beds of Diarmuid and Grainne."

CHECKING IN/EATING OUT

Towers Situated in the heart of Glenbeigh, this vintage inn has 37 guestrooms (all with private baths), many of which offer lovely views of the surrounding countryside. Also on the premises are a seafood restaurant and a lounge with nightly entertainment (also see *Pub Crawling* in DIVERSIONS). Closed November through March. Glenbeigh (phone: 66-68212; 800-447-7462 from the US; fax: 66-68260). Moderate.

En Route from Glenbeigh The main road to Cahirciveen, 17 miles away, encompasses some of the most memorable scenery along the Ring of Kerry. The road rises to Mountain Stage, so called because it was once a station for stagecoaches, and hugs the side of Drung Hill (2,104 feet), providing wonderful views of Dingle Bay and the mountains of the Dingle Peninsula beyond. A cairn near the top of Drung Hill is reputed to be the grave of St. Finian, a major leader of the great religious movement of the 6th and 7th centuries. The road continues high over the sea to Kells, a small resort on Kells Bay, and then descends to a broad valley running on to Cahirciveen. A mile before the town, just beyond the sharp turn left indicated by a series of striking yellow arrows, are the ruins of Carhan House. Daniel O'Connell, the national leader known as the Liberator who achieved emancipation for Irish Catholics, was born here in 1775.

CAHIRCIVEEN Set on the River Valentia at the head of Valentia Harbour, Cahirciveen (also spelled "Cahersiveen") grew up in the early 19th century. Its most notable building is the O'Connell Memorial Church on Main Street. Although intended to honor the centenary of Daniel O'Connell's birth in 1775, construction on the structure was not begun until 1888 when the cornerstone, sent by Pope Leo XIII from the catacombs in Rome, was laid. Across the bridge, about 2½ miles northwest of town, are the remains of Ballycarbery Castle, the magnificent 15th-century castle of MacCarthy Mor, once guarded by the old Gaelic O'Connell family. Cromwell's forces destroyed the castle in 1652 and drove the O'Connells to County Clare, though they later returned to the area. The ruins of an ancient stone forts Cahergal and Leacanabuaile are nearby. The latter, dating from the 9th or 10th century, is one of few stone forts to have been excavated. Inside, the remains of three stone beehive houses, once occupied by a poor farming community, were found, along with a square house apparently added later. Note the *souterrain,* originally an escape hatch, a place of refuge, and a storage space.

Valentia Harbour was well known in the 18th century as a smuggling port and hiding place for privateers. British naval vessels often anchored here too, but the smugglers earned their tolerance with judicious gifts of brandy. Valentia Island is in the harbor, joined to the mainland by a bridge at Portmagee (there's a good view of the harbor from the bridge).

En Route from Cahirciveen The Ring of Kerry route, N70, turns inland across the tip of the Iveragh Peninsula to Waterville, 11 miles away. Two detours along the way are possible: to Valentia Island (where there's good deep-sea fishing), and to the tiny village of Ballinskelligs. The turnoff for Portmagee and the bridge to Valentia Island is 4 miles southwest of Cahirciveen onto R565, and the turnoff for Ballinskelligs is 2 miles beyond that onto R566.

VALENTIA ISLAND The inhabitants of this tiny island (7 miles long and 2 to 3 miles wide) live by fishing, farming, and some tourism. The island is one of the most westerly points in Europe, and the first transatlantic telegraph cable, which came to Valentia in 1866, remained in use for 100 years. Knightstown, at Valentia's eastern end, consists of one main street and a lovely harbor and waterfront, and is a popular holiday resort renowned for its deep-sea fishing.

On the waterfront, directly across the bridge from Portmagee, is the entrance to the *Skillig Experience,* a new visitors' center. The building boasts a windowless façade, with grassy mounds and stone walls outside on the grounds. Inside, through a series of displays and audiovisuals, the center seeks to present an in-depth look at the Valentia area, and in particular the neighboring Skellig Rocks, two small islands off the coast (see below). The displays describe the long history of the Skelligs, focusing primarily on the 6th-century monks who inhabited the islands and founded a monastery there. The monastery survived for over 600 years and was widely recognized as a benchmark in the development of the early Christian church in Europe. For a closer look at the islands, visitors can then board a boat at Valentia and take a 1½-hour narrated cruise. The trip does not permit passengers to disembark on the island, but the boats cruise close enough for folks to see, hear, and smell the Skellig world, which includes thousands of indigenous sea birds and rare plant life. Open daily, May through September; limited schedule in April. There's an admission charge for the center and a separate fee for the cruise (phone: 64-31633).

SKELLIG ROCKS These two small islands, actually pyramids of rock, are 7 and 8½ miles off the coast of Bolus Head. Little Skellig (445 feet high), the smaller of the two, is a bird sanctuary with thousands of seabirds, especially gannets, nesting on its precipitous stone peaks. Bird life — puffins, razorbills, kittiwakes, gannets, and more — is also abundant on Great Skellig (714 feet high), or Skellig Michael, but this island is better known for the remains of the simple monastic settlement that existed here for 6 centuries. Founded, according to tradition, by St. Fionan and occupied by hermit monks between the 6th and the 12th centuries, the monastery has survived in almost perfect condition, probably because of the absence of frost in this mild westerly climate. The ruins, on a rock shelf 550 feet above the sea, consist of 6 beehive huts, 2 oratories that are early forms of the boat-shaped style that was used at Gallarus on the Dingle Peninsula, a ruined medieval church, a number of crosses and graves, and tiny patches of imported earth behind retaining walls where the monks may have attempted to grow something to vary their diet of seaweed, birds, and fish. Three steep stone stairways, corresponding to the three separate landing places (each one suitable for a different type of weather), lead to the settlement. Because the Skellig Rocks are slippery and hazardous, there are no organized boat trips that allow visitors to walk around the islands. Sightseers are encouraged to take the cruise that leaves from the visitors' center on Valentia Island and circles the rocks (see above).

BALLINSKELLIGS The blessing of a 4-mile beach along the western shore of Ballinskelligs Bay has made this tiny, partly Irish-speaking village a seaside resort. It is part of the Kerry Gaeltacht, and in the summer an Irish language school for children is conducted here. The ruins of a 16th-century MacCarthy castle are west of town, not far from the remains of an Augustinian monastery that was probably founded in the 12th or 13th century by monks returning from the monastic settlement of Skellig Michael. The ruins date from the 15th century and have been much eroded by the sea.

En Route from Ballinskelligs Follow the signposts back to N70 and Waterville; the right turn onto the main route 6 miles northeast of Ballinskelligs is just above the bridge over the River Inny, 2 miles north of Waterville.

WATERVILLE This small, unspoiled village lies on a strip of land between the Atlantic Ocean and beautiful Lough Currane, on the eastern shore of Ballinskelligs Bay. Mountains rise from the east and south of the lake. In addition to Lough Currane, there are many smaller lakes in the vicinity, making Waterville a famous angling center. Fishing for salmon, sea trout, and brown trout is free on Lough Currane and some of the smaller lakes, and by permit (available from any of the hotels) on still other lakes and the River Inny. There's also boating and bathing on the fine sandy beach on the bay shore. Resolute landlubbers can play golf on the championship *Waterville* golf course (phone: 66-74102; also see *Great Golf* in DIVERSIONS.)

Many early Christian ruins are scattered around Lough Currane, and the remains of a 12th-century Romanesque church can be found on a small island in the lake, known, not surprisingly, as Church Island. (It may be reached by boat, which can be hired in Waterville.) Waterville and Ballinskelligs Bay figure in many legends. According to one, Noah's son and granddaughter landed here after having been excluded from the Ark. According to another, the alignment of four stones on the skyline to the left of the road a mile south of town is the burial place of Scéné, wife of one of the eight leaders of the Milesians in the last, and greatest, of the legendary invasions of Ireland.

CHECKING IN

Butler Arms A well-known fishing hotel in town, this rambling, crenelated white house has been run by the same family for three generations and was a favorite haunt of Charlie Chaplin. Its restaurant, specializing in shellfish, is quite good. There are 29 rooms, all with private baths. Open April through October. Waterville (phone: 66-74144; 800-447-7462 from the US; fax: 66-74520). Expensive.

Club Med Situated on the outer reaches of the Ring of Kerry, bordered on one side by the Atlantic and on the other by Lough Currane, this resort (formerly the *Waterville Lake* hotel) is the first Club Med member in Ireland. There are 80 guestrooms with private baths, telephones, and TV sets, and 6 suites with fireplaces and balconies. A restaurant, piano bar, pub, bridge room, and shop are on the property. Sporting facilities include an indoor swimming pool and fitness center with a gym, saunas, and sunbeds, as well as three all-weather tennis courts. Bicycles also are available. There's fishing in the lake for salmon and brown trout, and in the ocean for sea trout (extra charge for boat and guide), and a free shuttle to the 18-hole championship *Waterville* golf course (greens fees are extra). Rates include meals with beer or wine, most sports, and nightly entertainment. Nightly reservations are accepted; weekly packages also are available. Waterville (phone: 66-74133; 800-CLUB-MED from the US; fax: 71-589-6086 via London). Expensive.

EATING OUT

Huntsman Furnished with dark oak priory tables and chairs, wrought-iron fixtures, and colorful hanging plants, this restaurant, owned by its chef, provides lovely waterside views with its seafood delights. Open daily for lunch, dinner, and light snacks; closed November through March. Reservations advised. Diners Club, MasterCard, and Visa accepted. In addition, there are 8 guestrooms, all with private baths. Waterville (phone: 66-74124; fax: 66-74560). Expensive to moderate.

Smuggler's The chef-owner of this renovated farmhouse with a nautical decor and panoramic views offers seafood specialties, as well as meat and poultry dishes. Selections from an extensive bar menu are also available. Open daily for lunch and dinner. Reservations advised for large groups. Major credit cards accepted. There are also 14 rooms for overnight guests. Cliff Rd., opposite the entrance to the golf course, Waterville (phone: 66-74330). Restaurant, expensive to moderate; guestrooms, inexpensive.

En Route from Waterville Heading south on N70, the road winds up to a height of 700 feet at the pass of Coomakista, affording superb views of the sharply rising (to 1,600 feet) inland mountains on one side and the lonely Skellig Rocks beyond the mouth of the bay on the other side. The road then descends in the direction of Derrynane Bay, separated from Ballin-skelligs Bay by a point of land called Hog's Head and from the River Kenmare by another point called Lamb's Head. Before the village of Caherdaniel, a signposted road to the right leads to *Derrynane House* (phone: 66-75113), ancestral home of the O'Connell family and now a museum. The O'Connells were a shrewd Irish family who lived by smuggling and importing embargoed goods. They also "exported" young Catholic Irishmen so they could obtain European educations and jobs denied them at home. Daniel O'Connell, the first Irish Catholic member of Britain's Parliament, inherited the Derrynane property from an uncle and lived here during his political life. The house, with a magnificent beach in front and a more sheltered beach at the side, has been restored and is open daily year-round, with O'Connell's personal possessions and furniture on display. It is part of Derrynane National Historic Park, which also includes a nature trail through lovely scenery. Open daily May through September; closed Mondays the rest of the year. There's an admission charge for the house.

Next along the route, near the shore of Derrynane Bay, is Caherdaniel. The village takes its name from a *caher,* or stone fort, possibly dating from the 6th century, which stands on the outskirts of town. Near it are the ruins of a much older fort and the remains of what seems to be an ancient road system used some 4,000 years ago. The route continues along the coast toward the small resort of Castlecove. Just before the village, a signpost points the way to the left for Staigue Fort, 2½ miles off the main road, beautifully positioned at the top of a valley that stretches to the sea.

CHECKING IN/EATING OUT

Derrynane This modern, 3-story, Best Western property in a secluded Gaelic-speaking area just off the main Ring of Kerry road offers wonderful views of the Atlantic Ocean. The 78 bedrooms have private baths and contemporary furnishings, TV sets, and telephones. There's a restaurant, lounge, gameroom, outdoor swimming pool, and access to a nearby beach; deep-sea fishing, horseback riding, windsurfing, and water skiing can be arranged at additional charge. Closed November to mid-March. Caherdaniel (phone: 66-75136; 800-528-1234 in the US; fax: 66-75160). Moderate.

STAIGUE FORT Nothing is known of the history of this circular stone fort, which could date as far back as 1000 BC. Though such forts are plentiful in the area, Staigue is one of the largest and most sophisticated, a masterly example of dry-stone construction (no mortar is used). It is also one of the best preserved of all ancient Irish structures. Little has been lost of the wall, which is up to 18 feet high on the north and west sides and 13 feet thick at the base and is scaled by sets of steps up to what was once a rampart. The area enclosed is 90 feet in diameter but contains no signs of houses, as at Leacanabuaile, leading to speculation that the fort — which has yet to be excavated — may have been occupied by nobility, who lived in wooden houses. Admire the quality of the fort's stonework, the sloping back of the walls, the massive lintels, and especially the architectural flourish of the steps inside. On the way back to Castlecove, look for a stone bridge with two spans on the left. Now in a field apparently going nowhere, it was once part of an old road system. Close by is an exposed rock with early copperworkers' writings.

En Route from Staigue Fort About half a mile beyond Castlecove village, an unnumbered road branches off the main road to White Strand, a particularly pleasant beach with beautiful views and good bathing. The main road then bends inland to Sneem, 13 miles from Caherdaniel, climbing through a low pass where there is a fine panorama of the Sneem Valley, with its great backdrop of mountains stretching as far as MacGillicuddy's Reeks.

SNEEM With its pink, green, bright red, robin's-egg blue, and even checkered houses freshly painted each year, this is a colorful and pretty village at the head of the River Sneem estuary. The town is divided in two by the river and has two village greens. Just before the narrow bridge between them, note the tiny Protestant church on the left, with its curiously Elizabethan air, a piece of 18th-century antiquarianism. Because Sneem is in fishing country (trout and salmon abound in the river and nearby mountain lakes), the church's weathervane sports a salmon. Stop just after the bridge to look at the river tumbling over the rocks below. Just beyond is an attractive 19th-century Italianate Catholic church on the right.

EATING OUT

Blue Bull A charming pub with three different rooms, each decorated with fascinating old prints of County Kerry scenes and, appropriately, a straw blue bull's head. This is a good stopping place, if only for a quick drink. In summer, a back room becomes a seafood restaurant, and there's music on most weekends throughout the year. Open daily for lunch and dinner from *Easter* to January 4. Reservations advised for dinner. Major credit cards accepted. Sneem (phone: 64-45231 or 64-45382). Restaurant, moderate; pub, inexpensive.

En Route from Sneem The Ring of Kerry route turns southeast toward the shore of the River Kenmare. A mile down the road, a detour signposted "Oyster Bed" (oysters thrive in this region) leads down to a pier where the weary can savor the calm of a garden spot before returning to the main road and driving the remaining mile to Parknasilla. Known for its lush trees, shrubs, and beautiful seascape, Parknasilla owes its subtropical vegetation to its position in a sheltered curve of coastline backed by the

895-foot Knockanamadane Hill. The *Great Southern* hotel (see *Checking In/Eating Out*), on the grounds of the onetime summer home of Charles Graves, Protestant Bishop of Limerick and grandfather of the poet Robert Graves, was a favorite holiday place of George Bernard Shaw. From Parknasilla, N70 runs east 12½ miles toward the upper end of the River Kenmare at Kenmare. Beyond Blackwater Bridge, in a forest on the right, is Dromore Castle, the seat of an old Gaelic family, the O'Mahonys, and the subject of a haunting lullaby. Also on the right, on a rock 2 miles out of Kenmare, are the ruins of Dunkerron Castle, a stronghold of the O'Sullivan family, branches of which occupied both sides of the River Kenmare from the early 13th century until they were driven out by the Cromwellians in the 17th century.

CHECKING IN/EATING OUT

Great Southern This luxury, 84-room hotel (not to be confused with Killarney's *Great Southern*), built in 1896 on the verdant grounds of a former private estate, is carefully and splendidly decorated in Victorian style. It has an excellent restaurant. Closed November through March. For additional details, see *Rural Retreats* in DIVERSIONS. Parknasilla (phone: 64-45122; 800-44-UTELL or 800-243-7687 from the US; fax: 64-45323). Expensive.

KENMARE This attractive town sits in a limestone niche, surrounded by old red sandstone, at the point where the River Roughty runs into the head of the sea inlet known as the River Kenmare. The location makes it an ideal base for touring either the Iveragh Peninsula to the north or the Beara Peninsula to the south. Kenmare is a planned landlord's town, laid out according to the instructions of the first Marquess of Lansdowne in 1775. A number of houses are built of the local limestone, and there is a fine Roman Catholic church with striking roof timbers. Next to it is the Convent of the Poor Clares, founded in 1861 and well-known because of its lace making school; the famous point lace and other types produced here are on display daily (phone: 64-41385). The town's oldest monument, the Druid's Circle, is beautifully set on the banks of the River Finnihy on the outskirts of the town and dates from the time of the Beaker folk, copper miners who arrived from Spain 4,000 years ago. The circle of 15 stones with a large boulder in the center is an example of a form frequently found in and mainly confined to this peninsula. Such circles were places of worship but may also have had secular, ceremonial uses as well as astronomical significance. There is even some evidence that they were the sites of human sacrifices.

Kenmare shares the mild climate common to the south coast, and the subtropical foliage evident at Parknasilla is seen here, too. There is swimming in the sheltered coves west of the town, extensive salmon and trout fishing, and opportunity for deep-sea fishing. In addition, a new 18-hole golf course is scheduled to be opened by this year. For additional information, contact the *Kenmare Golf Club* (phone: 64-41291).

CHECKING IN

Park Widely acclaimed as one of the country's finest hotels, this century-old, 50-room château sits on its own palm-tree–lined grounds on Kenmare Bay, just at the top of the village. There's a highly rated restaurant (see *Eating Out*), and 11 acres of gardens with walking paths, as well as tennis, croquet, and an adjacent golf course. Open April through early January. For additional details, see *Rural Retreats* in DIVERSIONS. Kenmare (phone: 64-41200; 800-525-4800 from the US; fax: 64-41402). Very expensive.

Sheen Falls Lodge Nestled on 300 acres of lawns and semitropical gardens beside the Kenmare Bay estuary and a sparkling waterfall, this 40-room hotel was developed around a home built in the 18th century for the Earl of Kerry. Although the interior is new, an Old World ambience is retained. Guest facilities include a restaurant, *La Cascade* (see *Eating Out*), an indoor leisure center, and outdoor sports. Closed early January through mid-March. For additional details, see *Rural Retreats* in DIVERSIONS. Kenmare (phone: 64-41600; 800-221-1074 from the US; fax: 64-48386). Very expensive.

Kenmare Bay Perched on a hill on the edge of town, this modern, 130-room Best Western affiliate has a delightful and warmly designed interior. Recently expanded and refurbished, its rooms all have private baths, color TV sets, telephones, and hair dryers; most have views of the Kerry mountains and countryside. Also on site are a good restaurant and a lounge that features traditional Irish music and dancing on many summer evenings. Closed November through February. Sneem Rd. (phone: 64-41300; 800-528-1234 from the US; fax: 64-41541). Moderate.

Hawthorn House A modern 2-story village home with attractive gardens, this superior bed and breakfast establishment is operated by the Murphy family. Each of the 8 bedrooms has a private bath and a distinctive decor. Open year-round. Shelbourne St. (phone: 64-41035). Inexpensive.

EATING OUT

Park This much-honored restaurant offers a blend of classic and progressive Irish fare in a romantic setting with bay views and candlelight. Featured dishes include salmon stuffed with spinach and wrapped in pastry, loin of lamb with oyster and walnut stuffing, and filet of rabbit with red wine sauce, as well as seasonal lobster and scallops from Kenmare Bay. All this, plus an elegant atmosphere and topnotch service. Open daily for breakfast, lunch, and dinner, April through early January. Reservations essential. Major credit cards accepted. *Park Hotel,* Kenmare (phone: 66-41200). Very expensive.

La Cascade Named for the cascading Sheen Falls that splash continuously beneath its windows, this restaurant is particularly romantic at night, when the waters are floodlit. The menu offers creative Irish cuisine, with choices such as sole with a mousseline of bell peppers in a shellfish cream sauce; sesame-flavored prawns with grilled seafood sausage; and wood-smoked and charbroiled filet of beef. Open daily for dinner. Reservations necessary. Major credit cards accepted. *Sheen Falls Lodge,* Kenmare (phone: 64-41600). Very expensive.

Lime Tree An old (1821) stone schoolhouse is the setting of another of Kenmare's highly acclaimed restaurants, next to the grounds of the *Park* hotel. Diners have a choice of the cozy downstairs area, with its warming fireplace, or the skylit gallery overhead. The menu includes poached monkfish, trout amandine, and rack of lamb with spicy plum sauce. Open April through October for dinner only; closed Sundays. Reservations advised. No credit cards accepted. Shelbourne St. (phone: 64-41225). Expensive to moderate.

Purple Heather Bistro Seafood is the specialty of the house, with snacks and meals served in the comfortable bar. Open for lunch and dinner; closed Sundays. Reservations unnecessary. No credit cards accepted. Henry St., Kenmare (phone: 64-41016). Moderate to inexpensive.

En Route from Kenmare Upon reaching Kenmare, travelers will have covered 90 miles of the Ring of Kerry route, excluding detours. From here, the most direct road back to Killarney, a distance of 21 miles, is N71 north, which winds over the mountains through Moll's Gap and via Ladies View, a lookout point with a panorama of the wonderful lakes of Killarney that is supposed to have gotten its name because it particularly pleased Queen Victoria's ladies-in-waiting. As alternatives, it's possible to turn south to Glengarriff or west to Coornagillagh and Lauragh for a tour of the Beara Peninsula (see the *West Cork* route).

Connemara and the Aran Islands

There's scarcely any other place in Ireland where it is possible to be so intimately in touch with the Irish past than in Connemara, that ancient landscape of bogland and mountains that stretches across west Galway to the rocky rim of the wild Atlantic. It is a domain much removed from the modern world, a haunted, mystical land, where the passage of time seems to have been halted.

Most Connemara people still speak the ancient Erse language, now called Irish, that is nearly extinct in other parts of Ireland. Connemara is home to Ireland's biggest Gaeltacht — a region where Irish still is spoken and where the Irish come to learn the ancient language. Since English is emerging as the international medium of communication, the preservation of Irish is increasingly threatened. The mother tongue does live, however, and any visitor to Connemara who has taken the trouble to learn a few Irish phrases will win an appreciative, warm welcome and won't go short of a drink.

It isn't merely the language that causes the echoes of bygone days to ring plangently through the glens and mountains of Connemara. Ever since the great mountains were sculpted against the western Irish sky and the glens were chiseled deep into the earth, the Connemara landscape has hardly changed, and humankind has barely fixed its stamp on it. It is a stark and unyielding place that has shaped its people into strong, independent individuals who cast a stoic and earthy eye on the rest of the world.

The land was always begrudging, requiring a fierce will to make it yield even a beggarly subsistence. But the Connemara peasants farmed every arable crevice of flinty earth. In the old days, they lived off potatoes, and when the horrendous potato blight fell upon Ireland during the 1840s, they suffered more than most others during the famine that followed. Since then, the region has been sparsely populated, the drain of young people through emigration continues today, although industrialization has finally slowed the once inevitable flight from this barren land.

The sea is the other mighty element with which Connemara people continuously wrestle, and their battles have inspired such writers as John Millington Synge and Liam O'Flaherty to powerful prose and poetry. Until recently, Connemara fishermen rode the Atlantic breakers in fragile *curraghs* to farm the sea. (The *curragh* is a boat of undefinable vintage that originally was made from hides but now is sheathed in tarred canvas.) It is possible to see *curraghs*, powered by sinew and oar, off the Connemara coast today. They look like black scimitar blades knifing through the waves, seemingly frail and vulnerable but in fact ingeniously crafted to ride out the angriest of storms. They are still widely used by the Aran Islanders.

If at all possible, a visit to Connemara should include a side trip to the Aran Islands. Stripped bare of trees by the Atlantic winds, these three rocky outcrops sit west of the mainland, facing the open mouth of Galway Bay. Their isolation has helped to preserve ancient traditions. The biggest island, Inishmore, attracts the preponderance of visitors and has developed commercial instincts, but the other two, Inishmaan and Inisheer, retain the ambience of an earlier age.

The rapidly developing technologies of the 20th century are only now taking root in Connemara. There are at last factories providing some jobs for the young people so that they no longer are inevitably forced onto emigrant ships. The fishing industry has gradually progressed beyond the *curragh* age. These developments, whether welcome or not, have brought a measure of affluence to the land. The old thatch-roofed cottages are in short supply, replaced by more comfortable, though less charming, bungalows.

But in Connemara the elemental link between humans, the earth, and the sea is still an undeniable force. Somehow humans seem inconsequential out on the Connemara landscape, with its great gnarled mountains rearing into the sky, lone and level bogs blending into desolate horizons, rivers racing toward the freedom of the sea, and valleys secluded from the outside world.

Our route starts in Galway City and heads northwest into Connemara territory. The road coils in a serpentine tour through valleys and mountains, at times verging on the Atlantic and going through most of the untamed and rugged areas of unsurpassed beauty that have made Connemara famous. The route circles back along the edge of Galway Bay to return to Galway City and then shoves off for the Aran Islands.

A word of caution: The roads here are, for the most part, narrow, winding, and roughly surfaced, and Irish drivers often display an unnervingly cavalier attitude at the wheel. So drive slowly and with the utmost care, keep way to the *left,* and at all times be prepared to encounter horse carts, flocks of sheep, or herds of cattle around the next bend.

Along this route, a double room at a hotel listed as expensive will cost from $80 to $150 per night, a room at a moderate establishment will cost $50 to $80, and at an inexpensive place, under $50. Dinner for two (excluding wine, drinks, or tip) will cost $50 or more in a restaurant listed as expensive; from $30 to $50 at places in the moderate category; and under $30 at an inexpensive spot. For each location, hotels and restaurants are listed alphabetically by price category.

EXTRA SPECIAL The magical combination of mountain, sky, and mist has brought generations of painters to Connemara. For those interested in making this landscape uniquely their own, two landscape painting workshops are offered in Connemara.

Both are held in weekly sessions and include studio and open air work; either studio will arrange accommodations for participants. The *Irish School of Landscape Painting* was founded by renowned Anglo-Irish painter Kenneth Webb, who teaches some of the classes. Students at all levels of expertise, including beginners, are welcome. Contact Miss C. Cryan, *Blue Door Studio* (16 Prince of Wales Ter., Ballsbridge, Dublin 4; phone: 1-686648). *Ballinakill Studios* was founded by American painter Ann O'Connor-Gordon, who now spends most of her time in the west of Ireland. Workshops for painters of all levels of experience are offered in July and August; classes emphasize personal growth and expression. For additional information, contact *Ballinakill Studios* (Connemara West Centre, Letterfrack; phone: 95-41044 or 95-41047; fax: 95-41112).

GALWAY CITY For a complete report on the city, its sights, restaurants, and hotels, see *Galway City,* THE CITIES.

En Route from Galway City Take N59 to the village of Oughterard (pronounced *Ook*-ther-ard), 17 miles away. This road runs almost parallel to Lough Corrib, a marvelous fishing lake. Most of the side roads to the right lead to the lakeshore, and it is easy enough to hire rowboats or power boats for pleasure trips or for fishing (see *Galway City* in THE CITIES).

OUGHTERARD Sixteenth-century Aughnanure Castle, about 2 miles southeast of the town (a signpost points the way); was the redoubt of the ferocious O'Flaherty tribe, who exhibited a sense of hospitality similar to that of the Borgias, once dispatching a dinner guest through a flagstone trap door into the river beneath the banquet hall. The castle (phone: 91-82214) has been restored and is open daily from June through mid-September. Guided tours are available; there's an admission charge.

The *Oughterard Golf Club* (phone: 91-82620) runs along part of the road to Aughnanure Castle; look for the signpost at the turnoff for the castle. Guests are welcome to play the rolling 18-hole course.

Angling is the life and soul of Oughterard. Wander into any of the pubs or hotels and the conversation inevitably concerns the great terminological inexactitudes of fishing lore. Anglers from all over Europe come here to pursue the trout and salmon of Lough Corrib. Stop by *Keogh's* (Bridge St.; phone: 91-82222) to buy a rod and creel, or at *Thomas Tuck* (Main St.; phone: 82335) for handmade flies, and then head for the lake for a great fishing experience.

One period of the year, about mid-May, is known as the "carnival of the trout." At this time, great clouds of newly hatched mayflies hover over the lake, and the trout go mad for them. Anglers capture masses of the mayflies, impale them on hooks, and "dap" them on the surface of the water; the trout all but jump out with their hands up (also see *Gone Fishing* in DIVERSIONS).

If other forms of wildlife interest you, stop at the *Corrib Conservation Centre* (Ardnasillagh; phone: 91-82519). Lectures and courses on the unique geography, flora, and fauna of the area are given here.

Outside the *Boat Inn* (see *Eating Out*) in the center of the village, a well-laden signpost shows the way to the Lake Drive along Lough Corrib and the Hill of Doon. This road along the Dooras Peninsula is a dead end, so travelers get two chances (the trips out and back) to enjoy the lovely views. As you leave the village, head toward Maam Cross. Watch for the waterfall nestled in a wooded glen, the last you'll see for miles.

CHECKING IN

Cloonabinnia House Built in the style of a large Swiss chalet, this family-run hotel overlooking Lough Corrib is immensely popular with anglers from all over Europe. It has 15 comfortable rooms (all with private baths), and excellent food is served in the restaurant, which is open to the public. Open March to October. Moycullen, 10 miles from Galway City on N59, turn right at the signpost (phone: 91-85555 or 91-85512; fax: 91-85640). Expensive.

Connemara Gateway A classy, modern motel with 62 comfortable rooms, a heated indoor swimming pool, an outdoor all-weather tennis court, attractive gardens, and a commendable restaurant featuring some homemade specialties. The staff is extremely friendly. On the main road from Galway City, just before entering Oughterard (phone: 91-82328; fax: 91-82332). Expensive.

Currarevagh House An aristocratic home on Lough Corrib has been converted into a peaceful and relaxing country house. The dining room is chiefly for registered guests, but others can call ahead to see if a table is free. Open April to October. Reservations necessary. For additional details, see *Rural Retreats* in DIVERSIONS. Signposted from the center of Oughterard and for the 4 miles to the lakeside. Oughterard (phone: 91-82312 or 91-82313; fax: 91-82731). Expensive.

Ross Lake House Rolling, unspoiled countryside and pretty gardens surround this Georgian-era house. There are 13 guestrooms, all with private baths; the 3 rooms in the old part of the house have the most period feeling. Guests can fish on nearby Ross Lake and Lough Corrib, or simply enjoy the quiet. Trout and salmon are specialties of the dining room. Signposted on the left, 14 miles from Galway City on N59. Rosscahill, Oughterard (phone: 91-80109; fax: 91-80184). Expensive.

Connemara Country Cottages For those who want to settle in for a week or more, here are five thatched, 2- and 3-bedroom houses with the charm of indigenous architecture and all the modern conveniences, including saunas, dishwashers, TV sets, and VCRs. The cluster of cottages is set well off the main road in rolling, sheep-dotted terrain, just a few miles from Oughterard. Leam East, Recess (phone: 91-82514; fax: 91-82462). Moderate.

EATING OUT

Water Lily A pretty, riverside restaurant serving local produce and fish cooked by the owner/chef. Open daily for lunch and dinner in summer; call for hours at other times. Bridge St., Oughterard (phone: 91-82737). Expensive.

Boat Inn Fresh fish from the nearby Lough Corrib and the Atlantic are the outstanding features of the menu in this friendly tavern with a mostly local clientele. Open daily for lunch and dinner in summer; bar lunches only in winter. Reservations advised for dinner. Major credit cards accepted. The Square, Oughterard (phone: 91-82196; fax: 91-82694). Moderate.

White Gables This attractive restaurant in a whitewashed old cottage in the center of the tiny village of Moycullen serves up country home-cooking, emphasizing fresh fish and local produce. An open fire, stone walls, and lace tablecloths make it an oasis on the road to Connemara. Open daily for lunch and dinner in summer; call ahead during the rest of the year. Reservations necessary. MasterCard and Visa accepted. Moycullen, 10 miles from Galway City on N59 (phone: 91-85744). Moderate.

En Route from Oughterard Continue traveling northwest on N59, which leads into Connemara. The land beyond Oughterard is desolate and bare, though in a valley to the left are a number of small lakes. Ten miles out, at Maam Cross, turn right onto L100, a precarious road that must be negotiated carefully — *very* carefully — on the way into the lonely valley of Maam.

Motorists should make it a point to stop often: to get out and sit on a rock, to stroll across a stone bridge, to talk with a passing farmer, and to immerse themselves in the atmosphere. There is also much to see *above* the land itself. Look upward, if only because generations of artists have come from many lands to do just that in Connemara. Unless there is heavy sea mist, fog, or impenetrable overcast, the sky above Connemara is a living mural of constantly changing cloud patterns, with an astonishing interplay of light, color, and shadow.

Five miles down L100, at Maam Bridge, turn left to head toward the village of Leenane, 9 miles away. This is the heart of the Maam Valley, with the craggy Maumturk Mountains that dominate the Joyce Country (see below) on the left and the hills of south Mayo to the right. There are two detours worth taking here. For the first, travel 5 miles along the road to Leenane, turn right at the signpost for Lough Nafooey, which lies 5 miles away in a sequestered valley of bogland grandeur. There are picnic spots set around the lovely lake. The second detour is a scenic route to Maumeen and St. Patrick's Well. From Maam Cross continue on N59, the direct route to Clifden. After about 12 miles, look for a small signpost on the right that says "Mamean" and turn into the narrow road. Drive over the silent bog dotted with little pools and grazing cattle for about 1½ miles until the road takes a sharp turn to the left and a rough parking area appears on the left. Leave the car and follow the pilgrims' path up the hill and through the gate (which also says Mamean), taking care to close it behind you. The gentle climb along a well-marked path is one of the best ways to experience the quiet of Connemara. Mountain sheep scamper by, little streams sparkle and rush along the way, and even a shower or mist won't obscure the wide, clearly marked trail. At the top, which is really a pass between the high-shouldered mountains on either side, there is a strong and simple statue of St. Patrick carved in limestone. It marks the spot where the saint is said to have rested. Nearby is Tobar Phaidrag, St. Patrick's Well, and all around are small Celtic crosses marking the Stations of the Cross. A tiny chapel usually is open and can provide shelter in case of a sudden shower. Pilgrimages take place on *Good Friday* and in August, but the site probably predates St. Patrick's time as a holy place, and the ancient magic lingers all year long.

Just up the road (N59) from Maumeen, a sign on the side of a long row of buildings proclaims "Beer Books Eggs Marble Wool." This is *Joyce's at Recess,* a shopping complex of sorts and the perfect place to relax after a walk up Maumeen. *Paddy Festy's* pub (phone: 95-34673) offers bar food all day and serves inexpensive dinners daily during the tourist season (from *Easter* to October). Local musicians gather twice weekly in summer and on Saturday nights throughout the year. A grocery store and filling station take care of life's necessities, and the *Connemara Marble Shop* (phone: 95-34604) contains a lovely collection of antiques, books, and high-quality crafts from jewelry to knitwear. As the sign outside the shop confidently states, "For those of you who like this sort of place, this is the sort of place you will like."

To rejoin the scenic high road, turn right at the signpost about a half-mile past the shops. This road winds through woodland and lakeside of the Inagh Valley and joins N59 near Kylemore. From here proceed to Leenane to continue on the route.

CHECKING IN

Lough Inagh Lodge A 19th-century hunting and fishing lodge that was part of the Martin estate of Ballynahinch has been converted to a small (12 rooms with private baths) hotel. Outside, beautiful Lough Inagh lies nestled between the mountains. Inside, a country elegance reigns. The restaurant is open to the public. Open *Easter* to October. Major credit cards accepted. Signposted from N59 at Recess or near Kylemore; the road connects the two loops of N59 (phone: 95-34706; fax: 95-34708). Expensive.

EATING OUT

The Gastronome Seafood and vegetarian dishes are the stars of the menu at this cozy inn by the side of the road in the middle of nowhere. Guestrooms are available. Open for lunch and dinner, May through October. Reservations advised. Major credit cards accepted. *Caher House,* N59, Recess (phone: 95-34617). Expensive to moderate.

Peacocks A sort of Celtic bazaar at Maam Cross, this establishment offers valuable services to tourists: a bar, a cafeteria, music on summer evenings, a shop with the whole bag of stereotypical Emerald Isle souvenirs, a small supermarket, a car accessories shop, and a filling station. There's even a replica of the cottage used in the 1952 movie *The Quiet Man,* which was filmed in the area. Maam Cross (phone: 91-82306 or 91-82374). Inexpensive.

JOYCE COUNTRY The Joyce Country, which covers much of the Maam Valley and the Leenane area, was named after the clan that ruled this wild territory from the 13th to the 19th centuries. Originally, the Joyces were of princely Welsh and English stock, remarkable for their tall, striking stature. Tom Joyce, the progenitor of the Irish sept, who came from Wales to Ireland and settled in Connemara during the reign of Edward I, is said to have been 7 feet tall. The clan eventually dispersed from the Joyce Country and resettled all over Ireland and, indeed, the world. The most revered Joyce in modern Ireland was the great writer James Joyce.

LEENANE This lovely village reposes at the bottom of a ring of mountains, one of whose peaks is called the Devil's Mother. Leenane also lies at the edge of Killary Harbour, the only true Scandinavian-style fjord to be found in Ireland. This long arm of water reaches deeply between giant mountains for 10 miles, and roads lining each side of the inlet provide dramatic panoramas of land and sea. Walk 3 miles up the road north from Leenane into Mayo for a view of the Aasleagh Falls on the River Erriff (setting of the dramatic fight scene in the 1991 film *The Field*). There's good salmon fishing in this area, too.

En Route from Leenane Head west on the road to Clifden, N59, which runs for a few miles along the shore of Killary Harbour. As the road bends inland, the Twelve Bens mountain range rises up ahead. In about 10 miles, Kylemore Abbey, a modern Gothic building, appears across a lake to the right. Built by a doctor in the 19th century as an adoring and lasting monument to his wife, Kylemore is now a prestigious school for girls, run by Benedictine nuns. The order also runs *Kylemore Pottery* (phone: 95-41113; fax: 95-41123). The large crafts shop adjacent to the school stocks the pottery and a range of other Irish products. The spacious tearoom can accommodate bus tours; it's open mid-March through October.

CHECKING IN/EATING OUT

Delphi Lodge This restored 1830s sporting lodge (there are 7 guestrooms) caters to serious fishing enthusiasts, but its idyllic setting makes it a haven for anyone looking for a bit of the quiet life. Most of the vegetables are homegrown and dinner includes the catch of the day. Leenane (phone: 95-42211; fax: 95-42296). Expensive.

Kylemore House Not to be confused with the *Kylemore Pass* hotel, this is a truly superior guesthouse, one of a number in the area. The 200-year-old country house has 6 guestrooms (all with private baths). Open April through October. For additional details, see *Rural Retreats* in DIVERSIONS. Three miles east of Kylemore Abbey on N59, the main Leenane–Clifden road (phone: 95-41143). Moderate.

RENVYLE About a mile west of Kylemore is a signpost on the right for Renvyle, 6 miles away. This road veers north of the main route to the precarious verge of the Atlantic, where the rocky headland juts defiantly out into the water. Out on the promontory is yet another ruined castle of the terrible O'Flahertys. There are some lovely, safe beaches all around this area. On the way into Renvyle, the route passes through a village called Tully Cross, where modern versions of the traditional thatch-roofed Irish cottages — fitted with comforts and conveniences unknown to the peasantry of yore — can be rented at moderate rates. Reservations made well in advance are essential. For information, call Aras Fáilte, the Galway Tourist Board (phone: 91-63081).

CHECKING IN

Renvyle House The decor is rustic and cozy at this elegant 56-room hostelry perched above the sea that offers plenty of sports and activities for the whole family. Closed January, February, and most of March. For additional details, see *Rural Retreats* in DIVERSIONS. Signposted on the right, 1½ miles north of Tully Cross, Renvyle (phone: 95-43511 or 95-43444; fax: 95-43515). Expensive.

Little Killary Adventure Center This establishment offers simple accommodations and a range of outdoor activities from sailing and canoeing to hiking and rock climbing in the wilds of Connemara. Closed mid-December to February 1. Meals are included in the rate. Salruck, Renvyle (phone: 95-43411; fax: 95-43411). Inexpensive.

LETTERFRACK About 8 miles from Renvyle back through Tully Cross is Letterfrack Village, a wide spot on the main road from Leenane to Clifden. Visit any of the pubs in the evening to hear some of the best genuine Irish music played on fiddle and tin whistle. The village also lies in the shadow of the towering range of mountains called the Twelve Bens. The Irish government has taken over 3,800 acres of this wild mountainous terrain and turned it into the Connemara National Park (phone: 95-41054). The entrance is only about 100 yards south of the Letterfrack crossroads. The park offers miles of wide-open spaces and Diamond Mountain looks over all. Self-guided walks lead over hill and vale, and the well laid-out visitors' center tells the story of this fascinating landscape. Here it is also possible to get a close look at the famous Connemara ponies, sturdy and tough little horses renowned the world over for their endurance, jumping power, and amiability.

Two excellent craftshops-cum-tearooms are in the Letterfrack area. *Connemara Handicrafts* (on N59; phone: 95-41058) has an excellent selection of tweeds, knitwear, pottery, paintings, and jewelry. The tearoom serves homemade goodies and sandwiches (open *Easter* through October). Farther up the road on the rise overlooking an expanse of bog and mountain, the thatched *Sweater Shop* (no phone) is crammed with sweaters as well as a range of souvenirs and crafts. Its tearoom looks over the stunning landscape and is particularly friendly and comfortable.

CHECKING IN/EATING OUT

Crocnaraw Country House This early-19th-century Georgian country residence, set in 20 acres of gardens and woods on the shores of the Atlantic, is a quiet country retreat. There are 6 guestrooms with private baths. Open May through October. Moyard on N59, 3 miles west of Letterfrack (phone: 95-41068). Expensive.

Rosleague Manor This gracious pink Georgian manor with 21 comfortable guestrooms, each with private bath, overlooks a quiet bay and serves superb food. Open *Easter* through October; dinner served daily. Reservations advised. Major credit cards accepted. For additional details, see *Rural Retreats* in DIVERSIONS. Two miles west of Letterfrack on N59 (phone: 95-41101 or 95-41102; fax: 95-41168). Expensive.

En Route from Letterfrack At the Streamstown crossroad make a sharp right turn onto the unnumbered road to Cleggan, 5 miles away.

CLEGGAN/INISHBOFIN The town of Cleggan is the embarkation point for Inishbofin Island, which in recent times has become a haunt of poets, philosophers, and artists from many lands. The M.V. *Aengus* sails to the island daily at 11 AM, 2 PM, and 6 PM. The fare is about $15 round trip. For information call 95-44750, 95-44640, or 95-44642 or the Galway or Clifden tourist offices. Tours of Inishbofin that trace its history — both natural and manmade — leave from Clifden in June, July, and August. Contact *Connemara Heritage Tours* (Market St., Clifden; phone: 95-21379; fax: 95-21845). Be aware that if a bad storm brews up, it is not unheard of to be marooned on the island for days (or even weeks), but in view of the hospitality and friendliness of the islanders, there are worse fates. The ruins of a 7th-century monastery are on the island, which was once in the possession of the menacing O'Flahertys. The daring sea queen of the western waters Grainne Ui Mhaille (pronounced *Grawn*-ya Ee *Whal*-ya and translated as Grace O'Malley) also found shelter for her warships here during her rebellion against the sovereignty of Queen Elizabeth I. The iron gauntlet of Cromwell fell on the island in 1652. The barracks where his Roundheads were billeted stands at the harbor entrance.

CHECKING IN/EATING OUT

Day's Overlooking the harbor on Inishbofin Island, this hotel has a friendly staff, an informal ambience, and 18 cozy, warm rooms (8 with private baths). Homemade soup, island lamb, crab, and lobster are served in the restaurant. Open April through September. Musical evenings are held during the summer. Major credit cards accepted. Inishbofin Island (phone: 95-45809 or 95-45829). Inexpensive.

Doonmore A small hotel that offers sea and shore angling facilities. It has 11 rooms (3 with private baths). Open April through September. Major credit cards accepted. Inishbofin Island (phone: 95-45804; fax: 95-45814). Inexpensive.

En Route from Cleggan Return to the main road (N59) and drive 4 miles southwest to Clifden.

CLIFDEN This town is cradled in a glen at the head of an Atlantic inlet into which a river rushes. Though it has a population of little more than 1,000, Clifden is called the capital of Connemara, a label that might be challenged by people in southern Connemara, where scarcely anything but Irish is spoken. Clifden is an English-speaking town, a legacy of the days when it was a favorite seaside summer resort of the British gentry.

The first wireless messages from Europe to America were sent from Clifden, and some of the transmitting masts are still standing. The inventor of the radio, Guglielmo Marconi, set up a station in Derrygimlagh Bog, 4 miles south of the town. The same bog has claim to another historical distinction: It was on its peaty surface in 1919 that the aviators John William Alcock and Arthur Whitten Brown landed their biplane, having flown from Newfoundland to complete the first nonstop transatlantic flight. A stone cairn marks the spot today, and nearby is a more imposing limestone monument in the shape of a plane's tail. These sites are well marked; travel about 4 miles out on the Ballyconneely road to reach them.

Any visitor to Clifden must ascend the dizzying heights of Sky Road. Signposted from the town's central square, the road is narrow and heart-stoppingly steep, requiring skilled gear shifting. The precipitous ascent affords a fabulous view of Clifden Bay and the savage rocky west coast as well as the small islands nestled like humpback whales in the Atlantic beyond. At the highest point, there's a walled-in parking lot.

There are plenty of opportunities for outdoor activities in the Clifden area. For information on sailing, windsurfing, and canoeing on Clifden

Bay, inquire at the *Clifden Boat Club* (Beach Rd.; phone: 95-21711). Golfers will want to play a round or two at the *Connemara Golf Club* (phone: 95-23502; fax: 95-23622), which has an 18-hole championship course beautifully situated right beside the Atlantic Ocean, with the Twelve Bens in the distance. The breezes make for an extremely lively round at this friendly club. It is a point of honor for regulars to play right through the hail and gale. Look for the signpost for the course near *Keogh's Pub* at Ballyconneely. Area stables offer horse lovers the chance to ride the famous Connemara ponies. *Errislannen Manor* (phone: 95-21134) is a well-run establishment that leads exhilarating treks along the hillsides of the Errislannen Peninsula for both novice and experienced riders. The *Cashel Equestrian Centre* offers riding and mountain trekking in Cashel and Cleggan (phone: 95-31082 for both locations).

To get a closer look at the land and learn some of its stories, spend a day with *Connemara Heritage Tours* (Market St., Clifden; phone: 95-21379; fax: 95-21845). This organization leads walking tours over bog and beach to some well-hidden points of historical and natural interest. Groups are small and guides are historians, archaeologists, and steadfast lovers of this special landscape. Tours are given from *Easter* to mid-September.

Less energetic visitors may want to spend a hour or two browsing through some of Clifden's many pleasant shops. The *Celtic Shop* (Main St.; phone: 95-21064) features all things Irish, including Claddagh rings, woolly scarfs, books, and music. *Fire and Fleece* (The Market Sq.; phone: 95-35955) specializes in sweaters, as well as a range of other Irish handmade goods. Traditional Irish tweed hats may be purchased at *Millars Connemara Tweeds* (Main St.; phone: 95-21038). There are also tweed ties, blankets, shawls, and scarfs; and the handsome rugged fabric, whose colors reflect the Connemara countryside, is sold by the yard. Upstairs is a small gallery of excellent local landscapes in oils and watercolors. Wonderful tweed items also are featured at the *Weavers' Workshop* (Main St.; phone: 95-21074), where Rory and Marianne Lavelle sell their own tweeds as well as the work of some of the Ireland's best weavers. You might catch them at the loom on a slow day. *Stanley's Shop and Art Gallery* (Market St.; phone: 95-21039) is a genuine country emporium with everything from Wellingtons and fishing tackle to tweed jackets in stock. The shop is all a jumble to the uninitiated, but anything you need is probably there somewhere. The art gallery is across the street. It deals mostly in local landscapes, many of them quite exquisite. For picnic supplies stop in at *Sullivan's Supermarket* (Main St.; phone: 95-21063), a small, well-stocked grocery store that always has a good selection of farmhouse cheeses.

In the last week of September, *Clifden Community Arts Week* attracts artists from across Ireland — and often from Europe and the United States. The festivities include concerts, workshops, and exhibitions. For details call Brendan Flynn (phone: 95-21184 or 95-21295); also see *Feis and*

Fleadh: The Best Festivals in DIVERSIONS. For information about all area activities and events, contact the Clifden Tourist Office (Market Sq.; phone: 95-21163), which is open May through September.

CHECKING IN Clifden is *very* quiet in winter; most hotels and restaurants and some shops close in December, January, and February. Call ahead in the off-season.

Abbeyglen Castle The name "castle" was added after architectural tinkering placed castellated turrets on what was a charming old mansion needing no such cosmetic surgery, but it's still a good place to stay, tucked away in a beautiful setting of gardens, waterfalls, and streams, with the monumental Twelve Bens forming a breathtaking backdrop. The 42 rooms (all with private baths) overlook the Atlantic, and the dining room features the (wonderful) standard Irish fare: beef, lamb, and seafood. Closed January and February. Major credit cards accepted. Sky Rd., Clifden (phone: 95-21201; fax: 95-21797). Expensive.

Ardagh This attractive, well-run establishment draws a continental and Irish clientele. Most of the 17 rooms (all with private baths) overlook Ardbear Bay, as does the handsome dining room. Watching the sun set while savoring the excellently prepared local catch is a real treat. Some of the best food in Connemara is served here (see *Eating Out*). Open March through October. Major credit cards accepted. A little over a mile from Clifden on L102, the Ballyconneely road (phone: 95-21384; fax: 95-21314). Expensive.

Rock Glen Manor House A converted 19th-century shooting lodge set amid sylvan glades and stony mountains on the edge of the Atlantic, this is a beautiful and restful retreat. Features include 25 comfortable guestrooms with private baths, a spacious drawing room decorated with watercolors of the local landscape, an old-fashioned billiards and snooker room, a small intimate bar, and a fine restaurant (see *Eating Out*). Open mid-March to late October. Major credit cards accepted. One mile south of Clifden on L102, the Ballyconneely road (phone: 95-21035 or 95-21393; fax: 95-21737). Expensive.

Alcock and Brown Named after the two flyers who made the first nonstop transatlantic flight from Newfoundland to Clifden, this family-owned and -operated hotel with a 1960s-style exterior is set right in the center of town. All the necessary creature comforts are provided in the 20 guestrooms with private baths. There is also a commendable dining table graced mostly by fresh fish and mountain lamb. Open most of the year; call ahead in winter. Market Sq., Clifden (phone: 95-21086; fax: 95-21842). Moderate.

Barry's An exceptionally friendly house where management and staff go out of their way to ensure the comfort of their guests, it has 18 small but pleasant rooms with private baths. Musicians gather nightly in the summer in the bar to play traditional music. Deep-sea fishing excursions can be arranged for guests. Open April through September. Main St., Clifden (phone: 95-21287; fax: 95-21499). Moderate.

Clifden Bay The oldest hotel in Connemara, this hostelry was built over 100 years ago. It was later a railway hotel, then the Foyle family took it over in the early part of this century. A place of warm informality, with 28 lovely rooms (each with private bath), fine food (lamb, salmon, and seafood are specialties), and music sessions many evenings. Headwaiter Paddy Davis has worked in the hotel since he was 14 and is a gold mine of stories about the place and the whole area. Open May through October. Main St., Clifden (phone: 95-21801; fax: 95-21458). Moderate.

Erriseask House This small (10 rooms), cozy hotel perched at the edge of Mannin Bay has one of the best views of the Twelve Bens. All rooms feature private baths, and most have a spectacular view of the bay and the mountains. The dining room serves superb local produce with a continental touch (see *Eating Out*). Open *Easter* to October. At Ballyconneely, signposted from the Clifden–Roundstone road (phone: 95-23553; fax: 95-23639). Moderate.

Failte The name means welcome and it is apt. Sean and Maureen Kelly serve award-winning breakfasts. Their modern home has 6 bedrooms (2 with private baths). Open March through October. About a mile from Clifden off L102, the Ballyconneely road (phone: 95-21159). Inexpensive.

Faul Farmhouse Kathleen Conneely and her family make guests feel right at home at this establishment, which has won an award from the Irish Farmhouse Association. All 6 rooms have private baths. The breakfasts are hearty, and Mrs. Conneely will prepare an evening meal if requested. Open March through October. Signposted from L102, the Ballyconneely road (phone: 95-21239). Inexpensive.

EATING OUT

Ardagh Some of the best meals in Connemara are served in this dining room overlooking Ardbear Bay. The setting is simple, but the fare is nothing short of exquisite — fresh Irish ingredients (lamb, salmon, oysters, mussels, and fish) prepared with a true continental touch. Open daily for dinner. Reservations advised. Major credit cards accepted. A little over a mile from Clifden on L102, the Ballyconneely road (phone: 95-21384; fax: 95-21314). Expensive.

Erriseask Fine food is accompanied by a view over Mannin Bay and the Twelve Bens at this popular dining spot, one of the best in Connemara. The dazzling local produce gets a continental touch from the Matz brothers, originally from Germany. Open daily for dinner. Reservations essential. Major credit cards accepted. At Ballyconneely, signposted from the Clifden–Roundstone road (phone: 95-23553; fax: 95-23639). Expensive.

O'Grady's Seafood All creatures great and small, shelled and unshelled, from the surrounding Atlantic are found on the tables of this quintessential fish house. Open for lunch and dinner; no lunch on Mondays; closed January and February. Reservations advised. MasterCard and Visa accepted. Market St., Clifden (phone: 95-21450). Expensive.

Rock Glen Manor House Good, plentiful Irish fare is served in a warm and charming atmosphere. Try the Irish cheese plate or the Bailey's ice cream. Open daily for dinner. Reservations advised. Major credit cards accepted. One mile south of Clifden on L102, the Ballyconneely road (phone: 95-21035; fax: 95-21737). Expensive.

Mainly Seafood A cozy, welcoming place that lives up to its name. Most of its ingredients come straight from the nearby ocean via the pier at the end of the road. Open for lunch and dinner mid-May to mid-September; closed Sundays. Reservations advised. MasterCard and Visa accepted. A mile and a half from Ballyconneely on the golf course road (phone: 95-23539). Expensive to moderate.

Atlantic Fishery A cornucopia of fresh fish is served up here at reasonable prices. Open daily for lunch and dinner from May through October. Reservations advised. MasterCard and Visa accepted. Main St., Clifden (phone: 95-21346). Moderate.

High Moors This place is a must-stop. Exceptionally fine dinners — with local lamb, fish, and homegrown vegetables — are served in a house with magnificent views of moor and bay. Open for dinner in June through August; closed Mondays and Tuesdays. Reservations essential. Visa accepted. Dooneen, Clifden, signposted three-quarters of a mile outside town on L102, the Ballyconneely road (phone: 95-21342). Moderate.

Mitchell's A lively restaurant and bar in the middle of town that serves food all day long in the summertime. Popular with crowds and families for dinner. Open daily for lunch and dinner from April through October. Reservations advised. Major credit cards accepted. Near Market Sq. (phone: 95-21867). Moderate.

Kelly's Coffee House Excellent coffee, homemade goodies, and an open fire make this an amiable gathering spot. Check out the old books upstairs. Open daily for breakfast, lunch, and tea. No reservations. No credit cards accepted. Church Hill, near Market Sq. (no phone). Inexpensive.

En Route from Clifden Head roughly 13 miles southeast on the "low road," L102, which hugs the jagged northern coast of the bay almost the whole way and leads quickly into the Gaeltacht area. Although most of the signposts are in Irish here, a traveler is not likely to get lost for any length of time, and most people can speak English well enough to direct a tourist back on the track.

ROUNDSTONE This is one of the loveliest sea villages in Connemara, and in summer it is crowded with tourists from across the globe. Its Irish name is *Cloch nah Ron,* meaning "rock of the seals," and in the evening the whiskered heads of seals can be seen bobbing in the bay. Two granite piers, built in the 19th century, jut into the bay to protect the fishing boats. Rising almost directly behind the main street is Errisbeg Mountain, which is easy to ascend; almost all of the west coast is visible from its summit. The two finest beaches in Connemara are off the main road, less than 2 miles west of the village. Nearby is a small crafts village on the site of an old monastery. Stop by *Roundstone Musical Instruments* (phone: 95-35808), where traditional Irish musical instruments are made. *Bodhráns* (Irish drums) are the specialty, but the factory also produces tin whistles and flutes. The factory and shop are open daily from 8 AM to 7 PM in April through September; weekdays from 9 AM to 5 PM during winter. *Sila Mag Aoide Designs* (phone: 95-35912), located in the tower of the old monastery, sells gold and silver hand-crafted jewelry adapted from old Irish designs.

CHECKING IN

Cashel House Often cited as one of Ireland's best hotels, offering 32 charming guestrooms and private baths, sheltered gardens, monastic quiet, and delicious food. It's advisable to book well in advance. For additional details, see *Rural Retreats* in DIVERSIONS. About 14 miles from Roundstone on the coast road to Galway City. Cashel Bay (phone: 95-31001; fax: 95-31077). Expensive.

Eldon's This small, family-run hotel located in the middle of this picturesque village has 13 comfortable rooms with private baths, some with views of the Twelve Bens and harbor. A lovely afternoon tea is served. Open March through October. Main St., Roundstone (phone: 95-35933; fax: 95-35921). Moderate.

Roundstone House Maureen Vaughan and her family run this small (14 rooms, all with private baths), friendly hotel, which has spectacular views of Roundstone Bay and the Twelve Bens mountain range. The food, with a distinctively maritime accent, is delicious. Open *St. Patrick's Day* through September. Main St., Roundstone (phone: 95-35864; fax: 95-35944). Moderate.

EATING OUT

Beola Lobster is king in this splendid restaurant, which also offers a feast of other viands fresh from the sea. Open daily for lunch and dinner in summer; closed in winter. Reservations advised. Major credit cards accepted. Main St., Roundstone (phone: 95-35871). Expensive to moderate.

En Route from Roundstone Continue on the coast road, L102, for 10 miles to Ballynahinch.

BALLYNAHINCH The splendid castle at Ballynahinch stands amid woodlands behind turreted gates. Here resided the powerful, albeit eccentric, Martin family, who were granted just about all of Connemara by the English king during the 18th century. (One of the Martins pledged the right allegiance to the right royal house at the right time.) The dispossessed O'Flahertys hated the Martins and put to the sword any who crossed their path, though the Martins themselves were quite competent swordsmen. One of them, Dick Martin, won notoriety as a duelist but redeemed his reckless reputation by founding the Society for the Prevention of Cruelty to Animals, thus earning the name Humanity Dick. The castle, now a hotel (see *Checking In/Eating Out*), has a magnificent setting among mountains, lakes, and woods. The Ballynahinch Fishery is world famous for salmon angling.

CHECKING IN/EATING OUT

Ballynahinch Castle Ancestral home of the Martin dynasty and now a hotel that echoes with history. It offers 28 rooms with private baths/showers, striking scenery, some of the best salmon fishing anywhere, and an excellent dining room. Weighing the catch of the day and celebrating take place in the *Fisherman's Pub*. Much frequented by American visitors. Open year-round. Ballynahinch (phone: 95-31006; fax: 95-31085). Expensive.

Zetland Set on wooded grounds, this hotel offers a hospitable welcome, complete with open fires, antiques-furnished lounges, and 19 cheerful, comfortable rooms with private baths. Fishing is big here on the hotel's own lakes, but there is tennis, croquet, billiards, and abundant scenic quiet for non-fishing types. The dining room specializes in seafood from nearby waters. Signposted from N59 between Recess and Ballynahinch (phone: 95-31111; fax: 95-31117). Expensive.

En Route from Ballynahinch After leaving Ballynahinch, double back on the road to reach the signpost for Cashel, then continue southeast along the coast once more. Lush with vegetation and shrubbery, Cashel provides a warm contrast to the stonier, starker face of the Connemara landscape. The view seaward is breathtaking. Carna is about 10 miles south of Cashel on L102.

CARNA This sea village is in the heart of the Irish-speaking district. If plans allow, come during July, when there are a number of maritime festivals. Carna is also a marvelous place to hear traditional Irish music. Visitors are welcome to join the informal sessions in the pubs or to go to an Irish dance known as a *céilí* (pronounced *kay*-lee). It's also worth taking a trip out to

MacDara's Island, the resting place of St. MacDara, protector of fishermen, who still dip their oars in salute as they sail past the island. *Connemara Heritage Tours* (Market St., Clifden; phone: 95-21379) offers guided trips to the island.

CHECKING IN/EATING OUT

Sceirde House Both the restaurant and the 12 guestrooms here are comfortable, pleasant, and quite affordable. The rooms all have private baths and come equipped with TV sets, telephones, and hair dryers. The food is nothing fancy, but it's fresh and wholesome, with particularly good lamb and fish. On weekends there's music, although it's not always traditional. Open daily for lunch and dinner year-round. Reservations necessary in summer. MasterCard and Visa accepted. Carna Village (phone: 95-32255 or 95-32279). Moderate.

En Route from Carna For the 20-mile drive to Carraroe, continue along the meandering L102 through Kilkieran to Gortmore and turn right at the signpost to Rosmuc. This isolated area is a place venerated in modern Irish history. It was in a cottage here that the mystic poet and philosopher Padraig Pearse, who led the 1916 rising against the British in Dublin, sought seclusion to contemplate Ireland's Celtic past and to dream of revolution and a free nation. After the rising, Pearse and the other leaders were shot, but their action led to independence for the southern part of Ireland within 5 years. The cottage is a national monument open to the public during the summer (no phone).

Returning to Gortmore, turn right on L102 and travel to Screeb, 3 miles away, then turn right onto L100 and continue on to Costelloe. From here detour southwest, following the signpost to Carraroe.

CARRAROE Set amid furze-clad hills and stony fields, this village is a place where the lingering charm of the past is at its strongest. Irish is the lingua franca, and the old traditional ways of cultivating the land are still used on the small farms. A number of pristine beaches are tucked away in niches along the rugged shoreline, including a small coral strand less than 2 miles from the village.

CHECKING IN

Ostan Cheathru Rua The name (pronounced *Oh*-shtawn Kah-roo Roo-ah) means "Hotel Carraroe." This 22-room establishment is comfortable and contemporary and offers good food. All rooms feature private baths/showers. Often there are enjoyable sessions of Irish music in the restaurant. Open from mid-May through mid-September. A highly visible signpost on the village's main street points the way. Carraroe (phone: 91-95116; fax: 91-95187). Expensive.

EATING OUT

An Ciseog A rarity in the area: This seaside eatery serves meals alfresco on the sandy beach when the weather permits. It's a popular rendezvous for beach-partying groups in summer. Open daily for lunch and dinner. Reservations unnecessary. No credit cards accepted. Carraroe Village (phone: 91-95222). Moderate.

En Route from Carraroe Return to Costelloe and head south on L100. Just before the village of Inverin, the road straightens and runs directly east to Galway City, 16 miles away, and for the entire run Galway Bay is on the right.

The town of Spiddal, 12½ miles from Galway City, is an excellent stop for crafts lovers. The *Craft Centre, An Spideal,* on the main road, is a complex of artisans' studios and shops that sits at the edge of the Galway Bay. Among the many places to browse are the *Stone Art Gallery,* which exhibits sculpture and paintings; *Roisin Comamara,* which produces tiny bouquets of wildflowers embedded in Lucite; and *One of Susan's,* which sells colorful mohair hand-knits. There's also a coffee shop. A mile farther down is *Mairtin Standun* (phone: 91-83108), which began as a small shop selling hand-knits and has expanded into a thriving center for all sorts of fine Irish goods. Sweaters are still a specialty and sell for reasonable prices; those with only tiny flaws are marked down for real bargains.

EATING OUT

Boluisce This charming, popular spot serves some of the most delicious food in the area. The menu features seafood, with lobster and prawns the specialties of the house. Open daily for lunch and dinner. Reservations necessary in summer. MasterCard and Visa accepted. Spiddal (phone: 91-83286; fax: 91-83285). Moderate.

ARAN ISLANDS

Cast adrift from the outermost rim of Europe, the Aran Islands stand guard at the entrance to Galway Bay — stony, immortal bastions of a past that dates from before the primal dawn of civilization. Hewn out of solid limestone and stripped bare of trees by the Atlantic gales, the three islands — collectively known simply as Aran — seem like geographical relics of the Stone Age. Over the centuries the islands have only grudgingly changed since they first emerged from the ocean thousands of years ago. The islands — Inishmore ("the big island"), Inishmaan ("the middle island"), and Inisheer ("the eastern island") — occupy a fascinating place in the lore of the east Atlantic. They have been linked in folk memory with

Atlantis, the lost continent, which in the Irish version of the story is known as *Hy Brasil,* the Isle of the Blest.

Whatever ancient mythologies surround Aran, it is certain that the islands were inhabited in prehistoric times, perhaps as far back as 3,000 years before Christianity. The pagan Fir Bolg ("men of the Belgae"), an early Celtic people from Europe, are believed to have been the first settlers on the islands. The cyclopean stone *duns* (pronounced *doons*), or forts, for which the islands are famous, may well have been built by the Fir Bolgs, though archaeologists have been unable to fix a definite date on the structures.

In the 5th century, Enda (a druid turned Christian), founded monasteries and built chapels all over the islands, establishing them as a center of monasticism and a fountainhead of religious teaching. Pilgrims from many lands made their way to Aran during the golden age of the early Irish church, which conducted its affairs quite independently of Rome. For more than 1,000 years, Aran flourished as one of the great holy places of the west, exerting an influence on the Christian world far out of proportion to its geographic size. Its renown as a sanctuary of cloistered piety and learning equaled that of Scotland's holy island Iona, and indeed the pioneering Scottish evangelist St. Columba (see *County Donegal* route) studied under Enda in Aran. One ancient scribe wrote: "There are more saints buried in Aran than are known to any but God alone."

Aran's position as a major monastic settlement began to wane during the 14th century, when it first came to the serious attention of the English, who sent a fleet of 50 ships to plunder the islands in 1334. It had been pillaged by the Vikings during the 11th century, but it still managed to hold on to its insular autonomy up to the time when Queen Elizabeth I mounted the throne of England.

Between the 11th and 16th centuries, the powerful O'Brien clan held sway over Aran. But Queen Elizabeth took possession of the islands in 1587 and handed them over to her countryman John Rawson, who erected Arkyne Castle on Inishmore and garrisoned it with a body of English soldiers. (Aran would not return to Irish rule until Ireland gained its independence in the 1920s.) In 1651, a small army of Cromwellian Roundheads took control of the islands after a year-long siege; they eventually became absorbed into the island population. Later, during the Protestant-Catholic struggle of the late 17th century, the islands fell to the forces of the Protestant King William, but those soldiers departed within a few years, and Aran remained Catholic and Irish-speaking.

The islands were largely forgotten until the middle of the 19th century, when anthropologists, archaeologists, and other researchers of Ireland's past began visiting Aran and letting the outside world know of this strange prehistoric relic in the ocean. They discovered that a way of life that had long since disappeared from almost every other part of Europe was still flourishing in Aran, unchanged over the centuries. The great Irish play-wright John Millington Synge was captivated by Aran, and his writings about it helped publicize the islands throughout the world. He spent his summers on Inishmaan in the early part of this century, building a stone "chair" on the edge of the cliffs, where he sat day after day gazing out into the Atlantic. In 1933, the American filmmaker Robert Flaherty made a celebrated documentary — *Man of Aran* — about the hard life on the islands, vividly depicting the rigors of wresting a subsistence from the stone-layered soil and the surrounding seas.

Aran is accessible by plane or boat from Galway City or by fast launch from the nearest point on the County Galway mainland, Rossaveal Harbour in Connemara. Two companies operate daily ferry service with several sailings per day in the summer, depending on weather conditions: *Aran Ferries* (in the tourist office, Eyre Sq., Galway City; phone: 91-68903; 91-92447 after 7 PM), and *Island Ferries* (Victoria Pl., opposite the tourist office, Galway City; 91-61767 or 91-72273). Both charge about $20 round trip for adults. The departure place for daily flights to the Aran Islands on *Aer Arann* is from Inverin, near Rossaveal (about $46 round trip). Flights are available to all three islands during daylight hours. Fly/stay packages are available as are bus transfers from Galway City. Call *Aer Arann* for current information and reservations (phone: 91-93034 or 91-93054; fax: 91-93238).

The most enjoyable way to explore Aran is to spend a few days on each island or to find a base on one island and make forays to the others. The three islands, only a few minutes' travel from each other, are linked by regular boat service (the schedule is entirely dependent on the weather). It is possible to skip from one island to the other in an *Aer Arann* plane, but under most circumstances that would scarcely be necessary. Available for purchase in any of the island shops or at Aras Fáilte, the Galway Tourist Board (off Eyre Sq.; phone: 91-63081, 91-65201, or 91-65202), is a superb detailed map of the islands called *Oileain Arann* ("the islands of Aran"), which pinpoints not only the numerous historic sites and monuments but nearly all the homes, with the names of the families occupying them. *Aran Walks*, guidebooks that accompany signposted walking trails on the islands, were being prepared at press time. Contact Pat Kearnsey (phone: 91-31974) for details.

Most accommodations on the islands are provided in private homes and are generally of high quality. Arrangements can be made for bed and breakfast or for partial board (includes dinner in the evening) or full board (includes both lunch and dinner). The *Oileain Arann* map has a fairly complete list of all the homes offering accommodations. Bed and breakfast accommodations for two average $38 to $50 a night; with partial board, $45 to $55; and with full board, about $60 to $70. A list of homes approved by Bord Fáilte, the Irish Tourist Board, is available at the Galway Tourist Board (see above). Dinner for two (excluding wine, drinks, and tips) will cost between $30 and $40 at places described as moderate, and under $30 at inexpensive eateries.

INISHMORE It's best to start a tour of Aran on the biggest island, Inishmore. All boats from the mainland berth at the principal port, Kilronan, where bicycles can be hired. This is perhaps the best way to sightsee in Inishmore, although the extremely steep hills can knock the breath out of those less fit. A more leisurely way of getting around, and certainly less strenuous, is by pony-drawn sidecar, or trap (which looks like a large dog cart). These can be hired, with driver; the cost depends on length of use or distance traveled. (Be prepared to bargain.) It also is possible to walk without too much stress: This island is about 10 miles long and little more than 2 miles wide at any point (but the hills are steep).

Inishmore is now geared to tourists, with numerous pony cart drivers, self-styled tour guides, and the like offering their services (sometimes aggressively) as visitors disembark. The tourism boom has somewhat diminished the island's former wild, remote atmosphere, although it has made it easier for visitors to find good restaurants and places to stay.

In 1992, Ionad Arann (locally known as the Centre) opened near the pier in Kilronan. It offers a helpful and interesting orientation for visitors, explaining the history, culture, and landscape of these remarkable islands. There is an adjoining coffee shop for light meals.

There are three great ring forts on Inishmore, the most impressive of which is Dun Aengus, prized as one of the most spectacular of megalithic monuments in all of Europe. It towers above the southwest cliffs of the island, some 6 miles west of Kilronan. About 4 miles east of Dun Aengus on the same coast is Dun Cuchathair, the Black Fort. Although much of it has fallen into the sea, it remains an awesome sight. At the western end of the island, south of the village of Eoghanacht, about 8 miles from Kilronan, is another massive fortress called Dun Eoghnachta, estimated to be 3,000 or more years old. At Killeany, beside the airstrip and about 1 1/2 miles southeast of Kilronan, is the most sacred reliquary in Aran — the ruins of the church built by St. Enda, where the saint is reputed to be buried. Beside Killeany pier are the ruins of Arkyne Castle, built by Queen Elizabeth I's countryman, John Rawson, and garrisoned by successive waves of invading soldiers from Elizabeth's time onward.

Shops at Kilronan harbor stock traditional Aran knitwear (also sold in many fine stores on the mainland), and tiny pubs, some of them roofed in thatch, are often scenes of merriment and song.

CHECKING IN

Cliff House A comfortable setting with plenty of delicious food from the kitchen of owner-chef, Mrs. Gill. All 7 rooms have private baths. Kilronan, Inishmore (phone: 99-61126). Inexpensive.

Johnston Hernon's Kilmurvey House A comfortable, pleasant 8-bedroom (4 with private baths) guesthouse, close to Dun Aengus. There's nothing pretentious on the menu, but the food is wholesome and usually includes excellent fresh fish. MasterCard and Visa accepted. Kilmurvey village, about 6 miles west of Kilronan, Inishmore (phone: 99-61218). Inexpensive.

EATING OUT

An tSéan Cheibh As might be expected, fish, in endless varieties, is the strong point of the house, although native lamb and beef dishes, conjured up with French flair or in traditional home-cooked style, are first-rate. The restaurant (whose name is pronounced Un Chan Cave, meaning "the old pier") is in the style of an Aran cottage, with lime-painted stone walls and an outdoor terrace overlooking the sea for alfresco dining. For quick meals, they also have a fast-food counter. Open from morning until late at night from May through September. Reservations unnecessary. MasterCard and Visa accepted. A 3-minute walk from the landing pier, Kilronan, Inishmore (phone: 99-61228). Moderate.

An tSéanDun Aonghusa Better known as the *Dun Aengus,* this is an atmospheric dining spot that serves good food in pleasant, old-fashioned surroundings. There are timbered stone walls and an enormous open fireplace. Fish dishes dominate the menu. Open daily for lunch and dinner in the summer only. Reservations advised. MasterCard and Visa accepted. Beside the landing pier, overlooking Galway Bay, Kilronan, Inishmore (phone: 99-61104). Moderate.

Gilbert Cottage The fish and smoked salmon served here are always well-prepared, and the mayonnaise, scones, and bread are homemade. Overnight accommodations are also available in the 7 guestrooms. Open daily for lunch and dinner. Reservations essential. No credit cards accepted. Oatquarter Kilronan, Inishmore (phone: 99-61146). Inexpensive.

En Route from Inishmore Take the boat from Kilronan to Inishmaan. (Tourism officials warn that trips to Inishmaan and Inisheer should be made only in the summer; the water can be rough during the rest of the year.)

INISHMAAN This is the most primitive-looking of the islands, rising sharply out of the ocean and blanketed in great gray slabs of limestone. Dry-stone walls, some of which were built many centuries ago, encircle the barren fields and form a jagged pattern of crisscrossed rocks right across the island. Here the hills are steepest of all and exhausting to negotiate on foot in the full heat of summer — and it is on foot that one has to travel, as bicycles or horse-drawn vehicles are hard to procure on Inishmaan. Still, it is a small island, no more than 4 miles by 2 miles, which means there isn't too much territory to cover. The only major road bisects the island, going from the landing pier on the east coast to the west coast. It's both a tortuous and torturous route but, blessedly, passes close to most of the sites worth seeing on the island. A mile inland, to the left of the road, is Dun Conchuir (Connor Fort). Rivaling Dun Aengus in breathtaking splendor, it alone is worth a visit to Inishmaan. The thatch-roofed cottage on the other side of the road, just before the fort, is where the playwright John Millington Synge stayed during the many summers he spent in Aran.

A little farther up the road is the island's museum, a traditional cottage where the furniture and fittings of a centuries-old peasant society are preserved intact, reflecting a lifestyle that has not changed much with the passing of time. Continue on the same road for another half-mile to reach the site of Synge's stone chair on the high cliffs overlooking Gregory's Sound. While sitting here, Synge was inspired to write *Riders to the Sea,* among the greatest one-act plays ever penned.

En Route from Inishmaan Inisheer is a 5-minute boat ride from Inishmaan.

INISHEER This is the tiniest of the Aran Islands, only about 2 miles by 2 miles and with fewer than 500 inhabitants. Bicycles can be hired at the pier, though some parts of Inisheer are not accessible on wheels, so walking is recommended. There's one formidable hill on the northeast side of the island; otherwise the terrain is flat, though rocky in parts. This is the best island for swimming (by an odd quirk of nature, the ocean waters around Aran are always a few degrees warmer than those at the mainland beaches). The sheer cliffs on the eastern side of the island provide a dramatic location from which to drop a fishing line into the roiling waters far below for deliciously edible mackerel or rock salmon. Nearby, a wrecked steamer, stranded on the rocks some years back, lies incongruously rusting away.

Inisheer does not boast the great forts found on the other two islands. The antiquities are practically all connected with the early church. Right beside the pier is an ancient circular graveyard from which bronze urns have been unearthed. A mile to the southeast is the island's most venerated holy place, the Church of St. Kevin, now almost completely buried in sand, even though it was in use as recently as 100 years ago. The remains of another early church — named after St. Gobnait, who is said to have been the only woman allowed into the monasteries of Aran — can be found about a quarter-mile south of the landing pier. Atop the high hill on the northeast side of Inisheer, the ruins of the O'Brien castle proudly tower above everything else on the island. Immediately south of the castle is an ancient cemetery called the Grave of the Seven Daughters, about which little is known.

CHECKING IN

Inisheer The only true hotel on Aran, with only 15 rooms (6 of which are suites with baths). The food is commendable, traditional, and with no frills. Major credit cards accepted. A few hundred yards south of the landing pier, Inisheer (phone: 99-75020). Inexpensive.

Strand House Mrs. Conneely runs this house with 9 rooms (6 have private baths). Her husband oversees the pub, which serves food. Inisheer (phone: 75002). Inexpensive.

EATING OUT

The Coffee Shop This is a good spot for scones and tea. Open in summer only. Just beside the pier, Inisheer (phone: 75049). Inexpensive.

Man of Aran Cottage This tea shop sits beside a lovely beach. It was one of the many local sites featured in Robert Flaherty's celebrated film *Man of Aran*. Kilmurvey, Inishmore (no phone). Inexpensive.

County Mayo

Above brooding Connemara, the Mweelrea and Partry mountains and the Sheeffrey Hills of southern County Mayo give way to a gentler landscape that wraps around beautiful, island-studded Clew Bay. Croagh Patrick, the stately mountain where St. Patrick is said to have prayed and fasted for 40 days for the salvation of the Irish people, is the dominant feature of the bay's southern shore, while Achill Island, Ireland's largest offshore island, guards the northwestern reaches of the bay. Inland, a series of lakes, most notably Lough Mask, which feeds into Lough Corrib near Mayo's border with County Galway, offer anglers excellent trout fishing. The more northerly regions of the county offer dramatic mountain and cliff scenery. Many Irish legends and historical figures remembered in story and song are associated with this region, and Mayo's natural riches and leisure facilities enable travelers to experience traditional Ireland at its best.

The coastline, with its succession of sandy beaches, rugged headlands, and dramatic cliffs, is steeped in legends of Grace O'Malley (Grainne Ui Mhaille), the 16th-century warrior sea queen who made herself ruler of the district that surrounds Clew Bay and its islands after the death of her father. Although some doubt the veracity of her legendary exploits, stories about her have been handed down in the spoken tradition of the islanders and written about in the historical novels *Queen of Men* by William O'-Brien and *Grania* by Morgan Llywelyn as well as in the more scholarly biography *Granuaile: The Life and Times of Grace O'Malley* by Anne Chambers.

In addition, while reliable Irish history reaches back no farther than the 7th century, the plain of Southern Moytura near Cong is said to have been the scene of the first battle between two mythical tribes believed to have ruled this area 3,000 years ago — the Fir Bolg, a race of small dark men, and the fair Tuatha De Danaan, said to be a race of magicians. Though the Danaan were victorious here, they were later overcome in the Celtic conquest. Legend says the defeated Danaan changed themselves into fairies and ever since have inhabited the hills, forts, and caves of Ireland. Beneath the rocks of Cong lie more than 40 dark, unearthly looking caves, and not a few locals will attest that many of the "little people" went to live there.

There is more historical certainty about the role that Mayo men played in the agitations of the Land League, formed in 1879 to help tenant farmers resist tyrannical landlords. Michael Davitt, one of the founders of the league, was born at Straid, near Castlebar, and Captain Charles Boycott, one of the league's targets, lived at Lough Mask House, on the shores of the southern Mayo lake.

The northern part of the county also has reverberated with historic clashes, most notably in 1798, when the French Revolution swept up on its shores. A force of more than 1,000 French soldiers sailed into Killala Bay and stormed ashore to join in the insurrection that had been stirred up by patriots, called the United Irishmen, in different parts of Ireland. What followed was a mixture of comic opera and bitter tragedy, all well reconstructed in a novel by the American writer Thomas Flanagan called *The Year of the French*. The French were joined by a ragtag band of Irish peasants who knew nothing about warfare but initially enjoyed a heady victory in Castlebar. Eventually, the makeshift army went down to inglorious defeat at the hands of the English.

Our County Mayo route originates in Galway City, from which it is a pleasant 20-mile drive into southern Mayo and the historic village of Cong. The route then skirts the western edges of Lough Mask, beneath the Partry Mountains, heading north to Castlebar. From this busy town in the heart of the limestone plain country, it turns north to the great salmon and fishing territory that encompasses the scenic lakes and rivers around Foxford, Pontoon, and Ballina. The route then follows the Atlantic cliffs to the bleak boglands of Erris and Belmullet and the wonderful seascapes beyond this wilderness. From there, the tour heads east and inland to Crossmolina, then south again and west to Newport and Achill Island. After an excursion to the island, it continues around Clew Bay, traveling through Westport and Louisburgh, then dips south into Joyce Country (described in the *Connemara and the Aran Islands* route) before returning to Cong or Galway. The route, a meandering 150 miles, can be covered comfortably in 3 to 4 days.

Expect to pay up to $240 a night for a double room at a hotel rated as very expensive; from $150 to $225 at establishments described as expensive; $75 to $150 at hotels rated as moderate; and less than $75 (sometimes considerably less at bed and breakfast establishments) at places listed as inexpensive. Dinner for two (excluding wine, drinks, and tips) at an expensive establishment will cost a minimum of $75; at a moderate place, two can dine well for $30 to $70; and dinner for two at an inexpensive spot will cost less than $30. For each location, hotels and restaurants are listed alphabetically by price category.

GALWAY CITY For a complete report on the city, its sites, hotels, and restaurants, see *Galway City* in THE CITIES.

En Route from Galway City Take N84 north around the eastern shore of Lough Corrib, passing through Cloonboo and Headford. The well-preserved ruins of 14th-century Ross Errilly Abbey are nearby. At Headford, pick up R334 northwest through Bunnafollistran and Cross. At Cross, bear west onto R346 to Cong, which is 20 miles from Galway.

CONG This tiny village, on an isthmus between Lough Mask and Lough Corrib, is best known for its ruins of the 12th-century Cong Abbey and the luxury hotel *Ashford Castle* (see *Checking In*). It may also be familiar to Americans as the setting for much of that quintessential Irish-American movie, *The Quiet Man*, which was filmed in these precincts.

Cong Abbey, founded in the 14th century for Irish Augustinians probably by Turlough O'Connor, King of Ireland, is considered one of the finest examples of early architecture in Ireland. The ruins include several doorways and windows of a transitional style, somewhere between Romanesque and Gothic, and are best seen from the cloisters' garth (yard). Behind the west end of the abbey garth is a small stone house constructed so that the River Cong flows through a gully beneath the floor. The structure is known as the Monks' Fishing House because monks from the abbey operated a fishtrap through a trapdoor in its floor.

The ruins of the abbey are beside one of the entrance gates to the lovely grounds of *Ashford Castle*. The oldest part of the castle was built in the 18th century, but the castellated towers and a bridge on the river's edge were added later by Sir Benjamin Guinness. The castle was converted into a hotel in 1939. Sections of the grounds are open to the public.

Besides the abbey, there are several interesting historical artifacts and monuments connected with Cong and its environs. The celebrated *Cross of Cong* (now in the *National Museum* in Dublin) was discovered in a chest in the village early in the 19th century. Made of oak plated with copper and decorated with beautiful gold filigree in a Celtic pattern, it is a masterpiece of 12th-century religious art. The little ruined church and the ancient Stone of Lunga on the low wooded island of Inchagoill in Lough Corrib belong to the age of St. Patrick. The stone is a 2½-foot-high obelisk that bears ancient Roman characters.

The stream connecting Lough Mask and Lough Corrib runs underground at Cong and is accessible from a number of caves that honeycomb the plateau of cavernous limestone between the lakes. The most accessible cave is the Pigeon Hole. To get there, turn right onto New Saw Mill Road, a mile west of the village. At the first cottage on the right, an iron gate opens to a field; a short way from the gate, 61 stone steps lead down to the underground chamber. Note: Those who choose to explore the cave do so at their own risk. If you decide to take a look, be careful when making the descent; the steps are slippery and the cave is dark.

Another local curiosity is the Dry Canal, which was built as a relief project during the Great Famine of 1846 with the idea of connecting Lough Corrib and Lough Mask to extend navigation. When it was completed, however, it was discovered that despite the cut-stone banks and locks, the canal was incapable of holding water due to its porous limestone bed.

About half a mile from the village on all three approach roads to Cong, you may notice small mounds of wooden crosses, called *crusheens*. For centuries, it has been the practice of funeral corteges to stop at these spots to say a prayer and add another cross to the pile.

Roughly 4 miles north of Cong, on a minor road along the shores of Lough Mask, are the ruins of a castle that belonged to Captain Charles

Boycott, a retired British army officer who was unpopular with his tenants. The name of Boycott came to stand for ostracism and isolation because workers refused to help him harvest his crops during the Land League agitation of the 1880s.

Cong is a center for hunting and fishing. Lough Mask is noted for large trout and pike; Lough Corrib — Ireland's second-largest lake — is renowned for brown trout, pike, and salmon. For additional details, see *Gone Fishing* in DIVERSIONS.

CHECKING IN/EATING OUT

Ashford Castle One of the finest castle-hotels in Europe. Each of the 83 rooms and 6 suites has a view of the lake or the hotel's formal gardens and wide lawns, and there is a 9-hole golf course on the grounds. The dining room serves elaborate French meals. Open daily for lunch and dinner. Reservations advised. Major credit cards accepted. For additional details, see *Rural Retreats* in DIVERSIONS. On 98A just east of Cong (phone: 92-46003; fax: 92-46260). Very expensive.

En Route from Cong The route north to Castlebar follows an unnumbered minor road via Clonbur and Finny along the western bank of Lough Mask, beside the Partry Mountains, passing through Tourmakeady, a small Irish-speaking village (shop at the woolen sweater factory here for bargains). At the village of Partry, take N84 about 3½ miles north, where a road on the right leads to the largely restored Ballintubber Abbey, which has been in almost uninterrupted use as a place of worship since it was founded by Augustinians in 1216. For a detailed description of the abbey, see *Ancient Monuments and Ruins* in DIVERSIONS. Return to N84 and continue north to Castlebar, which is approximately 25 miles from Cong.

CASTLEBAR The administrative capital of County Mayo, Castlebar is a thriving commercial center that began as a settlement near a castle built by the de Barra family. It became famous during the 1798 rebellion when a joint Irish-French force routed a superior British force here. So fast did the British calvary retreat that the event came to be known as the Races of Castlebar — though, sadly, it was a short-lived victory. The remains of John Moore, President of the Republic of Connaught, which the victors established after the battle, are buried in the town's pleasant, tree-lined mall. The Castlebar Tourist Board (phone: 94-21207) is open only in the summer. In late June or early July, the town hosts the *International Four Days' Walks,* a series of noncompetitive, well-supervised treks through the countryside. For details, see *Feis and Fleadh: The Best Festivals* in DIVERSIONS.

CHECKING IN

Breaffy House An elegant Georgian mansion with modern additions, it's set on 60 acres of wooded parkland. There are 43 pleasantly appointed rooms, and evening entertainment is scheduled during the summer months. Two miles from Castlebar on the Castlebar–Claremorris road, N60 (phone: 94-22033; fax: 94-22033). Moderate.

EATING OUT

Castle Bistro Seafood is a specialty at this attractive restaurant and bar reminiscent of a French bistro. Open daily. Reservations unnecessary. Major credit cards accepted. Castle St., Castlebar (phone: 94-22809). Moderate.

Davitt Excellent steaks, vegetarian dishes, and other straightforward fare are served in this well-run open-kitchen eatery. Open daily for lunch and dinner. Reservations advised. Major credit cards accepted. Rush St., Castlebar (phone: 94-22233). Moderate.

En Route from Castlebar In the village of Turlough, 3 miles northeast of Castlebar on N5, is a well-preserved round tower beside the ruins of a 17th-century church. The tower is slightly unusual, being lower and fatter than most such structures. It commands a fine view of the surrounding plains. Look for the signpost on N5. Head northeast from Turlough on N5 and turn north onto N58 at Bellavary village to reach Foxford and Pontoon.

FOXFORD About 14 miles from Castlebar, the River Moy flows through Foxford on its way into the Atlantic at Killala Bay. The Moy is an outstanding river for salmon fishing and, in its heyday around the turn of the century, constantly recorded the biggest annual catches of any salmon water in Ireland or Britain. Today it still provides magnificent fishing and is a must for salmon enthusiasts. The little town of Foxford (or nearby Pontoon; see below) is an ideal base from which to fish the mighty Moy. For information, contact Gerry Coleman at *Moy View Estate,* Foxford (phone: 94-56421).

Foxford is also renowned for the woolen mills established alongside the Moy by an order of nuns in 1892. Visitors are welcome to tour the newly opened tourist center which depicts life in rural Ireland over the last century. Open daily; admission charge (phone: 94-56756; fax: 94-56415). A bronze bust in the town honors one of its most illustrious sons, Admiral William Brown, the man who founded the Argentine Navy.

PONTOON Take the left fork just outside Foxford and travel 4 miles along R318 to Pontoon on Lough Conn. The name of the town comes from the bridge that was built to span the narrow stretch of water that links Conn with the smaller Lough Cullen. Both lakes are superb salmon waters, and Pontoon, situated in the midst of forests and majestic mountains fringing the lake shores, is an idyllic setting for anglers.

CHECKING IN/EATING OUT

Healy's A small (10 rooms), good hotel set amid lush woodland at the foot of a mountain, between loughs Conn and Cullen. Warm personal attention is given to all visitors, and a high standard of cooking is consistently maintained, with a welcome emphasis on traditional Irish fare. Guests may golf for free at Castlebar. Open year-round. Pontoon (phone: 94-56443; fax: 94-56572). Moderate.

Pontoon Bridge Perched on the edge of Lough Conn, this place, owned and operated by the Geary family, is a favorite haunt of anglers because it provides boats and tackle, along with ghillies (angling guides), for fishing trips (see *Gone Fishing* in DIVERSIONS). Two- and 4-day courses in landscape painting for beginners and experienced painters also are offered. Some of the 18 bedrooms (all with private baths) have striking views of the lake. The dining room has an excellent reputation. Open April through October. Pontoon (phone: 94-56120 or 94-56156; fax: 94-56120). Moderate.

BALLINA The 12-mile drive north to Ballina on R310 offers some of the loveliest lake scenery in Ireland. Ballina is Mayo's largest town and one of its most attractive (it's also the hometown of Ireland's president, Mary Robinson). Designed and founded by a local landlord in the mid-18th century, the town straddles the Moy at the point where the river broadens before entering the estuary leading to Killala Bay. It's famous for its salmon fishing and in particular for the Ridge Pool, just above the Ham Bridge. In summer, the Ridge teems with salmon. It is not unknown for an angler to hook 20 salmon or more during a day on the Ridge. The best months to fish here are June to September. For salmon fishing, contact the Fishery Manager at the *Moy Fishery* (phone: 96-21332). There is also a run of sea trout in the Moy from July through September. The locals take boats onto the estuary and use strips of mackerel as bait to catch these delectable fish in huge numbers. For sea trout fishing and boats, contact Judd Ruane (*Riverboat Inn,* The Quay, Ballina; phone: 96-22183).

Shoppers visiting Ballina will want to stop in at *Clarke's* (O'Rahilly St.; phone: 96-22484). It looks like a newsstand from the outside, but inside holds a treasure trove of unlikely items: Meissen porcelain, Crabtree & Evelyn toilet water, music boxes, Haitian folk art, and more, all under the watchful eye of owner Loretta Clarke, herself one of the most vivid attractions of the place.

CHECKING IN

Downhill This comfortable, long-established hotel on the banks of the River Bunree is a cozy and popular place among the locals. There are 52 guestrooms; try to get one overlooking the river, as they have more character.

There's a heated indoor swimming pool, squash courts, a sauna, a sun deck, a Jacuzzi, and a studio gym with an instructor. Guests also can fish on the lake or river for salmon, trout, and sea trout. The dining room fare is quite good, and there's late-night merriment at *Frogs Piano Bar and Disco*. Bunree, Ballina (phone: 96-21033; fax: 96-21338). Expensive.

Mount Falcon Castle Guest House Tucked away on 100 acres of forested parkland, this authentic, period country residence preserves the ambience of a past age. Log fires warm the rooms, and produce from the castle gardens and farm is served in the hotel dining room, celebrated for its home cooking. Dinner is particularly memorable — guests sit around one large, elegant table and are served by the (ancient) lady of the house, who is a real character. The Aldridge family, who own the castle, also hold the rights to one of the best fishing stretches on the Moy, which meanders through the grounds. Guests can book a day's angling for a fee. Closed around *Christmas* and in February and March. Mount Falcon, on N57 south of Ballina (phone: 96-21172; fax: 96-21172). Expensive.

Imperial A century-old hotel in the middle of town, its 35 rooms have been refurbished to handsome, modern standards, yet they still retain much of their original charm. The cuisine is of a high order, with superb fresh salmon in season. Pearse St., Ballina (phone: 96-22200; fax: 96-21005). Moderate.

Friarstown House This farmhouse has 3 large rooms (all with private baths). Each room has a gorgeous view of either the mountains or the lake. In addition to breakfast, the Dowdican family will provide guests with a picnic lunch or an evening meal. Friarstown, Knockmore (phone: 94-58270). Inexpensive.

Kingfisher Lodge A friendly bed and breakfast place that has 6 rooms, 4 with private baths. Run by the Gallagher family, it's only 275 yards from the River Moy. Mount Falcon (phone: 96-22718). Inexpensive.

EATING OUT

Swiss Barn The Swiss chef-owner of this rustic continental restaurant dispenses tasty dishes, among the most noteworthy of which are fondue *bourguignon*, lobster thermidor, and steak tartare; vegetarian dishes are also served. Open for dinner only; closed Mondays. Reservations essential. Major credit cards accepted. On N57, Foxford Rd. (the road is narrow, but forge ahead!), Ballina (phone: 96-21117). Moderate.

ARDNAREE Just east of Ballina on R294, on the east bank of the River Moy, is the village of Ardnaree ("the hill of the execution" in Irish), where legend tells that four brothers were hanged for the murder of a bishop in the 7th century. Because the murderers were princes, they were given a royal burial despite their foul deed, and a dolmen (megalithic tomb) marks the place where they are interred at Knockleagh, close to the railway station in the southwestern part of the town. Ardnaree was the scene of another hanging during the French invasion of 1798, when a scout for the French forces, Patrick Walsh, was captured by the British and executed on the spot. Also in Ardnaree are the ruins of a 14th-century Augustinian abbey and the 19th-century Catholic cathedral of St. Muredach, which has some beautiful stained glass windows.

En Route from Ballina R314 runs north from Ballina for 7 miles along the western edge of Killala Bay to the village of Killala and then turns northwest along the Atlantic cliffs almost to Belmullet and the Mullet Peninsula before it joins R313. Travelers who wish to omit this part of the drive can proceed directly west from Ballina on N59 for 8½ miles to Crossmolina and, from there, south to Newport and Achill Island (see "Crossmolina" and "En Route from Crossmolina" below).

KILLALA A sleepy, lovely seaport, Killala was at one time the seat of an influential bishopric, and the most important ecclesiastical center in Mayo. The Church of Ireland (Protestant) still maintains a cathedral built during the 17th century above the ruins of the original Catholic cathedral. According to legend, none other than St. Patrick himself established the first church here. Moreover, there is also a local belief that it was from Killala that the young Patrick made his escape from Ireland, where he had been taken and enslaved as a boy (he returned years later to convert the island).

Standing above the harbor is one of the best preserved round towers in Ireland, built by monks as a bell tower and refuge against pillagers. At Carricknass, just west of the village, are the ruins of a medieval castle built by the Burke clan, who were among the most powerful Anglo-Norman families to settle in Ireland during the 12th century.

Killala's most memorable moment in history came on an August morning in 1798 when three French men-of-war sailed into the bay and anchored off Kilcummin strand, just north of the village. A force of 1,067 French soldiers were rowed ashore in relays of longboats to take part in Ireland's revolution against England, engineered by the radical United Irishmen. The French were commanded by the swashbuckling General Humbert, a confrere of Napoleon. They had been led to believe that a well-armed and sternly disciplined band of Irish rebels was ready to join them when they came ashore, but instead they found ill-clad and ill-fed Irish peasants, who had no knowledge whatsoever of war and could speak only Gaelic. This motley army met little resistance at the start, and both Killala and Ballina were taken in a matter of hours. They then marched to Castlebar to achieve a famous victory over the British garrison there. However, they encountered superior English forces at Ballinamuck, in

County Longford, and were speedily defeated. The French were chivalrously treated as prisoners of war; the Irish were summarily executed, their supporters and families in Mayo also slaughtered.

En Route from Killala Resume the tour north on R314, driving 9 miles to the village of Ballycastle.

BALLYCASTLE A charming, old-fashioned village, Ballycastle still has one or two thatch-roofed cottages on its main street. (Thatch-roofed cottages are available for rent nearby. Contact the Galway Tourist Office; phone: 91-63081.) Linger here awhile and walk along the side road that leads to Downpatrick Head, a sheer promontory that has legendary connections with St. Patrick. Exercising great caution, walk to the edge of the precipice and peer down at Dun Briste ("the broken fort"), a huge rocky chunk of land that seems to have been severed from the mainland and cast adrift in the Atlantic. According to folklore, Dun Briste was the home of a pagan god, Crom Cruach, and St. Patrick cut it off from the mainland with a blow of his staff, thus isolating paganism from Ireland forever. The pleasant River Ballinglen, flowing through Ballycastle, holds a plentiful supply of lively brook trout. Stop in at *John Walkin* (Tone St., Ballycastle; phone: 96-22442), a shop that can provide fishing licenses, tackle, and other necessities. Outside the village, there's a beautiful crescent of sandy beach, ideal for swimming when the weather is hot.

Recent excavations at the nearby Ceide Fields (look for signposts) have unearthed evidence of enclosed farmland dating back to 3000 BC. The information center has a video explaining the site, the world's oldest known farming settlement. Ancient ring forts also dot the area and an ancient standing stone is in the Doonfeeney section of Ballycastle, off R314, about 2 miles northwest of the town center.

CHECKING IN

Humbert Lodge Run by the Hynes family, this place offers 4 comfortable rooms. Banagher, Carrowmore, Lacken, near Killala (phone: 96-32179). Inexpensive.

EATING OUT

Doonfeeny House Perched on wooded cliffs above the Atlantic, this is a superb restaurant whose talented owner-chef specializes in fresh fish and game in season. It's a small, hushed, candlelit place, with a respectable wine cellar to complement the excellent viands. Open daily for dinner. Reservations advised. No credit cards accepted. Signposted from Ballycastle, about 2 miles northwest on R314 (phone: 96-43092). Moderate.

En Route from Ballycastle Heading west 32 miles to Belmullet Town, R314 passes through some of the most deserted countryside in all of Ireland, with miles and miles of furze-covered bogland stretching to the south. On the northern side, sheer cliffs plunge vertiginously down to the wild Atlantic, and small remote beaches beckon from among the rocks.

BELMULLET This quaint old town, with a rather fetching down-at-the-heels appearance, is the gateway to the Mullet Peninsula, a large, desolate tract of land that juts out into the Atlantic. It's possible to tour the peninsula on its one good road in an hour or so. The most interesting part is at the southern tip, where a splendid lighthouse rises from the rocky shore at Blacksod. The area is steeped in history and legend. At Cross Point, near a lake 5 miles southwest of Belmullet, are the remains of an abbey that is thought to be connected with St. Brendan the Navigator, the adventurous sea voyager and holy man whom the Irish believe discovered the New World many centuries before Columbus. Two miles out in the ocean from Cross Point is the island of Inishglora, where in Celtic mythology the Children of Lir, who had been changed into swans by their evil stepmother, dwelt for hundreds of years, waiting for the sound of a church bell to return them to human form.

The Mullet forms the western shore of Blacksod Bay, regarded as one of the finest natural deep-water harbors in Europe, though it is little used nowadays. At the bottom of the bay, the largest of the galleons that sailed with the Spanish Armada — *La Rata* — has been lying since 1588, when it went down in a storm while trying to make its way back to Spain after being routed by Queen Elizabeth's naval forces. *La Rata* and a smaller ship, the *Nuestra Señora de Begona,* sought sanctuary in Blacksod, anchoring offshore and sending emissaries into the Mullet in a bid to stir up a local rebellion against the British. Getting no response, the Spanish were forced to sail on southward in the teeth of fierce Atlantic gales. *La Rata* sank as it was leaving the bay, but the *Nuestra Señora* made it safely home to Spain.

On the peninsula, 8 miles south of Belmullet, the derelict remains of the whaling station that once flourished in Elly Harbour are still visible. Until the close of the 19th century, the Elly station was one of the busiest in Europe, and the bay was often crowded with tall-masted whalers waiting to unload their catches. Small fishing boats still sail out of Elly and, oddly enough, a doll factory now occupies one of the warehouses where the whales once were processed.

En Route from Belmullet Travel 12 miles east on R313 to Bangor Erris and from there take N59 farther east (not south) 20 miles to the village of Crossmolina. This route passes through the tiny hamlet of Bellacorick, the location of one of Ireland's most intriguing "believe it or not" oddities. The coping stones on the north side of the bridge that crosses the River Oweninny send out musical notes when vigorously rubbed or hit hard with a rock, a phenomenon that no one has been able to explain satisfactorily.

CROSSMOLINA This is another premier angling center with plenty of large brown trout in the River Deel, which flows through the village. Bordering Crossmolina are the northern shores of Lough Conn. It's easy to hire a boat to go out on the lake; contact Daniel Hiney (Mullinmore St., Crossmolina; phone: 96-31202). On the lake shore, southeast of town, are the remains of Errew Abbey, built for the Augustinians in the 15th century. Near the point where the Deel enters the lake are the remains of 16th-century Deel Castle.

CHECKING IN

Enniscoe House Guests at this 7-room Georgian house, on the shore of Lough Conn, can take advantage of the fishing and boating here, or they can simply enjoy the restful atmosphere. There's a private boat landing on Lough Conn, and guests can be supplied with fishing gear; the establishment's fishing manager also offers patient instruction. The house is furnished with fine antiques and paintings, and meals are ample. Proprietress Susan Kellett also handles inquiries about the *North Mayo Family History Research Centre,* the local branch of Ireland's national genealogical project. Those interested in tracing their roots in this region may contact her at the hotel; a registration fee (about $13) is charged. Closed October to *Easter.* Castlehill, 2 miles south of Crossmolina on the R315 (phone: 96-31112; fax: 96-31773). Expensive.

En Route from Crossmolina From Crossmolina, head south on L140 for 5 miles and take the right fork onto L137. At the L136 T-junction, turn left and travel 10 miles south to Beltra. Here, turn right onto the continuation of L137 for 6 miles, which runs into Newport, another good angling village. The ruins of Garrighowley Castle, said to be the original home of pirate Grace O'Malley (Grainne Ui Mhaille), are in Newport (look for signs). The *Furnace Lakes and Salmon Research Agency* (phone: 98-41107) also has a small visitors' center in town that explains the agency's work charting the life cycle of salmon and sea trout, both vital to this fishing community. From Newport, drive 12 miles northwest on N59 as far as Mulrany, the entrance to Corraun Peninsula, and pick up R319, which bridges Achill Sound to Achill Island.

CHECKING IN/EATING OUT

Newport House A 19-room, white Georgian house with Regency decor, this beautiful bayside place is especially geared to the needs of fisherfolk. The chef prepares superb food, with fresh ingredients from the hotel's own gardens, farm, and fishery. For additional details, see *Rural Retreats* in DIVERSIONS. Newport (phone: 98-41222; fax: 98-41613). Expensive.

Mulrany Bay Ideally situated overlooking the bay, this hotel offers 39 rooms, 36 with private baths, plus tennis courts, a swimming pool, and a playroom and playground. The food is adequate. Mulrany (phone: 98-36222; fax: 98-36266). Moderate

---

ACHILL ISLAND The largest of Ireland's offshore islands, Achill is a popular holiday center, though it's little known to foreign visitors. It is dominated by three mountains, and its coast is marked by dramatic cliffs as well as several charming resort villages with long, broad, sandy beaches. The village of Achill Sound, just across the bridge from the mainland, is the island's principal shopping center. It also has facilities for swimming, boating, and fishing. Beyond Achill Sound, the Atlantic Highway bears left off L141, the island's main road, and passes a keep of the O'Malleys. Black-faced sheep dot the rolling bogs and occasionally block the winding road. Dooega, a small village at the mouth of a valley on the west side of Minaun Mountain, is a convenient place from which to climb the mountain or the Minaun Cliffs, rising to 800 feet.

Just before reaching Keel, the island's main resort town, the route passes the spectacular Cathedral Rocks, water-carved cliffs that resemble a Gothic cathedral jutting up from the ocean. Keel, on a curving bay sheltered by Slievemore Mountain on the north and Croghun Mountain on the west, is a center for surfing and diving. In addition to its 3-mile-long sandy beach, it has a 9-hole golf course and tennis courts.

Two miles beyond Keel are the whitewashed cottages of Dooagh, on a bay famous for salmon netting. Keem Bay, which has a narrow, fine-sand beach sheltered by the steeply rising Moyteoge Head, is 3 miles farther west. Basking sharks occasionally visit Achill waters in spring and are trapped in nets at Keem Bay and then killed with lances by island crews working from small canvas-covered *curraghs*. A steep hiking trail leads from Keem Bay to the summit of Croaghaun Mountain, with a 4-mile line of superb cliffs reaching as high as 2,000 feet above the ocean.

On the way back through Keem Bay, a road to the left leads north across the island to Dugort, a north shore village. From here, boatmen take visitors to the Seal Caves that extend far into the cliffs under Slievemore Mountain.

In addition to sea angling, there is fishing for trout in Achill's lakes and the River Dooega, and in recent years the island has become a popular locale for mountain climbing, windsurfing, canoeing, orienteering, and scuba diving. (For diving information, contact John P. O'Malley at the post office in Keel; phone: 98-43125.) The Achill Tourist Information Office is open in July and August only (phone: 98-45384).

CHECKING IN/EATING OUT

Achill Adventure & Leisure Island Holidays Along with simple hotel accommodations, outdoor excursions including canoeing, hill walking, rock climbing, and surfing are conducted with instruction. The chef takes special requests. Dugort, Achill Island (phone: 98-45384). Inexpensive.

Achill Outdoor Education Centre This place offers rustic hostel-style lodgings and a restaurant. Lessons are given with all outdoor activities. Cashel, Achill Island (phone: 98-47253). Inexpensive.

En Route from Achill Island N59 follows the curve of Clew Bay south from Mulrany to Westport, 8 miles below Newport.

EATING OUT

Boley House Good seafood is featured at reasonable prices. Open daily for lunch and dinner March through October; open occasional weekends the rest of the year. Reservations advised. MasterCard and Visa accepted. Keel, Achill Island (phone: 98-43147). Inexpensive.

WESTPORT This charming seigneurial town, in a hollow on the arm of Clew Bay, was planned for the Marquess of Sligo by James Wyatt, a famous British architect of the Georgian period. Its main street, known as the Mall, runs along both sides of the gentle River Carrowbeg, which is crossed by several picturesque stone bridges and sheltered by a colonnade of lime trees. Westport is an important center for sea angling and was the site of a meeting at which the Irish Land League was formed in 1879. The town also provided the setting for a number of novels by George A. Birmingham, the pen name of James Owen Hannay, rector of the Church of Ireland here from 1893 to 1913. A mile and a half west of the town center is Westport House, a fine Georgian mansion that was the home of the Marquess of Sligo. The house is open to the public from mid-May to mid-September (phone: 98-25141 or 98-25430). Designed by the German architect Richard Cassels in 1730 and altered 50 years later by Wyatt, it houses fine collections of old English and Irish silver, paintings by Sir Joshua Reynolds and James O'Connor, Waterford crystal, and fine old furniture. The attractive marble staircase was built by Italian artisans brought here specifically for that purpose. The basement area contains a warren of shops, an amusement arcade, and a tea shop. Outside, horse caravans (no longer in use) are on display.

Just outside the gates to the grounds of Westport House is Westport Quay, where boats can be rented for boating and fishing on Clew Bay. On Collanmore Island in the bay, there is a sailing center that offers instruction for beginner and intermediate sailors. For information, contact *Glenans Irish Sailing Centres* (28 Marion Sq., Dublin 2; phone: 1-767775 or 1-611481). Nearby Bertra Beach is a nice place for a swim, and the *Westport Golf Club* (3 miles from town; phone: 98-25113) has an 18-hole, par 73 championship course across the bay from Croagh Patrick.

A walking tour of Westport is offered by the Westport Tourist Information Office (The Mall; phone: 98-25711) and takes about an hour. In addition, outings to suit nearly any interest — from archaeology to horseback riding to sailing and fishing — may be arranged through Pauline McDermott (Main St., Newport; phone: 98-41647; fax: 98-26709). For visitors seeking their Irish roots, the *Clew Bay Heritage Centre* (The Quay; phone: 98-26852) provides genealogical information. It's open from 3 to 6 PM Sundays and from 10 AM to 1 PM the rest of the week.

Each June, a 4-day international sea angling festival takes place in Westport. For those who plan to linger in the area, *Westport House Country Estates* (Westport; phone: 98-25430) rents holiday homes and has a campground.

CHECKING IN

Olde Railway An old-fashioned, friendly hostelry on a tree-shaded street overlooking the river. The 20 rooms are comfortable, and the food is good (see *Eating Out*). The Mall, Westport (phone: 98-25166; fax: 98-25605). Moderate

Westport The highest standards are maintained at this modern, 49-room hotel. The staff is exceedingly friendly, and the food is first-rate. Westport, across the bridge at the bottom of James St., entering Newport Rd.; take the first left turn (phone: 98-25122; fax: 98-26739). Moderate.

Westport Woods Set on wooded grounds beside the lake, it offers 56 modest rooms. A restaurant offers tasty Irish dishes. Westport, on the road from town to The Quay (phone: 98-25811; fax: 98-26212). Moderate.

EATING OUT

Ardmore Specializing in fresh seafood, this small, intimate, candlelit restaurant overlooks Clew Bay. Owner-chef Pat Hoban prepares excellent continental and Irish dishes, while his wife, Noreen, supervises the dining room. Open for dinner only; closed Sundays. Reservations advised in summer. Major credit cards accepted. Rosbeg, Westport, 1 mile from the town center (phone: 98-25994). Moderate.

Asgard Owner-chef Michael Cadden specializes in seafood. The dining room, supervised by his wife, Mary, is candlelit and intimate. A lunch menu is available daily in the pub. Closed Monday evenings. Reservations advised. Major credit cards accepted. The Quay, Westport (phone: 98-25319). Moderate.

The Moorings Another cozy harborside spot. The Cordon Bleu–trained chef prepares fresh fish and meat dishes. Open for dinner only; closed Sundays. Reservations advised in summer. Major credit cards accepted. The Quay, Westport (phone: 98-25874). Moderate.

Olde Railway A family-run hostelry with Old World character and a popular pub where visitors can enjoy excellent seafood crêpes or just order a Guinness and mix with the locals. Open daily for dinner. Reservations advised. Major credit cards accepted. The Mall, Westport (phone: 98-25166). Moderate.

Quay Cottage Clams, lobster, mussels, and other shelled denizens of the deep are served all day in this quaint seaside inn. There is also a vegetarian menu. Open daily for lunch and dinner. Reservations advised. Major credit cards accepted. The Quay, Westport (phone: 98-26412). Moderate.

En Route from Westport Head west on the Louisburgh road. Four miles from Westport, look for the turnoff to N59 and the signpost for *Brackloon Weavers* (phone: 98-26236). Those seeking souvenirs might want to take a short detour to the shop, which features handwoven shawls, rugs, throws, and scarfs. It's closed Sundays. The graceful Croagh Patrick, Ireland's holy mountain, 5 miles west of Westport off R335, is one of the most impressive landmarks in the west of Ireland. Its 2,510-foot summit offers an inspiring view of the island-dotted bay, making the 2-hour climb worth the effort. The climb is over a pile of shifting boulders, however, so be careful and wear good walking shoes (although devout pilgrims traditionally made the ascent barefoot and some still do). Also, try not to disturb those pilgrims who are praying as they climb. St. Patrick is said to have spent 40 days and 40 nights in prayer and fasting atop the mountain in AD 441, and each year Catholics make this pilgrimage to the mountain on the last Sunday in July. The route up the mountain begins near Murrisk Abbey, which was built in the 14th century for the Augustinians and has a notable east window.

Eight miles farther west is Louisburgh, a pleasant fishing village at the mouth of the River Bunowen. There are several good sandy beaches nearby at Old Head, Carramore, Berta, Carrowniskey, and Thallabawn. In addition to three small hotels and guesthouses, there are ten self-catering cottages available; for details, contact the tourist board (Eyre Sq., Galway; phone: 91-63081). A minor road west from Louisburgh leads to Roonagh Quay, where boats are available for trips to Clare Island. In summer a ferry to Clare Island runs four times daily. For information, contact Chris O'Grady (phone: 98-26307).

CLARE ISLAND Steeped in the legends of the 16th-century sea queen Grace O'-Malley, Clare Island guards the entrance to Clew Bay and offers visitors a sense of peace and remoteness. Grace O'Malley's massive square castle, on the east coast of the island above the harbor, was converted into a coast guard station more than 150 years ago and is not particularly interesting. Tradition says that the ferocious Grace was interred in Clare Abbey, a small 15th-century church about a mile and a half southwest of the harbor.

There is only one small hotel on the island — Chris O'Grady's 13-room *Bayview* (phone: 98-26307) — but day-trippers can take advantage of several good beaches for bathing or picnics. A colorful regatta is held at Clare Island every July. Dr. Peter Gill has a restaurant on the island called *An Fulacht Fiadh* (the Irish name for ancient cooking places, still found in many parts of Ireland, that are associated with the warrior band, the Fianna). Gill will meet travelers at Roonagh Pier and take them to the island, where he provides a guided tour. Following afternoon coffee, the good doctor escorts visitors back to Roonagh. For information about the restaurant or the tour, call 98-25048.

En Route from Clare Island Back on the mainland, the 20-mile stretch south on R395 from Louisburgh to Killary Harbour, crosses a desolate moor and climbs past the village of Cregganbaum before descending to the Delphi Valley, which has a series of lakes and is flanked by the Sheeffrey Hills (2,504 feet) on the left. A sharp turn south leads to the northern shore of Killary Harbour and to the handsome waterfall where the River Erriff comes down from the mountain. At Leenane, a sparse fishing village at a bend in the Killary, the road to the right, R345, leads through Joyce Country (see the *Connemara and the Aran Islands* route), along the northern banks of Lough Corrib, and back to Cong (a distance of 14 miles). The 1990 movie *The Field* was filmed in this region. Alternatively, follow R336 from Maam Cross, then pick up N59 and drive 10 miles south to Galway City.

Antrim Coast

Northern Ireland's 70-mile stretch of northeastern coastline between Larne and Portrush offers some of the most exceptional scenery in Europe. Along the eastern edge of the Antrim Coast, as far north as Ballycastle, drivers also will be tempted to turn inland and explore the Glens of Antrim, a series of nine lovely valleys formed 20,000 years ago by retreating glaciers. The coastline, a veritable textbook illustration of geological history, has rock layers of red sandstone, white chalk, black basalt, and blue clay jutting out from beneath ancient lava flows.

Antrim has been inhabited for at least 5,000 years and probably a great deal longer than that. In Glenballyeamon, near Cushendall, stone "ax factories" dating from the Neolithic period have been discovered, and it is known that some of the tools made here of the local stone, diorite, were "exported" from Ireland to other countries. A Harvard University archaeological expedition has uncovered several layers of flint tools in a cliff face at Cushendun, which they think may be the key to the Irish Stone Age. In fact, so many ancient artifacts have been found near the ruins of Olderfleet Castle in Larne that fragments from Ireland's Stone Age are termed "Larnian." In addition, some archaeologists believe that this area is a prime example of the development of post–Ice Age society.

Although not part of the Roman Empire, Antrim was visited by the Romans, and trade developed with Roman settlements in Britain. Upon the decline of the empire and the weakening of its defense, Irish kings launched raiding parties on Roman holdings to steal booty and capture slaves. One of the most famous of these slaves, Patrick, son of a Roman centurion, who was later to become Ireland's patron saint, spent 7 years in captivity as a swine herd on Slemish Mountain (1,437 feet) in County Antrim before he escaped to Gaul (France).

Many Irish missionaries who set out to convert Europe to Christianity hailed from the north of Ireland, most notably St. Columbanus and St. Gall, who went to Germany, Switzerland, and Italy, and St. Columba, who went to Scotland. Because of the proximity of Ireland and Scotland (they're only 12 miles apart at the closest point), there always has been much traffic between the two countries. Besides Christianity, Ireland gave Scotland its Gaelic language, shared with it the game of hurling (called shinny or shinty in Scotland), and even sent over the famous bagpipes.

Two Scotsmen, Robert the Bruce and his brother Edward, who had freed their country from English rule, also attempted to emancipate Ireland, but succeeded only briefly. Edward was declared King of Ireland in 1316, but his death 2 years later threw Ireland back into its feud with the English crown. The wars continued until the end of the 16th century, culminating in the conquest of the north by the soldiers of Queen Eliza-

498

beth I. To tighten English control, a new policy — the "plantation of Ireland" — was devised. This plan for introducing Scottish and English Protestant settlers into the area was quite effective. A few Plantation manor houses still exist in Antrim today and can be seen along this route in Ballygally, on Rathlin Island, and elsewhere.

The first stop on our Antrim Coast route is Carrickfergus on the east coast, 9 miles northeast of Belfast. From Carrickfergus, the route hugs the northeastern shore of Ireland. The road from Larne to Cushendall (25 miles) was a great engineering feat when it was constructed in the 1830s. The magnificent east coast curves around the base of steep headlands between which the nine green glens of Antrim open to the sea. Torr Head is the northeasternmost point of the mainland. Westward along the coast is the Giant's Causeway, a curious basalt rock formation that is Ireland's most celebrated natural wonder and a UNESCO World Heritage Site. Portrush forms the western boundary of the Antrim Coast and County Antrim. The tour ends at the walled city of Londonderry.

Generally, hotels in Northern Ireland are clean and congenial, and most have dining rooms. Food is fresh and hearty and occasionally haute cuisine. Accommodations listed here as expensive will cost $100 or more for a double room with bath and full breakfast; those listed as moderate will run $60 to $100; and those listed as inexpensive will cost $60 or less. Guesthouses generally charge $35 to $50 a night. A meal for two, including VAT and service charge (but not beverages), will cost $50 or more at restaurants listed as expensive; from $35 to $50 at places in the moderate category; and less than $35 at eateries described as inexpensive. For each location, hotels and restaurants are listed alphabetically by price category.

BELFAST For a full report on the city's sites, hotels, and restaurants, see *Belfast* in THE CITIES.

En Route from Belfast Take M5 to Newtownabbey, then pick up A2 to Carrickfergus, a total distance of about 9 miles.

CARRICKFERGUS Said to be one of the oldest towns in Northern Ireland, Carrickfergus was named for Fergus, Gaelic king of the ancient kingdom of Dalriada. It was the north's main port and principal town until Belfast began to expand in the 17th century. The town's proud history is personified by its castle, built on a spit of basalt rock standing watch over the harbor. Northern Ireland's largest and best-preserved Norman castle, Carrickfergus recently has been authentically refurbished, and visitors can view a 10-minute introductory video on the castle's history; enjoy various changing exhibits; and inspect the banqueting halls, an old castle well, and the impressive dungeon. The castle is open Mondays through Saturdays from 10 AM to 6 PM, and Sundays from 2 to 6 PM in April through September; Mondays through Saturdays from 10 AM to 4 PM, and Sundays from 2 to 4 PM the rest of the year. There's an admission charge (phone: 93-51273). For detailed information, see *Ancient Monuments and Ruins* in DIVERSIONS.

Sections of Carrickfergus's town wall remain; the North Gate is particularly well-preserved due to restoration work in 1911. The four walls of the old County Antrim Courthouse on High Street, which date from 1613, are now the exterior walls of the Town Hall. Also on High Street are some attractive 18th-century houses. Just off the marketplace is St. Nicholas Church, built in 1185. Although most of the present structure dates from the 17th and 18th centuries, it retains some of its original 12th-century arcades and other features added in the 14th century. The 16th-century Flemish John the Baptist window in the nave is possibly the oldest stained glass in Ulster. The pretty churchyard is entered through a reconstruction of a distinctive, early-19th-century archway and bell tower. One mile east of town is Boneybefore, where the grandparents of Andrew Jackson (seventh President of the United States) lived. A monument marks the site of their home, while a reconstruction of their late-18th-century thatch-roofed, dirt-floor cottage, which contains period furnishings and exhibits, stands nearby. It's open May through October, weekdays from 10 AM to 1 PM and 2 to 6 PM, weekends from 2 to 6 PM. There's an admission charge (phone: 93-64972).

LARNE Continue north on A2 for 8½ miles to Larne. Second only to Belfast in its importance as a port in Northern Ireland, Larne is the closest point in Ireland to Britain, and the ferry trip from there to Stranraer, Scotland, takes just a bit over 2 hours. Huge freight ships as well as smaller pleasure craft dock in the harbor. A 95-foot tower is Larne's landmark. Modeled after the traditional Irish round tower, it was built to honor James Claine, a member of Parliament who so loved the harbor's view that he was buried upright so he "would never lose sight of it."

En Route from Larne The road to Ballygally, A2, passes Ballygally Head, a cluster of irregular rock pillars formed by lava that bubbled to the surface some 70 million years ago. Overlooking Ballygally Bay is *Ballygally Castle,* a Plantation manor house built in 1625 by a Scottish landowner, James Shaw, and turned into a hotel in 1948 (see *Checking In/ Eating Out*).

At Glenarm, the first and oldest of Antrim's nine glens, turn left on B97 for a scenic detour that takes our route (temporarily) inland. Behind the village is Glenarm Castle, completed in 1636 and today the residence of the 13th Earl of Antrim. The ancient estate, which includes Glenarm Forest, a lovely public park, is divided in two by the Glenarm River. The castle, not open to the public but visible from several points on the road, has been greatly altered over the years and now bears a striking resemblance to the Tower of London.

After passing the castle, follow B97 south and then west, turning onto

A42, passing through the tiny hamlet called The Sheddings. To the south is a solitary extinct volcano, Slemish Mountain (1,437 feet). Legend holds it was on the slopes of Slemish that a young slave, Patrick, served his master Miluic as a swine herd. Years later, in his *Confessio,* Patrick described himself as but "a beardless boy" of 16 when Irish pirates carried him away (ca. AD 389) from his family, who were Romans, probably living in what today is Wales. On Slemish Mountain, Patrick supposedly received divine visions urging him to ready himself for a life of Christian missionary activity; after 7 years of hardship and loneliness he escaped from Ireland to Gaul to fulfill those visions. For centuries since, Slemish has been a popular destination for pilgrimages on *St. Patrick's Day.*

At Broughshane, head 2½ miles northeast to the dramatically situated ruins of Skerry Hill Old Church, built on the supposed site of the *rath* (ring fort) of Miluic, Patrick's master. Just outside the church is a "footmark" in rock, which legend holds to be that of the Angel Victor, made as he ascended to heaven after one of his earthly visits to Patrick. From here head back on the A42 through Glencloy, a valley crosscut by streams and splashed by waterfalls, to Carnlough on the coast.

CARNLOUGH An old limestone quarrying town embraced by a sandy bay, this is a popular summer vacation spot. In season, the picturesque limestone harbor is abob with pleasure boats. In the center of town is a bridge over the main street that was built by the Marquess of Londonderry in 1854 to carry the small railway that transported limestone from the quarries in the hills above the harbor. Other limestone landmarks in the town include a square clock tower, the former Town Hall, and the harbormaster's office.

En Route from Carnlough North from Carnlough is Garron Point, which offers visitors the chance to savor the hillsides of one of the most scenic of Antrim's glens, Glenariff. At the foot of Glenariff is Red Bay, which takes its name from the sloping red sandstone cliffs.

At the end of Waterfoot, the bay's straggling shorefront village, turn left on A43 for a 5-mile drive up the side of Glenariff to the Glenariff Forest Park (phone: 266-37232). The park has a visitors' center, a café, a shop, restrooms, a ranger office, and picnic tables. Signposted walking trails offer wonderful views that range from a half-mile to 4 miles; foremost is the spectacular glen walk with 3 waterfalls. The park is open daily from 10 AM; closing hours vary and are posted. There's a parking lot fee. From here head back toward the coast.

CHECKING IN/EATING OUT

Ballygally Castle A 17th-century manor house with a 20th-century addition, this hotel has lovely views of Ballygally Bay and 30 modern bedrooms with private baths. The dining room, enclosed by picture windows facing the sea, is a good choice for coffee, tea, or a moderately priced lunch or dinner. The fresh fish is especially well prepared. Open daily. Reservations advised for dinner. Major credit cards accepted. 274 Coast Rd., Ballygally (phone: 574-583212; fax: 574-583681). Expensive.

Fenaghy House A $4-million renovation has transformed this mid-Victorian country house into a fine 23-room hotel (all with private baths), located near Skerry Hill Old Church. The property offers many amenities, including an equestrian center and a good restaurant. 136 Fenaghy Rd., Cullybackey, near Ballymena (phone: 266-881001; fax: 266-880080). Expensive.

Drumnagreagh This cliff-top hotel offers 16 comfortable rooms, each with private bath and either a sea or glen vista. Fish is a specialty at the two restaurants; both are open daily for lunch and dinner. Reservations advised. Major credit cards accepted. Three miles north of Ballygally on Coast Rd. in Glenarm (phone: 574-841651; fax: 574-841651). Moderate.

Londonderry Arms Built in 1848 by the Marchioness of Londonderry, this ivy-covered hotel retains its cozy Georgian coaching-inn air. There are 21 rooms (all with private baths) and an Irish crafts shop. Excellent food — morning coffee, lunch, afternoon tea, and dinner — is served. Dinner reservations advised on weekends. Major credit cards accepted. For additional details, see both *Pub Crawling* and *Rural Retreats* in DIVERSIONS. 20 Harbour Rd., Carnlough (phone: 574-885255 or 574-885458; fax: 574-885263). Moderate.

CUSHENDALL/CUSHENDUN The next stop on A2 is Cushendall, just 5 miles from Glenariff Forest Park, a bustling town whose streets are lined with stately Georgian and Regency houses. In the village center is a structure called Curfew Tower, a jail built in 1809. Cushendall is a holiday center, offering swimming, boating, and fishing.

A few miles west of Cushendall, on an unnumbered country road, are signs for Oisín's Grave, a court cairn, or burial mound, made of stones. The Oisín in question was a poet-warrior in the 3rd century, the supposed son of the mythological Irish hero Finn MacCool. Be warned that it's not an easy climb up the lower slopes of Tievebulliagh Hill to the grave. Return to A2, and it's 3 miles on to Cushendun.

Threaded by the River Glendun, Cushendun occupies a lovely sandy crescent of shore washed by the bay and anchored by sandstone cliffs at either end. The Cornish-style cottages on the north side of the river were designed by Clough William Ellis, an imaginative and innovative architect whose most famous work is at Portmeirion in Wales. Cushendun's white-washed stone cottages and the surrounding countryside are now maintained by the National Trust, which operates an information center, gift shop, and tea shop in the village. This area has been much painted by artists, and in summer they are often found busy at work. Despite tourist traffic, the village remains delightfully tranquil. Boats are available for hire, and the many caves in the sandstone cliffs are open for exploration. One of these is 20 miles deep and leads to Cave House, once the vacation home of the poet John Masefield and now owned by the Catholic church. The famous Irish chieftain Shane O'Neill (Shane the Proud), an opponent of Queen Elizabeth I and a leader of an Ulster revolt against England, was decapitated by the MacDonnells in Cushendun in 1567.

En Route from Cushendun For a pleasant side trip, take A2 slightly east, then north, over the Glendun Viaduct, an 82-foot-high bridge that crosses the River Glendun and offers an impressive panorama of the area. Across the bridge, the road continues to Loughareema, called locally the "vanishing lake": When there is a downpour, the lake rises, then falls dramatically because of the permeable chalk bed underneath. Near Loughareema is Ballypatrick Forest with a 4½-mile scenic drive. It's also a good spot for picnicking, pony trekking, or just walking.

Return to Cushendun, then take the Torr Road 12 miles along the coast to Fair Head.

CHECKING IN

Villa Up a steep lane is this 19th-century hilltop guesthouse with 3 rooms (2 with private baths) and a truly spectacular view of sheep grazing on startlingly green fields, with the sea far below. Morning coffee, afternoon tea, and in season strawberries and cream are served in the garden by owner Mrs. Scally. Open April through October. 185 Torr Rd., Cushendun (phone: 266-74252). Inexpensive.

FAIR HEAD A short detour off the Torr Road leads to the summit of this impressive 636-foot-high cliff. This area was much loved by Roger Casement, the Irish patriot and international philanthropist, and a monument to him stands here. The descent to Murlough Bay is steep, although the road is in good condition. Be sure to sound your horn on blind curves. Return to the Torr Road, drive west to Ballyvoy, and rejoin A2 for 4 miles to Ballycastle.

BALLYCASTLE At the mouth of the River Glenshesk and in the shadow of 1,696-foot-high Knocklayd Hill, Ballycastle is actually two towns linked by Quay Road, a pretty avenue lined with trees and Georgian and Victorian homes. Lower Town is a seaside resort with facilities for swimming, tennis, boating, golf, and fishing. Upper Town, the older of the two, has restaurants, shops, and many fine houses. The center of Upper Town is called the Diamond, where, centuries ago, the Scottish MacDonnell family's castle, for which the town was named, stood. Standing at the castle site today are the Greek-style Holy Trinity Church, built in 1756, and a memorial to George O'Connor, one of the town's patrons. The Diamond also is the scene of the annual *Ould Lammas Fair,* a kind of large flea market where all sorts of new and used articles are sold. It's held the last Monday and Tuesday in August (also see *Feis and Fleadh: The Best Festivals* in DIVERSIONS). Along the side streets leading from the Diamond are various shops.

On the outskirts of town is the Franciscan Bonamargy Friary, founded by the MacQuillan family in 1500. Damaged by fire in 1589, it was refurbished and occupied until 1642, after which it gradually fell into decay; the friary was restored again in 1931. Note the family tomb of the Earls of Antrim (the MacDonnells).

The town of Ballycastle has mythological as well as religious associations, for it was in the nearby Sea of Moyle that the tragic Children of Lir, who were changed into swans by their jealous stepmother, had to spend 300 of their 900 years' transmutation.

RATHLIN ISLAND A visit to Rathlin Island can be a delightful interlude in a driving journey, for cars must be left behind and the island explored on foot. The 6-mile crossing of Rathlin Sound from Ballycastle takes 50 minutes by motorboat (year-round, weather permitting, departing at 10:30 AM daily, and returning at 4 PM, 3 PM in winter); contact *Rathlin Venture* (phone: 265-763917) and *Iona Isle* (phone: 265-763907 or 265-763915). The approach to Rathlin Harbor at Church Bay provides a good view of the steep, 200-foot-high white limestone cliffs that surround most of the island. Fishing is the main occupation. To arrange an individual angling expedition, talk to one of the local fishermen.

With a population of only about 100 — down from 1,000 a century and a half ago — people are a minority here. The island's primary inhabitants are the thousands of sea birds that nest on Rathlin's crags and cliffs. The best vantage point for bird watching is West Lighthouse, on the western end of the island. At Kebble Nature Reserve there is a breeding ground for the island's puffin, kittiwake, and razorbill colonies. There's a minibus to Keeble that meets ferries in summer.

Although tiny, Rathlin has seen much history. The island's most famous landmark is Bruce's Cave, on the eastern end, to which Robert the Bruce retreated in 1306 with 3,000 of his men after his defeat at the hands of the English at Perth, Scotland. A favorite Irish legend holds that in the spring of 1307, while sitting in the cave brooding over his military loss, Bruce spied a spider, subsequently referred to by Winston Churchill as "the most celebrated in history." While Bruce watched, the spider repeatedly tried to ascend to the cave's roof by a gossamer strand. Seven times Bruce saw the spider attempt to hook its web from one rock to another before it finally succeeded. Inspired by the spider's persistence, Bruce returned to Scotland to fight again, and eventually gained the Scottish throne at the Battle of Bannockburn.

At Knockans are the ruins of an Irish sweathouse, a primitive version of the sauna, for which steam was produced by pouring water on heated stones. In the center of the island, Brockley is the site of a Stone Age ax factory, and, slightly north, Doonmore once was the site of an ancient hill fort. Near the harbor is an 18th-century manor house built by Viscount Gage.

CHECKING IN

Rathlin Guest House At the harbor a few minutes' walk from Tony McCuaig's pub is a small guesthouse with a reputation for hearty breakfasts. Operated by the McCurdy family, it has 4 rooms, none with private bath. Snacks, soup, and sandwiches are available; dinner is by arrangement. The Quay, Rathlin Island (phone: 265-763917). Inexpensive.

En Route from Rathlin Island The coastal road (B15), west of Ballycastle and leading to the Giant's Causeway, provides about a dozen miles of some of the Antrim's most charming sites. Kinbane Castle, one of the least known but most picturesque ruin sites, is poised on a white chalk pinnacle surrounded by the sea. The ruins here are what remain of a 16th-century castle built by Colla MacDonnell. His brother Sorley Boy, the first Earl of Antrim, was an active foe of Queen Elizabeth I. From the parking lot, there is a steep path. Ascend with care — though there's a handrail, the path can be slippery. At the end of the climb is a fine view across to Rathlin Island.

At the turnoff for Carrick-a-Rede ("rock in the road") Island, proceed to the parking lot and then follow the National Trust footpath to the coast. There, a swaying 63-foot wooden plank bridge with a wire handrail provides the only means for salmon fishermen and tourists to cross over the narrow 80-foot-deep chasm between the mainland and Carrick-a-Rede Island. Once on the island, salmon fishermen lower and hoist their boats from the rocky peak with a derrick. The bridge, dismantled annually in mid-September and re-erected early each May, swings in the winds, even in summer, but the superb coastal scenery is worth the perils of crossing. The site, open at all times, is a 15-minute walk from the Larrybane parking lot (there's a parking fee). The bridge visitors' center (phone: 265-731159) is open during the *Easter* holiday period; on weekends in May, June, and early September; on bank holidays; and daily from 11 AM to 6 PM in July and August.

Slightly farther along the coast, follow a snaking S-curve road down to Ballintoy Harbor. The place is a photographer's dream, with the sea set between white piers, a white beach beneath a sheer black volcanic cliff, and an archipelago of small jagged islands. There is a picnic site in the area, and a café is open in season. A pretty white church at a bend in the road down to the harbor was used as a refuge by Protestants during the 1641 rebellion.

Just past Ballintoy Harbor is White Park Bay, a lovely mile-long crescent of white sand with a backdrop of dunes and cliffs. Leading from the beach are footpaths to Ballintoy Harbor and the Giant's Causeway. At the western end of White Park Bay is Portbraddon, a hamlet of a half-dozen houses tucked into a cleft in the cliffs. It's also home to Ireland's smallest church, measuring 12 feet by 6½ feet.

GIANT'S CAUSEWAY After visiting White Park Bay take B146 off A2 to the Giant's Causeway — now in the care of the National Trust, and included on UNESCO's official World Heritage list of sites. It was at the end of the 17th century that writings about the peculiar beauty of the Causeway — with its roughly 40,000 basaltic "stepping stones" (mostly six-sided) which fit together so exactly that the natural volcanic wonder looks like the work of human hands — first attracted attention. However, stories concerning Northern Ireland's most famous sight date back to ancient times. One tale has it that the giant, Finn MacCool, champion of Ireland, was much aggrieved at the insolent boasting of a certain Caledonian giant, who had claimed he could beat all who challenged him in Scotland. The Caledonian sent word to Finn that if it wasn't for getting himself wet in the sea, he would swim over to Ireland and give MacCool a thrashing. Finally, Finn constructed a stone causeway to Scotland, and when it was completed, the Scot giant walked over the water to Ireland to fight Finn. By this time, however, Finn had become somewhat frightened at the thought of confrontation with the Caledonian. In a hastily hatched plot, his wife helped him don baby clothes and when the Scot giant arrived for battle she pointed to Finn saying, "This is the baby; you should see his father." At that the Caledonian giant fled back to Scotland, destroying the Causeway behind him. Lending credence to this tale are similar rock formations found off the Scottish Isle of Staffa, at Fingal's Cave, named in honor of Finn.

The more prosaic explanation for the Causeway's existence is that it was formed by the quick-cooling lava that burst to the earth's surface in the early Cenozoic era about 70 million years ago. Altogether there are about 40,000 basalt columns packed together in shapes so regular that they seem constructed by craftspeople rather than by nature. Some sections of the lava were naturally molded into unique designs that have been given nicknames such as Lady's Fan, Lord Antrim's Parlour, the Giant's Horseshoe, the Grand Causeway, and the Giant's Coffin. Another, called the Giant's Organ, is an astonishing 60-yard series of pillars of incredible regularity. Providing a backdrop to the Causeway are large basalt pillars called the Chimney Tops; in 1588, the retreating ships of the Spanish Armada aimed an attack on these columns, thinking they were part of Dunluce Castle. Past these stacks is Port Na Spania Bay, where one of the Spanish galleons, the *Girona,* was shipwrecked. In recent years, the wreckage of the sunken ship was explored, and the items that were recovered are on display at *Ulster Museum* in Belfast (see *Belfast* in THE CITIES).

The *Giant's Causeway Interpretation Centre* houses entertaining and educational exhibits, from a size 25 shoe marked "Finn MacCool's boot (?)" — the question mark is there — to detailed geological explanations of the area. Also on view are exhibits about local flora and fauna, the fishing industry, and the interesting history of tourism at the Causeway. Mark Twain visited here in the 19th century during an era when local guides were spinning a blatant brand of blarney about the origins of the Causeway. An excellent 25-minute multimedia presentation on all aspects of the Giant's Causeway is shown in the center's 56-seat theater. There's an admission charge for the show. The center is open from 10 AM to 7 PM during July and August; it closes as early as 4 PM the rest of the year, depending on the season. The tearoom and National Trust shop are both open from *St. Patrick's Day* through October (phone: 265-731855). There's free access to the Causeway at all times. A minibus (with a wheelchair lift) regularly runs from the interpretation center to the Grand Causeway formation daily from March through October.

The adventurous can hire a boat and a boatman to wander through the nearby caves of the Causeway; one called the Runkerry is 700 feet long.

En Route from the Giant's Causeway Bushmills, a pleasant hamlet 2 miles southwest on A2, is the home of the well-known Old Bushmills Distillery Co. Ltd., the oldest licensed distillery in the world, established by Thomas Phillips in 1608 and still in operation. Visitors to the distillery have included Peter the Great of Russia, who declared (in 1697), "Of all beverages the Irish is the best." Today's visitors are welcome Mondays through Thursdays from 9 AM to noon and 1:30 to 3:30 PM; and Fridays from 9 to 11:45 AM; mini-tours are conducted during the last 2 weeks in July when the plant is not in operation. The distillery is closed to visitors *Christmas Eve* through *New Year's Day*, July 12 and 13, and on some bank holidays. The tour, which takes about an hour, covers each stage of the triple distillation whiskey-making and bottling process, ending at the visitors' center where tourists can sample the product and browse in the gift shop. Since the company is small, appointments are suggested during the summer and are essential on inclement summer days (phone: 265-731521).

CHECKING IN

Bushmills Inn A recently refurbished 200-year-old coaching inn, it has 11 rooms, all with private baths and country-style decor. The common rooms have pine wood, peat fires, and Ulster charm. The hotel's formal restaurant features French provincial fare and a carvery. There's also a less formal brasserie. Open daily for lunch and dinner. 25 Main St., Bushmills (phone: 265-732339; fax: 265-732048). Expensive.

Causeway Perched above the sea close to the Giant's Causeway, the 16 rooms (all with private baths) in this wonderfully situated, owner-managed hotel have all been upgraded in recent years. Afternoon tea and a set dinner are served daily. 40 Causeway Rd., Giant's Causeway (phone: 265-731226). Moderate.

Hillcrest House Located near the Giant's Causeway, with views of the sea from many rooms, this guesthouse has 3 rooms (all with private facilities) and is personally run by resident owners Mr. and Mrs. McKeever. The attached restaurant is popular locally. It serves afternoon tea and dinner daily. Closed January. 306 Whitepark Rd., Giant's Causeway (phone: 265-731577). Moderate.

White Gables Country House This modern guesthouse with a panoramic Antrim Coast view near Dunluce Castle has 3 bedrooms with private baths and a comfortable guest lounge with a TV set. Dinner is available for guests only; no liquor license. Open April through October. No credit cards accepted. 83 Dunluce Rd., Portballintrae (phone: 265-731611). Inexpensive.

EATING OUT

Sweeney's Wine Bar Diners can enjoy chargrilled steaks, ribs, or vegetarian dishes in sight of the sea. Open daily for lunch and dinner. Reservations unnecessary. No credit cards accepted. 66 Seaport Ave., Portballintrae (phone: 265-731279). Inexpensive.

DUNLUCE CASTLE Two miles west on A2 is Dunluce Castle, built by Richard de Burgh, Earl of Ulster, in about 1300. On a breathtaking site — a basalt rock jutting from the sea — the structure is reached by a wooden walkway (which replaced the former drawbridge) and has five towers linked by a curtain wall. Since its builders thought — with some justification — that the fortress was impregnable, the castle doesn't have a keep. A cave passage through the rock beneath the castle, however, served as a secret exit and entryway by the sea. Dunluce was held for centuries by the de Mandevilles (also called the MacQuillans). In 1584, the Irish MacDonnells captured Dunluce from its English occupants when one of their countrymen employed in the castle hauled men up the cliff in a basket by night. In about 1595, with proceeds from the sale of treasure salvaged from the Spanish Armada galleon *Girona,* which had been wrecked nearby in 1588, the MacDonnells reconstructed Dunluce Castle, adding a magnificent banqueting hall. One stormy night in 1639, as the kitchen staff was engrossed in preparations for a splendid repast in the hall, the entire kitchen tumbled without warning into the sea 100 feet below. Of the staff, only a tinker mending pans in a window embrasure is thought to have survived. From that night, the Countess of Antrim refused to live at Dunluce. Over the centuries Dunluce gradually fell into decay, and today is one of Ireland's most romantic ruins. It's open Mondays through Saturdays from 10 AM to 7 PM and on Sundays from 2 to 7 PM, April through September;

Tuesdays through Saturdays from 10 AM to 4 PM and Sundays from 2 to 4 PM, October through March. There are guided tours in July and August; admission charge (no phone).

Continue on A2 3 miles west to Portrush. This resort town has long sandy beaches and facilities for tennis, boating, and fishing. It is most famous, however, for the outstanding links courses at *Royal Portrush Golf Club* (phone: 265-822311; fax: 265-823139), the only Irish club to have hosted the *British Open* (in 1951). *Royal Portrush*'s two 18-hole courses and one 9-hole course are located on 480 acres of wildflower-covered dunes (see *Great Golf* in DIVERSIONS). Guests are welcome, but the course is closed to non-members on Wednesday and Friday afternoons.

At this point, the route veers inland from Portrush 5 miles to Coleraine via A29.

EATING OUT

Ramore A chic harborside restaurant offering sophisticated, award-winning food and service. Open Tuesdays through Saturdays for dinner only. An adjacent wine bar is open for lunch and dinner; closed Sundays. Reservations necessary. Major credit cards accepted in the restaurant only. The Harbour, Portrush (phone: 265-823444). Expensive.

COLERAINE A 17th-century Plantation town at the head of the River Bann estuary, Coleraine was established by the London Company on land granted by James I in 1613. But Coleraine's roots reach far deeper than the 17th century — nearby archaeological excavations have indicated that there were settlements here as early as 7000 BC. A mile south of Coleraine, on the east bank of the Bann, is Mountsandel, the ruin of a fort once held by an early King of Ulster and later by the de Courcys. This is also where the Mesolithic artifacts thought to be the earliest traces of civilization in Ireland were discovered. In more recent times Coleraine has become a bustling industrial center engaged in whiskey distilling and in linen trade; it is a good regional shopping center. Its newest structures are the modern concrete and brick buildings of the University of Ulster, a few miles north off Portrush Road.

From Coleraine, take the coast road, A2, 7 miles to Downhill.

CHECKING IN/EATING OUT

Blackheath House About 7 miles south of Coleraine, this charming country guesthouse has 5 Georgian period bedrooms, all with private baths. The restaurant, *MacDuff's,* serves continental dinners featuring elegantly prepared local country produce, fresh salmon, and game in season. The restaurant is open for dinner Tuesdays through Saturdays. Reservations necessary. MasterCard and Visa accepted. 112 Killeague Rd., Blackhill (phone: 265-868433). Moderate.

DOWNHILL Most historians consider Downhill the private domain of the colorful Bishop Frederick Augustus Hervey, fourth Earl of Bristol, who in 1779 began his reign in Derry, the second wealthiest of Ireland's church districts. A man of extremes, he lived extravagantly, collected art avidly, and traveled extensively. He always took a large group of attendants on his journeys, and hotel owners were so eager for his business that they sometimes named their establishments in his honor, hence the many Bristol Hotels throughout Europe. Hervey's ostentatious lifestyle included running horse races for the pleasure of his clergymen at Magilligan Strand, the 6-mile-long beach (Ireland's longest) below the castle. Hervey, however, was not all frivolity. His more serious accomplishments include putting into practice the Catholic Relief Act of 1791, leading a private army on horseback to the Volunteer Convention in Dublin, and supporting demands and rallies for an Irish Parliament.

No fewer than four different architects were employed in designing the bishop's splendid estate. The castle's interior was destroyed by fire in 1851 and refurbished in 1876, but the restoration bore little resemblance to the original. The parts of the estate still standing are the Bishop's Gate, an arched portal with Doric columns; the Lion Gate, a sandstone structure carved with the two animals that are on the Bristol coat of arms; and the Mussenden Temple, a circular structure with Corinthian columns built in 1783 by Michael Shanahan and modeled after the Italian temples of Vesta. Established as a memorial to Hervey's cousin — some say mistress — the temple also served as the bishop's library. To reach the windswept temple, perched on a cliff above the sea, visitors can walk up a garden path at the Bishop's Gate, over a stile, across fields where sheep graze, and past the ruins of the former bishop's castle. Allow at least 45 minutes for the walk there and back, and wear sturdy shoes. Maintained by the National Trust, the temple is open from noon to 6 PM daily in July and August, and on weekends and holidays only in April through June and in September (phone: 265-848728).

At Magilligan Point (the west end of the 6-mile Magilligan Strand) stands a Martello tower, one of the many early 19th-century fortresses built in response to Napoleonic invasions. From Magilligan Point it's 1 mile across the mouth of Lough Foyle to County Donegal in the Irish Republic.

En Route from Downhill Take the steep-climbing Bishop's Road (yet another creation of Frederick Hervey) to Limavady. Along the scenic 9-mile road, stop at Gortmore, a picnic site and lookout point offering a wonderful, far-reaching view of the mountains of Donegal, the Foyle estuary, and the Magilligan Plain, a flat triangle of sand dunes and farmlands. Farther along Bishop's Road the scenery varies from treeless, high moorland to deep forests. The road ends at B201; turn right to Limavady.

LIMAVADY This old Georgian town set in the valley of the River Roe is perhaps best known as the place where in 1851 Jane Ross heard and transcribed the traditional Irish tune "Londonderry Air" (widely recognized as the melody to which the lyrics of "Danny Boy" are sung) as it was played by a wandering fiddler named MacCormick. (The original composer is believed to have been Rory O'Caghan, a blind 16th-century harpist.)

En Route from Limavady Two and a half miles west of Limavady, on A2 to Londonderry, the route passes through Ballykelly Forest. Sometimes called Walworth Wood, it was planted in the 17th century to honor Sir William Walworth, head of the London Fishmongers' Company in the late 14th century. Walworth House, on the grounds, is now in ruins except for a few of its towers.

Continue along A2 for 10 miles to Londonderry.

LONDONDERRY For a complete report on the city, its history, sights, restaurants, and hotels, see *Londonderry* in THE CITIES.

County Down and the Mountains of Mourne

With its distinctive mixture of mountains, sea, and green-growing fields, County Down, in the southeast corner of Northern Ireland, long has been the subject of stories and songs. The Down town of Newcastle, for example, is rhapsodized in the popular melody "Where the Mountains of Mourne Sweep Down to the Sea," while Irish courting customs are evoked in the ballad "Star of the County Down." More serious reflections on the landscape can be found in the novels and theological essays of C. S. Lewis, a native of north Down; the skyscape has been immortalized in the writings of such well-traveled authors as H. V. Morton, who described it as "the most dramatic in Europe."

The 19th-century novels of the three Brontë sisters — Charlotte, Emily, and Anne — whose father, Patrick, was a native son, are perhaps the best-known literary works inspired by County Down. Episodes, characters, and landscapes in *Wuthering Heights, Jane Eyre,* and all the Brontë books owe something to stories of his youth in County Down. The Brontë Homeland Route, included in this driving tour, gives travelers a sense of the powerful impact the ancestral soil and soul had on these writers' works.

With the inclusion of the city of Armagh, our driving tour also encompasses aspects of Ireland that led it to become known as the "land of saints and scholars." St. Patrick's roots are deeper in Ulster than anywhere else on the island, and nowhere as deep as in Armagh and Downpatrick. This area was inhabited, however, well before Patrick's 5th-century Christian missionary work. The earliest settlements in County Down date from the Mesolithic period (about 7000 BC). Later, in the Neolithic period (4000–2000 BC), inhabitants practiced rudimentary farming; then, around 700 BC, the Celts arrived from central Europe with their iron weapons. In existence nearly until the time of St. Patrick, their settlements were *raths,* or ring forts, circular earthen fortifications, usually on hilltops, where individuals or entire communities could live in relative safety. The principal northern stronghold for the Celts, a society of warriors ruled by high kings, was Emain Macha, today's Navan Fort, just outside Armagh.

Monks in the early centuries of the Christian era were the chroniclers of Down history, especially of the warfare among Irish chieftains. The remains of the monasteries and fortified homesteads of the period survive in great numbers (some 1,300 are said to exist in County Down alone). From the 9th to the 11th centuries, Viking raids on the exposed Down coast were numerous and merciless. During the 12th century, the Anglo-

Normans invaded and conquered the area. The Norman era was followed by Elizabethan attempts to rule through the policy of Plantation, so the 17th century saw the settlement of Northern Ireland, including Down, by tens of thousands of English and Scottish immigrants. The Scots, more numerous and mostly Presbyterian, were fine farmers. Granted the best agricultural land, they set about building houses, towns, and roads. Their efforts gave Northern Ireland much of the character it retains today. During the 19th century, the Industrial Revolution began to take hold in north Down, although the country remained significantly agricultural. Shipbuilding and linen manufacturing created far more prosperity for the north than for the south of Ireland.

Dominating County Down are the almost impenetrable Mourne Mountains: No road reaches their center — often called the Wilderness — so they naturally beckon the walker. Within an area of 25 miles, 15 summits rise above 2,000 feet. Slieve Donard (a mountain named for one of St. Patrick's disciples, a hermit who spent his life on its slopes), near Newcastle, has the highest peak, at nearly 2,800 feet. Roads ringing these Inner Mournes provide the motorist with a constantly changing panorama. C. S. Lewis wrote of the Mourne vista: "Imagine the mountains. . . . Sometimes they are blue, sometimes violet; but quite often they look transparent — as if huge sheets of gauze had been cut into mountainous shapes and hung up there."

The Mournes are "young" mountains, but much worn down by glaciers. Five varieties of granite — from gray to pink — were created during volcanic action about 75 million years ago. Over the centuries, Mourne granite provided the ballast for many ships. As the stonecutting industry developed, Mourne blocks were used to pave many an English city street. Light-gray granite boulders strewn throughout the rich Down soil have always made plowing difficult. For generations, the boulders have been dug up by farmers and built into miles of dry-stone walls that mark the boundaries of some 15,000 small fields in the Mourne region. Smaller stones left in the fields provide the good natural drainage necessary for potatoes — an important product here.

Agriculture still is the main industry in southeast Northern Ireland, but there is considerable forestry and sea fishing as well. Because of the lack of good land routes through the Mournes, the sea often compensates as the major means of commercial transportation. While timber and "taties" (potatoes) are shipped out from the seaside towns and villages of County Down and the Ards Peninsula, fish are hauled in to local harbors. Since the growing season in altitudes above 700 feet is too short to be economical, much of the higher Mourne land is given over to sheep grazing. In addition to the grass and scrub growth on which the sheep feed, mountain vegetation includes bristly brilliant yellow gorse (whin), several hues of heather, bog cotton, purple moon grass, fuchsia, and reddish bracken.

Our driving route begins and ends in Belfast, starting in a southwesterly counterclockwise direction — with a detour to Armagh — then heading down to the Irish Sea and along the coast, looping around the main mass of the Mournes (except for scenic inland incursions), then heading northeast to St. Patrick country around Downpatrick. It returns by way of the Ards Peninsula, sampling the best of both its coastlines. The approximate distance from west to east (Armagh to Portaferry) is 55 miles; north to south (Belfast to Rostrevor), 45 miles. While the distances are short, this beautiful region is best explored at a leisurely pace; plan to devote 3 or more days to this tour.

An expensive hotel in the area will charge $125 or more for a double room with private bath and breakfast. Accommodations in a moderate hostelry will cost $75 to $125, and inexpensive places will charge less than $75 a night. Staying at a guest- or farmhouse can be considerably less expensive. A three-course meal for two, including service charge and VAT (but not beverages), will cost $50 or more in an expensive restaurant, $35 to $50 in a moderate one, and less than $35 at a place listed as inexpensive. For each location, hotels and restaurants are listed alphabetically by price category.

BELFAST For a complete report on the city, its sights, hotels, and restaurants, see *Belfast,* THE CITIES.

En Route from Belfast Take M1 southwest from Belfast. After the Lisburn bypass, pick up A1 south for Hillsborough. Follow the signs off A1 into Hillsborough. The total distance from Belfast is 12 miles.

HILLSBOROUGH This architecturally elegant town is a fashionable suburb of Belfast and the capital of Northern Ireland's antiques trade. It was little more than forest and moorland when Moyses Hill, a native of Devon, England, arrived in Ireland in 1573. He served as an officer in the army of the Earl of Essex, sent by Elizabeth I to subdue the rebellious O'Neills. When the wars were over, Hill remained, holding important offices under the Crown, yet identifying himself with the Irish by marrying Alice, sister of Sorley Boy MacDonnell, the first Earl of Antrim and foe of Elizabeth I. Over generations, the Hill family became among the wealthiest landowners in Ireland. This town was named after them when Charles II chartered it as a borough in 1662.

The Hillsborough Parish Church (Church of Ireland, Episcopal), a beautifully situated town landmark, was enlarged from an earlier edifice at enormous expense to Wills Hill, Earl of Hillsborough and first Marquis of Downshire, who completed the improvements in 1773. The church remains one of the finest examples of Gothic Revival architecture in Ireland. From the church's sturdy tower, which houses a peal of 10 bells, rises a graceful 120-foot spire. The 1772 organ by John Snetzler, the most famous organ builder of the 18th century, and the 1795 small organ by George Pike England frequently are used for concerts. The State Chair is used by

Northern Ireland's secretary of state, who resides in Hillsborough Castle, or by members of the royal family. By the entrance gates, facing each other across the gracious tree-lined mall that leads to the church, are the sexton's house and the parish room, which were the girls' and boys' schools, respectively, when built in 1773.

On rising ground next to the church is Hillsborough Fort, built in 1630. It has been much altered since then, but the well-preserved stone structure retains many of its original architectural details. After the Restoration, Charles II made it a royal fort and named Arthur Hill the hereditary constable. The title carried with it the responsibility, as well as the expense, of maintaining a private garrison of 20 armed men. Called the Castlemen, the garrison was employed well into the 20th century. King Billy (England's William III) spent 4 nights in Hillsborough Fort in 1690 on his way to victory at the Battle of the Boyne. The fort is open Tuesdays through Saturdays from 10 AM to 7 PM, and Sundays from 2 to 7 PM, in April through September; it closes at 4 PM October through March. The park is open daily from dawn to dusk. There's no admission charge. A lake behind the fort has a footpath around it.

At the top of steep Main Street, handsomely lined with Georgian buildings, is Hillsborough Castle on the Square, completed in 1797. Formerly known as Government House, the castle was the official residence of the governor of Northern Ireland from 1925 until the termination of the office in 1973. Today, in addition to housing the official representative of the queen, it accommodates visiting members of the royal family and foreign diplomats. The ornamental ironwork entrance gates, built by the brothers Thornberry in 1745, are the finest example of their kind surviving in Northern Ireland. The Georgian Market House on the square is preserved as a historic monument.

CHECKING IN

White Gables This medium-size full-service hotel, the only one in Hillsborough, is on the outskirts of town. It has 31 double rooms with private baths, landscaped gardens, good facilities for children, and opportunities for fishing. There's also a fine restaurant (see *Eating Out*). 14 Dromore Rd., Hillsborough (phone: 846-682755; fax: 846-689532). Expensive.

EATING OUT

Hillside Bar The bar menu includes a salad bar and homemade pâté and soups, while the à la carte dinner menu features spareribs, salmon mayonnaise, and beef *chasseur*. The bar serves lunch and dinner; the award-winning restaurant serves dinner only; both are closed Sundays. Reservations advised. Major credit cards accepted. 21 Main St., Hillsborough (phone: 846-682765). Moderate.

White Gables A well-appointed restaurant in the hotel of the same name, it features fine French fare prepared with fresh, locally grown vegetables and game in season. All desserts and pastries are baked on the premises. Open daily for lunch and dinner. Reservations necessary on weekends. Major credit cards accepted. 23 Dromore Rd., Hillsborough (phone: 846-682755). Moderate to inexpensive.

Marquis of Downshire Dine on grilled meat, scampi, and salads in a comfortable pub atmosphere. Open for lunch and dinner; pub grub is served from 11:30 AM to 11 PM; closed Sundays. Reservations advised on weekends. Major credit cards accepted. 48 Lisburn St., Hillsborough (phone: 846-682095). Inexpensive.

Plough Inn For those who seek local character, this is the place for drinks and tasty pub grub such as homemade soups, pies, seafood dishes, and sweets. Open daily for lunch; dinner served Wednesdays through Sundays. Reservations advised. Diners Club, MasterCard, and Visa accepted. On the Square, opposite Hillsborough Castle (phone: 846-682985). Inexpensive.

En Route from Hillsborough Return to A1 and continue 6 miles southwest to Banbridge.

BANBRIDGE A pleasant market and industrial town on the upper River Bann, Banbridge has a main thoroughfare (Bridge and Newry St.) that's split into three sections, with dignified shop-lined terraces on each side. An underpass through the center of the steep street, the Banbridge "cut," was made in 1834 out of consideration for the horses that pulled carriages up the steep hill of the town, then an important stop on the Belfast–Dublin stagecoach route. In the center of the road, near where a bridge crosses the Bann, is the Crozier Monument, featuring four polar bears in stone. It stands in remembrance of Captain Francis Crozier, born in a house opposite, who went with Admiral Peary to the Arctic and died on the tragic expedition to Greenland.

En Route from Banbridge Take A50 northwest from Banbridge to Gilford; from there, pick up A51 to Armagh, a total of less than 20 miles.

ARMAGH With a population of about 15,000, Armagh is the ecclesiastical capital of Ireland. It has two cathedrals — one Church of Ireland (Anglican), the other Roman Catholic — both named for St. Patrick, who founded his principal church here in AD 445.

Armagh's story starts long before St. Patrick, however. It lays claim to being Ireland's oldest recorded settlement. Ptolemy, the 2nd-century geographer who produced a map of the then-known world, included a specific place in Ireland identified as Isamnion, which most scholars consider a form of Emain (meaning "palace") Macha (a warrior queen in Ulster who lived about 300 BC). Two miles west of present-day Armagh, the 18-acre drumlin (glacial hill) surrounded by farmland was the principal settlement in Ireland during the time of Christ. Excavation at Emain Macha, now more popularly known as Navan Fort, has revealed traces of occupation from the late Stone Age (about 2000 BC). The most important ruins found on the site are those of a circular, thatch-roofed building, nearly 45 yards in diameter, with a center oak post. Using highly accurate tree-ring dating, archaeologists from Queen's University, Belfast, have determined that the structure dates back to a settlement by the Celts in the late Bronze Age (about 700 BC). It is believed that this building served as a ceremonial, spiritual, and political center of Ulster.

Navan Centre (Killylea Rd.; phone: 861-525550), which opened on the site in mid-1993, depicts and interprets the rich Celtic history, archaeological finds, and mythology associated with Emain Macha/Navan Fort. Nestled into the side of a green slope at Navan, the building incorporates Celtic design elements. It's open Mondays through Saturdays from 10 AM to 7 PM, and Sundays from 11 AM to 7 PM, in April through September; Mondays through Saturdays from 10 AM to 5 PM, and Sundays from 11 AM to 5 PM, in October through March. *Navan Centre* also details Emain Macha's history as one of the central settings of the Ulster Cycle, the ancient record of the legendary deeds of Cu Chulainn and the Red Branch Knights. The cycle has been compared by many scholars to Homer's epics. One of the stories describes how the Connaught champion hurled a ball (the calcified brain of the King of Leinster) at Conchobor mac Nessa, King of Emain Macha. Conchobor was seriously wounded, with the ball lodged deep inside his head. The king's physicians stitched up the wound, leaving the ball inside, and advised the king to rest. However, upon hearing of the death of Christ, Conchobor became so enraged that the ball burst out of his head, and he died in AD 33. Since the king died in reaction to Christ's death, he was regarded as the first Irish martyr and the first pagan in Ireland to reach heaven.

The death of Conchobor marked the passing of the old pagan order in Ulster legend. Many historians believe that Emain Macha fell in AD 332, when the last of the traditional Ulster kings, Fergus Fogha, was killed in battle with the three *collas* (warriors) from the south, who afterward burned Emain Macha. But some believe that Emain did not fall until about 450. This theory would support another popular belief, that St. Patrick, drawn to this political center of Ulster, came here to preach Christianity and establish his principal church. The past glory and political importance of pagan Emain Macha provided symbolism and authority acceptable to early Irish Christians and, along with its early association with the Christian movement, fostered the rise of Armagh as the Christian capital of Ireland, which it remains today.

Although at first denied the hilltop site he wanted for his principal church in Armagh, Patrick eventually acquired the land from the chieftain Duire. Once his headquarters in Armagh was established, Patrick founded over 700 other Christian communities throughout Ireland. Patrick's era earned Ireland a reputation as the "land of saints and scholars." Around

Patrick's church in Armagh there grew a school of monastic learning that became famous throughout Europe during the Dark Ages, until the Danes destroyed it during the 9th and 10th centuries. Some 1,200 scholars were based in Armagh in 807, when *The Book of Armagh* — the first section of which is the *Life of Patrick* — was hand-lettered and illuminated here. The ornamented portions are contemporary with, and equal in importance to, the famous *Book of Kells*. Both books are in the library of Trinity College in Dublin.

On the hill where Patrick's stone church once stood is now the Church of Ireland cathedral, with its squat, square Norman tower. The exterior is essentially 12th century, although it has been rebuilt at least 17 times — most recently in 1912 — and it shows a strong Victorian influence inside and out. The sexton on the premises assists visitors on weekdays; ring the bell at 3 Vicar Hill for access on weekends. A marker in the west wall of the lovely cathedral close indicates the grave of Brian Ború, first king of all Ireland, who drove out the Norse invaders in 1014. Treasures in the cathedral library (open afternoons, Mondays through Saturdays) include a copy of *Gulliver's Travels* annotated by its Irish author, Jonathan Swift. Streets surrounding the cathedral follow the rings of the Celtic *rath* (ring fort), which originally stood on the site that Patrick selected for his church.

On a hilltop across town is the twin-spired Catholic cathedral, begun in 1840. The interior is almost Byzantine in its use of mosaics, carvings, and colors. On the pale blue ceiling and walls are represented every Irish saint and a multitude of angels.

Armagh has many graceful Georgian Regency buildings, a legacy of native son Francis Johnston, the distinguished 18th-century architect who also left his mark on Georgian Dublin. Encouraged by Archbishop Robinson and other wealthy patrons, Johnston and his contemporaries created The Mall (a rectangular town green on which cricket is played on weekends), as well as the architecturally noteworthy courthouse, market house, observatory, Royal School, Bank of Ireland building, and Charlemont Place. The buildings were built in the warm-colored local yellow limestone that makes the city glow even on the dullest day. The doorsteps and pavement around The Mall glow pink, from polished red limestone called Armagh marble. Most streets retain a historical character, especially in the area of the Shambles, which features antiques shops and a Friday livestock market.

Armagh County Museum (The Mall; phone: 861-523070) is one of the finest small museums in the country. Exhibits include prehistoric implements and artifacts, Irish lace and linen, carved Black Bog oak jewelry, displays and documents on Viking raids and natural history, and paintings by George Russell. It's open daily, except Sundays and holidays, from 10 AM to 1 PM and 2 to 5 PM. There's no admission charge. The Sovereign's House, also on The Mall, contains the *Royal Irish Fusiliers Regimental Museum* (phone: 861-522911). Museum hours are usually 10 AM to 1 PM and 2 to 4 PM, but it's best to call ahead; no admission charge. The *Astronomy Centre* (on College Hill; phone: 861-523689) includes a public observatory, a planetarium, and a hall of astronomy. It's open daily, except Sundays, from 2 to 4:45 PM; no admission charge. There are planetarium shows daily, except Sundays and holidays, in July and August, and on Saturdays the rest of the year; advanced booking is advised. There is an admission charge.

Because of its surrounding fertile farmland, Armagh is often called "the garden of Ireland." In May and June, signposts guide motorists on scenic routes through beautifully blooming orchards. Outside the city, a traveler may be lucky enough to come across a game of "road bowls" or "bullets." Played only in the Irish counties of Armagh and Cork, the game involves throwing an iron ball along a winding road, the object being to cover a set course of several miles in the fewest shots. Competitions are held in July and August.

CHECKING IN

Charlemont Arms The only hotel in the center of Armagh, it's situated between the two hilltop cathedrals and convenient to most of the other major sites. There are 14 rooms, 9 with private baths, and a restaurant. 63 English St., Armagh (phone: 861-522028). Inexpensive.

EATING OUT

Archway Homemade soup, sandwiches, and pastries are served in a cozy tearoom atmosphere. Morning coffee, lunch, and tea are available from 10 AM to 5 PM; closed Sundays, Mondays, and the month of July. Reservations unnecessary. No credit cards accepted. On The Mall, 5 Hartford Pl., near the *Armagh County Museum,* Armagh (phone: 861-522532). Inexpensive.

En Route from Armagh Backtrack east on A51 to Tandragee. Turn south on A27 and, after a couple of miles, east into Scarva, a hamlet on the now unused Newry Canal. Scarva is noted for its annual "sham fight," a colorful pageant held each July 13 in which the Battle of the Boyne (1690) is re-enacted in full dress, with pipe, brass, and silver bands from many of Northern Ireland's Orange Lodges performing. Follow B10 from Scarva to Banbridge and watch for signposts for the Brontë Homeland Route.

BRONTE HOMELAND ROUTE This signposted driving route extends over 8 square miles between Banbridge and Rathfriland to the southeast. Numerous relatives of novelists Charlotte, Emily, and Anne Brontë lived in this area. The scenic, serene, and remote river valley sprawls over gently rolling hills, with the Mountains of Mourne rising romantically in the distance.

The future father of the famous sisters was born on *St. Patrick's Day,* 1777, in Emdale. The house was a thatch-roofed, 2-room stone cottage, the foundations and walls of which are preserved and marked by a plaque.

Patrick Brunty (the original patronym) was the eldest of 10 children. Although apprenticed to a blacksmith and then a linen weaver, Patrick was also encouraged to educate himself, and local clergymen instructed him and lent him books. By the time he was 16, Patrick was teaching in the Presbyterian school at Glascar, and had started writing the *Cottage Poems* (published in 1811). Patrick later taught at the parish school of Drumballyroney, and also served as tutor to the children of the rector of Drumballyroney parish church. Today, visitors are welcome at the hilltop parish church and school. Six of Patrick's brothers and sisters are buried in the church's lovely little cemetery. In 1802, Patrick entered St. John's College, Cambridge University. Whether by confusion in university records or by choice — perhaps influenced by the fact that the King of Naples had made Admiral Nelson the Duke of Brontë in 1800 — from this period onward Patrick was known by this grander version of his family name. Patrick took his degree in 1806, and in 1812 he married Maria Branwell. The couple had six children, the last, Anne, was born in 1820, the year Patrick was appointed to the incumbency at Haworth, Yorkshire. Sadly, his wife died the following year, but from that time on, Haworth remained the Brontë family home.

Although Patrick returned to Ulster only once, he filled his daughters with tales of his youth in County Down. Episodes in all the Brontë novels owe something to the father's memories of the hills near Rathfriland. The character of Heathcliff in Emily's *Wuthering Heights* is said to be her wild great-uncle Welsh, who, like Heathcliff, was an adopted child. Patrick's brothers and sisters were said to recognize many of their father's old stories of Ulster in *Jane Eyre.* Patrick outlived all his children and died at the age of 84.

The 8 miles of small rural lanes that compose the Brontë Homeland Route may sometimes seem to lead in circles, but there could hardly be a prettier, more welcoming countryside in which to get slightly lost. If exploration doesn't uncover the main sites — the Brontë cottages at Emdale and Drumballyroney (1 mile south of Ballyroney, which is on B7, 3 miles northeast of Rathfriland) — ask directions from any of the friendly farmers along the roadside. The cottages are open daily, March through November; no admission charge. For further information on the sites, visit the tourist center (phone: 820-662991), 9 miles southeast of Bainbridge, off A1 and A50. It's open daily from 10 AM to 6 PM in March through September.

Return to B7 and follow it southwest into Rathfriland.

RATHFRILAND This hilltop Plantation-era market town has marvelous views of the Mourne mountain range and an appealing country Irish atmosphere. Steep streets lead to a pleasing square with an old market house in the middle. People from the surrounding countryside crowd the square on Wednesdays for the general market and on Tuesdays for livestock sales. *Graham's,* near the square, is a favorite local stop for homemade ice cream.

En Route from Rathfriland For the 24½-mile journey to Rostrevor, take B25 south from Rathfriland to Hilltown, named for the Hill family of Hillsborough renown, who founded it in 1766. A pretty parish church built in 1776 and a Georgian market house sit on the tree-lined main square. For its small size (population about 600), Hilltown is particularly well endowed with pubs, a legacy from the 18th century, when it was the main distribution point for spirits being smuggled via the "Brandy Pad" path from Kilkeel on the coast inland over the Mourne Mountains.

From Hilltown, scenic roads reach out in all directions. Follow B8 in the direction of Newcastle (to the left); then take B27 (toward Kilkeel) for 4 miles to Spelga Dam in the midst of the Mournes and Rostrevor.

ROSTREVOR Nestled in the lee of the mountains facing Carlingford Lough, a tidal inlet, this is the most sheltered spot in Northern Ireland, with palms and mimosas thriving in the open. The village square of this pretty resort features ancient trees. A turn onto Bridge Street reveals a lovely stone bridge over the little River Kilbroney. Flowing down the Fairy Glen Valley, the river is bordered by sylvan paths past small waterfalls. A signpost in the village identifies Forest Drive, which climbs up to a parking lot with an information office. From there, proceed on foot for about a half-mile to gain a panoramic view of Lough Carlingford and the mountains. A more strenuous extension of the path continues to Cloghmore (meaning "big stone"), a peculiar boulder moved by a glacier which, according to myth, is supposed to have been thrown at an enemy by Finn MacCool, the legendary Irish giant. Across Lough Carlingford are the Carlingford Mountains, locally called the Cooley Mountains, because Finn MacCool is supposed to be buried there. At the western edge of Rostrevor, near a tiny quay, is a granite obelisk in memory of Major General Robert Ross, a British soldier who, during the War of 1812, captured Washington, DC, and burned the White House.

If there's time for a side trip, upon reaching the main coastal road, A2, turn right and head northeast on a short drive to the *Narrow Water Castle Gallery* (Warrenpoint; phone: 693-753940), housed in the vaulted ceiling cellars of the handsome 1840 Tudor Revival–style home of the Hall family, residents of the town since the 17th century. The gallery, open Tuesdays through Saturdays from 2 to 6 PM, has changing exhibits of works by Irish and international artists. The castle is signposted to the right off A2, opposite the picturesque waterside ruins of Old Narrow Water Castle, which date from 1560. Return to Rostrevor via A2.

EATING OUT

Cloughmor Inn An enjoyable, casual eatery, featuring hamburgers and meat or savory pies. Open for lunch only; closed Sundays. Reservations unnecessary. No credit cards accepted. 2 Bridge St., Rostrevor (phone: 693-738007). Inexpensive.

En Route from Rostrevor Take A2 southeast from Rostrevor in the direction of Kilkeel, which is 6 miles away. At the River Cassy Water, a signpost proclaims "Welcome to the Kingdom of Mourne." This area extends to St. Patrick's Stream, south of Newcastle, and inland to the tops of the mountains. Tradition holds that in Celtic times the region was ruled by a cowherd king, Boirche, from the summit of Slieve Binnian, which overlooks the whole area.

Just past the walled wooded estate of Mourne Park, seat of the Earls of Kilmorey, turn left onto Ballymageogh Road for an exceptionally lovely ride. The road leads upward to a lookout point with a splendid semicircular view of brilliantly green fields that rise to become heathered moorlands that, still higher, become the barren peaks of the Mournes. Follow the road downhill, turn right, and drive through the hamlet of Attical, the last place in the Mournes where the Irish language was spoken. A short distance beyond the hamlet, turn right onto B27, which heads into Kilkeel, 4 miles away.

KILKEEL Kilkeel is the main fishing port on the south Down coast, sometimes called "the capital of the kingdom of Mourne." A bustling, cheerful commercial center of some 3,000 inhabitants, the town has a harbor constructed in 1866. Quayside auctions are interesting to watch.

CHECKING IN

Wyncrest Guest House A quality hostelry on a small working farm with 5 guestrooms, 2 with private baths. Irene Adair, the proprietor, offers a four-course dinner (for guests only) that features fresh local produce. No liquor license. No credit cards accepted. On A2, 3 miles northeast of Kilkeel. 30 Main Rd., Ballymartin (phone: 693-763012). Inexpensive.

EATING OUT

Fisherman This longtime coastal favorite recently relocated to a terraced house. Specialties include pâté, stuffed mushrooms, and fresh local seafood. Open for dinner daily in July and August, Thursdays through Sundays the rest of the year. Reservations advised. MasterCard and Visa accepted. 68 Greencastle St., Kilkeel (phone: 693-762130). Moderate.

En route from Kilkeel Retrace the route inland on B27 to a right turn marked Silent Valley (Head Rd.). Silent Valley serves as a reservoir for the Belfast area, supplying 30 million imperial gallons of water a day. Built between 1923 and 1932, it is half a mile wide and 2½ miles long and can hold 3 billion gallons. Silent Valley, which comprises beautiful parkland as well as the reservoir, is the only place from which the inner Mournes can be reached by car. The catchment area is encircled by the Mourne Wall, a massive dry-stone wall 6 feet high and 22 miles long that ascends and descends the 15 peaks of the inner Mournes.

Head Road itself runs through the foothills of the Mournes, parallel to the sea, which is visible in the distance below. The green fields of the small tidy farms on either side of the road host a maze of gray granite dry-stone walls, termed "ditches" locally. Follow Head Road to the end and turn right. At the main road, turn right again into Annalong.

ANNALONG Just 4 miles northeast of Kilkeel on A2, Annalong is a small, picturesque harborside village. It's best to park at the Annalong Cornmill and Marine Park, where there are public toilets, a café and gift shop, an exhibit on the village's mills, and an herb garden. Guided tours of a fully restored, water-powered corn mill from the early 1800s are available from 2 to 6 PM daily in June through September (phone: 396-768736). Use the free, self-guiding *Annalong Marine Park Trail* brochure for a more complete exploration by foot, and be sure to take the short path over the River Annalong, which powers the mill, to Annalong Harbor.

During the early 1900s, Annalong was one of the area's chief ports, exporting Mourne granite and Down potatoes. Only a small fleet of skiffs, used to catch herring and mackerel, now remains. Near the Annalong corn mill are several granite mills where Mourne granite is still cut and polished.

CHECKING IN

Glassdrumman Lodge This converted farmhouse offers unrivaled views of the Mourne Mountains and the Irish Sea. Situated on a 30-acre working farm, it has 8 tastefully decorated rooms, each with bath. Guests can collect their own eggs for a hearty farm breakfast. 85 Mill Rd., Annalong (phone: 396-768451; fax: 396-767041). Expensive.

EATING OUT

Glassdrumman House A complex of new and restored buildings that includes the *Kitchen Garden,* a reasonably priced eatery that serves everything from morning coffee or afternoon tea to three-course meals, and an elegant French restaurant, *Memories,* which serves dinner nightly. The complex is open from noon to 9:30 PM; closed Sundays. Reservations advised for dinner. MasterCard and Visa accepted. In addition, several shops here provide the makings of a perfect picnic — bread and pastries from the bakery; meat, salads, cheeses, and homemade pickles and preserves from the deli. Signposted on A2, 224 Glassdrumman Rd., Annalong (phone: 396-768585). Expensive to moderate.

Harbour Inn In a sturdy stone building at the quaint harbor, this spot serves fresh fish, steaks, shepherd's pie, and good desserts. Open for lunch Mondays through Thursdays; dinner on Fridays and Saturdays. No reservations. Major credit cards accepted. 6 Harbour Dr., Annalong (phone: 396-768678). Inexpensive.

En Route from Annalong Head north 4 miles on A2, with the Irish Sea on the right and the Mourne Mountains on the left.

NEWCASTLE An attractively situated seaside resort, Newcastle stretches in a broad crescent along a 5-mile sandy shore on the Irish Sea. The beauty of the town's setting inspired Irish songwriter Percy French to compose the well-known "Where the Mountains of Mourne Sweep Down to the Sea." A fountain in the seafront promenade gardens commemorates the composer. The Mournes' highest summit, barren-peaked Slieve Donard (2,796 feet), less than 2 miles away, dominates Newcastle with its mysterious and distinctive shape.

Nature has endowed Newcastle with beautiful scenery and fine forests, and there are plenty of opportunities for walking, pony trekking, and rock climbing. The *Mourne Countryside Centre* (phone: 396-724059), on the Central Promenade at Newcastle, informs visitors about anything to do with Mourne country, from geology to flora and fauna to the best routes into — and out of — the mountains by foot or car. It's open daily from 9 AM to 5 PM in September through June; 9 AM to 8 PM in July and August. Tollymore Forest Park (phone: 396-722428) has a number of hiking trails, as well as a café and an exhibition center in the Clanbressel barn (ca. 1730). Nearby, the Barbican Gate — a Gothic architectural folly — leads to a long avenue of Himalayan cedars. The park is open daily from 10 AM to dusk.

Tropicana (phone: 396-722222), a recreational facility on Newcastle's Central Promenade, has a heated outdoor seawater pool and a sheltered sunbathing patio. Other recreational features of the town include a putting green, a bowling green, tennis courts, and a boating lake. Rolling nearly into the center of Newcastle is the magnificent *Royal County Down Golf Club,* which noted golf professional Gene Sarazen voted the number one course in the world (see also *Great Golf* in DIVERSIONS). To make arrangements to play, contact the club secretary (Newcastle; phone: 396-723314; fax: 396-726281). The club's *Centenary Room* serves light lunches and is open to visitors weekdays from 9 AM to 6:30 PM.

CHECKING IN

Burrendale Offering the most modern comforts in the area, this property, surrounded by trees and gardens, has 50 guestrooms (4 executive suites), each with private bath, plus a health club and spa with a heated swimming pool, saunas, a solarium, Turkish steamrooms, Jacuzzis, an exercise room, a massage room, a beauty salon, and a refreshment bar. The restaurant features fresh local produce and seafood at moderate prices. The *Cottage Bar,* with its interior thatch roof and open fire, is a cozy retreat for inexpensive pub lunches, high tea (supper), and drinks. Just outside town at 51 Castlewellan Rd., Newcastle (phone: 396-722599; fax: 396-722328). Expensive.

Slieve Donard This attractive, atmospheric, turn-of-the-century hotel, built to be convenient to the former railway station nearby, occupies a wonderful site on the Irish Sea, with views of Slieve Donard and other Mourne peaks sweeping down to the shore. Extensively renovated, it has a health club, a heated indoor swimming pool, 2 outdoor tennis courts, and 6 acres of grounds that back up to the *Royal County Down Golf Club*. Just steps from the front door are several miles of beach. All 120 rooms have private baths; request a front room, preferably one with bay windows that take in both the sea and the Mournes. There's a lobby bar/lounge, and the fine *Percy French Grill Bar* (see *Eating Out*) is located on the hotel grounds. Downs Rd., Newcastle (phone: 396-723681; fax: 396-724830). Expensive.

EATING OUT

Enniskeen The dining room at this 12-room country-house hotel set at the foot of the Mourne Mountains offers wonderful views. A reasonably priced table d'hôte lunch is served, and for dinner an à la carte menu offers sweetbreads, fresh vegetables, locally caught salmon, chicken, and vegetarian dishes. Open daily for lunch and dinner; closed December through February. Reservations advised for window views at dinner. MasterCard and Visa accepted. 98 Bryansford Rd. (phone: 396-722392). Moderate.

Percy French Grill Bar On the grounds of the *Slieve Donard* hotel, overlooking the beach, this Tudor-style eatery offers pub fare for lunch and an à la carte menu in the evening. Dinner specialties include vegetarian dishes, lamb, steaks, roast duckling, shrimp scampi, and salmon. Open daily. Reservations advised for dinner on weekends. Major credit cards accepted. Newcastle (phone: 396-723175). Moderate to inexpensive.

Strand A 50-year-old establishment overlooking the sea, it serves pancakes, sandwiches, home-baked goods, and ice cream. Open daily in summer 10 AM to 11 PM; limited hours during winter. Reservations unnecessary. Major credit cards accepted. 53 Central Promenade, Newcastle (phone: 396-723472). Inexpensive.

CASTLEWELLAN For another rewarding side trip, take A50 inland 4 miles to Castlewellan, a picturesque market town nestled between the High Mournes and the Slieve Croob hills of central Down. Spires from the Church of Ireland and the Roman Catholic church rise at the eastern and western ends of the wide main street, which passes through two squares shaded by chestnut trees. Market day is Monday.

Signposted immediately north of town is Castlewellan Forest Park, 1,500 acres that once were a nobleman's estate. The park surrounds Lake Castlewellan, more than a half-mile long, where boats can be hired in season. The Scottish baronial-style castle overlooking the lake was built in 1856 to replace an earlier mansion of the Earls of Annesley, who once owned most of the Mournes. The farmstead was built around 1720 and includes courtyards, a barn, and a belfry in superb Queen Anne style. The *Grange Coffee House* offers quiche, salads, and pizza (phone: 396-778664; open daily 10:30 AM to 6:30 PM, *Easter* through September). Perhaps the finest feature of the park is the National Arboretum. Begun in 1790, it contains trees and plants from around the world. Some of the outstanding plantings are Scotch pine, beech, Irish yew, and a variety of cypress called Castlewellan Gold. A guidebook is available at the information office (phone: 396-778664). The park is open daily from 10 AM to dusk; there's a parking fee.

For an overland excursion to the Legananny Dolmen, considered one of Ireland's finest Neolithic tombs (ca. 2000 BC), pick up A50 outside Castlewellan Forest Park and head west toward Banbridge. In about 3 miles, a small sign for Legananny Dolmen indicates a right turn; from here, the antiquity is 5½ miles away, over well-paved but rural roads. Though it may not always seem so, the route is accurately signposted. The monument finally is visible off Dolmen Road, up a dirt lane to the right past a small farm. Beyond this unusually tall, tripod dolmen, standing at an altitude of 850 feet on Cratlieve Mountain, is a magnificent view over the Mournes. Bring stout shoes for hiking in this beautiful, virgin setting. Retrace the route to Newcastle.

En Route from Newcastle The 12-mile drive to Downpatrick is scenic. Heading northeast of Newcastle on A2 toward Dundrum, look for a sign on the right for the Murlough Nature Reserve. The National Trust has provided paths, notice boards, and an information center so that visitors can learn about the birds, flowers, and geology of the dunes and heath. The boardwalk-type path from the parking lot to the beach is about a half mile long.

Next, follow signs for Dundrum Castle. The remains of this Norman stronghold, built about 1177 by John de Courcy, rest strikingly on a 200-foot hill that offers splendid views of the mountains and the sea. The castle was taken by the English King John in 1210 and was bombarded by Cromwell's troops in 1652. The grounds are open at all times; the keep is open Tuesdays through Saturdays from 10 AM to 7 PM, and Sundays from 2 to 7 PM, from *Easter* through September; Saturdays from 10 AM to 4 PM, and Sundays from 2 to 4 PM, in October through March; closed 1 to 1:30 PM daily for lunch (no phone).

From Dundrum, take A24 north through Clough to Seaforde, where the Tropical Butterfly House at Seaforde Nursery (phone: 396-87225) is located. Over 30 species of free-flying tropical butterflies are here, as well as tropical insects and reptiles from four continents. Open Mondays through Saturdays from 10 AM to 5 PM, and Sundays from 2 to 6 PM, from *Easter* through September. From here, continue on A2 to Clough, and turn right (east) on A25 for Downpatrick.

EATING OUT

Woodlands This acclaimed dining place offers such specialties as Strangford scallops, game in season, and hazelnut and apricot meringue. Open for dinner Thursdays through Saturdays. Reservations necessary. Master-Card and Visa accepted. At Clough, head north on A24 to Ballynahinch. 29 Spa Rd., Ballynahinch (phone: 238-562650). Expensive.

DOWNPATRICK The administrative center for the rural, largely agricultural Down District of southeast Northern Ireland, Downpatrick obtained its name from close association with St. Patrick and from a local landmark, the great fort, or *dún,* of the Red Branch knight Celtair, thought to have been located on what is now Cathedral Hill. Although vulnerable to Viking raids for 300 years or more, Downpatrick grew in importance as a religious center. In 1176, English King Henry II granted the counties of Down and Antrim to John de Courcy, a Norman knight. De Courcy established a stronghold in Downpatrick and then secured his territory by dividing it into administrative units controlled by minor English overlords. To placate the Irish, de Courcy enshrined the local relics of St. Patrick, St. Brigid, and St. Columba, but the Anglo-Normans imposed their ways on the local population by replacing existing churches and clergy with their own orders of monks in elaborate religious houses. The picturesque ruins of Inch Abbey (see below) still stand outside the town on the banks of the River Quoile, and records reveal the existence of 6 other religious establishments in Downpatrick from that era, although no traces of these remain.

During the Middle Ages, Downpatrick suffered at the hands of the Scots and English, who burned and plundered many of its buildings, but by the early 18th century stability and prosperity had returned. This was especially due to the influence of the Southwells, a Bristol family who acquired the Manor of Downpatrick through marriage in 1703. Much of the development of the town can be attributed to the work of the family, who erected a quay on the River Quoile and encouraged markets and fairs and the building of hotels and houses. English, Scotch, and Irish Streets — old thoroughfares with distinguished architecture, much of it Georgian — meet at the center of Downpatrick, which is dominated by the fanciful tall clock tower and arcade of the assembly house. The layout and naming of these streets typifies the Elizabethan system of dividing settlements into ethnic quarters. Buildings of note include the Southwell charity schools and almshouses (1733), the imposing courthouse and County Hall, and the judges' residence, all on English Street.

Down Cathedral (Cathedral Church of the Holy Trinity) stands at the top of English Street, on the great *dún,* the onetime royal residence of the mighty Ulster chief Celtair, who may have predated St. Patrick by 400 or more years. By the 6th century, a great church stood on this site, although during the next several centuries it was regularly pillaged by the Danes. The site was occupied by monks of the order of St. Augustine until the 1172 Anglo-Norman invasion headed by John de Courcy, when the Augustinians were replaced by Benedictine monks from Chester. In 1245, the church was destroyed by an earthquake. In 1316, it was burned by Edward Bruce, brother of Robert the Bruce of Scotland. In 1538, it was destroyed yet again, this time by the English, and from then, it lay in ruins for more than 250 years. In 1790, restoration of the cathedral began, arranged through an Act of Parliament. The features of the ancient structure were retained as much as possible, and the restored building was erected on the walls and arches of the abbey choir that probably was built during the 14th century. The cathedral was reopened for services in 1818, and most recently was renovated in 1987.

Approaching from English Street, visitors first see the east door of the cathedral; in front of it stands a badly weathered 10th-century High Cross. From the west door are distant views of the Mournes. In the cemetery at the side is a great Mourne granite slab marked "Patric" that was placed here in 1900 as a reminder that Ireland's patron saint is traditionally believed to be buried close to the cathedral. (It is also thought that St. Brigid and St. Columba were later buried with St. Patrick.) The most striking interior features of the cathedral are the capitals, which are decorated with carved vine leaves, oak leaves with acorns, animals, birds, clusters of berries, and human heads. Some are genuine 14th- and 15th-century works, while others are by 18th-century restorers. The choir screen with stalls underneath is the only one of its kind remaining in Ireland. Down Cathedral possesses one of the two largest, most complete and original 18th-century organs in Ireland (the other is in Hillsborough, see above).

Just down English Street from the cathedral is the *St. Patrick Heritage Centre,* located in the gatehouses of the late 18th-century former Down County Gaol (jail). The center depicts the story of Ireland's patron saint through large-scale illustrations and other displays, emphasizing the strong links between southeast Ulster, Patrick, and early Irish Christianity. Sharing space in the gaol is the *Down County Museum,* which features exhibits on the area's natural history and archaeological past. Both are open weekdays from 11 AM to 5 PM, and weekends from 2 to 5 PM, from July through mid-September; Tuesdays through Fridays from 11 AM to 5 PM, and Saturdays from 2 to 5 PM, from mid-September through June. There are special events on *St. Patrick's Day* (March 17). No admission charge (phone: 396-615218).

EATING OUT

Rea's An atmospheric bar-restaurant with dark wood paneling and working fireplaces, where everything from soup to sauce is homemade or from fresh produce. Fresh seafood is the specialty of the house. Open weekdays for lunch only. Major credit cards accepted. 78 Market St., Downpatrick (phone: 396-612017). Moderate.

———————————

INCH ABBEY Take A7 toward Belfast for about half a mile, then turn left at the signpost for Inch Abbey. Set in a lovely rural area on an island in the River Quoile, the extensive ruins here are remains of a Cistercian abbey founded in the 1180s by John de Courcy, who built it in atonement for having destroyed in war another abbey south of Downpatrick. The abbey was built on the foundations of an ancient church that was devastated by a Viking raid in AD 1001. Although within sight of Downpatrick Cathedral across the river, the island site ensured the monks a degree of seclusion. Inch was a center of English influence; Irishmen were not allowed to enter the community. The abbey burned in 1404, and was replaced with a smaller structure; monastic life here ended in 1542. Nineteenth-century illustrations show the ruin ivy-covered and buried deep in fallen rubble. In 1910, the ruins were placed in the care of the state, and in 1980 a larger area — embracing most of the medieval precinct — was annexed. Within the precinct is the site of a 5th-century Celtic monastery, possibly connected to St. Patrick. Inch Abbey, accessible by a short walk from the parking lot, is open Tuesdays through Saturdays from 10 AM to 7 PM, and Sundays from 2 to 7 PM, from *Easter* through September; Tuesdays through Saturdays from 10 AM to 4 PM, and Sundays from 2 to 4 PM, in October through March. There's an admission charge (no phone). Return to Downpatrick.

En Route from Downpatrick Head northeast on A25, following the sign for Strangford. After about a mile, turn right for Saul and Saul Brae. Look for the gray granite church with a distinguishing replica of a Celtic round tower. The church was erected in 1932 to commemorate the 1,500th anniversary of Patrick's return to Ireland; it is open to the public daily.

SAUL Patrick received religious training in France, where he was consecrated as a bishop by Germanus of the See of Auxerre and directed to return to Ireland to Christianize the heathens. Landing at Wicklow in AD 432, Patrick proceeded to Ulster, site of his early years as a slave on Slemish Mountain in Antrim (see the *Antrim Coast* route). Working his way up the east coast of Ireland by ship, strong currents propelled him instead into Strangford Lough, where he landed at the mouth of the River Slaney. Coming ashore, Patrick and his company were met by a good-natured heathen named Dichu. When Dichu saw Patrick, he "became gentle, and believed." Patrick baptized his first convert, and, in return, Dichu gave Patrick a barn for his first church in Ireland. The area has since been known as Saul, a form of the Irish word for barn, *sabhal,* and is considered one of Ireland's holiest sites. Patrick always loved Saul, and it was here he came to rest after his travels throughout the rest of Ireland. It is said that when Patrick neared death, the angel Victor told him that Saul was the appointed place for him to die, and it was at Saul that Patrick received his last Eucharist from a bishop named Tassach. Many towns and monasteries vied for the honor of burying Patrick. According to tradition, an angel advised that a pair of untamed oxen be harnessed to a cart bearing Patrick's body; the oxen should "proceed wherever they wish, and where they shall rest let a church be founded there in honor of his body." The oxen supposedly stopped at Cathedral Hill in Downpatrick.

During his lifetime, Patrick founded Saul Abbey, placing it in the care of St. Duminius. For more than 300 years, the abbey existed unmolested. Eventually, however, it was raided and burned by the Danes. It was rebuilt by the Bishop of Down as an Augustinian priory but it again was destroyed by Edward Bruce in 1316. After this, the site was neglected for centuries. In 1788, a new church, a simple whitewashed building, was erected. In 1932, the Church of Ireland replaced it with the present structure, a replica of an ancient Celtic church. It is the parish church for a small number of neighboring families; services are held each Sunday at noon. Special services are held on *St. Patrick's Day* (March 17), when many modern pilgrims make their way to Saul. In the graveyard is one remaining wall of the original Saul Abbey and two small corbeled cells, one of which was used as a tomb, the other for prayer and meditation. Decorative stones from the original abbey can be viewed at the back of the present church.

On the commanding slope of nearby Slieve Patrick is a 33-foot granite statue of Patrick, also erected in 1932. Its base is decorated with bronze panels depicting scenes from the saint's life. Leading up the mountain to an open-air altar are the 12 Stations of the Cross, small altars commemorating the final events in Christ's life.

En Route from Saul Return to A25 and drive 4 miles toward Strangford. On the western outskirts of town, turn left for Castle Ward (phone: 396-86204), a National Trust property on 800 acres overlooking Strangford Lough. The stately 3-story residence of Bath stone was built between 1762 and 1768 for Bernard Ward, the first Lord Bangor, and his wife, Lady Anne. Owing to the differing and uncompromising architectural tastes of Lord and Lady Bangor — he preferred classical, she the then-fashionable neo-Gothic — Castle Ward has a southwest façade that is Palladian, while the northeast is Gothic. The same dichotomy of style is maintained throughout the interior. Lady Bangor's eccentric boudoir is one of the most peculiar rooms in Ireland, featuring ornate plasterwork, paneling, and painted doors. Perhaps not surprisingly, the couple later separated. The house is surrounded by beautiful gardens with walks. Also on the grounds are a Victorian laundry, an 18th-century summer house, a crafts workshop, and a tearoom that serves lunch, scones, and cakes. The grounds are open morning to dusk year-round. The house and tearoom are open daily except Thursdays from 1 to 6 PM in May through August;

weekends and holidays from 1 to 6 PM in April, September, and October. There's an admission charge for the house; parking is extra.

STRANGFORD Strangford is a pretty village along a double cove on the western shore of Strangford Lough narrows, through which St. Patrick sailed in 432. Some 400 million tons of water pass through the narrows during each tidal change. The powerful current so impressed raiding Vikings in the 10th century that they named the lough "strong fjord," hence its present name. A walking path along the shore passes Strangford Castle (a tower house from the 16th century) and the defensive tower of Old Court (residence of Baroness de Ros, Premier Baroness of Great Britain, a title created in 1264).

EATING OUT

Lobster Pot A highly recommended restaurant for lobster, clams, and fresh salmon. Open daily for lunch and dinner. Reservations advised. Major credit cards accepted. 11 The Square, Strangford (phone: 396-86288). Moderate.

En Route from Strangford Strangford village is one of the terminals for the Strangford Lough car ferry that sails to Portaferry, on the opposite shore, eliminating the 50-mile land route around the lough. The ferry carries 24 cars and runs year-round from each port every half hour or so from 7:30 AM to 10:30 PM weekdays; 8 AM to 11 PM Saturdays; and 9:30 AM to 10:30 PM Sundays (phone: 396-86637). The one-way fare for car and driver is very inexpensive. The lough, a large inlet of the Irish Sea, is 18 miles long and an average of 3½ miles wide. It is noted for multitudes of birds and marine creatures — nearly 700 species have been spotted here.

PORTAFERRY On the picturesque narrows opposite Strangford, Portaferry seems pleasantly removed from modern life. The long waterfront has Scottish-style cottages and some Georgian and early Victorian houses. The town, which has several interesting churches, rises steeply up a hill. The *Northern Ireland Aquarium* (Rope Walk, Castle St.; phone: 247-728062), with lots of interactive and audiovisual displays, recently completed a major expansion. It's open Mondays through Saturdays from 10 AM to 6 PM, and Sundays from 1 to 6 PM, in April through August; Tuesdays through Saturdays from 10:30 AM to 5 PM, and Sundays from 1 to 5 PM, in September through March. A tearoom serves snacks from noon to 5 PM daily in summer; weekends only the rest of the year. There's an admission charge.

CHECKING IN/EATING OUT

Portaferry Nearly opposite the car ferry slip, this establishment has 14 double rooms, each with private bath, and two restaurants: A cozy neighborhood-style bar/lounge facing the water serves pub grub lunches; a more formal, though reasonably priced, restaurant specializes in seafood. Open daily for lunch and dinner. Reservations advised. Major credit cards accepted. The Strand, Portaferry (phone: 247-728231; fax: 247-728999). Moderate.

En Route from Portaferry Head northeast on A2, up the North Down Ards Peninsula, to Cloghy and a 2-mile sweep of beach and dunes on the open Irish Sea. Continue to Portavogie, a classically pretty harbor with a colorful fishing fleet. In Portavogie, boats are built, sailed, and discussed night and day. The inhabitants are markedly Scottish in speech and traditions. Continue north to Ballywalter, then turn west onto B5 to Greyabbey on the lough side of the peninsula, which has a noticeably different feeling from the sea side. It's 7½ miles from Portaferry.

GREYABBEY This graceful village is most noted for its well-preserved ruins of a Cistercian abbey, founded in 1193 by Affreca, daughter of the King of the Isle of Man and wife of John de Courcy, the Norman conqueror of Ulster. The abbey, which has lovely grounds, was used as a parish church until 1778. An effigy tomb in the north wall of the choir may be that of Affreca. Open Tuesdays through Saturdays from 10 AM to 7 PM, and Sundays from 2 to 7 PM, from *Easter* through September; Saturdays from 10 AM to 4 PM, and Sundays from 2 to 4 PM, from October through March. Greyabbey village also is noted for its antiques shops.

En Route from Greyabbey About 3 miles north on A20 is an abrupt right turn, marked with a signpost, into the Mount Stewart House and Gardens (phone: 247-74387), a National Trust site. The house was the birthplace of Lord Castlereagh, England's foreign secretary during the Napoleonic Wars. The house is overshadowed by its gardens, which are among the finest in the British Isles. Laid out during World War I by Edith, Lady Londonderry, they offer unrivaled collections of plantings and vistas: topiary in the Shamrock Garden, a Temple of the Winds, an 18th-century folly that is a copy of an Athenian temple, and unusual locally carved animal statuary. A detailed guide is available at the entrance. The house is open from 1 to 6 PM, the gardens from 10:30 AM to 6 PM, daily, except Tuesdays, in May through September; weekends only in April and October. The shop and tearoom are open daily from 1:30 to 5:30 PM from June through August; weekends and holidays in April, May, September, and October. There's an admission charge. Continue northwest on A20 for 2 miles to Newtownards.

NEWTOWNARDS This is a flourishing commercial center, with Ulster's finest Georgian Town Hall and an old stone Market Cross. Just southwest is steep Scrabo Hill, made conspicuous for miles by its 135-foot-high tower (122 steps to the top), built in 1857 as a memorial to the third Marquis of Londonderry, one of Wellington's generals. The tower is now a countryside center (phone: 247-811491) with information and visual displays. It's open daily except Mondays from noon to 5:30 PM in June through September; at other times by arrangement. There's no admission charge. The views of north Down from both hill and tower are exceptional.

En Route from Newtownards The most direct route to the center of Belfast is A20 west. Alternatively, drive north on A21 to the seaside suburban town of Bangor, then west and south on A2, passing Cultra and the *Ulster Folk and Transport Museum* (see *Belfast* in THE CITIES).

Fermanagh Lakelands

Fermanagh is famous for its lakes — one-third of the county is water — and for its mountain-and-moor loveliness. The largest lake, the 50-mile waterway of Upper and Lower Lough Erne — separated by the island town of Enniskillen, ancient seat of the Irish Maguire chieftains — refreshes the entire region. Vantages like Lough Navar Viewpoint provide sweeping perspectives. In 1609, Sir John Davies, attorney general to Queen Elizabeth I, wrote that Fermanagh is "so pleasant and fruitful, that if I should make a full description thereof it would be taken as a poetical fiction."

In addition to lake scenery, other sights attract travelers: plantation-period castles, splendid stately houses, traditional crafts factories, pagan and early Christian monuments. Overall, life proceeds at a relaxed pace in this quiet corner of Ulster; the region is particularly known for that most leisurely of sports, fishing. The town of Enniskillen is one of Europe's angling capitals. Those who don't actively participate can sample the catch in local restaurants. Fermanagh's lakes are also perfect for cruising — cabin cruisers can be hired from several companies (most have a 1-week minimum) — and for canoeing, sailing, water skiing, swimming, painting, photographing, or simply contemplating.

During early Christian times, the islands in Lough Erne were populous ports of call. Churches and monasteries, built in Fermanagh since the 6th century, were especially concentrated on the islands and shores of Lough Erne. Built not only as retreats for religious contemplation, they made excellent way stations for travelers along the inland waterway. The Erne was important for centuries as a route of pilgrimage northwest to St. Patrick's Purgatory. (Located just over the border in Donegal near Lough Derg, this is the spot where St. Patrick is said to have had a vision of purgatory.) In the Middle Ages Fermanagh's population was three times the 50,000 it is today, and many of the 154 Lough Erne islands that now are uninhabited supported substantial numbers of residents and their parish churches. The lakes and islands offer the same scenic peace and serenity to 20th-century travelers that they did to 7th-century monastics.

Throughout the late 16th century, Queen Elizabeth's attempt to subjugate the Irish — ostensibly because of her fear that Spain would attack England through Ireland — was challenged by the leaders of the Gaelic aristocracy. Nowhere were her generals more fiercely opposed than in west Ulster by the O'Neills, O'Donnells, and Maguires. Her successor, Protestant King James I, used the Flight of the Earls (the escape of defeated Irish chieftains) in 1607 as an excuse to confiscate large parcels of land, which James then granted to English and Scottish "Planters," on the condition that they build settlements and provide strongholds loyal to him. The

Planters, mainly English and Lowland Scottish opportunists, built defenses against the hostile native population — about ten sturdy stone castles were added to Fermanagh's existing fortresses during the Plantation era. The castles now are mostly in ruins, but the remains (remarkably well preserved, considering their turbulent history) are among the principal attractions for visitors to west Ulster.

The history of the region in the post-Plantation 18th and 19th centuries is one of large-scale emigration to the New World, as illustrated by the stimulating displays at the *Ulster–American Folk Park* outside Omagh in County Tyrone (the northernmost portion of our route).

The following driving tour, which begins west of Belfast and ends south of Londonderry, is primarily in County Fermanagh, with some sites farther north in County Tyrone. From Dungannon in the east to Belleek in the west, the drive is about 70 miles; from Enniskillen in the south to Omagh in the north, it's about 30 miles. The overall mileage of this route, however, is difficult to calculate since it loops back on itself several times as it covers a concentration of sites around Lough Erne. The area can be sampled in depth, including side trips and walks, in 4 to 5 leisurely days.

Along the way, a double room with private bath and full breakfast will cost $100 or more in hotels listed as expensive, from $50 to $100 at places described as moderate, and less than $50 at inexpensive establishments. A three-course meal for two, including 10% service charge and VAT (but not beverages), will cost $50 or more at restaurants in the expensive category, $35 to $50 at places in the moderate category, and under $35 at eateries described as inexpensive. For each location, hotels and restaurants are listed alphabetically by price category.

BELFAST For a complete report on the city, its sites, hotels, and restaurants, see *Belfast,* THE CITIES.

En Route from Belfast Leave Belfast on M1 west, following the sign for Lisburn, for the 16½-mile drive to Dungannon. Or from Belfast International Airport, take A26 south and pick up M1 west at the attractive village of Moira. At Exit 12 (about a 30-minute drive from Belfast), turn onto B196, which loops north through Maghery and then back south to M1.

Residents of Maghery claim that emigrants from their town, a former fishing village on Lough Neagh, named New York's Coney Island after the wooded islet at the mouth of the River Blackwater. (Residents of Sligo City in the Republic of Ireland also claim this distinction for their island in Sligo Bay.) Today, a greater contrast between places would be hard to imagine. The Maghery Coney Island, now owned by the National Trust, has no inhabitants except birds, especially waterfowl. A monument near the ruins of an ancient circular church declares that St. Patrick often "resorted to this island" for prayers and meditation in the 5th century.

During the rule of Elizabeth I, Coney Island was a penal settlement; the execution mound can still be traced in the dense undergrowth. The island, accessible by boat from Maghery, is open at all times.

Lough Neagh is Ulster's inland sea, the biggest lake in the British Isles (20 miles long and 11 1/2 miles at its widest), nearly as large as Switzerland's Lake Geneva. Local lore accounts for its origin in this way: The Irish giant Finn MacCool, in a rage during a fight with rival giants, tore up a vast fistful of earth and hurled it toward England, but the piece of Irish sod thrown by Finn fell short. It landed in the Irish Sea and became known as the Isle of Man; the "hole" left in Ulster soil became Lough Neagh. This tale is supported by the remarkable similarity in shape and size of Lough Neagh and the Isle of Man. A more scientific explanation is that Lough Neagh is a "glacial puddle" that formed following the melting at the end of the last Ice Age.

Continue on B196 past Peatlands Park, which has more than 900 acres of peat faces (peat bog surfaces from which bricks of turf are cut), and a characteristic bogland ecosystem. There are also a visitors' center and a narrow-gauge railway. The park is open daily from 9 AM to dusk; the railway operates Saturdays, Sundays, and holidays from 2 to 6 PM from *Easter* through September (phone: 762-851102). One mile south of the park, follow signs to rejoin M1 west to Dungannon. At Exit 15, the end of the motorway, take A29 north for about 2 miles into the town center.

DUNGANNON The mound above Market Square in Dungannon, now surmounted by two towers from a castle built in 1790, was for centuries the site of the castle and seat of the O'Neill Kings of Ulster and the Earls of Tyrone. Once the most powerful of the four ancient Irish kingdoms, Ulster adopted as its emblem the O'Neill Red Hand. The story of the Red Hand survives from a distant era, when rivals from an unknown land sailed to Ireland for the purpose of conquering it. Nearing the Ulster coast, the shipboard warriors agreed that whoever touched Irish soil first would be lord over it. One daring chief, whose landing boat was lagging behind the others, cut off his left hand and threw it onto the shore, thus claiming he had touched land first. From this man descended the O'Neills, the royal race of Ulster. The last of the great O'Neills was Hugh, Earl of Tyrone, who alternately warred with and submitted to Elizabeth I until his escape to France in 1607 in the notorious Flight of the Earls.

Dungannon's noteworthy Tyrone Crystal Ltd., producers of mouth-blown, hand-cut, full-lead crystal, was opened in 1970. Despite its relatively recent origins, Tyrone Crystal, which is owned by a local cooperative and employs 150 people, has become well established among the world's foremost crystal manufacturers. Visitors may observe the cut-crystal production process — melting, blowing, cooling, cutting, washing, and polishing — during which some 30 people handle each piece.

To get to the factory (Oaks Rd.; phone: 868-725335; fax: 868-726260) from Dungannon town center, take the turn for Cookstown; at the "roundabout" (traffic circle) soon afterward, exit at about "5 o'clock" onto the Coalisland Road. It's less than 2 miles down the road on the right-hand side. Free 45-minute tours are available year-round, Mondays through Saturdays from 9:30 AM to 3:30 PM. Reservations are necessary. The factory is closed 2 weeks during mid-July. The shop sells top-quality items at retail prices, and "imperfects" at about one-third less than prevailing retail prices in Northern Ireland, which in turn are about 50% less than prices in the US. Shop hours are 9 AM to 5 PM; closed Sundays, *Easter* weekend, and July 12 and 13. There's also a restaurant on the premises.

CHECKING IN

Grange Lodge This Georgian country house on 20 tree-shaded acres offers 3 double rooms (2 with private baths), a good restaurant (closed Sundays; reservations necessary), a tennis court, table tennis, and darts. From M1 Exit 15, take A29 south for 1 mile and turn left at the sign for the Grange Meeting House. 7 Grange Rd., Dungannon (phone: 868-784212 or 868-722458; fax: 868-723891). Moderate.

EATING OUT

Dunowen Inn Set lunches, pub grub, and à la carte dinners are served here. Open for lunch and dinner; closed Sundays. Reservations unnecessary. Master-Card and Visa accepted. Market Sq., Dungannon (phone: 868-723144). Moderate to inexpensive.

En Route from Dungannon Leave Dungannon on A29 south and pick up A4 west for Enniskillen. At Ballygawley, about 15 miles from Dungannon, a left turn at the signpost leads to President Ulysses S. Grant's ancestral home, 4 miles east in the hamlet of Dergina (phone: 662-527133). In addition to a gift shop and a visitors' center, which offers a video on Irish immigration to North America and tells President Grant's family story, the site includes interesting exhibits of rural Irish life. The 10-acre farm is still worked by 19th-century methods; the livestock are purebred Irish goats, "mountainy" cattle, and poultry. It's open April through September, Tuesdays through Saturdays from 10 AM to 6 PM, Sundays from 2 to 6 PM. There's an admission charge.

Ballygawley is one of several villages along or just off A4 located in the 18-mile-long Clogher Valley along the River Blackwater. This gentle green region is rich in antiquities. Just northwest of Augher, off B83, is Knockmany Forest, the site of prehistoric ruins. On the summit of a steep wooded hill (650 feet) is the now enclosed Late Stone Age Knockmany chambered burial cairn, Northern Ireland's best-known example of a passage grave, with excellent specimens of rock-carved art. Elaborate designs, akin to those at the New Grange site in the Irish Republic's Boyne Valley, include concentric circles and zigzag and "snake" patterns. Queen Aine of the 6th-century kingdom of Oriel supposedly is buried at Knockmany.

The next village down the road, Clogher, also occupies an ancient site. The diocese of Clogher — the oldest bishopric in Ireland — is believed to have been established by St. Patrick himself; its first bishop was his disciple St. MacCartan. The small classical-style Church of Ireland cathedral (1744) is named for MacCartan. From the square tower, there is a good view of the Clogher Valley. Ask at the rectory for access.

It is a bit more than 5 miles from Clogher to Fivemiletown, so named because it's located 5 Irish miles from each of the neighboring villages. Just west of Fivemiletown, the route passes from County Tyrone to County Fermanagh, the most western of the 6 counties of Northern Ireland. Follow A4 the rest of the way to Enniskillen (a total of 46 miles from Dungannon).

CHECKING IN/EATING OUT

Blessingbourne Owned by the same family for 300 years, this striking Victorian Gothic country home, set on a 500-acre estate, has original fittings and furnishings. There are only 4 rooms — none with private bath, one with a four-poster bed. The baronial dining room overlooks the lake. Other amenities include tennis courts, fishing, and a library. Reservations essential. Turn right off A4 at Fivemiletown; continue about one-quarter of a mile, and turn right onto the estate at the gate lodge entrance (phone: 365-521221). Expensive.

ENNISKILLEN Situated on an island in the River Erne, a 50-mile natural waterway that connects Lower and Upper Lough Erne, Fermanagh's county seat is by far its largest town, with 13,000 inhabitants. Enniskillen, whose origins predate recorded history, was a mid-lake link of great strategic significance on the main route between the ancient Irish kingdoms of Ulster and Connaught. It was the medieval seat of the Maguires, chieftains of Fermanagh, who once policed the loughs with a private navy of some 1,500 boats.

The town was at the center of Irish resistance to Tudor domination; its history in the 16th century was one of siege, capture, burning, and battering by the Maguires, the rival O'Neill clan, and the English. During the closing stages of the war between Elizabeth I and Hugh O'Neill, the Maguires' Enniskillen Castle was severely damaged, partly by the Maguires themselves, to prevent the English from using it against them. When Planter Captain William Cole arrived as constable of the royal fort of Enniskillen soon after the Flight of the Earls in 1607, he found only a crumbling wall enclosing the burned-out shell of a tower house. Cole succeeded in creating a working fort out of the ruins of the Maguire castle, adding the Watergate, which remains a picturesque Enniskillen landmark.

When William Cole (by then a knight) died in 1658, he left his family rich in lands in Enniskillen and beyond. The Coles lived in Enniskillen Castle until the 18th century when, as the Earls of Enniskillen, they moved to Florence Court (see below). From the 17th century, the town of Enniskillen was known mainly for the Royal Inniskilling Fusiliers and the Inniskilling Dragoons, regiments raised in the area who participated in the battles of the Boyne, Waterloo, and the Somme.

The *Regimental Museum* within the castle contains the brilliant uniforms, arms, colors, regimental plate, Napoleonic battle trophies, metals, engravings, and photographs that trace the history of the famous Royal Inniskilling Fusiliers. A prized possession on display is the bugle that sounded the charge at the bloody Battle of the Somme (1916). The *Fermanagh County Heritage Centre and Museum,* also within the castle, evokes the history and folklife of Fermanagh from the Middle Stone Age to the end of the early Christian period through archaeological finds, realistic dioramas, and large-scale models and displays, among which are fiberglass copies of the famed White Island figures (see below). Excellent audiovisual programs on the Maguire chieftains, the Elizabethan wars, and the Plantation period are featured. The castle and its museums are open Mondays and Saturdays from 2 to 5 PM, and Tuesdays through Fridays from 10 AM to 5 PM in May through September; also Sundays from 2 to 5 PM in July and August. There's an admission charge (phone: 365-325000).

Enniskillen's interesting history and architecture are reflected in its winding main street, which carries six different names between the bridges at either end. The street is Fermanagh's major shopping center, with a lively Thursday market and numerous specialty stores, including outlets for arts, crafts, and antiques. Aran sweaters, Irish lace, handmade jewelry, and local pottery are good buys. Some of the best stores are *L. W. N. Hall, Booksellers* (10 High St.; phone: 365-324341), which sells maps and guides; *Armstrong & Kingston's* (8 High St.; phone: 365-322113), the place for men's quality tweeds, knitwear, and outerwear; *Fermanagh Cottage Industries* (14 East Bridge St.; phone: 365-322260) for handmade lace, other crocheted items, and hand-embroidered table and bed linen; and the *Enniskillen Craft and Design Centre* (Down St.; phone: 365-324499), a complex of 20 crafts workshops and a central gift shop, located in the historic heart of town. North of the main street, between Water and Market Streets, is a warren of alleys, including Corn and Butter markets (alleys where these products once were sold), that retain some of the architectural atmosphere of Old Enniskillen.

Two churches dominate the town. On Church Street, Enniskillen's large, rather plain Gothic-style St. MacCartan's Cathedral (1842) incorporates a font, north porch, and tower from a 17th-century church. One of the ten bells of the tower's carillon was cast from cannon captured at the Battle of the Boyne. The fine interior galleries house old colors of the

Enniskillen regiments, and there is a pulpit preserved from the 1688–89 Siege of Derry. Almost opposite the Cathedral is St. Michael's Catholic Church, completed in 1875 in the French Gothic style. An exterior view of the rear section, built on sloping ground, emphasizes the massive proportions. A third church, the Convent Chapel (Belmore St.), built in 1904 in the Byzantine style, features 15 windows by Michael Healy, Lady Glenavy, and Sarah Purser, noted Irish stained glass artists of the Dublin School.

Because it is on an island, Enniskillen offers varied views of the River Erne. The best are from the Watergate, the Broadmeadow (at which the *Lakeland Forum,* a public recreational facility, has a swimming pool, squash, aquatic sports, and many other recreational facilities), and the Round O landing stage (departure point for cruises).

Lakeland Visitor Centre (Shore Rd.; phone: 365-323110), by the town center parking lot, provides comprehensive area tourist information, accommodation booking services, information on major sites, crafts sales, and in summer, walking tours of Enniskillen. The center is open weekdays from 9 AM to 5 PM (6:30 PM in the summer), and Saturdays from 10 AM to 5 PM in June through September; Sundays from 10 AM to 2 PM in July and August. The center may be closed from 1 to 2 PM for lunch from October through May.

Overlooking the town from the east is Fort Hill Park, which features a Victorian bandstand topped by an elaborate clock. At the top of the hill, reached via Belmore Street in town, is Cole Column, a monument surmounted by a statue of General Sir Galbraith Lowry Cole, a descendant of William Cole, founder of Plantation Enniskillen. The later Cole fought in the Peninsula Wars and became governor of the Cape Colony in South Africa. The 108-step column can be climbed for a panoramic view of Fermanagh's lakes and mountains. It's open May through September on weekdays from 4 to 6 PM, and weekends from 2 to 6 PM; other times by appointment (phone: 365-325050). There's an admission charge.

Portora Royal School (Derrygonnelly Rd.; phone: 365-322658), established by decree of James I in 1608, lies to the west of town on a hill above the River Erne. The ruins of the 1619 Portora Castle, partially blown up in 1859 by experimenting chemistry students, are on the grounds. Colonnades and wings added to the main building in 1837 give the school an imposing appearance worthy of its history. "Old Boys" (graduates) of Portora include Oscar Wilde and Samuel Beckett.

The entrance to Castle Coole is opposite the *Ardhowen Theatre Centre,* on the Dublin road, a half-mile southeast of Enniskillen. The castle, a National Trust property considered to be the finest neo-classical house in Ireland, reopened in 1988 after the most extensive renovation ever undertaken by the National Trust in the UK. Castle Coole's restrained white splendor startles the eye, as was the intention of its builder, the first Earl of Belmore. It took 9 years (beginning in 1789) and vast sums of money to realize the earl's fantasy. All of the Portland stone for the structure was transported from England by sea and then by bullock and cart from Ballyshannon. Today, Castle Coole is a showpiece. Many of the handsome Regency furnishings were designed for the exact locations they occupy today. The estate lake is a breeding colony for greylag geese, and the *Enniskillen* golf course runs through the grounds. The visitors' center (phone: 365-322690) at the parking lot has a gift shop and exhibits on the restoration. The house is open from 2 to 6 PM daily except Thursdays in June through August; weekends and holidays only in April, May, and September. There's an admission charge. The grounds are open daily from dawn to dusk; no admission charge, but there's a small parking fee.

The *Ardhowen Theatre Centre,* beautifully set on the Dublin road on a hill overlooking Upper Lough Erne and its wooded shoreline, is a focal point for the arts in Fermanagh. The center includes a 300-seat theater, an outdoor terrace, a marina, picnic facilities, and a restaurant that is a popular coffee and lunch spot. The restaurant is open Mondays through Saturdays from 11 AM to 4 PM (phone: 365-325254). The box office is open Mondays through Saturdays from 10 AM to 4:30 PM and from 6 to 8 PM on performance evenings (phone: 365-325440).

CHECKING IN

Killyhevlin A well-appointed hotel on Upper Lough Erne, it has 22 rooms (each with private bath; some with lake views), and 14 self-catering 2-bedroom lakeside chalets. The welcoming, many-windowed lounge overlooks the lake; the *Oak Bar* exudes a pleasant spirit. The restaurant and lounge offer a broad menu (see *Eating Out*). Signposted on A4 near the *Ardhowen Theatre Centre,* on the Dublin road, Enniskillen (phone: 365-323481; fax: 365-324726). Expensive.

EATING OUT

Franco's This eatery offers pasta, pizza, and kebabs in a cozy, fireside atmosphere. Open for lunch and dinner; dinner only on Sundays. Reservations unnecessary. American Express accepted. Queen Elizabeth Rd., just off High St., Enniskillen (phone: 365-324424). Moderate.

Killyhevlin The restaurant in the eponymous hotel offers an extensive à la carte dinner menu and friendly service. Carvery luncheons (roasts, cut to order) are a specialty on Sundays. A luncheon buffet, with salad bar, is served in the lounge, which offers scenic views of Lough Erne. Open daily for lunch and dinner. Reservations advised. Major credit cards accepted. On the Dublin road, Enniskillen (phone: 365-323481). Moderate.

Blake's of the Hollow A fine late-Victorian pub that is a favorite with locals. Serves sandwiches and pub grub. Open for lunch and dinner; closed Sundays. Reservations unnecessary. No credit cards. Also see *Pub Crawling* in DIVERSIONS. 6 Church St., Enniskillen (phone: 365-322143). Inexpensive.

Detours from Enniskillen Before heading to Monea Castle and the village of Belleek, consider a detour to any one, or all three, of the following: Devenish Island, Florence Court House, or Marble Arch Caves.

DEVENISH ISLAND The most extensive remains of early and medieval Christian settlements in Northern Ireland are 2 miles north of Enniskillen, on a 70-acre island in Lower Lough Erne. The monastery on Devenish was founded by St. Molaise in the 6th century and remained functional as late as the 16th century. The most conspicuous landmark is an 82-foot, 12th-century round tower, the best preserved in Ireland, with a richly decorated cornice incorporating four carved heads. The Teampull Mor (Great Church), nearest the ferry jetty, dates from about 1225 in its first phase. It has a fine roll-molded south window characteristic of the transition from Romanesque to Gothic architecture. The south chapel was added later as a mausoleum for the Maguires, whose coat of arms is still visible. Other interesting sites include the house of St. Molaise, which faces the round tower; St. Mary's Abbey, the largest and most recent (1449) of the ecclesiastical buildings on the island; the stone High Cross in the cemetery south of the abbey; and a small museum that contains artifacts from the island. The best view is downslope from the east end of St. Mary's Abbey.

A 2-hour narrated cruise of Lough Erne stops at Devenish Island. The boat, which has a covered deck and a snack bar, sails from Round O jetty at Brook Park on the west bank of the River Erne. Departure times: in May and June, Sundays, and bank holidays at 2:30 PM; in July and August, daily at 10:30 AM, 2:15 PM, and 4:14 PM, with additional departures on Tuesdays, Thursdays, and Sundays at 7:15 PM; in September, Tuesdays, Saturdays, and Sundays at 2:30 PM. Reservations unnecessary. Contact *Erne Tours Ltd.* (phone: 365-322882).

Visitors who want more than a short stopover on Devenish, but no guided tour, can take the ferry from Trory Point jetty, about 3 miles north of Enniskillen, signposted off B82 toward Kesh. The ferry operates Tuesdays through Saturdays, *Easter* through September, 10 AM to 7 PM; Sundays, 2 to 7 PM. Contact *Devenish Island Ferry* (phone: 365-322711, ext. 230).

FLORENCE COURT Some 8 miles southwest of Enniskillen is Florence Court (Swanlinbar Rd.; phone: 365-82249), one of Ulster's most important historic houses. It oversees extensive parklands on the northeast shoulder of Cuilcagh Mountain. Head west on A4 (the Sligo road) for 3 miles, turn south onto A32, and follow the signposts to Florence Court Forest Park.

The park includes woodlands of 200-year-old oaks, moorland, and farmland. Look for the famous 220-year-old Florence Court Yew, the parent of all Irish yews worldwide. Walks from the parking lot are labeled according to difficulty and duration. The park is open daily from 10 AM to 1 hour before dusk.

Florence Court House, a National Trust property since the 1950s, is a fascinating example of Irish Georgian (mid-18th-century) architecture. It is also one of the most beautifully situated houses in Northern Ireland, with mountain peaks visible in three directions. In about 1710, Sir John Cole, then Mayor of Enniskillen, decided that cold, comfortless Enniskillen Castle was not a worthy home for his adored wife, Florence, so he built this country estate for her. Florence Court is best known for its intricate and charming plasterwork, the handiwork of Dublin stuccadore Robert West, who unified a mélange of interior architectural styles by placing flamboyant plaster cherubs, birds, flowers, and foliage everywhere. The plasterwork on the dining room ceiling is thought to be the finest in Ireland. It is original, unlike some of the other ceilings in the house, which had to be restored following a serious fire in 1955. The Venetian Room, with its gorgeous white-on-gray plaster ceiling of various birds and flowers, is just one example of how carefully the house was restored. From this delightful room a visitor can look out to the "ha-ha," a dry moat that kept cattle off the main lawn but allowed them to graze close enough to the house to be picturesque. Tours of the house are self-guided (reading materials provided), which allows lingering appreciation. In addition to a "pleasure ground" of plants and shrubs cultivated for the connoisseur, the National Trust has acquired additional working parts of the estate, including an icehouse, an eel bridge, a forge, a weighbridge, a sawmill, and a carpenter's shop. There is a gift shop and a café. Open daily, except Tuesdays, from 1 to 6 PM in June through August; weekends and holidays only from 1 to 6 PM in April, May, and September. There's an admission charge.

MARBLE ARCH CAVES When rejoining Swanlinbar Road outside Florence Court Forest Park, turn left (west), then left again (south) onto Marlbank Scenic Loop, a semicircular drive that crosses the Cuilcagh plateau, the finest caving area in Ireland, and ends near Marble Arch Caves.

The Marble Arch Caves are the best known in the subterranean labyrinth of Cuilcagh. The 1½-hour tour begins with a cruise across an underground lake, ending at the "junction," the spot where, in 1895, the earliest documented exploration and survey of the caves was begun by Edouard Martel, an eminent French speleologist. The caves developed in Darty limestone, a sedimentary rock 600 feet thick that was deposited about 330 million years ago. The huge cave system has been formed by three acidic underground streams that, over time, have etched away millions of tons of limestone, creating an entire underworld of lakes, rivers, waterfalls, passageways, lofty chambers, and reflecting pools. The Showcave, at the center of the system, is special for its size and for the variety of its formations. The caves offer the kind of exploration experience formerly available only to serious spelunkers. A path about two-thirds of a mile long winds past an array of fascinating formations: stalactites, mineral veils, rimstone pools, and cascades of cream-colored calcite coating the walls with a Belleek-like sheen. Wear shoes appropriate for wet surfaces, and bring a sweater and waterproof jacket. The Marble Arch Cave site has refreshment facilities, a shop, and exhibits. It's open daily mid-March through September from 11 AM; closing times vary according to the duty officer's discretion. It is advisable to check in advance to ensure date and time of choice (phone: 365-828855). There's an admission charge.

Return to A32 toward Enniskillen. Turn right (east) toward Arney and Bellanaleck and, if desired, follow signposts for the *Sheelin* restaurant (see *Eating Out*) on A509. Or return to Enniskillen via A509.

CHECKING IN

Tullyhona House On a working sheep-and-cattle farm, this guesthouse offers 7 rooms (4 with private baths), plus a sun-room and a lounge with a TV set. Open year-round. No credit cards. About 1 1/2 miles from Marble Arch Caves, on Marble Arch Rd., Florence Court (phone: 365-82452). Inexpensive.

EATING OUT

Sheelin Set in a 200-year-old, thatch-roofed, whitewashed cottage, this restaurant serves superb food. Special set-menu dinners on Saturdays feature such dishes as Chinese marinated steaks, lamb with orange and cream, and caramelized peaches. Open for breakfast, lunch, and dinner from 10 AM to 9:30 PM Tuesdays through Sundays in June through September; 10 AM to 6 PM Mondays through Saturdays the rest of the year. Dinner reservations essential. Major credit cards accepted. A crafts shop on the premises sells hand-crocheted woolen caps, scarves, shawls, ties, traditional hand-knit and tweed clothing, and soft toys. Rt. A509, Bellanaleck (phone: 365-82232). Dinner, expensive; lunch, inexpensive.

En Route from Enniskillen From Enniskillen head northwest on A46, then turn left onto B81 and travel west for about 3 miles. Turn right at signs for Monea Castle.

MONEA CASTLE Here is one of Northern Ireland's largest and best-preserved examples of a Plantation castle. Believed to be the site of a 15th-century Maguire stronghold and headquarters of that clan before Enniskillen became its capital, Monea's present ruins date from a 1618 castle built for Malcolm Hamilton, rector of Devenish, who later became archbishop of Cashel. The castle rises on a rocky bluff, surrounded on three sides by swampy ground. Just to the south is a small lake with a *crannóg,* an artificial island built for defense, suggesting prehistoric settlement of the site. Monea Castle is built of limestone with sandstone dressings. It has two 3-story towers with Scottish-style corbeling and crow-stepped gables. Part of the defensive *bawn* (ramparts) remains. Even in its relatively decayed state, Monea's strength and Scottish architectural ancestry are apparent. The castle was captured by the Maguires in 1641 but was quickly retaken by the Planters. In 1688, it was held by Gustavus Hamilton, Governor of Enniskillen. Abandoned after an 18th-century fire, Monea reverted to state care in 1954. It is open at all times; no admission charge (no phone).

En route from Monea Castle Return to B81 and turn right (north) for Derrygonnelly, a small village with a pleasant green and a Plantation-period church ruin. Follow signs for Glennasheevar Road for another 4 1/2 miles west to the Lough Navar Forest Scenic Drive. Continue on this drive for 7 miles through a wild forest of conifers; it is possible to stop along the way to enjoy self-guided nature trails and footpaths. At the far end of the semicircular scenic drive is a parking lot, beyond which is Lough Navar Viewpoint, an overlook affording one of the grandest views in Ireland. From here, you can see the steep sandstone Cliffs of Magho and nearly the whole of Lower Lough Erne and its islands. On a clear day, the mountains of several counties are visible, as well as the Atlantic shore of Donegal Bay to the west. The colors of lake, mountain, and sky are most impressive at sundown. For information, call the head forester at 365-64256.

Complete the scenic drive, then turn right onto the main (unnumbered) road. After driving about 4 miles through moorland and bog, turn right onto B52 and follow signs to Belleek.

BELLEEK A border village whose western outskirts lie in County Donegal, Belleek is known far and wide for its lustrous parian ware, a fine, white, decorative porcelain. The pottery was established in 1857 by John Bloomfield, owner of Caldwell Castle on Lower Lough Erne. On the grounds of his estate, Bloomfield found a superior quality of feldspar, an important ingredient of porcelain. His curiosity about the feldspar was initially aroused by the distinctive brilliance of the whitewash of his tenants' cottages. Originally the pottery produced earthenware, but by 1863 the formula for parian ware had been perfected by William Bromley, who came from England to work at Belleek. Bromley achieved Belleek's renowned eggshell thinness by refining the casting process. By 1869, prestigious orders, such as a tea service for the German royal family as a gift from Queen Victoria, were being received for the parian ware. Today, Belleek china, with its delicate, translucent ivory tint and painstakingly detailed decoration, appears in many museums and private collections worldwide.

The factory (phone: 365-65501; fax: 365-65625), which employs 140 people from both sides of the Irish border, is on A47 by the River Erne, just across the bridge at the entrance to Belleek. Tours begin with the raw materials: china clay, feldspar, ground flint glass, frit, and water. These are ground and mixed into a thick, creamy substance called "slip." After the slip is sieved, visitors can see it poured into plaster of Paris molds, which absorb the water. When dry, the shaped pieces begin their journey through many stages of decoration and firings. A piece that emerges less than perfect from any stage is destroyed — the Belleek factory allows no "seconds."

The factory welcomes visitors year-round. Tours are given weekdays from 9:30 AM to 12:15 PM and from 2:15 to 4:15 PM; the last tour on Fridays is at 3:15 PM. There is a small charge for tours, which last 20 minutes and depart about every half hour. The factory has a visitors' center (open daily), with a museum of unique pieces and a shop that has the world's most complete stock of Belleek. Prices are the same as in local shops, approximately 50% less than in the US. The shop is open weekdays from 9 AM to 6 PM, Saturdays from 10 AM to 6 PM, and Sundays from 2 to 8 PM, in March through June and in September; weekdays from 9 AM to 8 PM, Saturdays from 10 AM to 6 PM, and Sundays from 2 to 8 PM, in July and August; and weekdays from 9 AM to 5:30 PM in October through February. The Belleek pottery tearooms are open Mondays through Saturdays from 9:30 AM to 6 PM, and Sundays from 2 to 5:30 PM.

EATING OUT

Cleary's Corner Bar Overlooking the River Erne, this spot serves pub grub Mondays through Saturdays from noon to 10 PM. Reservations unnecessary. No credit cards accepted. Near the Belleek factory; 5 Main St., Belleek (phone: 365-65403). Inexpensive.

En Route from Belleek Take A47 east of Belleek, on the northern side of Lower Lough Erne. Once across the bridge to the west end of 5-mile-long Boa Island, watch for signs on the right indicating the old cemetery of Caldragh, site of two of Ireland's oldest and strangest stone figures, perhaps dating from the 1st century. The so-called Janus statues have a face on each side. (Janus was a Roman god with two faces; he could see the past and the future.) A hollow in the top of the Janus figure may have been used to hold drink or blood offerings to the gods. It is necessary to walk over rough ground to reach the stones.

About 10 miles from Belleek, A47 joins A35 north of Kesh. Bear south into Kesh on A35, and then bear right onto B82, which leads to Castle Archdale Forest and Marina (phone: 365-621731). Ferries to White Island operate June through September, Tuesdays through Saturdays from 10 AM to 7 PM, Sundays from 2 to 7 PM, and at other times on request (no service Mondays). The ferry trip is about $3.50. Also at Castle Archdale are the *Drumhoney Stables* (phone: 365-621892), which offers guided pony treks by Lough Erne, and old-time horse-drawn cart rides. There's a café on the premises.

WHITE ISLAND This 74-acre island was once the site of an early monastery. Eight inscrutable statues, found here at various times over a period of several decades, the last in 1958, have long attracted archaeologists, historians, and travelers from around the world. The figures, now placed side by side on a wall of the ruined 12th-century church in which they were discovered, are impressive for their scale (the tallest is about 4 feet high), powerful modeling, and the individuality of the faces. Each is distinct, but they share similarities: All stare fixedly forward; all have small hands and feet; and all wear a tunic with a bottom hem. Why the figures were concealed, whether they are pagan or Christian, and what they represent have been the subjects of much discussion. The church itself, a ruin since 1600, was restored in 1928. Its fine south door is the only intact Romanesque door surviving in Northern Ireland.

En Route from White Island Once back on the mainland, take B72 for 2 miles northeast, then connect with A35 southeast to Irvinestown. From Irvinestown, drive 20 miles northeast on A32 through Dromore to Omagh.

CHECKING IN/EATING OUT

Mahon's A family-run hotel for three generations, it has 18 rooms, each with private bath. The cozy bar is noted for its cocktails and entertainment. The restaurant is open daily for lunch, snacks, and dinner. Reservations unnecessary. MasterCard and Visa accepted. Enniskillen Rd., Irvinestown (phone: 365-621656; fax: 365-621945). Hotel moderate; restaurant inexpensive.

Jamestown Country House For an overnight stay at a hostelry that is well worth a detour, once back on the mainland from White Island, continue south from Castle Archdale on B82 toward Enniskillen. At Trory, make a sharp left (northeast) onto A32, then a right (east) onto B46 toward Ballinamallard and Errington. About a mile beyond the Fish Farm past Ballinamallard, turn left into a residential driveway marked "Jamestown." The house, which dates from 1760, has a projecting central bay and a handsome stableyard. There are 3 double guestrooms (all with private baths). Grounds include a tennis court and a croquet lawn. Guests are sometimes escorted on fishing or shooting expeditions on the estate by owner Arthur Stuart. In the evening, a gathering in front of the drawing room fire is followed by a gracious dinner (guests only) featuring local produce and game in season. Picnic lunches are available on request. Magheracross, Ballinamallard (phone: 365-81209). Moderate.

To resume the route from the hotel, follow B46 northeast through Kilskeery, Trillick, and Ballyard to Dromore. There, pick up A32 to Omagh.

OMAGH The capital and principal market town of County Tyrone, Omagh occupies open fertile country where the Carnowen and Drumragh rivers meet to form the Strule. All three rivers are good for fishing; the Strule is also noted for its mussel pearls. Omagh is a pleasant town with lovely river views, but little architectural distinction, since it was completely destroyed by fire in 1743. It does have some Georgian-style and late-19th-century houses, and the main thoroughfare, High Street, has a classical-style courthouse at its height. Omagh's most notable building is the Catholic cathedral, the Church of the Sacred Heart, designed by William Hague, which has Gothic-style steeples of unequal height, particularly lovely when viewed approaching the town. During the warmer months, Omagh hosts various festivals, agricultural and livestock exhibitions, and show jumping and gun dog trials. Souvenirs of the area include locally made linen, crochet lace, and turfcraft — plaques and statues of Irish mythological figures molded from compressed peat from the nearby Black Bog.

ULSTER–AMERICAN FOLK PARK Three miles north of Omagh on the Newtownstewart road (A5) in Camphill is the *Ulster–American Folk Park* (phone: 662-243292), which commemorates Ulster emigration to America. The 26-acre park features original and reconstructed buildings of the kinds in which Ulster natives lived and worked on both sides of the Atlantic, as well as exhibition galleries. The visitors' center has a café and a crafts/gift shop. The park is open Mondays through Saturdays from 10:30 AM to 6:30 PM, and Sundays and holidays from 11:30 AM to 7 PM, from *Easter* through September; weekdays from 10:30 AM to 5 PM from October to *Easter;* closed *Christmas, New Year's Day,* and *St. Patrick's Day.* Last admission is 1½ hours before closing; there's an admission charge. For detailed information on the park, see *Marvelous Museums* in DIVERSIONS.

CHECKING IN/EATING OUT

Mellon Country Inn Conveniently sited opposite the *Ulster–American Folk Park,* this rustic restaurant serves traditional food with French influences. The bar serves over 150 types of whiskey. (Also see *Pub Crawling* in DIVERSIONS.) Open for lunch and dinner; closed Sundays. 134 Beltany Rd., Omagh (phone: 662-661224). Expensive to moderate.

Royal Arms Centrally located on the main thoroughfare, this hostelry has 16 double rooms and 5 singles, all with private baths. Its restaurant offers morning coffee, afternoon tea, and a full lunch and dinner menu daily. Reservations advised for Saturday dinner and Sunday lunch. MasterCard and Visa accepted. 51 High St., Omagh (phone: 662-243262; fax: 662-245011). Moderate.

En Route from Ulster–American Folk Park Return to A5 and continue 30 miles north to Londonderry, passing through Strabane (see *Londonderry* in THE CITIES). Alternatively, take A5 south to Ballygawley, then A4 east to its junction with M1; drive east approximately 75 miles to Belfast.

Index

Oyster festivals, 139, 256–57

Package tours, 18–22
  for disabled travelers, 24–25
  for older travelers, 27
  for single travelers, 25–26
Park (Kenmare, County Kerry, Irish Republic), 268
Parknasilla, County Kerry, Irish Republic, 454–55
  hotels and restaurants, 455
Passports. *See* Entry requirements and customs
Pighouse Collection (Cornafean, County Cavan, Irish Republic), 292
Plane, traveling by. *See* Airplane travel
The Point (Dublin, County Dublin, Irish Republic), 121
Polo, 235
Pontoon, County Mayo, Irish Republic, 486–87
  hotels and restaurants, 487
Pontoon Bridge fishing hotel and school (Pontoon, County Mayo, Irish Republic), 344, 348, 487
Portaferry, County Down, Northern Ireland, 531–32
  hotels and restaurants, 531–32
Portballintrae, County Antrim, Northern Ireland, 508
  hotels and restaurants, 508
Port-na-Blagh, County Donegal, Irish Republic, 428–29
  restaurants, 429
Powerscourt Estate and Gardens (Enniskerry, County Wicklow, Irish Republic), 281
Public holidays. *See* Special events
Pubs, 255–56, 260–65
  See also pubs *entry under names of specific places*
Punchestown, County Kildare, Irish Republic, horse trials, 320

El Rancho Horse Holidays riding establishment (Tralee, County Kerry, Irish Republic), 322
Rare-book dealers, 286
Rathfriland, County Down, Northern Ireland, 520–21
Rathlin Island, County Antrim, Northern Ireland, 504–6
  hotels, 505
Rathmullan, County Donegal, Irish Republic, 425–26
  hotels and restaurants, 274–75, 425–26
Rathmullan House (Rathmullan, County Donegal, Irish Republic), 274–75
Religion. *See* Houses of worship
Rental accommodations, 29–30
Renting a car, 18
Renvyle, County Galway, Irish Republic, 465

hotels, 465
Renvyle House (Renvyle, Connemara, County Galway, Irish Republic), 275, 345, 465
Restaurants. *See* restaurants *entry under names of specific places*
Ring of Kerry, Irish Republic, route, 446–57
River and canal cruising. *See* Ship, Traveling by
River Bann, Northern Ireland, cruising, 333
River Shannon, Irish Republic, cruising, 332
Riverview Club tennis courts (Clonskeagh, County Dublin, Irish Republic), 316
Rock of Cashel (Cashel, County Tipperary, Irish Republic), 57–58
Rose of Tralee International Festival (Tralee, County Kerry, Irish Republic), 301
Rosguill, County Donegal, Irish Republic, 427
Rosleague Manor (Connemara, County Galway, Irish Republic), 275
Ross Lake House fishing hotel (Oughterard, County Galway, Irish Republic), 346
The Rosses, County Donegal, Irish Republic, 430–31
Rostrevor, County Down, Northern Ireland, 521–22
  restaurants, 521
Round Ireland Race sailing championship (Wicklow, Wicklow County, Irish Republic), 329
Roundstone, County Galway, Irish Republic, 472–73
  hotels and restaurants, 472
Royal County Down golf course (Newcastle, County Down, Northern Ireland), 315
Royal Dublin Society Concert Hall (Dublin, County Dublin, Irish Republic), 121
Royal Portrush golf course (Portrush, County Antrim, Northern Ireland), 315
Rugby, 76
Ruins, 259, 305–12
Rural retreats, 266–75
Ryan's fishing hotel (Cong, County Mayo, Irish Republic), 348

Sailing, 50, 76, 142, 221, 235, 327–31
  clubs, 328
  events, 328–29
  schools, 329–31
St. Patrick's Week, 302
Salmon, fishing for, 338–40
Saltee Islands, County Wexford, Irish Republic, 244–45
Saul, County Down, Northern Ireland, 529–31
Schull, County Cork, Irish Republic, 440–41
  hotels and restaurants, 441
Sea angling, 341–43
Sea View House (Ballylickey, Bantry,